# Visual C++™ Object-Oriented Programming

# Visual C++™ Object-Oriented Programming

*Mark Andrews*

SAMS PUBLISHING

A Division of Prentice Hall Computer Publishing
11711 North College, Carmel, Indiana, 46032 USA

*To Cindy and Michelle*



FIRST EDITION



International Standard Book Number: 0-672-30150-4

Library of Congress Catalog Card Number: 92-62685

96 95 94 93 4 3 2 1

Interpretation of the printing code: the rightmost double-digit number is the year of the book's printing; the rightmost single-digit, the number of the book's printing. For example, a printing code of 93-1 shows that the first printing of the book occurred in 1993.

*Composed in Palatino and MCPdigital by Prentice Hall Computer Publishing*

*Printed in the United States of America*

### Trademarks

**Publisher**
*Richard K. Swadley*

**Associate Publisher**
*Jordan Gold*

**Acquisitions Manager**
*Stacy Hiquet*

**Acquisitions Editor**
*Gregory S. Croy*

**Development Editor**
*Phillip Paxton*

**Production Editors**
*Erik Dafforn*
*Melba Hopper*

**Copy Editors**
*Anne Clarke Barrett*
*Michael Cunningham*
*Carolyn Linn*

**Editorial Coordinators**
*Bill Whitmer*
*James R. Welter II*

**Editorial Assistants**
*Sharon Cox*
*Molly Carmody*

**Technical Reviewers**
*Tim Moore*
*Greg Guntle*

**Marketing Manager**
*Greg Wiegand*

**Cover Designer**
*Tim Amrhein*

**Director of Production and Manufacturing**
*Jeff Valler*

**Production Manager**
*Corinne Walls*

**Imprint Manager**
*Kelli Widdifield*

**Book Designer**
*Michele Laseau*

**Production Analyst**
*Mary Beth Wakefield*

**Proofreading/Indexing Coordinator**
*Joelynn Gifford*

**Graphics Image Specialists**
*Tim Montgomery*
*Dennis Sheehan*
*Sue VandeWalle*

**Production**
*Carla Hall-Batton*
*Lisa Daugherty*
*Mitzi Foster Gianakos*
*Dennis Clay Hager*
*Howard Jones*
*Sean Medlock*
*Mike Mucha*
*Juli Pavey*
*Angela M. Pozdol*
*Linda Quigley*
*Tonya Simpson*
*Michelle Self*
*Barbara Webster*
*Dennis Wesner*
*Donna Winter*
*Alyssa Yesh*

**Indexers**
*John Sleeva*
*Suzanne Snyder*
*Tina Trettin*

Inside OLE 2.0
Microsoft Press

# Overview

# Contents

# About the Author

Mark Andrews, an experienced computer programmer and writer living in Santa Clara, California, has written over 15 computer books.

# Introduction

It's difficult to talk about Visual C++ without sounding like you work for Microsoft, which I don't; but I consider Visual C++ the best thing that's happened in years to object-oriented programming, C++ programming, and programming in general. If you don't have Visual C++, my suggestion is that you go right out and buy it. Then, go straight to Chapter 1, "Microsoft Visual C++," and start reading. I think you'll be glad you did.

Visual C++ is a programming environment that enables you to write object-oriented programs in C++ without facing the drudgery of designing a user interface by hand every time you create an application. With Visual C++, you click one menu command—the AppWizard command—and the Visual C++ system creates an executable Windows application framework, complete with a menu bar and one window. Then, with Visual C++'s excellent Windows-based source code editor—the first Windows-based editor to be made available with a C or C++ compiler—you can build on AppWizard's foundation to create your own object-oriented application. (The editor works like a Windows-based word processor. It has a built-in source line debugger that you can run without leaving the editor, and it automatically color codes the syntax in your files for readability and easy code maintenance.)

## What You Get with Visual C++

When I received my beta release of Visual C++ from Microsoft, I already knew from the grapevine that it featured a C++ application generator and a Windows-based editor, so that did not surprise me. But I am surprised—make that amazed—by the many other Visual C++ features. They include the following:

- *Microsoft Foundation Class library, Version 2.0.* This is a collection of more than 100 C++ classes, totaling more than 60,000 lines of source code, that are specially designed to work seamlessly with the interactive tools that come in the Visual C++ package.

- *Windows-based, graphics-oriented programming tools.* This set of impressive tools includes the following:

- A source code browser that helps you navigate through your C++ classes and implementation code in order to identify and track relationships among member functions, structures, variables, types, and macros.
- App Studio, an integrated Windows resource editor, that enables you to use standard mouse-driven editing techniques to create and edit bitmaps, cursors, dialog boxes, icons, menus, and strings with precise control of properties.
- ClassWizard, an interactive tool that enables you to connect, or bind, your C++ code with Windows messages and class member functions.
- QuickWin libraries that enable you to write text-based applications with Visual C++. With QuickWin, you can test code and prototype programs quickly without bothering to write full-fledged Windows interfaces, and you can quickly update existing DOS-based applications by porting them into the Windows environment.
- Precompiled headers (and precompiled source files) that make you more productive by decreasing compilation time.

- *Sample code and online help*. This includes more than 20 complete sample applications demonstrating major features of the Microsoft Foundation Class library, more than 30 technical notes that describe Visual C++, implementation techniques in detail, and a wealth of documentation provided both online and in book form.

# What Visual C++ Doesn't Do

Despite all that Visual C++ offers, there is one thing it doesn't do. It doesn't turn programming novices into C++ experts overnight. Although Visual C++ can build you an application framework and can help you produce better C++ code more efficiently, it can't teach you the intricacies of the C++ languages, and it can't write the code that implements the functionality of your applications. No matter what kind of programming environment you use, you must write your programs yourself. That's where this book comes in.

A lot of books have been written about C++, but this one is a little different. It focuses not only on Visual C++—which is pretty well documented in the online and offline manuals that come with the Visual C++ package—but also on object-oriented programming with C++. In 24 carefully written, graded chapters supplemented with thousands of lines of hands-on programming examples, this book teaches you everything you need to know about Visual C++ in order to program in Visual C++—from the basic fundamentals covered in Chapter 1 to the graphics capabilities of the Visual C++ introduced in Chapter 23, "Windows and Views."

# This Book and You

This book is not written for programming novices; it is for people who have at least some programming experience—preferably in C—and who know something about the Windows programming environment. Even within this potential audience, however, programming expertise varies. Some C programmers are more fluent in the language than others, so this book defines briefly, and often illustrates, the most important C, C++, and Windows terms and concepts when they are first mentioned.

This book goes into more detail when it starts exploring some of the murky corners of C and C++ that many programmers—even experienced programmers—may not completely understand. This book should meet the needs of people who are somewhat familiar with C and Windows and who want to learn how to write programs in Visual C++.

Because this is not a book for beginners, if you don't have a rudimentary understanding of C or some other programming language, I suggest that you study a good introductory text on C before plunging into this volume. On the other hand, if you are a highly advanced C programmer, you may find that you can skip some sections of the book or that you can scan them to refresh your memory. Throughout the book, I have tried to strike a sensible balance between saying too little and saying too much in order to make this book appropriate for as wide an audience of C programmers as possible.

In case you do find parts of the book rough going, a number of good introductory books on C and C++ are listed in the Bibliography.

# What You'll Need to Use Visual C++

To compile and use the programs provided in this book and on the program disk that comes with it, you'll need an IBM personal computer system or a PC that is compatible with the following:

- An 80386 or higher microprocessor (a fast 80486 is strongly recommended).
- At least 4M of RAM (8M is better, and 16M or more is better still).
- At least one hard disk drive with a minimum of 8M of free space. More disk space is highly desirable. One modestly sized Visual C++ project, with all the source and object code that goes with it, requires too much memory to fit on a 1.4M floppy disk; and when you start making backups, you can quickly run out of disk space. I don't know how many hundreds of megabytes you'll wind up needing; you can never be too rich, too thin, or have too big a hard disk drive.
- At least one 3.5-inch 720K floppy disk drive; at least one 3.5-inch 1.2M floppy disk drive; or both.
- A good VGA color monitor and a mouse.

# Software Requirements

This is the software you'll need to develop Microsoft C/C++ programs:

- MS-DOS Version 3.3 or later.
- Version 3.0 or later of Microsoft Windows (Version 3.1 or later is recommended) or Version 0.9 or later of a DPMI (DOS Protected Mode Interface) server.
- Your Visual C++ package.

# Installing Microsoft C++

The Visual C++ development package includes a setup program. It prompts you for information about your computer system and about your personal preferences and then installs Visual C++ and its supporting tools, online help and documentation in accordance with the answers that you have provided.

Some of the choices that you can make when you run the setup program are as follows:

- The kind of "memory model" you want to use when you write C/C++ programs. To choose a memory model, take into account the amount of memory you have available and whether you think you'll be writing small, "compact," medium-sized, or large programs. If you're not sure of the answers to those questions, refer to Chapter 9, "Managing Memory."
- Whether the programs you write will support floating-point math and, if so, how you plan to implement floating-point support.
- The kinds of C++ Windows libraries you will use, if any. When in doubt, choose the defaults.

If you make a mistake in choosing a setup option or if you expand your computer system or change your mind about an option later on, you can select a different set of options at any time by running the setup program again.

It is beyond the scope of this introduction to describe the Visual C++ setup program in detail. For more information on the setup program and how to run it, see the documentation that comes with the Visual C++ package.

When you have installed Microsoft Programmer's Workbench (PWB), make a copy of the bonus disk that comes with this book and then store your original disk for safekeeping. If you want to compile and execute the programs on your bonus disk as you read this book rather than type the programs yourself, you might find it convenient to create a directory for the programs on your hard disk and then copy all the sample programs into that directory.

## Getting Started

Many authors list the contents of their books in their introductions, but I don't like to do this. For a list of the chapters in this book, please refer to the Table of Contents. To find out more about what's in each chapter, please turn to the page the chapter starts on and start reading. I'd rather let you read the book than tell you what it contains.

That ends this introduction. Now you're ready to turn to Chapter 1 and start learning to write object-oriented programs in Visual C++.

# I

# Visual C++

Chapter 1

# Microsoft Visual C++

Visual C++ is one small step in the C++ learning curve, but it is one giant leap in the evolution of object-oriented programming. It may be the most important new tool for object-oriented programming since Bjarne Stroustrup, the inventor of C++, christened and named his language in 1983.

With Microsoft Visual C++, it's as easy to develop Windows-based programs for the IBM Personal Computer and PC-compatibles as it is to write text-based programs using old-fashioned implementations of C++. In fact, I think it's even easier, because Visual C++ comes with a powerful set of prewritten classes that can greatly simplify the writing of Visual C++ programs.

The class library that comes with Visual C++ is Version 2 of the Microsoft Foundation Class (MFC) library. MFC2 is more than a library of C++ classes; it is designed specifically to support a brand new visually oriented system for developing Microsoft C++ programs.

With the classes that are provided in the Visual C++ MFC library and the interactive tools that come with Visual C++, you can actually create a working C++ application without writing a line of code; all you have to do is tell the Visual Workbench what kind of application you want by selecting menu items and clicking controls in dialog boxes. You then can use the VWB editor and other Visual C++ tools to write the code required to complete your application.

This book has a twofold purpose: to introduce you to Microsoft Visual C++ and Version 2 of the Microsoft Foundation Class (MFC) library and to show you how to use those two tools to write object-oriented programs. This chapter introduces the Visual C++ package, and Part III—which begins with Chapter 21—focuses on writing programs that make use of the MFC library. The middle chapters—the bulk of the book—are designed to help you learn how to write object-oriented programs using Microsoft Visual C++ as a programming environment.

## About Visual C++

Visual C++ is more than just a new tool for developing C++ applications. It has a host of noteworthy new features, including:

- The Visual Workbench (VWB). An integrated development environment that includes the Visual C++ editor, a powerful source-line debugger, a browser, and an interactive make utility, all under one shell. The VWB editor replaces the text-based Programmer's WorkBench editor that came with Microsoft C++ Version 7.

- AppWizard. An application generator that can create a complete C++ software project at the touch of a mouse button. By selecting the AppWizard command from the Visual Workshop's Project menu, you can generate a working C++ application that comes equipped with one window and a menu bar. Then, using other Visual C++ tools, you can add your own code and resources to expand AppWizard's application into exactly the kind of program you want. AppWizard relieves you of the tedium of getting a Windows application up and running before you can start developing a software project. With AppWizard, you can create C++ applications interactively using the classes provided by the MFC library and the interactive, graphics-based tools that are built into the Visual Workbench.

- AppStudio. An interactive graphics tool for creating and editing Windows resources. With App Studio, you can design resources such as dialog boxes, menus, icons, bitmaps, and cursors by editing them onscreen with the mouse. App Studio automatically generates resource files for the resources you create. Then, if you like, you can fine-tune the resources you've created by editing their ASCII files with the Visual Workbench editor. More information about App Studio is presented in Chapter 22, "The Visual Workbench."
- ClassWizard. An interactive tool that lets you create new classes, map messages to class member functions, and map controls to class member variables. To create a class with ClassWizard, you simply select a base class from a list of available classes and then type in the name of a derived class. ClassWizard automatically creates the source files needed to define and implement the new class. ClassWizard then binds the new class to the program being developed. During program development, you can use ClassWizard to create the classes you need for your program, including message handlers and message maps (tables used to locate the code that handles messages).
- The Visual Workbench Browser. This can be used to search for information about the relationships among modules, constants, macros, variables, symbols, and classes. With the Browser, you can view class hierarchies, function call trees, and symbol definitions and references.

This chapter offers only a brief introduction to the development tools that come with Visual C++. Many of the development tools provided with Visual C++ are described in more detail in Part III of this book, which focuses on developing Visual C++ programs using the Microsoft Foundation Class library. For detailed descriptions of the Visual Workbench tools that are provided with Visual C++, see the Microsoft *Visual Workbench User's Guide.*

## Other Visual C++ Features

Besides the development tools described under the previous heading, Visual C++ provides these features:

- A set of runtime libraries.
- A set of Windows libraries.

- Online documentation for the Windows Software Development Kit (SDK).
- A Windows-based source line debugger that can be invoked at any time during the development of a program. You can enter the debugger from the Visual Workbench simply by selecting the Go command from the Debug menu. Then, without interrupting program development, you can do the following:
  - Set, use, and delete breakpoints.
  - Step into, over, and out of functions.
  - Test and change the values of variables.
  - Monitor variables and expressions through a watch window.
  - Check the values of CPU registers and flags.
  - Trace the execution of a program, keeping track of all functions that have been called and have not returned.

Figure 1.1 shows the commands that you can select from the VWB editor's Debug menu. The *Visual Workbench User's Guide,* which comes with Microsoft Visual C++, provides detailed instructions for using the Visual C++ debugger.

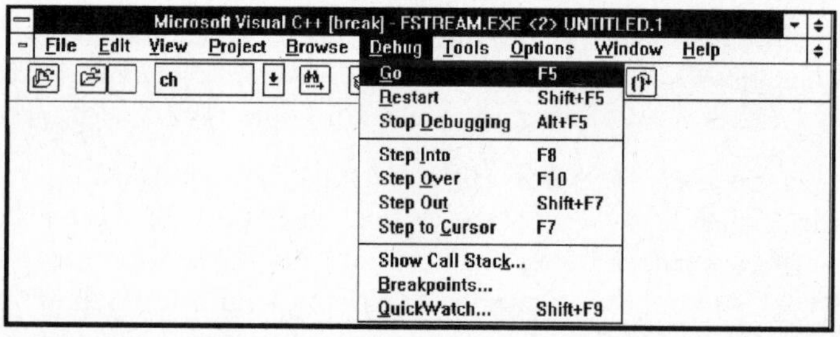


*Figure 1.1. The Visual Workbench Debug menu.*

# The Visual Workbench Editor

If you've used any products with Windows-based text editors, you should have no trouble getting accustomed to the Visual Workbench editor. It's a standard-variety Windows-based editor, with a pull-down menu bar from which you can select menu commands with a mouse. The editor also is equipped with a toolbar, from which you can execute commands by clicking icons. Figure 1.2 shows the main screen of the VWB editor.

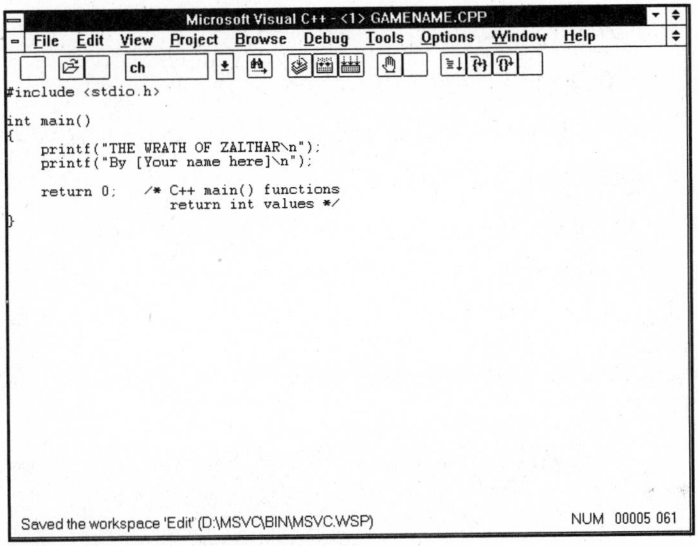
Microsoft Visual C++ - <1> GAMENAME.CPP
File Edit View Project Browse Debug Tools Options Window Help
ch
#include <stdio.h>
int main()
{
printf("THE WRATH OF ZALTHAR\n");
printf("By [Your name here]\n");
return 0; /* C++ main() functions
return int values */
}
Saved the workspace 'Edit' (D:\MSVC\BIN\MSVC.WSP)
NUM 00005 061

*Figure 1.2. The Visual Workbench editor.*

## The File and Edit Menus

The VWB editor has File and Edit menus from which you can select commands that perform standard file and editing operations. You can use standard command-key equivalents for many commonly used menu commands.

For example, you can copy a selected block of text to the clipboard by typing Ctrl-C, move a selection to the clipboard by typing Ctrl-X, and paste a selection from the clipboard into a document by typing Ctrl-V. Other keyboard commands are listed in Table 1.1.

**Table 1.1. Visual Workbench editor keyboard commands.**

| *To* | *Press* |
|---|---|
| Move one word to the left | Ctrl+left arrow |
| Move one word to the right | Ctrl+right arrow |
| Move to the first indentation of the current line | Home |
| Move to the beginning of the current line | Home, then Home |
| Move to the first indentation of the next line | Ctrl+Enter |
| Move to the end of the current line | End |
| Move to the beginning of the file | Ctrl+Home |
| Move to the end of the file | Ctrl+End |
| Undo the last edit | Ctrl+Z |
| Undo the last edit | Alt+Backspace |
| Redo the last edit | Ctrl+A |
| Delete to the end of the word | Ctrl+T |
| Copy text to the clipboard | Ctrl+C |
| Copy text to the clipboard | Ctrl+Ins |
| Cut text to the clipboard | Ctrl+X |
| Cut text to the clipboard | Shift+Del |
| Paste text from the clipboard | Ctrl+V |
| Paste text from the clipboard | Shift+Ins |
| Move to the matching brace | Ctrl+] |
| Insert a tab | Tab |
| Toggle display of tab symbols | Ctrl+Alt+T |

## Special Features of the VWB Editor

Besides its standard-variety features, the Visual Workbench editor has a number of special features. For example:

- *Color text highlighting.* The VWB editor highlights language keywords, identifiers, comments, and strings in different colors. That makes it easy to identify blocks of text, such as loops and comments, in source-code programs.
- *A toolbar.* This contains icons for 14 frequently used operations, such as a search-and-replace tool and several useful debugging functions. From the toolbar, you can set and clear breakpoints, open a window for monitoring variables, and jump over, into, or out of functions during debugging.
- *"Smart" dialog boxes.* The Open File and Save As dialogs, which are accessible from the File menu, remember the filename types that were previously typed in. This feature saves typing when you want to look for a particular type of file more than once during an editing session.
- *File searching.* The VWB editor has a powerful search-and-replace utility. You can match whole words, perform case-sensitive searches, and search for regular expressions. You can search for text both forward and backwards through a file. And you can move to a specific line in a file by selecting the Line command from the View menu.
- *Bookmarks.* You can set, clear, toggle, and move to bookmarks by selecting bookmark commands from the View menu.
- *Debugging.* The Visual Workbench has a source-line debugger that you can use (without leaving the VWB editor) by selecting commands from the Debug menu. If you own the Professional Edition of Visual C++, you can launch the CodeView debugger from the Tools menu. By selecting the Debug command from the Options menu, you can specify options that the VWB debugger uses when it debugs programs.
- *Launching VWB tools from the editor.* The VWB debugger isn't the only tool that you can launch from the VWB editor. By selecting commands from the VWB menu, you can launch the three tools we discussed earlier, plus a few new ones:
    - App Studio, an interactive graphics-based tool that can be used to create resources such as menus, dialog boxes, bit maps, and icons.
    - AppWizard, which can create a working Visual C++ application in a single step. You then can expand the starter application created by AppWizard into a full-scale Windows program.
    - ClassWizard, a tool that can generate and manage classes and can automate the creation and editing of code to handle messages and data used by dialog boxes.

    - The VWB Browser, which you can use to search for information by viewing class hierarchies, function call trees, symbol definitions, and symbol references.
    - The VWB Help tool, which offers online help on almost any topic related to Visual C++ or the VWB development environment.
- *Customizing the editor.* You can customize many parts of the Visual Workbench to suit your own preferences and programming needs. For example, you can add commands to the Tools menu, set directory paths used by the Visual Toolbox, set the font and typeface used in the VWB text window, and change the colors used to highlight source text.

For more information on the tools that can be accessed from the VWB editor, see the Microsoft *Visual Workbench User's Guide.*

## The Standard and Professional Editions

Microsoft Visual C++ comes in two versions: a Standard Edition and a Professional Edition. The Professional Edition is the successor to Microsoft C++ Version 7. The Standard edition is the successor to Microsoft Quick C.

The Professional Edition and Standard Edition contain the same software for developing Windows-based applications. The main difference between the two editions is that the Professional Edition supports the building of programs that can be run under Windows and MS-DOS while the Standard Edition can be used only to develop Windows programs.

This book focuses on the building of Windows-based programs, so you can use it with either edition of Visual C++.

### Extra Features of the Professional Edition

Besides the features that come with both editions of Visual C++, the Professional Edition has some extra features. For example, the Professional Edition includes the following:

- Support for several kinds of projects that are not supported by the Standard Edition. With the C++ Professional Edition, you can develop MS-DOS applications, MS-DOS overlaid applications, MS-DOS .COM applications, and P-code applications. (P-code is a special kind of code that takes up less space than machine code, but it runs more slowly.) For comparison, with the Standard Edition you can develop only Windows-based programs (including QuickWin programs).

- The Microsoft CodeView debugger. (Although the Standard Edition doesn't come with CodeView, it does include the Visual Workbench source line debugger.) The Visual C++ Professional Edition comes with a CodeView debugger that you can install on the Visual Workbench menu.
- Hard-copy documentation for command-line tools.
- Sample software development kit (SDK) programs and hard-copy documentation for SDK tools.

### USING VBX CONTROLS WITH VISUAL C++

Many custom controls, sometimes referred to as *VBX* (Visual Basic) controls, have been developed for the Microsoft Visual Basic environment. With a package called the Microsoft Visual Control Pack, available as a separate product, you can use custom controls in your Visual C++ programs.

A *custom control* is an extension to the Control Palette in the Visual C++ App Studio (or in the Microsoft Visual Basic Toolbox). When you install a custom control in the App Studio, you can use that custom control the same way you would use any standard, built-in control. When you add a custom control to an application written in Visual C++, the control becomes part of the application, and the user of the program can use it just like any other control.

The Microsoft Visual Control Pack contains a set of controls that has a 3-D look: an animated button (one that moves when you click it); a set of dialogs that can be used for various purposes, such as to load and save files and manage communications; a control that can be used to design many kinds of graphs; and a number of other controls.

To use VBX controls with Visual C++, you must install them into the App Studio resource editor and make them part of the App Studio environment. You then can use ClassWizard to define message maps for the controls you've installed. You also can use ClassWizard to initialize the properties of the controls.

# Installing Visual C++

Microsoft Visual C++ comes with a Setup program that automatically installs Visual C++. All you have to do is insert the Visual C++ installation disk in a disk drive and execute the Setup program. The Setup program displays an Installation Options dialog window that can install Visual C++ in whatever configuration you specify. Figure 1.3 shows the Installation Options dialog window.

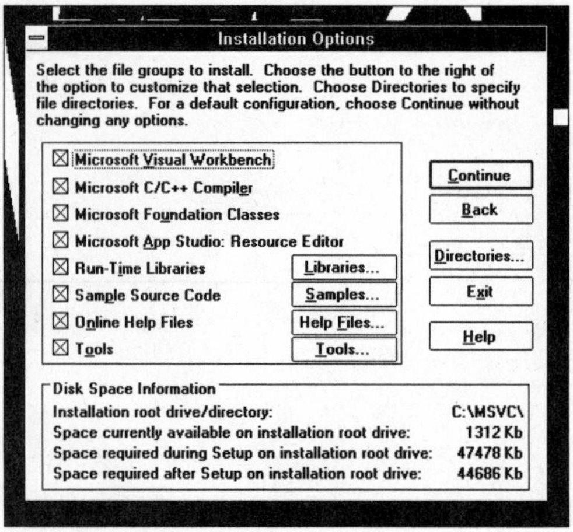


*Figure 1.3. Installation Options dialog box.*

## What You Need to Install Visual C++

The minimum hardware and software requirements for installing Visual C++ are the following:

- An IBM Personal Computer or a 100 percent IBM compatible PC, running an 80386 or higher processor.
- MS-DOS Version 5.0 or later.
- A VGA monitor.
- Four megabytes of available memory (although six megabytes are recommended).
- A hard disk with enough disk space to hold all the options you need. The Visual C++ Setup program lets you select installation options and then

informs you of the disk-space requirements for the options you selected. Setup then checks to make sure you have enough space before copying files.

- A 1.2M, 5.25-inch disk drive, or a 1.44M, 3.5-inch disk drive.
- Version 3.1 of Microsoft Windows or Microsoft Windows for Workgroups, running in enhanced mode. If you own the Professional Edition of Visual C++, you can configure your computer system to compile and link Visual C++ commands from MS-DOS command lines (see Chapter 7, "Compiling Visual C++ Programs"). But you need Windows to install Visual C++.

## One-Step and Multi-Step Installation

You can install the complete Visual C++ package in one installation session, or you can install a smaller configuration and update it later by installing more libraries, sample programs, help files, or other components.

During installation, you can obtain online help at any time either by pressing the F1 key or clicking the Help button in a dialog box.

Complete instructions for installing Visual C++ are provided in the *Visual Workbench User's Guide* that comes with the Microsoft Visual C++ package.

# The Visual Workbench

The Microsoft Visual Workbench is an integrated, Windows-based programming environment that runs under the Microsoft Windows operating system. It has six components, all of which run in Windows under a single shell. The six components of the Visual Workbench are:

- A powerful Windows-based text editor. When you launch Microsoft Visual C++, the Visual C++ editor appears on-screen, ready and waiting for you to type a program or to select a menu or toolbar command.
- The Visual Workbench graphical browser, a Windows-based version of the text-based Microsoft Source Browser accompanying Microsoft C/C++ Version 7. With the Visual Workbench graphical browser, you can find related symbols in a program and examine their relationships. The browser uses a database that contains information on where each symbol

is defined and used and that describes the relationships among the modules, constants, macros, variables, functions, and classes used in a program.

- The Visual C++ compiler. The Visual C++ Professional Edition comes with an optimizing compiler, while the Visual C++ Standard Edition comes with a standard compiler. The Professional Edition compiler can compile Windows P-code applications and MS-DOS applications, while the Standard Edition compiler cannot. (For more information about P-Code, see Chapter 8, "Linking Visual C++ Programs.") You can set options for the Visual C++ compiler from a dialog window called the C/C++ Compiler Options dialog box.

- A linker. The Visual C++ linker is controlled from a dialog window called the Linker Options dialog box. For more information about the Visual C++ linker, see Chapter 8.

- A brand new source line debugger. This runs under Windows, and you can use it without leaving the editor. The Visual C++ debugger is described earlier in this chapter, in the section titled "About Visual C++."

- A make utility. Before you create a Visual C++ application, you must create a project that contains the source files, resources, and libraries that make up a program, plus a makefile that includes the compiler and linker commands that are needed to build the program. You can create a project from the Visual Workbench simply by selecting the New command from the Project menu. The Visual C++ make utility then can build your application at any time you wish, at the touch of a menu command. Visual C++ projects are described in more detail in the next section, "Using Visual C++."

- A Help database. Online help is available at any time from the Visual Workbench: just select the subject that you need help with from the Help menu. Figure 1.4 shows the choices offered by the Help menu.

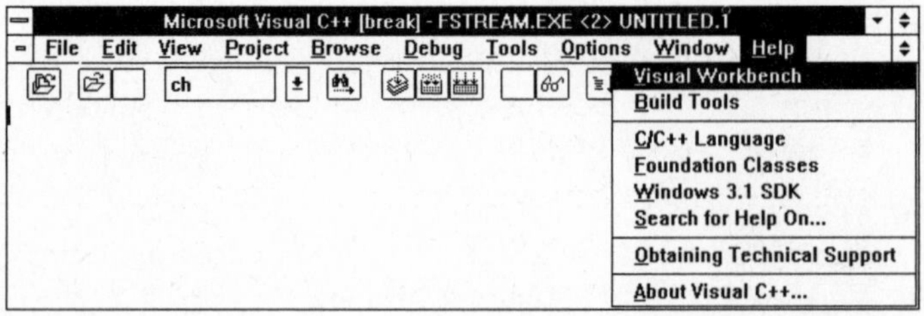


*Figure 1.4. The Help menu.*

**NOTE—NON-VISUAL C++**

Because Visual C++ is designed primarily to be used with the Visual Toolbox, the Setup program doesn't ordinarily configure your system to compile and link Visual C++ programs by executing commands from an MS-DOS command line. However, if you own the Professional Edition of Visual C++, you can make some changes in your AUTOEXEC.BAT file that will let you build Visual C++ programs from MS-DOS command lines. (You can't do that with the Standard Edition because the Standard Edition is not compatible with MS-DOS.) For instructions on how to build Visual C++ programs nonvisually, see Chapter 7, "Compiling Visual C++ Programs."

## Using Visual C++

Most of the applications you write with Microsoft Visual C++ probably will be Windows-based. In fact, with the Standard Edition of Visual C++, Windows-based programs are the only kind you *can* write. With the Professional Edition, you can write MS-DOS programs if you like (see the note just before this section, titled "Non-Visual C++"), but Visual C++ is designed primarily for people who want to write Windows-based programs.

You can write two kinds of Windows-based programs with Visual C++:

- Full-scale Windows applications that can be equipped with all the trimmings to which Windows users are accustomed: multiwindow support, dialog boxes, click-and-drag icons, and any other Windows goodies that you want to build into your programs.
- QuickWin programs, which are what you get when you cross Windows applications with MS-DOS applications. Programs are written using a special library called the QuickWin library. A QuickWin application puts a window and a menu bar on the screen, but little else. QuickWin programs do not support dialog boxes, the use of icons, or many of the other interactive tools that most Windows applications offer. Instead, the window that's displayed by a QuickWin program works like a video monitor: the user can type text in the window, and can perform input and output operations with standard MS-DOS input and output routines.

Because QuickWin applications are easy to create, they can be useful during program development; they're convenient for prototyping code and for doing quick jobs that don't justify the development of a full-blown Windows interface.

Figure 1.5 is the screen display of a QuickWin program. In the next section, "Writing a C++ Program," you'll get an opportunity to write and build a QuickWin application. Then you'll know how to use QuickWin to compile the example programs in Parts I and II of this volume.

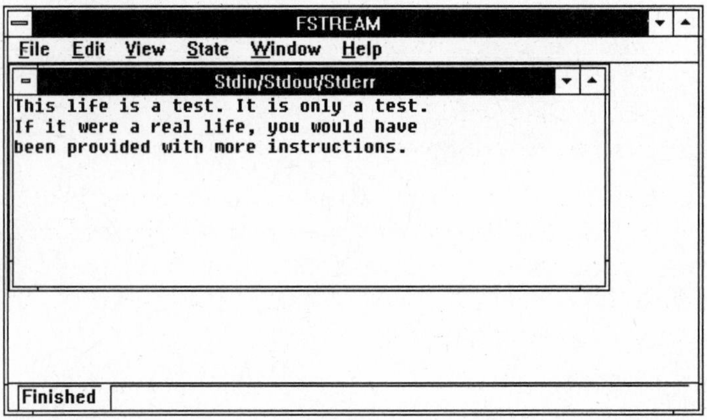


*Figure 1.5. The QuickWin screen display.*

# Writing a Visual C++ Program

The example programs in Parts I and II of this book are short applications that were developed with the QuickWin library. The easiest way to study them, therefore, is to compile and run them in the QuickWin environment.

At the end of this section there's a tutorial that will give you an opportunity to write and build a simple QuickWin application. When you've written and compiled the program presented in this section, you'll be able to compile the rest of the example programs in Parts I and II quickly and easily, using the QuickWin library.

As you compile, edit, and run the example programs in Parts I and II, you'll get valuable practice using the Visual Workbench and the other tools in the Microsoft Visual C++ development environment.

Then, when you get to Part III, you'll be able to advance beyond the QuickWin environment and start creating full-scale Windows applications using the classes in the MFC library. Procedures for compiling full-fledged Windows applications with Visual C++ are presented in Chapter 23, "Windows and Views."

## About QuickWin

A QuickWin application is a program that runs under the Windows operating system but interfaces with the user using text-based I/O, much like programs that run under MS-DOS. A QuickWin program displays a multiple document interface (MDI) window on the screen; the user then interacts with the program by typing text in the window, in the same way that a user interacts with text-based programs that run under MS-DOS.

Because QuickWin programs work like standard text-based programs, they can manage I/O using the `printf()` and `scanf()` family of functions defined in the STDIO.H header file, as well as the C++ `iostream` classes defined in the header file IOSTREAM.H. (The classes in the IOSTREAM.H library are described in detail in Chapter 20, "Streams.")

Because QuickWin programs and MS-DOS programs use the same kind of text-based I/O, software developers can port existing MS-DOS programs to Windows quickly and easily by recompiling the programs using the QuickWin library.

The QuickWin library can handle most I/O operations that are used in MS-DOS programs, including programs that use the MS-DOS GRAPHICS.LIB library. However, QuickWin can't handle programs that use hardware-specific DOS procedures, such as BIOS interrupts or procedures that manipulate video memory directly.

**NOTE—STANDARD VISUAL C++ SUPPORTS QUICKWIN**

Although you can't write MS-DOS programs with the Standard Edition of Visual C++, the Visual C++ Standard Edition does support QuickWin. So, if you own Standard Edition Visual C++ and want to write MS-DOS-style programs, you can write them with the QuickWin libraries. You then can run them under Windows, in the same way you can run any Windows-based application.

## Visual C++ Projects

Before you can write and build a QuickWin program—or any Visual C++ program—you must create a *project*. Every application written in Visual C++ is built around a project. A project contains all the source files, resources, and libraries that make up a program, along with the compiler and linker commands needed to build the program.

Projects simplify program development by giving you an easy way to keep track of the files and libraries that are needed to build a program or a library. Projects also provide storage space for important information about compiler and linker options.

Finally, projects streamline the build process; they speed up software development by recompiling only files that have changed since the program's last compilation or build. For example, if a project has five source files and you edit only one of them between builds, that one is the only file the Visual C++ compiler recompiles before the program is linked. Alternatively, if you want to rebuild all files from scratch, you can select a menu command that performs a full build.

**NOTE—VISUAL WORKBENCH WORKSPACES**

To help you manage projects, C++ supports the use of a tool called a *workspace*. A workspace is a mechanism for saving and restoring an arrangement of windows associated with a project.

When you're working on a project in the Visual Workbench editor, the window arrangement that appears on the screen is considered the current workspace. By selecting the Workspace command under the Options menu, you can save up to three workspaces in addition to the current workspace. When you save a workspace, it's stored in a special project file called a *workspace file*.

When you close a project or exit the VWB editor, the current workspace automatically is saved in a workspace file.

When you're developing a project using the VWB editor, you can open any saved workspace automatically by selecting the Workspace command from the Options menu. The workspace that you have selected then becomes the current workspace. For more information on workspaces, see the Microsoft Visual C++ user's guides.

This section is designed to get you off to a fast start programming in Visual C++, so it explains very briefly how you can create a simple project that contains one file. For a closer look at projects and how they work, please see Chapter 8, "Linking Visual C++ Programs."

> **USING PWB PROJECTS FROM VISUAL C++**
>
> Visual C++ project files are different from project files you may have created with the Microsoft Programmer's WorkBench (PWB) in Microsoft C/C++ Version 7. However, if you have projects that were created with PWB, you can use them from the Visual Workbench by loading them into the Visual Workbench as *external projects*. For more information on loading external projects and using them from Visual C++, see the Microsoft *Visual Workbench User's Guide*.

## Building a Sample QuickWin Program

To build a QuickWin program, you must have the QuickWin library installed in your Visual C++ folder. If you didn't install QuickWin when you installed Visual C++, you can rerun the Visual C++ Setup program to install the QuickWin library.

When you have made sure that you have the QuickWin library installed, you can create and build a QuickWin program by following these steps:

1. From the Windows File Manager, create a directory on your hard disk for projects that contain the example programs in *Visual C++ Object-Oriented Programming*.
2. From the Windows Program Manager, launch Visual C++.
3. When the Visual Workbench editor appears on the screen, type this program:

```
#include <stdio.h>

int main()
{
    printf("THE WRATH OF ZALTHAR\n");
    printf("By [Your name here]\n");
```

```
        return 0; /* C++ main() functions
                     return int values */
}
```

(You might wish to refer back to Figure 1.2 to see how this should look on your screen.)

You probably recognize this program as a variation on that old C standard, "Hello, world." The program works in both C and C++. However, there are new and improved ways to write it in Visual C++, as you'll see in later chapters of this volume.

4. Select Save As from the File menu, and save the program in your example-programs folder. Name the program GAMENAME.CPP. (If you're already in your example-programs folder, you can save the program by selecting the Save menu item instead of Save As, as shown in Figure 1.6.)

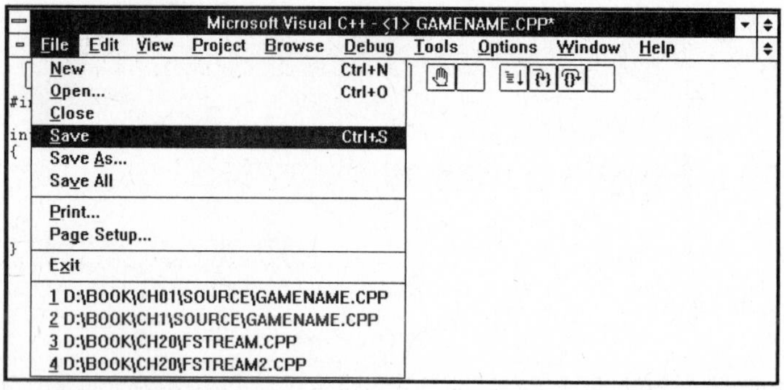


*Figure 1.6. Saving a source code file.*

5. From the Project menu, select New, as shown in Figure 1.7.
6. When the New Project dialog window appears, type GAMENAME in the text box labeled Project Name, as shown in Figure 1.8.
7. Open the list box labeled Project Type. Then select QuickWin application (.EXE) as a project type, as shown in Figure 1.9. (The list box in the illustration is the one displayed by the Professional Edition of C++; if you own the Standard Edition, fewer application types are displayed.)

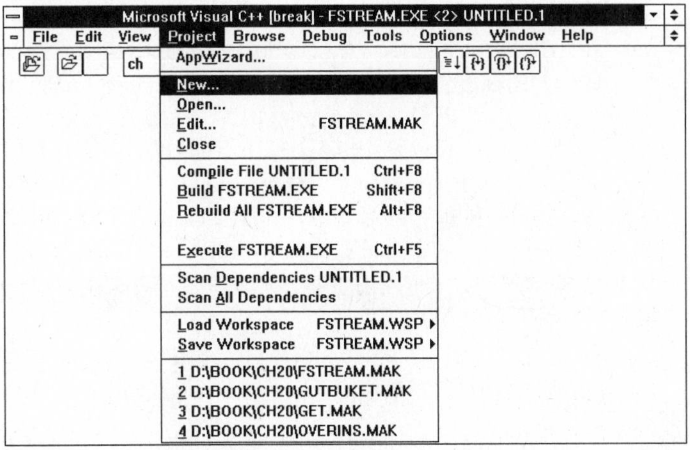
Microsoft Visual C++ [break] - FSTREAM.EXE <2> UNTITLED.1
File Edit View Project Browse Debug Tools Options Window Help
ch
AppWizard...
New...
Open...
Edit... FSTREAM.MAK
Close
Compile File UNTITLED.1 Ctrl+F8
Build FSTREAM.EXE Shift+F8
Rebuild All FSTREAM.EXE Alt+F8
Execute FSTREAM.EXE Ctrl+F5
Scan Dependencies UNTITLED.1
Scan All Dependencies
Load Workspace FSTREAM.WSP
Save Workspace FSTREAM.WSP
1 D:\BOOK\CH20\FSTREAM.MAK
2 D:\BOOK\CH20\GUTBUKET.MAK
3 D:\BOOK\CH20\GET.MAK
4 D:\BOOK\CH20\OVERINS.MAK

*Figure 1.7. Choosing New from the Project menu.*

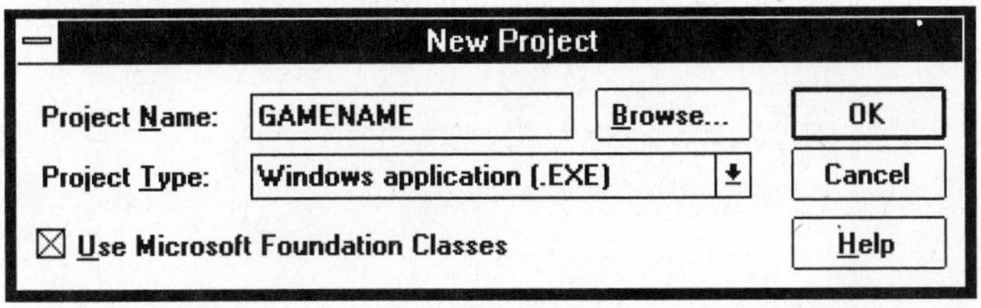
New Project
Project Name: GAMENAME
Browse...
OK
Project Type: Windows application (.EXE)
Cancel
Use Microsoft Foundation Classes
Help

*Figure 1.8. Naming a project.*

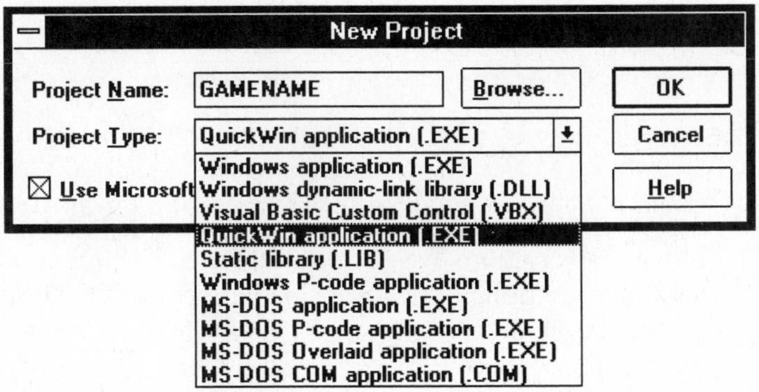
New Project
Project Name: GAMENAME
Browse...
OK
Project Type: QuickWin application (.EXE)
Cancel
Use Microsoft
Help
Windows application (.EXE)
Windows dynamic-link library (.DLL)
Visual Basic Custom Control (.VBX)
QuickWin application (.EXE)
Static library (.LIB)
Windows P-code application (.EXE)
MS-DOS application (.EXE)
MS-DOS P-code application (.EXE)
MS-DOS Overlaid application (.EXE)
MS-DOS COM application (.COM)

*Figure 1.9. Selecting a project type.*

8. Close the New Project dialog box. The Visual Workbench then opens another dialog window—the Edit dialog box for the Project option. By browsing through the directories and files listed in the list box labeled Directories, find the name of the GAMENAME.CPP program you wrote in Step 3. Then either double-click the GAMENAME.CPP icon or select it and click the Add button. Notice that the name of the program then appears in the list labeled Files in Project, as shown in Figure 1.10.

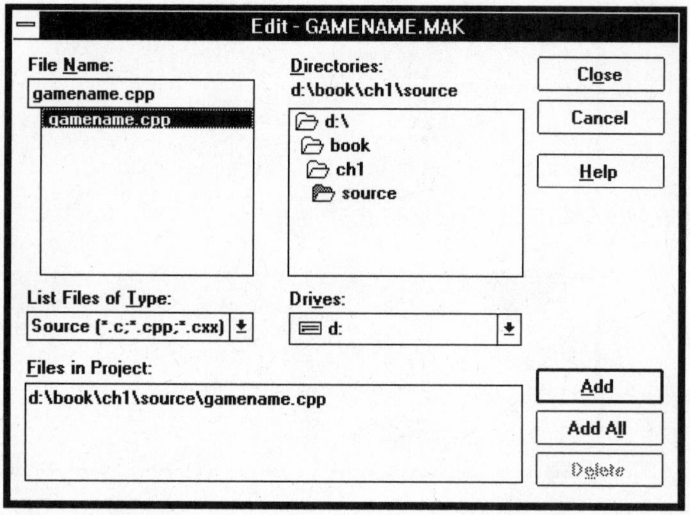


*Figure 1.10. The Browse dialog box.*

9. Close the dialog by clicking the Close button.

10. Compile the GAMENAME.CPP program by selecting Build or Rebuild All from the Project menu. In response to the Visual Workbench's dialogs asking you whether you really want to rebuild the program, click Yes.

11. Execute the program by selecting the Execute command from the Project menu. If everything has worked properly, Visual C++ now launches the GAMENAME.CPP program as a QuickWin application, as illustrated in Figure 1.11.

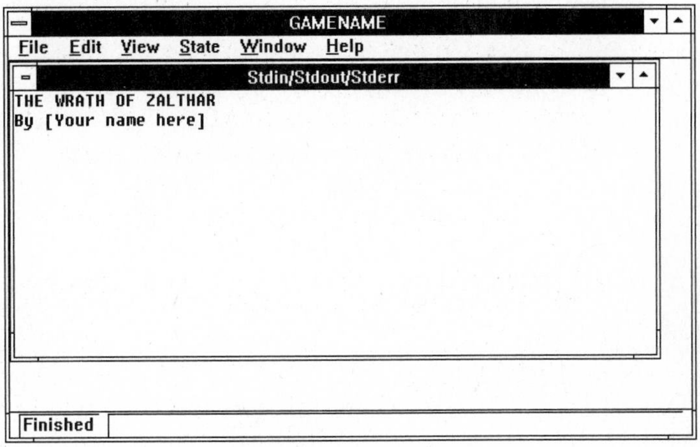


*Figure 1.11. Executing a QuickWin program.*

> **TIP—GETTING HELP FROM THE VISUAL WORKBENCH**
>
> The New Project dialog box—like most of the other dialog boxes the Visual Workbench displays—has a Help button that can provide you with an extraordinary amount of online help about almost any subject related to Visual C++. To use the Help button, simply click it. The Help button then displays a window labeled Visual Workbench Help. The Visual Workbench Help window is shown in Figure 1.12.
>
> The Visual Workbench Help window contains menus, buttons, and hypertext controls that you can use to navigate to the category of help you need. To obtain information about the Visual Workbench Help tools, press F1 while the Visual Workbench Help window is on the screen.

# Summary

You have seen the future of object-oriented programming, and it is Visual C++.

This chapter introduced Microsoft Visual C++, described its components, and gave you an opportunity to write and build a simple program using the tools that make up the Visual C++ programming environment. One important tool introduced in this chapter is the QuickWin library, a Visual C++ library that software designers often use to test code and to prototype programs.

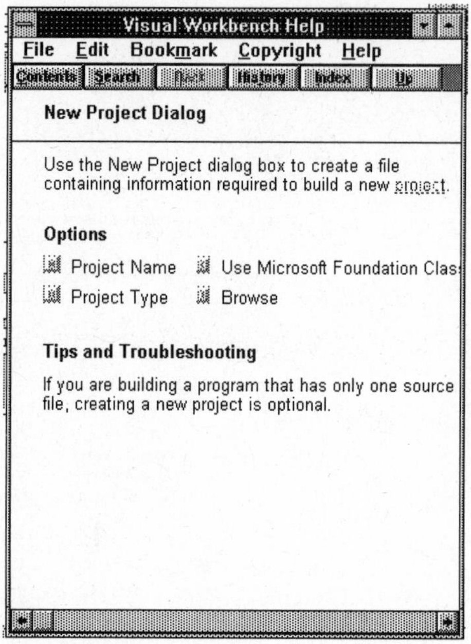


*Figure 1.12. The Visual Workbench Help window.*

All of the example programs presented in Parts I and II—which span Chapters 1 through 20—were written and built using the QuickWin library. So if you have mastered the contents of this chapter, you have all the information you need to compile and link all the example programs that are presented in the first 20 chapters of this volume.

As you study the first 20 chapters of this book, you also can use the tools introduced in this chapter to create and build your own Visual C++ programs. So when you reach Chapter 21, you'll be ready to start developing more complex applications using the C++ classes in the Microsoft Foundation Class (MFC) library.

Chapter 2

# A Better C—Plus

What do you get when you cross a procedural language with an object-oriented paradigm? When Bjarne Stroustrup did that, what he came up with was C++. And C++—part procedural language, part object-oriented language—quickly became the most important language to come along since C.

C++ is a synergy of improvements and extensions to C. The enhancements and additions you hear the most about are those that make C++ an object-oriented language, that is, a language that tries to solve problems in a new and better way by dividing programs into objects that have meaningful relationships with each other rather than into largely unrelated aggregations of functions and data.

But C++ is not just an object-oriented language. It's a hybrid language with two different kinds of characteristics. Half of them are traditional features of ANSI C, some of which have been enhanced and expanded. The other half are features that have improved and enhanced C to make it a suitable foundation for object-oriented languages.

This chapter covers the differences between C and C++ that are either unrelated or only incidentally related to object-oriented programming. Features of C++ that are related to object-oriented programming are covered in the remainder of this volume.

Other differences between C and C++ are covered in Chapters 3 through 9. Part II, which focuses on object-oriented programming, begins with Chapter 10.

It may seem odd to start a book on an object-oriented programming language with a chapter on the nonobject-oriented features of the language. If that bothers you, just remember that the additions and enhancements to C that are described in this chapter are improvements that strengthened the framework provided by C so that C++'s object-oriented extensions could be added to the C language in a seamless and sensible manner.

Also, remember that many of the topics covered in this chapter may be more related to object-oriented programming than you think; some of the nonobject-oriented features of C++ open gateways to other features that make the addition of object-oriented features possible. Even new features that are incidental to object-oriented programming are sure to come in handy in your day-to-day programming tasks. So don't skip or merely scan this chapter; be patient, and you'll be glad you were.

# A Brief History of C++

Even before its new features were added, C had the potential for being a framework for a very powerful object-oriented language. For example, because of C's low-level view of the world, it was easier to add a set of object-oriented features than it would have been if C had been a higher-level language. (As engineers at Apple found out, expanding Pascal into an object-oriented language was not nearly as successful an effort.)

On the down side, improvements were needed in areas such as C's notoriously lax type checking—and C also needed a few new features, such as inline functions, overloaded functions, and smart linkage.

So, as important as its object-oriented features are, C++ has a long list of additions and enhancements that are incidental to object-oriented programming. These elements, some of which have now been incorporated into the ANSI C standard, come in many shapes and sizes. Some perform important tasks, such as tightening up C's data-typing system. Others eliminate minor annoyances and major deficiencies that have plagued C programmers ever since Brian Kernighan first typed "Hello, world" on a computer console. Still others provide useful features that have never been a part of the C language.

> **NOTE—THE EVOLUTION OF VISUAL C++**
>
> The first implementation of C++, pioneered by AT&T, used a two-step (not a three-step) process for building programs. First, a module called a *translator* converted C++ source code into ordinary C code. This translator module, called CFront, was created by AT&T. Many implementations of C++ still use CFront to translate C++ source code into C-language source code for further processing.
>
> When CFront finishes translating C++ source code into C-language source code, an ordinary C compiler takes over and compiles the translated C code into object-code modules. That completes the compilation process; the compiled object code can then be linked, producing an executable object-code program.
>
> Microsoft—to its credit, I believe—resisted the temptation to license AT&T's CFront translator as a fast and easy way to produce a C++ compiler. Instead, Microsoft started from scratch and designed an integrated compiler that can compile a C++ program from start to finish, without going through the extra step of translating the program's source code into C with someone else's C++-to-C translator.

# Learning C++

Brian Kernighan, the author of C, created a monster when he wrote a trivial little program that printed the greeting "Hello, world" on a computer screen. "Hello, world" was the first code sample that Kernighan presented in *The C Programming Language*—the standard reference work on the language—and since then, countless students have started their journey toward becoming C programmers by typing and trying to compile the "Hello, world" program.

Because this book isn't aimed at beginning programmers, it doesn't start with the familiar "Hello, world" greeting. Instead, it begins with Listing 2.1, a slightly more ambitious program that illustrates several of the most important nonobject-oriented features of the C++ language.

Listing 2.1 doesn't illustrate the use of object-oriented features of C++, such as objects and classes. Those features are covered in later chapters of this volume.

> **A SAMPLE C++ PROGRAM**
>
> The program in Listing 2.1 is based on part of an adventure-game program named The Wrath of Zalthar. I designed The Wrath of Zalthar specifically for this book, to illustrate the most important principles of Visual C++ and object-oriented programming.
>
> As you study this book, you will see The Wrath of Zalthar grow into a framework for a fairly sophisticated adventure-game program before your very eyes. As the game evolves, it will demonstrate the use of many features of Visual C++ including classes and objects, constructors and conversion functions, function and operator overloading, inheritance and polymorphism, arrays and linked lists, streams, and the Microsoft Foundation Class library, which contains an enormous number of classes and functions that can help you write graphically oriented (as well as text-oriented) Windows programs.
>
> By the time you finish this volume, you'll know how all of these features work, and you'll be on your way to creating your own C++ programs.

**Listing 2.1. The WRATH.CPP program.**

```
// 0201.CPP
// Illustrating the basics

#include <iostream.h>

struct  PlayerData {
     int  strength;
     int  charisma;
     int  dexterity;
     int  intelligence;
};
```

```
// Function prototypes

void     GetData();

// two versions of an overloaded function
void     PrintData(PlayerData);
void     PrintData(const char *lineToPrint);

int main()
{
     // struct definition; note that 'struct' keyword is not used
     PlayerData myPlayerData = { 24, 29, 12, 2 };

     const char *title = "\nTHE WRATH OF ZALTHAR";
     const char *copyrightLine = "Copyright 19XX, [Your Name Here]";

     // first version of overloaded function
     PrintData(title); // program title
     PrintData(copyrightLine);

     // second version of overloaded function
     PrintData(myPlayerData);

     // well-behaved c++ main() functions return an int value
     return 0;
}

// version 1 of overloaded function
void PrintData(PlayerData myPlayerData)
{
     cout << "\nStrength: " << myPlayerData.strength << '\n';
     cout << "Charisma: " << myPlayerData.charisma << '\n';
     cout << "Dexterity: " << myPlayerData.dexterity << '\n';
     cout << "Intelligence: " << myPlayerData.intelligence << "\n\n";
}

// version 2 of overloaded function
void PrintData(const char *lineToPrint) // called by main()
{
     cout << lineToPrint << "\n"; // stream statement
}
```

If you know C but are new to C++, the program in Listing 2.1 may contain a few elements and constructs you aren't familiar with. Some examples:

- *One-line comments.* All comments in C programs are delimited by the character combinations `/*` and `*/`. C++ also supports one-line comments that start with the character combination `//`. This construct lets you nest comments in C++ programs, something that isn't allowed in C. This program contains several C++-style comments. For example:

```
// 0201.CPP
// Illustrating the basics
```

- *Function prototypes.* In C++, every function that is called in a program must have a forward declaration, or *function prototype.* Function prototypes, suggested in ANSI C and required in C++, were created to reduce programming errors by enforcing type-checking. Listing 2.1 contains these function prototypes:

```
void      GetData();
void      PrintData(PlayerData);
void      PrintData(const char *lineToPrint);
```

- *Function overloading.* In C++, multiple functions in the same scope can have the same name, provided their argument lists are different. This feature is known as *function overloading.* In Listing 2.1, `PrintData()` is an overloaded function. These are the two versions of `PrintData()` in the WRATH.CPP program:

```
void      PrintData(PlayerData);
void      PrintData(const char *lineToPrint);
```

- *The `const` modifier.* The `const` modifier is a type qualifier that turns variables into constants. Unlike the preprocessor directive `#define`, which creates constants by using simple macro expansion, the `const` modifier lets you give a constant a data type as well as a value and a name. That makes `const` objects subject to type-checking, which reduces the chance of programming errors. It can also make debugging easier, because a `const` that has a name and a data type can be treated as a full-fledged item by a debugger. Because of these capabilities and other capabilities of `const` variables—which are examined more closely in Chapter 3—you should use `const` variables in your C++ programs rather than constants created by the `#define` directive.

- *Input and output streams.* C++ has a brand-new set of alternatives to the `printf()` and `scanf()` family of functions used for input and output in C. In C++, instead of using functions such as `printf()` and `scanf()`, you can handle I/O operations with a set of classes that are defined in the

IOSTREAM.H file. These stream classes, called *iostream classes*, are easier to use than the C-style I/O functions defined in the STDIO.H file. They also provide type-checking mechanisms that can reduce programming errors. In this program, the two functions named `PrintData()` use the `iostream` class `cout` to print text to standard output (normally, the screen). The keyword `cout` is followed by the character combination <<, which is called an *overloaded operator* in C++. Operator overloading, still another new feature of C++, is the topic of Chapter 16.

The following code fragment illustrates how the C++ iostream operators work. As you can see, this code uses the `cout <<` construct rather than the `printf()` construct that you find in a C program. The C++ iostream operators are covered in much more detail in Chapter 20, "Streams."

```
void PrintData(PlayerData myPlayerData)
{
     cout << "\nStrength: " << myPlayerData.strength << '\n';
     cout << "Charisma: " << myPlayerData.charisma << '\n';
     cout << "Dexterity: " << myPlayerData.dexterity << '\n';
     cout << "Intelligence: " << myPlayerData.intelligence << "\n\n";
}

// version 2 of overloaded function
void PrintData(const char *lineToPrint) // called by main()
{
     cout << lineToPrint << "\n"; // stream statement
}
```

# C++ Comments

If programmers were asked to list the most frustrating features of C, one complaint that would certainly land near the top of the list is the construct for placing comments in C programs. This is, of course, the construct that forces comments to be delimited with the character combinations `/*` and `*/`.

There's nothing especially wrong with using the symbols `/*` and `*/` to delimit comments. What's annoying is that comments enclosed in these delimiters cannot be nested—and the frustration factor is increased because the delimiters themselves seem to have a natural kind of camouflage that often seems to render them almost invisible in source text.

Consequently, C programmers constantly run into situations in which they try to comment out portions of code that already contain comments. When that happens, C compilers inevitably choke and return compilation errors. What usually happens is that the compiler starts a comment with a `/*` symbol, ignores the next `/*` symbol, ends the comment with the first `*/` symbol that it encounters, and then informs you that the next `*/` symbol doesn't have a match.

C programmers learned long ago that they could remedy this situation with a simple hack. You can nest C comments—in a manner of speaking—by sprinkling the preprocessor directives `#if ... #endif`, `#ifdef ... #endif`, and `#ifndef ... #endif` liberally throughout your programs. These directives don't exactly comment out unwanted code, but they do force the compiler to ignore blocks of code that already contain comments. As you know, preprocessor directives were never really intended to serve as comment delimiters—but, hey, it works, and it's the only thing that's worked until now.

## A Better Way

Now, fortunately, C++ has come up with a better way. In C++, you can write one-line comments that are preceded by the two-character combination `//`. And you can nest as many one-line comments as you like inside the block-comment delimiters `/*...*/`. You can start a comment that begins with `//` anywhere on a line, and you never have to worry about balancing a `//` symbol with another `//` symbol. Unless you specify otherwise, a one-line comment always ends at the end of the line it's on.

When C programmers first learn about C++'s new `//` comments, they usually start using them immediately. One-line comments eliminate nested-comment compilation errors forever, and they help prevent the abuse of preprocessor directives.

**WARNING—BE CAREFUL WITH BACKSLASHES**

You can turn a one-line comment into a multiline comment by placing the line-continuation character \ at the end of the line on which the comment appears. But if you do that, be careful; placing the symbol \ between the end of a one-line comment and a newline character can produce results that you might not expect. For example, consider the following code segment:

```
printf(" The amount is %d", // \
     6);
```

When you compile this code, the two slash marks in the first line `//` cause all further text on the same logical line to be regarded as a comment. The backslash character at the end of the first line `\` then joins that line to the next line. Consequently, the characters `6);` on the second line are regarded as part of the comment that begins on the first line. That means the line being compiled has no ending parenthesis and no terminating semicolon, so compilation fails.

Because of effects such as this, the safest rule to follow is to avoid the use of the line-continuation character `\` in any line that includes a one-line comment.

## Mixing C-Style and C++-Style Comments

Because C++ is a superset of C, both old-style C comments and new-style C++ comments work in C++ programs. The program in Listing 2.2 shows how. The Visual C++ compiler ignores all comments when it compiles this program, so all the program does is print two lines of text to standard output (normally, the screen).

### Listing 2.2. Varieties of C/C++ comments.

```
// 0202.CPP
// The Wrath of Zalthar

/******* THIS IS THE WRATH OF ZALTHAR PROGRAM ******/
/* ======== THIS CODE IS NOT COMMENTED OUT. ====== */

// THE WRATH OF ZALTHAR
// A Sample C++ Program

#include <iostream.h>
```

*continues*

**Listing 2.2. continued**

```
// Function prototype
void Display(char *lineToPrint);

int main()
{
      Display("THE WRATH OF ZALTHAR"); // program title
      Display("Copyright 19XX, [Your Name Here]");
      return 0;
}

void Display(char *lineToPrint)     // called by main()
{
      cout << lineToPrint << "\n"; // stream statement
}

/* ---------------------------------------------*/
```

# Keywords

There are 32 reserved words that have special meanings in C. These 32 words are called *keywords*. All 32 of the keywords used in C are also used in C++, and C++ has 16 new keywords.

Five C++ keywords are not implemented in Visual C++. Conversely, the Visual C++ compiler recognizes 20 special keywords that are not official C++ keywords and that may not be recognized in other implementations of the language.

## C++ Keywords: The Complete List

Table 2.1 lists all keywords that are defined in C++. The 16 keywords that are used in C++ but not in C are printed in **boldface**. The 5 keywords that are not implemented in Visual C++ are printed in *italics*.

**Table 2.1. C++ keywords.**

| *Keyword* | *Type* | *Description* |
|---|---|---|
| ***asm*** | special | Identifies assembly language code in a source code program. Not used in Visual C++; included in the Visual C++ list of reserved words only for compatibility with other implementations of C++. In Visual C++, use the `__asm` keyword instead. |
| auto | specifier | Specifies that a variable is automatic, or local. |
| break | statement | Causes a jump to the statement following the innermost `do`, `for`, `switch`, or `while` statement. Also used to exit from a `switch` statement. |
| case | label | Marks labels in a `switch` statement. |
| ***catch*** | statement | Specifies that a function is willing to try to handle an exception. |
| char | type specifier | Identifies a `char` type. |
| **class** | type specifier | Identifies the `class` data type. |
| const | type qualifier | Identifies a `const` object. |
| continue | statement | Begins the next iteration of a `do`, `for`, or `while` loop. |
| default | label | Marks code in a switch statement that executes when no `case` label matches the `switch` expression. |
| **delete** | operator | Deallocates memory. |
| do | statement | Forms iterative loops when used with `while` statement. |
| double | type specifier | Identifies a `double` data type. |
| else | statement | Identifies an expression to be executed when an `if` expression is false. |
| enum | type specifier | Identifies an `enum` data type. |

*continues*

**Table 2.1. continued**

| *Keyword* | *Type* | *Description* |
|---|---|---|
| extern | specifier | Identifies an object that is defined in another translation unit or in an enclosing scope. |
| float | type specifier | Identifies a `float` data type. |
| for | statement | Executes a statement a specified number of times, based on the value of an expression. |
| **friend** | access specifier | Permits a specified object to have access rights to private and protected members of another object. |
| goto | statement | Transfers control to a specified statement identified with a label. |
| if | statement | Causes code to execute if an expression is true. |
| **inline** | specifier | Identifies a function as an `inline` function. |
| int | type specifier | Identifies an `int` data type. |
| long | type specifier | Identifies a `long` data type. |
| **new** | operator | Allocates memory. |
| **operator** | specifier | When used with an operator, overloads the operator or specifies that the operator is overloaded. |
| **private** | access specifier | Identifies members of a class as having `private` access. |
| **protected** | access specifier | Identifies members of a class as having `protected` access. |
| **public** | access specifier | Identifies members of a class as having `public` access. |
| register | specifier | Identifies a variable as a `register` variable. |
| return | statement | Stops executing the current function and returns control to the calling function. |

| *Keyword* | *Type* | *Description* |
|---|---|---|
| short | type specifier | Identifies a `short` data type. |
| signed | specifier | Specifies that a variable is `signed`. |
| sizeof | operator | Computes the size of a block of data. |
| static | specifier | Specifies that a variable is `static`. |
| struct | type specifier | Identifies a `struct` data type. |
| switch | statement | Performs a multiple branch, depending on the value of an expression. |
| ***template*** | specifier | Specifies how to make a family of related classes. |
| **this** | specifier | The name of a special pointer to an object for which a member function is called. |
| ***throw*** | statement | Offers an exception to any function that may be able to handle the exception. |
| ***try*** | statement | Identifies a function as a function that is willing to try to handle an expression. |
| typedef | specifier | Identifies a user-defined data type. |
| union | type specifier | Identifies a `union` data type. |
| unsigned | specifier | Specifies that a variable is `unsigned`. |
| **virtual** | specifier | Identifies a function as being `virtual`. |
| void | type specifier | In a function definition, specifies that a function passes no parameters or has no return type. When the `void` keyword is used in a pointer definition, as in `void *pvData;`, that denotes that the pointer points to an arbitrary typed object. Any valid pointer can be cast as or passed as a parameter of type (`void*`). It can then be cast back to any valid pointer type. |
| volatile | type qualifier | Identifies a `volatile` object. |
| while | statement | Executes a statement until an expression evaluates to 0. |

> **NOTE—WHEN UNDERSCORES PRECEDE KEYWORDS**
>
> Notice that every Microsoft-specific keyword in Table 2.1 is preceded by two underscore characters (__). The use of two underscore characters preceding a keyword is reserved for use by Visual C++. When you create your own keywords, you should refrain from using a single underscore followed by a lowercase letter to avoid possible conflicts with current or future keywords reserved for use by the compiler. For more information on leading underscores, see the section in this chapter titled "Using Underscore Characters with Microsoft Keywords."

## Keywords Not Implemented in Visual C++

Five keywords that are part of the C++ language are not implemented in Visual C++. These five keywords were not included in the original version of C++, but were subsequently added to the language. They may be implemented in future versions of Visual C++.

One keyword not implemented in Visual C++ is the specifier `template`, which identifies a family of related classes. The other C++ keywords not implemented in Visual C++ are `catch`, `throw`, and `try`, three statements used in exception handling (situations in which errors are detected). When exception-handling keywords are used in a program, functions in the program can attempt to handle the exception that has arisen rather than immediately returning an error message.

Instead of relying upon the `catch`, `throw`, and `try` keywords defined in other implementations of C++, Visual C++ provides three exception-handling macros that are defined in the Microsoft Foundation Class (MFC) libraries. These three macros—named `CATCH`, `THROW`, and `CException`—are described in the *Class Libraries Reference* manual that comes with the Visual C++ compiler.

Table 2.2 lists the C++ keywords not implemented in Visual C++.

**Table 2.2. Keywords not implemented in Visual C++.**

| *Keyword* | *Type* | *Description* |
|---|---|---|
| *asm* | special | Identifies assembly language code in a source code program. |
| catch | statement | Specifies that a function is willing to try to handle an exception. |
| template | specifier | Specifies how to make a family of related classes. |
| throw | statement | Offers an exception to any function that may be able to handle the exception. |
| try | statement | Identifies a function as a function that is willing to try to handle an expression. |

**NOTE—USING UNDERSCORE CHARACTERS WITH MICROSOFT KEYWORDS**

In your C++ programs, every keyword that is unique to Visual C++ should be preceded by two underscore characters. For backwards compatibility, Visual C++ does support single-underscore versions of Microsoft-specific keywords. However, the ANSI C standard requires double underscores to precede non-ANSI keywords, so the double-underscore format for Microsoft-specific keywords is preferred.

Six Microsoft-specific keywords—`near`, `far`, `huge`, `cdecl`, `fortran`, and `interrupt`—can be written with no leading underscores at all. Again, however, the double-underscore format is preferred.

In programs compiled with the `/Za` (ANSI compliance) compiler option, every Microsoft-specific keyword must be preceded by a double underscore.

## Keywords Unique to Visual C++

The keywords in Table 2.3 are recognized by Visual C++, but are not standard C++ keywords and may not be recognized by other C++ compilers.

**Table 2.3. Microsoft-exclusive C++ keywords.**

| *Keyword* | *Description* |
|---|---|
| `__asm` | Embeds assembly language in a C or C++ program. Used in Visual C++ instead of the standard C++ keyword `asm`. |
| `__based` | In 16-bit compilations. Used as an address qualifier when a data item or a function is declared; specifies that the address of the item is expressed as a 16-bit offset within a specified base segment. In 32-bit compilations. Types that are based on a pointer are considered 32-bit offsets to a 32-bit base. |
| `__cdecl` | Identifies a function or variable that uses the C naming and calling conventions. (During function calls, arguments are pushed on the stack from right to left; names are case-sensitive and an underscore prefix is added to each name.) |
| `__emit` | Embeds machine code in a program. (Strictly speaking, `__emit` is not a keyword; rather, it is a pseudo-instruction for the Visual C++ inline assembler. It is not supported for 32-bit compilations.) |
| `__export` | Identifies a function or data item that is exported from a dynamic link library (DLL). |

| *Keyword* | *Description* |
|---|---|
| `__far` | An address qualifier indicating that full 32-bit segment:offset addressing is used for a function or a variable. |
| `__fastcall` | Identifies a function that uses the `fastcall` calling convention, which passes arguments in the registers for faster function calls. |
| `__fortran` | Identifies a function or variable that uses the FORTRAN and Pascal calling conventions. (In the FORTRAN/Pascal-style calling convention, arguments are pushed on the stack from left to right and names are converted to all uppercase.) FORTRAN and Pascal calling conventions are identical, so this keyword has the same effect as the `__pascal` keyword. |
| `__huge` | Identifies a data item that may exceed 64K in size and must be addressed using 32-bit segment:offset address. |
| `__inline` | Identifies an `inline` function. (Used in C but not in Visual C++. In Visual C++, use the `inline` keyword instead.) |
| `__interrupt` | Identifies a function as an interrupt handler, forcing the compiler to generate entry and exit code that meets the requirements of interrupt handlers. |
| `__loadds` | Forces the compiler to load the 80X86 data segment register (the DS register) with a specified value before calling a function. (The previous value of DS is restored before the function returns.) |
| `__multiple_inheritance` | When a pointer to a member of a class is declared before the class is defined, the class can be declared as a `__multiple_inheritance` class. This lets you control code that the class declaration generates on a class-by-class basis. |

*continues*

**Table 2.3. continued**

| *Keyword* | *Description* |
|---|---|
| `__near` | Identifies a function or a data item that is in "near" address space, and therefore must be accessed using only its 16-bit offset address. |
| `__pascal` | Identifies a function or variable that uses the Pascal and FORTRAN calling conventions. (In the FORTRAN/Pascal-style calling convention, arguments are pushed on the stack from left to right and names are converted to all uppercase). Pascal and FORTRAN calling conventions are identical, so this keyword has the same effect as the `__fortran` keyword. |
| `__saveregs` | Forces the compiler to generate code to save all CPU registers before a function is executed and to restore the registers when the function ends. |
| `__segment` | Identifies a variable that is capable of holding a 16-bit segment address; a Microsoft-specific data type. |
| `__segname` | Specifies the name of a segment. |
| `__self` | Name of the segment where a based pointer is stored. |
| `__single_inheritance` | When a pointer to a member of a class is declared before the class is defined, the class can be declared as a `__single_inheritance` class. This lets you control the code that the class declaration generates on a class-by-class basis. |
| `__stdcall` | Identifies a function that follows a standard calling convention (similar to the `__cdecl` keyword, except that a `__stdcall` function contains built-in capabilities for type-checking arguments). |

| *Keyword* | *Description* |
|---|---|
| `__virtual_inheritance` | When a pointer to a member of a class is declared before the class is defined, the class can be declared as a `__virtual_inheritance` class. This lets you control the code that the class declaration generates on a class-by-class basis. |

# Identifiers

In C++, as in C, *identifiers* are the names that you supply for variables, types, functions, and labels in a program. In other words, an identifier is a word that is used to identify a specific instance of typed data. Specifically, an identifier is a sequence of characters that can specify the following things:

- A variable name.
- A class, structure, or union tag.
- An enumerated type.
- A member of a structure, union, or enumeration.
- A function.
- A typedef name.
- A label name.
- The name of a macro.
- The name of a macro parameter.
- In object-oriented programs, a class, an object that belongs to a class, a member variable, or a member function.

Some identifiers in this list are treated differently in C++ than in C. Identifiers that are handled differently in C and C++ are examined in this chapter—except for classes, objects, and members of objects, which are object-oriented topics and are examined in later chapters.

Identifiers have several properties, including types, storage classes, and scopes. Data types are examined in this chapter; storage classes and scopes are covered in Chapter 5.

> **NOTE—LENGTHS OF IDENTIFIERS IN VISUAL C++**
>
> The physical lengths of C and C++ data types are machine-specific, so some of the data types used by Visual C++ to program MS-DOS computers are different from corresponding types used in other programming environments.
>
> In Visual C++, identifiers can be extraordinarily long; although it seems incredible, the first 247 characters of an identifier in Visual C++ are significant. However, in function identifiers, this restriction applies to the function's "mangled" name; that is, the extended name that the compiler assigns to function identifiers so that it can distinguish between overloaded functions that have the same name. In Visual C++, when the compiler has "mangled" a function name, the mangled name can be no more than 247 characters long.

# Data Types

C++ supports all the fundamental data types that are standard in C—plus several more. Also, C++ uses some of C's familiar data types in new and different ways. For example, an enumeration (`enum`) is a full-fledged data type in C++. That means that once you initialize an enumerator, you can refer to it by its identifier name alone, without bothering to use the `enum` keyword.

Structures have also been enhanced in C++. In C, a `struct` is not a data type, but merely a template that makes it more convenient to group sequences of data. In C++, a `struct` is a distinct data type. So, once you define a `struct` in C++, you can refer to it solely by its identifier name, without having to use the `struct` keyword. Examples of enumerators and `struct` variables are provided later in this section.

Another data type that has new capabilities is the `union` type, which now has a new subtype called an *anonymous union*. This enhancement to the `union` data type is described under the heading "Unions" in this section.

## Classes

The single most important feature of C++ is its use of a new, user-defined data type called a `class`. Classes are modeled after `struct` types, but they have a host of new features. For example, classes can contain functions as well as data; they can conceal data from functions that are defined in other classes or in other parts of a program; they can inherit behaviors from other classes; and they can pass behaviors down to other classes.

The `class` data type—the key to object-oriented programming—is introduced in Chapter 10, "Object-Oriented Programming." Classes are not covered in detail in this chapter because it focuses on the non-object-oriented features of C++.

## char Types

C++ has corrected a fairly serious deficiency of C by improving and clarifying the handling of character data. In C, as you may know, a `char` never was really a full-fledged data type. One shortcoming of C is that it has no such thing as a true character constant. In C, although the constant `'c'` looks like a character constant, it's really an integer constant. Consequently, in C, the expression `sizeof('c')` and the expression `sizeof(1)` produce the same result—which, in a 16-bit implementation, is not 1 but 2. A more familiar shortcoming of C, perhaps, is the automatic promotion of all `char` types to `int` types when they are passed to functions or used in expressions.

### Enhancements to char Types in C++

C++ has eliminated these shortcomings. In C++, character constants really are character constants: `sizeof('c')` produces a result of 1, and `char` expressions and `char` arguments never lose the `char` types; they are never automatically elevated to `int` types.

Another improvement is that in C++ there are three character types: `unsigned char`, `signed char`, and `char`. This enhancement lets designers of compilers implement `char` optimally for specific machines. But no matter how `char` is implemented, in C++ `char` is a distinct type.

When you aren't concerned with the arithmetic properties of character data—which is probably the case most of the time—you can simply use the `char` type. But when you do care about arithmetic properties, you can use either a `signed char` or an `unsigned char` type—your choice—and be assured that your programs will be portable and predictable.

### char Types in Visual C++

In Visual C++, `char` and `signed char` are the same data type: specifically, a 1-byte type that stores the ASCII value of a typed character. Visual C++ also supports the `unsigned char` type. In Visual C++, the `char` (or `signed char`) data type uses seven bits to store character data and uses one bit as a sign bit. Therefore, the `char` data type can represent 128 typed characters.

In the Microsoft implementation of C++ , the `unsigned char` data type uses 8 bits to store character data and doesn't have a sign bit. Therefore, the `unsigned char` data type can represent 256 characters: the basic 128-character ASCII character set and an extended character set that is available on IBM Personal Computers and PC-compatibles.

The basic and extended character sets that are available in IBM PCs and PC-compatibles are listed in Appendix A.

## Integer Types

Visual C++ has four integer types: `int`, (or `short int`), `unsigned int`, `long`, and `unsigned long`. Table 2.4 lists the sizes of these types and the ranges of values that each type can store.

**Table 2.4. `int` data types.**

| *Type* | *Size* | *Range* |
|---|---|---|
| int (or short int) | 2 bytes | –32,768 to 32,767 |
| unsigned int | 2 bytes | 0 to 65,535 |
| long | 4 bytes | –2,147,483,648 to 2,147,483,647 |
| unsigned long | 4 bytes | 0 to 4,294,967,295 |

## Floating-Point Types

Visual C++ has three floating-point data types: `float`, `double`, and `long double`. These three types comply with IEEE (Institute of Electrical and Electronics Engineers) specifications.

### Type float

The `float` data type holds a 4-byte, single-precision value consisting of:

- A sign bit.
- An 8-bit, excess-127 binary exponent.
- A 23-bit mantissa.

The mantissa represents a number between 1.0 and 2.0. Because the high-order bit of the mantissa always is 1, that bit is not stored. This representation yields a range of approximately $3.4 \times 10^{-38}$ to $3.4 \times 10^{38}$, with at least seven digits of precision.

### Type double

The `double` data type stores a double-precision value that is eight bytes long. The `double` type contains 64 bits: one for the sign, 11 for the exponent, and 52 for the mantissa.

The format of the `double` data type is similar to the format of the `float` type, except that the `double` type has an 11-bit, excess-1023 exponent and a 52-bit mantissa, plus the implied high-order 1 bit. This format yields a range of approximately $1.7 \times 10^{-308}$ to $1.7 \times 10^{308}$, with at least 15 digits of precision.

### Type long double

In Visual C++, the `long double` data type has 80 bits: one bit for the sign, 15 bits for the exponent, and 64 bits for the mantissa. The range of type `long double` is $3.4 \times 10^{-4932}$ to $1.2 \times 10^{4932}$, with at least 19 digits of precision.

## Aggregate Types

In C++, aggregate data types include arrays, `enum` types, structures, unions, and classes. All of these data types except classes are described under the headings that follow. The `class` type is introduced in Chapter 10, "Object-Oriented Programming."

## Enumerations

Enumerations have been around a long time, but they not have been very popular among C programmers. That isn't surprising; there isn't much value in using enumerations in a weakly typed language such as C. But enumerations are enhanced in C++ and actually are quite useful in C++ programs.

In both C and C++, an *enumeration*—declared with the keyword `enum`—is a list of consecutive integer constants, each one of which has a user-assigned variable name. When the name of one of the fields in an `enum` variable appears in a program, the compiler substitutes the field's integer value for the specified field name.

Listing 2.3 is a simple example of the use of enumerators. In this example, `customer` is an enumerator in which the fields `domestic`, `Canadian`, and `Japanese` equate to the integers 0, 1, and 2, respectively.

### Listing 2.3. An `enum` variable in C.

```
// 0203.CPP
// A Sample C++ Program

#include <stdio.h>

enum customer {domestic, Canadian, Japanese};

int main()
{
    enum customer myCustomer;

    printf("The customer's nationality is Nationality No. %d.\n",
          Japanese);

    return 0;
}
```

In the program in Listing 2.3, the field `domestic` equates to the integer 0, the field `Canadian` equates to the integer 1, and the field `Japanese` equates to the integer 2. Therefore, the program prints the following line on-screen:

```
The customer's nationality is Nationality No. 2.
```

Although the program in Listing 2.3 works in both C and C++, the C++ language once again offers a better alternative. In C, when you declare you want to define an instance of an enumerator variable, you must precede its name with the keyword `enum`. This is not necessary in C++. In C++, you can write the program shown in Listing 2.3 as shown in Listing 2.4.

#### Listing 2.4. An enum variable in C++.

```
// 0204.CPP
// A Sample C++ Program

#include <iostream.h>

enum customer {domestic, Canadian, Japanese};

int main()
{
    customer myCustomer;
    int n = Japanese;
    cout << "The customer's nationality is Nationality No. "
       << n << ".\n";

    return 0;
}
```

Listing 2.4 also shows how you can convert an enumeration into an integer. However, you cannot convert an integer to an enumerator unless you use a cast.

The main difference between C-style enumerators and C++ enumerators is that in C++, the tag name of an enumeration is a type name. This feature lets you use an `enum` tag name to declare an enumeration variable, in the same way that you can use a `struct` tag name to declare a structure. Furthermore, in C++, each enumeration is its own type—which makes the `enum` a type-safe tool in C++.

The program in Listing 2.5 is a more ambitious illustration of how `enum` can be used in a C++ program.

#### Listing 2.5. Using an enumerator.

```
#include <iostream.h>

enum playerClasses { WARRIOR, GNOME, WIZARD };
char *className [3] = { "WARRIOR", "GNOME", "WIZARD" };

char *PrintClassStr(int playerClass)
{
     return className[playerClass];
}

int main()
{
```

*continues*

**Listing 2.5. continued**

```
     char *aString = PrintClassStr(WIZARD);
     cout << aString << '\n';
     return 0;  // In Visual C++, the main() function
                // returns an integer value
}
```

The first line of Listing 2.5 declares an `enum` variable named `playerClasses`. The `playerClasses` variable is an enumerated list of names. When the `enum` list is compiled, the compiler assigns the name `WARRIOR` a value of 0. The name `GNOME` is assigned a value of 1, and the name `WIZARD` is assigned a value of 2.

In the second line of the program, an array of strings named `className[]` is declared. In this array, `className[0]` is the string `"WARRIOR"`, `className[1]` is the string `"GNOME"`, and string `className[2]` is the string `"WIZARD"`.

The first function in the program, named `PrintClassString()`, takes an integer variable as a parameter and returns a pointer to a string. Because the `enum` variable named `playerClasses` has assigned integer values to the names `WARRIOR`, `GNOME`, and `WIZARD`, any of those three names can be passed in lieu of literal numbers to `PrintClassString()` function.

For example, the `main()` function of the program passes the identifier `WIZARD` (which has a value of 2) to `PrintClassString()`. In response, `PrintClassString()` prints the word `WIZARD` to standard output (normally, the screen).

Another difference in the way that `enum` types are handled in C++ and the way they're handled in C is that C++ has tightened the rules governing what you can do to enumerators. In C++, you can perform only one operation on an `enum`: an assignment. That means that you cannot perform arithmetic operations on `enum` types in C++.

The following short program shows a typical use of `enum` that is legal in C but *not* in C++. Some C++ compilers—for example, the Apple Macintosh MPW (Macintosh Programmer's Workshop) compiler—issue a warning but build the program. The Visual C++ compiler happily compiles the program in C, but doesn't compile it at all in C++; instead, it balks and generates error messages.

```
// ENUM.C
// Works in C, but not in C++!!

enum abils {
     strength, dexterity, charisma, intelligence};
```

```
int main()      /* this code works in C, but not in C++! */
{
     enum abils s = strength;
     s--;
     s = 4;
     return 0;
}
```

In this C-language function, the arithmetic operations `s--` and `s = 3` are allowed, but this is not necessarily good news. A close examination reveals that each of these arithmetic operations gives s an illegal value; both `s--` and `s = 4` result in a value for `s` that lies outside the range of the `abils` enumerator.

Fortunately for enumerator fans, this situation cannot arise in a C++ program. If there's some reason that you must perform arithmetic on a value that's part of an enumeration, you must perform a type-casting operation to let the compiler know what you're doing. For example, this is how you might write the program shown in the previous example:

```
enum abils {
     strength, dexterity, charisma, intelligence};

int main()
{
     abils s = strength:     // enum keyword not needed; in C++,
                             // abils is a type name
     inti = s;
     i --;
     i = 4;
     return 0;
}
```

If you use a technique like the one shown in the last example to change the value of an enumerator item, be careful; explicitly casting an integer into an enumeration is not guaranteed to be safe. If the integer you want to assign is outside the range of the enumeration, or if the enumeration contains duplicate values, the result of the cast is left undefined.

## Arrays

In C++, as in C, an *array* is a set of variables made up of a collection of elements with the same type. You can initialize an array by specifying a list of values, with the values separated by commas and the whole list enclosed in curly braces. For example:

```
int myArray[12] = {3, 9, 4, 93, 297};
```

The first element in an array has an offset of 0, the second element an offset 1, and so on, with the offset of each consecutive element incrementing by one. Thus, in this example, the first element (the number 3) in `myArray` is `myArray[0]`, the second element (the number 9) is `myArray[1]`, and the fifth element (the integer 297) is `myArray[4]`.

In C++, you can allocate memory for an array with the `new` operator, and you can free the memory when it is no longer needed by using the `delete` operator. The `new` and `delete` operators are described in more detail in Chapter 9.

## Structures

In C, a *structure* (declared with the keyword `struct`) is not a data type, but is merely a template for storing a collection of data that can have various types. In C++, however, a structure is an actual data type.

This difference has important effects on the way structures are referred to in C and C++ programs. In C, when a structure is declared, subsequent references to the structure must include the keyword `struct`. In C++, once a structure is declared, it can be referred to by its name alone, without the keyword `struct`.

There is one other important difference between C++ and C structures: in C, a structure can hold only data; in C++, a structure can hold functions as well as data. In this respect, a C++ structure is similar to a C++ class. Classes are examined more closely in Part II, which begins with Chapter 10.

### Declaring and Referring to Structures in C and C++

In both C and C++, a structure has this general form:

```
struct tag {
     type variableName
     ...
};
```

In C, the keyword `struct` identifies this kind of declaration as a structure declaration. The word *tag*, which is optional, assigns a unique name to the particular structure being declared. Next comes a list of variable declarations specifying the collection of data that the structure contains.

## NOTE—DECLARATIONS AND DEFINITIONS

In C++, as in C, a *declaration* introduces a name to the compiler and tells the compiler something about that name.

This is a structure definition:

```
struct AnExample
{
   int aField:
   int anotherField;
};
```

This is a structure declaration:

```
AnExample JustTesting;
```

A *definition*, in contrast, is a complete description of an element in a program. A definition tells the compiler everything there is to tell about a name, leaving nothing unsaid. Every name that is used in a program must have a complete definition, but must be defined only once.

This is a definition of a variable:

```
x = 24;
```

Sometimes a declaration can also be a definition. This statement declares and defines a variable in one step:

```
int x = 24;
```

It is important to note that in C++, a definition does not always reserve space in memory. Although the definition of a variable or a function does reserve space in memory, just as it does in C, a definition of a class, a `struct`, a `union`, or an `enum` does not. In C++, the memory needed for a class, a `struct`, a `union`, or an `enum` is allocated not at compilation time (when the class is defined) but at runtime, when objects that are members of the class are created. Objects are covered in more detail in Part II, which begins with Chapter 10.

`Unions` and `enum` data types are described under their own headings in this section.

In C, when you declare a `struct`, the result is a structure *template* that can be used from that point on as a type specifier. In C++, the declaration creates a variable with the data type `struct`. This new data type can then be used to declare a variable of the new type (and the appropriate storage is allocated).

Unless a structure contains functions—which is possible in C++, but not in C—the declaration of a C structure looks just like the declaration of a C++ structure. For example, this structure definition is valid in both C and C++:

```
struct date {
     int month;
     int day;
     int year;
};
```

In a C program, the structure created by this declaration can be referred to in any of these ways:

```
static struct date = {7, 4, 1776};
struct date dates[15];
struct date *datePtr = dates;
```

Note that in each of these three declarations, the keyword `struct` is used.

In a C++ program, because `struct` is an actual data type, you can refer to the `date` structure without using the `struct` keyword, as these examples show:

```
static date = {7, 4, 1776};
date dates[15];
date *datePtr = dates;
```

### Adding Functions to C++ Structures

In C++, a structure can hold functions as well as data. Listing 2.6 shows how a structure containing a function can be used in a C++ program.

#### Listing 2.6. Adding a structure to a function.

```
// 0206.CPP
// Adding a structure to a function

#include <iostream.h>

struct Birthday {
    int month, day, year;
    void display(void); // a function to display the date
};
```

```
void Birthday::display(void)
{
    static char *mon[] =
    {
     "January", "February", "March", "April", "May",
        "June", "July", "August", "September", "October",
        "November","December"
    };

    cout << mon[month-1] << ' ' << day << ", " << year;
}

int main()
{
    static Birthday theDate = {7, 4, 1776};
    cout << "The nation was born on ";
    theDate.display();
    return 0;
}
```

## Storing Bit Fields in struct Variables

Both C and C++ provide a syntax that lets you store sequences of unformatted bits in `struct` variables. A sequence of unformatted bits stored in a struct is called a *bit field*.

You can declare a bit field in a `struct` using the following syntax:

```
struct TimeStamp {
     unsigned day   :    6;
     unsigned month :    5;
     unsigned year  :    8;
     unsigned time  :    16;
};
```

This code fragment reserves six bits in memory for a `struct` element named `day`; five bits for an element named `month`; eight bits for an element named `year`; and 16 bits for an element named `time`. When a structure such as the one shown in the code has been defined, you can access any of its bit fields with the dot operator (`.`) or the arrow operator (`->`), in the same way that you would access any `struct` element. For example, you can access the bit field named `TimeStamp.day` as follows:

```
TimeStamp stamp;
cout << stamp.day << '\n';
```

This statement uses the IOSTREAM.H variable `cout` to print the bit field `stamp.day`, followed by a return character, to standard output (normally, the screen).

For more information on using bit fields in Visual C++, see the Microsoft documentation on Visual C++.

> **NOTE—SCOPE RESOLUTION IN C++**
>
> In Listing 2.6, note that the declaration of the `display` function uses the syntax `Birthday::display`. The character combination `::`—known in C++ as the *scope resolution operator*—is an assignment operator for functions that are declared in structures. You can use the scope resolution operator in the same way that you use a dot (`.`) as an assignment operator for an element in a structure, or the character combination `->` as an assignment operator for a pointer to an element in a structure.
>
> These three operators—the dot (`.`), the scope resolution operator (`::`), and the pointer operator (`->`)—are used in C++ classes in the same way that they're used in C++ structures. You'll learn more about this topic in Part II, which begins with Chapter 10.

### How the Program Works

In Listing 2.6, the `main()` function declares a `Birthday` structure named `theDate` and initializes it with a value. The `main()` function then calls the `Birthday::display` function. Finally, the `Birthday::display` function displays this message:

```
The nation was born on July 4, 1776.
```

Besides the features described in this section, C++ structures have several other enhancements—for example, the access specifiers `private`, `protected`, and `public`. These are covered in Part II, which begins with Chapter 10.

## Unions

The `union` data type permits data of more than one length to be stored in the same memory space. When you define a `union`, the memory assigned to it is long enough to hold the longest data element that the union can contain. This is a declaration of a union:

```
union EPluribusUnion {
     short shortVal;
     long longVal;
     double doubleVal;
};
```

The declaration of a union looks much like the declaration of a struct. However, the declaration of a union and the declaration of a struct have different results.

## How Elements of a union Are Stored

When you declare a struct, each element in its member list has a different starting address in memory, and all of its elements can reside in memory at the same time. When you declare a union, each element in its member list has the same starting address, and only one element can reside in memory at any given time. The data type a union contains can be an array or a class, as well as a simple data type.

Figure 2.1 shows how the elements of a union are stored in memory. The union shown in the illustration has three elements: a short data type named shortVal, a long data type named longVal, and a double data type named doubleVal.

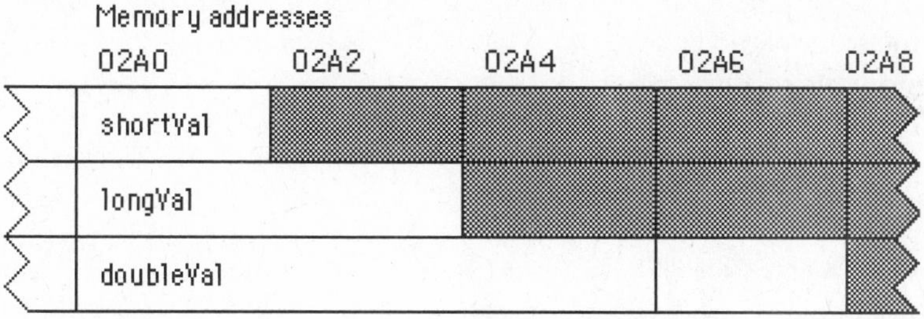


*Figure 2.1. A* union.

In an object-oriented program, a union such as the one shown in Figure 2.1 can have many of the features of a class, including member functions, access restrictions, constructors, and destructors. (These features of classes are described in Part II.) Members of a union cannot have constructors or destructors (described in Chapter 14). If a class is a member of a union, that class cannot have constructors or a destructor.

A union cannot be derived from a class, and it cannot serve as a base class. (Classes and base classes are described in Part II.)

## Anonymous unions

Besides the ordinary unions described under the previous heading—the kind of unions with which C programmers are familiar—C++ provides a special kind of union called an anonymous union. The most obvious difference between an anonymous union and an ordinary union is that an anonymous union doesn't have a tag name. However, there are other differences between ordinary unions and anonymous unions that are important. This is a declaration of an anonymous union:

```
union    {          // anonymous union
    int anInt[2];
    div_t div_result;
};
```

The anonymous union declared in this code fragment—like an ordinary C-style union—has two elements, only one of which can reside in memory at any one time. However, as you can see, this anonymous union has no tag name. One of the union's elements is an integer array named anInt[]. The other element is a structure of type div_t—a type defined in the MATH.H file that's provided with Visual C++.

A div_t structure is made up of two short integers: one named div_t.quot and the other named div_t.rem. The MATH.H function div() uses div_t structures to store the results of division operations. When you call div() to divide two numbers, the function stores the quotient of the division operation in div_t.quot. The remainder is stored in div_t.rem.

### Using Anonymous unions

In object-oriented programs, anonymous unions are more suitable for use in classes and struct variables than are ordinary unions. When you declare an anonymous union, you're declaring an object—not just a data type. Thus, in an object-oriented program, there are no surprises in the behavior of an anonymous union; they behave just like other classes.

Because an anonymous union has no tag name, you can access the variables it contains directly, without having to specify the name of the union—it has none—and without having to use the dot operator (.) syntax or the arrow operator (->) syntax, both of which you must use when you want to access the elements of an ordinary union. Because the names of the elements in an anonymous union can be used by themselves in a program, they are not allowed to conflict with other identifier names that are defined in the same scope.

### Restrictions on the Use of Anonymous Unions

Other restrictions of anonymous unions:

- An anonymous `union` must be declared as `static` if it is global; that is, if it is declared in file scope.
- In an object-oriented program, a `union` can have only public members; declaring private or protected members in an anonymous `union` can generate compilation errors.
- An anonymous `union` cannot have member functions.

Listing 2.7 is an example of how an anonymous`union` can be used in a C++ program.

#### Listing 2.7. An anonymous `union`.

```
// 0207.CPP
// Using anonymous unions

#include <iostream.h>
#include <stdio.h>

int main()
{
    union    {       // anonymous union
        int anInt[2];
        div_t div_result;
    };

    cout << "Enter an integer: " << '\n';
    cin >> anInt[0];            // number to be divided

    cout << "Divide by: " << '\n';
    cin >> anInt[1];            // divisor

     div_result = div(anInt[0], anInt[1]);

    cout << "Quotient: " << div_result.quot << '\n';
    cout << "Remainder: " << div_result.rem <<  '\n';

    return 0;
}
```

Listing 2.7 uses the MATH.H function `div()` to divide two numbers. The program then prints out the results of the division operation.

The numbers to be divided are stored in the memory locations named `anInt[0]` and `anInt[1]`. When the `div()` function divides the two numbers, it stores the results of its division operation in the memory locations named `div_t.quot` and `div_t.rem`—which have the same addresses as the locations `anInt[0]` and `anInt[1]`.

Thus, when the division operation is complete, its results are stored in the same memory locations that held the numbers to be divided before the division operation began.

## Pointer Types

In both C and C++, a *pointer* is a variable that holds the address of an object. Because of the peculiarities of the MS-DOS development environment, Visual C++ has some very special rules about pointers. In Visual C++, the physical length of a pointer can vary, depending on the *memory model* of the program. The memory model in which a program is written affects not only the length of the pointers used in the program, but also the format in which addresses are stored in pointers.

For more information on memory models and how they affect the use of pointers, see Chapter 9, "Managing Memory."

## Reference Types

A *reference*—a new data type introduced with the premiere of C++—is a 16-bit or 32-bit quantity that holds the address of an object but behaves syntactically not like a pointer, but like an ordinary variable. In other words, a reference is a pointer that can be treated as a variable in a C++ program. A reference contains an address, just as a pointer does. However, you can use a reference without having to be concerned with using the indirect kinds of constructs that you must use when you work with pointers.

In C++, you can define a reference in this fashion:

```
int anInteger = 20;
int& aReference;
```

After this code has been executed, you can use the reference `aReference` in the same way that you would use the value 20 or the variable *`anInteger`*. The reference `aReference` doesn't contain the value 20; instead, it contains the address of the variable *`anInteger`*. But you can use it in the same way that you would use the variable *`anInteger`*.

References are so important in C++ that a major section in Chapter 4 is devoted to describing them.

# Type void

The `void` data type has several uses. This data type can be used in function headers, or it can be used to create *generic pointers,* that is, pointers that are undefined or have arbitrary values.

In C++, as in C, you can use the `void` data type to specify that a function returns no value. For example, this function declaration specifies that `AFunction()` returns no value:

```
void AFunction(int x):
```

This declaration states that `AFunction` is a function that takes an `int` argument and does not return a value. When you define `AFunction` using this syntax, the body of `AFunction` can contain a return statement but can't contain a return expression. If the declaration had specified that `AFunction` return a non-`void` result, the function would have to return a value, not simply return.

## Specifying void as a Function Parameter

In C++, the `void` data type also clears up an ambiguity that has always existed in function declarations written in C. In the C language, the following function declaration may seem ambiguous because it is a legal C/C++ function prototype:

```
int AFunction();
```

This declaration is ambiguous in C because the function being declared may or may not take parameters. Although an empty pair of parentheses follows the name of the function, that doesn't mean anything in a C program. To a C compiler, it could simply mean that the author of the program didn't bother to type in the parameters that `AFunction` requires.

This ambiguity is not allowed in C++. In a C++ program, when you follow the name of a function with an empty pair of parentheses, that syntax has a specific meaning; it means that the function being declared *does not have* parameters. If a function does take parameters, you must place their data types and names between the parentheses that follow the name of the function being declared, so the C++ compiler will know what the function's parameters are.

When you declare a function that takes no parameters in C++, you can place the word `void` between the parentheses that follow the name of the function, or you can leave it out. Either way, it's clear that the function takes no parameters. Thus, in C++, neither of the following two function declarations takes parameters, and the two declarations are equivalent:

```
int AFunction();
int AFunction(void);
```

In these declarations of `AFunction()`, the keyword `void` inside the parentheses is optional. Many C++ programmers use the word `void` for an argument list when they declare functions that take no arguments because this makes it clear to anyone reading the program that the function *does* take no arguments. This practice is technically not necessary, but it makes the meaning of the function declaration unmistakably clear.

## Using void Pointers

Some specific rules govern the use of `void` in C++. For example, you can't declare an ordinary variable to be a `void` data type, because a variable must have a value. Hence, this kind of statement is not allowed:

```
void x;    // this statement is meaningless and not allowed
```

However, when you declare a pointer, you *can* declare its data type to be void. For example, the following declaration creates a generic pointer—that is, a pointer that can subsequently be set to point to any type of data:

```
void *aPointer;     // declares a generic (void) pointer
```

When you use the syntax shown here to create a `void` pointer, you can set the pointer to point to any data type. For example, you can create a `void` pointer named `aPointer` and then set the pointer to point to an integer variable:

```
void *aPointer;     // declare a generic pointer
int x;           // declare an integer variable
aPointer = &x; // pointer now points to integer variable
```

You also can create a `void` pointer and then assign it the value of another pointer, which can point to any data type. For example:

```
double *doublePtr;         // declare a double pointer
double doubleNr = 4.1416;      // declare a double variable
doublePtr = &doubleNr;         // pointer points to a double
void *aPtr;                    // declare a generic pointer
aPtr = doublePtr;              // now it also points to double
```

In C++, you can perform a casting operation to convert any pointer to a `void` pointer. You then can perform another casting to convert the pointer that had been cast to a `void` back into its original type. If the pointer holds an address when you perform these conversions, C++ guarantees that you can perform the operations without losing the information stored in the pointer. Thus, when you execute this program:

```
// FUN WITH POINTERS

#include <iostream.h>

int main()
{

     double *doublePtr;              // declare a double pointer
     double doubleNr = 4.1416;       // declare a double variable
     doublePtr = &doubleNr;          // pointer points to a double
     void *aPtr;                     // declare a generic pointer
     aPtr = doublePtr;               // now it also points to double
     doublePtr = (double *)aPtr;     // cast double pointer to void
     cout << *doublePtr;
     return 0;
}
```

The following result is printed out:

```
4.1416
```

### NOTE—UNDERGROUND PROGRAMMING NOTES

By stretching the envelope of operations such as those described, C++ programmers have come up with various unauthorized programming techniques that involve the use of `void` pointers. For example, this is a commonly used technique for adding a value to a `void` pointer by using a "cast to `char`" construct:

```
voidPtr = (char *)voidPtr + 1;
```

And this is a construct that you can use to assign a value by dereferencing a `void pointer`:

```
*(doublePtr *)voidPtr = 4.1416
```

Techniques such as these generally are not recommended for mainstream program development, but they can come in handy when you're writing such things as debuggers, browsers, and test tools—and want more control over the tools you're developing than ordinary programming techniques provide.

## The typedef Declaration

In a C or C++ program, you can create a new data type by using the keyword `typedef`. With a `typedef` declaration, you can specify an alternative name for any type already defined by C or C++, or for any type you choose to declare. When you declare a `typedef`, the data type you specify becomes a new type.

The simplest syntax for a `typedef` definition is:

```
typedef type_name alternate_name;
```

where *`type_name`* is an exiting type name and *`alternate_name`* is an alias for *`type_name`*.

This is an example of a simple `typedef` statement:

```
typedef int COUNT;
```

This declaration lets a program use the name `COUNT` as a more descriptive alias for data type `int`. For example, this statement:

```
COUNT n1, n2, n3, total;
```

is a more customized equivalent for this statement:

```
int n1, n2, n3, total;
```

In C, `typedef` declarations often are used to assign names to struct templates. For example, the following declaration creates a `struct` of a new type named `Abils`:

```
typedef struct abilities {
     int strength;
     int dexterity;
     int charisma;
     int intelligence;
} Abils;
```

Once this declaration has appeared in a program, you no longer have to use the keyword `struct` to refer to the variables that are elements in the `struct` named `Abils`. Instead, you can refer to them directly, as in this `main()` function:

```
int main()
{
     Abils myAbils;
     Abils *myAbilsPtr = &myAbils;
     myAbils.strength = 24;
     myAbilsPtr->dexterity = 23;
     return 0;
}
```

This example works just as well in C++ as it does in C. However, there is no need to use a `typedef` declaration in this way in C++. In C++, `struct` already is a full-fledged data type, so you don't need to use the keyword `struct` to refer to the elements in a `struct` variable anyway. The only reason you might want to `typedef` a `struct` in C++ is to maintain backwards compatibility with old code written in C.

# Summary

Although most people who've heard of C++ think of it as an object-oriented language, C++ actually is a hybrid language—part object-oriented language and part C. This chapter focused on the new features of C++ that aren't directly related to object-oriented programming: one-line comments, new keywords, new identifiers, new data types, and data types that may look familiar but are handled in new ways in the C++ language.

In Chapters 3 through 9, many of the topics that were introduced in this chapter are covered in more detail. You'll start learning about the object-oriented features of Visual C++ in Part II, which begins with Chapter 10.

Chapter 3

# Type Qualifiers

C++ has many data types, but only two *type qualifiers:* `const` and `volatile`. A variable that is designated `const` cannot be modified (even though it's technically still a variable), and a variable that is designated `volatile` can be protected from being unexpectedly changed by procedures that are not under the control of the executing program—for example, interrupt service routines.

The `volatile` qualifier works the same way in C++ as it works in C. However, the `const` qualifier has been enhanced in C++ and is much more important in C++ than it is in C.

The `const` modifier can be used to define the constants that appear in a C++ program, in much the same way that constants in C programs are defined with the preprocessor directive `#define`. In C++, the `const` qualifier is a better mechanism for declaring constants than is the `#define` directive because `const` variables have data types and therefore are subject to type-checking—and that, of course, reduces the likelihood of programming errors.

This chapter describes the `const` and `volatile` type qualifiers and explains how they're used in C++ programs.

# The const Qualifier

A `const` is a value (to avoid confusion, I won't call it a variable), which, once set, cannot be modified.

When you create a `const` object, there are two equally important rules you must follow:

- First, you *must* initialize a `const` when you declare it (that makes sense; a `const` without a value would be quite useless).
- Second, once a `const` is initialized with a specified value, its value cannot be changed.

Another thing to remember: You can create a constant variable in C++, but you can't create a variable constant. By preceding a variable declaration with the `const` keyword, you can turn the variable into a `const`. However, once a `const` has been declared and initialized, it cannot be modified. Therefore, there is no such thing as a variable constant.

The program presented in Chapter 2 in Listing 2.1, contains a number of `const` objects. For instance, `lineToPrint` is a pointer to a string that is a constant:

```
void      PrintData(const char *lineToPrint);
```

Note that, in this example, the string to which `lineToPrint` points is a constant, but the pointer that's named `lineToPrint` is not a `const`; `lineToPrint` is free to point to another string, but the string that it points to can't be changed.

## Uses of the const Qualifier

You can use the `const` qualifier to declare:

- Any fundamental or aggregate data type.
- A pointer to an object of any type.
- A data type created with `typedef` declaration.

If you don't specify a data type when you create a `const` object, the compiler creates an integer `const` by default.

## const Objects in C and C++

The `const` qualifier isn't really an innovation of C++. In both C and C++, the `const` qualifier is used to initialize constants. It has always existed in C, but has been considerably enhanced in C++.

As you'll see in Chapter 7, "Compiling Visual C++ Programs," you can define constants in both C and C++ with the preprocessor directive `#define`. However, constants created with `#define` directives have no specific data type and therefore cannot be type-checked by the compiler. In contrast, with the `const` qualifier, you can create constants that do have data types and therefore can be type-checked, reducing programming errors.

Once you declare a `const`, it appears in your program's symbol table, complete with a name, a type, and a value. That can reduce the chance of programming errors, because it means that the compiler can perform type-checking on a `const` object—something it cannot do with a constant created with the `#define` directive.

Using `const` objects also can make debugging easier because a debugger can easily find a `const` whose name and characteristics appear in a program's symbol table.

Because `const` objects are more powerful in C++ than constants created with the `#define` directive, you should *not* create the constant by invoking the preprocessor's define directive, as you would in C:

```
#define A_VALUE 100;      // don't do it this way in C++
```

Instead, this is the way to create a constant in a C++ program:

```
const int STRLEN = 255;  // this is the way to create a constant
```

This statement declares an integer `const` named `STRLEN` and initializes the `const` with a value of 255.

## Advantages of Using const Objects

These are some other advantages of using `const` objects in C++ programs:

- A `const` has a specific data type and can therefore be type-checked by the compiler, reducing the likelihood of compilation errors.
- You can access a `const` object with pointers.
- Constants declared with the `const` qualifier are accessible to the CodeView symbolic debugger.

**Listing 3.1. Using a constant to specify the size of an array.**

```
// 0301.CPP

// THE WRATH OF ZALTHAR
// A Sample C++ Program

#include <iostream.h>

#define POPEYE true


int main()
{
    char *const NL = "\n";
    const int size = 32;

    cout << "THE WRATH OF ZALTHAR" << NL;
    cout << "Copyright 19XX, [Your Name Here]" << NL;
    return 0;
}
```

## Enhancements to const Objects

The `const` qualifier is not new in C++: it also exists in C. However, because of several important differences, constants created with the `const` qualifier are much more powerful in C++ than they are in C.

Because C++ has added new capabilities to `const` objects, constants created with the `const` modifier can be used in C++ programs in place of constants created with the preprocessor directive `#define`.

In C, the primary purpose of the const modifier is to create constant identifiers that can be placed in read-only memory (ROM) because it is guaranteed that the values of these identifiers will not be changed.

When you declare a const in C, the compiler merely stores it in a special area of memory where read-only data is stored. This treatment prevents you from using a const in certain ways; for example, in C, you can't initialize a const with a variable returned by a function. In C++, you can.

## New Features of const Objects

Here are the main differences between const objects declared in C++ and const objects declared in C:

- In C++, the default linkage for a const variable is internal. That means, unless you specify otherwise, a const object is recognized only inside the source file in which it is defined. Because the default linkage for a const variable is internal, you can place const declarations in header files, the same way you can place a #define directive in a header file. In C, placing a const directive in a header file generates a linker message if the header file is included by more than one module in a program.
- You can declare an array to be a const in C++—another practice that is not allowed in C. Once you declare and initialize a const array, the values of the elements in the array cannot be modified.
- In C++, you also can use const variables in pointer declarations. For example, this statement declares that a const named strPtr is a pointer to a constant string:

  ```
  const char *strPtr = aStr;
  ```

- You can use const variables in many other ways in C++. For example, this declaration of a function named SafeFunc prevents the function from modifying one of the parameters that is passed to it:

  ```
  int SafeFunc(const struct protectedStruct *protectedStructPtr);
  ```

- In C, you can't substitute a constant for an expression. But C++ treats a const as if it were a true constant expression. So in C++, wherever you can use a constant expression, you can use a const variable.
- Because you can't substitute a constant for an expression in C, you can't use a const variable in place of an expression for a purpose such as

specifying the size of an array. So this pair of statements, which would not be allowed in C, works fine in C++:

```
const int STRLEN = 255;
char sl[STRLEN];
```

## Initializing a const with a Function

In C++, you can initialize a `const` with a value returned by a function. So this short program works in C++:

```
int GetValue()
{
    return 500;
}

int main()
{
    const int x = GetValue();
    return 0;
}
```

Once you execute this program, you can't modify the variable `x` because it's a constant. Any attempt to modify `x`—for example:

```
x++        // NO! x is a const!
```

generates a compilation error.

## Functions That Return const Objects

Functions can return `const` objects in C++. For example:

```
const int ReturnAVal()
{
    return 5000;
}

int main()
{
    int hey = ReturnAVal();
    hey++;
    return 0;
}
```

When this program has been executed, the variable hey can't be modified because it's a constant. Any attempt to modify hey—for example, this statement:

```
hey++              // ERROR! hey is a const!
```

generates a compilation error.

## Passing a const Array to a Function

You can pass a const array to a function. For example, this statement declares a function that takes a const array as an argument:

```
void DisplayArray(const double myArr[], int n);
```

In this function declaration, myArr[] is a pointer that points to const data. This means you can pass the DisplayArray() function an array named myArr[]. The myArr[] array can contain any number of elements you like. However, you cannot later change the number of elements in the array. For example, this code fragment sets up a three-element myArr[] array and calls the DisplayArray() function:

```
double myArr[] = { 1000, 2000, 3000 };
DisplayArray(myArr[], 3);
```

The first of these statements creates myArr[] and initializes its elements to the values 1000, 2000, and 3000. Once that initialization has taken place, the values of the elements in myArr[] cannot be modified. Hence, after these statements are executed, the following statement generates a compiler error:

```
myArr[1] += 5000;    // ERROR! myArr[1] is a constant!
```

## How the const Modifier Works

Because the default linkage for const objects is internal, a declaration of a const object written in this format:

```
const int SIZE = 37;
```

is equivalent to a statement written in this format:

```
static const int SIZE = 37;
```

This means that the const object named SIZE is accessible only inside the current file.

This limited accessibility is usually just what you want. Because a `const` object has internal linkage, you can place the declaration and initialization of a `const` object in a header file. You then can include that header file in several source files in the same program.

After the preprocessor includes the contents of the header file in each source file, each source file contains its own copy of the `const` object's declaration and initialization. Because a `const` object can't be modified once it's defined, this scheme works fine; each source file gets a copy of the `const`, and there are no linking errors.

## Altering the Linkage of a const Object

If you want to override this process and give a `const` object `extern` linkage so it will behave like a global constant, C++ provides a mechanism that allows you to do just that. But be careful; the results may not be what you expect.

To change the linkage of a `const` object from internal to external (so the `const` will be accessible to a file other than the one in which it is declared), all you have to do is explicitly use the storage class specifier `extern` when you declare the `const`. For example:

```
extern const int SIZE = 37;
```

By substituting the keyword `extern` for the keyword `static`, this statement declares the `const` named `SIZE` to be exportable. That makes `SIZE` accessible from other translation units but causes linking errors if you place the definition of the `const` in a header file and then try to include that header file in multiple source files.

The reason: If you declare a `const` to be external and the preprocessor places a copy of the declaration of the `const` in more than one source file, the following definition winds up in multiple source files:

```
extern const int SIZE = 37;
```

If the `const` named `SIZE` has internal linkage—which it has, by default—none of the source files can see the definition of the `const` that appears in the other source files. However, if the `const` is declared to have external linkage—as in this initialization—all the source files can see the copies of the definition that are included in the other source files. And, because C++ allows a `const` object to be initialized only once, the result is a linking error.

# Using a const in a Pointer Declaration

In C++, you can initialize a `const` in much the same way that you would initialize any variable; you can even initialize a `const` by making the constant a pointer, as shown in Listing 3.2.

## Listing 3.2. Using `const` in a pointer declaration.

```
// 0302.CPP

// THE WRATH OF ZALTHAR
// A Sample C++ Program

#include <iostream.h>

char *const NL = "\n";

int main()
{
    cout << "THE WRATH OF ZALTHAR" << NL;
    cout << "Copyright 19XX, [Your Name Here]" << NL;
    return 0;
}
```

When you use the `const` qualifier in a pointer declaration, the placement of `const` is significant. That's because the placement of the qualifier helps determine whether the pointer will point to a `const`, or will itself be a `const`.

For example, the following code fragment declares `myPtr` as a `const` that is a pointer to a string:

```
char *const myPtr = buffer1;  // myPtr is a constant pointer to a string
*myPtr = 'c';                 // It's legal to change the string
myPtr = buffer2;              // ERROR! Trying to change a constant
```

You can modify the string to which `myPtr` points, but because `myPtr` is a `const`, you cannot modify `myPtr` itself by making it point to another string.

The following code fragment is different from the previous one because it declares `myPtr` to be a pointer to a constant that's a string:

```
const char *myPtr = buffer1;  // myPtr is a pointer to a constant string
myPtr = buffer2;              // It's legal to change the pointer
*ptr = 'c';                   // ERROR! Trying to change a constant
```

In this case, you can modify `myPtr` so that it points to another string, but you cannot modify the string to which `myPtr` points because that string is a constant.

## Using Constants with Pointers

Using constants with pointers can be tricky because you can use the `const` keyword with pointers in two different ways:

- One way is to make a pointer point to a constant object. This prevents a program from using the pointer to change the *value* to which it's pointed.
- Another way is to make the pointer itself constant. This prevents you from changing the *address* to which it's pointed.

## When Is a const Not a const?

When you use this syntax to create a pointer that points to a constant:

```
int weight = 315;
const int *ptr = &weight;
```

the value the pointer points to isn't actually a `const`; it's just a `const` as far as the pointer is concerned. For instance, in this example, the pointer named `ptr` points to an integer variable named `weight`. To the pointer named `ptr`, `weight` is a constant because it's referred to as a `const` in the second line of the example. Actually, though, `weight` is only an integer variable because it's defined this way in the first line of the example:

```
int weight = 315;
```

Because `weight` is only an ordinary `int` variable that looks like a `const` to `ptr`, you can change the value of `weight` directly with a statement like this:

```
weight = 715;  // OK, because weight is really just an int variable
```

But, as you have seen, you can't change the value of `weight` indirectly through the `ptr` pointer:

```
*ptr = 714;     // NOT! because ptr points to a constant integer
weight = 124;  // OK! because weight is not declared as a const
```

## Pointing to the Address of a const

A different situation arises when you assign the address of a `const` variable to a pointer that points to a `const`:

```
const float height = 5.20;
const float *ptr = &height;
```

In this example, `ptr` is a pointer that points to an integer `const` named `height`. Because `height` is declared as a constant, it is a true constant. So you can't change the value of `height` directly, and you can't change it through its pointer:

```
height += 1.14;          // CAN'T DO THIS—height is a constant
*ptr = 6;                // NO!!! ptr points to a real constant
```

This is something else you can't do:

```
const float height = 4.50;    // INVALID
float *ptr = &height;         // INVALID TOO
```

C++ doesn't allow these statements because they could let you do tricks that you shouldn't be permitted to do. If you could assign the address of `height` to the pointer named `ptr`, you could use `ptr` to alter the value of `height`. That would violate the `const` status of `height`, so C++ doesn't let you assign the address of a `const` to a pointer that points to something that isn't a `const`.

When you have mulled over that point, consider these statements:

```
int strength = 28;
const int *ptr = &strength;
```

When these statements have executed, you can't change the value of the variable `strength` through its constant pointer, as you have seen. However, you can change the value of `ptr` by making it point to a new address. So this is okay:

```
int charisma = 24;
ptr = &charisma;            // okay; ptr now points to a new address
```

Remember, however, that you still can't use `ptr` to change the value that it points to (which is now 24).

## Where to Put a const

By repositioning the `const` keyword in a statement, you can prevent a program from changing the value of a pointer to the constant:

```
int pumpkin = 18;
const int *pp = &pumpkin;      // pointer to const int
int *const pp2  = &pumpkin;    // const pointer to int
```

In the second of these two lines, pp is declared as a pointer to a constant integer. In the third line, pp2 is declared as a constant pointer to an integer. As you might guess, these two declarations are not the same—and have very different results.

The point to ponder in this example is that the keyword const occupies different positions in the second and third lines of the example. After the code has executed, pp2 can point only to pumpkin because pp2 is a const pointer to an integer. However, you can use pp2 to alter the value of pumpkin because pumpkin is an integer variable.

The declaration in the second line of the example does not allow you to use pp to alter the value of pumpkin, but it does permit you to make pp point to another location. In short, pp2 and *pp both are constants, but *pp2 and pp are not constants, so the results of all these operations are predictable.

## A const Pointer to a const Object

As a final illustration, these statements declare a const pointer to a const object:

```
double duty = 4.0E28;
const double *const roster = &duty;
```

After these statements execute, roster can point only to duty, and roster cannot be used to change the value of duty because both roster and *roster are constants.

# The volatile Qualifier

When you write a routine that can be accessed from outside your program—for instance, by an interrupt routine—you may want to protect variables in your program from being unexpectedly modified by procedures that are not under your program's control.

By declaring a variable to be volatile, you can prevent the compiler from optimizing your code (that is, from making any assumptions about the value of a variable from one line of code to another). That can safeguard variables in your code from being changed by procedures that are not in your program.

When you want to safeguard an identifier from being included in the optimization process—to prevent its value from being changed unexpectedly from one line of code to another—declare the variable using the `volatile` qualifier, as in these examples:

```
volatile char delicateChar;
volatile int  delicateInt;
volatile int *delicateIntPtr;
```

Once you declare the variables `delicateChar` and `delicateChar` to be volatile, as in these examples, you can be sure the compiler won't depend on their being set to specific values when it optimizes the code that contains the variables.

## How volatile Works

The `volatile` qualifier warns the compiler that the value associated with the name that follows can be modified by actions other than those contained in the currently executing user-written program. Therefore, the `volatile` keyword can be useful when you want to declare objects in shared memory, which can be accessed by multiple processes, or in global areas used for communication with interrupt service routines.

When the state of an object can change unexpectedly, the only way a program can ensure predictable performance is to declare the object to be `volatile`.

In Visual C++, when an identifier is declared to be `volatile`, the value of the identifier is reloaded from memory each time the identifier is accessed by the program, even when this operation has no effect. This system greatly reduces the kinds of optimizations that the compiler can make in user-written code when the code is compiled.

The `volatile` qualifier has usage rules that are similar to those of the type qualifier `const`. The qualifier `volatile`, like the qualifier `const`, can appear only once in a declaration and must be placed after the type it qualifies.

When you declare an identifier using the `volatile` qualifier, the qualifier tells the controller that the identifier's value may be changed without notice by something that is beyond the control of the program in which the identifier appears, such as a concurrently executing thread or an interrupt servicing routine.

Declaring an object to be `volatile` can have a significant effect on how much the code that contains the value can be optimized. However, when the state of an object can change unexpectedly, declaring the object to be `volatile` is the only way that you can ensure the integrity of your program.

## Declaring an Object to Be Both const and volatile

You can declare an identifier to be both `const` and `volatile`. This combination guarantees that the identifier cannot be changed in any way—either from the currently executing user-written program, or by actions that are beyond the control of the currently executing user-written program.

The following code fragment shows how identifiers can be declared both `const` and `volatile`:

```
// make aChar a const
const char aChar = 'C';

// make aCharRef a const reference to a const
const char * const aCharRef = &aChar;

// pointer is volatile, object is const
const char * volatile VolPtrConstObj;

// pointer is const, object is volatile
volatile char * const ConstPtrVolObj;

// object and pointer are both volatile
volatile char * volatile aCharRef;
```

# Summary

In C++, the keywords `const` and `volatile` are known as *type qualifiers*. In C++, as in C, a variable that is designated `const` cannot be modified, and a variable that is designated `volatile` can be protected from being unexpectedly changed by procedures that are not under the control of the executing program—for example, interrupt service routines. To take advantage of the capabilities of a `volatile` variable, the compiler must reload the value from the `volatile` variable from memory when it is referenced.

The `volatile` modifier is used the same way in C++ as in C. But the `const` modifier has been enhanced in C++ and can be used to define the constants that are used in a program, much like the `#define` preprocessor directive is used in C++. In C++, it's better to define constants with `const` than with `#define` because `const` variables have a data type and therefore are subject to type-checking. Constants defined with the `#define` directive have no particular type and therefore are more likely to cause programming errors.

This chapter described the `volatile` and `const` type qualifiers and explained how they're used in C++. More differences between C and C++ that are not directly related to object-oriented programs are covered in Chapters 4 through 9.

Chapter 4

# Variables

Variables and constants are the most basic elements of the C++ language. In C++, as in C, variables and constants are manipulated by operators to form expressions, and expressions are grouped together to form functions.

Variables and constants were introduced in Chapter 2, "A Better C—Plus," and constants were examined in more detail in Chapter 3, "Type Qualifiers." This chapter focuses on variables.

In C++, as in C, a *variable* is an identifier with a value that can change during the execution of a program. There are several differences between the way variables are handled in C++ and the way they're handled in C. For example:

- In C, you must declare all automatic (local) variables at the beginning of the function in which they appear. In C++, local variables don't have to appear at the beginnings of functions; they can appear at the point at which they first are needed in a program.

- In C, there is no clear distinction between *initialization* (giving a variable an initial value) and *assignment* (assigning a value to a variable later on). In C++, this distinction is clear—and important.

Another important new feature of C++ is the addition of a brand new type of variable called a *reference*. In C++, a reference is a variable that holds the address of an object but behaves syntactically as if it were a nonpointer variable. References can provide you with many of the advantages of pointers, but without the extra overhead and code clutter that can result from using pointers.

This chapter focuses on C++ variables. It covers the declaration of variables in C++, the differences between initialization and assignment of values to variables, and the use of references in C++ programs.

# Declaring Variables in C++

In a C++ program, local variables don't have to be declared at the beginnings of functions; they can appear where they first are needed in the program, if the programmer feels that's more convenient. For example, consider the variable *n* in Listing 4.1:

### Listing 4.1. Declaring a variable in C++.

```
// 0401.CPP
// Declaring a variable in C++

// This program lists your system's environment variables.
// If you use the /n command-line option, the program also
// prints line numbers.

#include <iostream.h>
#include <string.h>

int main(int argc, char *argv[], char *envp[])
{
     int nrOfLines = 0; // Default is no line numbers.

     if(argc == 2 && strcmp(argv[1], "/n") == 0)
          nrOfLines = 1;

     int n = 0;
     while (envp[n] != NULL) {
```

```
        if(nrOfLines)
         cout << n;
        cout << ": " << envp[n++] << "\n";
    }
    return 0;
}
```

In this example, the variable *n* is declared where it first appears—just before the `while` loop inside the `main()` function, and not at the beginning of the `main()` function, where it would have to be declared in a C program.

C++ permits this kind of declaration because it often makes more sense to declare a variable where it's needed than it does to declare all of the local variables that are going to appear in a function at the beginning of a function. When you're forced to declare all of a function's local variables at the beginning of a function, it's easy to lose track of where the variables first appear. That can make your source code hard to understand.

Also, when you delete a section of code from a function, you can easily forget to remove any variables that may be used only in that section—and, as a result, you can wind up with useless variables that take up valuable space in a program without doing anybody any good.

Unfortunately, declaring variables where they first appear can lead to pitfalls, too. If you declare every variable in a function where the variable first turns up, you can wind up with code that's sprinkled with variable declarations. When that happens, it can become a task to track down the places where important variables are declared.

The best way to resolve this dilemma is simply to use common sense. A good rule of thumb is to declare all of the *important* local variables in a function in the same place—at the beginning of the function—and to declare less important variables, such as those that can be used in short loops and then discarded, where they first appear.

**NOTE—BY THE WAY**

In some versions of C, you declare a global variable more than once, although that doesn't make much sense and isn't a good programming practice. In C++, you can declare a global variable only once, which is as it should be.

# Initialization and Assignment

In C++, as in C, *initialization* is the initial assignment of a value to a variable or a constant. Initialization can take place only once: when an identifier is first declared.

*Assignment* is a different kind of operation. An assignment occurs when the value of an existing variable is changed. Because the value of a constant can't be changed, a constant can't be the target of an assignment operation.

In C, the difference between initialization and assignment is sometimes muddled. For example, in C, these two operations have the same effect, and therefore have traditionally been regarded as being two versions of the same thing:

```
/*** first example ***/
int x;
x = 5;

/*** second example ***/
int x = 5;
```

In C++, these two examples are quite different. The first example declares an integer named x and then *assigns* a value of 5 to x. The second example *initializes* the variable x with a value of 5.

## Initializing Constants and References

The initialization of a const provides a good illustration of how initialization is used in C++. In C++, when a constant is created using the type qualifier const (covered in Chapter 3, the const *must* be initialized to hold a specific value—and that requirement makes sense because a constant that holds no value is useless.

Another rule mandated by C++ is that once a const has been initialized, it cannot be assigned a new value. This is also a sensible rule because a const would not be a constant if its value could be changed.

## Initializing a Reference

In most cases, a reference must be initialized when it is created. (References are described in their own section later in this chapter.) That's because a reference can't exist without a variable to which to refer and cannot be manipulated as an independent entity. Therefore, when you declare a reference, you normally initialize it so it has something to refer to.

There are some exceptions to this rule, however. Specifically, you don't have to initialize a reference when that reference:

- Is declared as a parameter in the declaration or definition of a function (which means that it is initialized when the function is called).
- Is declared as the return type of a function (which means that its value is set when the function returns).
- Is declared as `extern` (which means that it is initialized elsewhere).
- Is a member of a class (which usually means that it is initialized in the class's constructor function; constructors are described in Chapter 14, "Constructors and Destructors").

For more about references, see the section about references later in this chapter.

## Initializing a const

Here's an example of the initialization of a `const`:

```
const int KID_AGE = 10;
```

In this example, once the `const` named `KID_AGE` has been initialized to hold the value 10, it cannot be changed to hold a different value.

## Initializing External Data

The most obvious difference between initialization and assignment is the fact that a `const`—which can be initialized only once—can be the target of an initialization but cannot be the target of an assignment. But there are other important differences between initialization and assignment. For instance, in C++, you can use full expressions to initialize external data (that is, data that is declared as `extern` or is external by default). In C, the only expressions you can use to initialize external data are constant expressions. Thus, expressions such as the following are valid in C++, but not in C:

```
const double e = exp(1.0);
const double pi = acos(-1.0);
```

This enhancement gives external identifiers the same flexibility that has always been available to local identifiers in C. For example, this short program is allowed in C++, but not in C:

```
#include <iostream.h>

inline long GetA() { return 666; }
const long globalConst = GetA();

int main()
{
     cout << globalConst;
     return 0;
}
```

The output of this program is

```
666
```

## Function-Style Initializations

In both C and C++, the = sign often is used to initialize data. That's confusing because the = operator often is called the *assignment operator*. Nonetheless, in C++ as well as C, all three of the following statements are initialization operations:

```
int x = 10;
float y = 141.16;
char c[] = "Zippy";
```

In C++, there's an alternate format for initializing variables that doesn't require the use of the = operator. This alternate syntax is based on a notation style used in Simula, one of the first popular object-oriented languages. The style lets you use parentheses to initialize identifiers. In C++, for example, you can substitute the following statements for the statements in the previous example:

```
int x(10);
float y(141.16);
char c[]("Zippy");
```

Although the first two statements in this example look like functions, they're actually initializations. The third statement, which initializes a character-string array, looks even more bizarre:

```
char c[]("Zippy");
```

## Examples of Function-Style Initializations

One advantage of this new format is that it lets you give multiple values to an object in a single statement—something you can't do in initialization statements that use the = operator. This isn't so important for built-in types, but it can be convenient when you're working with operations involving classes, which often are initialized with several values. For example, if a program contained a `Complex` class type made up of a pair of doubles, like this:

```
Complex n = Complex(2.5, 3.7);
```

you could initialize an object of the `Complex` class with this statement:

```
Complex n(2.5, 3.7);
```

Of course, you're responsible for providing the code implementing your `Complex` class.

Another example of the use of function-style initialization is this short program, which uses the new format to initialize a `struct` named `myCust`:

```
#include <iostream.h>

struct Customer {
     char *name;
     char *address;
     Customer(char *nm, char *addr)
          { name = nm, address = addr; }
};

int main()
{
     Customer myCust("Dr. Strangelove", "USAF\n");
     cout << myCust.name << ", " << myCust.address;
     return 0;
}
```

In this example , the structure named `myCust` is initialized in this statement:

```
Customer myCust("Dr. Strangelove", "USAF\n");
```

This construct is a shortcut for the following style, which is rarely seen:

```
Customer myCust = Customer("Dr. Strangelove", "USAF\n");
```

## Using Function-Style Initializations

Although the function-style initialization syntax can be used to initialize any data type, it's used most often to initialize objects. In the following statement, for example, the string enclosed in parentheses is passed as an argument to the constructor of a class named `FileNameClass`:

```
StringFileNameClass("MYFILE.DAT");
```

(Constructors are described in Chapter 14.) You also can use the function-style initialization format with the new operator. For example:

```
Rect *myRect new Rect(20, 20, 32, 97);
```

## Function-Style Initializations in Function Headers

C++ provides a special syntax for using the function-style initialization format to initialize identifiers used in functions. To use this technique, all you have to do is follow the function's parameter list with a colon and a list of function-style initialization statements. For example, this function header initializes four variables by assigning them values in its header:

```
int strength, charisma, dexterity, intelligence;

InitAbils() : strength(24), charisma(12), dexterity(15),
     intelligence (12)
{
     count++;
}
```

This function definition has the same effect as the following more conventional definition:

```
InitAbils()
{
     strength = 24;
     charisma = 12;
     dexterity = 15;
     intelligence = 12;
     count++;
}
```

When you use function-style initializers to initialize the variables in a function header, you can substitute variables for the literal numbers used in the previous example. For instance:

```
InitAbils(int stren, int charis, int dext, int intel) :
     strength(stren), charisma(charis), dexterity(dext),
```

```
    intelligence (intel)
{
    count++;
}
```

Writing function headers using this format may seem odd until you get used to it, but many C++ programmers like the technique because it separates the initialization of variables and constants from the body of a function.

### When Not to Use Function-Style Initializations

There are many other ways to use function-style initializations in C++ programs. For example, as you'll see in Chapter 16, "Operator Overloading," you can use function-style initializers to write *copy constructors* (which make copies of objects) and to create special functions that can convert back and forth between data types, including user-defined classes. As you will see in later chapters, you also can use function-style initializers to initialize variables in function headers.

Although it's possible to use the function-style syntax to assign values to simple data objects, that practice is not generally recommended. A function-style initialization statement has the same effect as a conventional C-style initialization statement (the kind that uses the = operator), but is less familiar to most programmers—and is even ambiguous because it looks like a function.

In nonobject-oriented operations, deciding when (and if) you should use function-style initializations is largely a matter of personal taste. Generally, you should stick with traditional-style initialization operations in traditional-style situations; I cannot think of a good reason to make an ordinary initialization look like a function, unless you want to win an obfuscated C++ contest. If that's what you want, you now know another obscurity you can add to your collection.

## References

A *reference* is a new data type that made its premiere with the introduction of C++. In C++, a reference is a variable that holds the address of an object but behaves syntactically as if it were a nonpointer variable. References can provide many of the advantages of pointers, but without the extra overhead and code clutter that can result from using pointers.

For example, when you want to pass a long data structure as a parameter to a function, passing the structure by value can slow down processing and consume a large amount of memory. An alternative is to pass the function a pointer to the data structure. But to work with pointers, you must use indirection, which adds overhead and complicates and clutters programs.

Sometimes (but not always), a better alternative is to pass a reference. This section tells when you should do that, when you shouldn't, and why.

## Defining a Reference

You can define a reference by following it with the unary operator `&`, as shown in this example:

```
int origValue = 20;
int& refValue = origValue;
```

In this code fragment, `origValue` is defined as an integer variable with a value of 20, and `refValue` is a reference to the variable `origValue`. When a program has executed this fragment, the program can use `refValue` in exactly the same way that it would use the integer variable `origValue`.

Listing 4.2 shows how you can reduce overhead and increase processing speed by using a reference to call a function.

### Listing 4.2. Using a reference in a program.

```
// 0402.CPP
// Reducing overhead with references

#include <iostream.h>

// a big object
struct bigStruct    {
    char longStr[1000];       // much ado about nothing
} structName = {"Pretend this string is a really big object."};

// -- two functions that have the same structure as a parameter
void snailspace(bigStruct vagueVar);        // call by value
void rocketship(bigStruct& vagueVar);       // call by reference

int main()
{
    snailspace(structName);    // have lunch while you do this
    rocketship(structName);    // instant processing
    return 0;
}
```

```
// Call-by-value function
void snailspace(bigStruct vagueVar)
{
    cout << '\n' << vagueVar.longStr;
}

// Call by reference function
void rocketship(bigStruct& vagueVar)
{
    cout << '\n' << vagueVar.longStr;
}
```

In Listing 4.2 a structure named `bigStruct` holds a character string named `longStr`. This string is 1,000 characters long. If the string were a much larger object, the program would show you that it's faster to execute a call by reference than it is to execute a call by value. As the program is currently written, you'll probably have to take my word for that (although you could increase the size of `bigStruct` and add some benchmarking tests). But as it stands, the program still can show you how a call by reference works.

Listing 4.2 contains two functions that print the string in `bigStruct`. Both of these functions are called from the program's `main()` function.

One of the functions that prints the string in `bigStruct` is named `snailspace`. When `main()` calls the `snailspace()` function, `main()` passes the complete 1,000-character string named `longStr` to the `snailspace()` function. The program then prints `longStr` on the screen. If `longStr` were a really big object, this could take some time.

The other function that prints the string in `bigStruct` is named `rocketship`. When `main()` calls the `rocketship()` function, `main()` passes a *reference* to the 1,000-character string named `longStr` to the `rocketship()` function. Again, if `longStr` were a very large object, this would be a much faster operation than passing the whole string to the `snailspace()` function.

If the `bigStruct` structure in Listing 4.2 were really a large object, the program would demonstrate two advantages of using references to call functions:

- Lower overhead (in terms of both processing speed and memory use).
- The elimination of the cluttered-looking, hard-to-understand programming style that indirection can cause when you use many pointers in a program.

The program in Listing 4.2 also illustrates one hazard of using references in a program. Notice that in the `main()` function, the `snailspace()` and `rocketship()` functions are called using the exact same syntax—event though the `snailspace()` function is called by value and the `rocketship()` function is called by reference.

This really isn't a problem in a short program, but it could be a serious problem in a longer program split into multiple files. And, when you bring the data-encapsulation features of C++ into the procedure, allowing a function to make a call by reference when it doesn't necessarily know that it's doing so could have serious consequences indeed—up to and including program crashes. That's why you must be careful when you use C++ references outside the realm of object-oriented programming.

## Capabilities of References

References were created to combine the simplicity of making calls by value with the speed and efficiency of calling by address. Reference variables offer advantages over pointers in many kinds of situations, but in other situations pointers still are preferred.

Because references combine the capabilities of ordinary variables with the capabilities of pointers, they are quite powerful—so powerful, in fact, that they can be dangerous unless you know what you're doing. (Fortunately, some bugs that used to make them even more powerful have been removed in Visual C++. See note titled "Defusing References," later in this section.) References can be dangerous because C's call-by-reference architecture was designed to help safeguard variables from being changed in ways that are unexpected and hard to track down—and references have the power to undermine that protection if they fall into unskilled hands.

Because of their built-in power, references generally should be used only with `struct` variables and C++ classes—not with the standard C/C++ data types. (An exception to this rule is the practice of using references to return values from functions, a capability that can come in handy no matter what kind of data you're referencing.)

There's another reason not to bother with references when you're working with small, fundamental data types. When you're working with small data types, you can't usually save any overhead by using references; it generally takes just as long to pass a reference as it does to pass the original data type. When you're working with classes, however, a big benefit of references is that they reduce the overhead required to pass parameters to functions.

## Initializing References

Because a reference is not a variable on its own, but merely an alias of a variable, a reference is useless unless it has been initialized.

Although a reference must always be implicitly initialized, there are some situations in which you do not have to initialize a reference explicitly. For instance, you do not have to initialize a reference explicitly if:

- The reference is declared as a parameter in a function declaration. In this case, the value of the reference is established by the caller's argument when the function is called.
- The reference is declared as the return type of a function. In this case, the value of the reference is established when the function returns.
- The reference is declared with the keyword `extern` because it is initialized elsewhere.
- The reference is a member of a class and therefore is initialized in the constructor function of the class. (Classes are covered in Part II, which begins with Chapter 10.)

When you start using references, you might want to keep this checklist handy so you'll know the circumstances under which a reference must be initialized.

**NOTE—DEFUSING REFERENCES**

In some versions of C++ (specifically, those based on Version 2.0 of AT&T C++), there was a hidden danger. Fortunately, this danger was removed in Version 2.1 of AT&T and does not exist in Visual C++.

The danger was this: If a reference type was different from the type of the object with which you initialized the reference, the compiler could not correctly associate the reference with the object. In such a case, the compiler created an object of the type with which the reference was initialized and then referred the reference to this "anonymous" object. This behavior was not what one would ordinarily expect, and almost certainly not what was desired.

Because of this quirk, in the version of C++ that preceded Visual C++, the compiler allowed operations like this:

```
int originalVar = 792;
long& anotherVar = originalVar;
```

As you can see, this example declares an int named originalVar and initializes it with the value `792`. In Version 2.0 of AT&T C++, this code caused the compiler to create a long reference named anotherVar and initialized it to refer to the int. The compiler then created a secret, anonymous long variable with the value `792`. Finally, anotherVar reference was set to refer to this nameless `long` variable.

When this kind of coding was allowed, the resulting reference referred to an integer but behaved like a long integer—a bizarre kind of behavior that could create unforeseen problems and would rarely be useful in a program.

Fortunately, this quirk does not exist in Visual C++. When you attempt this kind of operation in Visual C++, the compiler generates Compilation Error No. C2607: "Cannot implicitly convert an int to a non-`const long&`."

Because of the AT&T 2.0 C++ compiler's willingness to create anonymous constants when there was no data for a reference to point to, the following kind of coding is allowed in some versions of C++:

```
int& nonexistentVar = 2;

nonexistentVar ++;
```

Because this is legal in antediluvian C++, some clever programmers use it as a hack when they want a distant function to modify a local variable. When you attempt such a trick in Visual C++, all you get is Compilation Error No. C2440, "Cannot convert from `const int` to `int near&`."

## References as Aliases

Because a reference is really just an alternate name for a variable, a reference is sometimes referred to as an *alias* for the variable with which it is associated. An alias is a good name for a reference because you can always use a reference in exactly the same way that you can use its associated variable.

However, a reference also has many of the characteristics of a pointer. Because a reference contains an address, just as a pointer does, you can define a reference to hold the same address as a specific pointer by using this syntax:

```
int aValue = 100;
int *aValuePtr = &aValue
int& aReference = aValuePtr;
```

When this code fragment has been executed, the reference named `aReference` holds the same address as the integer pointer named `aValuePtr`. However, because `aReference` is an alias for `aValue`, you can use `aReference` in your program in the same way that you would use `aValue`—for example, both of the following lines increment the value of `aValue`:

```
aValue++;
aReference++;
```

You can accomplish the same result using `aValuePtr`, but you must use indirection:

```
*aValuePtr++;
```

**NOTE—REFERENCES AND OTHER ALIASES**

Although a reference sometimes is referred to as an alias, it actually is a full-fledged data type—not the same kind of alias as the kind you can create by using the preprocessor statement `#define`. The purpose of using a reference is to gain the benefits of using a pointer without requiring the kind of dereferencing notation that pointers require.

Although a reference behaves much like an alias created with the `#define` alias, an alias actually is a real variable. You can tell it's a real variable because, at different times in the execution of a program, a reference can be initialized to refer to different objects.

Listing 4.3 is a more detailed illustration of how you can use `refValue` the same way that you would use `origValue` in a program:

**Listing 4.3. Using a reference variable.**

```
// 0403.CPP
// Using a reference variable

#include <iostream.h>

void main()
{
     int origValue = 100;
     int &refValue = origValue;

     cout << "origValue = " << origValue << ".\n";
     cout << "refValue = " << refValue << ".\n\n";

     cout << "Incrementing refValue.\n";
     refValue++;

     cout << "origValue = " << origValue << ".\n";
     cout << "refValue = " << refValue << ".\n\n";


     cout << "Incrementing origValue.\n";
     origValue++;

     cout << '\n' << origValue;
     cout << '\n' << refValue;
}
```

As Listing 4.3 illustrates, when you perform an operation on a reference—such as `refValue`—the operation has the same effect on the value that it would have if performed on the variable associated with the reference—in this case, `origValue`.

When you execute the program in Listing 4.3, it displays the following output, showing that `refValue` and `origValue` are simply two names for the same item:

```
origValue = 100.
refValue = 100

Incrementing refValue.
origValue = 101.
refValue = 101.

Incrementing origValue.
origValue = 102.
refValue = 102.
```

## Passing References as Parameters to Functions

One of the most important features of references is that they provide a new way to pass arguments to functions. In C (as noted in Chapter 6, "Functions") there are two ways to pass an argument to a function: either by its value or by its address. In C++, there is a third way to pass an argument: by reference.

> **NOTE—A C++ FEATURE**
>
> In C, as you may know, passing an argument to a function by address has traditionally been referred to as passing the argument by reference—but now, in C++, passing an argument by reference has a new (and more precise) meaning. In C++, what once was referred to as passing an argument by reference now is referred to as passing an argument by its address (or, alternatively, by its pointer).
>
> This change in terminology is necessary because the C++ language now has a data type called a reference. A reference is a data type that holds an address—like a pointer—but behaves syntactically as if it were a nonpointer variable. Furthermore, you can pass a reference as an argument to a function in the same way you would pass any other data type. In C++, this is what "calling by reference" means.

## Passing an Argument by Value

In both C and C++, when you pass an argument to a function by its value, the compiler makes a copy of the value specified by the argument and passes the copy, not the original value, to the function. Therefore, the called function cannot modify the actual value that's stored in memory; it can modify only the copy of the value that is passed to it. When you pass an argument to a function by value, you can be assured that the actual value is safe.

Listing 4.4 illustrates a simple call by value. In the example, when the `main()` function calls the function `IncrementCoords()`, it passes the variables `x` and `y` by value. Because the call is by value, `IncrementCoords()` is not granted access to the actual variables `x` and `y`. Instead, `IncrementCoords()` receives copies of `x` and `y` and alters those copies. Run the program and you'll see that when `IncrementCoords()`

has been executed, the x and y variables defined in the main() function are unchanged.

**Listing 4.4. Passing arguments to a function by value.**

```
// 0404.CPP
// Passing arguments by value

#include <iostream.h>

// forward declaration

void IncrementCoords(int a, int b);

main()
{
      int x = 0;
      int y = 0;

      cout << "x = " << x << "\n";
      cout << "y = " << y << "\n\n";

      cout << "Calling IncrementCoords(int x, int y)";
      cout << 'n\';
      IncrementCoords(x, y);

      cout << "Now x = " << x << "\n";
      cout << "and y = " << y << ".\n";

      return 0;
}

void IncrementCoords(int a, int b)
{
      a = a + 20;
      b = b + 20;

      cout << "a = " << a << "\n";
      cout << "b = " << b << "\n\n";
}
```

## Passing an Argument by Address

When you pass an argument to a function by address, the compiler does not make a copy of the argument and pass it to the called function. Instead, the compiler passes the *address* of the actual value stored in memory to the called function. The function then can modify the value that's stored in memory by referencing the data indirectly, through its pointer.

As an example, suppose you wanted to write a function that would increment the x and y coordinates of a window. Using pointers, you could pass the coordinates to a function by their addresses, and the called function then could alter the coordinates by changing the contents of their addresses. Listing 4.5 illustrates this operation.

### Listing 4.5. Passing arguments to a function by address.

```
// 0405.CPP
// Passing a value by address

#include <iostream.h>

// forward declaration

void IncrementCoords(int *a, int *b);

main()
{
      int x = 0;
      int y = 0;

      cout << "x = " << x << "\n";
      cout << "y = " << y << "\n\n";

      cout << "Calling IncrementCoords(int &x, int &y) \n";"
      IncrementCoords(&x, &y);

      cout << "Now x = " << x << "\n";
      cout << "and y = " << y << ".\n";

      return 0;
}

void IncrementCoords(int *a, int *b)
{
      *a = *a + 20;
      *b = *b + 20;
}
```

In Listing 4.5, the addresses of the window's x and y coordinates are passed to the function IncrementCoords(). The IncrementCoords() function then changes the x and y coordinates by changing the contents of their addresses.

## Passing an Argument by Reference

In C++, instead of passing an argument to a function by its value or by its address, there's a third alternative: You can pass it as a reference, as shown in Listing 4.6.

### Listing 4.6. Passing arguments to a function by reference.

```
// 0406.CPP
// Passing arguments by reference

#include <iostream.h>

// calling by reference, c++ style

// forward declaration

void IncrementCoords(int &a, int &b);    // a and b are now references

main()
{
      int x = 0;
      int y = 0;

      cout << "x = " << x << "\n";
      cout << "y = " << y << "\n\n";

      cout << "Calling IncrementCoords(x, y)"
      IncrementCoords(x, y);   // no longer need the & operator

      cout << "Now x = " << x << "\n";
      cout << "and y = " << y << ".\n";

      return 0;
}

void IncrementCoords(int &a, int &b)
{
      a = a + 20;    // don't need the * prefixes
      b = b + 20;
}
```

In Listing 4.6, `IncrementCoords()` is defined as a function that takes two reference variables (`&a` and `&b`) as parameters. Therefore, when the variables `x` and `y` are passed, `IncrementCoords()` treats them as reference variables.

The results of this operation are the same as the results of the operation shown in Listing 4.5: Because the addresses of the window's `x` and `y` coordinates are passed to `IncrementCoords()` by reference, the `IncrementCoords()` function can change the `x` and `y` coordinates by changing the contents of their addresses.

> **NOTE—BY THE WAY**
>
> Niklaus Wirth, the Zurich professor who created the Pascal language, was once asked whether his name was pronounced *Worth* or *Veert.*
>
> He replied: "If you call me by reference, it's *Veert.* If you call me by value, it's *Worth.*"

## How Not to Use References

Although Listing 4.6 shows how a function can alter parameters that are passed to it by reference, it isn't usually a good idea to pass parameters to a function by reference simply so they can be changed. It fact, this can be a dangerous practice. Look carefully at the call to the `IncrementCoords()` function in Listing 4.6, and you'll see why:

```
IncrementCoords(x, y);    // no longer need the & operator
```

Except for the comment at the end of this line of code, there's no way to tell that the statement is a call by reference to the function `IncrementCoords()`. In fact, if this statement were encountered by a C programmer who didn't know anything about C++-style calls by reference, the programmer naturally would assume that the call `IncrementCoords(x, y)` is an ordinary call by value. And, of course, because a function cannot alter a parameter that's passed to it by value, the programmer also would assume that the variables `x` and `y` are safely protected from being altered by the `IncrementCoords(x, y)` function. However, as you saw in Listing 4.6, this assumption is false; because `IncrementCoords()` is a function that's called by reference, `IncrementCoords()` can very easily alter the values of `x` and `y`. And that's where the danger lies.

Because calls by reference look exactly like calls by value—but can alter the parameters that are passed to them—they're fraught with danger. If you start calling functions by reference simply because references are easier to use than pointers, sooner or later someone will mistake one of your calls by reference for a call by value and will write a section of code that inadvertently changes the contents of an apparently safe variable. As you know, that could spell real trouble in a program.

The best way to prevent this kind of error is to resist the temptation to start using references everywhere you once used pointers. As you'll see in later chapters, references are designed primarily to be used in object-oriented programs, in situations where the code clutter and complex indirection rules that result from the use of pointers make pointers difficult to use. In ordinary situations in which it would be almost as easy to use a pointer as to use a reference, you're generally better off using a pointer.

It's also helpful to remember that references are not intended to make it easier to alter arguments that are passed to functions. Therefore, when you write a function that's called by reference (and could therefore endanger variables that are passed to it), you can safeguard those variables simply by declaring them as constants, as in this example:

```
// protecting referenced variables by making them constants
void PrintCoords(const int &x, const int &y);
```

If you take this precaution when you call a function by reference, the function cannot change the contents of its parameters.

## Accessing Elements of a Referenced Structure

When you use a reference to identify a structure, you access elements in the structure with the direct member selection operator (`.`) instead of the pointer member selection operator (`->`). Listing 4.7 shows how to access elements of a referenced structure.

#### Listing 4.7. Accessing elements of a referenced structure.

```
// 0407.CPP
// Accessing elements of a referenced structure
```

```
#include <iostream.h>

void PrintCoords(myRect& a);

struct myRect {
     int xCoord;
     int yCoord;
} theRect = {10, 20};

main()
{
     int x, y;

     x = theRect.xCoord;
     y = theRect.yCoord;

     PrintCoords(x, y);
     return 0;
}

void PrintCoords(myRect& a)
{
     cout << "Rect X =:" << a.xCoord << '\n';
     cout << "Rect Y =:" << a.yCoord << '\n';
}


int main()

{

     PrintCoords(theRect);

}
```

## Writing a Function That Returns a Reference

In C++, a function can return a reference. Listing 4.8 shows how a function that returns a reference might be used in a program that lists certain qualities of characters in the game. To run the program, enter a value ranging from 1 through 5 on the command line (or, if you're using the Visual Workbench, select the Debug command from the Options menu. Then, in the Program Arguments text box, enter an argument ranging from 1 through 5).

### Listing 4.8. Writing a function that returns a reference.

```
// 0408.CPP
// A function that returns a reference

#include <iostream.h>
#include <stdlib.h>

struct qualities {
    int strength, stamina, charisma;
};

// forward declaration
qualities& GetQuals(int n);

qualities playerQuals[] = {
    { 1, 16, 33},
    { 2, 22, 32},
    { 3,  6, 49},
    { 4, 12, 48},
    { 5, 19, 40},
};

int main(int argc, char *argv[])
{
    if (argc > 1)    {
     qualities& quals = GetQuals(atoi(argv[1]));
     cout << quals.strength << '/' << quals.stamina
          << '/' << quals.charisma;
    }
    return 0;
}

qualities& GetQuals(int n)
{
    return playerQuals[n-1];
}
```

When a function returns a reference, the action has a side effect that you might not expect: it lets you use a function on the left side of an assignment statement. Listing 4.9 shows how a reference returned by a function can be used as an `lvalue`.

### Listing 4.9. Using a reference returned by a function as an `lvalue`.

```
// 0409.CPP
// Using a lvalue reference
```

```
#include <iostream.h>

// forward declaration
char &replace(int n);

char str[80] = "Hello, xorld";

main()
{

     replace(7) = 'w'; // replace x with w

     cout << str;;

     return 0;
}

char &replace(int n)
{
     return str[n];
}
```

When you write a function that returns a reference, the function cannot return a reference to a local variable that is defined within the function. For this reason, the following example is not legal:

```
qualities& GetQuals(int n) {
     qualities quals = {6, 14, 33};
     return quals;        // ERROR! Reference to an auto variable
}
```

The problem here is that the variable `qual` goes out of scope when the function returns. Therefore, the function returns a reference to a variable that no longer exists. The Visual C++ compiler may not complain when you execute this kind of function, but the results of calling the function are unpredictable. Sometimes the call may work because the stack location where the automatic variable is stored is still intact when the reference is returned. However, the program can fail if an interrupt servicing routine changes the stack.

## Using References with const Objects

When you combine the `const` qualifier, a reference, and a pointer in a single declaration statement, the syntax can get confusing. In this statement, the pointer is a `const`:

```
int *const x = &y;
```

However, in the following statement, the value the pointer points to is a `const`:

```
const int *x = &y;
```

And, in this statement, both the pointer and the value to which it points are constant:

```
const int *const x = &y;
```

# Summary

This chapter covered some of the differences between the way variables are used in C and the way they are used in C++. For example:

- In C++, you don't have to declare automatic (local) variables at the beginnings of functions. If it seems appropriate, you can declare a variable at the point in a function where it first appears.
- The difference between initialization of a variable and the assignment of a value to a variable is more important in C++ than it is in C—and there are some new techniques for initializing variables in C++.
- C++ has introduced a new data type called a *reference*. A reference is a variable that can be treated as a nonpointer variable but behaves like a pointer. References can provide you with many of the advantages of pointers, but without the extra overhead and code clutter that can result from using pointers. However, because of the way references behave, there are some things that you can't do with references. For example, you cannot:
  - Modify a reference.
  - Perform arithmetic operations on a reference.
  - Assign a value to a reference.
  - Obtain the address of a reference.
  - Compare references.
  - Point to a reference with a pointer.

Chapter 5

# Properties of Variables

Although many of the example programs in this book are so short that they occupy just one file, most C++ programs are made up of a large number of files. To create variables that work together correctly in a program made up of multiple files, you must understand certain important properties of C++ variables, such as *storage class*, *scope*, *linkage*, and *duration*. Those properties are the topic of this chapter.

Two important properties of a variable are its *storage class* and its *scope*. The storage class of a variable determines its lifetime (sometimes called its *duration*), its form of initialization and, in certain cases, its linkage. (The linkage of a variable determines whether it can be accessed from another file.)

The *scope* of a variable specifies the portions of program text from which the name of the variable can be recognized. Thus, the scope of a variable determines where a variable can be used in a program, and where in a program the variable has meaning.

This chapter examines the storage-class and scope properties of variables. It also covers the duration and linkage properties of variables.

# Storage Class

There are four storage classes for data in C++: the *external*, *static*, *automatic*, and *register* storage classes. The storage class that is assigned to an identifier determines three important properties that every variable has: *scope*, *duration*, and *linkage*. These concepts are discussed in the following pages.

The keyword `typedef` sometimes is linked with the storage-class specifiers, but only for convenience. The real purpose of the `typedef` specifier is to create user-defined names for new or existing data types.

If you're an expert C programmer, you may already be familiar with the material in this chapter. However, storage classes, scope, and linkage are so important in object-oriented programs that they are covered here in some detail. Even if you know the material, it probably wouldn't hurt to scan it—just to refresh your memory—before you move on to later chapters.

## The External Storage Class

In C++, just as in C, an *external* (`extern`) *variable* is a variable that can be recognized not only in its own translation unit, but also from any translation unit in a program. An external variable is assigned memory space when a program starts executing, and the variable keeps that storage space for the duration of the currently executing program. In other words, an external variable is a *permanent* variable that doesn't go out of existence until the program quits.

When you declare a variable outside any function, that variable is assigned the external storage class by default. However, to access the variable from a translation unit other than the one in which it is declared, you must also declare it inside that translation unit, and you must precede this external declaration with the variable modifier `extern`, as shown in Table 5.1.

**Table 5.1. Using an external variable.**

| *File A* | *File B* |
|---|---|
| | `#include <iostream.h>` |
| `int a = 25896;` | `extern a;` |
| `char *tinyStr = "Hi!";` | `extern tinyStr;` |
| `int main()` | `void testFunct()` |
| `{` | `{` |
| `...testFunc();` | `cout << a << "\n";` |
| `return 0;` | `cout << tinyStr << "\n";` |
| `}` | `}` |

You also can use the `extern` modifier in the initial declaration of the variable (in Table 5.1, that's the declaration in File A). But this is not a common practice because it's confusing; when you precede a variable's initial declaration with `extern`, there's no way to distinguish it from the variable's external declarations.

In Table 5.1, `a` and `tinyStr` are external variables because they are declared outside any function in File A and are redeclared using the `extern` modifier in File B. When the program runs, it prints the following lines to standard output (normally, the screen):

```
25896
Hi!
```

## The Static Storage Class

A *static variable* is a permanent variable that is recognized only inside its own function or its own file. A static variable that is declared outside any function is a *static global variable*. A static variable that is declared inside a function is a *static local variable*.

You can declare any global or local variable to be static by preceding the variable's declaration with the storage class modifier `static`, as in this example:

```
static int myStaticVar;
```

When you declare a variable to be static, the compiler allots permanent storage to the variable, and that same storage remains allocated to the variable for the duration of your program. This is true for both static global and static local variables.

## Static Global Variables

If you declare a variable outside any function and if you do not make the variable accessible to other translation units by also declaring it in those other translation units with the `extern` modifier, the compiler treats the variable as static by default.

If you want to make sure a global variable is treated as static—and making sure is the preferred method, because it's a better programming practice than trusting your luck to the compiler—you can explicitly declare the variable to be static by preceding the variable's definition with the `static` keyword:

```
static int globalStaticVar;
```

## Static Local Variables

To make a local variable static, you must explicitly declare it to be static by preceding it with the static keyword, as in this example:

```
main()
{
static int localStaticVar;
static int localStaticVar2 = 10;
...
}
```

When you declare a local variable to be static, the compiler creates permanent storage for the variable, just as it does for a global static variable. However, a static local variable is known only inside the block in which it is declared. (A *block* is any segment of code delimited by curly brackets.) In other words, a static local variable is a local variable that retains its value between function calls.

Static local variables are frequently used in C and C++ programs because they are often desirable to preserve the value of a local variable between calls. For example, a static variable might be used to keep track of a number that increments each time the function is called. If static variables were not available, you could use global variables for this kind of operation. However, a global variable can be altered by any function in a program, so local static variables are better repositories for delicate and frequently changing data.

Here's an example of a function that makes use of a local static variable:

```
int IncrementerFunc()
{
static int numberToHike = 1;

     return(numberToHike++);
}
```

In this code fragment, the variable `numberToHike` starts out at 1 and increments by 1 each time the function `IncrementerFunc()` is called.

## The Automatic Storage Class

Any variable defined inside a block is said to have *automatic* (or `auto`) storage, unless the variable is explicitly declared to be `extern` or `static` with the `extern` or `static` keyword.

The `auto` storage class is the default storage class for all local variables—that is, for all variables declared within blocks. If you wish, you can explicitly declare a variable to be automatic by preceding its declaration with the modifier `auto`. However, because all local variables have `auto` storage class by default, you don't have to use the `auto` keyword to make a local variable automatic. In fact, because local variables are automatic by default, you rarely see the `auto` modifier in a C or C++ program.

Ordinarily, Visual C++ stores automatic objects and variables on the stack of the executing program. When the compiler optimizes code, it can put automatic variables in registers. However, a Visual C++ program always behaves as if automatic variables are allocated on the stack.

## The Register Storage Class

You can declare any variable to be a *register variable* by preceding its declaration with the modifier `register`, as in this example:

```
register int myRegisterVar;
```

When a variable has been declared as a register variable, the compiler stores the variable in a CPU register if there is a suitable register available.

If the compiler can't find an available register for a register variable, it treats the variable as an automatic variable. If the compiler can't provide register storage for a variable that is declared to have `register` storage class, the compiler gives the register variable preference over automatic variables the next time it allocates register storage.

If the compiler does manage to store a register variable in a register, operations on the variable are speeded up significantly because memory access is not needed to determine or change the value of a variable stored in a register.

You can assign the register storage class only to function arguments and local variables. A register variable, like an automatic variable, has a lifetime that lasts only until the end of the function in which it is declared.

**BY THE WAY**

In the days before ANSI C, the register storage class could be used only for integer and character variables. In ANSI C and C++, a variable of any type can be declared as a register variable. The longer a register variable is, the less certain you can be that the variable will actually be stored in a register. However, declaring a `long`, a `double`, or a `float` as a register variable can't hurt, so you might as well try.

# Scope

*Scope* is a property that determines where in a program you can use an identifier, and where in a program the identifier has meaning. The scope of an identifier can be limited to the block, function, file , or prototype in which it appears.

## Local Scope

A *block*—a programming unit that has always existed but has become more important with the introduction of C++—is simply a section of code enclosed by curly brackets. Thus, a function can also be called a block. In this code fragment, the code between the brackets is a block:

```
while (envp[n] != NULL) {
    if(nrOfLines)
     cout << n;
    cout << ": " << envp[n++] << "\n";
}
```

Blocks can be *nested*; that is, blocks can appear inside other blocks. For instance, in this example, the block that follows the keyword `while` appears inside the block that comprises the `main()` function.

When an identifier is declared inside a block, it is said to have *local scope*. This means that the identifier is recognized only in the block in which it is declared, and only after the point at which it is declared. Thus, in Listing 5.1, the variable *n* is recognized only inside the set of curly brackets that follows the keyword `while`.

**Listing 5.1. Identifier with function scope.**

```
// 0501.CPP
// Function scope

// This program lists your system's environment variables.
// If you use the /n command-line option, the program also
// prints line numbers.

#include <iostream.h>
#include <string.h>

int main(int argc, char *argv[], char *envp[])
{
     int nrOfLines = 0; // Default is no line numbers.

     if(argc == 2 && strcmp(argv[1], "/n") == 0)
          nrOfLines = 1;

     int n = 0;
     while (envp[n] != NULL) {
         int i = n;
         if(nrOfLines)
          cout << i;
         cout << ": " << envp[n++] << "\n";
     }
     return 0;
}
```

Because the variable *n* is declared inside a block, it has a short duration. It is created at the point at which it is declared. When the block in which it appears ends, the variable goes out of scope, unless it's a static variable, and then it goes out of existence, too. If the block is used again—and in this case it is, because it's part of a `while` loop—the variable is re-created.

## Function Scope

The only kind of identifier that can have *function scope* is a label. (A label, as you may recall from C, is an optional identifier that can be placed inside a function, so that section of the function can be accessed from a `goto` statement inside the same function.) A label can appear anywhere within a function and is accessible from anywhere in the function, before or after the point at which it appears. However, a label cannot be accessed from outside the function in which it appears.

In Listing 5.1, the identifier `nrOfLines` has function scope.

## File Scope

If an identifier is declared outside any function, it has *file scope*. An identifier that has file scope is accessible from any point in the file that follows the identifier's declaration—that is, from all subsequent blocks in the file.

A variable that has file scope is also known as a *global variable*. An external variable has file scope and therefore must be declared outside any function. A static global variable also has file scope. In Listing 5.2, the variable `nrOfLines` has file scope.

#### Listing 5.2. Variable with file scope.

```
// 0502.CPP
// File scope

// This program lists your system's environment variables.
// If you use the /n command-line option, the program also
// prints line numbers.

#include <iostream.h>
#include <string.h>

int nrOfLines = 0; // Default is no line numbers.

int main(int argc, char *argv[], char *envp[])
{
     if(argc == 2 && stricmp(argv[1], "/n") == 0)
          nrOfLines = 1;

     int n = 0;
     while (envp[n] != NULL) {
         int i = n;
```

```
            if(nrOfLines)
             cout << i;
            cout << ": " << envp[n++] << "\n";
        }
        return 0;
}
```

## Prototype Scope

When you declare an identifier inside a function prototype, the identifier has *prototype scope*. An identifier that has prototype scope is recognized only inside the function prototype in which it is declared. An identifier that has prototype scope is used only in the forward declaration of a function, not in the function definition and not in the function itself. Later in the file, when the function appears, the identifiers that actually are used as the function's arguments are declared.

In this line, taken from Listing 6.1, the variable `myStr` has prototype scope:

```
// function prototype
void Display(char *myStr);
```

## Resolving Conflicts in Names of Identifiers

One consequence of the scope rules used in C++ is that multiple variables with the same name can appear inside a C++ function, provided they are declared in different blocks. This means that, within a function, conflicts in the names of local variables can arise.

Fortunately, when variable names are duplicated in a function, their name conflict is easy to resolve. All you have to remember is that a variable that's declared inside a block takes precedence over a variable that's declared outside the block, and that a local identifier takes precedence over a global identifier with the same name.

For example, if both a local identifier and a global identifier are named `x`, every occurrence of `x` while the local identifier is in scope is recognized as the local identifier `x`, not the global identifier `x`. Thus, as long as the local identifier `x` is in scope, the global identifier `x` is effectively invisible. When the local identifier `x` goes out of scope, the global identifier `x` comes into scope again.

The same principle applies to local identifiers declared within blocks and identifiers that are declared inside smaller, nested blocks. If a variable named *x* is declared at the beginning of a function and another variable named *x* is declared in a smaller block inside the function, the variable *x* that's outside the nested function is effectively invisible for as long as the variable that's declared in the nested block is in scope. When the identifier *x* that is declared inside the nested block goes out of scope, the identifier *x* that's declared in the outer block comes into scope again.

## How Scope Precedence Works

Listing 5.3 shows how scope precedence works in C++.

**Listing 5.3. Precedence of variables in C++.**

```
// 0503.CPP
// Scope precedence

#include <iostream.h>
#include <string.h>

int strLen = 128;

int main()
{
     int strLen = 32;
     int n = 0;

     // some code is skipped here ...

     while (n == 0) {
         n++;
         int strLen = 12;
         cout << "The string length is " << strLen << ".\n";
     }
     return 0;
}
```

In Listing 5.3, the variable `strLen` is declared three times: once globally, once at the beginning of the `main()` function, and once inside the nested block that follows the keyword `while`. The declaration at the beginning of the `main()` function takes precedence over the global declaration, and the declaration inside the nested block takes precedence over the declaration at the beginning of the `main()` function. Therefore, by the time the program reaches the `cout` statement inside the `while` loop, `strLen` has a value of 12, and the `cout` statement prints this message:

```
The string length is 12.
```

## The Point of Declaration

If an identifier is initialized at the same time it's declared, it is considered to be declared immediately after its declarer but prior to the appearance of its initializer. That might not seem important at first glance, but it can have significant effects on the way a program works. For example, consider this code fragment:

```
int strLen = 12;
int AFunction()
{
     int myVar = strLen;
}
```

In this example, what's the value of `myVar`? If you said it's undefined, you're right. If `strLen`'s point of declaration were *after* its initialization, `myVar` would be initialized to 12, the value of `strLen`. However, because that isn't the case, `myVar` is initialized to an undefined value.

## The Scope Resolution Operator

When you're inside a block in a C++ program and a local variable has the same name as a global variable , you can override the normal precedence rules of C++ and instruct the compiler to recognize the global variable instead of the local variable. All you have to do is prefix the name of the local variable with the *scope resolution operator* `::`, as shown in Listing 5.4.

### Listing 5.4. Overriding a global variable with a local variable.

```
// 0504.CPP
// Overriding a global variable with a local variable

#include <iostream.h>
#include <string.h>
```

*continues*

**Listing 5.4. continued**

```
int strLen = 32;

int main()
{
     int n = 0;

     // some code is skipped here ...

     while (n == 0) {
         n++;
         int strLen = 12;
         cout << "The string length is " << ::strLen << ".\n";
     }
     return 0;
}
```

In the `cout` statement in Listing 5.4, the name of the variable `strLen` is preceded by `::`, so the compiler treats `strLen` as a global variable and the `cout` statement prints this message:

```
The string length is 32.
```

Note that, if a function contains nested local scopes, the scope resolution operator doesn't provide access to variables in the next outermost scope; it provides access only to global variables.

# Duration

The storage class of a variable determines whether it has a *global* or a *local* duration. In C and C++, a variable with a global lifetime is called a *static* variable, and a variable with a local lifetime is called an *automatic*, or `auto`, variable.

The duration of a variable determines when memory is allocated for the variable. A static variable has a value throughout the execution of a program. An automatic variable is allocated new storage each time execution control passes to the block in which it is defined. When execution returns, the variable no longer has a meaningful value.

Variables declared in functions are automatic by default. When a function is called, memory is allocated for the function's `auto` variables. When the function ends, the memory allocated for its `auto` variables is released.

Static duration is the default duration for variables with file scope. A static variable is always available, because the memory allocated for it is not freed until the program ends. You can declare any variable in a function to have static duration by preceding the variable's declaration with the keyword `static`.

# Linkage

*Linkage* is a word that describes the way that objects and functions are shared between translation units. Names of objects and functions can have three kinds of linkage: *internal linkage, external linkage,* and no linkage. The linkage of a variable determines whether and how it can be accessed from another source file.

## Internal Linkage

A variable declared outside any function in a source file is said to have *internal linkage.*

A variable with internal linkage is recognized only inside the source file in which it is defined, and is accessible only inside its own translation unit. Therefore, it has *file scope.* A variable that is declared using the `static` modifier also has internal linkage. This declaration gives the variable `externVar` internal linkage:

```
static int externVar; // static keyword ensures internal linkage.
```

## External Linkage

An object or function that is accessible inside its own translation unit and is also accessible to other translation units is said to have *external linkage.* For example, a global variable that's declared using the `extern` modifier has external linkage. The following declaration gives the variable `externVar` external linkage:

```
extern int externVar;
```

An object that is static merely because it is declared outside a block has internal linkage unless it is specified as external with the `external` keyword.

You can force a `const` identifier to have external linkage by preceding the declaration of the constant with the `extern` storage class modifier, like this:

```
const extern int externVar;
```

In Visual C++, if a function name with file scope is explicitly declared as *inline*, it has external linkage. An object that is static merely because it is declared outside a block also has external linkage.

### No Linkage

An identifier that is defined inside a block is not accessible outside its own block, so it is said to have no linkage. A variable with no linkage ordinarily is visible only within the block in which it is declared. However, you can make an object that has no linkage accessible to other translation units by passing a pointer to a function in the other translation unit.

Automatic variables have no linkage; neither do enumerator names nor `typedef` names.

## Summary

This chapter covered four important properties of variables: storage class, scope, linkage, and duration. To sum up:

- The *storage class* of a variable determines its lifetime (sometimes called its *duration*), its form of initialization, and, in certain cases, its linkage.
- The *scope* of a variable specifies the portions of program text from which the name of the variable can be recognized. Thus, the scope of a variable determines where a variable can be used in a program, and where in a program the variable has meaning.
- *Linkage* describes the way objects and functions are shared between translation units. The linkage of a variable determines whether it can be accessed from another source file. Names of objects and functions can have three kinds of linkage: internal linkage, external linkage, and no linkage.
- A variable that is declared outside any function in a source file is said to have *internal linkage*. A variable with internal linkage is recognized only inside the source file in which it is defined, and is accessible only inside its own translation unit. Therefore, it has *file scope*.

- An object or a function that is accessible inside its own translation unit and also is accessible to other translation units is said to have *external linkage*. For example, a global variable that is declared using the `extern` modifier has external linkage.
- An identifier that is defined inside a block is not accessible outside its own block, so it is said to have no linkage. A variable with no linkage ordinarily is visible only within the block in which it is declared. However, you can make an object that has no linkage accessible to other translation units by passing a pointer to a function in the other translation unit.
- Automatic variables have no linkage. Neither do enumerator names nor `typedef` names.

Chapter 6

# Functions

Classes are the building blocks of C++, but the *function* is the fundamental building block of C—and is still the main *procedural* component of C++. A function usually is designed to perform a specific task, and its name often provides a clue about what that task is. Subtasks are performed by *statements* inside the function. In C++, a function also can contain declarations and definitions of variables, classes, and objects.

In both C and C++, all program activity takes place inside functions. Functions let you define and code the tasks in a program separately, so your programs can be modular. In large, complex programming projects, this ability to create standalone functions is important because it helps to ensure that one programmer's code does not accidentally affect code written by another programmer.

Another tool that C provides for structuring and compartmentalizing programs is the *code block*, often referred to simply as a *block*. In both C and C++, a block is a logically connected group of program statements that is treated as a unit. From a syntactical point of view, any sequence of source code enclosed in curly brackets is a block. Thus, the body of a function is a block.

Blocks can be nested, as this code fragment shows:

```
int main()
{                                    // the main() segment is a block
    int x;
    for (x = 0; x < 10; x++)
        if (x < 5) {                 // this is a nested block
            cout << "x < 5";
            cout << '\n';
        }
}
```

C++, with its object-oriented approach to programming, has taken the modularity of C programming even further by introducing classes and objects, which can be defined and declared either inside or outside functions. In C++, classes and objects are important, but functions are still more important. You can write a program without classes and objects, but you can't write a program without functions in C++ or C!

Classes and objects are introduced in Chapters 21 and 22 and are covered in more detail throughout the rest of Part 2. This chapter focuses on functions.

## The main() Function

In traditional style C++ programs, as in C, every program has a primary function that must be named `main()`. (Windows-based C++ programs have a different kind of structure, as you'll see in Chapters 22 through 24.) Execution of a C or C++ program normally begins and ends with the translation unit that contains the function `main()`. During the program, the `main()` function calls other functions to perform specific tasks.

**NOTE—A C++ FEATURE**

In C, although it is unusual, the `main()` function can be called from other functions in a program. In C++, this questionable practice is not allowed.

When `main()` calls another function, it passes execution control to the called function, so that execution of the task begins at the first statement in that function. A function returns control to `main()` at the first `return` statement the function encounters, or at the end of the function.

**NOTE—A MICROSOFT FEATURE**

In Visual C++, the `main()` function should always be declared as data type `int`. That's because the `main()` function of a Visual C++ program always returns an integer value to DOS. If the `main()` function does not contain a return statement, or if the return statement does not specify a value, the compiler returns a warning message (No. C4508).

When `main()` returns a value, DOS can check the value for errors in the executing program. An application's `main()` function should return a value of zero if no problems are encountered. If an error is detected in executing the `main()` function, `main()` should return a nonzero value.

You can use the constants `EXIT_SUCCESS` and `EXIT_FAILURE`, which are defined in the standard include file STDLIB.H, to return a value informing DOS of the success or failure of your program. For more details on the `EXIT_SUCCESS` and `EXIT_FAILURE` constants, see the Visual C++ *Run-Time Library Reference* that comes with the professional edition of Visual C++.

A program ordinarily stops executing at the end of its `main()` function, although it can terminate at other points for a variety of reasons. For example, when an error is encountered in the execution of a program, you can force the program to terminate by calling:

- The `exit` function, which allows the normal C-language termination processing to take place, and then returns a specified value to the operating system as the program's return code or exit code.

- The `abort` function, which forces a program to terminate immediately, without letting the normal C-language termination processing to take place.
- The `assert` function, which lets you insert a conditional failure code in a program to assist in debugging.
- The `return` function. Executing a `return` function from `main()` is functionally equivalent to calling the `exit` functions.

All of the termination functions that can be executed from `main()` are declared in the header file STDLIB.H. They are described in more detail in the *Run-Time Library Reference* that comes with the professional edition of the Visual C++ compiler.

## Defining a Function

When a function appears in a program, the complete function—including its name, its argument list, and its source code—is formally known as a *function definition*. Clearly, then, every function in a program must have a function definition. A function definition contains:

- a *declaration specifier*, which tells what data type the function returns.
- a *declarator*, which contains the name of the function and its formal arguments. The function's formal arguments are enclosed in parentheses.
- the *function body*, which is the code that executes when the function is called.

This is an example of a function definition:

```
void AFunction(char *myStr, int strLen)
{
    // This is the function body.
}
```

The *body* of the function shown in the preceding example contains only a comment enclosed in curly brackets. The function's *declaration specifier* is `void` (because the function does not return a value; if the function returned, for example, an integer, the declaration specifier would be `int`).

The *name* of the function is `AFunction`. The function's *argument list* is `(char *myStr, int strLen)`. And the function's *declarator* is made up of the name of the function plus the function's argument list: `AFunction(char *myStr)`.

## NOTE—A MICROSOFT FEATURE

In Visual C++, when you write a function that uses the arguments `argc` and `argv`, a user who calls the function can use two wildcard characters—the question mark (`?`) and the asterisk (`*`)—to specify filename and pathname arguments on the function's command line. You can use this feature in DOS-based programs that allow users to type command lines.

In Visual C++, command-line arguments are handled by a routine named `_setargv`. By default, `_setargv` does not expand wildcards into separate strings in the `argv` string array. However, by linking a program with a library file named SETARGV.OBJ, you can replace the default `_setargv` routine with a different routine that does accept wildcards. When you link a program with SETARGV.OBJ, the program interprets wildcards typed by a user in the same way wildcards are interpreted by the DOS shell when they appear on DOS command lines.

When you build a program with the Visual Workbench, you can link the program with SETARGV.OBJ, simply by adding the library to your project. If you compile your program manually with the CL command, you can link the program with SETARGV.OBJ by specifying the library's name on the CL command line. In either case, you must specify the option `/NOE` (no extended dictionary search) when you link the program to avoid multiple-definition errors when the linker searches for the `_setargv` function.

To set the `/NOE` option, select Project from the Visual Workbench's Options menu and then click the Linker button in the Project Options dialog box. When the Linker Options dialog box appears, check the box labeled "Prevent Use of Extended Dictionary."

When you compile a program with this kind of CL command, and a user communicates with your program by typing in a command line, your program will recognize commands that contain wildcards the same way they would be recognized if they were typed as an MS-DOS command line.

Enclosing a command-line argument in quotation marks (`"  "`) suppresses wildcard expansion. Within quoted arguments, you can represent quotation marks literally by preceding the double quotation mark with a backslash (`\`). If no matches are found for a wildcard argument, the argument is treated literally.

For a more detailed explanation of how command-line wildcards work in DOS, refer to your MS-DOS user's guide.

# C++-Style Function Definitions

When the ANSI specification for C was established, the kind of function definition shown in the previous example replaced an earlier kind, which now is obsolete. The following code fragment shows what a function definition looked like before the ANSI C standard for function definitions was established:

```
AFunction(myStr)      // WARNING: This kind of function declaration ...
char *myStr           // ... is not recommended in Visual C++!
int  strLen
{
     // This is the function body.
}
```

Here's the same function definition rewritten in the style mandated by ANSI C and required in Visual C++ programs:

```
void AFunction(char *myStr, int strLen)
{
     // This is the function body.
}
```

As you can see, the old-style function definition uses a different syntax for declaring arguments than that established by the ANSI standard. These are the differences in the two examples:

- The old-style definition does not have to include a `void` declaration specifier if the function returns no value. The new-style definition must include a void declaration specifier if the function returns no value.
- In the old-style definition, the data types of the formal parameters are not part of the declarator. Instead, they are placed between the definition and the body of the function. The new-style definition requires the data types of all parameters to be specified.

Visual C++ supports old-style function definitions, but you should still use the new-style syntax for defining functions. When you use the new syntax, the compiler can (and does) check your code to make sure that it uses correct data types. The old-style syntax does not permit the checking of data types and increases the likelihood of errors.

# Function Prototypes

In C++, a function must be declared before it is defined. Declaring a function before you define it is called *function prototyping*. A function prototype is sometimes called a *forward declaration*.

A function prototype, or forward declaration, looks just like a function definition without a function body. The compiler uses a function's prototype to compare the types of arguments in subsequent calls to the function. The compiler also uses function prototypes to convert the types of function arguments whenever necessary.

A function declaration, like a function definition, includes:

- A *declaration* specifier, which tells what data type the function returns.
- A *declarator*, which contains the name of the function and its formal arguments. The function's formal arguments are enclosed in parentheses.

Because there is no function body in a function declaration, the declaration ends with a semicolon.

## An Example of Function Prototyping

This is an example of a function prototype:

```
void AFunction(char *myStr, int strLen);
```

To illustrate function prototyping, Listing 6.1 has both a `main()` function and a second function that is prototyped. The prototyped function, named `Display`, has a forward declaration that appears in the fifth line of a program. The function itself is called from inside the `main()` function, and is defined at the end of the program.

### Listing 6.1. Using a function prototype.

```
// 0601.CPP

// THE WRATH OF ZALTHAR
// A Sample C++ Program

#include <iostream.h>
```

*continues*

**Listing 6.1. continued**

```
// function prototype
void Display(char *myStr);

char *const NL = "\n";
int const STRSIZE = 32;

int main()
{
    char playerNameStr[STRSIZE];

    cout << NL;
    Display("THE WRATH OF ZALTHAR");
    Display("Copyright 19XX, [Your Name Here]");
    cout << NL;

    cout << "Player's name: ";
    cin >> playerNameStr;

    cout << "Your player's name is ";
    cout << playerNameStr << "." << NL << NL;

    return 0;
}

void Display(char *myStr)
{
    cout << myStr << NL;
}
```

In the pre-ANSI C era, function prototypes were permitted, but they weren't required and weren't widely used. When the ANSI C standard was established, function prototyping was suggested but still was not required.

Today, some ANSI C compilers return warning messages when you fail to declare prototypes, and other compilers can be set to terminate compilation and return fatal errors when functions are not prototyped. But C++ has escalated the demand for function prototyping to a new level. In C++, in most cases, function prototypes are required.

## Rules for Function Prototyping

In Visual C++, you must prototype any function that is called before it is defined—and it is best to prototype every function in a program except for the `main()`

function. (The `main()` function of a program does not require a prototype because it's never called by any other function.)

If a function is defined before it's called, it is not strictly necessary to write a prototype for the function: the function isn't called until it is defined, and its definition can therefore serve as its prototype. However, function prototypes help the Visual C++ compiler check functions for correct data typing, an ability missing from standard C—and that's why it's a good idea to prototype all functions used in a program.

You are allowed to place a function prototype anywhere in a source file, as long as the prototype appears before the function is defined and before any calls are made to the function. By convention, however, the function prototypes in a source file usually are grouped together near the beginning of the file.

> **NOTE—FUNCTION PROTOTYPES IN C**
>
> The requirement that all functions have prototypes is one of the few areas in which C++ is not backwards-compatible with standard C. If you have an old C program in which function prototypes are not used, you'll have to write prototypes for all functions in the program before you can compile it on the Visual C++ compiler.

# Overloading Functions

In C++, two functions that are in the same scope can have the same name, provided each function has a distinctive parameter list. This would be disastrous in C, but it's fine in C++ because C++ permits *function overloading*.

In C++, when you create multiple functions that have the same name, the compiler distinguishes between them by comparing the number and types of their parameters.

Giving more than one function the same name is called *overloading* the functions. Functions that are in the same scope and have the same name—but different argument lists—are called *overloaded functions*.

An overloaded function usually is named after some similar function, and usually performs some operation that's similar—but not identical—to whatever its namesake does. If overloaded functions had been around when the C language was written, functions such as `strcpy` and `strncpy`—which perform similar operations but require different argument lists—could have been given the same name.

## Using Function Overloading

Overloaded functions can be useful in object-oriented programs because classes that are derived from other classes often have functions, called *member functions,* that are slightly different from member functions of their base class (more information about classes and class hierarchies is presented in Chapters 21 through 23). Function overloading also can be useful in situations that aren't directly related to object-oriented programming, as Listing 6.2 illustrates.

### Listing 6.2. Overloaded functions.

```
// 0602.CPP
// Overloaded functions.

#include <iostream.h>

// function prototypes
void PrintAddress(char *nameVar, char *hometownVar);
void PrintAddress(char *nameVar, char *hometownVar, char *countryVar);

void main()
{
   PrintAddress("Beth", "New York");
   PrintAddress("Mieko", "Tokyo", "Japan");
}

void PrintAddress(char *nameVar, char *hometownVar)
{
   cout << nameVar << ", " << hometownVar << "\n";
}

void PrintAddress(char *nameVar, char *hometownVar, char *countryVar)
{
   cout << nameVar << ", " << hometownVar << ", " << countryVar<< "\n";
}
```

Listing 6.2 is a simple program that could serve as a model for an international address book. In the program, there are two different functions named `PrintAddress`. One of these `PrintAddress` functions prints domestic addresses, and the other prints foreign addresses. The domestic `PrintAddress` function prints the name of a person and the person's home town. The foreign `PrintAddress` function prints the name of a person, the person's home town, and the person's country.

The `main()` function of the program prints two address-book entries: one domestic entry and one foreign entry. As you can see, you can print either a domestic entry or an international entry by calling the same function: `PrintAddress`. You don't have to call one function to print a domestic address and call another function to print a foreign address. Instead, you can use the same function for both kinds of addresses, because the compiler can tell which function to call from the argument list that's passed to the function.

Function overloading is described in much more detail in Chapter 15.

## Name Mangling

In both C++ and C, the linker resolves references to functions by storing the names of functions in a *symbol table*. In a C program, every function has a different name, so the symbol table holds the names of all variables and symbols in the module being compiled. In a C++ program, because functions can be overloaded, the symbol table contains not only the name of each function in a program, but also the number and types of the function's arguments. Storing all of this information in the symbol table usually is referred to as *name mangling*.

Because C++ is derived from C, it would be reasonable to assume that existing C language libraries and header files could be linked with a C++ program and called by the C++ functions in the program. Unfortunately, because C++ mangles symbols, including a C library in a C++ program isn't quite that simple. Before you can mix C++ files and C files in the same program, you must take some kind of action to *unmangle* the names of the functions used in the C++ files.

C++ programmers often want to import C libraries into C++ programs, so the designers of Visual C++ created a tool that makes it relatively painless to mix C++ files and C files in the same program. This tool, called an *alternate linkage specification*, is covered in Chapter 8, "Linking Visual C++ Programs."

# Inline Functions

As you'll see in Chapter 7, "Compiling Visual C++ Programs," you can use the preprocessor directive `#define` to place *macros*—short routines that run faster than functions—in C and C++ programs. But macros created with the `#define` directive have serious flaws: they can't be type-checked to prevent programming errors, and they are subject to undesirable, unexpected, and often erratic side effects that can sneak elusive bugs into programs.

Because of the shortcomings of the `#define` directive, the designers of C++ came up with a new and better tool for doing the job that macros have traditionally done. This new tool is called the *inline function*.

Inline functions are short, fast, efficient routines that can be used the same way macros are used in C. Inline functions run much faster than ordinary functions, usually at the cost of a slight increase in program size. When you want to write a short routine that a program can call without the stack-manipulation overhead that functions require, write the routine as an inline function.

To write an inline function, all you have to do is precede the function with the function qualifier `inline`, like this:

```
inline EvenNum(myVar) myVar % 2 ? FALSE : TRUE;
```

**OOP TIP**

In object-oriented programs, you don't have to use the modifier `inline` to define inline functions that are members of classes. When you define a function inside a class definition, the compiler checks to see if the function is short enough to be compiled as an inline function. If it is, the compiler automatically makes it an inline function. Class-member functions are described in more detail in Part II.

Once you define an inline function, the compiler does not call the function using the standard C++ calling convention, in which local variables are placed onto the stack. (Calling conventions are described in Chapter 8, "Linking Visual C++ Programs.") Instead, if possible, the compiler makes a verbatim copy of the function each time the function is called in a program and places that copy at the point in the source code from which the function is called. Then the compiler executes the function *inline*, without touching the stack.

If the function is too long to be pasted into the program at each point where it's called, the compiler doesn't expand the function inline even if the function is declared with the `inline` qualifier. Instead, the compiler makes just one copy of the function and calls the function each time it appears, using a stack-based calling method similar to the standard C++ calling convention. Therefore, to obtain the maximum advantage of using inline functions, you should use the `inline` qualifier only to call short functions—preferably just one line long, and certainly no longer than two or three lines.

You should declare `inline` functions in a function prototype, in the same way that you write a forward declaration for any function. If you plan to call an inline function in more than one source file, you should put its declaration in a header file. And any time you modify the body of an inline function that appears in more than one file, you must recompile the files that call that function.

# Default Function Arguments

In C++, you can specify *default values* for arguments in a function's argument list. If you specify a default value for an argument to a function, you don't have to pass that argument to the function when you call the function. Instead, each time you call the function, the compiler executes the function using the argument's default value.

In C++, using default function arguments can increase the flexibility of a program. If you often call a function using a specific value for one (or more) of the function's arguments, you can make that value the default value for the argument. You then can call the function as many times as you like without bothering to supply its default argument (or arguments).

To define a default value for a function argument, you must place the default value in the argument list that's declared in the function's prototype. For example, this function prototype supplies a default argument list for a function named `DisplayString()`:

```
zvoid DisplayString(int strLen = 128, float points = 1228.3,
    long pixels = 33489);
```

In this example, the default values defined for the arguments to `DisplayString()` are 128, 1228.3 , and 33489. If you want to use those default values for the function's arguments when you call the function, you can simply pass the function an empty argument list when you call it:

```
void DisplayString();
```

When you call `DisplayString()` in this fashion, the result is the same as if you had passed the default arguments to the string when you made the call:

```
DisplayString(128, 1228.3, 33489);
```

## Overriding Default Function Arguments

When you define a default value for a function argument, you aren't forced to use the default value every time you call the function. You can override the default value any time you like.

To override a default function value, all you have to do is pass an alternate value for the argument when you call the function. The compiler then uses the argument's alternate value instead of its default value when it executes the function. In the previous example, you could override all three of `DisplayString`'s default arguments by calling the function in this way:

```
DisplayString(23, 984.6, 12847);
```

This call replaces the default arguments 128, 1228.3, and 33489 with the arguments 23, 984.6, 12847.

## Overriding Selected Arguments

When a function has more than one default argument, you can override some of its default parameters while not overriding others. For example, consider this call:

```
DisplayString(23, 984.6);
```

This call overrides `DisplayString`'s first and second arguments by defining them as 23 and 984.6, respectively, but it allows the compiler to use the default value 33489 for the function's last parameter.

When you override some default arguments of a function, but don't override others, there is one important rule to remember: If you omit one of a function's default arguments, you also must omit all default arguments that follow the default argument you omitted. In other words, you cannot omit a default argument unless you omit all default arguments to its right. For example, this function call is illegal:

```
void AFunction( , , 65535);   // WARNING: This doesn't work!
```

This syntax is not allowed because it's hard to read and increases the likelihood of errors.

# Variable Argument Lists

In C++, you can declare a function that takes an unspecified number of arguments. An argument list that has one or more unspecified arguments is called a *variable argument list*. Once you declare a function with a variable argument list, you can fill in the unspecified arguments in the function's argument list when you call the function.

Variable argument lists are not a new idea in C/C++ programming. In C, such familiar functions as `printf` and `scanf` have variable argument lists. However, they're more common in C++ than in C.

## Variable Argument Lists in C

When a C or C++ function has a variable argument list, the list ends with three periods (...). If a C function has a variable argument list, at least one actual argument must precede this ellipsis. Thus, in C, the following function declaration is legal:

```
void MyFunc(int x, int y);
```

but this declaration is *not* allowed:

```
void MyFunc(...);          // NOT legal in C!
```

## Variable Argument Lists in C++

In C++, it is perfectly legal to declare a variable argument list that contains no arguments. Thus, in C++, the following function declaration is allowed:

```
void MyFunc(...);          // This is OK in C++!
```

Alternatively, you can define one or more arguments in a function's argument list, but leave other arguments unspecified:

```
int FuncWithVarArgs(char *var 1, int var2, ...);
```

**NOTE—A MICROSOFT FEATURE**

In Visual C++, when you declare a variable argument list that contains at least one specified argument, you must precede the ellipsis at the end of the list with a comma, in this fashion:

```
int MicrosoftFunc(char *var 1, int var2, ...);
```

In some other variations of C++, this final comma is not required.

By the way, when a function has a variable argument list, Visual C++ does not perform type-checking on the variables that are left unspecified.

## Writing Variable Argument Lists

When you call a function that has a variable argument list, you must find a way to tell the compiler how many parameters the argument list contains, and what their data types are. If you don't provide that information, the compiler has no way of knowing when it should stop pushing arguments onto the stack and start executing the program.

### Specifying Variable Arguments with Format Strings

One way to tell the compiler how many arguments a function has, and what their data types are, is to pass the function a *format string*. When a function requires a format string, the format string must be the first argument in the function's argument list.

If a format string is followed by other arguments, special symbols embedded in the format string tell the compiler how many more arguments there are and the data types of their arguments. These special symbols are called *conversion specifiers*.

A conversion specifier consists of two characters: a text character, called a *conversion character*, and an escape symbol, called an *introducer*. In the following example, `d` and `f` are conversion characters, and the introducer that precedes each conversion character is `%`:

```
void PrintIt(int x, float y)
{
    printf("The amounts are %d and %f.\n", x, y);
}
```

In this example, the conversion character `d` tells the compiler that it can expect the variable `x` to be a decimal value. The next conversion character, `f`, tells the compiler that it can expect the variable `y` to be a floating-point value.

This statement calls the `PrintIt()` function in the preceding example:

```
PrintIt(5, 6.1416);
```

This statement prints the line

```
The amounts are 5 and 6.1416.
```

to standard output (normally, the screen).

## Specifying Argument Lists with Terminating Values

You also can specify the variables in a variable argument list by including a *terminating value* in the argument list. When an argument list contains a terminating value, that value is not used in the function but is placed at the end of the variable argument list to signal the compiler that the last argument in the argument list has been pushed onto the stack.

An example:

```
TermValFunc(char *str1, char *str2, int 0);
```

In this example, the argument list passed to the function `TermValFunc()` has two string arguments and a terminating value of 0. When the C++ parser encounters the terminating variable in the `TermValFunc()` argument list, it knows that it has read all the arguments that the function requires.

Ending an argument list with a terminating value has one shortcoming: all of the arguments in the list must have the same data type. This is necessary because different data types require different numbers of bytes for storage, and the terminating-value technique for writing a variable argument list does not provide the compiler with any information about data types.

# The STDARG.H Functions

In C++, there's a another way to supply arguments to functions that have variable argument lists. You can provide the compiler with all the information it needs about a variable argument list by supplying a prewritten set of variables that tell the compiler how many arguments the list contains and what their data types are.

Three macros that you can use for this purpose are defined in a header file named STDARG.H. The macros are named `va_start()`, `va_arg()`, and `va_end()`.

The macros in the STDARG.H file have two useful features:

- The macros in the STDARG.H file have been written for you, and are versatile enough to be used in a variety of ways.
- The STDARG.H macros provide a portable way to pass variable arguments. That's because two versions of the macros are available: the macros defined in STDARG.H conform to the ANSI C standard, and the macros defined in the header file VARARGS.H are compatible with UNIX System V.

Listing 6.3 shows how the `va_start()`, `va_arg()`, and `va_end()` macros can be used in a program. The STDARG.H macros used here are described under the headings that follow the listing.

### Listing 6.3. Using the STDARG.H macros.

```
// 0603.CPP
// Using the stdarg.h macros

#include <iostream.h>
#include <stdarg.h>

int Compute (int first, ...);

int main()
{
      cout << (Compute(2, 15, -1)) << '\n';
      cout << (Compute(5, 5, 5, -1)) << '\n';
      cout << (Compute (17, 897, 2, 165, -1)) << '\n';
      return 0;
}

int Compute (int first, ...)
{
      int count = 0, sum = 0, i = first;
      va_start marker;
```

```
        va_start (marker, first);
        while (i != -1) {
              sum += i;
              count++;
              i = va_arg(marker, int);
        }
        va_end(marker);
        return sum;
}
```

In Listing 6.3, in the function named `Compute()`, a `va list` variable named `marker` is declared. The `Compute()` function starts reading the contents of the `va list` variable at the point where the macro `va start()` is called. The function stops reading the contents of `va list` at the point where the macro `va end()` is called. The list is read in a `while` loop. When a value of –1 occurs in the list, the `while` loop ends, and the reading of the list ceases. The `Compute()` function is called in the `main()` segment of the program. Each call to the `Compute()` function uses a different number of parameters. The `va start()` and `va end()` macros, along with the `va list` variable, make the function work correctly each time it is called.

## The va_list Data Type

The `va_list` macro is a data type that equates to a list of variables. Once you define a `va_list` variable, you can use it as a parameter to the `va_start()` and `va_end()` macros.

## The va_start() Macro

Here is the syntax of the `va_start` macro:

```
void va_start(va_list arg_ptr, prev_param);
```

The `va_start()` macro sets `arg_ptr` to point to the first optional argument in a variable argument list passed to a function. If the function's argument list contains parameters that have been specified in the function's declaration, the `prev_param` argument to `va_start ()` provides the name of the specified function argument that immediately precedes the first optional argument in the argument list.

When the `va_start ()` macro is executed, it causes the `arg_ptr` parameter to point just beyond the argument specified by `prev_param`.

The arg_ptr argument to the va_start() macro must have va_list type. The va_start () macro must be executed before either the va_arg() macro or the va_end() macro can be called.

If prev_param is declared with the register storage class, the va_start() macro's behavior is undefined.

## The va_arg() Macro

This is the syntax of the va_arg() macro:

```
void arg(va_list arg_ptr, type);
```

The va arg() macro has a twofold purpose:

- First, va_arg() returns the value of the object pointed to by the argument pointer arg_ptr.
- Second, va_arg() increments arg_ptr to point to the next item in the variable argument list of the function being called, using the size type to determine where the next argument starts. The type specified in the va_arg() macro's parameter list tells va_arg() what type of data is being read. The type argument tells va_arg() whether the data pointed to is an integer, a double, or some other type. The type argument also provides va_arg() with the information that is needed to update arg_ptr correctly.

You can use the va_arg macro any number of times within a function to retrieve arguments from the function's argument list.

## The va_end Macro

Here's the format of the va_end macro:

```
void va_end( va_list arg_ptr);
```

The va_end() macro performs the housekeeping chores that are necessary for the called function to return correctly. When all arguments are read, va_end() resets arg_ptr to NULL. If va_end() is not called after all of a function's variable arguments have been read, strange and undefined errors can afflict the program calling the macro.

# Passing Arguments to Functions

In C++, as in C, you can pass an argument to a function by either the argument's *value* or by its *address*. To pass an argument to a function by its value, simply place the argument in the called function's argument list, as this code fragment illustrates:

```
int aValue = 5;
CalledFunction(aValue);
```

> **NOTE—ASKING FOR REFERENCES**
>
> Before the advent of C++, passing an argument to a function by its address was usually referred to as passing the argument by reference—but now, a new data type, called a *reference*, has been created, so passing an argument by reference now means something else entirely. Passing arguments by reference is covered in Chapter 4, "Variables."

## Passing Arguments by Value

In both C and C++, when you pass an argument to a function by value, the compiler makes a copy of the value specified by the argument and passes the copy, not the original value, to the function. When you pass an argument to a function by value, the called function cannot modify the actual value; it can modify only the copy of the value that is passed to it. Therefore, when you pass an argument to a function by value, you can be assured that the called function cannot modify the actual value, which is in memory.

## Passing Arguments by Address

In C++, as in C, you can pass an argument to a function by its address. To do that, you place a *pointer* to the argument in the function's argument list, in this fashion:

```
int aValue = 5;
CalledFunction(&aValue);
```

When you pass an argument to a function by its address, the compiler does not make a copy of the argument and pass it to the called function. Instead, the *address* of the actual value stored in memory is passed to the called function. The function then can modify the value stored in memory by referencing the data indirectly, through the pointer that points to the value.

## Safeguarding Data Passed to a Function

In C, the usual practice is to pass data to a function by its address if you want the function to be able to modify the data, and to pass data to a function by its value if you want to safeguard the data from being modified by the function.

When you want to prevent a function from modifying data that is passed to it, the technique of passing the data by value works fine if the amount of data being passed to the function is small. However, if you want to pass an argument that represents a large data structure to a function, and you want to protect the data from being modified by the called function, it can be costly in terms of both time and memory to make a copy of the data and to pass the copy to the function.

## Declaring an Argument to Be a Constant

In C++, you can pass a large amount of data to a function and protect the data from being modified by the function. Here's how: Place a pointer to the data in the function 's argument list, but also declare in the argument list that the data being pointed to is a constant. Then, even though a pointer is passed to the function, the function cannot modify the data that the pointer refers to.

This is a safeguard that you can use in C++ when you want to make absolutely certain that a function doesn't make unwanted changes in an argument that is passed to the function by its address.

The following prototype shows how you can prevent a function from changing the contents of a pointer by passing to the function an argument that is a pointer to a constant:

```
int SafeFunction(const struct delicateStruct *ptrToStruct);
```

Once you write a function prototype that contains a pointer to a constant, as shown in this example, you can be assured that no matter what the declared function does with the pointer passed to it, it won't be able to change the data pointed to because that data is a constant.

Listing 6.4 shows how `SafeFunction()` protects the contents of the structure `delicateStruct`.

**Listing 6.4. Safeguarding data passed by reference to a function.**

```
// 0604.CPP
// Protecting data passed by reference

#include <iostream.h>

// function prototype
int SafeFunction(const struct delicateStruct *ptrToStruct);

int main()
{
    const struct delicateStruct *ptrToMyStruct;

    SafeFunction(ptrToMyStruct);
    return 0;
}

int SafeFunction(const struct delicateStruct *ptrToStruct)
{
    struct delicateStruct *badStructPtr;      // ordinary pointer
    badStructPtr = ptrToStruct;     // ERROR! trying to modify a constant
}
```

In Listing 6.4, there's no way that `SafeFunction()` can modify `delicateStruct` because `delicateStruct` is a constant. If you try to execute the program, the compiler returns Compilation Error 2446: "Could not convert between specified types."

## Calling a Function to Initialize a const

You can initialize a constant to a value that is returned by a function call, using a format such as this:

```
const int myFunc();
```

You then can use the value that the function returns as you would any constant—and that means, of course, that you can't change its value. Listing 6.5 shows a function that returns a constant.

**Listing 6.5. A function that returns a constant.**

```
// 0605.CPP
// A function that returns a constant

const char* GetString();

int main()
{
     const char* lulu = GetString();
     return 0;
}

const char* GetString()
{
     return "Lulu";
}
```

Ordinarily, initializing a `const` by making a call to a function causes no problems. However, if you're generating code for a ROM, you can run into trouble because the constant being initialized must be placed in the code segment, and its value is not known until runtime. To overcome this difficulty, you can initialize the `const` by using a reference to the constant in the constant's declaration:

```
const int& newConst = constVal();
```

When you declare a constant using a reference, the compiler puts the reference in the data segment, but does not allow the reference to point to anything but a `const`. (References are described in detail in Chapter 4.)

# Summary

This chapter covered functions, the building blocks of C++. Topics that were addressed in this chapter included:

- *The `main()` function.* Always returns an integer value in Microsoft Visual C++.
- *Function definitions.* ANSI C mandated a new style for writing function definitions, and you must use that style in your Visual C++ programs.

- *Function prototypes.* In Visual C++, you must declare functions before you define them. Therefore, a list of function declarations often appears at the beginning of a C++ source file. Declaring a function before you define it is called *function prototyping.* A function prototype sometimes is called a *forward declaration.*
- *Function overloading.* A C++ mechanism that enables you to give more than one function the same name. Function overloading is an important feature of C++.
- *Inline functions.* Execute faster than ordinary functions because they use less overhead.

Chapter 7

# Compiling Visual C++ Programs

When you've written a C++ program, what can you do with it? Not much, until you learn how to turn your source-code masterpiece into an executable program.

To make an application out of a source-code program, you must (1) compile your source code into object-code modules, and then (2) link those object-code modules into an executable program. This two-part process is called *building* a program.

When you develop an application using Microsoft Visual C++, you can compile and link your program simply by selecting commands from the Visual Workshop's Project menu. (If you own the Professional Edition of Visual C++, you also can compile and link programs from an MS-DOS command line.)

This chapter explains how the Visual C++ compiler does the work of compiling source-code files into object-code modules. Chapter 8, "Linking Visual C++ Programs," explains how the Visual C++ linker performs the linking operations that transform object-code modules into executable programs.

# Building a Visual C++ Program

Figure 7.1 shows how the Visual C++ preprocessor, compiler, and linker work together to generate an executable Visual C++ program.

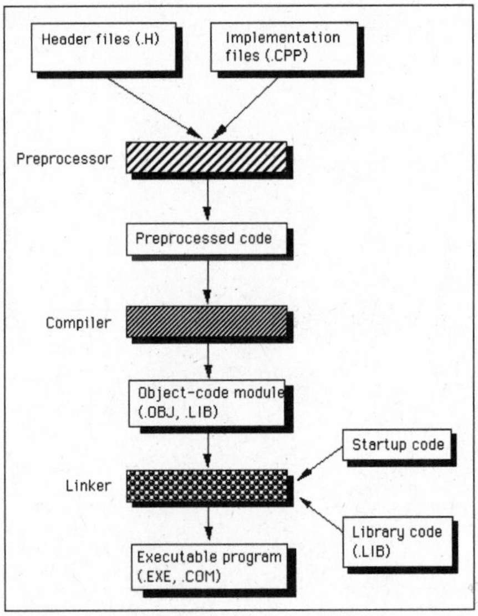


*Figure 7.1. Building a C++ program.*

As Figure 7.1 shows, the generation of a Visual C++ program can be broken down into three phases:

1. First, the Visual C++ *preprocessor* prepares your source code for compilation. The source code sent to the preprocessor usually has the suffix .CPP (for your main source files) and .H (for header files, also called headers). The C++ preprocessor is a text processor that breaks C++ source code down into *tokens* in order to locate macro calls. The preprocessor also executes preprocessor directives, which can perform such tasks as blocking the compilation of specified portions of source code and performing text-expansion and text-substitution operations.
2. When your source code has been prepared by the preprocessor, it is sent to the Visual C++ *compiler,* which compiles the code into object-code modules. Object-code modules generated by the compiler usually have the suffixes .OBJ (for modules compiled in ordinary fashion) or .LIB (for static library modules).
3. Finally, these modules go to the linker, which links them with other code—such as object-code libraries and standard startup code modules—which must be combined with your code to produce an executable program. During this process, your code can be linked with standard libraries that perform such everyday functions as handling I/O and performing arithmetic operations. Microsoft also provides an enormous set of library functions that can perform window-related tasks and many other kinds of exotic operations. The result of this step usually is an executable file such as an .EXE file or a .COM file.

### NOTE—THE STANDARD C LIBRARY AND THE MFC LIBRARY

The features of C++ that are covered in Part I of this book—that is, the nonobject-oriented features of the language—are implemented in the standard C libraries and in the runtime library supplied with Visual C++. The object-oriented features of C++ are covered in Part II, which focuses on object-oriented programming, and in Part III, which introduces the Microsoft Foundation Class (MFC) library.

# Compiling a Visual C++ Program

When the preprocessor finishes its work on a file, the result is an interim source file called a *translation unit*. A C++ program can contain a single translation unit, but usually is made up of one or more translation units linked together.

Typically, a translation unit contains a source file (with comments intact) and all of the header files that have been included in the file with the `#include` directive. A translation unit does not contain code that conditional compilation directives have deleted from the program.

When the preprocessor has created a translation unit, it sends the translation unit to the Visual C++ compiler. The compiler converts the code in the translation unit to a set of object-code modules, which can be stored either as object-code files or object-code libraries.

## Speeding Up Compilation

The Visual C++ compiler runs fast, but there are ways to make it run even faster. For example, you can use precompiled files, as explained in a moment. Other ways to speed up processing include using the fast compile option, using a disk-caching program, and using a RAM disk program. Each of these are explained in this chapter.

## Using Precompiled Files

The compiler spends much of its time processing header files, so precompiled header files can speed compilation significantly, especially when you combine them with the fast compile option. This speed increase is particularly important when you include large header files such as WINDOWS.H or the Microsoft Foundation Class (MFC) header files.

Three compiler options let you take advantage of precompiled header files:

- `/Yc` (create precompiled header).
- `/Yu` (use precompiled header).
- `/Yd` (include debugging information).

You can control the generation and use of precompiled headers from the Compiler Options dialog box that is accessed through the Visual Workbench Project menu. For details, see the Visual C++ *Programming Techniques* manual. See also the heading "Precompiled Headers and Precompiled Files" later in this chapter.

## Using the Fast Compile Option

The compiler spends considerable time optimizing your code to make it faster. When you're developing an application and execution speed isn't as important as compilation speed, you can significantly speed up compilation by using the fast compile option (`/f`).

The fast compile option deactivates some of the optimizations that the compiler normally performs, thereby saving time. Later, when your program nears the final build stage, you can stop using the fast compilation option to reactivate code optimization and speed up execution.

There are two other compiler options that set the fast compile option automatically:

- The `/O` option turns off all optimizations, and therefore results in a fast compile.
- The `/Od` option disables optimizations, again resulting in a fast compile.

## Using a Disk-Caching Program

Disk-caching programs can speed up the execution of programs—including compilation programs—by moving code and data stored on disks into memory, where it can be accessed faster. The Visual C++ Setup program installs a disk-caching program named SMARTDRV. A new version of the SMARTDRV program, Version 4.0, started shipping with the introduction of Visual C++ Version 7. Version 4.0 of SMARTDRV is considerably improved over earlier versions. If you have an earlier version, you should replace it with Version 4.0.

## Use a RAM Disk Program

A RAM disk program can improve compilation speed by storing the compiler's intermediate files in RAM instead of on disk. One RAM disk program that you can use is the RAMDRIVE.SYS, which is supplied with MS-DOS. When you run the Visual C++ Setup program, it suggests a RAMDRIVE size appropriate to your system.

If you use SMARTDRV (described under the previous heading), you don't need to use the RAMDRIVE.SYS program unless you have a lot of extra memory in your system. If you use both RAMDRIVE.SYS and SMARTDRV, it's usually best to allocate more of your available memory to SMARTDRV than you assign to RAMDRIVE. That's because SMARTDRV 4.0 manages memory more efficiently than RAMDRIVE. If you allocate too much memory to RAMDRIVE.SYS, you may limit the amount of memory that can be assigned to your SMARTDRV cache.

To use RAMDRIVE.SYS, you must specify a drive by placing the drive's designator in the TMP environment variable. For more information about setting environment variables, see the documentation that comes with the Visual C++ compiler.

## Identifiers

When the Visual C++ preprocessor sends a translation unit to the Visual C++ compiler, the translation unit can contain many kinds of elements, including declarations, definitions, and identifiers. (The word identifier is an all-purpose description that includes the constants, variables, data types, and functions). The compiler combines all these elements into object-code modules that then can be linked into executable programs.

The identifiers recognized by the Visual C++ compiler were introduced in Chapter 2, "A Better C—Plus." Some identifiers are described in more detail in that chapter and in Chapter 4, "Variables."

## Compiling Programs in P-Code

One special feature of the Visual C++ compiler is that it lets you compile your code into *P-code*—a special kind of code that takes up less space than machine code, but runs more slowly. When you compile a code segment into P-code, a small interpreter is placed in your program. It translates the P-code in your program into machine language when the code is accessed at run time.

Most compilers translate programs into machine code that a computer can execute directly. The Visual C++ compiler works that way, too—but it also lets you compile your source code into P-code.

Because code segments compiled into P-code take up much less memory space than segments that are compiled into machine language, they can come in handy when you want to write a very small program and don't mind sacrificing a little execution speed. Microsoft makes that tradeoff quite frequently; some of Microsoft's most sophisticated and best-selling software was written using P-code.

To compile a program in P-code from the Visual Workbench, do the following:

1. Choose the Options menu from the menu bar.
2. Select Project... from the menu.
3. The Project Options dialog box appears. The program types are listed in a combo box. Press the arrow at the right of the combo box and choose the P-code option (either Windows or DOS) from the list.

Be sure that C or C++ is selected in the Run-Time Support list. Then, from the Project Template list, select either DOS P-Code EXE or Windows P-Code EXE.

To compile a program in P-code from a command line, just specify `/Oq` as the first option on the command line.

For more information on compiling programs in P-code, see the Visual C++ *Programming Techniques* manual.

# C and C++ Compilers

The compilation process can be divided into two main phases:

- A *preprocessing* phase, during which preprocessor directives are implemented. Preprocessor directives—such as `#include`, `#if`, and `#endif`—are special instructions that are carried out by a preprocessor built into the Visual C++ compiler. The Visual C++ compiler, like all C and C++ compilers, carries out all preprocessing directives contained in a source-code file before compilation takes place.
- A compilation phase, during which preprocessed code is compiled into object code modules.

There are some differences between the way programs are preprocessed and compiled by C compilers and the way they are preprocessed and compiled in C++. One difference is that C++ compilers have extra type-checking mechanisms that reduce programming errors and enhance the reliability of compiled programs. The type-checking mechanisms of C++ are examined closely in this chapter.

Another feature of many C++ compilers is that they don't generate machine code, but produce C-language source code that must then be compiled by a conventional C compiler. This two-stage technique for compiling C++ programs is called *translation*.

During the early stages of the development of the C++ language, all C++ compilers actually were translators that generated C-language source code, which then had to be compiled into machine code by C compilers. This process was used only because stand-alone C++ compilers were not available.

Some implementations of C++ still produce executable code using a two-phase translation process. The Microsoft Visual C++ compiler does not. The Visual C++ compiler is a one-step compiler that transforms C++ code into object code in one step, without having to rely on a separate C compiler. That makes the Visual C++ compiler faster, more efficient, and more reliable than the compilers used in many other implementations of C++.

(Alternatively, the Professional Edition of Visual C++ can compile programs in P-Code. For more information about P-Code, see the heading "Compiling Programs in P-Code" earlier in this chapter.)

# Compiling Programs with the Visual Workbench

It's easy to compile and link Visual C++ programs from the Visual Workbench. All you have to do is select a command from the Project menu (Figure 7.2). If you want to compile a program without linking it, you can select the Compile command from the Project menu. To compile and build a program in a single step, you can select the Build command or the Rebuild All command.

The Build command performs a more efficient build than the Build All command because it compiles only files that have changed since the last build. The Rebuild All command compiles all files—those that have not changed as well as those that have.

**NOTE—PROFESSIONAL AND STANDARD EDITION DIALOGS**

The Professional Edition of Visual C++ can build more kinds of applications than can the Standard Edition, so the New Project and Project Options dialog boxes displayed by the Professional Edition have more choices than those displayed by the Standard Edition. Specifically, the Professional Edition supports the building of MS-DOS applications and applications written in P-code (see the heading "Compiling Programs in P-Code," later in this chapter, for more information). The dialog boxes displayed by the Standard Edition do not offer MS-DOS or P-code build options.

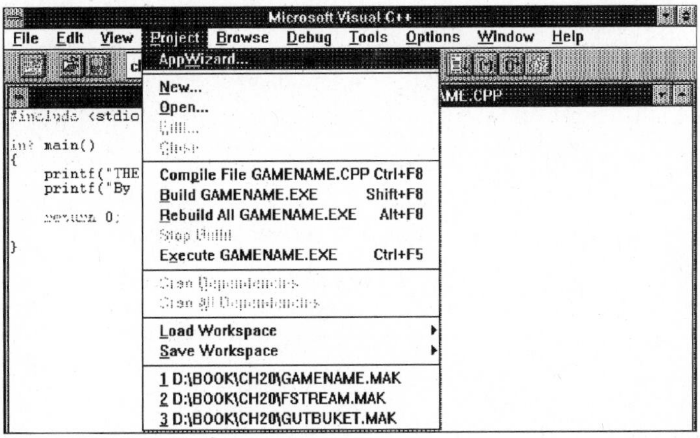


*Figure 7.2. The Project menu.*

## The New Project Dialog Box

As noted in Chapter 1, "Microsoft Visual C++," the first step in writing a Visual C++ program is to create a *project*. A project contains all the source files, resources, and libraries that make up a program, along with the compiler and linker commands that are needed to build the program.

You can create a project from the Visual Workbench by selecting the New command from the Project menu. The Visual Workbench then displays a dialog box that you can use to specify the kind of application that you want to create.

In Chapter 1, you created a QuickWin application—a simple text-based program that runs under Windows, inside a document window displayed on a Windows screen. In Part III, which begins with Chapter 21, you'll have an opportunity to create a full-scale Windows application.

## Components of a Project

As you've seen over and over as you built the programs in Chapters 1 through 6, every application written in Visual C++ begins its life as a project. Specifically, the components of a Visual C++ project are:

- A *makefile*, which builds the project. The makefile that builds a project always has the same name as the project itself, plus a filename extension (.MAK) that identifies the file as a makefile. Makefiles for Visual C++ applications are compatible with the Microsoft Program Maintenance Utility (NMAKE).
- A *status file*, which contains information needed by the Visual Workbench. The status file associated with a project always has the same name as the project itself, plus a filename extension (.VCW) that identifies the file as a project file.
- The source files, object files, and resource files needed to compile and execute the project.

> **NOTE—ONE-FILE PROJECTS**
>
> If your program consists of only one file—as many of the example programs in this book do—you can compile and run it without explicitly creating a project. (For QuickWin programs, the make utility even includes the module-definition file automatically.) However, it's always a good idea to create a project anyway—especially if your program has special compiler or linker settings. If the program is not registered as a project, its compiler and linker settings are lost when another project is loaded or Visual Workbench is restarted.

## Project Files You Supply

When you create a project using the New Project dialog box, the Visual C++ build utility generates the project's makefile and status file. Besides those two files, you must supply:

- The *source code* needed to compile the program. Although a small C++ program can contain only one source file—many of the small sample programs in this book do contain just one file—most commercial-quality

C++ programs contain a great number of files. Each source file in a C++ program contains some of the source code needed to build the application.

- A set of *header files* that contain function declarations, data structures, and data definitions. In C++, header files also contain definitions and declarations of classes; definitions and declarations of class member functions; constant and macro declarations and definitions; and declarations and definitions of external variables.
- A set of object-code *libraries* that contain implementations of functions and (in object-oriented programs) implementations of classes and class member functions. Visual C++ supports many kinds of libraries, including the standard libraries shipped with C, the runtime library supplied with Visual C++, the Microsoft Foundation Class (MFC) library of C++ classes, and even dynamic-link libraries (DLLs), which let different applications share common object code when multiple applications are running simultaneously.

## QuickWin Programs and Other Applications

Once you specify what kind of application you want to create, you can create a project that contains the files your application requires.

If you want to create a QuickWin application, as you did in Chapter 1, all you have to do is write one source-code file and then build it by selecting the Build command or the Build All command from the Project menu. To create a Windows application (an .EXE file) or a Windows Dynamic-Link Library (a .DLL file), you can select the AppWizard command from the Project menu.

Procedures for building a QuickWin program were outlined in Chapter 1. Creating a Windows application requires a few more steps. You'll learn what they are in Chapter 21, "The Microsoft Foundation Classes."

## The Project Options Dialog Box

Once you decide what kind of application you want to write and select an application type from the New Project dialog box, you can specify various options that you want the Visual C++ compiler and linker to use when they compile and link your program.

To set compiler and linker options, select the Project command under the Options menu. The Visual C++ Workbench then displays a Project Options dialog box like the one shown in Figure 7.3.

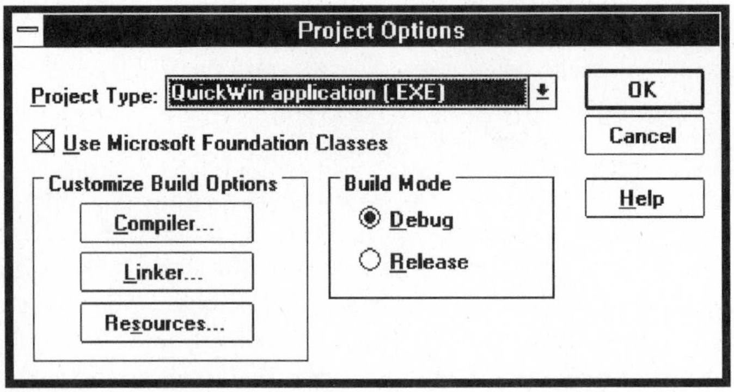


*Figure 7.3. Project Options dialog box.*

> **NOTE—COMMAND-LINE COMPILATION**
>
> If you own the Professional Edition of Visual C++, you can compile and link Visual C++ programs by typing and executing MS-DOS command lines. However, before you can build programs by executing command lines, you must make some special modifications to your AUTOEXEC.BAT file, as noted under the heading "Configuring Your System for Command-Line Compilation," later in this chapter.

## The Debugging and Release Buttons

To use the Project Options dialog box, you must set the list box labeled Project Type to match the type of application you want to create. You also can select one of the radio buttons in the Build Mode group to specify whether you want to build a debug version or a release version of the program that you're writing.

If you select Debug, the Visual Workbench places debugging symbols in your program so that you can debug them using the Visual C++ source line debugger.

Debugging symbols lengthen the size of an application by a small amount and slightly increase execution time. Once you debug your application, you can recompile it without debugging symbols by returning to the Project Options dialog box and selecting the Release button.

## The Compiler Button

In the lower left-hand corner of the Project Options dialog box, there is a radio-button group labeled Customized Build Options. There are three buttons in the group: Compiler, Linker, and Resources. The results of clicking the Linker and Resources buttons are described in Chapter 8, "Linking Visual C++ Programs." This section explains what happens when you click the Compiler button.

When you click the button labeled Compiler, a dialog box labeled Compiler Options appears on the screen. The Compiler Options dialog window is shown in Figure 7.4.

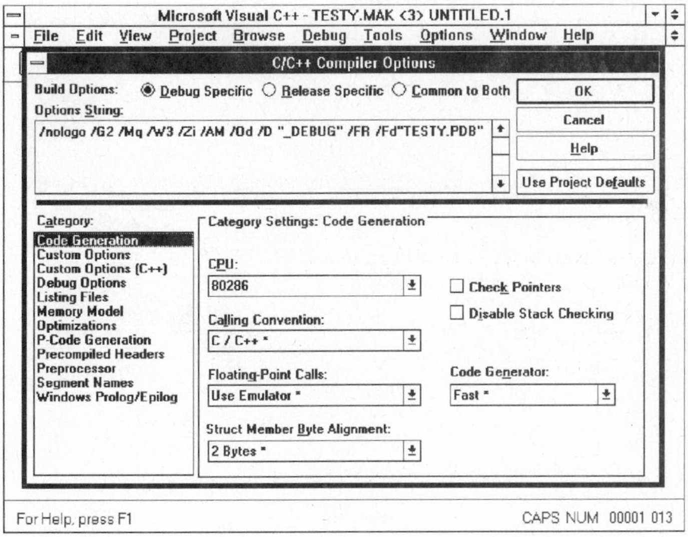


*Figure 7.4. The Compiler Options dialog box.*

## Using the Compiler Options Dialog Box

The Compiler Options dialog box is divided into two parts: one part occupying the top third of the box and a bigger part occupying the area below it. The controls in the top part of the window work like the controls in any Visual C++ dialog window. But you can change the appearance of the bottom part of the window by selecting command-line items in the list box labeled Category.

For example, when you select the option category Custom Options, the layout of the lower right-hand part of the Compiler Options window changes to show you more options, as shown in Figure 7.5. You then can select various customized compiler options by clicking the controls shown in the Category Settings section of the Compiler Options window.

## NOTE—USING DEFAULT COMPILER OPTIONS

The Visual C++ Setup program installs a set of default compiler options when you install Visual C++. When you choose compiler options using the Compiler Options dialog box, your new choices override your default choices. When you're selecting new compiler options using the Compiler Options dialog box, you can restore your default compiler options at any time by clicking the button labeled Use Project Defaults.

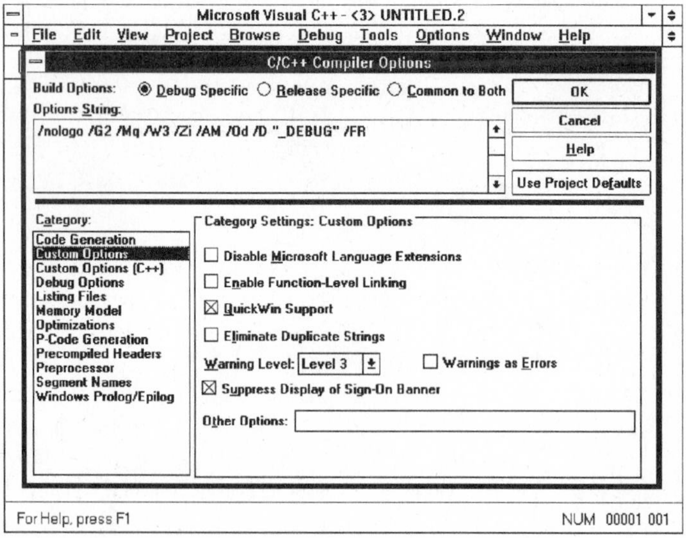


*Figure 7.5. Selecting a compiler option.*

When you select a command-line option from the list box in the lower left-hand corner of the Compiler Options dialog box, the change that you make is shown in the upper half of the window, in the text box labeled Options String.

When you close the Compiler Options dialog and compile your program, the Visual C++ compiler executes the command line that was displayed in the Options String text box when the Compiler Options dialog box was closed.

> **NOTE—INTERPRETING THE OPTIONS STRING**
>
> The string shown in the Options String text box is not an actual command line, but merely a representation of a command line, designed to show you the compiler options that currently are selected. If you own the Professional Edition of Visual C++, and want to compile a program by executing an MS-DOS command line, the string shown in the Options String text box might not work. For instructions on compiling a program by executing a command line, see the documentation that comes with the Professional Edition of Visual C++.

### Getting Help with Command-Line Options

The Visual C++ compiler accepts an enormous number of options—many more than can be described in this chapter. There are so many options that Microsoft provides a special kind of Help mechanism to help you choose the ones you want when you compile Visual C++ programs.

To obtain help information about a specific option, just highlight the option in the text box labeled Options String (or simply place the insertion point on the option) and press F1. The Visual Workbench then displays a window containing Help information about the option you have selected.

## Configuring Your System for Command-Line Compilation

Because Visual C++ is designed primarily to be used with the Visual Toolbox, and because the Standard Edition does not support MS-DOS command lines, the Standard Version Setup program doesn't ordinarily configure your system to compile and link Visual C++ programs by executing commands from an MS-DOS command line. In fact, you cannot build programs by executing command lines if you own the Standard Version of Visual C++. With the Standard Version, you must compile and link programs using the Compiler Options and Linker Options dialog boxes.

However, if you own the Professional Edition of Visual C++, you can make some changes in your AUTOEXEC.BAT file that will let you run the Visual C++ compiler, the Visual C++ linker, and other build tools such as `NMAKE` from MS-DOS command lines.

If you own the Professional Edition of Microsoft Visual C++, you can follow these steps to modify your AUTOEXEC.BAT for MS-DOS command-line tools:

1. Launch any text editor that is compatible with MS-DOS. (You can use the Visual C++ editor.)

2. Open your AUTOEXEC.BAT file.

3. To the directories shown on the PATH line of your AUTOEXEC.BAT file, add the name of the directory in which Microsoft Visual C++ is stored. Separate the name of your Visual C++ directory from the previous directory with a backslash (\). For example, if Visual C++ is stored in a directory named MSVC:

   ```
   C:\MSVC\BIN
   ```

4. To your AUTOEXEC.BAT file, add a line that specifies two directories for your C-language INCLUDE files. Those two directories are:

   - The INCLUDE directory inside the directory in which Visual C++ is stored.
   - The MFC directory inside the Visual C++ (MSVC) directory.

   For example, if Visual C++ is stored in a directory named MSVC on drive C: add this line to your AUTOEXEC.BAT file:

   ```
   SET INCLUDE = C:\MSVC\INCLUDE;C:\MSVC\MFC\INCLUDE
   ```

5. To your AUTOEXEC.BAT file, add another line that specifies two directories for your C-language .LIB files. Those two directories are:

   - The LIB directory inside the directory in which Visual C++ is stored.
   - The MFC directory inside the MSVC directory.

For example, if Visual C++ is stored in a directory named MSVC on drive C: add this line to your AUTOEXEC.BAT file:

```
SET LIB = C:\MSVC\LIB;C:\MSVC\MSVC\LIB
```

6. In order to execute the `CL`, `LINK`, `NMAKE`, `CVPACK`, and `BSCMAKE` commands, either they must be in the same directory as the file DOSXNT.EXE, or DOSXNT.EXE must be on their path. Also, you must place a command like the following in the [386Enh] section of the SYSTEM.INI file (this command assumes that Visual C++ is installed in the C:\MSVC directory:

```
DEVICE = C:\MSVC\BIN\DOSXNT.386
```

7. Finally, the file DOSXNST.386 must be in the BIN directory inside the directory in which Visual C++ is installed. For example, if Visual C++ is stored in a directory named MSVC on Drive C, DOSXNST.386 must be in the C:\MSVC\BIN directory. That's where the Visual C++ Setup program places the DOSXNT.386 file.

Once you configure your system to build programs from MS-DOS command lines, you can manually execute the commands `CL`, `LINK`, `NMAKE`, `CVPACK`, and `BSCMAKE` (provided, again, that you own the Visual C++ Professional Edition). These are all 32-bit MS-DOS-extended programs that must be executed on an 80386—or better—processor, running in protected mode.

Once your system is configured to accept MS-DOS build commands, you can execute the `CL`, `LINK`, `NMAKE`, `CVPACK`, and `BSCMAKE` commands from any MS-DOS session running under Windows, as well as from outside Windows at the MS-DOS prompt.

# The Visual C++ Preprocessor

When you compile a Visual C++ program, the Visual C++ preprocessor runs transparently. Before the compiler compiles your source code into object-code modules, your code passes through the compiler's preprocessor. When you compile a Visual C++ source file, a preprocessor that's built into the Visual C++ compiler carries out all preprocessor directives that the source file contains. The compiler then compiles the file into object-code modules.

A preprocessor directive always begins with the symbol #, optionally preceded by spaces and tab characters. The symbol # always is followed by a preprocessor directive.

There are two kinds of preprocessor directives:

- Directives that cause text to be inserted into a source-code file before the file is compiled. The process of placing text in a file in accordance with a preprocessor directive is called *macro expansion*. When a preprocessor directive causes macro expansion to take place, the preprocessor directive is removed and replaced by a text string. The contents of the text string are determined by rules that govern the use of preprocessor directives. For detailed information on how macro expansion works in Visual C++ programs, see the documentation that Microsoft supplies with C++.
- *Conditional compilation* directives such as `#if`, `#ifdef`, `#ifndef`, and `#endif`. When the Visual C++ preprocessor encounters a directive that starts a conditional compilation—such as `#if`, `#ifdef`, or `#ifndef`—any source code that follows the directive is either compiled or not compiled, depending on whether the word that follows the directive has been or has not been defined. Normal compilation resumes at the next matching `#endif` directive.

### NOTE—THE PREPROCESSOR PARADOX

While the C++ preprocessor has many wonderful new features, the C++ language also has a host of new features that make preprocessors less useful than they were in C. In fact, there are some preprocessor directives that you should avoid using in your C++ programs altogether because the C++ language now offers better and safer alternatives, for example:

*Constants created with the `#define` directive.* In C++, objects declared as `const` can be used in constant expressions. That means that, in a C++ program, you can declare constants that have type and value information and are stored in your program's symbol table. Defining a constant with the preprocessor `#define` directive is not as precise. Constants created with `#define` have no type or data information, so they can't be type-checked and can't be tracked down as easily during debugging. For more about C++'s enhancements to `const` objects, see Chapter 3, "Type Qualifiers."

*Function-type macros.* Instead of using function-type macros in C++ programs, you should now use *inline functions*. Inline functions are better than preprocessor macros because:

> Inline functions are subject to the same kind of type-checking as ordinary functions. In contrast, function-style macros are not type-safe.
>
> Inline functions have no undesirable side effects. When the compiler processes an inline function, it evaluates expressions supplied as arguments before it compiles the body of the function. This procedure eliminates side effects caused by expressions in the argument list. In contrast, function-style macros often have surprising and unwanted side effects.
>
> For these reasons, it's usually better to create a constant with the `const` modifier than relying on the `#define` directive, and it's usually better to write an inline function than it is to write a function-style macro.

Programmers often use preprocessor directives to make source programs easy to change and easy to compile in different execution environments. For example, the preprocessor can replace tokens in source text, insert the contents of other files into a source file, or suppress the compilation of specified parts of a file by removing sections of text.

When you write a statement that contains a preprocessor directive, the number sign (#) must be the first non-white-space character on the line that contains the directive. (White-space characters can precede the number sign and can appear between the number sign and the first letter of the directive.)

A statement that includes a preprocessor directive extends only the line of source text on which the directive appears, unless the line ends with the line continuation character. If you insist, you can use the line-continuation (backslash) character to continue a preprocessor statement to the next line.

Preprocessor directives can appear anywhere in a source file, but they apply only to the remainder of the source file.

Here are two examples of preprocessor directives (note that a semicolon does not appear at the end of a line containing a preprocessor directive):

```
#define STR_SIZE 28
#include <iostream.h>
```

A preprocessor directive applies only to the portion of a source file that follows the directive.

> **NOTE—ANALYZING PREPROCESSED CODE**
>
> If you'd like to see exactly what the Visual C++ processor does to your code, you can get a listing of your code after it has been preprocessed by compiling your code with the `/E` or `/EP` compilation options. Both options invoke the preprocessor, which then sends a text file to standard output—normally the screen. The difference between the two options is that the `/E` option generates `#line` directives, while `/EP` does not.

# Header Files

The basic routines and data for the C and C++ language are supplied in a standard default library that's built into the Visual C++ compiler. You don't have to include any special files in your source programs to call the functions and use the data types provided in this built-in C/C++ library; your compiler accesses them automatically.

However, you cannot write a robust C++ program if you limit it to the functions and data types that are available in your compiler's standard built-in library. That library does not contain any functions for managing I/O operations, graphics, or Windows-related operations, and it lacks many other kinds of functions that almost every C++ program requires. So you'll need to include procedures implemented in external libraries in most of your C++ programs.

More than 550 useful (or essential) C and C++ functions are provided in the run-time library shipped with Visual C++. Many other routines, including most Windows-related procedures and many other functions that can be used in non-Windows programs, are supplied in the Microsoft Foundation Class (MFC) library. The MFC library also contains an enormous number of classes and member functions that you can use in object-oriented C++ programs.

## Using Header Files

Every library that Microsoft supplies with Visual C++ is associated with a specific *header file*. A header file is a source-code file that defines the functions implemented in a particular library, and provides data and data structures that the library requires. Visual C++ uses header files when it compiles a program, and uses library files when the program is linked.

Before you can access a function, class, or member function that is implemented in a library, you must know what header file is associated with the function so you can include the appropriate header file in your program.

You can find out what header files are associated with which libraries by consulting the library manuals that come with Visual C++. Once you know what header file you need in a program, you can include the header file in your program by placing the `#include` preprocessor directive in the source-code file where the call to the function appears. For example, if you look up the `printf()` function in the *Run-Time Library Reference* available from Microsoft, you'll find that `printf()` depends on the STDIO.H header file. So, before you use `printf()` to print a program, your source code must include a line similar to this:

```
#include <stdio.h>
```

Once you include this directive in a source-code program, the Visual C++ compiler inserts the contents of the header file STDIO.H into the program's source code when the program is compiled. Your program then can call the `printf()` function, just as if `printf()` were declared in the file being compiled. For example, this short program calls the `printf()` function to print a line of text to standard output (normally, the screen).

```
#include <stdio.h>
int main()
{
     printf("THE WRATH OF ZALTHAR\n");
     return 0;
}
```

## Contents of Header Files

Header files not only contain declarations of functions; they also can contain declarations, constants, and type definitions, and other kinds of information on the libraries to which they may require access. For example, header files can contain declarations of external variables and complex data types. Therefore, if you have a collection of constant and macro definitions that you want to include in a program, you can place them in header files and use the `#include` directive to add your definitions to any source file.

## Nesting Header Files

You can *nest* include files; that is, you can place an `#include` directive in a file that is included in a program by another `#include` directive. For example, if you include a file named MYFILE2 in a file named MYFILE1, MYFILE2 can include another file named MYFILE3. In this case, MYFILE1 is the *parent* of MYFILE2, and MYFILE1 is the *grandparent* of MYFILE3.

## Bracketed and Quoted #include Directives

In C, as in C++, there are two formats for including files in programs. When you want to include a standard Visual C++ header file—for example, the file IOSTREAM.H or the file STDIO.H—the conventional practice is to enclose the name of the file to be included in brackets. When you want to include a header file that you have written yourself—for example, a file that contains declarations of your own variables, constants, and data types—the convention is to enclose the name of the included file in double quotation marks.

These two lines show the two styles for including files in a C or C++ program:

```
#include <iostream.h>
#include "myfile.h"
```

There is no official requirement for you to follow the convention of using two styles for including header files—but it's a good idea because it saves compilation time.

## How the Preprocessor Finds Header Files

If a filename that follows an `#include` directive is enclosed in angle brackets—in the format `#include <iostream.h>`—the preprocessor starts searching for the specified header file in the directories in which Visual C++ header files reside; that is, in the directories specified by the DOS INCLUDE environment and the path specified by the `/I` compiler option. If that search fails, the preprocessor starts another search, beginning with the current directory.

If the filename that follows an `#include` directive is enclosed in quotation marks—in the format `#include "myfile.h"`—the preprocessor begins its search in the current directory.

If the file isn't in the current directory, the search moves to the current directory's *parent directory*, that is, the directory that contains the current directory. If the desired file is still not found, the preprocessor searches the *grandparent directory*, that is, the directory that contains the parent directory.

If the file being sought is not in the current directory, the parent directory, or grandparent directory, the preprocessor starts searching the standard Visual C++ library files, as if the filename were enclosed in angle brackets.

### NOTE—#INCLUDE STATEMENTS IN VISUAL C++

When a pathname enclosed in quotation marks appears in an `#include` statement, Visual C++ handles the search for the specified file in a way that's different from the procedures used by other C and C++ compilers.

In most versions of C and C++, when you include a file in a program using the style `#include "myfile.h"`, the preprocessor starts searching for the file in the current directory. If that search fails, the preprocessor immediately moves its search to the directory in which standard header files reside. In Visual C++, as you have seen, the search moves next through parent and grandparent directories, and only then does it continue to the directories where Visual C++ header files reside.

There's another important difference between the way in which Visual C++ handles quoted include files and the way in which they're handled by most other kinds of C and C++ compilers. In Visual C++, an `#include` statement written in the quotation-mark format can contain a complete, unambiguous pathname called a *fully qualified* pathname.

A fully qualified pathname is one in which the first character is a forward slash (`/`) or a backslash (`\`) or the second character is a colon (`:`) For example, `C:\MSVC\BOOK\SOURCE\CH1` is a fully qualified pathname. Therefore, in Visual C++ (but *not* in most other varieties of C or C++), this kind of `#include` statement is legal:

```
#include "C:\MSVC\BOOK\SOURCE\CH1\myfile.h"
```

When an `#include` statement is followed by a fully qualified pathname enclosed in quotation marks, the specified path is the only one that is searched by the preprocessor.

## Precompiled Headers and Precompiled Files

When you include a header file in a C or C++ program, the source code in the header normally is recompiled every time the compiler encounters a module that includes the header. When a program contains many header files, this recompilation of header files can take a long time. Therefore, Visual C++ provides a method for precompiling header files to speed up the compilation process.

In fact, when you program with Visual C++, you aren't limited to precompiling header files; you also can precompile executable source files. That can speed up compilation significantly because a precompiled file does not have to be compiled every time the program that contains the file is built.

When you use precompiled files to build a program, each precompiled file is compiled only once. Each time a source-code file that includes a precompiled header file is compiled, the precompiled copy of the header is used, and the header is not recompiled.

When you use precompiled header files, the first compilation of your code—the one that creates the precompiled header file—takes a little longer than a normal compilation. Subsequent compilations are speeded up by the existence of precompiled include files.

### Using Precompiled Files with Visual C++

The Visual C++ compiler isn't the only compiler that supports precompiled header files. However, the Microsoft implementation of precompiled headers is different from the system used by most other compiler manufactures. The difference is that the Visual C++ compiler can precompile executable code, not just declarations. This approach is particularly well suited to C++ programs, which typically place many definitions of classes and member functions in header files.

> **NOTE—USING PRECOMPILED TYPES WITH THE CODEVIEW DEBUGGER**
>
> Besides supporting precompiled header files, Visual C++ lets you use *precompiled types,* which apply the same general technique used in precompiled headers to the generation of debug information required by CodeView (supplied only with the Professional Edition of Visual C++).

> In early versions of Microsoft C++, the C++ compiler generated debugging information for each header file in a program every time it compiled a module that contained the header file. Now, if you choose, you can instruct the Visual C++ compiler to save all CodeView information from header files in a separate object file, and can add the information to each object module at link time, rather than at compile time. As a result, compile time during the debugging cycle also is greatly reduced. For more information on using the CodeView debugger, see the CodeView Debugger User's Guide and Tools manual that comes with the Professional Edition of Visual C++.

## Precompilation Commands

The most efficient way to use precompilation is to precompile header files that frequently are used in a program. Precompilation is most useful when:

- Header files make up a significant portion of your source code.
- You change the executable code in your source files more often than you change program's header files.
- Your program has multiple modules, all of which use a standard set of include files.

In the last of these three cases, if all your modules use the same compilation options, you can precompile all of your include files into one precompiled header and save even more compilation time.

The easiest way to take advantage of Visual C++'s precompilation capabilities is to specify automatic precompiling. You can do that by selecting the `/YX` compiler option and letting the compiler decide when to create and use precompiled files.

Alternatively, you can manually compile a program with a precompiled header file by using the `/Yc` ("create") compiler option. The compiler then precompiles the program's header files and assigns them filenames that end with the suffix .PCH.

You might want to use manual precompiling when, for example, an application's source files use common sets of header files but don't include them in the same order. Or, you might use precompiling when you want to include your source code in your precompilation.

When you use precompiled header files in a program, you can speed up the compilation of the program even more by using the fast compile (`/f`) option, which is the compiler's default setting. The `/f` option saves the state of a compilation, including CodeView information, after header files have been processed. In later compilations, the compiler simply restores the saved compilation state from a precompiled header .PCH file, rather than recompiling the unchanged header files.

For more information on precompiled header files, see the Microsoft documentation that comes with the Visual C++ package.

# The #define Directive

The Visual C++ preprocessor does its work by performing simple text substitution on the source code that it preprocesses. Because this text-replacing process results in the creation of macros, it sometimes is referred to as *macro expansion*.

You can instruct the preprocessor to perform macro expansion by using the `#define` directive, which has this syntax:

```
#define identifier token_string
```

where *`identifier`* is a symbolic name for a constant and *`token_string`* is a text string. When you execute a `#define` directive using this format, the preprocessor creates a symbolic name for the *`identifier`* variable and associates that name with a string variable that is specified in the *`token_string`* field. From that point on, the compiler substitutes the string specified in *`token_string`* variable for the string specified in *`identifier`* every time the word *`identifier`* appears in the source file.

## Creating Constants with #define

You can use the `#define` directive to create symbolic names for constant values, as in this example:

```
#define SIZE 32
```

When the C/C++ preprocessor encounters this directive , it creates the symbolic name `SIZE` and associates the name `SIZE` with the *text string* (not the integer) 32. From that point on, whenever the word `SIZE` occurs in the source file being preprocessed, the preprocessor replaces the word `SIZE` with the text string 32—that is, the number 32 expressed as a string of two digits. After the source file is preprocessed, it looks just as it would look if the number 32 had been typed instead of the word `SIZE` everywhere the word `SIZE` originally appeared.

There's also an `#undef` directive that removes an assignment of a value from a constant.

> **NOTE—THE CONST MODIFIER VERSUS THE #DEFINE DIRECTIVE**
>
> Although you can create constants in C++ with the `#define` keyword, there is a better way. With the `const` modifier, which turns variables into constants, you can declare `const` variables that are much more versatile than constants that are created with `#define`. For more about how the `const` creates constants in C++, see Chapter 3, "Type Qualifiers."

## What the #define Directive Doesn't Do

Because a `#define` directive is not a declaration or a directive, but merely a text-substitution facility, there is no way to assign a data type to a constant that is declared and defined with the `#define` directive. When you create a constant with the `#define` directive, you can use the constant any way you like: as an integer, a string, a Boolean value, or any other basic data type. For example, place this line in a source file:

```
#define POPEYE true
```

and the preprocessor happily replaces all subsequent occurrences of the word `POPEYE` with the word `true`, which the compiler then interprets as a Boolean value. In this case, when preprocessing is finished, the Boolean value `true` appears everywhere that the word `POPEYE` originally appeared in the source file.

Because the `#define` directive doesn't care what data type a constant has when it defines the constant, the compiler has no way to perform data-checking to ensure that the constant is used correctly. Consequently, defining constants with the `#define` directive can be a risky practice.

Fortunately, a safer way to define constants was introduced with the premiere of C++: the `const` modifier, which is covered in Chapter 3.

> **NOTE—PREPROCESSING WITHOUT COMPILING**
>
> When you compile a Visual C++ program, your source code ordinarily is preprocessed before it is sent on to the compiler. However, you also can invoke the preprocessor directly without sending preprocessed code to the compiler. That way, you can examine the preprocessor's output without compiling a program.
>
> To get a listing of your source code after it is preprocessed but before it is compiled, all you have to do is execute the compile (CL) command with the `/E` or `/EP` option. Both options invoke the preprocessor and send its output to the standard output device (normally, the screen). The difference between the two options is that `/E` prints a line number at the beginning of each line of the preprocessor's output, while `/EP` does not print line numbers.

## Creating Macros with #define

As noted earlier, the text-substitution operations that are performed by the `#define` directive sometimes are referred to as macro expansions. The results of these text-substitution operations often are referred to, logically enough, as macros.

With the `#define` directive, you can create two kinds of macros: *object-like macros* and *function-like macros.*

### Object-Like Macros

An object-like macro is a macro that replaces a name with a specified text string. Here is the general syntax you must use to create an object-like macro with the `#define` directive:

```
#define name replacement_text
```

where *`name`* is the name of a macro and *`replacement_text`* is the text that is to be substituted for the name of the macro in all subsequent source text.

When you define a constant using the `#define` directive, the statement in which the constant is defined is an object-like macro. For example,

```
#define SIZE 32
```

is an object-like macro. So, the preprocessor substitutes the number 32 for the word `SIZE` everywhere the word `SIZE` originally appeared in the file.

This `#define` statement creates a macro named `RANGE_ERR` that equates to the string `"Error: Value out of range"`:

```
#define RANGE_ERR "Error: Value out of range"
```

Once you define the `RANGE_ERR` macro in this fashion, you can type `RANGE_ERR` instead of the message `"Error: Value out of range"` every place you want the message to appear in a program. For example, this statement prints a range-error message to standard output:

```
if (myVar > maxVar) {
     cout << RANGE_ERR << /n;
}
```

## Function-Like Macros

The `#define` statement also can create macros that take parameters, and are consequently sometimes called *function-like macros*. In C programs, for the sake of speed and efficiency, function-like macros often are used in place of short functions. By using a macro in a program instead of a function, you often can reduce overhead because the compiler does not have to call a function by manipulating values on the stack. Instead, the precompiler simply replaces each occurrence of the macro with its expanded textual equivalent. The result is an increase in program speed, usually at the expense of slightly increased program size.

Here is the syntax of a `#define` directive that creates a function-like macro:

```
#define name (identifier_list) replacement_text
```

where *`identifier_list`* equates to a list of identifiers that look and work almost exactly like a set of arguments you pass to a function. When you use the `#define` directive to create a function-like macro, you supply a formal parameter list, just as you'd provide a formal argument list in declaring a function. When you call the macro in your source code, you pass arguments to it, in much the same way that you would if the macro were a function. For example, this sequence of directives defines a macro named `EVEN_NUM`:

```
#define FALSE 0
#define TRUE 1
#define EVEN_NUM(num) (((num) % 2) ? FALSE : TRUE)
```

If `EVEN_NUM` is defined this way in a program, you can call it with a statement like this:

```
if (EVEN_NUM(7) == TRUE)
     cout << "The number is odd\n.";
else
     cout << "The number is even.\n";
```

Because the number 7 is odd, this code fragment prints

```
The number is odd
```

to standard output.

## Side Effects

You may have noticed in the previous macro definition that parentheses are used quite liberally. That's because macros are subject to unwanted *side effects*. A side effect, as you may know, is an action that occurs as a result of executing a statement. Programmers often write statements not for their primary effects but for their side effects, for example, storing a value, clearing the screen, and so on. However, sometimes side effects are accidental, not deliberate—and accidental side effects can produce undesirable results.

Assume, for example, that the macro definition shown in the previous example is written using fewer parentheses, like this:

```
#define EVEN_NUM(myVar) myVar % 2 ? FALSE : TRUE
```

Now assume that you call the macro with this statement:

```
x = 2;
y = 4;
if (EVEN_NUM(x + y) == TRUE)
     cout << "The number is odd\n.";
else
     cout << "The number is even.\n";
```

In this case the expression `(x + y)` evaluates to 2 + 4, or 6, so you would expect the `EVEN_NUM` macro to return the Boolean value `TRUE`. However, because of an unexpected side effect, the macro returns `FALSE`.

This is the problem: If `EVEN_NUM` evaluated the expression as

```
(x + y) % 2
```

as you might expect, the result would be true because 2 + 4 reduces to 6, an even number. However, `EVEN_NUM` actually evaluates the expression

```
x + y % 2
```

which evaluates to 2 + 0, or 2, yielding a result of `FALSE`.

There are other precautions you must take when you write macros. For example, there can be no white space between the left parenthesis of a macro and the first character that follows the parenthesis . That's because the preprocessor looks for white-space characters after the macro name to determine where the replacement text begins. If the preprocessor encounters a left parenthesis in the name string without intervening space, it assumes that a parameter list follows and regards everything up to the next closing parenthesis as part of that list.

> **NOTE—A C++ FEATURE**
>
> Because of the shortcomings of macros, C++ offers a new kind of function—called an *inline function*—that provides all of the advantages of function-like macros without the disadvantages.
>
> Inline functions are described in Chapter 6, "Functions."

# Conditional Compilation Directives

*Conditional compilation directives* are preprocessor directives that can permit or prevent the compilation of specified portions of a source file, depending upon whether certain conditions are true. Software developers often use conditional compilation directives to write programs that can be compiled in different versions for different machines.

Conditional compilation directives always occur in pairs. The first directive in the pair starts conditional compilation, and the second directive terminates conditional compilation. The following example shows how conditional compilation directives—in this case, the directives `#if` and `#endif`— typically are used in C and C++ programs:

```
#if defined(BATMAN)
ConditionalFunction();
#endif
```

In this example, if a constant named `BATMAN` has been defined in an executing program, a function named `ConditionalFunction()` is called. If `BATMAN` is not defined when the compiler encounters this code fragment, `ConditionalFunction()` is not called.

By placing conditional compilation directives in a program in this manner, you can instruct the compiler to compile specified code segments only if specified variables are defined. Then, by either defining the specified variables in header files or leaving them undefined, you can compile different versions of the same source-code program . This can be a useful technique when you want to write a program that can be compiled with different compilers or can be executed on different systems.

Conditional compilation directives, like all preprocessor directives, are compiler-specific. Conditional compilation directives recognized by Visual C++ include the directives `#if ... #endif`, `#ifdef ... #endif`, or `#ifndef ... #endif`.

A conditional compilation directive always is followed by a constant or a constant expression that has a value of true (a nonzero value), or false (a zero value). If the expression that follows the directive is true, the source code that follows the expression is passed on to the compiler. If the expression is false, the source code that follows the expression is intercepted by the preprocessor and is not sent on to the compiler.

## Writing Comments with Compilation Directives

Although conditional compilation directives were designed primarily to help make source code more portable, many C programmers also use conditional compilation directives to place comments in programs. This is a usage that arose out of frustration; traditional C-style comments can't be nested, so C programmers often use conditional compilation directives to "comment out" portions of code that already contain comments.

It isn't necessary to use conditional compilation directives to write C++ comments because—as you saw in Chapter 2—comments that can be nested are now available to C/C++ programmers. For more information on placing comments in C++ programs, see the section on comments in C++ programs in Chapter 2.

## The #if Directive

In both C and C++, the truth of an `#if` directive often depends on whether a constant has previously been defined. You can prevent a portions of code from being compiled by following an `#if` directive with a statement that you know to be false. The preprocessor then will intercept the source code that follows the statement and will not send it on to the compiler.

When you use an `#if` or `#ifdef` directive, it's important to remember that you must balance it with a closing `#endif` directive, as in this code fragment:

```
#if defined(POPEYE)
MyFunction();
#endif
```

This example sends `MyFunction()` to the compiler if the constant `POPEYE` has been defined in the program being preprocessed. If `POPEYE` has not been defined, the line that follows the `#if defined` statement is not sent to the compiler, and `MyFunction()` is never called.

The preprocessor directive `#ifdef` is equivalent to the directive `#if defined`. Therefore, the previous example could also be written as:

```
#ifdef POPEYE
MyFunction();
#endif
```

The preprocessor directive `#ifndef` sends the code that follows it to the compiler if a specified constant has *not* been defined. For example, this statement causes `MyFunction()` to be sent to the compiler if the constant `POPEYE` has not been defined:

```
#ifndef POPEYE
MyFunction();
#endif
```

## The #else and #elif Directives

Between the `#if` directive and its matching `#endif` directive, you can place other directives, such as `#else` or `#elif`.

You can use any number of `#elif` directives between the `#if` and `#endif` directives, but only one `#else` directive is allowed. If you use an `#else` directive, it must be the last directive before `#endif`.

The `#if`, `#else`, and `#elif` directives work like the `if`, `else if`, and `else` directives in C. For example:

```
#if defined POPEYE
OneFunction();
#elif defined SWEETPEA
SomeOtherFunction();
#else
PrintError();
#endif
```

In this example:

- If the constant POPEYE is defined, OneFunction() is sent to the compiler.
- If POPEYE is not defined but the constant SWEETPEA is defined, SomeOtherFunction() is sent to the compiler, but OneFunction() is not.
- If neither POPEYE nor SWEETPEA is defined, only the function PrintError() is sent to the compiler.

## Combining the #ifdef and #else Directives

Listing 7.1 shows how the #ifdef, #else, and #endif directives can be used in a program. In this example, if the constant POPEYE is defined, the stream variable cout sends two lines of text to standard output (normally, the screen). If POPEYE is not defined, the STDIO.H statement printf sends the same text to standard output.

### Listing 7.1. Using conditional compilation directives.

```
// 0701.CPP

// THE WRATH OF ZALTHAR
// A Sample C++ Program

#include <iostream.h>
#include <stdio.h>

#define POPEYE true

int main()
{
    #ifdef POPEYE
    cout << "THE WRATH OF ZALTHAR\n";
    cout << "Copyright 19XX, [Your Name Here]\n";
    #else
    printf("THE WRATH OF ZALTHAR\n");
    printf("Copyright 19XX, [Your Name Here]\n");
    #endif
    return 0;
}
```

**NOTE—USING CONDITIONAL COMPILATION IN HEADER FILES**

C and C++ programmers often use conditional compilation directives to make sure that header files are included in a program only once, because including a header file more than once can cause compilation errors.

The standard technique for ensuring that a header file is included only once is to check to see if a user-created variable has been defined. If the variable has not yet been defined, the header file is included in the program and the variable is then defined. If another attempt is made to include the header file in the program, the precompiler detects that the variable has now been defined, and the header file is not included in the program again.

Here's how this conditional compilation technique works in the MATH.H file supplied with Visual C++:

```
#ifndef _INC_MATH

// ... function declarations in the MATH.H file ...

#define _INC_MATH
#endif  /* _INC_MATH */
```

This code prevents the MATH.H file from being included in a compiled program more than once.

# Other Preprocessor Directives

Other preprocessor directives recognized by the Visual C++ processor are:

- `#error`. A directive prints an error message and aborts compilation if an error is detected.
- `#pragma`. A directive that can provide a C or C++ program with machine-specific features without affecting code portability. In Visual C++, for example, the directive `#pragma data_seg` specifies the segment used for data in a program. For a complete listing of Visual C++ pragmas, and explanations of how they're used, see Microsoft's Visual C++ documentation.
- `#line`. A directive that controls the placement of line numbers in listings.

# Special Features of the Visual C++ Preprocessor

Visual C++ supports several special features that C-language preprocessors lack. These new features are *charizing, stringization, token concatenation, string concatenation, trigraph replacement*, and *predefined macros*. These are described in the next few sections.

## Charizing

In Visual C++, the C++ `#define` directive can convert parameters of macros into character constants. To use this feature, you must place the symbol `#@`, followed by an alphabetical character, in an expression that is used as a parameter of the `#define` statement. When you use the `#@` symbol in this way, it represents a character constant.

Between the `#define` directive and the expression that contains the `#@` symbol, you must place a macro that takes a character as a parameter. The character that follows the `#@` symbol must match one of the arguments in the macro's parameter list, as in this example:

```
#define CharIt(x) #@x
```

When you use the `#@` symbol in this way, it's known as the *charizing* operator.

When the macro is expanded, the compiler places single quotation marks around the parameter in the macro that the charizing operator represents.

This short program shows how the charizing operator works:

```
// CHARIZE.CPP
// The Charizing Operator

#include <iostream.h>

#define CharIt(x) #@x

int main()
{
     cout << CharIt(c) << CharIt(a) << CharIt(t)
          << CharIt(.) << '\n';
     return 0;
}
```

In this example, each character passed to the macro named `CharIt()` is charized. This means that when the preprocessor expands the `CharIt()` macro, it places single quotation marks around the character inside each pair of parentheses. Thus, when the `Display()` macro is expanded, the statement

```
cout << CharIt(K) << CharIt(a) << CharIt(t)
     << CharIt(.) << '\n';
```

is expanded to:

```
cout 'K' << 'a' << 't' << . '\n';
```

Therefore, the output of the program is:

```
Kat.
```

## Stringizing

The Visual C++ `#define` directive can convert parameters of macros into string constants. To use this feature, you must place the symbol `#`, followed by an alphabetical character, in an expression that is used as a parameter of the `#define` statement. When you use the `#` symbol in this way, it represents a string constant.

When you use the `#` symbol in this way, it is known as the *stringizing* operator. Using the stringizing operator is called stringizing, or *stringization*.

Between the `#define` directive and the expression that contains the `#` symbol, you must place a macro that takes a character string as a parameter. The character that follows the `#` symbol must match one of the arguments in the macro's parameter list, as in this example:

```
#define Display(x) cout << #x << '\n';
```

When you call a macro that uses the stringizing operator as an argument, you can substitute a string for the stringizing operator in macro argument. You should not enclose the string in quotation marks, because the stringizing operator places quotation marks around the string when the macro is expanded.

Also, if any character in the string must be preceded by an escape character (`\`) in order to be printed properly, the stringization operator inserts the escape character into the string when the macro is expanded.

This short program shows how the stringizing operator works:

```
// STRNGIZE.CPP
// Stringizing

#include <iostream.h>

#define Display(x) cout << #x << '\n';

int main()
{
     Display(Play "Misty" for me.);
     return 0;
}
```

In this example, the argument passed to the macro named `Display()` is stringized. This means that when the preprocessor expands the `Display()` macro, it places double quotation marks around the string that is passed as an argument. Also, the stringizing operator places an escape character around the quotations inside the string. Thus, when the `Display()` macro is expanded, the statement

```
Display(Play "Misty" for me.);
```

is expanded to:

```
cout << "Play \"Misty\" for me." << '\n';
```

Therefore, the output of the program is:

```
Play "Misty" for me.
```

## Token Concatenation

In a macro definition in Visual C++, you can use the *## operator*—sometimes called the *token-pasting operator* or the *merging operator*—to join a pair of tokens into a single token. With this technique, you can create lists of identifiers with similar names.

In C++, as in C, a *token* is the smallest element of a program that is meaningful to the compiler. In a preprocessor statement, elements such as keywords, identifiers, constants, string literals, operators, and punctuators are recognized as tokens. In a macro definition, the token-pasting operator can *paste* any two tokens together into a single token.

In the following preprocessor statement, the token-pasting operator combines the string literal `Error` with the character constant `n` to form a single token:

```
#define Error(n,txt) char Error##n[] = "Error " #n ": " txt;
```

This statement also makes use of the stringizing operator (#, described under a previous heading), which can convert macro parameters into string constants. To invoke this preprocessor directive, you can place this declaration in a program:

```
Error(1, "Elvis sighted.");
```

You then can place this statement in your program:

```
cout << Error1 << '\n';
```

When the preprocessor encounters this statement, it expands the statement into this form:

```
Error 1: Elvis sighted.
```

The statements shown in these examples all appear in this short program:

```
// TOKNPAST.CPP
// Token-pasting

#include <iostream.h>

#define Error(n,txt) char Error##n[] = "Error " #n ": " txt;

Error(0, "Edge of earth encountered.");
Error(1, "Elvis sighted.");
Error(2, "UFO landed.");

int main()
{
    cout << Error0 << '\n';
    cout << Error1 << '\n';
    cout << Error2 << '\n';
    return 0;
}
```

When you execute the program, this is its output:

```
Error 0: Edge of earth encountered.
Error 1: Elvis sighted.
Error 2: UFO landed.
```

**NOTE—PREPROCESSOR STRING CONCATENATION**

The C++ preprocessor can concatenate adjacent string constants—and, although you don't hear much about it, preprocessor string concatenation is one of the neatest features of the C++ language.

To take advantage of this feature, all you have to do is place the string constants next to each other in the macro's formal parameter list, enclosed in quotation marks and separated by whitespace characters. You can use this mechanism to divide a long string into segments, which you can then place in a preprocessor directive. Combining string concatenation with token stringization can produce interesting results.

This little program shows how you can use string concatenation in a program:

```
// STRCAT.CPP
// Token-pasting

#include <iostream.h>

int main()
{
    cout << "Harry\n" "Snake\n" "Amy\n";
    return 0;
}
```

Here's the output of this program:

```
Harry
Snake
Amy
```

## Trigraph Replacement

If you ever need to write software on a foreign-language computer keyboard that doesn't contain some of the symbols that C and C++ require, Visual C++ lets you substitute certain three-character combinations for the missing symbols.

A trigraph always begins with two question marks (`??`). Table 7.1 shows the trigraphs recognized by the Visual C++ processor, and the symbols they represent:

**Table 7.1. Trigraphs.**

| *Trigraph* | *Equivalent Symbol* |
|---|---|
| `??<` | { |
| `??(` | [ |
| `??-` | ~ |
| `??>` | } |
| `??)` | ] |
| `??!` | ¦ |

# Predefined Macros

Visual C++ recognizes six predefined ANSI C/C++ macros, and has added several more. Although there are exceptions (see Table 7.2), the name of a predefined macro usually begins with a single or double underscore. The name of every predefined ANSI macro begins with a double underscore. Most names also end with a double underscore.

When you place a predefined macro in a C++ program, the preprocessor expands the macro into a predefined string. For example, the following program contains the predefined macro `__DATE__`, which prints the current date to standard output (normally, the screen):

```
// MCROTEST.CPP
// Using a predefined macro

#include <iostream.h>

int main()
{
     cout << __DATE__ << '\n';;
     return 0;
}
```

This program prints the current date in the format Mmmm DD YYYY, as in this example:

```
Jul 6 1993
```

Predefined arguments take no arguments and cannot be redefined.

Table 7.2 lists the six standard ANSI C/C++ predefined macros recognized by Visual C++. Predefined macros recognized by Visual C++ are listed in Microsoft's Visual C++ documentation.

**Table 7.2. ANSI C/C++ predefined macros.**

| *Macro* | *Definition* |
|---|---|
| `__cplusplus` | If this macro is defined, the program is compiled as a C++ program. Otherwise, the program is compiled as a C program. |
| `__DATE__` | The translation date of the current source file. The date is a character string of the form `"MMM DD YYYY"`. The quotes are included to form a proper C++ string. |
| `__FILE__` | The name of the current source file. |
| `__LINE__` | The current line (a numeric value). |
| `__STDC__` | Specifies full compliance with the ANSI C standard. `__STDC__` is defined as the integer constant 1 only if the `/Za` command-line option is used; otherwise, the macro is undefined. |
| `__TIME__` | The current time (a string literal in HH:MM:SS format). |

# Summary

This chapter introduced the user interface of the Visual C++ compiler, and explained how to compile Visual C++ programs in two ways: by selecting menu commands from the Visual Workbench editor, and (if you own the Professional Edition of Visual C++) by executing MS-DOS commands from command lines.

The chapter also explained how the Visual C++ preprocessor works, and described special features of the Visual C++ compiler that C-language compilers do not have. Some of the special features of the Visual C++ compiler are:

- *Precompiled files*. When you create Visual C++ programs, you can precompile executable files as well as header files to speed up the compilation process.
- *Charizing*. In Visual C++, the C++ `#define` directive can convert the parameters of macros into character constants. When the macro is expanded, the compiler places single quotation marks around the parameter in the macro that the charizing operator represents.
- *Stringizing*. The Visual C++ `#define` directive can convert parameters of macros into string constants. To use this feature, you must place the symbol `#`, followed by an alphabetical character, in an expression that is used as a parameter of the `#define` statement. When you use the `#` symbol in this way, it represents a string constant.
- *Token concatenation*. In a macro definition in Visual C++, you can use the *## operator*—sometimes called the *token-pasting operator* or the *merging operator*—to join a pair of tokens into a single token. With this technique, you can create lists of identifiers with similar names.
- *Trigraph replacement*. With Visual C++, you can write software on a foreign-language computer keyboard that doesn't contain some of the symbols that C and C++ require. For those symbols, you can substitute certain three-character combinations (each of which begins with two question marks) for the missing symbols.

Once you compile a C++ program, the next step is to build it. Chapter 8, "Linking Visual C++ Programs," covers the building process.

Chapter 8

# Linking Visual C++ Programs

A project full of C++ source code files can't do you any good until you compile and link them into an executable program. The process of compiling and linking a program is often referred to as *building* the program.

Every implementation of C++ comes with two build tools: a *compiler*, which compiles code into object code modules, and a *linker*, which links those modules into an executable program. Visual C++ has a compiler and a linker that you can access from the Visual Workbench editor—or, if you own the Professional Edition of Visual C++, from an MS-DOS command line.

Chapter 7 "Compiling Visual C++ Programs," explained how the Visual C++ compiler does the work of compiling source code files into object code modules. This chapter explains how the Visual C++ linker performs the linking operations that transform object code modules into executable programs.

This chapter also tells how the Visual C++ preprocessor, compiler, and linker work together to generate an executable Visual C++ program.

## Creating a Project

As you may recall from Chapter 7, the first step in writing a Visual C++ program is to create a *project*: a group of files grouped together to make it easier to compile and link a Visual C++ application. Projects simplify program development by giving you an easy way to keep track of the files and libraries needed to build a program or a library. Projects also provide storage space for important information about compiler and linker options.

As noted in Chapter 7, you can create a project by selecting the New command from the Project menu. The Visual Workbench then displays a series of dialogs that walk you through the process of creating a new project, adding whatever source code files you like to the project and using the project to build and execute a Visual C++ program.

When you select the New command from the Project menu, the Visual Workbench then displays a New Project dialog box that you can use to specify the kind of application you want to create. This process is described in more detail in Chapter 7.

When you have decided what kind of application you want to write and have selected an application type from the New Project dialog box, you can specify various options that you want the Visual C++ compiler and linker to use when they compile and link your program.

You can set compiler and linker options by selecting the Project command under the Options menu. The Visual C++ Workbench then displays a Project Options dialog box like the one shown in Figure 8.1.

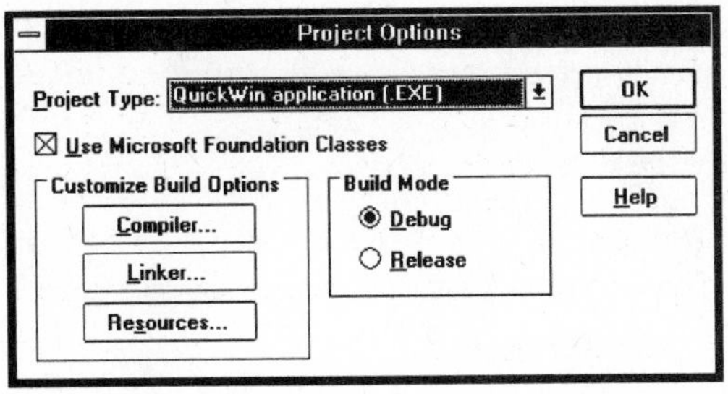


*Figure 8.1. Project Options dialog box.*

> **COMMAND-LINE LINKING**
>
> With the Professional Edition of Visual C++ (but not with the Standard Edition), you can link Visual C++ programs by typing and executing MS-DOS command lines. But before you can link programs by executing command lines, you must make some special modifications to your AUTOEXEC.BAT file, as in Chapter 7.

## The Linker Button

To select options for linking Visual C++ programs, click the Linker button in the button group labeled Customize Build Option. Visual C++ then displays a dialog box labeled Linker Options. The Linker Options dialog window is shown in Figure 8.2.

## Using the Linker Options Dialog Box

The Linker Options dialog box—like the Compiler Options dialog box described in Chapter 7—is split into two parts. The controls in the top part of the window work like the controls in any Visual C++ dialog window. But you can change the appearance of the bottom part of the window by selecting command line items in the list box labeled Category.

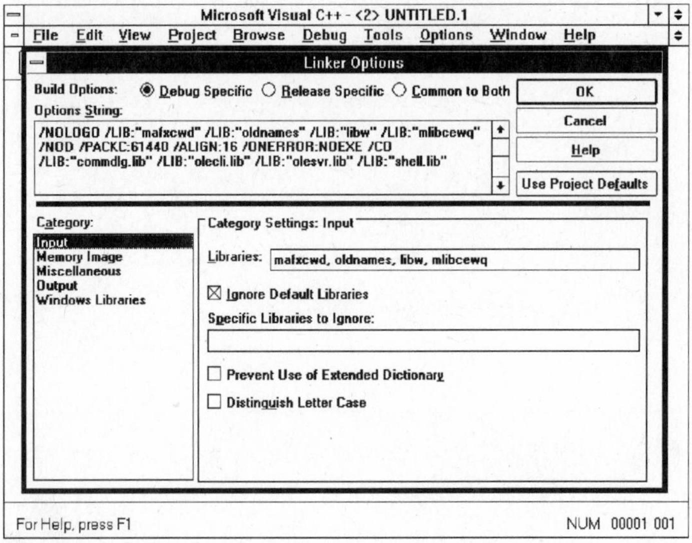


*Figure 8.2. The Linker Options dialog box.*

For example, when you select the option category Windows Libraries, the layout of the lower-right part of the Linker Options window changes. Then, from the list box labeled Import Libraries and DLLs, you can select any Windows libraries and Dynamic Link Libraries (DLLs) that you want to import into your program at link time.

When you select a command line option from the list box in the lower-left corner of the Linker Options dialog box, the change that you have made is shown in the upper half of the window in the text box labeled Options String.

When you close the Linker Options dialog and compile your program, the Visual C++ compiler executes the command line that was displayed in the Options String text box when the Linker Options dialog box was closed.

It's important to note, though, that the text shown in the Options String text box is not an actual command line, but merely a representation of a command line, designed to show you the linker options that are currently selected. If you own the Professional Edition of Visual C++ and want to link a program by executing an MS-DOS command line, the string shown in the Options string text box might not work. For instructions on linking a program by executing a command line, see the documentation included with the Professional Edition of Visual C++.

> **USING DEFAULT LINKER OPTIONS**
>
> When you install Visual C++, the Visual C++ Setup program installs a set of default linker options. When you choose linker options using the Linker Options dialog box, your new choices override your default choices. With the Linker Options dialog box, you can restore your default linker options at any time by clicking the button labeled Use Project Defaults.

## Getting Help with Command-Line Options

Because the Visual C++ linker recognizes many options—more than can be described in this chapter—Visual C++ provides a special kind of Help mechanism to help you choose those that you want when you link Visual C++ programs.

You can obtain help information about a specific linking option by highlighting the option in the text box labeled Options String (or by placing the insertion point on the option) and pressing F1. The Visual Workbench then displays a window containing help information about the option you have selected.

# Linking a C++ Program

When a source code program has been compiled into object code modules, as described in Chapter 7, the program is sent to the Visual C++ linker. The linker resolves external references in the object code modules and links the modules with each other and with any external libraries that they require, producing an executable program.

> **STATIC LINKING, DYNAMIC LINKING, AND DLLS**
>
> The process of linking code modules using a linker is known as *static linking*. C++ also supports code that links at runtime instead of at link time. The process of linking code modules at runtime is called *dynamic linking*.

Dynamic linking is used to link programs with dynamic link libraries, or DLLs. A DLL is an object code library that can be accessed by multiple applications simultaneously. DLLs are often used in Windows-based programs; in fact, the Windows operating system is implemented as a set of DLLs.

When two applications are written in such a way that they can use common object code libraries, the libraries that they share can be stored in memory as a DLL. DLLs can conserve memory by eliminating the need to allocate memory for multiple copies of the same code. DLLs can also increase the execution speed of programs.

When you compile a source file, the file that the compiler generates is an object file with a name that ends in the suffix .OBJ. A program's .OBJ file contains the name of every function that the program calls, whether the function is defined inside the program or not.

When the Visual C++ linker links a compiled .OBJ file, the linker resolves all external references to functions that are defined inside the .OBJ file and then searches any library (.LIB) files that are needed to create an executable file, such as an .EXE file, a .DLL file, or a .VBX file (a Visual Basic custom control file). If the program contains any functions that are not defined inside the program, the linker searches for those functions in the library files that are used in the link.

If the linker finds the object code for all of the functions that are needed in the link, the linker includes that code in the program's final executable file. If the linker fails to find the object code for any function in the program, it returns an error message.

## Libraries Provided with Visual C++

With the header files that you include in your programs, you can access two huge library collections that are provided with the Visual C++ compiler: the Visual C++ runtime library and the Microsoft Foundation Class (MFC) libraries.

The Visual C++ runtime library contains more than 550 useful (or essential) functions that are not built into the C or C++ languages. These functions include input and output routines, memory allocation routines, process control routines, graphics routines, and many other kinds of functions. The runtime library also includes the `iostream` library, a streamlined new replacement for the old C-language I/O library, STDIO.H. The `iostream` library is described in detail in Chapter 20, "Streams."

The Microsoft Foundation Class (MFC) library provides an object-oriented framework for managing Windows-related graphics functions. The MFC library also provides a number of classes that are not directly related to windows. The MFC library is examined more closely in Part III, which begins with Chapter 21.

## The Runtime Library

The documentation that comes with Visual C++ lists all the 550-plus functions in the Visual C++ runtime library and tells what header file you must include to access each function.

The easiest way to ensure that the linker can find any library that you may need in your programs is to let the Setup program create a set of *combined libraries* when it installs Visual C++. If you choose the option that lets the Setup program install a set of combined libraries, the linker will know where to find every function in the runtime library, and you'll never have to worry about explicitly linking a runtime library with your programs. Instructions for using the Setup program are provided in the *Getting Started* manual included with the Visual C++ compiler.

If you choose not to let Setup create a set of combined libraries, there are some libraries that you must tell the linker about if you want to use them. One such library is the Microsoft C graphics library, which contains many graphics functions that range from functions that create simple shapes to procedures that can help you create ambitious graphics presentations. If you use graphics at all in your applications, you'll probably want to have access to the graphics library.

You can find out more about the Microsoft C graphics library and how to access it by consulting the Visual C++ *Run-Time Library Reference* and the Visual C++ *Programming Techniques* manual.

## The MFC Library

The Microsoft Foundation Class (MFC) library contains an extensive set of C++ classes that are specifically designed for developing Windows applications. Along with Windows-related classes, the MFC library contains many general-purpose classes that can help you manage collections, files, memory management, persistent storage, exceptions, diagnostics, strings, and timing.

The Windows-oriented functions included in the MFC library include routines that handle menus, windows, dialog boxes, icons, bitmaps, and even string and text functions designed specifically for the Windows environment. The MFC library also contains procedures that implement the Windows Multiple Document Interface (MDI), which can manage multiple windows running simultaneously.

Procedures provided by the MFC library that aren't directly related to Windows include functions for runtime typing, serialization, file I/O, and exception handling and functions for handling strings, dates, and collections.

The MFC library is examined in more detail in Part III of this volume, which begins with Chapter 21.

# Mixing C++ with Other Languages

Because C++ is a relatively new language, there may be situations in which you want to build a C++ program that contains code modules written in other languages. You may have a library of valuable routines written in other languages, or you may want to insert some time-critical assembly language—such as a device driver or an interrupt service routine—which you want to insert in a C++ program.

The designers of Visual C++ knew that needs such as these would arise, so they provided a number of mechanisms for combining source code written in Microsoft C and C++ with source code written in other languages.

One such mechanism is called *external linkage specifications*. For situations in which external linkage specifications don't suffice, Visual C++ provides a set of modifiers that can combine source code written in Microsoft C and C++ with source code written in other languages. These modifiers—`__cdecl`, `__pascal`, `__fortran`, and `__asm`—are described later in this section.

This section presents a general introduction to combining C++ source files with source files written in C, Pascal, and assembly language. For a detailed examination of mixed-language programming with Visual C++, see the *Programming Techniques* manual included with the Visual C++ compiler.

## Name Mangling

Although C++ is derived from C, there are significant differences in the way in which programs written in the two languages are compiled. The main reason you can't mix C and C++ translation units is that C++ supports *overloaded functions,* which are functions with the same name but different argument lists.

To prevent ambiguities in the names of overloaded functions, the Visual C++ compiler modifies the name of each function in a program when the function is declared. Along with the function's name, the compiler stores the number of arguments and the types of the arguments that are passed to the function. If the function is part of a class, the compiler makes a record of that fact also.

When the compiler adds all this data to the name of a function, the name is said to be *mangled*—and it is this mangled name that the compiler stores in the program's object file.

When the C++ compiler has "mangled" a function's name by adding information to it, the C++ linker can use the function's mangled name to verify that calls made to the function from other translation units use the correct number and types of arguments. If the number of arguments or the types of arguments passed to the function are wrong, the linker knows that another function that has the same name is being called, or that an error has been made in the call. Resolving external references in this manner is called *type-safe linkage.*

Because C functions cannot be overloaded, C compilers do not mangle function names; mangled names are generated only by C++ compilers. Therefore, when you call a C function from a C++ code module, you must tell the C++ compiler that the function you are calling is in a C-language module and therefore doesn't have a mangled name.

## Alternate Linkage Specifications

To inform the C++ linker that a C function is being called, you can use a technique called an *alternate linkage specification*. In C++, the term *linkage specification* refers to the protocol for linking functions or procedures written in different languages. For example, you can use an alternate linkage specification when you have a function that is written in C and you want to insert the program in a program written in C++.

## The extern Keyword

In programs written in Visual C++, you can use the keyword `extern` to identify a block of code that you want to compile and link using an alternate linkage specification. For example, if you want to insert a block of C-language code in a C++ program, you can precede the code with the linkage specification `extern "C"`, as in this example:

```
extern "C"
{
     void TestFunc();
}
```

This code fragment declares `TestFunc()` to be a function that must be compiled and linked as if it were a C function. Once this declaration has appeared in a program, any calls that are made to `TestFunc()` use C-style calling and linking methods.

You can also use linkage specifications to call functions that are written in languages other than C. To call a non-C function from a C++ program, merely write a C-style linkage specification that declares the function using the appropriate language modifier. For example, to call the Pascal function `PascalFunc()`, you could declare it as follows:

```
extern "C" {
     int __pascal PascalFunc( int n );
}
```

This example declares `PascalFunc()` to be a function with the Pascal calling convention.

### THE __CPLUSPLUS MACRO

You can determine whether a program is being compiled in C or C++ by checking the value of a predefined macro named `__cplusplus`. If the `__cplusplus` macro is defined, the compiler is compiling in C++. If the macro is not defined, the compiler is compiling in C.

All of the standard include files provided with Visual C++ are written in C, so they contain conditional compilation directives to determine whether a program is being compiled in C or C++. These directives use the `__cplusplus` macro to check the language in which the program is being compiled. If the program is being compiled in C++, the external specification `extern "C"` is included in the code to make sure that the functions declared in the file are compiled in C. For example, the MATH.H file supplied with Visual C++ contains this code:

```
#ifndef __cplusplus
extern "C" {
#endif

// function declarations

#ifdef __cplusplus
}
#endif
```

The `__cplusplus` macro is one of a number of predefined macros supplied with Visual C++. All the predefined macros provided in the Visual C++ package are listed in the Visual C++ *Language Reference* manual. All predefined macros are preceded by two underscores. They take no arguments and cannot be redefined.

## Effects of Linkage Specifications

In Visual C++, linkage specifications affect these calling conventions:

- The order in which arguments are expected on the stack.
- The responsibility for adjusting the stack after a function returns. (In C, the calling function is responsible for cleaning up the stack after a function call. In Pascal, the called function is responsible for balancing the stack before returning to the caller.)
- The passing of hidden arguments. (When a member function is called in C++, a special pointer called the `this` pointer is secretly passed as a hidden argument. The `this` pointer points to the object that contains the member function being called and can be used by the function to access that object. For more information about the `this` pointer, see Chapter 12, "Objects.")

- The case sensitivity of names.
- The "decoration" of names. The Microsoft C compiler prefixes names with an underscore, sometimes referred to as "decoration." In C++, name decoration is used to retain type information through the linkage phase. (For more information on this topic, see the Visual C++ *Language Reference* manual.)

## Function Modifiers

Name mangling is not the only challenge that the Visual C++ compiler faces when it encounters non-C++ code in a program. Another problem is that different languages use different *calling conventions* and when a program contains sequences of code that use different calling conventions, all of the calling sequences that are used in the program must be resolved.

To resolve the differences between code sequences that are written in languages that use different calling conventions, Visual C++ provides a set of *function modifiers* that can precede the names of function declarators to change the way that functions are executed. To use a function modifier, all you have to do is place the modifier before the name of any function. Visual C++ then executes the function in accordance with its function modifier.

All function modifiers supplied with the Visual C++ package are specific to Microsoft C and Visual C++. Other implementations of C++ may use different function modifiers.

In Visual C++, every function modifier is preceded by two underscores. Some function modifiers are not supported in 32-bit compilations.

These are some of the function modifiers used by Visual C++:

- There are five function modifiers that let you combine source code written in Microsoft C and C++ with source code written in other languages. These modifiers—`__cdecl`, `__pascal`, `__fortran`, `__fastcall`, and `__asm`—are described later in this section.
- With the function modifiers `__near`, `__far`, `__huge`, and `__based`, you can override the addressing specified by the compile-time memory models. `near`, `far`, `huge`, and `based`. (For descriptions of these memory models, see Chapter 9, "Managing Memory.")

- You can export a function from a DLL to Windows using the `__export` function modifier.
- The `__inline` function modifier speeds up processing by instructing the compiler to compile a function as an inline function. (Inline functions are described in Chapter 6, "Functions.")
- The `__interrupt` function modifier specifies that a function is an interrupt handler.
- You can customize loading procedures and the saving of registers with the function modifiers `__segment`, `__segname`, `__based`, `__loadds`, and `__saveregs`.

All Microsoft-specific modifiers are described in the Microsoft *C Language Reference* and *C++ Language Reference* manuals.

## The C Calling Convention

When you compile a program in C, the Microsoft C compiler uses the C-language calling convention by default. (Surprisingly, C++ programs do not ordinarily use the C calling convention, but use the Pascal/FORTRAN calling method, except for functions with variable-length argument lists, as explained later in this section.) Fortunately, you do not have to be concerned with this idiosyncrasy because the compiler ensures that the C++ code is compiled correctly.

The functions in the Visual C++ runtime library are written in C and therefore use C calling conventions. You don't have to worry about this fact, either, because the compiler uses external linkage specifications to ensure that functions in the runtime library are called using the correct conventions.

The C calling convention is relatively inefficient because C supports functions that have a variable number of parameters. Because argument lengths of varying lengths are allowed in C, the arguments in a C function are pushed onto the stack in the opposite order from the order in which they appear in the function's argument list—that is, from right to left. If they were pushed onto the stack from left to right, it would be more difficult for the compiler to determine how many arguments the argument list contains.

Another characteristic of the C calling convention is that the calling function is responsible for restoring the stack to its original state after the called function returns. In contrast, when you call a procedure using the Pascal/FORTRAN calling convention, the called function is responsible for cleaning up the stack before it returns to the caller.

Because the Visual C++ compiler uses the `__cdecl` calling method by default when it's compiling in C, you don't have to specify the `__cdecl` calling method when you compile a C program. If you write a program in a language other than C and want the program compiled using the C calling convention, you can force the compiler to compile the code using C calling methods throughout by executing the CL (compilation) command with the `/Gd` option.

By using other options with the CL command, you can compile C programs using non-C calling conventions. For example, you can compile a C program using register calling conventions by executing the CL command with the `/Gr` option.

When you are compiling a C-language source file using a non-C calling convention, you can switch back to the C calling convention on a function-to-function basis by using the function modifier `__cdecl`, as in this example:

```
int __cdecl SampleFunc(int x, char *y);
```

## The Pascal/FORTRAN Calling Convention

When you precede the name of a function that you're calling with the keyword `__pascal` or the keyword `__fortran`, Visual C++ calls the routine using the Pascal/FORTRAN calling convention. (Since Pascal and FORTRAN use the same calling convention, these two keywords produce identical results.)

The `__fortran` and `__pascal` keywords are not supported in 32-bit compilations.

The Pascal/FORTRAN calling convention is more efficient than the C calling convention. In the Pascal/FORTRAN calling convention, the arguments in a C function are pushed onto the stack in the order in which they appear in the function's argument list—that is, from left to right. Another characteristic of the Pascal/FORTRAN calling convention is that the called function is responsible for restoring the stack to its original state before it returns to the caller. In contrast, when you call a function using the C calling convention, the calling function is responsible for cleaning up the stack when the function is complete.

As noted earlier, Visual C++ uses the Pascal/FORTRAN calling convention by default—except for functions with variable-length argument lists, which use the C calling convention by default. Therefore, it is not necessary to use the keyword `__pascal` or the keyword `__fortran` to call a Pascal or FORTRAN routine from a C++ program.

> **THE RUNTIME LIBRARY, WINDOWS.H FUNCTIONS, AND FUNCTION MODIFIERS**
>
> The functions in the Visual C++ runtime library are written in C. But you don't have to be concerned with that, even if you're programming in C++, because the `__cdecl` keyword is used with the appropriate precompiler directives in the runtime library header files to ensure that the functions in the libraries compile correctly.
>
> On a related topic, the Windows-related functions in the WINDOWS.H file are defined using the `__pascal` function modifier. Therefore, WINDOWS.H functions are compiled using the Pascal/FORTRAN calling convention. You don't have to worry about this, either, because the `__pascal` function modifier is used with appropriate precompiler directives in the WINDOWS.H file to make sure that the functions in the file are compiled correctly, whether you're compiling in C++ or C. All you have to do is include the appropriate header files, and Windows takes care of the details.

Parameters to functions that use the FORTRAN/Pascal calling convention are placed on the stack in the same order in which they appear in the routine's argument list—that is, from left to right. For this reason, procedures with variable-length parameter lists—such as the `printf` function—cannot use the Pascal/FORTRAN calling convention. However, the Pascal/FORTRAN calling convention produces smaller, faster programs than the C calling convention.

Another characteristic of the Pascal/FORTRAN calling convention is that the called function is responsible for cleaning up the stack before it returns to the caller. In contrast, when you call a function using the C calling convention, the calling function is responsible for restoring the stack to its original state after the called function returns.

Although any C function can be declared with the FORTRAN/Pascal calling method, FORTRAN/Pascal convention is used mainly to call Pascal or FORTRAN routines from within C programs.

To call a C++, Pascal, or FORTRAN routine from a C program, you must precede the function's declaration with either the keyword `__pascal` or the keyword `__fortran`, as in these examples:

```
int __pascal SampleFunc(int x, char *y);

int __fortran SampleFunc(int x, char *y);
```

By compiling a source file with the CL option /Gc, you can force the Visual C++ compiler to make all routines in the file observe the FORTRAN/Pascal calling convention.

## The Register Calling Convention

When program speed is very important, you can speed up the execution of a function by passing arguments to the function in registers rather than on the stack. You can enable the register calling convention on a function-by-function basis by declaring time-critical functions with the __fastcall keyword, in this fashion:

```
int __fastcall SampleFunc(int x, char *y);
```

By executing the CL command with the /Gr command-line option, you can force the Visual C++ compiler to use the register calling convention for an entire file.

The register calling convention yields the greatest speed benefits in programs that spend a significant amount of time performing function calls, such as recursive programs or programs that call functions from within loops. If you use the /Gr option, you should use it to compile only small programs. In larger programs, you should restrict your use of the __fastcall modifier to selected functions.

When you call a function using the register calling convention, only the first three arguments in the function's argument list are actually stored in registers. The rest are passed to the function using the FORTRAN/Pascal calling convention. That's because the 80x86 processor has a limited number of registers and must use some of them for processing!

Because the Visual C++ compiler maintains separate registers for passing arguments and for performing processing operations, the register calling convention does not conflict with regular CPU processing, or with any register variables that you may have declared.

However, you should observe caution in using the register calling convention with routines that are written in inline assembly language. That could conflict with the compiler's use of registers for storing parameters.

## The __asm Modifier

There are two ways to place assembly language source code in Visual C++ programs. You can:

- Use the `__asm` modifier to invoke an inline assembler that is built into the Microsoft C compiler.
- Write stand-alone assembly language code modules using the Microsoft Macro Assembler (MASM), and then use the link your assembly-language source code to your C/C++ source code.

If you are an experienced assembly language programmer, own the Microsoft Macro Assembler, and want to incorporate robust assembly language code modules into your C/C++ programs, you'll probably want to write your assembly language code using the MASM and then link it to your C/C++ programs. But when you need to insert just a small amount of assembly language code in a C/C++ program, you'll probably find that's easier and more convenient to invoke your C compiler's inline assembler with the `__asm` keyword.

To insert a block of assembly language code in a Visual C++ program, simply precede the block of assembler code with the `__asm` keyword, as shown in this example (which sounds a beep by sending the beep character—ASCII 7—to standard output):

```
__asm
{
mov ah, 2
mov dl, 7
int 21h
}
```

Alternatively, you can place the `__asm` keyword in front of each assembly instruction, like this:

```
__asm mov ah, 2
__asm mov dl, 7
__asm int 21h
```

Still another alternative is to place all of your assembly language instructions on the same line. This technique works because `__asm` is a statement separator:

```
__asm mov ah, 2  __asm mov dl, 7  __asm int 21h
```

To use the inline assembler that's built into the Visual C++ compiler, you do not have to be concerned with assembly language calling and naming conventions because the inline assembler produces inline C-compatible code automatically. For complete instructions on using the inline assembler, see the Microsoft *Programming Techniques* manual. Instructions for writing assembly language code with the Microsoft Macro Assembler are provided in the MASM documentation.

Chapter 9

# Managing Memory

It's been a long and winding road from the 8086 chip and MS-DOS to the 32-bit, 486 processor and Windows-based programs written in Visual C++. And we aren't at the end of the road yet.

Someday, everyone who uses an older-model PC-compatible may trade up to a machine equipped with a 386 chip, a 486 chip, or something even newer. Then C++ programmers can start writing 32-bit programs designed to run under 32-bit operating systems such as Windows NT. But Visual C++ is designed for programmers who want to write software that runs under 16-bit Windows operating systems. So, when you write programs in Visual C++, you'll have to contend with the 640K memory barrier that PC-compatibles are infamous for—and the complexities of segmented memory.

This chapter describes the memory architecture of 386- and 486-based computers and explores the various memory configurations that you can use when you write programs in Visual C++. For supplementary information on the memory architecture of the 386 and 486 family, see Appendix B, "The 80X86 Chip Family."

# About This Chapter

This chapter examines several areas of memory management that pose a special challenge to Visual C++ programmers. The main topics explored in the chapter are:

- *Segmented memory*. The segmented memory architecture of IBM PCs and PC-compatibles have complicated the lives of programmers since the day the first IBM PC was unveiled. The first section of this chapter demystifies segmented memory. Appendix B is a closer examination of the memory architecture of the 80X86 family of chips, which powers the IBM PC and PC-compatibles.

- *Memory modes*. You can compile programs for IBM PCs and PC-compatibles in four memory modes: real mode, protected mode, standard mode, and enhanced mode. When you install the Visual C++ Visual Workbench, you can select a default memory mode for your compiler. Later, if you want to use another mode, you can interactively override your compiler's default setting. You can also select a memory mode for an individual compilation by choosing the Windows Prolog/Epilog category from the Compiler Options dialog box. For instructions on using the Compiler Options dialog window, see Chapter 7, "Compiling Visual C++ Programs."

- *Memory models*. You can compile Visual C++ programs using six memory models: tiny, small, medium, compact, large, and huge. When you install Visual C++, you can select a default memory model. Later, if you want to use another mode, you can interactively override your compiler's default setting. You can also select a memory model for a compilation by placing a memory-mode option on your command line. You can choose a default memory model for your copy of Visual C++ when you run the Visual C++ Setup program. You can select a memory model for an individual compilation by selecting the Memory Model category in the Compiler Options dialog box. Procedures for using the Compiler Options dialog window are outlined in Chapter 7.

- *Pointers*. Because of the segmented memory architecture of the IBM PC and PC-compatibles, the Visual C++ compiler generates three different kinds of pointers—`near`, `far`, and `huge`—depending on the memory model of the program being compiled. When you write a program, you can override the procedure that the compiler uses to assign pointers, depending on your program's specific needs. This chapter examines the three kinds of pointers used in Visual C++ and tells how they are used. More points on pointers are presented in Appendix B.
- *The `new` and `delete` operators*. To allocate and deallocate memory, C++ has two new operators: `new` and `delete`. The `new` and `delete` operators were introduced in Chapter 2, "A Better C—Plus," and are examined more closely in this chapter. You'll encounter them again in Chapter 16, "Operator Overloading."
- *Memory management under Windows*. Programs for Windows use special memory-management procedures and have special memory-management needs. These topics are the focus of the section "Memory Management Under Windows," which you can find later in this chapter.

# Segmented Memory

IBM PCs and PC-compatibles present special challenges to software designers because different models of IBM PCs and PC-compatibles are powered by different kinds of microprocessors. All the microprocessors used to power IBM PCs and PC-compatibles belong to the 80X86 family of chips, but different members of the 80X86 family have different addressing requirements. These requirements evolved as the family of 80X86 chips and their grandparents evolved from 8-bit processors to 32-bit processors, with a number of steps in between.

As the 80X86 chip family evolved—and as the memory capacity of personal computers grew—IBM and other PC manufacturers continued to improve the chips and the processing capabilities of their products, while making sure that each new model was compatible with its predecessors. The result of this process was the evolution of a memory architecture that is now known as the *segmented memory model*.

# How Segmented Memory Works

The Intel 8086 microprocessor, from which the 80X86 family of chips evolved, is a 16-bit integrated circuit. Normally, a 16-bit computer chip can address 65,536 different memory locations . But the designers of the 8086 microprocessor found a way to make it address 1,048,576 different locations. They performed this seemingly impossible task by creating a segmented memory-addressing system.

Segmented addressing creates many challenges for creators of software designed to be run on IBM PCs and PC-compatible machines. For example, when you use pointers in a Visual C++ program, you must take care to ensure that they point to the correct memory locations. You must also consider memory segmentation when you link a Visual C++ program.

In the segmented memory model, memory is not viewed as being contained in one contiguous block of RAM with consecutive memory addresses, but is divided into 64K segments. The segment is a fundamental unit in Intel's 808X and 80X86 series of microprocessors; in IBM PCs and PC-compatibles, everything revolves around segments.

In IBM PC and PC-compatible programming, a segment is a contiguous area of memory containing from one to 65,536 bytes. A segment must begin at a memory location whose address is a multiple of 16. Addresses that are multiples of 16 are called *paragraph boundaries*. So a segment must begin on a paragraph boundary.

The block of memory that extends from one paragraph boundary to the next is called a *paragraph*. A paragraph always begins on a paragraph boundary and extends up to—but does not include—the next paragraph boundary. So a paragraph is a contiguous area of memory that is 16 bytes long.

In an IBM PC or a PC-compatible, the first paragraph of memory extends from Memory Address Zero (zero is a multiple of 16) to Memory Address 15, inclusive (it is 16 bytes long). The second paragraph of memory begins at Memory Address 16 and extends through Memory Address 31. This pattern, which continues through Memory Address 65,535, provides a method for numbering every paragraph of memory between Address 0 and Address 65,535. The system for numbering paragraphs of memory is as follows:

The paragraph that extends from Memory Address zero to Memory Address 15, inclusive, is Paragraph 0. The paragraph that extends from Memory Address 16 to address 31, inclusive, is Paragraph 1. This pattern continues until no more paragraphs of memory are available, for example, Paragraph 4,096, which extends from Address 65,536 to Address 65,551, inclusive.

The highest possible paragraph number is 65,535. That's because 65,535 is the largest number that can be represented in 16 bits. Paragraph 65,535 extends from memory address 1,048,560 to memory address 1,048,575.

# Memory Segments and Paragraph Boundaries

Although every memory segment must begin on a paragraph boundary, a segment is always at least 64K long. That means a segment is always longer than a paragraph. Therefore, a memory segment always extends across a number of paragraph boundaries. However, since every memory segment starts on a paragraph boundary, every segment in memory can be uniquely identified by the paragraph number of the memory location at which the segment begins.

The number that identifies a memory segment is known, logically enough, as a *segment number*. A segment number is the paragraph number identifying the memory location where the segment begins.

# The 80X86 Chip's Segment Registers

To keep track of segment addresses, every chip in the 80X86 family has four registers that are dedicated to holding the segment numbers of areas of memory that are frequently accessed:

- The CS *(code segment)* register contains the segment number of the location of the code for the current executing program.
- The SS *(stack segment)* register contains the segment number of the location of the current stack.
- The DS *(data segment)* register contains the segment number of frequently used data.
- The ES *(extra segment)* register is a spare register that is used as necessary.

The 80X86 microprocessor, unless instructed otherwise, always fetches program code from the segment pointed to by the CS register, accesses stack-based data from the segment pointed to by the SS register, and updates program data in the segment pointed to by the DS register. The ES register is used only for carrying out certain special hardware instructions.

After a segment register is loaded with a value, all subsequent accesses to that segment of memory do not need to supply the segment portion of a complete address. Only the 16-bit offset portion of the address is required. The type of memory access determines which segment register supplies the segment portion of the address.

In a program written for an 80X86-powered computer, you can refer to a memory location in one of two ways:

- If the program is less than 64K long, the whole program can fit in one memory segment. Therefore, you can refer to any memory location in the program by specifying a 16-bit address.
- If a program is more than 64K long, you can access any location in memory by using what is known as a *segment:offset address*, or a *fully specified address*—that is, a 16-bit segment number and a 16-bit offset within that segment. By supplying a fully specified address, a program can always access any location in memory. However, this procedure requires twice as much storage per address as supplying only an offset value, and it also takes longer.

An address that consists of only an offset is called a near address. A pointer to a near address is called a `near` pointer. A completely specified address—that is, one that consists of both a segment and an offset—is called a far address. And a pointer to a far address is called a `far` pointer.

# Near Calls and Far Calls

When a program needs to call a subroutine that lies within its own code segment, or memory segment, it can call the subroutine by specifying only the offset of the subroutine's address within that segment. This kind of function call is known as an *intra-segment call*, or a *near call*.

When a program needs to call a subroutine in a different code segment, or memory segment, the program must specify the segment and the offset of the subroutine. This kind of call is known as an *inter-segment call*, or a *far call*.

# How Segments Overlap

A segment is a unit that defines a logical mapping over a range of memory. One idea that may be difficult to grasp is that segments can overlap, that is, that multiple segments can contain the same memory location, depending on where each segment starts and stops.

Because a segment can start at any address that is an integral multiple of 16 and because a segment is always at least 64K long, a single memory address can lie inside a number of segments. This overlapping is caused by the way the microprocessor generates addresses, by the way these addresses are interpreted by the software that is running, and by the computer's operating system.

A segment can be defined by its starting address, its ending address, and certain properties that it has—such as read-only, read-write, execute-only, execute-write, and so on. Segments can contain code, data, and Windows resources.

# Segment:Offset Addressing

To access a memory address in a given 64K memory segment, you must use segment:offset addressing. As mentioned earlier, you must use two values to access a memory address using segment:offset addressing: a segment value, which specifies the beginning of a 64K memory segment, and an offset value, which specifies a distance, or offset, into that segment.

For more information on segment:offset addressing, see Appendix B.

# Memory Modes

The 80X86 family of processors can operate in two different memory states, or modes: *real mode* and *protected mode*. There also are two memory modes that were created specifically for use by Windows programs: *standard mode* and *enhanced mode*.

All but the earliest members of the 80X86 microprocessor family can be operated in either real mode or protected mode. Real mode is the memory mode that all 80X86 computers "wake up" in when they are powered on or reset. Protected mode is a more powerful mode that provides access to more memory and protects the memory used by multiple programs running simultaneously.

# Real Mode

Real mode provides 1M of addressable linear memory and uses a 64K segment size. Real mode derives its name from the fact that all addresses accessed are in physical, or "real," memory. DOS is an example of a program that runs only in real mode.

Real mode was originally designed for computers powered by an 8086 or 8088 chip. When such machines are running in real mode, they can address 1M (1,024K) of memory. That's because the 8086 and 8088 chips have only 20 address lines, so they have no way to access any address value larger than 20 bits.

Generally, a system running under real mode is limited to 640K of conventional memory—the only 640K that was available on the earliest MS-DOS PCs. If an 80286 chip is being used, real mode also grants access to some extra high-memory addresses (HMA).

In real mode, the CPU treats linear addresses as physical addresses. Segment addresses are referenced directly by a static value—not looked up in a descriptor table as they are in protected mode.

Windows uses real mode as a kickstarter to get into protected mode (described under the next heading), which can be entered only when a global descriptor table has been created and initialized with the appropriate structures.

# Protected Mode

Protected mode, introduced with the 80286 microprocessor, permits access to the processor's entire linear address space. Also, it affords memory protection to programs when more than one program is running at a time, hence its name.

In protected mode, the 80X86 processor steps in to prevent programs from carrying out operations that may endanger other programs—such as I/O. When a program wants to carry out an operation that might endanger another program, it must issue a call to a supervisor program, which then performs the task on the executing program's behalf.

Protected mode also prevents programs from overwriting memory being used by other programs.

In protected mode, linear addresses are generated indirectly by a selector pointing to an entry in a set of processor-protected segment tables called *descriptor tables.* These tables are not addressed directly, as they are in real mode. If an application tries to access a segment that is not in one of these tables, the application is terminated.

Another feature of protected mode is that it greatly extends the idea of segments. In real mode, a segment is any 64K region of memory that starts at an address that is an integral multiple of 16 and lies within the first 1,088K of memory. In protected mode, a segment is a region of memory that can start anywhere within 16M of address space and can have any length ranging from a single byte up to 64K.

In protected mode, each memory segment contains some bits that hold special information called access rights. These bits are used to limit what application can access the memory segment for what purposes and when a program that is in the segment can perform I/O operations.

There are actually two versions of protected mode—16-bit protected mode and 32-bit protected mode. The 80286 chip runs in 16-bit protected mode, and the 386 and 486 chips run in 32-bit protected mode. The differences between 286 protected mode and 386/486 protected mode stem naturally from the fact that the 286 chip uses 24 bits for addressing and 16 bits for data, whereas the 386 and 486 chips use 32 bits for address and 32 bits for data.

These two varieties of protected mode use different kinds of selectors for code and data segments. When 16-bit protected mode code is running, 64K code and data segments are used. When 32-bit protected mode code is executed, all segments are assumed to be 32 bits wide.

# Standard Mode and Enhanced Mode

Besides the real and protected memory modes used by the 80X86 family of chips, there are two special memory modes used only by Windows programs: standard mode and enhanced mode. You can run Windows 3.0 in real mode, standard mode, or enhanced mode; Windows 3.1 runs only in standard mode and enhanced mode.

On a computer built around the 8086 chip— or on an 80286 or 386 machine with less than 1M of memory—Windows 3.0 runs in real mode. In this mode, Windows and its applications occupy an upper area of the basic 640K of memory known as conventional memory, above MS-DOS and any RAM-resident programs that may be loaded.

## Standard Mode

On a PC that's powered by the 80286 processor and that has at least 1M of memory—or on a 386 PC with less than 2M of memory—Windows runs in 286 standard mode. In this mode, Windows can use up to 16M of conventional memory and extended memory.

Standard mode adds several features to real mode, including memory protection, a 16M linear address space and 1M allocable blocks from the global heap. A Windows program running in enhanced mode can address up to 64M of memory.

Standard mode was designed to run on PCs equipped with 80286 microprocessors. It assumes that you may not have any upper-memory RAM, so it uses lower and expanded memory for itself and for all Windows applications.

If you have an extended memory manager installed and you run Windows in standard mode, Windows won't use it, and neither will any Windows applications. However, Windows does run fast in standard mode—about 15 percent to 20 percent faster than it runs under 386 enhanced mode, assuming the same hardware is used.

## Enhanced Mode

On a 386-powered PC with at least 2M of memory, Windows runs in 386 enhanced mode. This mode is essentially the same as standard mode with two extra features. One extra feature is that Windows uses the paging registers of the 386 processor to implement virtual memory. Each 386 page is 4K long. In 386 enhanced mode, Windows can swap these pages to disk and reload them when necessary. This page-swapping is something that is ordinarily transparent both to the user and to the creator of Windows applications.

The other additional feature of 386 enhanced mode is that it supports multiple virtual DOS machines. This feature does not ordinarily affect the Windows programmer.

# Memory Models

In the world of IBM PC and PC-compatible programming, *memory model* is a term used to describe the architecture of a program. By designing a program to fit a particular memory model, you can ensure that your application runs as efficiently as possible. Six different memory models are available for programs designed for IBM PCs and PC-compatibles: tiny, small, medium, compact, large, and huge.

When you write a Microsoft C or C++ program, you can specify a memory model for your program, depending upon the size of the program and the kinds of CPUs with which you want the program to be compatible. If you don't specify what memory model you want to use for your programs, Visual C++ defaults to the small memory model.

If you wish, you can specify a default memory model for your programs. If you set up a default memory model and then want to build a program that uses another memory model, you can switch memory models from the Visual Workbench menu by following this procedure:

First, choose the Project command from the Options menu. When the Project Options dialog box appears, press the compiler button in the Customize Build Options group box. When the C/C++ Compiler Options dialog appears, choose the Memory Model entry in the Category list box. The Memory Model combo box will appear in the lower-right corner of the dialog box.

# How Memory Models Work

Every Visual C++ program has at least two segments: a code segment, which contains the implementations of functions, and a data segment, which contains variables and constants.

The memory model that you select for a program determines the maximum size of the program's code and data segments and also determines the machine-language instructions that are used to access the code and data. This, in turn, determines the execution speed of the program.

In general, the larger a memory model you use, the larger and slower is your executable program. You can build programs that use only one segment and are therefore very fast, but a one-segment program cannot be larger than 64K. You can build larger programs that use multiple segments, but multisegment programs execute more slowly than one-segment programs.

# Memory Models and Pointers

To access memory locations in programs based on the six available memory models, Visual C++ provides three kinds of pointers: `near` pointers, `far` pointers, and `huge` pointers. A `near` pointer is always 16 bits long. Pointers of the `far` and `huge` configurations are 32 bits long.

Tiny-model programs use only `near` pointers. Small-model programs use only `near` code pointers and `near` data pointers. Compact-model and medium-model programs use both `near` and `far` pointers. Large-model and huge-model programs use only `far` pointers.

When you run a tiny-model program, the address references stored in the 80X86 segment registers never change. When you run a small-model program, the CS, SS, and DS registers remain the same during execution (unless the program references something outside the program). The exception is the ES register, which changes depending on whether it's being used in a code or data operation. In a compact- or medium-model program, the address references stored in some segment registers must be changed from time to time, but others can remain unchanged throughout the program's execution. When a large- or huge-model program is executed, the address references stored in the 80X86 segment registers are subject to frequent changes.

Because of the time it takes to recalculate addresses, small-model, compact-model, and medium-model programs run slower than tiny programs but faster than large-model and huge-model programs.

When you have selected the memory model that you want to use for a program, the Visual C++ compiler automatically configures every pointer in your program to work properly with the memory model you have chosen.

However, if you encounter a special situation in which you want to use a different kind of pointer, you can declare any pointer in a program to be configured in a special manner by using three special modifiers: `__near`, `__far`, and `__huge`. One situation in which you might want to use a customized pointer is to access a particularly large block of data in a program (for example, a very large array).

# Overlays and the MOVE Utility

You can also build programs using mixed memory modes; in fact, you can even design programs that are divided into parts called *overlays*. When you create a program that has overlays, parts of the program can be called and run as needed, even if the whole program won't fit into memory all at one time.

When you create a program that uses overlaying, one part of the program—called the *root*—stays in memory throughout the execution of the program, while other pieces of the program that are stored on disk are moved into and out of RAM from disk as the need arises. Typically, the root of a program is the part that contains the program's `main()` function.

When a program uses overlays, they occupy a block of conventional memory not occupied by the root. If enough RAM is available, more than one overlay can be loaded into memory at the same time. When a program calls a function that is not currently in RAM, the overlay that contains the function is copied from disk into a block of memory called the *overlay heap*. If the overlay heap does not contain enough RAM available for the new overlay, the least recently used overlay in memory is discarded.

With the premiere of Visual C++, Microsoft introduced a new utility for creating overlaid programs. This tool, called the Microsoft Overlaid Virtual Environment (MOVE), allocates a heap in conventional memory for overlays that are in use. MOVE can also allocate a cache in extended or expanded memory.

Key new features of MOVE include:

- *Support for both code and data*. Both code and data (not just code) can be overlaid, giving the software designer control over how the program is organized. This feature makes it easy to overlay C++ objects, and it is particularly useful with programs that contain large data spaces.

- *Multiple RAM-resident overlays*. More than one overlay can reside in memory at one time, and up to *65,535* overlays can be used by a single program. This feature lets MS-DOS programmers build programs of virtually unlimited size.

- *Inter-overlay calls.* A function in one overlay can call a function in another overlay through a pointer to the external function.
- *Overlay caching.* MOVE can cache discarded overlays, providing quick access to the overlay if it is discarded and called again.
- *Function- and segment-level control.* MOVE gives program designers precise control over the contents of their overlays. Any combination of functions, segments, or object files can be placed in an overlay.

To build an overlay program using MOVE, you must create a text file known as a module definition (.DEF) file that describes the overlays. The linker uses the module definition file to determine the memory layout of the code and data of the overlay program. Normally, you don't need a module definition file to link a MS-DOS program, but the linker needs a module definition file when it links an overlaid DOS program.

# Deciding on a Memory Model

Although using the correct memory model can increase the efficiency of a program, using one memory model instead of another always involves certain tradeoffs. For example, programs that use the smaller memory models—and therefore make more use of `near` pointers—take less space and can run faster than programs written for larger memory models and thus require the use of `far` pointers. However, the code for a program that uses only `near` pointers cannot consume more than 64K of memory. Also, the program's data segments and its stack cannot exceed 64K each.

These limitations are fine for small programs, but a program with 70K of code soon runs into trouble. Because the program's code must be split into two segments—for example, one 64K segment and one 6K segment—references to the code in the separated segment must be accessed with far (inter-segment) calls.

Suppose, however, a program with 70K of code needs only 64K or less of memory space for its data. Because 80X86 chips access code and data using different segment registers, a program with less than 64K of data can use `near` pointers for all data references, even though it might have to use `far` pointers to access some code routines.

Of course there are programs that require more than 64K of memory for their code segments and also require more than 64K of memory for their data. Programs that large must use `far` pointers to access both code and data, which means that they require larger memory models.

# Advantages of Using Memory Models

The main advantage of using memory models is that they tell the Visual C++ compiler what kind of pointers it should use for code and what size pointers it should use for data. Therefore, the memory model that you choose tells the computer what form of addressing you want to use for each application you write.

However, the six standard memory models that are available in Visual C++ do not always produce the most efficient code. So, even when you have selected a memory model, you still might have to use the `__near`, `__far`, and `__huge` modifiers to set up special kinds of pointers for special situations—for example, when you want to access memory addresses in a very large block of data, such as a very long array.

Also, there are certain restrictions in using certain memory models. For example, you can't use the tiny memory model to write Windows applications.

# The Six Memory Models

A program that uses the *tiny* memory model can be no more than 64K long—including both code and data. A *small*-model program can occupy up to 128K: 64K for code and 64K for data. A *medium*-model program has no memory limitations on code size, but its data must fit into a 64K segment. A *compact*-model program has no memory limitations on its data size, but its code must fit into a 64K segment.

A *large*-model program has no memory limitations on its code or data, but its data arrays cannot cross 64K segment boundaries. A *huge*-model program has no memory limits on its code or data, and its data arrays can span segment boundaries.

# The Tiny Memory Model

The smallest kind of Visual C++ program—the tiny-model program—takes up less than 64K of memory when its code, data, and stack are combined. Tiny-model programs can be run only under DOS ; the tiny-model program is not compatible with Windows.

Tiny-model programs offer the fastest processing speed available because all four segment registers in the 80X86 chip always point to the same memory-segment address and because all of the memory addresses in a tiny program can be accessed by 16-bit pointers with no offsets. So you can use the tiny memory model when you:

- Want to write a very short program (such as the example programs you've seen so far in this book) that doesn't require Windows but runs under DOS.
- Want your program to use as little memory space as possible.
- Plan to convert your program to a .COM file (a file that runs fast but has to fit in less than 64K of RAM). To generate a .COM file from a tiny-model program, you can compile the file with the CL (compilation) option /AT. Then you can link your program with the CRTCOM.LIB library using the /TINY link option.

## The Small Memory Model

In the small memory model, a program has separate code and data segments. The stack is included in the data segment. In a small-model program, up to 64K of memory is available for code, and another 64K is available for data. Therefore, neither the code segment nor the data segment in a small-model program can be larger than 64K.

Small-model programs use 16-bit pointers for both code and data. To make a 16-bit pointer point to an actual memory address in a small-model program, the value stored in the pointer must be combined with the contents of a segment register. However, because all the program's code is in one segment and all the program's data is in another, the values stored in the code and data segment registers never change. This means that a small-model program can execute almost as fast as a tiny-model program.

If you don't explicitly specify a memory model when you build a program, Visual C++ defaults to the small model, allotting up to 64K for the program's code and another 64K for the program's data.

# The Medium Memory Model

Programs written under the medium memory model use `far` (32-bit) pointers to access code addresses and use `near` (16-bit) pointers to access addresses and data. The code used in a medium model program can occupy up to 1M of memory, but the data used by the program is limited to 64K.

The medium model can come in handy when you want to write large, complicated programs that do not use much data.

# The Compact Memory Model

The compact memory model is a mirror image of the medium model—it uses `near` pointers to access code addresses, but uses `far` pointers to access data. When you build a program using the compact memory model, the program's data can occupy up to 1M of memory, but the program itself is limited to 64K. The compact memory model can be useful when you want to write relatively short programs that use large amounts of data.

# The Large Memory Model

The large memory model is designed for large programs that contain large amounts of data. Programs written under the large memory model use `far` pointers to access both code and data. Therefore, a program written under the large memory model can contain as much as 1M of code and as much as 1M of data. However, static data in the large memory model is limited to 64K.

# The Huge Memory Model

The huge memory model, like the large memory model, uses `far` pointers to access both code and data. However, the huge memory model removes the large model's 64K limit on static data. You can use the huge model for your largest programs.

# Using Pointers in Visual C++

As noted in the previous section, Visual C++ provides three kinds of pointers to access memory locations: `near` pointers, `far` pointers, and `huge` pointers. A `near` pointer is always 16 bits long. Pointers of the `far` and `huge` configurations are 32 bits long.

## near Pointers

When you write a tiny-model program or a small-model program, every address in the program's code segment and every address in the program's data segment can be accessed with a 16-bit pointer. For this reason, a 16-bit pointer is called a `near` pointer, and 16-bit addressing is called *near addressing*.

Because of its limited length, a 16-bit pointer can access only 64K of memory. To access an actual memory address, a `near` pointer must be combined with a value stored in a segment register. As noted in the first section of this chapter, the value in a segment register always contains or points to the beginning of a memory segment. The value of a pointer is always an address that specifies a memory location within a memory segment.

When you access an address with a pointer, the kind of segment register used to calculate the address depends on what type of object the pointer points to. When a `near` pointer points to a function, the CS (code segment) register provides the pointer's segment address. When a `near` pointer points to a data object, the DS (data segment) register provides the segment address.

In a tiny-model program, which uses only `near` pointers, the arithmetic operations that must be performed to create 32-bit pointers are never necessary. Also, the addresses stored in the CS and DS segment registers never have to change. Thus, even though programs that use only `near` pointers are limited in length, they run faster than larger programs.

Because `near` pointers do not store segment values, they can be directly compared. This is not often possible with `far` pointers because `far` pointers with different values can point to the same physical memory location. Also, arithmetic operations on `near` pointers are easier because calculations with `near` pointers do not have to handle segment values.

# far Pointers

When a program requires more than 64K for its code or its data, at least some of the pointers used in the program must be 32-bit pointers, or *far pointers*. Accessing an object with a `far` pointer is called *far addressing*.

A `far` pointer is a 32-bit pointer that contains both a segment value and an offset value. Therefore, you don't have to use a value stored in a segment register to calculate an address using a `far` pointer.

All programs larger than 64K must use either `far` pointers or `huge` pointers, which are described under the next heading.

A program that uses `far` pointers executes more slowly than a program that uses only `near` pointers. Also, `far` pointers consume twice as much memory as `near` pointers. However, `far` pointers can access any available memory location—up to four gigabytes in a 386 or 486 machine.

One disadvantage of using `far` pointers is that they cannot be directly compared. As noted earlier in the chapter, one physical memory location can be represented by 4,096 different segment:offset values. Obviously, these 4,096 values are not mathematically equal, although they point to the same memory location. So, if you need to perform logical comparisons on the values of pointers, you must use `near` pointers or `huge` pointers rather than `far` pointers.

It's also difficult to perform arithmetical operations on addresses stored in `far` pointers. If you ever have an occasion to perform an arithmetic calculation on a value stored in a `far` pointer, remember that you can't safely perform the operation on just the pointer's offset value; you must also consider the value in the segment part of the pointer.

Although a `far` pointer is 32 bits long, it can point only to a code or data segment that lies completely within a 64K segment. Therefore, a `far` pointer cannot keep track of a data segment that crosses a 64K boundary. (In Visual C++, a code segment cannot cross a 64K boundary, but a data segment can. Code must always be broken down into 64K segments.) If a program has a data segment that spans a 64K boundary, the data must be accessed with `huge` pointers, which can access more memory addresses but require slower and more complicated pointer arithmetic.

# huge Pointers

A `huge` pointer is the only kind of pointer that can access memory locations in data segments longer than 64K. You can't use a `huge` pointer to access addresses in a code segment because 80X86 code segments cannot be longer than 64K.

A `huge` pointer—like a `far` pointer—contains 32 bits, expressed as a segment value and an offset value. The distinguishing feature of a `huge` pointer is that the address stored in the pointer is *normalized*.

To normalize the address stored in a `huge` pointer, the 386/486 chip performs a special mathematical conversion on the address stored in the pointer. The address is manipulated in such a way that as much of the address as possible is stored in the segment part of the pointer. When this operation is complete, the offset part of the pointer contains only a value ranging from 0 to 16—or from 0 to F in hexadecimal notation.

A normalized `huge` pointer has two advantages over a `far` pointer. First, `huge` pointers that point to the same memory location are always equal, so you can logically compare the values of `huge` pointers. Second, you can perform mathematical operations on `huge` pointers more easily because the segment value of a `huge` pointer rolls over when an arithmetic operation requires the segment value to change.

The main disadvantage of using `huge` pointers is that the pointer arithmetic required to create and manipulate `huge` pointers requires extra overhead. Pointers of the `huge` variety therefore reduce processing speed.

For more information on how addresses in `huge` pointers are normalized, see Appendix B.

# Pointers to void

A variable defined as a pointer to `void` can point to an object of any type. However, for most kinds of operations to be performed on a pointer or to the object to which it points, the type of object to which it points must be explicitly specified for each operation.

# Pointers to Undeclared Data Types

You can declare a pointer to a structure, a union, or an enumeration type before the structure, union, or enumeration type is defined. This kind of declaration is allowed because the Visual C++ compiler does not have to know the size of an aggregate type to which a pointer points in order to allocate space for the pointer variable.

# The new and delete Operators

To allocate memory in C, you must visit an inelegantly named area of memory called the *heap*. C++ treats you nicer; it lets you go pick out the memory you want at a more friendly sounding place named the *free store*.

In C, as you may know, programs frequently call the `malloc()` and `free()` functions to allocate and deallocate memory from a block of memory called the system heap. The `malloc()` function allocates memory using a technique often called *dynamic allocation* because it can manage memory during the execution of a program.

C++ offers a new and better method for managing dynamic memory management. In a C++ program, instead of calling a function to allocate or deallocate memory, you invoke an operator. C++ provides two memory-management operators—the `new` and `delete` operators—that allocate and deallocate memory from a memory supply called the *free store*.

The `new` and `delete` operators are more versatile than `malloc()` and `free()` because they can associate the allocation of memory with the way you use it. They are also more reliable because the compiler performs type-checking each time a program allocates memory with `new`.

### WHAT NEW CAN'T DO

Although the `new` operator does some type-checking when you attempt to allocate memory—to make sure, for example, that a pointer to a `double` isn't initialized to the address of an integer—you are still responsible for writing code that makes sense. For example, it's still possible for your program to overrun the amount of memory you have allocated, to

> attempt to free memory that hasn't been allocated, and to make other mistakes in dynamic memory allocation. So you must still stay alert when you're carrying out memory-allocation operations.

Another advantage stems from the fact that `new` and `delete` are implemented as operators, not functions. That means `new` and `delete` are built into the C++ language itself, so programs can use `new` and `delete` without including any header files.

Still another important feature of the `new` and `delete` operators is that they never require type-casting—and that makes `new` and `delete` easier to use than `malloc()` and `free()`.

# How the new Operator Works

When you call the `malloc()` function in a C program, you pass a size to `malloc()` and the function returns a `void` pointer, which you must cast to whatever data type you want. For example, to allocate memory for a `struct` named `myAbils` in a C program, you can write these statements:

```
struct Abilities myAbils;     // define the structure

myAbils = (struct Abilities*)malloc(sizeof(struct Abilities));
```

The above statement returns a `void` pointer, which you must then cast to a pointer to an `Abilities` structure.

Using the `new` operator is much simpler. The `new` operator is not a function, so it has no parameter list. To obtain memory from an object-oriented program, you don't even tell `new` how much memory you want; `new` automatically finds out how much memory you need by checking the size of the object you are initializing.

The `new` operator returns a pointer, but it isn't a `void` pointer, so you don't have to cast the pointer to the data type for which you have obtained the memory. Instead, the compiler returns the kind of pointer you have requested.

To illustrate how the `new` operator is used, suppose you want storage for an array of 100 integers. You can obtain that memory with the `new` operator by writing these statements:

```
int *memBlock;
memBlock = new int [100];
```

If you want to be more concise, you can write:

```
int* memBlock = new int [100];
```

Both of the above examples declare a pointer named memBlock and initialize it to the address returned by new. If a pointer of the requested size is available, new returns a pointer to the beginning of a block of memory of the specified size. If there is not enough dynamic storage available to satisfy a request, new returns a zero (in Visual C++, a null pointer has a value of 0 instead of the value NULL).

Each time you execute an expression that invokes the new operator, the compiler performs a type check to make sure that the type of the pointer specified on the left-hand side of the operator is the correct type for the memory being allocated on the right. If the types don't match, the compiler issues an error message.

When you have invoked the new operator, you can find out whether new has succeeded in fulfilling your request for memory by simply checking the value that the new operator returns. The new operator returns a pointer value. If a zero value is returned, memory allocation has failed.

# Initializing Memory with a Value

When you allocate memory with the new operator, you can place an initialization value or expression inside parentheses at the end of the expression that invokes the new operator. C++ then initializes the memory you have allocated to the value you have specified.

For example, this statement initializes and allocates storage for an integer, initializes the storage that is allocated to a value of 0, and then saves a pointer to the allocated memory block in the pointer variable memPtr:

```
int *memPtr = new int (0);
```

Strangely, you can't use the above syntax to initialize storage for each element of an array. Thus, this construct is not permitted, even though it would probably be more useful:

```
int *memPtr = new int [100] (0);    // NO! This doesn't work
```

Although the above syntax doesn't work, you can, of course, write your own routine to initialize memory locations. One way to do that is to overload the new operator (operator overloading is covered in Chapter 16).

# Using the new Operator

You can use the new operator with a pointer to a data type, structure, or array. The new operator allocates as much memory as the specified pointer needs and assigns the address of that memory to the pointer that it returns. (In object-oriented programs, new also can allocate memory for user-defined objects such as classes, as you'll see in Part II of this book.)

You can also use the new operator to create an object that belongs to a class. When a C++ program instantiates a class object, the statement that instantiates the object often contains both a call to a constructor and a new operator. In fact, as you will see in Chapter 14, "Constructors and Destructors," that's the most common method for instantiating class objects.

Typically, a statement that instantiates a class has this syntax:

```
AClass *anObject = new AClass;
```

When you allocate memory for a class object by using both the new operator and a constructor, as shown above, the new operator does not override the object's constructor; the constructor is still invoked (constructors are introduced in Chapter 12, "Objects," and are examined more closely in Chapter 14).

When you use both the new operator and a constructor to create a class object, it is not necessary to delete the object using the delete operator when the object is no longer needed. When an object is instantiated with both a constructor and a new operator, the object is deleted automatically and its memory is deallocated automatically when it is no longer needed.

For more information on using the new operator with constructors, see Chapter 14.

The program in Listing 9.1 uses the new operator to obtain some memory for an instance of a structure. Then it initializes the new structure with a famous date—the nation's birthday. The program prints this message:

```
The nation's birthday is 7/4/1776
```

### Listing 9.1. Using the new operator.

```
// 0901.CPP
// Using the new and delete operators

#include <iostream.h>
```

```
struct theDate {          // theDate structure
    int mo;
    int da;
    int yr;
};

int main()
{
    theDate *independenceDay = new theDate;  // allocate memory
    independenceDay->mo = 7;     // assign a value to the theDate
    independenceDay->da = 4;
    independenceDay->yr = 1776;
    cout << "The nation's birthday is " // print the theDate
      << independenceDay->mo << '/'
      << independenceDay->da   << '/'
      << independenceDay->yr;
    delete independenceDay;       // return memory to the free store

    return 0;
}
```

This is the output of the program in Listing 9.1:

```
The nation's birthday is 7/4/1776
```

When the program finishes its job, it disposes of the memory it has allocated by using the `delete` operator.

# Allocating Memory for an Array

Listing 9.2 shows how you can use the `new` operator to allocate memory for an array. The program prints a message to standard output, normally the screen. The message is similar to the one printed by the program in Listing 9.1.

### Listing 9.2. Obtaining memory for an array.

```
// 0902.CPP
// Obtaining memory for an array

#include <iostream.h>

int main()
{
```

*continues*

**Listing 9.2. continued**

```
    int *independenceDay = new int[3]; // obtain memory for an array
    independenceDay[0] = 7;    // assign a value to the date
    independenceDay[1] = 4;
    independenceDay[2] = 1776;
    cout << "The nation's birthday is still " // print famous date
      << independenceDay[0] << '/'
      << independenceDay[1] << '/'
      << independenceDay[2];
    delete []independenceDay;     // return memory to the free store
    return 0;
}
```

The output of Listing 9.2 is:

```
The nation's birthday is still 7/4/1776
```

# Allocating Memory Interactively

The program in Listing 9.3 shows how you can invoke `new` to allocate memory for an array. When you run the program, it prompts you to type the size of an array. When you respond, the program prints your array, which contains the number of consecutive numbers that you have requested.

**Listing 9.3. Obtaining memory for an array.**

```
// 0903.CPP
// Allocating an array's memory dynamically

#include <iostream.h>
#include <stdlib.h>

int main()
{
    cout << "How many entries in your array? ";
    int sz;
    cin >> sz;             // prompt for input
    int *myArray = new int[sz];      // allocate a sz-sized array
    for (int n = 0; n < sz; n++)
     myArray[n] = n + 1;   // fill the myArray
    for (n = 0; n < sz; n++)    // print the myArray
```

```
    cout << '\n' << myArray[n];
   delete []myArray; // return the myArray to the free store
   return 0;
}
```

You can also use new and delete operators to obtain memory for an array and then dispose of the memory when it is no longer needed. Listing 9.3 illustrates this usage of the new and delete operators.

# Allocating Memory for an Array of Unknown Size

You can invoke the new operator to obtain memory for an array even if you don't know in advance how much memory the elements of the array require. All you have to do is invoke the new operator using a pointer to the array. If new can't calculate the amount of memory that you need when your statement is compiled, new waits until runtime, when the size of the array is known, and allocates the necessary memory then. For example, this code fragment allocates memory for an array of six strings at runtime:

```
myString *myText;
myText = new myString[6];
```

# Deallocating Memory Assigned to Arrays

When you allocate an array of strings with the new operator and then want to deallocate the array with the delete operator, you must place a pair of empty brackets after the delete operator to specify that an array is being deleted:

```
delete [] myText;   // use this syntax to delete an array
```

If you forget to place the braces after the delete operator, the compiler assumes that you want to deallocate memory for just one string. The memory allocated for the rest of the array is not deallocated—and if your application later assumes that the memory has been deallocated, the consequences can be serious. So *don't* use this syntax when you want to deallocate an array:

```
delete myText; // this statement deletes just one string!
```

To sum up: When you have allocated memory for an array with the `new` operator and you want to deallocate the memory with the `delete` operator, always use the `delete []` syntax. You must use the brackets, but `new` can figure out the value that they should contain.

**BY THE WAY**

In early versions of C++, when you called `delete`, you were required to specify the size of the array within the brackets, like this:

```
delete myText[6];    // the old way; no longer used
```

Furthermore, if you specified a different size than that used in the call to `new`, the compiler returned an error. Today, C++ compilers remember the sizes of all arrays that are allocated with the `new` operator and ignore any number that you might place between the brackets that follow the `delete` operator. In Visual C++, no matter how long an array you want to delete, use this syntax:

```
delete []myText;     // the new way; do it like this now
```

## Allocating Memory by Calling a Function

When you allocate memory for an array with the `new` operator, you can call a function to compute the dimension of the array. Listing 9.4 shows you how.

### Listing 9.4. Allocating memory by calling a function.

```
// 0904.CPP
// Allocating memory by calling a function

#include <iostream.h>
#include <stdlib.h>
#include <string.h>

int compare(const void *a, const void *b);

int main()
{
```

```
    cout << "Maximum number of words: ";
    int maxwords;
    cin >> maxwords;
    char **words = new char *[maxwords];
    char *word = new char[80];
    for (int wordcount = 0; wordcount < maxwords; wordcount++)    {
     cout << "Enter a word (type 'end' if done before "
          << maxwords << " words): ";
     cin >> word;
     if (strcmp(word, "end") == 0)
            break;
     words[wordcount] = new char[strlen(word)+1];
     strcpy(words[wordcount], word);
    }
    qsort(words, wordcount, sizeof(char *), compare);
    for (int i = 0; i < wordcount; i++)
     cout << words[i] << '\n';
    for (i = 0; i < wordcount; i++)
     delete words[i];
    delete word;
    delete words;
    return 0;
}

int compare(const void *a, const void *b)
{
    return strcmp(*(char **)a, *(char **)b);
}
```

The program in Listing 9.4 prompts the user for a series of strings. When the user finishes typing entries, the program sorts the strings by calling the C function `qsort` and then displays the strings the user has typed in their sorted order.

Notice that this program uses the `new` operator for two different kinds of operations. First, the program allocates an array of character pointers named `words`. The size of this array is the value stored in the variable `maxwords`—a value that you have set in response to a prompt. In the words array, the program stores a series of strings. Each of these strings is stored in a memory buffer sized to fit that string plus the zero terminator. For each word you type, the program allocates a memory buffer that is the length of the word plus one character for the zero terminator. When you type the number of names stored in `maxwords`—or when you type the word "end" to signify that you're finished—the program sorts and displays the words you have typed.

# Using the delete Operator

The `delete` operator is very easy to use—but it also can be dangerous. If you make a mistake in a complex string of memory-related operations and attempt to delete a block of memory that has not been allocated, the bug that results may be a show-stopper that doesn't show up right away and is difficult to track down.

One way to make `delete` operations a little safer is to initialize every pointer to `NULL` value and to assign addresses to your pointers later in your program. For example, this constructor function initializes three string pointers to NULL values:

```
Player() { name = NULL; weapon = NULL; magic = NULL; }
```

This function definition appears in the version of The Wrath of Zalthar program that you'll find when you get to Chapter 14. Later in that version of the Zalthar program, a function named `DuplicateString()` assigns real addresses of strings to at least two of the four string pointers that are initialized to `NULL` values in the above statement. In some cases, though, one string pointer—the one named `magic`—is never assigned an actual address. As you'll see in Chapter 14, that's because some objects in the program don't make use of a `magic` string.

At any rate, when the program ends, this destructor function (destructor functions are introduced along with constructors in Chapter 14) invokes the `delete` operator to deallocate the memory that has been allocated to each string:

```
~Player() { delete name; delete weapon; delete magic; }
```

Because the `delete` operator has the ability to crash programs, the preceding statement would be an invitation to disaster if the three pointers had not been assigned `NULL` values earlier in the program. That's because memory for one of the pointers—the one named `magic`—may not have been allocated. But, because the `magic` pointer has been assigned a `NULL` value, calling the `delete` operator to delete the memory assigned to it can do no harm. The `delete` operator is always safe when its target is a `NULL` pointer.

## Handling Low-Memory Conditions

As you may know, the C function `malloc()` returns `NULL` when it cannot allocate a requested amount of memory. For this reason, C programmers know that it's a good practice to check for a `NULL` return value every time `malloc()` is called. That doesn't create more memory, but it can warn an application about a low-memory condition so that the program can take alternative measures (such as advising the user to close windows or simply terminating gracefully when there is no other alternative), instead of unexpectedly crashing as a result of trying to dereference a `NULL` pointer.

The C++ new operator normally returns 0 (the NULL value in C++) when the operator cannot allocate a requested amount of memory. So in C++, you can check for a nonzero return value each time you call new. In C++, though, there is a more convenient way to deal with low-memory conditions.

C++ extends the power of the new operator by providing a global function named _set_new_handler(). In a C++ program, you can use the _set_new_handler() function to install an error handler for the new operator. If you want to use such an error-handling function, you must write the code for it yourself.

When new cannot allocate the amount of memory requested, it checks to see if the _set_new_handler() function has been used to install an error handler. If the _set_new_handler() has not been used to install an error handler, new simply returns 0 when it can't allocate a requested amount of memory. But, by writing a _set_new_handler() function, you can force the new operator to call an error-handling function instead of simply returning 0.

# The _set_new_handler( ) Function

The _set_new_handler() function, defined in the header file NEW.H, takes a function pointer as an argument. When you call _set_new_handler(), the pointer that you supply is set to point to an error-handling function—which you also supply. Subsequently, if the new operator finds that it can't allocate a requested amount of memory, it doesn't simply return 0. Instead, it calls your error-handling function. When you write an error-handling function for the new operator, it's called a *new handler*.

When you write a new handler and implement it with a _set_new_handler() function, you don't have to check the return value of new every time you call new. Instead, you can write just one function to handle low-memory conditions, and the compiler calls your new handler whenever it's needed.

Listing 9.5 illustrates the use of a new handler that prints an error message and exits the currently executing program.

**Listing 9.5. A low-memory error-handling function.**

```
// 0905.CPP
// The _set_new_handler function
```

*continues*

**Listing 9.5. continued**

```
#include <iostream.h>
#include <stdlib.h>
#include <new.h>

int exhausted(size_t size);

void main()
{
    _set_new_handler(exhausted);
    long total = 0;
    while (1)    {
     char *hogMem = new char[10000];
        total += 10000;
     cout << "Got 10000 bytes for a total of " << total << '\n';
    }
}

int exhausted(size_t size)
{
    cerr << "\n\aThe free store is empty\n";
    exit(1);
    return 0;
}
```

The program in Listing 9.5 executes a loop that consumes memory in increments of 10,000 until it runs out of memory to allocate. Then, it stops allocating memory and displays the total amount of memory currently allocated and prints the message, "`The free store is empty.`"

> **IMPORTANT**
>
> Notice that the `exhausted` function in Listing 9.5 takes a parameter of type `size_t`, which represents the size of the block requested when `new` failed. Also notice that `exhausted` returns an integer. When you write an error-handling function for the new operator, it always must take a parameter of type `size_t` and always must return an integer.

# How new Allocates Memory

The `new` operator allocates memory from an area of memory called the *free store*. The C++ free store corresponds to the heap in C; it provides the memory for objects created at runtime.

In a Visual C++ program, the location of the free store depends on the memory model of the program being compiled. In a tiny-model, small-model, or medium-model program, `new` obtains memory from the program's default data segment. In compact-model, large-model, and huge-model programs, `new` allocates memory that lies outside the default data segment.

The address space from which the `new` operator obtains memory depends on the memory model under which the executing program was compiled. For example, in a program compiled under the `tiny`, `small`, or `medium` memory model, `new` allocates memory in the near address space by default, and the data type returned by `new` is a 16-bit pointer. In a compact-model, large-model, or huge-model program, `new` allocates memory in the far address space, and the data type returned by `new` is a 32-bit pointer.

# The Near, Far, and Based Memory Spaces

When the address space from which memory is allocated lies inside the default data segment, it is called the *near address space* because it can be accessed with `near` pointers. Memory that spans one or more segments outside the default data segment is called the *far address space*. The far address space can be accessed only with `far` pointers.

Besides the address spaces that are based on memory models, programs can also allocate memory from a *based address space*—that is, a single memory segment that lies outside the default data segment. In the `malloc()` family of memory-allocation functions, based address space routines generally have the same names as standard memory routines, but begin with `_b`. For instance, `_bmalloc()` allocates a memory block from a based address space, and `_bfree()` frees a block allocated from a based address space.

Using a based address space offers some advantages over using address spaces that correspond to the memory models of programs. For example, based address spaces let you group related data in a single segment. This can simplify the management of related data.

Using the based address space can also speed up pointer arithmetic. Although a based address space lies in the `far` data segment, pointers to its data items are the same size as `near` pointers. Thus, pointer arithmetic on items in a based address space is faster than pointer arithmetic on items in the far address space.

One disadvantage of using the based address space is that programs that make use of it do not comply with ASCII standards and are therefore not portable to other platforms.

For more details about the based address space and how it is used by `malloc` and related routines, see the *Run-Time Library Reference* available from Microsoft.

# Overloading the new and delete Operators

C++ provides a technique that programs can use to change the default behavior of the `new` and `delete` operators. This technique, a powerful and frequently used feature of C++, is called *operator overloading*.

# The operator new( ) and operator delete( ) Functions

To overload operators such as `new` and `delete`, C++ provides a special keyword—`operator`—that can be placed before the name of a function in a function declaration. When the `operator` keyword is used with a function name in this fashion, the function can change the behavior of the specified operator in any way the writer of the function desires. For example, the program in Listing 9.6 modifies the behavior of the `new` and `delete` operators.

**Listing 9.6. Overloading new and `delete`.**

```
// 0906.CPP
// Overloading the new and delete operators

#include <iostream.h>
#include <stdlib.h>
#include <stddef.h>

// function prototypes
```

```
void *operator new(size_t bufSize);
void operator delete(void *voidPtrType);

int main()
{
    int *stuffVal = new int[16];
    for (int n = 0; n < 16; n++)
        cout << " " << stuffVal[n];
    delete [] stuffVal;

    return 0;
}

void *operator new(size_t bufSize)
{
    void *retVal = calloc(1, bufSize);
    return retVal;
}

void operator delete(void *voidPtrType)
{
    free(voidPtrType);
}
```

The program in Listing 9.6 overloads the `new` operator to overload a block of memory. Then, it stuffs the allocated memory with zeroes, prints the zeroes, and deallocates the memory that has been allocated by using the `delete` operator. These two functions create customized versions of the `new` and `delete` operators:

```
void *operator new(size_t bufSize);
void operator delete(void *voidPtrType);
```

Visual C++ overloads the `new` and `delete` operators in this same way—by calling customized global functions named `operator new()` and `operator delete()`. These customized functions are what give Visual C++ the capability of using different memory-allocation procedures for different memory models.

In Listing 9.6, the `operator new()` function presented calls the C function `calloc()` to allocate a block of memory and initialize it to zero. The `operator free()` function in Listing 9.6 calls the `free()` function that C provides.

These examples are worth studying because support of overloaded operators is a powerful and important capability of C++ that you can use to modify the behavior of operators in your own programs. For example, suppose you want `new` to allocate a block of memory and then initialize the block's contents to zero before returning its address. You can force the `new` operator to initialize the contents of a memory block to zeroes by overloading the `new` operator as shown in Listing 9.6.

> **HOW OPERATOR OVERLOADING WORKS**
>
> Operator overloading is a powerful feature of C++. You can use operator overloading not only to modify the behavior of the `new` and `delete` operators, but also to change the behavior of common arithmetic operators to suit your own purposes. For example, you can overload the arithmetic addition operator (`+`) to add the members of two `struct` variables instead of merely adding two numbers.
>
> For more information about the overloading of the `new` and `delete` operators, see Chapter 16.

# The size_t Type

Notice that in Listing 9.6, the `new` operator takes a parameter of type `size_t`. The `size_t` data type, defined in the header file STDDEF.H, holds the size of an object.

In the preceding example, the `bufSize` parameter of the `operator new` function holds the size of the object being allocated, and the compiler automatically sets the value of the `bufSize` variable whenever you use the `new` operator. Also note that the `new` operator returns a `void` pointer. Any `new operator` function that you write must be passed a parameter of type `size_t` and must return a `void` pointer.

In Listing 9.6, the `delete` operator takes a `void` pointer as a parameter and has a `void` return type. The `void` pointer passed to `delete` points to a block of memory to be deallocated. The return type of the `delete` function is `void` because `delete` does not return a value. Any `delete` operator you write must be passed a `void` pointer as a parameter and must have a `void` return type.

# Adding Parameters to the new Operator

By using operator overloading—described in Chapter 16—you can redefine the `new` operator to take additional parameters. For example, the program in Listing 9.7 defines a `new` operator that allocates a memory block and fills it with a character specified by the user.

**Listing 9.7. Adding parameters to the new operator.**

```
// 0907.CPP
// Overloading the new and delete operators

#include <iostream.h>
#include <stdlib.h>
#include <string.h>
#include <stddef.h>

// function prototypes
void *operator new(size_t dataSize, int filler);
void operator delete(void *type);

int main()
{
    // allocate a zero-filled array
    char *cp = new ('0') char[10];

    // display the array
    for (int i = 0; i < 10; i++)
     cout << ' ' << cp[i];

    // release the memory
    delete cp;
    return 0;
}

// overloaded new operator

void *operator new(size_t dataSize, int filler)
{
    void *rtn;
    if ((rtn = malloc(dataSize)) != NULL)
     memset(rtn, filler, dataSize);
    return rtn;
}

// overloaded delete operator

void operator delete(void *type)
{
    free(type);
}
```

In Listing 9.7, you may notice that the additional argument passed to `new` is enclosed in parentheses, in this fashion:

```
char *cp = new ('0') char[10];
```

This is an unusual construct, but in the current version of C++, this is the way it's done. Because C++ is a young language that is still evolving, odd syntax requirements such as this one may change in future versions.

## Using new to Change Memory Pools

Under rare circumstances—for example, when you're writing a program that runs in mixed memory modes—a situation may arise in which you don't want memory allocated from an address space other than your program model's default address space. In such a case, you can overload the `operator new` function to force it to allocate memory from a nondefault address space. To illustrate, this declaration forces the `operator new()` function to allocate memory from the far address space:

```
void __far *operator new(size_t);
```

For more details on overriding the operator new and operator delete functions, see the *Visual C++ Reference*.

In Visual C++, the `operator new` function is the only function that can be overloaded solely on the basis of return type. Furthermore, it can be overloaded only in certain ways.

The `delete` operator causes the `operator delete()` function to be called, which frees memory back to the available pool.

For more information about how to customize the address space used by the `operator new()` function, see the Visual C++ *Run-Time Library Reference*.

## Overloading _set_new_handler( )

The default behavior of the `_set_new_handler()` function, which was introduced earlier in this section, is simply to return `0`. But in Visual C++, there is an alternative: you can force the `_set_new_handler()` function to return a pointer to the current new handler before invoking another new handler.

If you overload `_set_new_handler()` in this way, you can reinstall the handler that it originally pointed to whenever you like. That means you can keep a whole collection of new handlers on hand, and you can implement any new handler you like at any time you like.

## Saving and Restoring a New Handler

For example, the following statement defines a `_set_new_handler()` function that installs a new handler named `MyNewHandler`. When `MyNewHandler` has been installed, the statement returns a pointer to the handler that `MyNewHandler` replaced (the `_PNH` data type used in this example will be explained momentarily).

```
_PNH old_handler = _set_new_handler(MyNewHandler);
```

When you finish using the new handler that this statement installs, you can reinstall the handler that the new handler replaced by executing this statement:

```
_set_new_handler(old_handler);
```

In the previous statement, which installed the handler named `MyNewHandler`, `_set_new_handler()` was defined as a function returning a `_PNH` data type. There are three kinds of values that a call to `_set_new_handler()` can return:

- `_PNH`. A pointer to a new handler that takes a single argument of type `size_t` and returns type `int`. This is the default type of the `_set_new_handler()` function. You can define `_set_new_handler()` to return a `_PNH` type when you want to trap a failure of memory allocation in a far or huge address space.
- `_PNHB`. A pointer to a new handler that takes arguments of type `__segment` (the number of elements) and type `size_t` (the segment base) and returns type `int`. You can define `_set_new_handler()` to return a `_PNHB` type when you want to trap a failure of memory allocation in the based address space.
- `_PNHH`. A pointer to a new handler that takes arguments of type `unsigned long` (the number of elements) and type `size_t` (the size of a given element) and returns type `int`. You can define `_set_new_handler()` to return a `_PNHH` type when you want to trap a failure of memory allocation in a far or huge address space.

These data types are described in more detail in the Visual C++ *Language Reference*.

## Returning _set_new_handler( ) to Its Default Behavior

When you have overloaded the `_set_new_handler()` function to implement a new handler, you can force `_set_new_hander()` to return to its default behavior—which is to return `0`—by calling it with an argument of `0`, like this:

```
_set_new_handler(0);
```

## Alternate _set_new_handler( ) Functions

Visual C++ provides several kinds of `_set_new_hander()` functions that let you trap memory-allocation problems in address spaces other than the default address space for the memory model being used by the currently executing program.

Under normal circumstances, the `_set_new_handler()` function automatically behaves as expected for the memory model used by the currently running program. However, by using Visual C++'s alternate `_set_new_hander()` functions, you can trap failures in memory-allocation operations in other address spaces.

For example, the function `_set_fnew_handler()` can trap failures in allocating memory in the far address space, and `_set_hnew_handler()` can trap failures in allocating memory in the huge address space. For more information on this topic, please refer to the Visual C++ *Language Reference*.

# Memory Management Under Windows

Windows applications do not strictly follow any of the memory models described in this chapter. Even if you write a Windows application using a standard memory model, the Windows API (application program interface) takes over your program as soon as you make a Windows call and immediately customizes the memory model that you have chosen. Because of this peculiarity, Windows programming is often called *mixed-model programming*.

As noted earlier in this chapter, the Microsoft C++ compiler provides two keywords, `near` and `far`, that you can use to specify the size of a pointer that you want to use to access a memory location or call a function. If the data or function that you want to access is in the memory segment currently being used, you can access the data or the function with a `near` pointer. If the data or function is in some other memory segment, you can access it using the `far` pointer.

Windows departs from the standard 80X86 memory models by starting with a standard model and then mixing in other memory references that are not standard for the model that has been chosen. In applications written under Windows, `far` pointers to data are not used in the small or medium memory models, and `far` calls to functions are not used in the small or compact memory models. However, Windows uses `far` pointers extensively to interface with applications that are running under Windows.

## How Windows Systems Work

The Windows 3.1 API contains more than 1,000 functions that are defined in a file named WINDOWS.H. This number increases when Windows extensions such as Pen Windows and Windows Multimedia are included in a program. The vast number of functions that Windows must access could not possibly fit into one segment along with your application. Because they must be in a different segment, they must be accessed using `far` (inter-segment) calls—no matter what memory model you have chosen.

Another consideration is that the 1,000-plus Windows functions included in the WINDOWS.H file amount to what really can be considered an independent application. For example, they have their own code and data segments.

When a Windows function needs to access a memory location or a function within your application, Windows must access the location or function using a `far` pointer. A `near` pointer passed to a Windows function would be interpreted as an offset within the Windows function's data segment, not as an offset within your application's data segment. In fact, unless a `far` pointer is passed, the Windows function has no idea where your data segment resides.

## Windows and Segment Registers

As noted earlier in this chapter, the 80X86 processor treats segment addresses as physical addresses when it is running in real mode. In real mode, segment addresses are referenced directly by a static value—not looked up in a descriptor table as they are in protected mode.

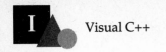

Because real mode treats segment addresses as physical addresses, the 80X86 chip's segment registers contain paragraph numbers only when the microprocessor is running in real mode. That's because the use of paragraph numbers to calculate addresses restricts the microprocessor to addressing 1M of memory. When Windows is running in either standard mode or in 386 enhanced mode, the processor is running in *protected mode*, which enables the microprocessor to address 16M of memory.

When an 80X86 processor is running under Windows in protected mode, the chip's segment registers contain *selectors* rather than segment numbers. The reason that segment numbers are called selectors in Windows protected mode is that a segment number has a direct correspondence to a physical memory location, whereas a selector value does not.

## Descriptors

To calculate the physical memory address of the start of a segment, you can multiply the segment number by 16. Under Windows, selectors provide an alternative, indirect method for specifying the physical memory address of a segment. When a Windows application is running, the microprocessor uses a selector as a subscript into one of two memory mapping tables to obtain a *descriptor*. This descriptor contains—along with other information—the linear (or virtual) memory location of the start of the segment. In standard mode, a linear address is the same as a physical address. In 386 enhanced mode, a linear address can be mapped to a different physical address.

Under Windows, segment numbers always reference regions of memory that are 64K long—whether or not there is actually memory at the referenced location. When a Windows application is running, selectors reference memory indirectly via descriptors, which can limit a segment to less than 64K.

Because of the way segment numbers work, you can compare two segment numbers and obtain meaningful results. The higher of two segment numbers always specifies a segment address that starts at a higher physical memory location than the location specified by the lower segment number.

In contrast, the result of comparing two selectors does not guarantee a meaningful result. When you compare two selectors, the selector with the higher value can specify an address that starts at either a higher or lower physical memory location than the location specified by the lower selector value. In fact, two different selector values can reference the same physical memory location.

When Windows is running in real mode, a program can use a `far` pointer to a 16K segment of memory and can freely access the 48K memory beyond its allocated length. In Windows protected mode, the microprocessor knows that the length of the segment is 16K and can prevent a program from accessing beyond that limit. Because of this extra checking, problems caused by dangling pointers are much easier to detect in Windows programs running in standard or 386 enhanced mode.

When you run a large-model program under Windows, all memory is addressable, so you don't have to keep track of what information is stored in which segment. So, generally speaking, the large memory model would seem to be the logical choice when you want to write a large Windows application. However, if a program is large because it uses multiple data segments, it might encounter unexpected restrictions when it is executed under Windows.

Here's where the potential problem lies: When you run a compact-model program, a large-model program, or a huge-model program under Windows, the program's data segment is fixed; that is, it cannot be moved around in memory. This can create a real obstacle for memory management, making it more difficult and more time-consuming.

Windows makes the memory positions of `far` data segments fixed because Windows has no way to redirect references to `far` data segments. For example, a program can save a `far` pointer to data in a far segment. If Windows, while running in real mode, moves the segment, the segment number portion of the `far` pointer will no longer be valid. The program does not know that the `far` data segment has moved, so it cannot update the `far` pointer. Windows knows the `far` data segment has moved but does not know that the program has stored a `far` pointer to the relocated data.

You won't encounter this problem when you run Windows in protected mode. In all operating modes, Windows loads only one instance of a program using multiple data segments. When Windows is running in protected mode, the address in the descriptor that is referenced by the selector portion of the `far` pointer is updated. Because the selector itself remains unchanged, all copies of the `far` pointer remain valid.

Generally, to avoid these restrictions, it is best to use the small or medium models for Windows programs. The small model limits applications to a maximum of 64K code, so most commercial-quality Windows applications are medium-model programs.

# Summary

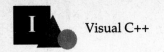

This chapter demystifies the memory architecture of the IBM Personal Computer and PC-compatibles—which are built around the 80X86 family of microprocessors—and explains how to write Visual C++ programs for 80X86 computers. Topics covered in this chapter include:

- The segmented memory architecture of 80X86-based computers.
- The six memory models that are used to write programs for 80X86 computers: tiny, small, medium, compact, large, and huge.
- The use of pointers in Visual C++ programs.
- The `new` and `delete` operators (which were introduced in Chapter 2 and will appear again in Chapter 16).
- Memory management under Windows: Special memory-management procedures that are used to write Windows-based programs, and the special memory-management needs of programs designed to be run under the Windows environment.

More information about Visual C++ memory management is presented in Appendix B.

II

# Object-Oriented Programming

Chapter 10

# Object-Oriented Programming

If you bought this book to learn about object-oriented programming, this is the chapter you've been waiting for. Part I, which ended with Chapter 9, "Managing Memory," introduced you to the Visual C++ interface and also to features of the C++ language that are not directly related to object-oriented programming. In Part II, which begins with this chapter, you'll learn how to write object-oriented programs in C++. Then you'll be ready to move on to Part III, which will teach you how to write commercial-quality Windows programs using Version 2 of the Microsoft Foundation Class (MFC) library.

This chapter tells you what object-oriented programming is, what it isn't, and why you made the right choice when you decided to learn how to design software using Visual C++.

Some of the topics examined in this chapter are:

- Object-oriented programming concepts.
- Benefits of programming in C++.
- Terms used in C++, such as encapsulation, abstraction, inheritance, multiple inheritance, and polymorphism.
- Features of C++.
- Elements of a C++ program, including classes, objects, member variables, and member functions.

# About Object-Oriented Programming

Object-oriented programming—sometimes fondly referred to as OOP—is a hot topic in the computer industry. That's because OOP appears to be—at least for now—a giant leap in the development of computer languages. Some programming experts call OOP at least as significant a step forward as the development of the first high-level computer languages 20 years ago. And the experts seem to be right. Computer technology moves fast, and nobody ever knows what will happen tomorrow or the day after. At the moment, however, it appears that object-oriented programming—and C++ programming in particular—is probably destined to dominate software development at least for the rest of this decade.

One reason that C++ seems to have a rosy future is that all the prominent R&D-oriented manufacturers in the personal computer industry—including IBM, Apple, Microsoft, Borland, and many other companies—are investing heavily in object-oriented technology in general and in C++ in particular. IBM and Apple are jointly developing new operating systems written in C++. Over the past year or so, Microsoft has rolled out a host of new products built around C++, including Visual C++, the Windows NT operating system, and the Win32 software development system. And where Microsoft goes, Borland either has already been or is sure to follow.

## Misconceptions

Most people don't know exactly what object-oriented programming is. That isn't surprising because a lot of misinformation is being passed around.

Some of this misinformation comes from unscrupulous peddlers whose products have no relationship whatsoever to object-oriented programming, but who have claimed quite falsely that they have climbed aboard the OOP bandwagon. These manufacturers, taking advantage of the public's naiveté about object-oriented technology, have hyped products as being object-oriented when the products are really only graphics-oriented. They have pointed to graphics-oriented "objects," such as buttons, icons, dialog boxes, and windows themselves, that often appear in Windows programs and then claimed that when you write programs that manipulate such objects, you're writing object-oriented programs.

Nothing could be further from the truth. As you'll see in this chapter and in the rest of this book, any perceived relationship between objects in windows and object-oriented programming is purely coincidental. Graphics-oriented products aren't necessarily object-oriented, and object-oriented programs aren't necessarily graphics-oriented. In fact, most object-oriented programs in Part I of this book are text-based programs that contain no graphics "objects" at all. On the other hand, most books that have been written about Windows programming—including the classic *Programming Windows* by Charles Petzold—don't contain object-oriented programs.

## The OOP Controversy

C++ has become an object of some controversy because, frankly, sweeping new technological developments cost a lot of money. And some software and hardware manufacturers, stung by technologies that didn't work out in the past, are skeptical about junking tried and true programming procedures and starting off on a trek toward new, heavy hyped horizons.

Their reluctance is understandable. Over the past 20 years, software and hardware manufacturers have invested billions of dollars in programs written in traditional procedural computer languages—and legions of software engineers are proficient in using procedural languages but know next to nothing about object-oriented programming. Because object-oriented technology requires sweeping changes in software design, OOP is going to have to prove its worth to some computer designers, software developers, and most of the people who handle the cash at hardware and software companies.

Advocates of object-oriented programming are confident that object-oriented languages offer such clear benefits over procedural languages that OOP is certain to overcome the objections of skeptics and to usher in a new era in computer programming. OOP boosters say that object-oriented programming will change the way software is developed, will change user expectations about software, will increase the range and the kinds of applications offered to the public, and will spell success for programmers and companies who can adapt most quickly to the exciting new field of object-oriented program design.

Many of the heavy hitters in the computer industry agree. Others are still trying to take a wait-and-see attitude.

## How It Works

What's so special about object-oriented programming? Briefly, instead of trying to shoehorn a problem into the structure of a program written in a procedural language, OOP attempts to fit the language in which programs are written to the problem that is at hand. When you write an object-oriented program, your first task is to design a data form that corresponds to the essential features of your problem. Then you must create a set of procedures, or methods, that manipulate that data to solve the problem.

If you're writing a program designed to solve more than one problem, you can create sets of data structures and methods that work together, and then you can arrange those structures and behaviors into relationships and hierarchies that also work well together. Simply stated, you can break a problem down into objects that have built-in data and built-in behaviors. Then you can group those building blocks into a sensible arrangement that seems to be suited to solving your problem.

If your first attempt to solve the problem doesn't work as well as you expected, you can rearrange the building blocks that make up an object-oriented program into a different arrangement. Object-oriented languages let you do that easily and conveniently because the objects that make up an object-oriented program are more independent than the procedures that make up a procedural program, and can therefore be rearranged and moved around more freely.

Furthermore, when you have designed an object-oriented program that works, you can reuse the program's code in other applications much more easily and conveniently than you can when you're working with procedural programs such as C and Pascal. Thus, when you write programs in an object-oriented language, you don't have to start from scratch every time you get a new program to write or a new problem to solve.

## How It All Began

To understand how C++ works and what it can do for you, it helps to know something about how the language evolved.

In the earliest computers, the language in which subtasks were programmed was machine language. To enter programs into the computer, operators had to toggle switches on the machine's front panel.

As long as programs were just a few hundred instructions long, this cumbersome approach worked well enough to meet most programming needs. As programs grew longer, the manual entry of machine-language programs gave way to programs written in assembly language. Assembly language—which used numbers and letters to represent machine instructions symbolically—was invented to help programmers deal with larger and increasingly complex programs.

## From COBOL to Simula

Beginning in the late 1940s and continuing through most of the 1980s, assembly language evolved into higher-level languages such as COBOL, FORTRAN, Basic, Pascal, C, and Ada. These and other higher-level languages were easier to understand and use than machine language and assembly language had been, but they didn't change the procedural programming paradigm: to divide programs into smaller tasks until a sequence of procedural operations could be performed.

Even as procedural languages were being developed, though, program designers were beginning to think in terms of objects. In computer science, an object is an abstract entity that embodies the characteristics of a real-world object. You don't need an object-oriented language such as C++ to create and manipulate objects. Objects are the result of a programming methodology, not the product of a specific programming language.

Development of languages with object-oriented features can be traced as far back as the 1960s. Simula, an Algol-like language, was designed in that decade as a language for writing simulations. In Simula, built-in data types are not objects, but objects can be created. Other languages—for instance, Smalltalk—are completely based on objects. Anything you manipulate in a Smalltalk program is some kind of object.

In the 1970s, Alan Kay, an engineer at the Xerox PARC (Palo Alto Research Center) in Palo Alto, CA, extended the concepts introduced in Simula and designed a language called Smalltalk. Smalltalk, still in use today, is a wholly object-oriented language; in Smalltalk, all data types—including such familiar types as integers—are objects. This uniform approach makes for great elegance, but it does have drawbacks—mainly, efficiency. Overuse of objects can impose runtime penalties that seriously degrade the performance of a program.

In the early 1980s, Bjarne Stroustrup of AT&T developed an extension to the C language called C with classes. C with classes became the foundation for C++, which in turn became the most popular object-oriented language.

> **NOTE—WHAT'S IN A NAME**
>
> The name C++ is derived from the C increment operator ++, which adds 1 to the value of a variable. C++ derives its name from the fact that it's an augmented version of C.

## The Debut of C++

Stroustrup tried to design C++ in a way that would take advantage of the most desirable features of objects but avoid the runtime disadvantages of a totally object-oriented language such as Smalltalk. In C++, many of the things you manipulate in a program are objects, but many aren't. For this reason (*not* because C++ is derived from C), C++ is said to be a *hybrid object-oriented programming language.*

Because C++ is not totally object-based, it fundamentally alters—but does not entirely replace—the old procedural programming paradigm. In a C++ program, as in any object-oriented program, a problem is broken down into subgroups of *related* parts. Each part takes into account both the code and the data that is related to it. During this process, these subgroups are organized into a hierarchical structure. Finally, the subgroups are organized into self-contained units, or *objects.*

C++ makes it possible to create reusable objects, but it uses procedural methods to build the objects. In fact, in C++ an object is actually a specialized instance of a traditional data type.

# Benefits of C++

Because of the way it uses classes and objects, C++ offers several solid benefits over procedural programming techniques—for example, object-oriented programming in C++ provides:

- *A more natural approach to programming.* Object-oriented programming languages provide a more natural way of looking at problem solving than traditional procedural programming languages. In an object-oriented program, fields of data and procedures that manipulate the data are grouped together in a construct called an *object*. In a procedural program, the data and data-manipulation methods that make up an object are often found in widely separated portions of a program.
- *Simplicity.* Because related data collections and methods are grouped together, object-oriented programs are easier to understand and easier to maintain than programs written in traditional procedural languages.
- *Code reusability.* In an object-oriented program, objects are specifically designed for reuse. Consequently, every time a program is written, code used in the program has the potential of being reused in future programs.
- *Reliability.* When code that was used successfully in one program is reused in another program, you can be sure that the code is reliable because it has already been tested. And as a block of code is used in more programs, it becomes more reliable.
- *Continuity.* Because C++ is derived from C, experienced C programmers can learn C++ quite easily. Furthermore, existing applications written in C can be upgraded to C++ without much difficulty. Because C is the most popular procedural language for writing commercial programs, continuity from C to C++ has helped to make C++ the most widely used OOP language.

## Code Reuse

One of the most important features of C++ is the way it facilitates code reuse. In procedural languages such as C, code reuse is possible but is often difficult. That's because code that is written for one program can rarely be used in another program without extensive modification.

To illustrate this difficulty, imagine that Terence, a few cubicles down from your office, has written a piece of C-language code for a project he is working on. When you examine it, you are delighted to discover that you also might be able to use it in your project.

Unfortunately, when you examine the code more closely, the next discovery you'll probably make is that Terence's code requires at least a few modifications or extensions before you can use it in your project. Furthermore, because Terence's code is not written in C++, you'll usually find that the data and functions used in his program are not grouped neatly together into objects, but are scattered throughout the program.

Nonetheless, you decide that it will be easier to modify Terence's code than it would be to write similar code from scratch. So you modify Terence's code and use it in your program.

That's Part 1 of this scenario. Part 2 begins six months later, when Terence walks into your office again and hands you a new file. He tells you that he has updated his program, fixed a few bugs, and added a couple of important features. Now you have another problem: If you want to upgrade your program as he has upgraded his, you must go through his code again, looking for his modifications in both your code and his, and incorporating his changes into your program.

Now consider how this scenario works if you and Terence are not C programmers, but are working in C++. The first time Terence walks into your office and hands you his code, you don't have to modify any code that he has written. Instead, you merely create some objects that inherit properties from his objects—duplicating properties that can be used without modification and modifying properties that must be changed.

Because Terence's program is made up of data and functions that are neatly grouped together as objects, you don't have to chase around in the program looking for functions that are widely separated from the data that they affect. In fact, thanks to data abstraction, you usually don't have to know anything about the member variables of objects at all; all you have to be concerned with is how to call the objects' member variables.

The second time Terence walks into your office, he does not hand you a new file that completely replaces his original file; instead, he hands you a new file that contains only the code for objects he has modified, and possibly some new header files that define some new objects. To incorporate his modifications into your program, you can probably simply recompile his program using his new objects—without making any other changes in the program at all.

## Zen and the Art of C++ Programming

Now that you know how object-oriented programs attempt to imitate life, it's time to add that this attempt is never fully successful. There are parallels between object-oriented programming, but they are never perfect parallels.

The view that an object-oriented program should parallel a real-life situation exactly is known as the *objectivist* view of object-oriented programming. But there's no one in the field of OOP who holds strictly to an objectivist programming philosophy. Examine any object-oriented solution to a programming problem, and you'll quickly see why.

Suppose, for example, that you wanted to write an object-oriented program that simulated the operation of an airport. From the very beginning of such a project, you'd probably feel overwhelmed by the enormous number of objects involved and the vast network of relationships among all the objects involved.

For a start, you'd be dealing with aircraft, flight patterns, runways, control towers, buildings, passengers, flight crews, and weather. Is weather an object? If so, what's the exact relationship between the weather and the pilot of an airliner? Will it make him late for work? Or is that question important enough to consider in the design of your program?

Consider other relationships. Is an airplane an object that flies in a flight pattern? Or is a flight pattern something that an airplane flies in? Are planes designed to roll down runways, or are runways designed for planes? That's an important factor to consider in designing an airport-simulation program because determining what kinds of objects determine the behaviors of other objects is one of the first decisions that you have to make when you start designing an object-oriented program.

If that sounds like bad news, the good news is that there are no right or wrong answers to questions such as these. If your answers result in a smooth-running program that makes sense to the people who run and maintain it, then your answers are correct. If they result in a jumbled-up program that no one can interpret or understand, then your answers probably weren't so good. In this respect, the object-oriented programming paradigm is like any other programming paradigm. If it's a great program, you've done a great job.

To illustrate how different teams of programmers can look at the same problem and come up with different programming models, a real-life example might be helpful. When programmers at Apple sat down to design a Macintosh object-oriented programming package called MacApp, they started with an object called a document—which can be a text document, a drawing, or anything else that can fit in a window—and then started listing all the properties that a document can have.

They soon discovered that a document can have a practically unlimited number of properties. Properties of a document can include text, fonts and styles, drawings, colors, sounds, icons, and windows—which, in turn, can have their own properties, such as scroll bars, title bars, and go-away boxes. This arrangement made sense to the programmers developing MacApp, so that's the way the package was designed.

When software engineers at Microsoft sat down to create a C++ library for Windows, they took a different approach from the one created by the designers of MacApp. Microsoft's programmers started with a window and then began listing the properties that a window can have. They decided that a window, like a document, can have a large number of properties, including scroll bars, title bars, go-away boxes, icons—and documents.

That's right. In MacApp, a document is a property of a window. In the Microsoft Foundation Class library, a window is a property of a document. Which hierarchy is correct? That's a matter of opinion. I favor the Microsoft approach because I think it makes more sense to put a document in a window than it does to place a window over a document. But then again, who's to say?

## A Wall Street Simulation

As an example of how objects and classes work, suppose you have designed an object-oriented program to simulate the operation of the stock market. In this program, each company listed on the stock exchange could be an object. The stock exchange itself could be another object. The ticker tape could be an object; each buy or sell order could be an object, and so on.

You could design this model so that when an order is completed, an object communicates that fact to the ticker-tape object, as well as to the object representing company whose stock was traded. The Dow Jones Industrial Average is an object that uses functions to communicate with all the companies whose earnings are averaged out to compute the Dow Jones average. As underlying stock prices change, so does the value of the Dow Jones Industrial Average object; thanks to the magic of object-oriented programming.

In our Wall Street OOP model, there are many objects, each specialized to carry out a particular task, and each modeled after an object in the real world. To simulate other kinds of real-world activities, you can create virtually unlimited varieties of other object-oriented models. Object-oriented programs simulate real life; when you design an object-oriented program to solve a problem, the best plan of attack is to create software objects that are based on real-world objects in the domain of the problem you are solving.

**NOTE—INTANGIBLE OBJECTS**

Students of C++ are sometimes surprised to learn that some "objects" used in C++ programs aren't tangible things, such as tables and chairs, but are things that you can't see: for example, the act of making a trade on Wall Street. But it's important to remember that in C++, intangible concepts—or even processes or procedures—can be used as objects. And there are precedents for this kind of thinking outside the field of object-oriented languages.

Consider this book, for example; it's divided into three parts. Part I focuses on Visual C++; Part II explores object-oriented programming in C++; and Part III covers the use of the Microsoft Foundation Class (MFC) library. Taking the point of view of this book into consideration, you then could say that using C++ is an object, and that using the MFC library is also an object.

Some of the chapters in this book are about intangible ideas and procedures too. For example, Chapter 1 is an introduction to Visual C++, and an introduction is another "object" that's intangible. Other chapters that focus on intangibles include Chapter 8, "Linking a C++ Program," which is about linking C++ programs; Chapter 9, "Managing Memory"; this chapter, "Object-Oriented Programming," and so on. So it would seem that viewing intangibles as if they were intangible objects is something we really are accustomed to in real life after all.

## A Factory Simulation

Because object-oriented programming was created to simulate the way things work in the real world, many other kinds of real-world situations are as well suited as Wall Street for object-oriented treatment. For example, suppose that you own a factory that manufactures chairs, stools, and tables. Then assume that you want to automate your factory's manufacturing procedures with a C++ program.

You might start by defining a class named `Furniture`. Once you have defined a furniture class, you can declare individual objects—that is, items of furniture—that meet the specifications of the `Furniture` class.

Because furniture is a general name that includes chairs, stools, and tables (and may include more items as your company grows), you might want to make `Furniture` a general kind of class called an *abstract class*—broad enough to encompass all the varieties of furniture that are (or may one day be) manufactured by your company.

One characteristic of an abstract class is that you can't create (or *instantiate*) objects that belong to the class. In this case, that's logical because you can't create "a furniture." Because "a furniture" is not an object that can be created, the only way you can use an abstract class is to create *derived* classes from it—that is, classes that inherit characteristics and behaviors of the abstract class, and from which actual objects can be created.

Figure 10.1 shows the abstract class `Furniture` and several concrete classes, or subclasses, that are derived from the `Furniture` class—specifically, tables, chairs, and stools. It makes sense to call `Furniture` an abstract class because you can't create an object that's "a furniture." However, you can create "a table," "a chair," or "a stool." Thus, they are concrete classes.

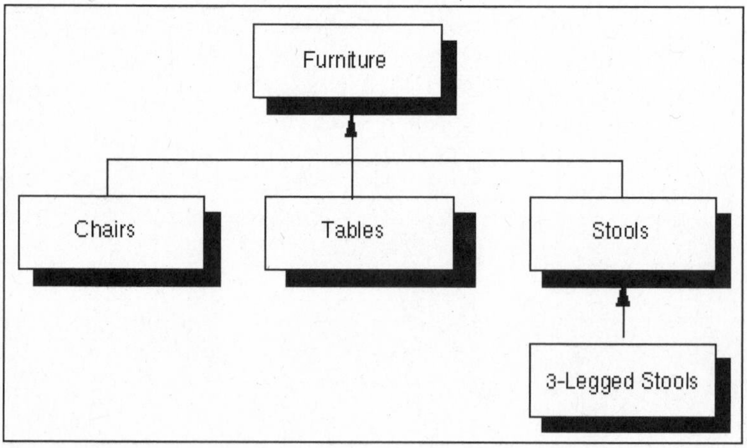


*Figure 10.1. The `Furniture` class.*

### NOTE—DATA MODELS

Figure 10.1 shows what's sometimes called a *data model.* In the field of object-oriented languages, a data model is a model that provides a general picture of how an object-oriented project will be organized. A data model doesn't go into many specifics—and that's where the fun begins. When you have decided that your model will include certain classes—in this case, the classes shown in Figure 10.1—you must start figuring out exactly what kinds of data and behaviors your classes (and the objects created from them) will contain.

In C++, classes (and the objects created from classes) can contain both data and behaviors. From the point of view of data, the `Furniture` class could contain data generally describing a universe of objects, probably made of wood, each with an array of legs (either three or four legs because you manufacture stools as well as tables and chairs).

As Figure 10.1 illustrates, three classes are derived directly from the `Furniture` class: `Chairs`, `Tables`, and `Stools`. Because `Chairs`, `Tables`, and `Stools` are all derived from the `Furniture` class, they inherit certain characteristics and behaviors from the `Furniture` class. That's quite logical in this case because chairs, tables, and stools are all pieces of furniture. As self-evident as this example may be, it demonstrates the object-oriented principle of *inheritance.*

### NOTE—GOING UP?

In Figure 10.1, notice that the arrows extending from subclasses to parent classes are drawn upside-down, pointing upward from the derived classes to the parent classes. The arrows point that way because a derived class is aware of its parent class, but a parent class is not aware of its derived classes.

Now notice that one class in Figure 10.1—the class labeled `3-Legged Stools`—doesn't inherit directly from the `Furniture` class. Instead, it is a subclass of the `Stools` class and therefore inherits from the `Stools` class.

The diagram doesn't show exactly what the `3-Legged Stools` class inherits from the `Stools` class, but let's assume that it inherits all the characteristics of the `Stools` class except one: specifically, having four legs.

If this is true—if the `Stools` class is defined as having four legs—then the class named `3-Legged Stools` actually does inherit the characteristic of having four legs. But in C++, the `3-Legged Stools` can *override* the inherited characteristic of having four legs and can replace it with a new characteristic: namely, the characteristic of having three legs.

This overriding of an inherited characteristic illustrates an object-oriented principle called *polymorphism*. In the field of biology, the word polymorphism means "having multiple forms"—and it has the same meaning in C++. In C++, a class can inherit characteristics from another class, but can then change them, or override them. That means a given set of class characteristics can be changed into other forms as it is passed on to derived classes and its various characteristics are overridden.

But what kinds of behaviors can you create for the `Furniture` class? That depends on what you want to use your program for. If you want to automate your manufacturing process, then the behaviors that you define for the `Furniture` class could include sawing, planing, the attachments of legs, and so on. On the other hand, if you were writing a program to handle invoicing and billing, you would define behaviors such as ordering goods, invoicing, managing a payroll, and the like.

## Problems in Project Planning

One of the nicest things about C++ is that once you develop an approach to a program that makes sense to you, you can use that approach and see if it works. If it doesn't, C++ supplies many kinds of tools and features that make it easy for you to alter your approach. For example, by taking advantage of the principle of data abstraction (described later in this chapter), you can experiment with objects, arranging them into different kinds of hierarchies until you discover what kinds of relationships between the objects in your program work best.

As you'll see when you start programming in C++, the language offers wonderful tools for sculpting classes into objects and then arranging and rearranging those objects until you have a smoothly working program.

Before I move on to the next heading, I'd like to emphasize one strong feeling that I have: Too much has been written about how much time and effort you have to spend plotting out the objects and methods you're going to use in a software project before you can start writing code. Of course, it's always good to plan ahead, and it's true that before you start coding, you should have some fairly solid ideas about what kinds of objects you'll be using in your program and what the relationships between those objects will be.

However, if your initial plans turn out to have flaws, it's much easier to correct those flaws and rethink your program's structure in C++ than in any procedural language I've ever encountered. Every class in a C++ program is a "black box" that contains an independent collection of data and functions, and it's much easier to rearrange the black boxes that make up a C++ program so that the program will work better than to move functions, procedures, and structures around when you redesign a procedural program.

As the evolution of The Wrath of Zalthar program in this book illustrates, a software project always changes as it grows, and it rarely winds up looking much like you thought it would when you started planning it. In that respect, a C++ project is much like any programming project. The difference is that C++ is easier to work with than any procedural language I've ever seen when you're forced to make extensive alterations in a program.

# The C++ Lexicon

Students of C++ sometimes feel intimidated by the large number of unfamiliar terms used to describe the characteristics and features of the language.

If you're a newcomer to C++, the jargon that's bandied about by C++ old-timers may sound like just an arrogant attempt to slap new and unnecessary labels on concepts already used in procedural programming. It may be true that C++ experts sometimes use more jargon than the language really requires, and it's also true that in some cases, better words could have been found than the ones the experts selected.

For example, OOP people talk about "instantiating an instance of a class," when "creating an object" means the same thing. An even more peculiar term is the word "overloading," which has a very negative meaning in the fields of audio and electrical engineering. In C++, however, "overloading" is used to describe a useful tool. (In C++, overloading is a feature that lets programmers call different but similar functions using the same name and that provides a technique for creating new arithmetic and logical operators. A better label for this capability might be "redesigning.")

These peculiarities aside, there really are valid reasons for learning and using most of the technical terms that make up the C++ vocabulary. Most of the odd-sounding words that have worked their way into the C++ lexicon really do describe ideas that are quite different from the concepts used in procedural programming.

One OOP-related word that's often heard these days is *paradigm*—a four-dollar word that simply means an example or model. In linguistics, a paradigm is a list of inflectional forms that illustrates a word's conjugation or declension. In the field of computer languages, a paradigm is a blueprint that illustrates ways of solving problems.

For almost 50 years now, software designers have used *procedural* and *structural* paradigms to create most kinds of computer programs. Procedural and structural paradigms take a top-down, or structured, approach to program design: A task is partitioned into subtasks; those subtasks are further partitioned into still smaller subtasks, and so on until the main task has been divided into subtasks that are simple enough to be programmed in a conventional procedural language.

According to some experts, object-oriented technology has brought about the first fundamental change in the programming paradigm in more than 40 years of software development. An object-oriented program is made up of reusable objects that are relatively independent of other objects, yet can have characteristics that are inherited from other objects and also have characteristics that can be passed on to other objects. This paradigm is said to have more in common with the standard paradigms used in other engineering disciplines than does the procedural paradigm that is used for program construction by conventional procedural languages.

It's important to note that OOP does not repudiate the procedural paradigm, but enhances it. Object-oriented programs make use of procedures, but those procedures are encapsulated within objects, along with the data that the procedures manipulate. Thus, object-oriented technology has fundamentally changed—but has not destroyed—the old procedural programming paradigm.

Other terms often encountered in OOP circles include these:

- *Objects.* An object is a user-defined data type that resembles a C-style `struct`, but contains both data and functions that can manipulate that data. The data fields contained in an object are usually called *member variables*, but are sometimes referred to as *data members*. The functions contained in an object are usually called *member functions*, but are sometimes called *methods*. In an object-oriented language, the data and procedures that are grouped together to form objects can be used together to create more objects. In C++, *inheritance* lets you create objects that inherit properties of other objects. And objects can access data and call functions that are members of other objects.

- *Classes.* In C++, every object is an instance of a user-created data type called a *class*. A class is a framework that sets up the architecture of an object. When a class is declared, no memory is allocated for objects that belong to the class. Memory is not allocated for an object until the object is created. An object is an *instance* of a class. Therefore, the act of creating an object is called *instantiating* the object.

- *Data encapsulation.* In C++, the member functions declared within the definition of a class can access all member variables that belong to the same class. However, an object can safeguard its member variables from being accessed or altered from elsewhere in a program. The ability that an object has to conceal its data from other parts of a program is called *data encapsulation*. Data encapsulation is an important feature of C++ because it prevents data members of a class from being inadvertently modified by functions defined outside the class.

- *Data abstraction.* When you design a class in C++, you can conceal the details of how data is represented and modified inside the objects that belong to a class. When a function outside a class requests an action or a piece of data from a member function of an object, the outside function does not need to know—and should not care—exactly how its request is fulfilled. All the requesting function has to know is what information it must pass to the member function that is being addressed and in what form the information being requested will be returned. Data abstraction is what lets the calling function ignore the details of how data types are represented inside objects and lets it concentrate instead on the job that it wants done.

- *Inheritance.* In an object-oriented language, you can create a new class from any existing class by modifying the properties of the existing class. The usual purpose for deriving one class from another is to create a more specialized class. The derivation of one class from another class is called *inheritance*. A class from which other classes are derived is called a *base class*, and classes that are derived from (or inherit from) a base class are called *derived classes*. The immediate base class of a derived class is called a *parent class*. In C++, a derived class can inherit more than one immediate base class. Then the derived class is said to be using *multiple inheritance*.

- *Multiple inheritance.* Some object-oriented languages—including C++—support *multiple inheritance*. In a language that supports multiple inheritance, an object can inherit properties from more than one class. More information about multiple inheritance is provided in Chapter 19.

  Classes can inherit behaviors from other classes, but a program can alter any of those properties if the program designer wishes. A class can inherit a routine—for example, a drawing routine—from a parent class. The class that inherits the routine can use the routine in the same way that the parent class does, or it can alter the routine and use it in its altered form. Thus, a derived class does not have to be an exact duplicate of a parent class. It can inherit some behaviors intact from its parent class; it can modify other behaviors to fit its own special requirements; and it can add unique behaviors of its own.

- *Polymorphism.* In biology, the occurrence of different properties in individual organisms, or in organisms in the same species, is called *polymorphism*. In a C++ program, polymorphism lets you create a family of classes with behaviors that vary, according to what is appropriate for each class. More specifically, polymorphism lets you use one function name to call multiple functions. If you call a member function of a particular object, your call may have one result, and if you issue the same call to a member function of another object, the result may be completely different.

  In a C++ program, just as in real life, inheritance creates families. In many cases, all classes in a family implement some version of a routine that has the same name in all the classes. Suppose, for example, that you create a class with a member function named `Display()` that prints text on the screen. Thanks to the magic of polymorphism, you can invoke the `Display()` function that belongs to a particular member of your program's family of classes, even if you don't know what the object's exact structure will look like at runtime. And your program will execute the `Display()` function that belongs to the appropriate object, even if that object's `Display()` function is different from other `Display()` functions in your program. You'll see how all this works in later chapters of this volume.

# Features of C++

The features of C++ outlined in the preceding list provide the language with some pretty impressive capabilities. For example, in a well-designed, object-oriented program, abstraction and encapsulation can create an interface that lets you access only the features and behaviors of an object that you're interested in and need to know, while ignoring all others.

An even more noteworthy benefit of C++ is that it lets you share code with other programmers—without giving them access to source code that you don't want them to have, or to classes, objects, data, or programming techniques that you don't want them to know about.

When you design a program in C++, you can make it available to other programmers by providing them with just your header files and your compiled object-code modules—while keeping your source code to yourself. Even without your source code, other programmers can access your classes (but only the classes, objects, data, and behaviors that you permit them to access) and can even derive classes from your classes. But, thanks to data encapsulation, you don't need to tell them any more about your program than they need to know.

In more technical terms, this is how data encapsulation works:

When you declare a member variable of an object, you can label the variable `public`, `private`, or `protected`. If the variable is public, any function can access it. If it's private, it can't be changed from outside the class in which it is defined. If it's protected, it can be changed from inside its class or from inside related (derived) classes.

### NOTE—WHAT C++ DOES AND DOESN'T DO

Although object-oriented programming is an important step in the evolution of programming, it is not a panacea. OOP does offer new and better ways of structuring the creation, designing, and writing of computer programs, and it does offer new benefits (or at least potential benefits), such as saving time and money in program development by offering new opportunities for the sharing and reuse of code. A badly written program, however, is not a better program if it happens to be written in an object-oriented language. Object-oriented spaghetti is no better than structured spaghetti or modular spaghetti—and sloppy programmers can program as sloppily in C++ as they can in any other language.

## Data Encapsulation and Data Abstraction

*Data encapsulation* is the ability that an object has to conceal its data from other parts of a program. In contrast, *data abstraction* is what lets the calling function ignore the details of how data types are represented inside objects, and lets it concentrate instead on the job that it wants done.

Although these two concepts are very different, the terms "data encapsulation" and "data abstraction" sound so much alike that it's easy to confuse them. Here's a way to tell them apart:

When you look at an X-ray of a person, you can see internal organs: the person's heart, lungs, and bones. Without an X-ray, you can't see these organs; the skin hides them. That's data encapsulation.

When you look at a person's driver's license, you can learn certain facts about the person, such as the person's weight, height, and address. But there are many other facts about the person that are too intimate to be printed on a driver's license. Thus, a driver's license can tell you what your state's government feels you are entitled to know about the person, but nothing more. That's data abstraction.

Figure 10.2 illustrates this comparison between data encapsulation and data abstraction.

In a C++ program, data abstraction streamlines the acquisition of information in an object-oriented programming, while concealing information that there's no need to reveal. Meanwhile, data encapsulation safeguards important data. Because of data abstraction, you don't have to plow through every detail of an object's implementation to obtain information that you need. And data encapsulation makes it more difficult for a function to make unwanted modifications in privileged data.

## Inheritance

When you have finished defining the member variables and member functions of the `furniture` class, you can start creating objects that belong to the class—such as chairs, tables, stools, and other kinds of furniture.

When you start declaring objects that belong to the `Furniture` class, each object that you create *inherits* from the `Furniture` class every member variable and every member function that the class definition contains. Therefore, when you create an object that belongs to a class, the object automatically has member variables and member functions that can be used to describe its finish, its manufacturing procedures, and so on.

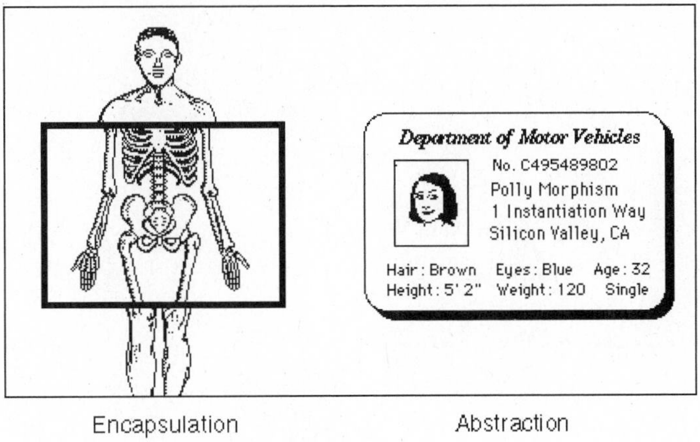


*Figure 10.2. Encapsulation and abstraction.*

## Multiple Inheritance

In C++, classes not only inherit data and behavior from other classes; classes also can contain new data and behaviors that can in turn be inherited by other classes. As you have seen, the ability of classes to inherit from other classes is called *inheritance.*

C++ also has a related feature some other object-oriented languages do not have. In C++, classes can inherit properties not from just one class, but from multiple classes. The ability of classes to inherit from multiple classes is called *multiple inheritance.*

Multiple inheritance is even more common in the biological sciences than it is in C++. Every animal that has both a mother and a father has characteristics that are obtained through multiple inheritance. If you have your mother's eyes and your Uncle Charlie's nose, you're a beneficiary (or a victim) of multiple inheritance.

One excellent example of multiple inheritance in the animal kingdom is provided by the duckbill platypus (Figure 10.3). The platypus inherits its mammalian qualities from the mammal class, but seems to inherit its bill, webbed feet, and egg-laying capabilities from the duck class—which descends, in turn, from the `bird` class.

*Figure 10.3. The Duckbill Platypus.*

Taking this chain of inheritance a step further, the `bird` class is a subclass of the `animal` class. Figure 10.4 illustrates this hierarchy.

Multiple inheritance is covered in much more detail in Chapter 19.

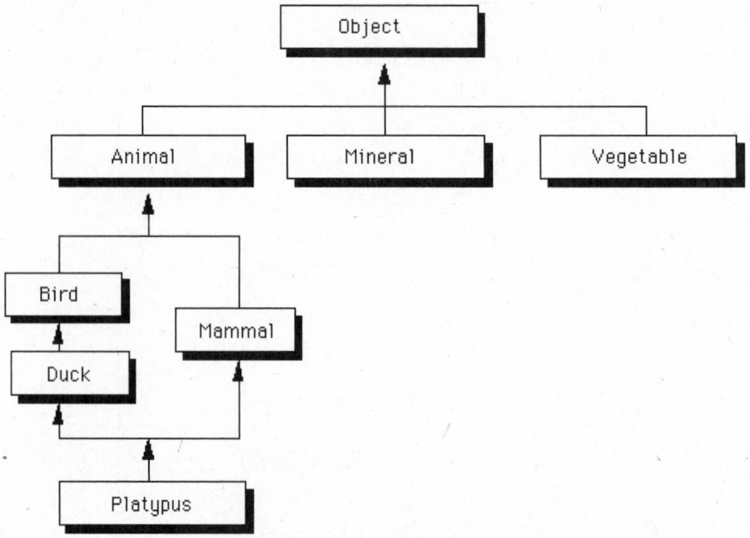


*Figure 10.4. Multiple inheritance.*

> **NOTE—GENERIC OBJECT CLASSES**
>
> You may notice that in Figure 10.4, classes `Animal`, `Mineral`, and `Vegetable` all descend from a generic class named `Object`. Generic classes from which all classes descend are common in class libraries, including the Microsoft Foundation Class (MFC) library, which is examined in Part III of this book.

## Polymorphism

In biology, when individual organisms or organisms in the same species have the same properties, that's called *polymorphism*. In the C++ language, polymorphism is what lets you create a family of classes with behaviors that vary, according to what is appropriate for each class.

In C++, thanks to polymorphism, you can write multiple functions that have the same name. If you call a member function when a particular object is being accessed, your call may have one result, and if you issue the same call to a member function when another object is being accessed, the result may be completely different.

Figure 10.5 illustrates the principle of polymorphism. The illustration is adapted from a segment of the multiple inheritance chart shown in Figure 10.4.

Referring to Figure 10.5, assume that you're a biology teacher writing an educational program about the reproduction of animals. Also assume that you have written two multimedia presentations: a presentation on bird reproduction that runs when you execute a function named `LaysEggs()` and one on mammal reproduction that runs when you execute a function named `BearsYoungAlive()`.

Now suppose you're writing your program in a procedural language—for example, C. To determine which of these routines executes in a C program, you might write a `switch` statement along these lines:

```
switch (bearsYoung) {
case MAMMAL:
     BearsYoungAlive();
     break;
case BIRD:
     LaysEggs();
     break;
/* more cases */
}
```

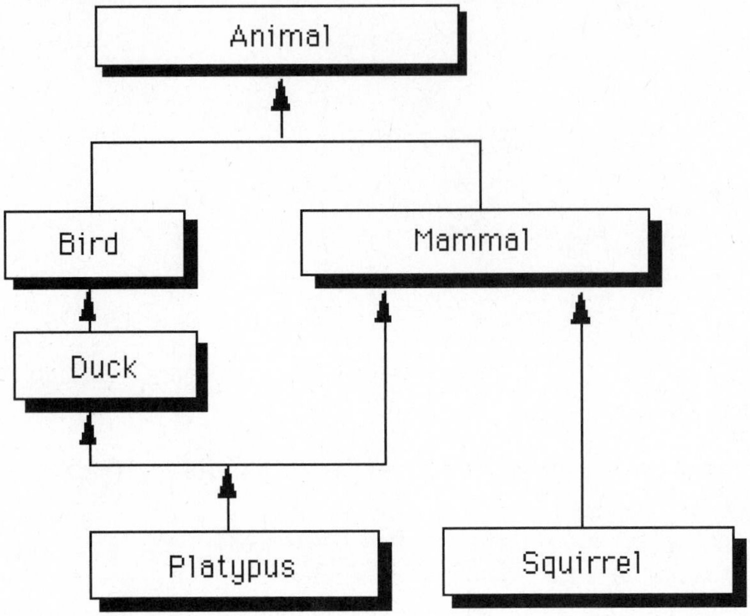


*Figure 10.5. Polymorphism.*

## An Alternative to the Switch Statement

Switch statements are useful in C, but in C++ there's an easier technique for checking a value to decide which of a group of functions should execute. In a C++ program, when you are presented with multiple functions and have to decide which function to call, you don't generally write a `switch` statement. Instead, you write a *virtual function*: that is, a function that lets a program perform one task when one object is being accessed and performs another task when another object is being accessed.

Leaving aside for a moment the question of what a virtual function looks like, let's just assume that you have decided to write a virtual function to replace the `switch` statement shown in the above code fragment. Here's how a virtual function works:

First, a virtual function doesn't depend on a switch statement. Instead, it determines what action should be taken by checking to see what kind of object is being accessed—in this case, what kind of object is being displayed on-screen.

If there's a picture of a bird on-screen, the virtual function mechanism causes the program to run a presentation about how birds lay eggs. If there's a picture of a mammal on the screen, the virtual function mechanism causes the program to execute a presentation about how mammals bear their young alive.

## Virtual Functions

That sounds like the same kind of thing you can do with a `switch` statement, but there's a big difference in the way you do it in C++. The virtual function equivalent of a switch statement doesn't require one function that's named `LaysEggs()` and another function that's named `BearsYoungAlive()`. Instead, the program contains two functions with exactly the same name—for instance, `Reproduction()`.

If you call the `Reproduction()` function while a picture of a bird is on-screen, a presentation about egg-laying runs. If you call the `Reproduction()` function while a picture of a mammal is on the screen, you get a presentation about how mammals bear their young alive.

Both functions have the same name—`Reproduction()`—but they perform different actions, depending on the picture that's on-screen when you call the function. This takes place automatically, without a `switch` statement. When the program calls a function named `Reproduction()`, the appropriate version of the `Reproduction()` function executes, depending upon what picture is currently on-screen.

## Combining Polymorphism with Multiple Inheritance

Figure 10.5 illustrates this process and extends it. As you have just seen, when you execute the `Reproduction()` function while a picture of a mammal is on-screen, you see a presentation about how mammals bear their young alive.

That means that if a picture of a squirrel is on-screen when the `Reproduction()` function executes, you see the presentation about mammals because a squirrel is a mammal—unless, of course, the `Squirrel` class has its own version of the `Reproduction()` function. If that's the case, a special `Squirrel` version of the `Reproduction()` function might execute.

Now assume that a picture of a platypus is on-screen when you execute the `Reproduction()` function. In this case, multiple inheritance, as well as polymorphism, comes into play. If the `Platypus` class inherits its reproductive behavior from the `Duck` class, then executing the `Reproduction()` function runs the presentation on egg-laying instead of the presentation on bearing young alive.

This whole process takes place automatically—without a switch statement—thanks to C++'s support of polymorphism and multiple inheritance. For more information on how C++ implements polymorphism and multiple inheritance, see the sections on those topics later in this chapter. For even more detailed coverage of both topics, see Chapter 19.

# Elements of a C++ Program

When you write a C++ program, almost everything you manipulate in the program can be defined as an object. During program execution, objects are constantly being created and deleted. In a C++ program, objects run the show, interacting with other objects and often joining together with other objects in groups, collections, arrays, lists, and so on. In an object-oriented program, there are many objects and kinds of objects, all capable of communicating with each other and each specialized to carry out a particular task.

## Classes and Objects

Every object in a C++ program is based on a user-defined data type called a class. A *class* resembles a C-style `struct`, but it can contain functions as well as data. Classes that are members of hierarchies can inherit behaviors and also can pass on behaviors to other classes. An *object* is a multielement, user-defined variable that is based on a class.

In case you'd like to see what a class looks like right now, here's a simple class definition:

```
class OneAbil {
private:
     int strength;
public:
     void SetStrength(int str) { strength = str; }
     int GetStrength() { return strength; }
};
```

The above class definition contains a declaration of one data element, or *member variable*, named `strength`. It also contains two *member functions*: `SetStrength()` and `GetStrength()`.

One important feature of a C++ class is that it can encapsulate data, or hide it from other functions and other parts of a program. In the above definition, the access specifier `private` conceals the member variable `strength` from other parts of the program. But the member functions `SetStrength()` and `GetStrength()` have `public` access; that means that they are accessible from other parts of the program.

More information about member variables, member functions, and access specifications are provided later in this chapter and in other chapters in Part II.

## Member Variables

In C++, the data elements that a class contains are called *member variables*, or *data members*. When you have defined a class, you can create member variables of that class in much the same way that you create elements in a `struct` in C.

If you're familiar with C, you know that a `struct` is not an actual object, but merely a template that describes the logical structure of an object. When you have defined a `struct`, you can create as many objects as you like that have the logical structure described by the `struct` that you have defined.

Similarly, in C++ a class is not an object, but rather a template that describes the logical structure of an object. Consider, for example, the `Furniture` class. Furniture, as you saw, cannot be instantiated into an object because you can't go out and buy "a furniture." Rather, you go out and buy a table, a chair, or a stool—all *objects* of the `furniture` class.

When you have defined a class, you can create as many objects as you like that have the logical structure described by the class that you have defined.

## Member Functions

When you start considering the kinds of member variables (elements) that you might want to include in the `Furniture` class, many possibilities come to mind. You might want a member variable that specifies the retail price of a piece of furniture, and you might want another that specifies the item's wholesale cost. You might create other member variables to specify the dimensions of the piece, its weight, and the date that it was manufactured.

Once you have finished creating member variables for the `Furniture` class, you can start creating procedures, or member functions that manipulate the class's member variables. One member function might describe the procedures used to manufacture a piece of furniture, and other member functions might describe distribution procedures, pricing procedures, procedures for inventory restocking, and so on. In a C++ program, the member functions of an object are implemented as code that the object executes.

An object might contain data that specifies what kind of wood the object is made of and data that specifies what kind of finish the object has. (Later, your factory may start manufacturing objects without legs—such as bookcases—but if you design your program well, that should prove to be no problem.)

# Summary

This chapter introduces Part II of this book, which teaches you how to write object-oriented programs in C++. Part II prepares you for Part III, which will complete your Visual C++ education by teaching you how to write Windows programs using Version 2 of the Microsoft Foundation Class (MFC) library.

This chapter introduces some important fundamentals of object-oriented programming and C++ in particular. Topics covered in this chapter include:

- Data encapsulation and data abstraction.
- Inheritance and multiple inheritance.
- Polymorphism.
- Classes and objects.
- Member variables.
- Member functions.

The purpose of this chapter is to familiarize you with C++ terminology and some of the concepts used in object-oriented programming. In Chapter 11, you'll start putting this information to use by writing your own object-oriented programs.

Chapter 11

# Classes

Classes are the basic building blocks of C++ programming. As one anonymous pundit put it, C++ has "a touch of class." As another remarked, C++ is "a classy language." But no matter how you say it, classes are probably the most important single feature of C++. They are the foundation of object-oriented programming in the C++ language.

The `class` is a descendent of the `struct`, a data framework widely used in C. But the C++ class did not evolve directly from the C-style `struct`. The `struct` itself was enhanced along the way. To understand how that happened, it helps to know something about how the data structure known as a `struct` works in C.

This chapter explains how C++ classes are derived from the data `struct` used in C, and tells how C++ objects are derived from classes. Many topics introduced in this chapter will be covered in more detail in later chapters. Topics introduced in this chapter include:

- Instantiating objects
- Accessing class members
- Member functions
- Access specifiers
- Class diagrams
- Abstract classes
- Subclassing
- Virtual functions
- Class libraries

# Enhancing the struct

A `struct` is a structure, or framework, that can store any kind of data. A `struct` can hold any kind of data—including `struct` frameworks—and can be almost any shape and size. But it's important to know that a `struct` has no physical existence until data is actually stored in it. Memory is never allocated for the data stored in a `struct` until that data is actually defined.

When data is placed in the framework provided by a `struct`, a block of memory is allocated for the stored data. The data is then stored in the memory that is allocated for it. The size of the `struct`, and the sequence of the data stored in the `struct`, are determined by the size and shape of the `struct` that holds the data. The data that is stored in the `struct` thus becomes an *object*, or an *instance* of the `struct`.

In the C language, the `struct` is not a full-fledged data type, but merely a *type specifier*—specifically, a framework in which data elements of various kinds can be stored.

Because the `struct` keyword is only a type specifier in C, you must use the `struct` keyword when you define a `struct` variable in C. For example, suppose this definition of a `struct` appears in a C program:

```
struct Birthday {   // defining a C-style struct
   int day;
   int mon;
   int yr;
};
```

After a struct named Birthday is defined, as in the above example, you must use the keyword struct to declare an instance of Birthday, as in this example:

```
struct Birthday myBirthday;    // declaring a C-style struct
```

## The C++-Style struct

In C++, the struct type specifier has been promoted to a full-fledged data type. So, after a struct is defined in C++, you can define an instance of the struct without using the struct keyword—in the same way that you would define an instance of any other variable. In C++, if this struct definition appears in a program

```
struct Birthday {    // defining a C++-style struct
   int day;
   int mon;
   int yr;
};
```

you can declare an instance of the struct without using the struct keyword, as in this example:

```
Birthday myBirthday;      // declaring a C++-style struct
```

Because the struct has been upgraded to a fundamental data type in C++, the syntax that governs the use of struct objects is simpler than it was in C. That makes the C-style struct easier to use—and because the class is an enhancement of the C++-style struct, that makes it easier to use classes in programs too.

## Storing a Function in a struct

C++ has enhanced the struct data type in several other important ways. In C++, for example, a struct can contain not only data, but also functions that can manipulate that data. A C++-style struct that contains a function can be defined in this fashion:

```
struct Birthday {    // defining a C++-style struct ...
   int day;
   int mon;
   int yr;
     void PrintBirthday(void);  // ... that contains a procedure
};
```

If a struct definition like the one shown above appears in a C++ program, an instance of the `struct` can be created with a statement like this:

```
Birthday myBirthday;
```

The `PrintBirthday()` function that appears in the definition of the `Birthday` structure can then be called using the dot (.) operator, as in:

```
myBirthday.PrintBirthday();
```

## Limiting Access to Data in a struct

Another new feature of the `struct` data type is that it has a mechanism for limiting access to the data that is stored in it. When a `struct` appears in a C++ program, every data element in the `struct` is, by default, designated `public`. That means that every element in the struct is as accessible from other parts of the program as the `struct` itself.

If you don't want an element in a `struct` to be publicly accessible, you can limit access to it by using a keyword called an *access specifier*. There are three access specifiers: `private`, `protected`, and `public`.

All data elements in a `struct` are designated `public` by default. So, if you create a `struct` that contains no access specifiers, all data elements in the `struct` are `public` by default.

### private and public Elements of a struct

If you declare a data element in a `struct` to be `private`, the element is not accessible outside the `struct`; it can be used only by functions that are declared inside the definition of the `struct`. For example, in this `struct` definition, the data elements `day`, `mon`, and `yr` are all designated `private`, but the function `PrintBirthday()` is designated `public`:

```
struct Birthday {
private:
   int day;
   int month;
   int year;
public:
     void PrintBirthday();
};
```

In the data structure that is defined above, the `PrintBirthday()` function is declared to be `public`, but the integer elements `day`, `month`, and `year` are declared to be `private`. So the `PrintBirthday()` has the same storage type as the `Birthday` structure, but the elements `day`, `month`, and `year` are accessible only to the `PrintBirthday()` function.

### protected Elements of a struct

If you declare an element in a `struct` to be `protected`, the element is accessible only to objects that are derived from the `struct` in which the element is declared. Hierarchies of `struct` objects are not often created in C++, so the `protected` access specifier is rarely seen in `struct` objects. But it is often used in classes, as you will see later in this chapter.

## From struct to class

The `class` data type has all the features of a C++-style `struct` data type, plus a few more. For example, the `class` data type has access-specifier rules that make it easy for a class to become a *parent class*, or a *root class*, from which other classes can be derived. In fact, C++ uses access specifiers to enforce class inheritance and polymorphism: two important properties of object-oriented programs. Class inheritance and polymorphism were introduced in Chapter 10, "Object-Oriented Programming," and are described in greater detail in Chapter 19, "Inheritance and Polymorphism."

You can tell by looking at the definition of a class that classes and C++-style `struct` variables have a lot in common. In fact, in C++, the only difference between a class definition and a `struct` definition is that a class definition is preceded by the keyword `class` instead of the keyword `struct`. This is a definition of a class:

```
class PlayerAbils {
     int strength;
     int charisma;
     int dexterity;
     int intelligence;
     char *armor;
};
```

A class, like a C++-style `struct`, is a full-fledged data type. So, once you have defined a class in a C++ program, you don't have to use the keyword `class` every time you refer to it. So, if the class definition shown above appears in a C++ program, you can create an instance of the `PlayerAbils` class without using the `class` keyword:

```
PlayerAbils myAbils;
```

When you define a class and then create an instance of the class, the instance you have created is called an *object*. The process of creating an object that is an instance of a class is called *instantiating* the object. The statement shown above instantiates an object named `myAbils`, which is an instance of the `PlayerAbils` class.

## Instantiating an Object

A class, like a `struct`, is a framework for storing data; it has no physical existence until data is actually stored in it. Memory is never allocated for a class until data is placed in the structure that the class provides. When data is placed in the framework provided by a class, a block of memory is allocated for the data, and the data that is stored in the framework described by the class becomes an *object*, or an *instance* of the class.

Because you must create a class before you can create an object that belongs to the class, the process of instantiating an object is a little different from the process of creating a variable that has a simple data type—such as an `int`, a `double`, or a `char`.

When you create a variable with a simple data type, such as an `int`, there are only two steps to follow. First, you must declare your intention to create a variable by writing a *declaration*, like this:

```
int x;
```

When you have declared a variable, you must define its contents by writing a *definition* in this format:

```
x = 10;
```

Because a class is a variable with a user-defined data type, it takes one extra step to create an object that belongs to a class. To create an object, these are the steps you must follow:

In C++, creating a class is a three-step process:

1. First, you must write a *class definition* . As noted earlier, a class definition does not declare a variable, but merely creates a template that you can use as a framework to create an object.

2. When you have defined a class, you can instantiate an object that has the logical structure that the definition of the class describes. To instantiate an object, you must write a *declaration* for the object. The compiler then allocates memory for the object that you have created.

3. A class can have two kinds of elements: data elements, which are called *data members* (or *member variables*), and function elements, which are called *member functions*. When you have defined a class and have instantiated an object of the class, you can define and manipulate the data members and member functions that are declared for the class.

# Object Instantiation Illustrated

Figure 11.1 shows the process of creating a simple variable and compares that process with the process of instantiating an object.

# Accessing Members of a Class

When you have defined a class and have instantiated an object, you can access members of the object by preceding the name of the field being accessed with the name of the struct and the dot operator (`.`), as follows:

```
myBirthday.month = 7;
```

Alternatively, you can declare a pointer to the class and then access the fields of the class with the arrow operator (`->`), in this fashion:

```
struct *myBirthdayPtr = &myBirthday;
myBirthdayPtr -> month = 7;
```

# Member Functions

A class, like a C++-style `struct`, can contain functions as well as data—as this example shows:

```
class Birthday {
public:
     int month, day, year;
     void PrintBirthday(void);  // a function to display the date
};
```

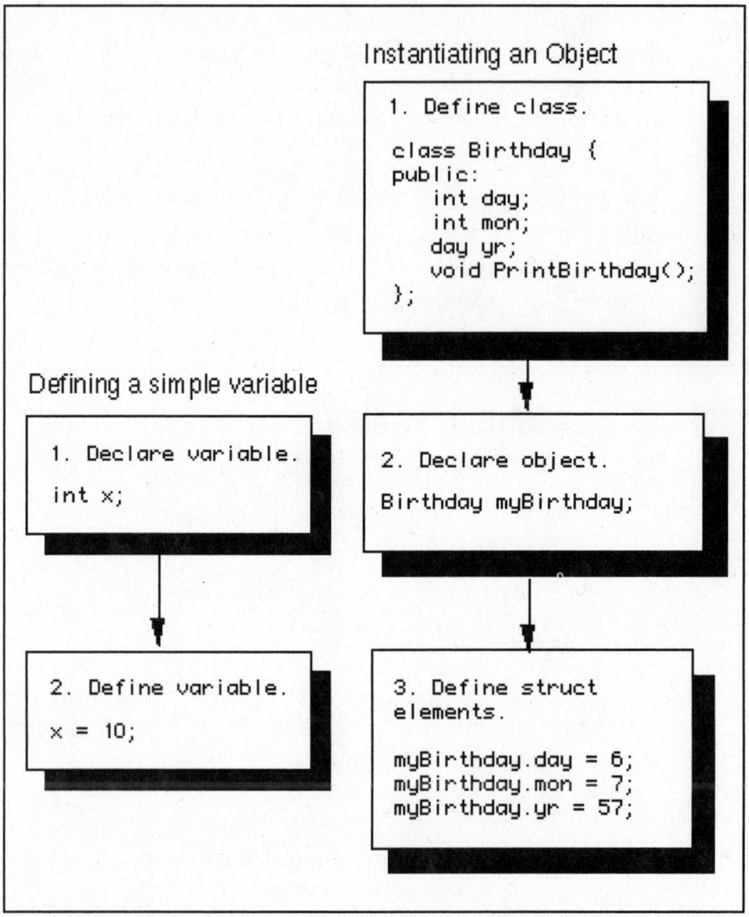


*Figure 11.1. Instantiating an object.*

The code fragment shown above defines a class named `Birthday`. The `Birthday` class contains three data members—named `month`, `day`, and `year`—and a member function named `PrintBirthday()`.

If you placed the above class definition in a C++ program, you could define the function `PrintBirthday()` in this fashion:

```
void Birthday::PrintBirthday(void)
{
     static char *mon[] = {
          "January","February","March","April","May","June",
          "July","August","September","October","November",
          "December"
     };
     cout << mon[month-1] << ' ' << day << ", " << year;
}
```

## The Scope Resolution Operator

Notice the character combination :: that appears in the first line of the preceding function definition. That symbol, known as the scope resolution operator, is often used in C++ programs. In the preceding example, it specifies the scope of the member function `PrintBirthday()`. The same symbol is often used to specify the scope of member functions of classes. For example, if the `Birthday` class were defined in a program as shown above, you could refer to the member function `int` as

```
Birthday::int;
```

Similarly, you could refer to the member function `PrintBirthday()` as

```
Birthday::PrintBirthday()
```

For examples of how the scope resolution operator is used in C++ programs, see Chapter 12, "Objects."

## Access Specifiers

Classes, like `struct` objects, can use *access specifiers* to limit access to the data they contain. There are three access specifiers for classes, just as there are for `struct` objects: `private`, `public`, and `protected`.

Public members of a class can be accessed from anywhere in a program. Private members can be accessed only by the class itself, and protected members can be accessed by the class and its derived classes. (Derived classes were introduced in Chapter 10 and are covered in detail in Chapter 19.) This is the mechanism that C++ uses to enforce the object-oriented principles of data encapsulation and data abstraction.

## Access Specifiers in struct Objects and Classes

There is one difference between the way access specifiers are used in classes and the way they are used in `struct` objects. In a `struct` definition, as you have seen, all elements are `public` by default. So, in a class definition, every member is `private` unless you explicitly specify that it is `public` or `protected`.

When you use the `private` access specifier in the definition of a class, all member variables and member functions that follow the keyword `private` are accessible only to the member functions within the structure definition. When you use the `public` access specifier in a class definition, all members that follow the word `public` are accessible to any function that is within the scope of the class.

For example, in this class definition, the integer variables `Birthday::month`, `Birthday::day`, and `Birthday::year` are private, whereas the member function `Birthday::PrintBirthday()` is public:

```
class Birthday {
private:
     int month, day, year;
public:
     void PrintBirthday(void); // a function to display the date
};
```

You can use the same access specifier more than once in the same class definition. For example, you could use the `private` specifier twice in the above class definition, like this:

```
class Birthday {
private:
     int month;
public:
     void display(void); // a function to display the date
private:
     int, day, year;
};
```

## Providing Indirect Access to Data Members

When you create a class, you must decide which members are kept private and which are made public. By keeping member variables of a class `private`, you can protect them from unwanted modification. However, a class can contain `public` member functions that manipulate `private` member variables.

For example, a program can call a public member function of a class, and that member function can change the value of a private member variable of the same class. This feature lets you provide *indirect* public access to the member variables of a class. Examples of how indirect public access works in C++ programs is presented in Chapter 12.

### friend Classes and friend Functions

When you have declared a member of a class to be `private` or `protected`, you can grant special access to that class member to specially privileged classes and functions. To grant special access to limited-access class members, you can use a special C++ mechanism: the `friend` keyword.

In C++, an object can grant *friendship* status to any function in a program by declaring that the function is a `friend`. Then the `friend` function can access all private and protected members of the object.

An object can also grant friendship status to another object. In this case, too, the object that has been named a friend then has access to the other object's private and protected members.

Friend functions and friend objects can be useful when you want to relax the access rules that ordinarily apply to `private` and `protected` member variables. For example, suppose you write a program that has to execute a public member function of a class repeatedly because it needs access to a certain private data member of a class.

The `friend` keyword and friendship status are described in more detail in Chapter 13, "Member Functions."

## Classes and Objects

As noted at the beginning of this chapter, when you define a class in a C++ program, the compiler does not allocate any memory for objects that belong to the class. To allocate memory for an object that belongs to the class, you must create an object that is an instance of the class. In other words, you must *instantiate* the object. Then memory for the object is allocated.

When you have defined a class, you can instantiate an object that belongs to the class by writing a statement such as this:

```
Warrior   aWarrior;
```

When you instantiate an object using the above syntax, you can use the dot operator (.) to access member variables and member functions. This statement calls the member function `Warrior::PrintData()` when a `Warrior` object has been created using the syntax shown above:

```
Warrior.PrintData();
```

Because a class is a data type, you can also instantiate a class object by creating a pointer to the object, like this:

```
Warrior   *aWarrior;
```

When you instantiate an object using a pointer, you can access members of the object using the arrow operator (->). This statement calls the member function `Warrior::PrintData()` when a `Warrior` object has been created using a pointer:

```
warriorPtr->PrintData();
```

Listing 11.1, this chapter's version of the adventure-game program, The Wrath of Zalthar, shows how classes can be created and how objects can be instantiated in C++ programs.

## COMPILING THE ZALTHAR PROGRAM

When you compile this chapter's version of the Zalthar program—and this also applies to most of the other example programs in this book that have more than one code segment—make sure that you use the linker option `/NOE`, which prevents the linker from using "extended dictionaries." An extended dictionary is a list of symbol addresses in a library created with the Microsoft Library Manager (LIB). When `/NOE` is turned on, the linker consults extended dictionaries to speed up searches. But in many programs, the `/NOE` option can cause the linker to generate errors complaining that symbols have been defined more than once. To use the `/NOE` linker option in Visual C++, choose Project from the Options menu. When the Project Options dialog box appears, click the button labeled Linker. Then check the box labeled "Prevent Use of Extended Dictionary."

### WHAT'S IN A GAME?

In Chapter 2, "A Better C—Plus," you were introduced to an adventure game called The Wrath of Zalthar: a program that was designed specifically for this book to illustrate the most important principles of Visual C++ and object-oriented programming. Since Chapter 2, parts of the game have appeared in code samples from time to time, but Listing 11.1 is the first listing to make substantial changes in the program. The program will continue to evolve—and will continue to be improved—in later chapters.

**Listing 11.1. The Wrath of Zalthar, Chapter 11 version.**

### ZALTHAR.H

```
// ZALTHAR.H
// The Wrath of Zalthar, Chapter 11 Version
// Copyright 1992 Mark Andrews.  All rights reserved.

#include <stdio.h>
#include <iostream.h>
#include <string.h>
#include <stdlib.h>

inline void FatalError()
{
    fprintf(stderr, "A fatal error has occurred\n");
    exit(1);
}

char *DuplicateString(char *aString)
{
    char    *aCopy;

    aCopy = new char[strlen(aString) + 1];
    if (aCopy == NULL)
        FatalError();
    strcpy(aCopy, aString);
    return aCopy;
}
```

*continues*

**Listing 11.1. continued**

```
class Player {
public:
     virtual void PrintData(void) = 0;

     virtual void PrintTitle(void)
          { cout << "\nPLAYER" << "\n"; }
};

class Warrior: public Player {
private:
     char *name;
     char *weapon;
public:
     void PrintTitle(void)
          { cout << "\nWARRIOR" << "\n"; }
     void SetName(char *playerName)
          { name = DuplicateString(playerName); }
     void PrintName(void)
          { cout << "Name: " << name << "\n"; }
     void SetWeapon(char *playerWeapon)
          { weapon = DuplicateString(playerWeapon); }
     void PrintWeapon(void)
          { cout << "Weapon: " << weapon << "\n"; }
     void PrintData(void)
          {
               PrintTitle();
               PrintName();
               PrintWeapon();
          }
};

class Gnome: public Warrior {
private:
     char *magic;
public:
     void PrintTitle(void)
          { cout << "\nGNOME" << "\n"; }
     virtual void SetMagic(char *playerMagic)
          { magic = DuplicateString(playerMagic); }
     virtual void PrintMagic(void)
          { cout << "Magic: " << magic << "\n"; }
     void PrintData(void)
          {
```

```
            PrintTitle();
            PrintName();
            PrintWeapon();
            PrintMagic();
        }
};
```

### MAIN.CPP

```
// MAIN.CPP
// The Wrath of Zalthar, Chapter 11 Version
// Copyright 1992 Mark Andrews.  All rights reserved.

#include <stdio.h>
#include "Zalthar.h"

int main()
{

    // Set up a pointer to an object

    Warrior aWarrior, bWarrior, *warriorPtr;
    Gnome aGnome, *gnomePtr;

    // print report
    warriorPtr = &aWarrior;
    warriorPtr->SetName("Bruno");
    warriorPtr->SetWeapon("Sword");
    warriorPtr->PrintData();

    warriorPtr = &bWarrior;
    warriorPtr->SetName("GayLynn");
    warriorPtr->SetWeapon("Crossbow");
    warriorPtr->PrintData();

    gnomePtr = &aGnome;
    gnomePtr->SetName("Glog");
    gnomePtr->SetWeapon("Broadsword");
    gnomePtr->SetMagic("X-ray vision");
    gnomePtr->PrintData();

    return 0;
}
```

## USING INLINE FUNCTIONS INSIDE CLASS DEFINITIONS

You may notice that in Listing 11.1, some member functions are defined inside class definitions. For example:

```
void PrintTitle(void)
     { cout << "\nWARRIOR" << "\n"; }
```

When you place a function definition inside a class definition, the compiler treats the embedded function as an inline function. An inline function, as noted in Chapter 2, is a function that is usually not called as an ordinary function is, but is compiled inline to reduce overhead and speed up processing.

Defining a function inside a function definition is equivalent to declaring an ordinary function to be an inline function by preceding the function's definition with the keyword `inline`.

Ordinary inline functions are described in more detail in Chapter 2. Inline functions that are defined inside class definitions are examined more closely in Chapter 13.

## HEADER FILES AND SOURCE FILES

C++ programmers often divide the source code into header files and source files, a practice that is illustrated by the version of the Zalthar program shown in Listing 11.1. As the program illustrates, header files usually have the suffix .H—in contrast to source files which have the suffix .CPP. Class declarations are usually placed in header files (in this case, ZALTHAR.H), whereas definitions of member functions are usually placed in source files (in Listing 11.1, the file named MAIN.CPP).

Usually, a C++ program uses one header file and one source file for each class that it contains. This rule may not be followed in programs that contain small classes or classes that are closely related. Sometimes, interfaces and implementations of related classes are placed in the same file.

> Generally speaking, a header file describes a class's interface, whereas a source file describes the class's implementation. It's important to follow this procedure when you write commercial C++ programs, because you can make your classes available to other programmers by distributing only your header files and your compiled object-code files—while keeping your source code private.
>
> There's another benefit in separating a class's header-file interface from its implementation file: When you separate your files in this way, you can make your classes largely self-contained, so they don't have to depend on each other's implementation details.

This is how the program in Listing 11.1 instantiates the objects `aWarrior`, `bWarrior`, and `aGnome`, and then declares pointers that can be set to point to the objects:

```
Warrior aWarrior, bWarrior, *warriorPtr;
Gnome aGnome, *gnomePtr;
```

When you have instantiated an object that is a member of a class, the new object can use any of the member variables and member functions that appear in the definition of the object's class. To access a member variable or a member function of its class, an object can use the familiar dot operator `.` (if the member being accessed is a nonpointer variable) or the arrow operator `->` (if the member being accessed is a pointer variable). For example, in the `main()` segment shown in Listing 11.1, the object `aWarrior` accesses its member variables and the member function `PrintData()` in this fashion:

```
warriorPtr = &aWarrior;
warriorPtr->SetName("Bruno");
warriorPtr->SetWeapon("Sword");
warriorPtr->PrintData();
```

In these statements, notice that the name of the object that calls the member function `PrintData()` is substituted for the name of the class that declared the functions. So, when you execute the program, this is the information about the `aWarrior`, `bWarrior`, and `aGnome` objects that the program prints on-screen:

```
WARRIOR
Name: Bruno
Weapon: Sword

WARRIOR
Name: GayLynn
Weapon: Crossbow
```

```
GNOME
Name: Glog
Weapon: Broadsword
Magic: X-ray vision
```

## Class Diagrams

C++ program designers often use *class diagrams* as graphical representations of classes and class members. In one popular graphics style that has been adapted for use in this book, classes are represented as shadowed boxes with the name of the class printed in bold type, instance variables printed in italic type, and methods in regular type.

Figure 11.2 is a diagram that shows a class and two objects that belong to the class. The class, named `Warrior`, is used in the adventure game named The Wrath of Zalthar. The two objects are `aWarrior` and `bWarrior`, which are derived to the `Warrior` class. The diagram is based on a version of The Wrath of Zalthar game that is shown in Figure 11.1.

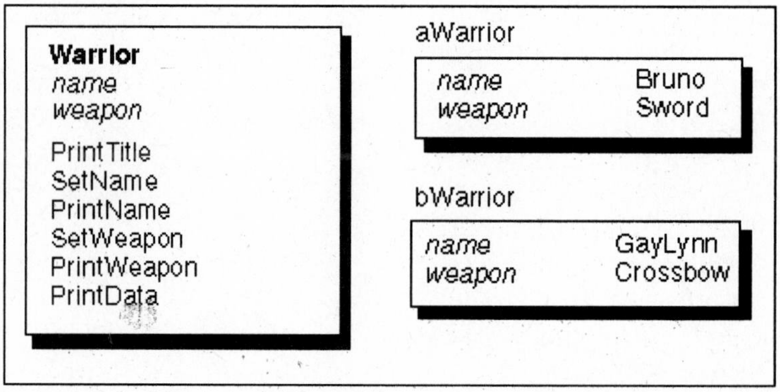


*Figure 11.2. Warrior class with two instances.*

In Figure 11.2, the `Warrior` class has two member variables: *name* and *weapon*. The `Warrior` class also has six member functions: `PrintTitle()`, `SetName()`, `PrintName()`, `SetWeapon()`, `PrintWeapon()`, and `PrintData()`.

When the program is executed, the member function `PrintTitle()` prints the word `WARRIOR` on-screen. `SetName()` and `SetWeapon()` are public member functions that obtain two private member variables: the name of a game character and the weapon that the character uses. Similarly, `PrintName()` and `PrintWeapon()` are public member functions that obtain and print the character's name and the name of the character's weapon on-screen. The `PrintData()` function calls `PrintTitle()`, `PrintName()`, and `PrintWeapon()` to write all information about a character to the screen.

> **RECOGNIZING VARIABLES AND FUNCTIONS IN CLASS DIAGRAMS**
>
> In Figure 11.2, notice that the name of the `Warrior` class is printed in boldface type, whereas the names of the member variables `name` and `weapon` are printed in italics, and the names of the class's member functions are printed in roman type.
>
> This is a standard system for representing names of classes, member variables, and member functions in class diagrams. When class diagrams are drawn in accordance with this system, you can tell at a glance what the name of a class is (it's printed in boldface), what its member variables are (they're printed in italics), and what its member functions are (they're printed in roman type).

The two objects to the right of the `Warrior` class represent two objects of the `Warrior` class. One of the warrior objects, named `aWarrior`, represents a game character who is named Bruno and uses a sword as a weapon. The other warrior object, named `bWarrior`, represents a character named GayLynn. Her weapon is a crossbow.

Both of the objects derived from the `Warrior` class inherit all member variables and all member functions that are owned by the warrior class. But `aWarrior` and `bWarrior` store different values in the member variables that they inherit from the `Warrior` class, and some of their member functions perform slightly different actions.

To clarify this point, both `aWarrior` and `bWarrior` have a `name` member variable and a `weapon` member variable. The string "Bruno" is stored in the member variable `aWarrior.name`, and the string "Sword" is stored in the member variable `aWarrior.weapon`. The string "GayLynn" is stored in the member variable `bWarrior.name`, and the string "Crossbow" is stored in the member variable `bWarrior.weapon`.

The objects `aWarrior` and `bWarrior` inherit all member functions of the `Warrior` class. The functions `aWarrior::PrintTitle()` and `bWarrior::PrintTitle()` perform the same action: both functions print the word `WARRIOR` on-screen. The other member functions obtain and print other information about aWarrior and bWarrior. In the same way, the main() function obtains and prints data about the Gnome object aGnome by calling member functions.

## Data Abstraction in the Zalthar Program

In a well-designed C++ program, classes usually keep most of their member variables private so that the variables won't be unexpectedly changed by functions in other parts of the program, causing surprising and usually undesirable results. Often, however, the designer of a C++ program wants to access a private member variable of a class from a function that is not a member function of the class. As you may have noticed by now, this often happens in the Zalthar program shown earlier in this chapter in Listing 11.1.

As you have seen in this chapter, C++ does offer a way to access private members of a class, but not directly. In C++, when you want to read or change a private member variable of a class from outside the class, you can often access the variable through a member function that has been defined as public. By offering access to private variables through public functions, a class can provide indirect outside access to selected member variables, while maintaining some protection over the contents of those variables.

In the Zalthar program, you have seen some demonstrations of how this data-protection system works. For example, in the definition of the Warrior class, the member variables name and weapon are declared to be private variables:

```
class Warrior: public Player {
private:
     char *name;
     char *weapon;
     ...
};
```

However, the Warrior class still provides functions throughout the program with access to the name and weapon variables. It does this by offering access to name and weapon through functions such as SetName() and SetWeapon():

```
void SetName(char *playerName)
     { name = DuplicateString(playerName); }
...
void SetWeapon(char *playerWeapon)
     { weapon = DuplicateString(playerWeapon); }
```

Besides providing valuable protection for the variables name and weapon, this system lets users of objects access the name and weapon variables without having to be concerned with how the variables are manipulated by the object's member functions. In fact, to make use of an object in a C++ program, you don't know anything about the object at all, except for the syntax that is needed to access its public member functions.

In C++, the ability to make use of an object without knowing how its data is represented internally is called *data abstraction*. Because of data abstraction, every object in a C++ program can be designed as a "black box" holding internal data that is accessible only through carefully selected public member functions.

Thanks to data abstraction, if the designer of a C++ program wants to rewrite an object to add features, fix bugs, or just make the object's code work more efficiently, the designer can change the object internally without having to inform anyone who uses the object that it has been redesigned.

As long as the designer makes sure that the object's member functions accept the same input as they previously did, and return the same results as they previously did, the redesign of an object does not have to have any functional effect (except, perhaps, for speedier processing) on any other part of the program.

## Abstract Classes

Sometimes a new class is not intended to be used in the exact form in which it was created, but is designed to be used only as a foundation for other new data types. If this is the only reason for creating the class, the new class is called an *abstract class*. You cannot create objects that belong to an abstract class, but you can derive other classes from it.

An *abstract class* is a class that is not instantiated in a program, but is used solely as a parent class from which other classes are derived. A class that is designed to be instantiated is sometimes referred to as a *concrete* class. In the Zalthar program, `Player` is an abstract class, and the `Warrior` and `Gnome` classes are concrete classes.

Abstract classes often provide only a rudimentary framework for other classes, that is, a framework that must be fleshed out to provide needed functionality. To use an abstract class, you must create a subclass. Often, you must also add new member functions or overload existing member functions.

When an abstract class has been defined in a program, classes that are derived from the abstract class can be declared. In Listing 11.1, the class `Player` is defined first, and then the concrete classes `Warrior` and `Gnome` are declared.

Figure 11.3 shows how the `Warrior` class is descended from the abstract `Player` class, and how the `Gnome` class is descended from the concrete class `Warrior`. Because of this derivation, you can call the `Warrior` class a *subclass* of the `Player` class, and you can call the `Gnome` class a subclass of the `Player` class.

Figure 11.3, like Figure 11.2, is based on The Wrath of Zalthar program that is shown in Listing 11.1.

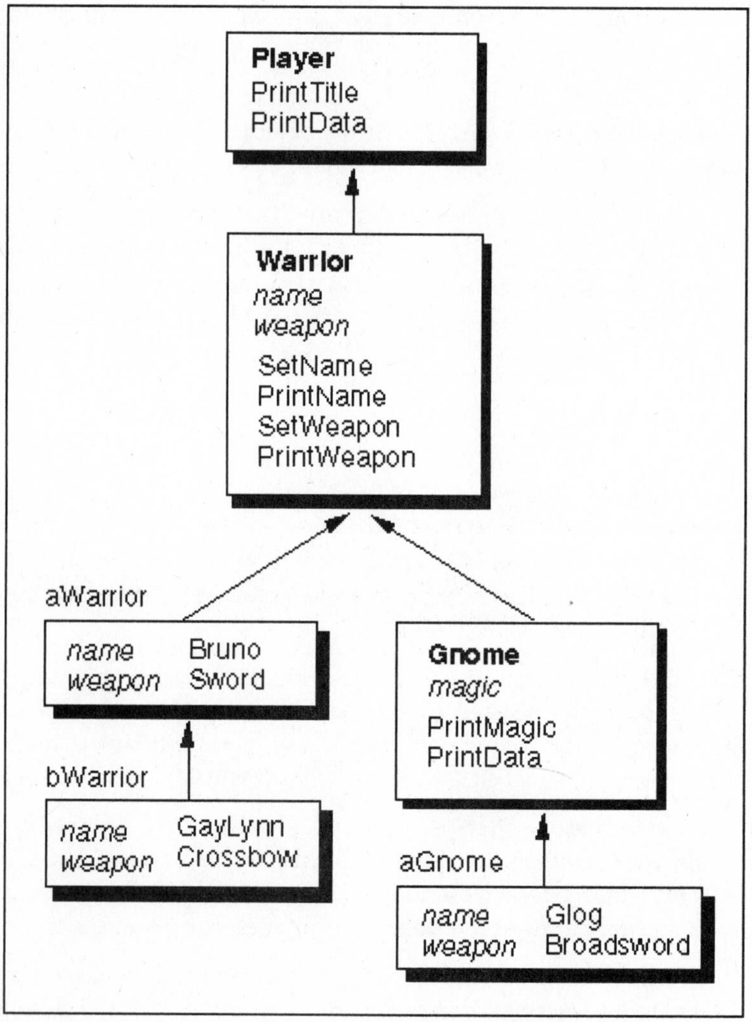


*Figure 11.3. Class derivation.*

## Subclassing

Figure 11.3 shows how you can create new classes that *inherit* from (or are *derived* from) existing classes. A class from which other classes are derived is usually called a base class, but is sometimes referred to as a *superclass*. A class that is derived from a base class is usually called a derived class, but is sometimes referred to as a *subclass*.

A class that lies immediately above a derived class in a program's class hierarchy is called a *parent class*. A class that lies immediately below a parent class in a program's class hierarchy is called a *child class*.

Deriving classes from other classes is sometimes called *subclassing*. By subclassing objects in a C++ program, objects can inherit member functions and customize them.

When you create a subclass, it inherits member variables and member functions from its parent class. The derived class can also add new member variables and new member functions to those inherited from its parent class. Furthermore, a derived class can redefine, or *override*, an inherited member function by providing entirely new code that is executed instead of the inherited code when the member function is called.

> **OVERLOADING AND OVERRIDING**
>
> Writing multiple functions that have the same name is called *overloading*. Replacing a member of a function of a class by writing another function with the same name in a derived class is called *overriding*. In C++, you can replace any member function of a base class by defining a function with the same name and the same parameter list in the instantiation of a derived object. The virtual function is then said to be *overridden*.

The `Warrior` class inherits two member functions from the `Player` class: `PrintTitle()` and `PrintData()`. The `Warrior` class also has four member functions that aren't inherited: `SetName()`, `PrintName()`, `SetWeapon()`, and `PrintWeapon()`.

The `Gnome` class inherits the six member functions owned by `Player` and `Warrior`, and adds two more: `SetMagic()`, which inherits a string that specifies a magical ability, and `PrintMagic()`, which prints this ability on-screen.

The `Gnome` class definition declares these functions because in the Zalthar game, gnomes have magical abilities, whereas warriors don't.

Two of the member functions inherited from the `Player` class are redefined—or *overridden*—by both the `Warrior` class and the `Gnome` class. The redefined member functions are `PrintTitle()` and `PrintData()`. The `Warrior` class overrides `PrintTitle()` to print the word `WARRIOR` on-screen, and the `Gnome` class overrides `PrintTitle()` to print the word `GNOME`. Both the `Warrior` class and the `Gnome` class override `PrintData()` to write customized information to the screen. The process of overriding an inherited function is described under the next heading, "Virtual Functions."

Because the overridden `PrintTitle()` function causes `Warrior` objects and `Gnome` objects to print different titles, and because `PrintData()` is overridden to print custom information, this is the output that you see when you execute The Wrath of Zalthar program:

```
WARRIOR
Name: Bruno
Weapon: Sword

WARRIOR
Name: GayLynn
Weapon: Crossbow

GNOME:
Name: Glog
Weapon: Broadsword
Magic: X-ray vision
```

## Virtual Functions

In Listing 11.1, two member functions of the `Player` class are redefined, or overridden. These two member functions are named `PrintTitle()` and `PrintData()`. If you examine the definition of the `Player` class back in Listing 11.1, you'll see that the person who wrote The Wrath of Zalthar (that's me) expected both `PrintTitle()` and `PrintData()` to be overridden when the `Player` class definition was written. The giveaway is this class definition, which appears in the file ZALTHAR.H:

```
class Player {
public:
     virtual void PrintData(void) = 0;
```

```
     virtual void PrintTitle(void)
          { cout << "\nPLAYER" << "\n"; }
};
```

Later in the program, these two class definitions appear:

```
class Warrior: public Player {
private:
     char *name;
     char *weapon;
public:
     void PrintTitle(void)
          { cout << "\nWARRIOR" << "\n"; }
     void SetName(char *playerName)
          { name = DuplicateString(playerName); }
     void PrintName(void)
          { cout << "Name: " << name << "\n"; }
     void SetWeapon(char *playerWeapon)
          { weapon = DuplicateString(playerWeapon); }
     void PrintWeapon(void)
          { cout << "Weapon: " << weapon << "\n"; }
     void PrintData(void)
          {
               PrintTitle();
               PrintName();
               PrintWeapon();
          }
};

class Gnome: public Warrior {
private:
     char *magic;
public:
     void PrintTitle(void)
          { cout << "\nGNOME" << "\n"; }
     virtual void SetMagic(char *playerMagic)
          { magic = DuplicateString(playerMagic); }
     virtual void PrintMagic(void)
          { cout << "Magic: " << magic << "\n"; }
     void PrintData(void)
          {
               PrintTitle();
               PrintName();
               PrintWeapon();
               PrintMagic();
          }
};
```

In the first of the preceding two code fragments, notice that both function definitions in the definition of the `Player` class begin with the keyword `virtual`. In C++, a function whose definition begins with the keyword `virtual` is known (logically enough) as a *virtual function*. A virtual function is a member function of a base class that the designer of a program expects to be redefined in one or more derived classes.

As noted earlier in this chapter, virtual functions are the key to polymorphism. When you call a member function of an object, and the function is declared also as a virtual function in the object's base class, C++ executes the derived class's version of the function. In contrast, if the function you call is declared as a nonvirtual function by the object's base class, the base class's version of the function is executed.

When you place a virtual function in a program, the compiler stores the function in a special memory location and then accesses the function through a table of pointers called a *v-table*. At runtime, when a program calls a virtual function, C++ consults the v-table to determine which version of the function it should call. The details of how v-tables work are spelled out in Chapter 19.

Virtual functions are what make polymorphism work in C++. When a member function of a class is declared to be `virtual`, you can issue exactly the same function call twice in a program and obtain two different results, depending on what object is in scope when you call the function.

Refer once more to the preceding two code fragments, and you'll see how virtual functions work. In the definition of the `Player` class, as you have seen, the member function `Player::PrintTitle()` is declared to be a virtual function. (The member function `Player::PrintData()` is a different kind of virtual function that works in a slightly different way, as you'll see later in this section.) This is the version of the `PrintTitle()` function that appears in the definition of the `Player` class:

```
virtual void PrintTitle(void)
     { cout << "\nPLAYER" << "\n"; }
```

The `Player::PrintTitle()` function is then overridden by two other member functions with the same name and the same parameter list (which, in this case, is `void`). One of these overriding functions appears in the definition of the `Warrior` class, and the other appears in the definition of the `Gnome` class:

```
void PrintTitle(void)
     { cout << "\nWARRIOR" << "\n"; }

void PrintTitle(void)
     { cout << "\nGNOME" << "\n"; }
```

The `PrintTitle()` function is called by a function named `PrintData()` function, which appears in two places in the program. `PrintData()` is a member function of both the `Warrior` class and the `Gnome` class:

```
void PrintData(void)
     {
          PrintTitle();
          PrintName();
          PrintWeapon();
     }
```

Because the `PrintTitle()` function that's defined by the `Player` class is overridden by the `Warrior` and `Gnome` member functions that have the same name, the version of the function that is defined by the `Warrior` class is the version that executes when a `Warrior` object is in scope. So, if you call `PrintTitle()` when a `Warrior` object is in scope, the compiler invokes this version of the function

```
virtual void PrintTitle(void)
     { cout << "\nWARRIOR" << "\n"; }
```

which prints the word `WARRIOR` to standard output, normally the screen.

As a result, the Zalthar program produces this output:

```
WARRIOR
Name: Bruno
Weapon: Sword

WARRIOR
Name: GayLynn
Weapon: Crossbow

GNOME
Name: Glog
Weapon: Broadsword
Magic: X-ray vision
```

Similarly, the version of the function defined by the `Gnome` class is the version that executes when a `Gnome` object is in scope. So, when you use a pointer to call `PrintTitle()` from a `Gnome` object, the compiler executes this version of the function

```
virtual void PrintTitle(void)
     { cout << "\nGNOME" << "\n"; }
```

and the word `GNOME` is printed on-screen.

Because virtual functions work in this way, you should always declare a member function of a base class as virtual when you expect the member function to be overridden by derived classes.

## Calling a Virtual Function

Because a virtual function is destined to be overridden, it's pretty clear that the `PrintTitle()` function defined in the `Player` class definition will probably never be called:

```
virtual void PrintTitle(void)
     { cout << "\nPLAYER" << "\n"; }
```

If you like, however, you can force the compiler to execute the base class's version of the function by using the scope resolution operator (`::`). For example, if you wanted to call the `Player` class's `PrintTitle()` function from a member function of the `Warrior` class, you could do that by writing this statement:

```
Player::PrintTitle();
```

To make the above call from a `Warrior` object, you could modify the `Warrior` version of the `PrintData()` function definition to look like this:

```
void PrintData(void)
     {
          Player::PrintTitle();
          PrintName();
          PrintWeapon();
     }
```

The `Warrior` version of the `PrintData()` function would then call the `Player` version of `PrintTitle()`, and the word `PLAYER` would be printed on-screen.

## Pure Virtual Functions

Sometimes you may want to write a base-class member function that will always be overridden. A member function that must be overridden is called a *pure virtual function*. A pure virtual function is never used in its default form, but it is always overridden.

Pure virtual functions often are used in C++ programs, especially in definitions of abstract classes. When you want to declare a base function in a class, and you know that the function will always be overridden, the most elegant way to write your code is to define the function as a pure virtual function.

To declare a pure virtual function, all you have to do is assign a zero value to a virtual function—effectively equating the function to a null pointer. In the Zalthar program, the `Player::PrintData()` function is declared to be a pure virtual function:

```
virtual void PrintData(void) = 0;
```

A pure virtual function is essentially a placeholder; its value cannot be defined in the base class in which it is declared, so it must be overridden in derived functions.

To sum up, when the definition of a base class contains a member function that you suspect will be overridden, you should declare the version of the member function that's declared in the base class to be a virtual function. If the following two conditions are also met, you should make the function a pure virtual function:

- You are sure that the member function will be overridden before it can be used.
- There is no reason for the base class to provide a definition of the member function.

More detailed explanations of how virtual functions work are presented in Chapter 17, "Conversion Functions," and Chapter 19.

## Another Example Program

The program in Listing 11.2 contains more illustrations of how data abstraction works in a C++ program. The program also illustrates inheritance and data encapsulation.

### Listing 11.2. Data abstraction in C++.

```
// 1102.CPP
// Using a class

#include <iostream.h>

class  PlayerData {
private:
     int  strength;
     int  charisma;
     int  dexterity;
     int  intelligence;
protected:
     char *armor;
public:
     void      GetData();
```

*continues*

**Listing 11.2. continued**

```
     void      PrintData();
     void IncrementStrength(){ strength++; }
};

void PlayerData::GetData()
{
     strength = 24;
     charisma = 29;
     dexterity = 12;
     intelligence = 2;
     armor = "chain mail";
}

void PlayerData::PrintData()
{
     cout << "\nStrength: " << strength << "\n";
     cout << "Charisma: " << charisma << "\n";
     cout << "Dexterity: " << dexterity << "\n";
     cout << "Intelligence: " << intelligence << "\n\n";
     cout << "Armor: " << armor << "\n\n";
}


int main()
{
     PlayerData     myPlayer;
     PlayerData     *playerPtr = &myPlayer;

     playerPtr->GetData();
     playerPtr->PrintData();
     playerPtr->IncrementStrength();
     return 0;
}
```

1102.CPP is a segment of code adapted from the adventure game program, The Wrath of Zalthar. The Zalthar game is played with fictional characters who not only have names and weapons, but also have races, abilities, and other characteristics. 1102.CPP is a block of code used during the development of the game to determine what kinds of attributes the characters in the game would have. As you shall see in later chapters, some of the elements demonstrated in 1102.CPP will be incorporated into later versions of the Zalthar program.

In the 1102.CPP program, the name, race, category, and characteristics of characters are stored as member variables of the abstract class `PlayerData`. In this version, `PlayerData` class also has three member functions: `IncrementStrength()`, `GetData()`, and `PrintData()`.

## Creating a PlayerData Object

Near the end of Listing 11.2, in the first line of the `main()` function, this statement *instantiates* an object, or creates an object that is an instance of the `PlayerData` class:

```
PlayerData      *playerPtr = &myPlayer;
```

## Data Encapsulation in the 1102.CPP Program

As you can see, all the member variables of the `PlayerData` class are private, but its three member functions are public. So the member variables of the `PlayerData` class can be accessed only from the class itself, or from objects (such as `myPlayer`) that belong to the class. But the member functions of the player class can be accessed from any function in the program—such as the `main()` function.

The function `PlayerData::GetData()` is a public member function of the `PlayerData` class, so it can access the `PlayerData` class's member variables and pass those values on to calling functions. The job of `PlayerData::GetData()` is to set the values of the private member variables of the `PlayerData` class while affording some privacy for those variables. (Notice that in the definitions of these two functions, the *scope resolution operator* `::` is used to identify `GetData()` and `PrintData()` as member functions of the `PlayerData` class. That's the standard format for defining member functions in C++ programs.)

The `PlayerData::PrintData()` function, like the `PlayerData::GetData()` function, is a member of the `PlayerData` class. So `PlayerData::PrintData()` can also access private member variables of the `PlayerData` class. The `PlayerData::PrintData()` function prints the program's output on-screen.

Because `PlayerData::GetData()` and `PlayerData::PrintData()` are public member functions, they can be accessed from any function in the program, including the `main()` function. When you execute the program, the `main()` function calls `PlayerData::GetData()` and `PlayerData::PrintData()` and prints this output:

```
Strength:       24
Charisma:       29
Dexterity:      12
Intelligence:    2
Armor:          chain mail
```

# Class Libraries

Although C++ has many advantages over C—its new and improved features have filled up ten chapters so far—the most powerful feature of C++ is that it supports classes that can be grouped into class libraries. C++ class libraries are reminiscent of C-language function libraries, but are much more powerful.

Function libraries for C programs, such as the STDIO.H libraries, have been around since the day the first C compiler went on the market. The C++ successor to STDIO.H—the class library named IOSTREAM.H—was released with the introduction of C++. And now, other C++ class libraries are widely available.

C++ class libraries are superior to C-style function libraries because they support the benefits inherent in object-oriented languages: benefits such as data encapsulation and abstraction, inheritance, and polymorphism.

These are some of the advantages that C++ class libraries have over the function libraries used in C:

- *Classes support data encapsulation and data abstraction.* C's function libraries increase the functionality of the C language, but without encapsulating the data that the functions manipulate, and without associating functions with their data. In C++, functions and their data are associated with each other for easy access, yet are afforded some protection from being inadvertently modified by functions outside the class in which the functions are declared.

- *New classes look like language extensions.* You can create objects from classes defined in libraries in the same way you create instances of the C++ built-in types. Thus classes, with their special constructors and overloaded operators, provide a natural programming interface.

- *Class libraries are better than "cookbooks."* If you need a new C-language function that is similar to one defined in a function library, you must copy the original function (if you're fortunate enough to have the source code) and then figure out how it works and change it to meet your needs. In contrast, when you need a class that resembles a predefined class, you can use all the original class's functions and data—or any part of it that you want—without any need to access the object's source code. Even better, you can modify the class in any way you like, and in as many ways as you like, easily and efficiently.

When you program in C, you can use function libraries obtained from various sources, or you can roll your own. Similarly, when you program in C++, you can write your own class libraries or choose from a variety of class libraries that are commercially available.

For example, Version 2 of the Microsoft Foundation Class (MFC) Library—which is designed specifically for use with Visual C++—is supplied by Microsoft with every Visual C++ compiler sold. Borland C++ comes with a competitive set of C++ class libraries. And, of course, you can design your own class libraries.

Part III of this book contains a tutorial on the Microsoft Foundation Class Library, and covers that library in detail.

# Summary

This chapter introduced classes, the foundation of object-oriented programming in C++. It explained how C++ classes evolved from the `struct` type specifier, how objects are derived from classes, and how classes are used in C++ programs. The chapter also introduced many topics—such as member functions, abstract classes, virtual functions, and class libraries—that will be examined more closely in later chapters, beginning with Chapter 12.

Chapter 12

# Objects

If classes are the blueprints of C++, as I asserted in the first sentence of Chapter 11, "Classes," objects are the structures built with those blueprints to create object-oriented programs. In C++, an object is an instance of a class. A class, like a C-style `struct`, is a framework that describes what an object will look like when it is created. When you build an actual structure in accordance with the directions provided by a class, that structure is an object.

In a C++ program, almost anything can be constructed as an object. Many of the tangible elements in C++ programs, such as the graphical elements in Windows-based programs, are implemented as objects. Elements that aren't visible, such as data structures and even procedures for doing things, also can be implemented as objects.

Objects are often grouped into larger objects, such as simple lists, linked lists, and arrays. And of course, in accordance with the principles of inheritance, objects can inherit behaviors from other objects and modify those behaviors, forming hierarchies of objects.

Classes were introduced in Chapter 10, "Object-Oriented Programming," and were described in a little more detail in Chapter 11. This chapter takes an even closer look at objects, what they are, how they are created, and what they do. It is a wide-ranging chapter that introduces such topics as:

- How memory is allocated for objects.
- Access specifiers.
- Public and private derivation of objects.
- Member functions and member variables.
- Accessing member variables.
- Static member variables and static member functions.
- Arrays of objects.
- Scope and linkage of objects.
- The `this` pointer.

Many of the topics introduced in this chapter are examined more closely in later chapters.

# From struct to Object

As you may recall from Chapter 11, classes are based on the `struct` variable—not the `struct` type specifier used in C, but the full-fledged `struct` data type introduced with the premiere of C++.

In the C language, as you learned in Chapter 11, you must use the keyword `struct` every time you declare an instance of a structure. Thus, if you define this `struct` in a C program

```
struct PlayerAbils {
     int strength;
     int charisma;
     int dexterity;
     int intelligence;
     char *armor;
};
```

you must use the keyword `struct` each time you declare an instance of the structure. For example:

```
struct PlayerAbils MyAbils;    // you must use this construct in C
```

In C++, a `struct` is a full-fledged data type. So after you have defined a `struct` in a C++ program, you don't have to use the keyword `struct` every time you refer to it. Thus, if you define this `struct` in a C++ program

```
struct PlayerAbils {
     int strength;
     int charisma;
     int dexterity;
     int intelligence;
     char *armor;
};
```

you can declare a `PlayerAbils` struct without using the `struct` keyword:

```
PlayerAbils MyAbils;      // this works in c++, but not in c
```

One way to become familiar with classes is to compare C++, the class data type, with the `struct` template used in C. For the sake of this comparison, suppose that you're a C programmer—not a C++ programmer—who is writing an adventure game such as The Wrath of Zalthar program that was examined in Chapter 11.

As you may recall, the Zalthar program is played with fictional characters who have qualities such as `strength`, `charisma`, `dexterity`, and `intelligence`. If you want to represent qualities such as these in a C program, you might create a `struct` type to represent these qualities and then start writing functions to manipulate and display the contents of your `struct`.

As you start designing your `struct`, it might look like this:

```
struct PlayerAbils {
     int strength;
     int charisma;
     int dexterity;
     int intelligence;
     char *armor;
};
```

In C, there is no tool that you can use to print all the elements in a `struct` as a block. Obviously, you cannot pass an entire structure to a library function that prints formatted output, such as `printf`. Of course, you can print each member of the structure individually, or you can write your own function to print the entire structure. The latter is shown in Listing 12.1.

**Listing 12.1. Printing the contents of a `struct`.**

```
/***1201.C***/
/*** Using a structure in C ***/

#include <stdio.h>

struct PlayerAbils {
     int strength;
     int charisma;
     int dexterity;
     int intelligence;
     char *armor;
};

struct PlayerAbils MyAbils;

int main()
{
     MyAbils.strength = 24;
     MyAbils.charisma = 29;
     MyAbils.dexterity = 12;
     MyAbils.intelligence = 2;

     MyAbils.armor = "chain mail";

     printf("\nStrength: %d\n", MyAbils.strength);
     printf("Charisma: %d\n", MyAbils.charisma);
     printf("Dexterity: %d\n", MyAbils.dexterity);
     printf("Intelligence: %d\n\n", MyAbils.intelligence);
     printf("Armor: %s\n\n", MyAbils.armor);

     return 0;
}
```

In Listing 12.1, the five `printf` functions in the `main()` segment print the contents of the `struct` named `PlayerAbils` that precedes the `main()` segment. This is the program's output:

```
Strength: 24
Charisma: 29
Dexterity: 12
Intelligence: 2

Armor: chain mail
```

When you have defined a C-style structure that contains a collection of data, you can start writing functions to manipulate that data in any way you wish. For example, you can write functions to accept the input of data from a user, as well as to print the data in various formats.

But in C, as you have seen, there is no direct way to associate functions that manipulate the data in the structure with the structure itself. Consequently, when a program contains a number of functions that access data in the same data structure, the functions are often widely separated from the structure that contains the data and from each other.

## Shortcomings of C-Style Structures

Often, if there are many functions in a C program that manipulate the data in the same structure, the functions themselves are scattered throughout the program. That can make it difficult to make changes in a program when you want to update the program, and it can make the prospect of porting code from one program to another extremely difficult.

Conventional techniques for accessing data in C-style structures also have other drawbacks:

- Because the data in a structure is separated from the functions that manipulate the data, there is no easy way to ensure that the data in the struct is valid. When you create a class that contains both member variables and member functions, you can easily call a member function that reports back on the validity of one or more member variables.
- The C language provides no techniques for creating structures that inherit data, variables, or functions from other structures. As you will see in this chapter, C++ does.

C++ offers some interesting ways to solve these problems, as you'll see in the remainder of this chapter.

### USING STRUCT VARIABLES IN C++

Even though C++ lets you place functions in `struct` variables, that doesn't mean you should. Generally speaking, it's best to use `struct` variables in C++ programs in the same way they're used in C: as collections of data elements, without functions. In my opinion, adding a function to a `struct` is confusing and offers no real benefits; if a `struct` becomes important enough to contain a function, you should probably consider promoting it to a class. Then, it will have all other features of a class, too, at no extra cost in overhead.

## Defining an Object's Contents

When you have instantiated an object, you can define its member variables and member functions by assigning values to them. For example, in Listing 12.1, these statements in the `main()` function define the variables `strength`, `charisma`, `dexterity`, and `intelligence` (which are integers) and the member variable `armor` (which is a string):

```
MyAbils.strength = 24;
MyAbils.charisma = 29;
MyAbils.dexterity = 12;
MyAbils.intelligence = 2;

MyAbils.armor = "chain mail";
```

# Using Objects

A C++ class, like a C++ `struct`, is a user-defined data type that can contain functions as well as data. A variable that is an element of a class is called a *member variable*. A function that is a member of a class is called a *member function*.

As noted earlier, a class is very similar to a `struct` in C++. In fact, there is only one fundamental difference between a C++-style `struct` and a C++ class.

The difference is this: All variables and functions that are elements of a C++-style `struct` are *public* by default. That means they can be accessed from any function that is inside the `struct` in which they are declared. In contrast, all member variables and member functions of a class are *private* by default. That means a member of a class can be accessed only from functions declared within its own class.

## How Objects Are Created

When you define the contents of a class, the compiler doesn't allocate any memory for objects that belong to a class. To create an actual object that belongs to the class, you must declare an instance of the class. That's called *instantiating* the object.

At runtime, when you create an instance of a class, C++ allocates memory for the object that you have instantiated.

The creation of classes and the instantiation of objects were introduced in Chapter 11, "Classes." Instantiating objects with constructors is the topic of Chapter 14, "Constructors and Destructors."

## Two Ways to Initialize Objects

When you create a class, C++ does not allocate memory for any objects that belong to the class. Memory is not allocated for an object until the object is instantiated. Then C++ allocates memory for the object that has been created. There are two ways to allocate memory when you create an object:

- You can instantiate the object by writing a special kind of function called a *constructor*. When you write a constructor that initializes an object, C++ automatically executes the constructor when the object comes into scope. When the object goes out of scope, C++ automatically deallocates the memory that was allocated to the object when its constructor executed. Thus, when you create an object using a constructor, you don't have to deallocate its memory when it is destroyed.
- You can create an object by simply declaring it, as if it were an ordinary variable. When you choose this method for instantiating an object, the compiler creates a constructor for you and then initializes the object with the constructor that it has created. But there's a disadvantage to this approach. When the compiler creates an object that doesn't have a constructor, the object is built by using a simple formula that does not provide all the capabilities of a properly constructed object. You'll learn more about the construction of objects in Chapter 14.

## Constructors

A *constructor* is a special kind of function that allocates memory for an object. It is not technically necessary to write a constructor for every object in a C++ program, but constructors offer so many benefits that most objects do have constructors. For example, a constructor can initialize data members of an object when the object is created and can ensure that member variables of an object being created are initialized with valid data.

Constructors also can perform special kinds of operations, such as converting data from one type to another and making copies of objects. Constructors are examined in detail in Chapter 14.

A constructor is always declared inside the definition of a class and always has the same name as the class in which it is declared. For example, this is a simple constructor for a class named `AClass`:

```
AClass() {}     // constructor
```

Some constructors take arguments, and some do not. When you invoke a constructor that takes no arguments, the statement that calls the constructor looks something like this:

```
AClass myObject;     // statement that calls a constructor
```

Notice that when you call a constructor function that has no arguments, there are no parentheses after the name of the constructor. Thus, when a statement in a program invokes a constructor that has no arguments, the statement has a closer resemblance to a declaration of a variable than to a statement that calls a function.

## Constructors That Take Arguments

You can pass arguments to constructors in the same way that you can pass arguments to ordinary functions. If you pass arguments to a constructor, the constructor can use those arguments that are passed to it to perform specified actions, such as initializing member variables and checking the contents of the variables to ensure that they are within acceptable ranges.

If you want a constructor to perform any user-defined actions, such as initializing or checking variables, you must provide the code that performs the specified actions. The program in Listing 12.2 demonstrates the use of a constructor that initializes a variable.

### Listing 12.2. A constructor that initializes a variable.

```
// 1202.CCP
// Demonstrating constructors

#include <iostream.h>

class ExampleClass {
public:
     int x;
     ExampleClass(int a) { x = a; }      // constructor
     ~ExampleClass() {}                 // destructor
};
```

```
int main()
{
     ExampleClass myTestObject(100);
     int n = myTestObject.x;
     cout << n << '\n';
     return 0;
}
```

This program defines a class named `ExampleClass`. Notice that `ExampleClass` has a constructor that takes one argument:

```
class ExampleClass {
public:
     int x;
     ExampleClass(int a) { x = a; }      // constructor
     ~ExampleClass() {}             // destructor
};
```

When `ExampleClass` has been defined, this program invokes the constructor for `ExampleClass`, passing the constructor an integer value as a parameter. The constructor sets the member variable `ExampleClass::x` to the value passed to the constructor.

In Listing 12.2, the `main()` segment of the program initializes an object named `myTestObject` and sets the `myTestObject.x` member variable to a value of 100:

```
int main()
{
     ExampleClass myTestObject(100);
     int n = myTestObject.x;
     cout << n << '\n';
     return 0;
}
```

## Function-Style Initializations in a Constructor Call

In Listing 12.2, this is the definition of the `ExampleClass` constructor:

```
ExampleClass(int a) { x = a; }      // constructor
```

The constructor shown here also could be written using this syntax:

```
ExampleClass(int a):x(a) {}
```

The two constructors shown here produce identical results. Each takes a parameter named `a`, and each assigns the value of that parameter to a member variable `x`.

The syntax of the first constructor is nothing new; it is the syntax of an ordinary C function. The second constructor is written in a new kind of C++ syntax that was introduced in Chapter 4, "Variables." In Chapter 4, you saw how you can use this new syntax to declare a member function of a class. As you can see by examining the second statement shown above, you can use this new format to write constructors, as well as to write member functions.

## Letting the Compiler Create a Constructor

Although most objects are created using constructors—and although the use of constructors is highly recommended—it is possible to instantiate an object that does not have a constructor. To create an object that has no constructor, all you have to do is declare the object, in the same way you would declare an ordinary variable.

When you declare an object for which a constructor is not available, the compiler steps in and creates a simple constructor for you. Then, it instantiates your object by invoking the constructor it created.

Listing 12.3 shows how a program can create objects without invoking a constructor.

### Listing 12.3. The Wrath of Zalthar, Chapter 12 version.

---

**ZALTHAR.H**

```
// ZALTHAR.H
// The Wrath of Zalthar, Chapter 12 version
// Copyright 1992 Mark Andrews.  All rights reserved.

#include <stdio.h>
#include <iostream.h>
#include <string.h>
#include <stdlib.h>

inline void FatalError()
{
    fprintf(stderr, "A fatal error has occurred\n");
    exit(1);
}

char *DuplicateString(char *aString)
{
    char    *aCopy;
```

```
    aCopy = new char[strlen(aString) + 1];
    if (aCopy == NULL)
        FatalError();
    strcpy(aCopy, aString);
    return aCopy;
}

class Player {
public:
     virtual void PrintData(void) = 0;

     virtual void PrintTitle(void)
          { cout << "\nPLAYER" << "\n"; }
};

class Warrior: public Player {
private:
     char *name;
     char *weapon;
public:
     void PrintTitle(void)
          { cout << "\nWARRIOR" << "\n"; }
     void SetName(char *playerName)
          { name = DuplicateString(playerName); }
     void PrintName(void)
          { cout << "Name: " << name << "\n"; }
     void SetWeapon(char *playerWeapon)
          { weapon = DuplicateString(playerWeapon); }
     void PrintWeapon(void)
          { cout << "Weapon: " << weapon << "\n"; }
     void PrintData(void)
          {
               PrintTitle();
               PrintName();
               PrintWeapon();
          }
};

class Gnome: public Warrior {
private:
     char *magic;
public:
     void PrintTitle(void)
          { cout << "\nGNOME" << "\n"; }
     virtual void SetMagic(char *playerMagic)
          { magic = DuplicateString(playerMagic); }
     virtual void PrintMagic(void)
          { cout << "Magic: " << magic << "\n"; }
     void PrintData(void)
          {
```

*continues*

**Listing 12.3. continued**

```
                PrintTitle();
                PrintName();
                PrintWeapon();
                PrintMagic();
            }
};
```

**MAIN.CPP**

```
// MAIN.CPP
// The Wrath of Zalthar, Chapter 12 Version
// Copyright 1992 Mark Andrews.  All rights reserved.

#include <stdio.h>
#include "Zalthar.h"

int main()
{

     // Set up a pointer to an object

     Warrior aWarrior, bWarrior, *warriorPtr;
     Gnome aGnome, *gnomePtr;

     // print report
     warriorPtr = &aWarrior;
     warriorPtr->SetName("Bruno");
     warriorPtr->SetWeapon("Sword");
     warriorPtr->PrintData();

     warriorPtr = &bWarrior;
     warriorPtr->SetName("GayLynn");
     warriorPtr->SetWeapon("Crossbow");
     warriorPtr->PrintData();

     gnomePtr = &aGnome;
     gnomePtr->SetName("Glog");
     gnomePtr->SetWeapon("Broadsword");
     gnomePtr->SetMagic("X-ray vision");
     gnomePtr->PrintData();

     return 0;
}
```

In Listing 12.3, three objects are created, and each one of them is created without invoking a constructor. The objects are initialized using these two statements, which appear in the `main()` segment of the program:

```
Warrior aWarrior, bWarrior, *warriorPtr;
Gnome aGnome, *gnomePtr;
```

The statements shown here instantiate three objects: `aWarrior`, `bWarrior`, and `aGnome`. The objects named `aWarrior` and `bWarrior` are instances of a class named `Warrior`, and the object named `aGnome` is an instance of the `Gnome` class.

Along with the objects named `aWarrior` and `bWarrior`, the program in Listing 12.3 creates a pointer to a `Warrior` object. This pointer is named `warriorPtr`. Along with the object named `aGnome`, the program creates a pointer to a `Gnome` object named `gnomePtr`.

When the objects `aWarrior`, `bWarrior`, and `aGnome` have been created, this block of code assigns values to member variables of the objects and then prints a simple report:

```
// print report
warriorPtr = &aWarrior;
warriorPtr->SetName("Bruno");
warriorPtr->SetWeapon("Sword");
warriorPtr->PrintData();

warriorPtr = &bWarrior;
warriorPtr->SetName("GayLynn");
warriorPtr->SetWeapon("Crossbow");
warriorPtr->PrintData();

gnomePtr = &aGnome;
gnomePtr->SetName("Glog");
gnomePtr->SetWeapon("Broadsword");
gnomePtr->SetMagic("X-ray vision");
gnomePtr->PrintData();
```

In this code fragment, the pointers declared in the previous example are initialized to the addresses of `aWarrior`, `bWarrior`, and `aGnome`. After the objects are instantiated and initialized, the function `PrintData()` is used to print the values of the objects' data members on-screen.

## Writing a Constructor for a Class

There's an easier way to instantiate the three objects created in Listing 12.3. It would take less work to instantiate the objects by invoking a constructor that takes arguments. For example, when you get to Chapter 14, you'll see this constructor for the `Gnome` class Listing 14.1:

```
Gnome(char *nm, char *wpn, char *mag) :
     Warrior(nm, wpn)
     { SetMagic(mag); }
```

Later in Listing 14.1, in the program's `main()` segment, this statement invokes the `Gnome` class's constructor to instantiate an object of the `Gnome` class:

```
Gnome aGnome("Glog", "Broadsword", "X-ray vision");
```

This is an easier technique than creating a `Gnome` object without a constructor and then writing a separate member function to initialize each one of the object's member functions.

Other benefits of using constructors to instantiate objects are outlined in Chapter 14.

## Destructors

Most classes used in C++ programs have a *destructor* as well as a constructor. A destructor—like a constructor—always has the same name as its class. But the name of a destructor is always preceded by the tilde, or the C++ bitwise `NOT` operator (~). This is a declaration of a simple destructor that destroys an object of the class `AClass`:

```
~AClass();
```

A destructor never takes arguments and never returns a value. And you are not permitted to specify a return type—not even `void`—when you define a destructor for a class.

When a class object is no longer needed, its destructor is called. When an object that has a destructor is deallocated, the job of the destructor is to deallocate any memory that has been allocated *by* the object.

If an object does not perform any memory-allocation operations, it does not really have to have a destructor, because no extra memory has to be deallocated when the object is deleted. But placing a destructor in an object's definition can never do any harm; if the destructor isn't needed, it doesn't do anything. So most class definitions contain destructors, even if the destructors aren't required.

More information on destructors is presented in Chapter 14.

# Member Variables

In C++, an object is a collection of the member variables and member functions that make up a class. A *member variable*—sometimes referred to as a *data member*—is a single data element in the collection of data elements that make up an object.

There are two kinds of member variables: *static member variables* and *non-static member variables*. A non-static member variable is a variable that is a member of a specific object in a class. A static member variable is a special kind of variable shared by all objects in a class.

Most member variables used in C++ are non-static member variables. Non-static and static member variables are described in more detail later in this section.

## Pointers to Member Variables

Although a class is not an object, C++ sometimes lets you treat a class like an object. For example, C++ lets you declare pointers to member variables of a class before any objects that belong to the class are created. That lets you plan ahead; when you create a pointer to a data member of a class and then instantiate an object that belongs to a class, your pointer will be in place, all set up and ready to access the data member that it points to.

As an illustration of how pointers to member variables can be used, consider a class named `TheClass`, which is defined in Listing 12.4.

### Listing 12.4. Pointers to member variables.

```
// 1204.CPP

#include <iostream.h>

class TheObject {
private:
     int a, b, c;
     // give SetValue() access to private data
     friend void SetValue(TheObject myObject, int x);
```

*continues*

**Listing 12.4. continued**

```
public:
     TheObject() {}
     ~TheObject() {}
};

void SetValue(TheObject myObject, int x)
{
     int TheObject::*memVarPtr;
     memVarPtr = &TheObject::a;
     myObject.*memVarPtr = x;
}

int main()
{
     TheObject myObject;
     SetValue(myObject, 100);

     return 0;
}
```

Listing 12.4 defines a class named `TheClass` and a global function named `SetValue()`. This is the first statement in the `SetValue()` function:

```
int TheClass::*memVarPtr;
```

The preceding statement, which may look strange at first glance, declares a pointer named `memVarPtr`. Then, it sets `memVarPtr` to point to an unnamed integer member variable of `TheClass`—even though no objects that belong to `TheClass` have been created yet and no member variables of any such objects have been defined.

Actually, what is stored in `memVarPtr` is the offset of the member variable `a` in an object of the class `TheClass`. (This offset is incremented by 1 so that `memVarPtr` won't have the same offset as a virtual function; virtual functions are described in more detail in Chapter 13, "Member Functions.") So `memVarPtr` is set to 1.

`TheClass` has three member variables that are integers, namely, the data members `a`, `b`, and `cmemVarPtr` can now be set to point to member variable `a`, member variable `b`, or member variable `c`. This operation also can be performed before any objects that belong to `TheClass` have been created and before any member variables of any such objects have been defined.

This statement in the second line in the `SetValue()` function sets `memVarPtr` to point to member variable `a`:

```
memVarPtr = &TheClass::a;
```

When `SetValue()` is called, it doesn't know anything about the object that it is working on, except that the object is a member of the class named `TheClass`. But `SetValue()` happily takes the reference passed to it, adds the index stored in `memVarPtr`, and in this way determines what the correct memory location will be when a `TheClass` object is defined.

Next, `SetValue()` uses indirection to give the member variable named `a` a value that has passed to `SetValue()` as a parameter.

When all the preceding operations have taken place, the `main()` segment of this program creates an object of the class named `myObject`:

```
TheClass myObject;
```

Then `main()` calls `SetValue()`, passing the function a copy of `myObject` and a value of 100:

```
SetValue(myObject, 100);
```

Finally, `SetValue()` uses indirection to set the value of `myObject:a` to 100:

```
myObject.*memVarPtr = x;
```

Pointers to member variables also can work in other ways. For example, you could substitute this `main()` segment for the `main()` segment in Listing 12.4:

```
// 1204.CPP

#include <iostream.h>

class TheClass {
private:
     int a, b, c;
     // give SetValue() access to private data
     friend void SetValue(TheClass myObject, int x);
     friend int main();
public:
     TheClass() {}
     ~TheClass() {}
};

void SetValue(TheClass myObject, int x)
{
```

```
    int TheClass::*memVarPtr;
    memVarPtr = &TheClass::a;
    myObject.*memVarPtr = x;
}

int main()
{
    TheClass *objPtr = new TheClass;
    int TheClass::*memVarPtr;
    memVarPtr = &TheClass:: a;
    objPtr->*memVarPtr = 200;

    return 0;
}
```

In the first line of the above `main()` segment, the `new` operator is used to instantiate an object of the class `TheClass`, and a pointer named `objPtr` is initialized to point to the new object:

```
TheClass *objPtr = new TheClass;
```

Next, a pointer named `memVarPtr` is set to point to an integer member variable of the class named `TheClass`:

```
int TheClass::*memVarPtr;
```

In the third line of the example, reference is used to assign the address of `TheClass::a` to a pointer named `memVarPtr`:

```
memVarPtr = &TheClass::a;
```

Finally, the arrow operator (`->`) is used to set the value of the member variable `a` to 200:

```
objPtr->*memVarPtr = 200;
```

Now that you know how all this works, you should be warned that working with pointers to member variables is a risky business that can lead to program crashes if there are any slip-ups, particularly when your pointers point to data that doesn't yet exist! So when you start passing pointers to member variables, make sure that they point where they're supposed to. These are dangerous waters.

## Arrays of Member Variables

In most ways, a member variable of an object can be treated like any other variable. For example, you can create an array of an object's member variables, in much the same way that you would create any array of variables. When you have set up an array of an object's data members, you can loop through the data members that belong to the object, reading member variables or writing to member variables as you iterate through the loop. In this way, with one short `for` loop, you can read or set all of an object's member variables (or, if you prefer, a particular set of the object's member variables).

Listing 12.5 shows how you can create and use an array of member variables.

**Listing 12.5. An array of pointers to member variables.**

```
// 1205.CPP
// An array of pointers to member variables

#include <iostream.h>

class Abils {
private:
     int strength;
     int dexterity;
     int charisma;
     int intelligence;
public:
     Abils() {}
     ~Abils() {}
     // give main() and SetVar() access to private members
     friend int main();
     friend void SetVar(Abils *object, int Abils::*member, int var);
};

void SetVar(Abils *object, int Abils::*member, int var)
{
     object->*member = var;
}

int main()
{
     int abilsArray[] = { 24, 19, 31, 22 };

     int Abils::*abilsList[] = {
          &Abils::strength,
          &Abils::dexterity,
          &Abils::charisma,
          &Abils::intelligence
     };
```

*continues*

**Listing 12.5. continued**

```
     Abils myPlayer;
     Abils *playerPtr = &myPlayer;

     for (int n = 0; n < 4; n++)
          SetVar(playerPtr, abilsList[n], abilsArray[n]);

     cout << "Strength: " << myPlayer.strength << '\n';
     cout << "Dexterity: " << myPlayer.dexterity << '\n';
     cout << "Charisma: " << myPlayer.charisma << '\n';
     cout << "Intelligence: "
             << myPlayer.intelligence << '\n';

      return 0;
};
```

Listing 12.5 defines a class named `Abils` that has these data members:

```
int strength;
int dexterity;
int charisma;
int intelligence;
```

In the `main()` segment of the program, these two statements instantiate an object of the `Abils` class named `myPlayer` and then create a pointer to the object:

```
Abils myPlayer;
Abils *playerPtr = &myPlayer;
```

Before the `myPlayer` object is created, an array containing one entry for each member variable of the object is defined. The array is named `abilsList`. This is the array:

```
int Abils::*abilsList[] = {
     &Abils::strength,
     &Abils::dexterity,
     &Abils::charisma,
     &Abils::intelligence
};
```

Next, this `for` loop is executed to initialize each data member of the `myPlayer` object:

```
for (int n = 0; n < 4; n++)
     SetVar(playerPtr, abilsList[n], abilsArray[n]);
```

The preceding statement calls a global function named `SetVar()`, which is a `friend` of the `Abils` class. The `SetVar()` function sets the value of each data member in the `abilsList` array:

```
void SetVar(Abils *object, int Abils::*member, int var)
{
     object->*member = var;
}
```

Finally, these four statements are executed to print the value of each member variable of the `myPlayer` object:

```
cout << "Strength: " << myPlayer.strength << '\n';
cout << "Dexterity: " << myPlayer.dexterity << '\n';
cout << "Charisma: " << myPlayer.charisma << '\n';
cout << "Intelligence: "
     << myPlayer.intelligence << '\n';
```

This is the output of the program:

```
Strength: 24
Dexterity: 19
Charisma: 31
Intelligence: 22
```

## Constant Member Variables

You can declare a member variable of an object to be a constant by preceding the name of variable with the `const` keyword. For example, in this code fragment, the member variable `x` is declared to be a constant:

```
class TestClass {
private:
     const int x;
public:
     TestClass() : x(100) {}
     ~TestClass() {}
     int GetX() { return x; }
};
```

When you have declared a constant member variable, you can initialize it by invoking an appropriate constructor for the object to which it belongs. (Constructors are the topic of Chapter 14.) For example, this constructor initializes the constant member variable declared in the preceding code fragment by giving the variable a value of 100:

```
TestClass() : x(100) {}
```

After you have declared and initialized a constant member variable, its value cannot be changed. Listing 12.6 is a short but complete program that declares and initializes a constant member variable and then prints its value to standard output, normally the screen.

**Listing 12.6. A constant member variable.**

```
// 1206.CPP
// A constant member variable

#include <iostream.h>

class TestClass {
private:
	const int x;
public:
	TestClass() : x(100) {}
	~TestClass() {}
	int GetX() { return x; }
};

int main()
{
	TestClass s;
	const int a = s.GetX();
	cout << a << '\n';
	return 0;
}
```

## Static Member Variables

A static member variable is a special kind of variable shared by all objects in a class. When a class has a static variable, only one copy of the variable exists, and that single copy of the variable is shared by all objects that belong to the class.

A static member variable can be useful when a program contains a value that can be changed from outside the definition of a class and when you want that value to be accessible to all objects in a class.

Static member variables are used in many ways in C++ programs. One typical use of a static member variable is to keep track of the number of objects in a list. Each time a program creates an object in the list, the static member variable can be incremented, and each time an object is destroyed, the variable can be decremented. In this way, the variable can always contain the number of currently active objects in the list.

Static member variables also can keep track of other kinds of changeable values, such as interest rates. When a static member variable is used to keep track of a value such as an interest rate, the value of the static member variable can be changed each time the interest rate changes. Thus, the current rate is always immediately accessible to any object that lies within the scope of the static member variable.

When you define a class, you can create a static member variable that belongs to the class by preceding the variable's declaration with the `static` keyword. For example, this statement declares a static member variable named `count`:

```
static int count;        // declare static member variable
```

If you do not declare a member variable to be static, it is non-static by default.

When you declare a static member variable in a program, a fixed memory location is allocated for the variable at link time; that location doesn't change for the lifetime of the program. In this sense, a static member variable resembles a global variable.

However, access to a static member variable is more limited than access to a global variable. After you have initialized a static member variable, functions outside its class can access it only by using the scope resolution operator (`::`) preceded by the name of the class in which the variable is declared.

For example, this statement assigns a value of `0` to a static member variable named `count` that is declared inside the definition of a class named `Dracula`:

```
Dracula::count = 0;
```

## Using a Static Member Variable

Listing 12.7 shows how a static member variable can be used in a C++ program.

### Listing 12.7. A static member variable.

```
#include <iostream.h>

class SampleClass {
```

*continues*

**Listing 12.7. continued**

```
public:
     static int staticVar;          // declare static member variable
     SampleClass() {}
     void SetStaticVar(int a) { staticVar = a; }
};

int SampleClass::staticVar;         // define static member variable

int main()
{
     SampleClass myObject;          // define local object
     myObject.SetStaticVar(100);    // initialize static data member
     cout << SampleClass::staticVar << '\n';
     SampleClass::staticVar = 200;
     cout << SampleClass::staticVar << '\n';
     myObject.staticVar = 300;
     cout << SampleClass::staticVar << '\n';
     return 0;
}
```

In Listing 12.7, a static member variable named `staticVar` is declared inside the class definition of a class named `SampleClass`. This is the declaration of `staticVar`:

```
static int staticVar;          // declare static member variable
```

## Defining a Static Member Variable

Because a static member variable is a hybrid object—a kind of cross between an ordinary member variable and a global variable—there are some peculiar rules that govern the creation and handling of static member variables. For example, a static member variable must be declared inside the definition of a class but must be defined outside its class's definition.

In Listing 12.7, the static member variable `staticVar` is defined in a line that appears outside the definition of `SampleClass`:

```
int SampleClass::staticVar;          // define static member variable
```

## Initializing a Static Member Variable

When you define a static member variable, you can initialize it at the same time if you like. This definition of a static member variable initializes the variable with a value of 100:

```
int ExampleClass::aStatVar = 100;
```

If you choose to initialize a static member variable after it has been defined, you can initialize it either directly or with a function, in the same way that you would initialize any member variable. In Listing 12.7, this public member function is called to initialize the static member variable named `staticVar`:

```
void SetStaticVar(int a) { staticVar = a; }
```

After you have declared and initialized a static member variable, you can access it from any member function of its class. If it is a public or protected member variable, you also can access it from other classes, or from outside any class, in accordance with normal access rules.

## Accessing a Static Member Variable

When you have defined and declared a static member variable, you can access it from inside an object of its class, in the same way you would access any member variable. In Listing 12.7, a class named `SampleClass` has a member variable named `SetStaticVar()` that can be called to set the value of the static member variable named `staticVar`:

```
void SetStaticVar(int a) { staticVar = a; }
```

This statement in the `main()` segment of the program sets the value of `staticVar` by calling the member function `SetStaticVar()`:

```
myObject.SetStaticVar(100);
```

Because access to `staticVar` is public, the `main()` segment also can set the value of `staticVar` by accessing the variable directly:

```
SampleClass::staticVar = 200;
```

Notice that in this statement, the scope resolution operator (`::`)—preceded by the name of `SampleClass`—is used to access `staticVar`.

```
myObject.staticVar = 300;
```

Another statement in the `main()` segment of Listing 12.7 accesses `staticVar` with the dot operator (`.`) preceded by the name of the object `myObject`. This construct is possible because a static member variable that has public access is accessible through any object that has access to it:

```
myObject.staticVar = 300;
```

In the `main()` segment of Listing 12.7, all three of the techniques shown in the three preceding examples are used to assign values to `staticVar`:

```
int main()
{
     SampleClass myObject;          // define local object
     myObject.SetStaticVar(100);    // initialize static data members
     cout << SampleClass::staticVar << '\n';
     SampleClass::staticVar = 200;
     cout << SampleClass::staticVar << '\n';
     myObject.staticVar = 300;
     cout << SampleClass::staticVar << '\n';
     return 0;
}
```

In the code fragment shown here, it's important to remember that because `staticVar` is a static member variable, only one copy of the variable exists. That means that each assignment statement shown in the preceding code fragment assigns a value to the same memory location, overwriting the previous value of `staticVar`.

## Private Static Member Variables

A static member variable, like any other member variable, can be public, protected, or private. If a static member variable is private, it cannot be accessed from a function outside its class unless access to it is specifically granted—for example, through friendship status or through a public member function.

Listing 12.8 shows how a program can use a private static member variable to keep track of objects that belong to a class.

### Listing 12.8. A private static member variable.

```
#include <iostream.h>

class LittleList {
private:
     static int ct;                    // declare static member variable
public:
     LittleList() { ct++; }
```

```
     ~LittleList() { ct--; }
     static int GetCount() { return ct; }    // static member function
};

int LittleList::ct = 0;             // initialize static member variable

int main()
{
     LittleList obj1, obj2, obj3;  // define local objects
     cout << "Number of objects: " << LittleList::GetCount() << '\n';
     return 0;
}
```

---

The name of the static member variable used in Listing 12.8 is `ct`. Although access to `ct` is private, the variable is initialized using the same technique that would be used to define any other static member. That isn't surprising because there is only one way to define a static member variable: from outside the variable's class in a statement that accesses the variable using the scope resolution operator (`::`):

```
int LittleList::ct = 0;             // initialize static member variable
```

With one exception, the format of this statement is the same as the format of the statement that initialized the static member variable `staticVar` back in Listing 12.7. The exception is that in the above definition, the value of the variable being defined is initialized with a specified value.

Of course this difference has nothing to do with whether the variable is public or private; any static member variable can be initialized when it is defined.

In Listing 12.8, the static member variable `ct` is used to keep a running count of three objects in a class named `LittleList`. The objects are named `obj1`, `obj2`, and `obj3`.

In the program, each time an object of the `LittleList` class is initialized, the object's constructor increments the `ct` variable:

```
LittleList() { ct++; }
```

Similarly, each time an object's destructor is called, `ct` is decremented:

```
~LittleList() { ct--; }
```

Because `ct` is a private variable and because no `friends` of the `LittleList` class are declared, the only way to access `ct` from outside its class is through a member function. In Listing 12.8, `ct` is accessed through a public member variable named `GetCount()`:

```
cout << "Number of objects: " << LittleList::GetCount() << '\n';
```

This statement—which appears in the `main()` segment of the program—accesses the member function `GetCount()` using the scope resolution operator (`::`).

The `main()` function could have accessed `GetCount()` through one of the objects of the `LittleList` class by using the dot operator (`.`) and the following syntax:

```
cout << "Number of objects: " << obj1.GetCount() << '\n';
```

However, this is not a recommended way to refer to a static member variable because there is no way to tell from looking at the statement that a static member variable is being accessed. It's considered better form to access static member variables using the scope resolution operator.

## Arrays of Static Member Variables

Static member variables can be grouped into arrays that work much like arrays of ordinary member variables. For example, you can use indirection—that is, addresses accessed through pointers—to set and read arrays of static member variables.

Listing 12.9 shows how you can create and use an array of static member variables in a C++ program.

#### Listing 12.9. An array of static member variables.

```
// 1209.CPP
// An array of static member variables

#include <iostream.h>

class Account {
private:
     static float mortgageInt;
     static float carInt;
     static float cardInt;
public:
     Account() {}
     ~Account() {}
     friend main();
     friend void SetVar(float *data, float interest);
};

class Mortgage: public Account {
private:
```

```
     static float mortgageInt;
};

class Car: public Account {
private:
     static float carInt;
};

class Card: public Account {
private:
     static float cardInt;
};

// initialize static member variables
float Account::mortgageInt = 5.4;
float Account::carInt = 12.9;
float Account::cardInt = 20.2;

void SetVar(float *data, float interest)
{
     *data = interest;
}

int main()
{
     // array of static member variables
     float* interestList [] = {
          &Account::mortgageInt,
          &Account::carInt,
          &Account::cardInt
     };

     cout << "Mortgage interest: "
          << *interestList[0] << '\n';
     cout << "Car interest: "
          << *interestList[1] << '\n';
     cout << "Credit card interest: "
          << *interestList[2] << '\n';

     SetVar(&Account::mortgageInt, 5.2);
     SetVar(interestList[1], 10.4);
     SetVar(interestList[2], 24.9);

     cout << "\nRevised mortgage Interest: "
          << *interestList[0] << '\n';
     cout << "Revised car Interest: "
          << Account::carInt << '\n';
     cout << "Revised credit card Interest: "
          << Account::cardInt << '\n';

     return 0;
};
```

The program in Listing 12.9 bears a strong resemblance to the program presented earlier in Listing 12.5. You shouldn't find that surprising because both programs show how to use arrays of member variables.

The program in Listing 12.9 defines a class named `Account`. The `Account` class has three static member variables that represent interest rates: `mortgageInt`, `carInt`, and `cardInt`.

The program instantiates three subclasses of the `Account` class. These three subclasses are named `Mortgage`, `Car`, and `Card`. Each subclass overrides one static member variable of the `Account` class. The `Mortgage` class overrides the static member variable `mortgageInt`, the `Car` class overrides the static member variable `carInt`, and the `Card` class overrides the static member variable `cardInt`.

When the `Mortgage`, `Car`, and `Card` classes have been defined, the static member variables `mortgageInt`, `carInt`, and `cardInt` are initialized:

```
float Account::mortgageInt = 5.4;
float Account::carInt = 12.9;
float Account::cardInt = 20.2;
```

In the `main()` segment of the program, an array is created to access the static member variables `mortgageInt`, `carInt`, and `cardInt`. The array, declared in this statement, is named `interestList`:

```
float* interestList [] = {
     &Account::mortgageInt,
     &Account::carInt,
     &Account::cardInt
};
```

When the preceding array has been declared, the contents of the array are printed. Then, these statements are executed to modify the values of the static member variables `mortgageInt`, `carInt`, and `cardInt`:

```
SetVar(&Account::mortgageInt, 5.2);
SetVar(interestList[1], 10.4);
SetVar(interestList[2], 24.9);
```

When the values of `mortgageInt`, `carInt`, and `cardInt` have been changed, their new values are printed. This is the output of the program:

```
Mortgage interest: 5.4
Car interest: 12.9
Credit card interest: 20.2

Revised mortgage interest: 5.2
Revised car interest: 10.4
Revised credit card interest: 24.9
```

## Special Rules About Static Member Variables

One of the oddest things about static member variables is the way they're initialized. Even if a static member variable is declared to be private, it can be (in fact, must be) initialized from outside the class in which it is declared.

There are also other nonstandard rules that govern the initialization of static member variables. These nonstandard initialization rules exist because a static member variable combines some features of a member variable with other features of a global variable:

- You can initialize a static member variable only once. If you attempt to initialize it again, the compiler returns a link error. However, once a static member variable is initialized, you can assign a new value to it as many times as you like during the execution of a program.
- You can't initialize a static member variable from within a constructor function. That's because a constructor can be called many times, and an object can be initialized only once in a C++ program.
- You can't initialize a static member variable from inside a header file because a header file might be included in a program more than once. Instead of being initialized in a header file, a static member variable must be initialized in the source module that contains the definitions of its class's member functions.
- Because of these rules, a private static member variable can be (in fact, must be) initialized from outside its class, in a stand-alone statement that appears outside any function. These same requirements apply to the initialization of *public* static member variables.
- Because you can't initialize a static member variable from inside a constructor or from inside a header file, some alternative had to be provided. That's why a private static member variable can be initialized in a stand-alone statement outside any class definition and outside any function.
- A static member variable can be accessed directly—without the need for a dot (`.`) or arrow (`->`) operator—from member functions of its class. But if you want to access a static member variable from outside its class, you must use the scope resolution operator (`::`), as in:

```
int LittleList::ct = 0;  // initialize static member variable
```

or:

```
cout << "Number of objects: " << LittleList::GetCount() << '\n';
```

### Features of Static Member Variables

To sum up, a static member variable is a member variable that:

- Exists for the lifetime of a program.
- Has only one instance shared by all objects that belong to a class.
- Exists even if there aren't any class objects. Thus, you can perform some operations on a static member variable—such as obtaining a pointer to it—even if no objects have been created for the variable's class.

## Static Member Functions

When a static member variable appears in a program, you can access the variable from a *static member function*. It is also possible to access a static member variable from a non-static member function. However, a static member function is specifically designed to access static member variables.

When you write a member function that accesses a static member variable, it's usually best to make the member function that accesses the variable a static member function. Then, when another programmer reads your code (or when you read it yourself after it gets cold), it's clear that the job of the function in question is to access a static member variable.

Refer back to Listing 12.8 and you'll see that a static member function named `GetCount()` is declared inside the definition of the `LittleList` class:

```
static int GetCount() { return ct; }      // static member function
```

In the program's `main()` function, this statement calls `GetCount()` to obtain the current number of objects:

```
cout << "Number of objects: " << LittleList::GetCount() << '\n';
```

Because `GetCount()` is a static member function, this statement uses the scope resolution operator (`::`) to access the function. As noted earlier in this section, `GetCount()` also could be accessed through any `LittleList` object using the dot operator (`.`), but the preceding syntax is preferred because it shows clearly that `GetCount()` is a static member function.

# Allocating Memory for Objects

There are two main ways to allocate memory for an object. You can create an object by calling the object's constructor from inside a function, or you can allocate memory for the object by invoking the `new` operator.

When an object is passed to a function as a parameter or is declared to be a local variable of a function, you can instantiate the object by invoking the class's constructor directly—that is, without using the `new` operator. Consider the definition of the class named `AClass` in Listing 12.10.

### Listing 12.10. Declaring an object as a local variable.

```
// 1210.CPP
// Declaring an object as a local variable

#include <iostream.h>

class AClass {
private:
     int x;
public:
     AClass() {}
     ~AClass() {}
     void SetX(int a) { x = a; }
     int GetX() { return x; }
};

void DoStuff()
{
     AClass myObject;

     myObject.SetX(500);
     int n = myObject.GetX();
     cout << n << '\n';
}

int main()
{
     DoStuff();
     return 0;
}
```

In the program in Listing 12.10, an object named `myObject` is instantiated as a local variable inside a function named `DoStuff()`. Because `myObject` is declared as a local variable, it has the same scope as any local variable; that is, the object is instantiated by the function that declares it (in this case, `DoStuff()`) and is destroyed when the function terminates.

Because `myObject` is instantiated as a local variable rather than through a pointer, the functions in the program can use the dot operator (`.`) to access members of `myObject`. For example, the `DoStuff()` function uses this statement to call the member function `myClass.GetX()`:

```
int n = myClass.GetX();
```

Obviously, this method of instantiating an object cannot be used to create objects that have global duration, unless the objects are declared in a program's `main()` function. When you want to create an object with a longer duration, you can instantiate it *dynamically*.

## Allocating Memory Dynamically

You can allocate memory for an object dynamically by allocating memory for the object with the `new` operator. The following program constructs an object by invoking the `new` operator:

```
class MyClass {
private:
     int x;
public:
     MyClass() {}                    // constructor
     ~MyClass() {}                   // destructor
     void SetX(int a) { x = a; }
};

int main()
{
     MyClass *myObject = new MyClass;
     myObject->SetX(100);
     // more code ...
     return 0;
}
```

You can use the preceding syntax to construct global objects, that is, objects that lie outside the scope of any function. When you want to create an object intended to last for the duration of a program, the best way to allocate memory for the object usually is to use the `new` operator.

When you construct an object dynamically, the `new` operator takes the name of a class as a target and returns a pointer to the specified class. So, when you initialize a class invoking the `new` operator, you must access members of the class through the pointer that the `new` operator returns.

When memory for an object is allocated dynamically, you can use the arrow operator (`->`) to access members of the object. For example, in the program shown above, this line calls the member function `SetX()`:

```
myObject->SetX(23);
```

## Frame Allocation

Calling an object's constructor directly, without using a pointer, is sometimes called *frame allocation*. When you create an object using frame allocation, you do not have to allocate memory for it using the `new` operator. You can simply call its constructor (if it has no constructor, the compiler will create one). Either way, you can instantiate the object using this syntax:

```
Birthday myBirthday;
```

When you create an object using frame allocation, you do not have to access the object through a pointer, so you do not have to create a pointer to the object. That means you can access members of the object using the dot operator (.) in this fashion:

```
myBirthday.PrintBirthday();
```

### How Frame Allocation Works

Frame allocation derives its name from a memory structure called a *stack frame* that is set up whenever a function is called. The stack frame is an area of memory on the stack that is set aside for use by a function when the function is called.

While the function is being executed, the stack frame created for the function holds the arguments passed to the function, as well as any local variables that the function requires. When the function terminates, the memory allocated for the stack frame is deallocated automatically.

Frame variables often are called *automatic variables* because the compiler automatically allocates the space for them.

When a program defines a variable that is local to a function, space for the variable is allocated on the stack frame when the function is called. If the parameters and variables required by the function are small and if there aren't many of them, the function's stack frame does not have to be very large. But if the function has a parameter or a variable that is a large array or a large data structure class, more space is required.

Fortunately, parameters and variables stored on a stack frame are automatically deleted when they go out of scope. Local variables declared by a function are deallocated when the function exits. But global variables also can be stored in a stack frame, and their scope lasts longer than the scope of local variables. And local variables declared inside blocks that are smaller than a function have a shorter scope than local variables.

When a C++ object is allocated on a stack frame, the procedure required to delete it is more complicated. When an object is declared using frame allocation, its constructor is automatically invoked when it is defined. When the object goes out of scope, its destructor is automatically invoked, deallocating the memory used by the object, along with any additional memory that the object may have allocated. (Destructors are described later under a separate heading.)

### Advantages and Disadvantages of Frame Allocation

The main advantage of creating objects on the stack frame is that you don't have to worry about deallocating them when you no longer need them. As soon as a function that contains a stack frame object terminates, the memory that has been allocated for the object is deallocated automatically. But you should be aware of the automatic calls being made, especially to the destructor.

The primary disadvantage of using frame allocation is that creating a large object on a stack frame can be quite costly in terms of memory requirements and execution speed. Generally speaking, creating large objects on stack frames is a bad habit. If you frequently create and delete stack frame objects during the execution of a program, the repetitive allocation and deallocation of memory that frame allocation causes can significantly denigrate the execution speed of the program.

Another fact to remember when you create an object using frame allocation is that frame variables cannot be used outside their scope.

## Heap Allocation

As mentioned earlier, you also can allocate memory for the object dynamically, by invoking the `new` operator (which is described in Chapter 9, "Managing

Memory"). When you create an object by invoking the `new` operator, space for the object is allocated on the *heap*—an area of memory, separate from the stack, where various kinds of objects required by applications are stored.

The heap is a section of memory that's reserved for the memory-allocation needs of the application that's being executed. So objects stored on the heap have a longer lifetime than objects stored in stack frames; they are not automatically deallocated every time a function terminates. That makes the heap a good place to store large objects. It's also a good place to store objects used by more than one procedure.

The technique of allocating memory for objects on the heap is sometimes referred to, quite logically, as *heap allocation*. To create an object using heap allocation, you can write this kind of declaration:

```
Birthday *myBirthday = new Birthday;
```

When you allocate memory for an object using heap allocation, you have to access the object through a pointer, so you do not create a pointer for it. Then, you can access members of the object using the arrow operator (`->`):

```
myBirthday->PrintBirthday();
```

For example, the C function `malloc()` allocates memory on the heap, and the C function `free()` deallocates heap memory. When you compile a Visual C++ program in Debug mode, the Microsoft Foundation Class (MFC) library provides modified (overloaded) versions of the `new` and `delete` operators to allocate and deallocate objects stored in the heap.

## Advantages and Disadvantages of Heap Allocation

The main advantages of heap allocation is that it requires less stack memory and makes programs run faster. The main disadvantage of heap allocation is that object variables stored in the heap aren't automatically deallocated when they're no longer needed. When you no longer need an object that's stored in the heap, you must remember to delete it by invoking the `delete` operator.

## The MFC Library's new and delete Commands

When you allocate and deallocate memory using the `new` and `delete` operators instead of relying on the C functions `malloc()` and `free()`, you can use certain debugging tools provided by the MFC library. That's because the versions of `new` and `delete` that the MFC library uses have built-in debugging support. The debugging tools provided by the MFC library's `new` and `delete` commands can be useful in detecting memory leaks. These tools are described in detail in the Visual C++ version of the Microsoft C++ *Class Library Reference.*

When you have finished debugging an application and are ready to build the Release version of the program, the `new` and `delete` operators provided by the Microsoft Foundation Class library are generally still the best way to allocate and deallocate memory for objects.

# Accessing Members of Objects

Beginning C++ programmers sometimes get confused about when to use the dot operator (`.`), the arrow operator (`->`), and scope resolution operator (`::`) to access objects and classes in class definitions, object declarations, and declarations of class members. If this topic still seems murky to you, the explanations in this section may help.

When you declare an identifier inside a class, you can access the identifier from outside the class by preceding it with the class identifier and either the dot operator (`.`), the arrow operator (`->`), or the scope resolution operator (`::`).

One important fact to remember is that the dot operator (`.`) and the arrow operator (`->`) are always used with names of objects, whereas the scope resolution operator (`::`) is always used with the name of a class.

## The Dot, Arrow, and Scope Resolution Operators

The dot operator and the arrow operator work the same way with member objects of classes as they do with elements of `struct` variables. The dot operator accesses an object directly, and the arrow operator accesses an object through a pointer.

For example, both of the following statements call member functions of objects. But the first statement calls a member function directly, whereas the second statement calls a member function through a pointer to an object:

```
int a = classy.VagueFunc();    // dot operator
int b = aPtr->VagueFunc();      // arrow operator
```

The scope resolution operator (`::`) is a new operator introduced by C++. It is used to access data members of an object not currently in scope. For example, this statement calls a member function of a class named `RealClass` when `RealClass` is not in scope:

```
int d = RealClass::VagueFunc();
```

Listing 12.11 illustrates several ways to use the dot operator (`.`), the arrow operator (`->`), and scope resolution operator (`::`) to access objects and classes.

### Listing 12.11. Operators for accessing classes and objects.

```
// 1211.CPP
// The scope resolution operator

#include <iostream.h>

int VagueFunc()
{
     return 2;
}

class RealClass {
public:
     int VagueFunc();
     int CallOtherVagueFunc()
          { return ::VagueFunc(); }
};

int RealClass::VagueFunc()
{
     return 1;
}

int main()
{
     RealClass classy;
     RealClass *aPtr = &classy;

     int a = classy.VagueFunc();     // dot operator
     int b = aPtr->VagueFunc();         // arrow operator
     int c = VagueFunc();              // not a member function
     int d = classy.CallOtherVagueFunc();

     cout << "\na = " << a << "\n";
     cout << "b = " << b << "\n";
     cout << "c = " << c << "\n";
     cout << "d = " << d << "\n";

     return 0;
}
```

In Listing 12.11, the statement

```
int a = classy.VagueFunc();    // dot operator
```

uses the dot operator (`.`) to call the version of `VagueFunc()` defined inside the definition of the class named `RealClass`. Then the statement assigns the value returned by `VagueFunc()` to variable `a`.

In this statement, a pointer named `aPtr` is set to point to the address of `classy`:

```
RealClass *aPtr = &classy;
```

Then the following statement uses the arrow operator (`->`) to call the member function `classy.VagueFunc()` and assigns the value returned by `classy.VagueFunc()` to the variable `b`:

```
int b = aPtr->VagueFunc();           // arrow operator
```

This statement

```
int c = VagueFunc();                // not a member function
```

contains no access operator, so it calls the version of `VagueFunc()` defined outside any block.

Next, this statement

```
int d = classy.CallOtherVagueFunc();
```

uses the dot operator to call the member function `classy.CallOtherVagueFunc()`. The `classy.CallOtherVagueFunc()` function then uses the scope resolution operator (`::`) to call the function `VagueFunc()`, which is not a member function of any class. This is the statement in which the member function `classy.CallOtherVagueFunc()` calls the nonmember function `VagueFunc()`:

```
int CallOtherVagueFunc()
    { return ::VagueFunc(); }
```

As you can see, the scope resolution operator is used alone in the statement shown here. So it calls the version `VagueFunc()` that is not a member function of a class.

Finally, the program prints this output to the screen:

```
a = 1
b = 1
c = 2
d = 2
```

## Using the (::) Operator in a Function Header

When you need to access a member function in a class outside the class's definition, you must have some way of telling the compiler what class the member function belongs to. You can do that by placing the scope resolution operator (::) in the header of the function, as follows:

```
int RealClass::VagueFunc()
{
     return 1;
}
```

Notice that in the header of this function definition, the scope resolution operator is placed between the name of the class that the function belongs to and the name of the function being defined. In other words, the scope resolution operator specifies the scope of the member function that you are defining.

To understand what this means, you must understand the concept of *class scope.* In C, as you may recall from Chapter 5, "Properties of Variables," objects have various kinds of scope. An object comes into scope when a program declares it, and an object goes out of scope when the program exits the block in which the object is declared (a *block* is any sequence of code inside curly brackets).

There are several kinds of blocks in C and C++, so objects declared in different kinds of blocks have different kinds of scopes. For example, objects in C++ programs can have local scope, function scope, file scope, prototype scope, and *class scope.*

In C++, all members of classes have class scope. For example, in the program presented in Listing 12.12, the class members `strength`, `charisma`, `GetAbils()`, and so on, all have class scope.

#### Listing 12.12. Creating multiple objects of a class.

```
// 1212.CPP
// Using a class

#include <iostream.h>

class  PlayerAbils {
```

*continues*

**Listing 12.12. continued**

```
private:
     int  strength;
     int  charisma;
     int  dexterity;
     int  intelligence;
protected:
     char *armor;
public:
     PlayerAbils() {}                   // constructor
     ~PlayerAbils() {}                  // destructor
     void      GetAbils();
     void      PrintAbils();
};

void PlayerAbils::GetAbils()
{
     strength = 24;
     charisma = 29;
     dexterity = 12;
     intelligence = 2;
     armor = "chain mail";
}

void PlayerAbils::PrintAbils()
{
     cout << "\nStrength: " << strength << "\n";
     cout << "Charisma: " << charisma << "\n";
     cout << "Dexterity: " << dexterity << "\n";
     cout << "Intelligence: " << intelligence << "\n\n";
     cout << "Armor: " << armor << "\n\n";
}


int main()
{
     PlayerAbils myPlayer;

     myPlayer.GetAbils();
     myPlayer.PrintAbils();
     return 0;
}
```

### HOW THE 1212.CPP PROGRAM WORKS

In the program shown in Listing 12.12, this statement initiates an object named `myPlayer` by creating an instance of the `PlayerAbils` class:

```
PlayerAbils myPlayer;
```

You could write similar statements to instantiate other objects of the `PlayerAbils` class. For example:

```
PlayerAbils yourPlayer;
PlayerAbils mikesPlayer;
PlayerAbils marjoriesPlayer;
```

The format used in these examples is not the only format for instantiating an object. Other formats for creating objects include the following:

```
PlayerAbils ourPlayers[6];          // creates an array of objects
PlayerAbils *dataPtr;               // creates a pointer to an
                                       object
PlayerAbils analyzeData(char *);    // creates a function prototype
```

Because each of these instantiations is different, each does, of course, have a different result. The preceding three instantiations create:

- An array named `ourPlayers`, which contains six `PlayerAbils` objects.
- A pointer named `dataPtr`, which contains the address of a `PlayerAbils` object.
- A prototype of a function named `analyzeData`. The `analyzeData` function takes a pointer to a `char` as a parameter, and returns a `PlayerAbils` object.

## How the Scope Resolution Operator Works

Because the scope resolution operator identifies the scope of a class member, the scope resolution operator must always be followed by the name of a class member. For example, if this class definition appears in a program

```
class RealClass {
private:
     int x;
public:
    int VagueFunc();
};
```

then you can define the member function `VagueFunc()` with the scope resolution operator, using this format:

```
int RealClass::VagueFunc()
{
     return 1;
}
```

If a scope resolution operator is preceded by an identifier, the identifier that precedes the operator must be the name of a user-defined type, usually a class. If you make a mistake and precede the scope resolution operator with the name of an object rather than the name of a class, the compiler generates an error.

Listing 12.13 shows how you can use the scope resolution operator in a C++ program.

### Listing 12.13. More uses for the (: :) operator.

```
// 1213.CPP
// Demonstrating class- and object-related operators

#include <iostream.h>

int VagueFunc()      // a function with file scope
{
     return 1;
}

class RealClass {
private:
     int x;
public:
    int VagueFunc();      // a function with class scope
};

int RealClass::VagueFunc()
{
     return ::VagueFunc() + 1;
}
```

```
RealClass classy;          // creating a RealClass object named classy

int main()
{
     RealClass myObj;

     int a = VagueFunc();            // calling function with block scope
     int b = myObj.VagueFunc();      // calling function with class scope

     cout << "\n" << a << "\n";
     cout << b << "\n";

     return 0;                      // what the main() function returns
}
```

## File Scope and Class Scope

In Listing 12.13, there are two functions named `VagueFunc()`. One version is defined outside any class, so it has file scope. The other version of `VagueFunc()` is defined inside the definition of the class named `RealClass`, so it has class scope.

The version of `VagueFunc()` defined outside any class returns a 1. And the version of the function declared inside the definition of `RealClass` calls the function that has file scope and adds 1 to the value that the function returns. `VagueFunc()` returns a value of 1, so the result of this calculation is 2.

When the statement

```
int a = VagueFunc();
```

is executed, the version of `VagueFunc()` that has file scope is called. Consequently, `a` is assigned a value of 1.

Next, the statement

```
int b = myObj.VagueFunc();
```

is executed. In this statement, the function identifier `VagueFunc()` is preceded by the name of a `RealClass` object named `myObj`. So the version of `VagueFunc()` that has class scope is called, and `b` is assigned a value of 2.

Thus, the program's output is:

```
1
2
```

# Access Specifiers

When you write a class definition, you can create member variables that are accessible only to objects that belong to the class. You also can create member variables that are accessible from all functions in a program—or from functions defined in derived classes.

To help you limit access to members of a class, C++ provides three special keywords called access specifiers. By placing access specifiers in the definition of a class, you can make any member of the class `private`, `public`, or `protected`—that is, somewhere in between.

When you declare a class member to be `private`, the member is accessible only from member functions of its own class or from member functions of other classes specifically declared to be *friends* of their own class (`friend` classes are described in more detail in Chapter 13.)

A `protected` member of a class is accessible from member functions of its own class and from member functions of classes derived from that class.

A `public` member of a class is accessible from member functions of its own class and from other functions that declare an instance of that class.

## Encapsulation

In C++, the keywords `private`, `public`, or `protected` provide the key to data encapsulation. They can help you ensure the integrity of the data encapsulated inside a class by making that data inaccessible to functions outside the class in which it is declared.

Members of a class are private by default, so you don't have to do anything to encapsulate a member variable of a class. Unless you specify otherwise, the default value of every member of a class is `private`, and the compiler enforces that privacy on your behalf.

Fortunately, though, you do have a say in this. When you design a class, you can specify data members that you want to hide so that they can't be inadvertently altered from functions inside the program that lie outside the class in which they are declared.

Listing 12.14 is a small program that shows how the access specifiers `private` and `public` can be used to support data encapsulation in a C++ program.

#### Listing 12.14. Using a class in C++.

```
/*** 1214 .CPP ***/
/*** Using a class in C++ ***/

#include <iostream.h>

class OneAbil {
private:
     int strength;
public:
     void SetStrength(int str) { strength = str; }
     int GetStrength() { return strength; }
};

OneAbil myAbil;

int main()
{
     myAbil.SetStrength(24);
     int str = myAbil.GetStrength();
     cout << '\n' << str << '\n';
     return 0;
}
```

The program named in Listing 12.14 defines a class named `OneAbil` and then declares an object of the `OneAbil` class. The name of the object is `myAbil`. The `myAbil` object is accessed from the program's `main()` function.

The `OneAbil` class contains one private member variable named `strength`. Because `strength` is a private member variable, it can't be accessed from the program's `main()` segment. However, the `OneAbil` class also defines two public member functions that the `main()` function can use to access the `strength` variable indirectly. They are named `GetStrength()` and `SetStrength()`

The functions `GetStrength()` and `SetStrength()` have access to the private member variable `strength` because both of those functions, like the `strength` variable, are member functions of the `OneAbil` class. Because `GetStrength()` and `SetStrength()` are public member functions of the `OneAbil` class, the `main()` function can access the `strength` variable indirectly by calling `myAbil.GetStrength()` and `myAbil.SetStrength()`.

When you execute the program, the `main()` function assigns a value of 24 to the `strength` variable by calling `myAbil.SetStrength()` and then obtains the value of the `strength` variable by calling `myAbil.GetStrength()`. That done, the `main()` function prints the value of the `strength` variable (24) to standard output, normally the screen.

Because `GetStrength()` and `SetStrength()` are both member functions of the object named `myAbil`, any function that is not a member of the `OneAbil` class must follow a rigid procedure to access the two functions. Specifically, a function that isn't a member of the `OneAbil` class cannot access either function unless it invokes the name of an object that belongs to the `OneAbil` class, followed by the dot access operator (`.`):

```
myAbil.SetStrength(24);
int str = myAbil.GetStrength();
```

The requirement to access an object's member functions in this fashion provides a measure of protection to private member variables. For example, even though the value of the private member variable `strength` can be changed indirectly through the public member function `myAbil.SetStrength()`, that is the only way that it can be changed.

## Using Access Specifiers

As mentioned earlier, class definitions begin with the `private` access mode as the default mode, so you can omit the `private` label if you list the `private` members of a class first. However, it's a good idea to use the *private* label because it makes your intentions clear to others who read your code.

You can use the `private`, `public`, and `protected` labels in any order and as often as you want in a class definition, but most programmers group the `private`, `protected`, and `public` members separately. The effect of an access specifier lasts until another access specifier appears in the class definition or the class definition ends.

The program presented earlier in Listing 12.12 provides another example of how access specifiers can be used in a C++ program. In Listing 12.12, the definition of the `PlayerAbils` class contains all three access specifiers:

```
class  PlayerAbils {
private:
     int  strength;
     int  charisma;
     int  dexterity;
     int  intelligence;
protected:
     char *armor;
public:
     void      GetAbils();
     void      PrintAbils();
};
```

As you can see, this program contains four member variables—`strength`, `charisma`, `dexterity`, and `intelligence`—and two member functions. The two member functions are `PlayerAbils::GetAbils()`, which obtain data to be printed, and `PlayerAbils::PrintAbils()`, which outputs the data that `PlayerAbils::GetAbils()` obtains.

In the `PlayerAbils` class declared at the beginning of the program, the member variables `strength`, `charisma`, `dexterity`, and `intelligence` are declared to be private; the member functions `PlayerAbils::GetAbils()` and `PlayerAbils::PrintAbils()` are declared to be `public`; and the member variable `armor` is declared to be `protected`:

Because all members of the class are private by default, you could eliminate the `private` label from the preceding code fragment without changing the access specifications of any of the class's members. The member variables `strength`, `charisma`, `dexterity`, and `intelligence` would still be `private` because the first members declared in a C++ class are private by default; the member functions `PlayerAbils::GetAbils()` and `PlayerAbils::PrintAbils()` would remain `public` because they are explicitly declared to be public.

## Interpreting Access Specifiers

The access specifiers used in the 1212.CPP can be interpreted as follows:

- The four integer variables declared to be `private` are accessible only from functions declared inside the definition of the `PlayerAbils` class. That means the variables `strength`, `charisma`, `dexterity`, and `intelligence` are accessible only through the public member functions named `GetAbils()` and `PrintAbils()`.
- The character-pointer variable named `armor` is declared to be `protected`. That means it can be accessed by the public member functions `GetAbils()` and `PrintAbils()` and also from any functions that may be declared inside the definitions of derived classes.
- The member functions `GetAbils()` and `PrintAbils()` are declared to be `public`. That means they can be accessed from any function in the 1212.CPP program.

Consider all these rules for a moment, and you'll see that although the member variables `strength`, `charisma`, `dexterity`, and `intelligence` can't be accessed from outside the `Player` class—because they're all declared to be `private`—they can be accessed *indirectly* from any function in the 1212.CPP program.

If a function outside the `PlayerAbils` class needs to obtain the value of one of the class's private variables, all the outside function has to do is call the public member function `GetAbils()`. Similarly, a function outside the `Player` class can print the value of any of the class's private members by calling the public member function `PrintAbils()`.

## The public Access Specifier

When you declare a member function or a member variable to be `public`, the member is accessible from any function in the program in which the class is declared. Although it might sound tempting to declare every member of every class public—because that would make it easy to access all members of every class—that really isn't a good idea. The purpose of access specifications is to safeguard the data members of classes from being accidentally changed—in the same way that global variables often are changed inadvertently in programs written in procedural languages. If you declared all members of all classes to be public, they would have no protection at all.

In programs written in C++, a common practice is to declare the member variables of a class private, but to provide indirect access to the data that they contain through member *functions* declared to be public. Later in this section, you'll see examples showing exactly how this technique works.

## The private Access Specifier

In a C++ program, private class members have the strictest access control. When a member variable or member function is explicitly assigned private access or has private access by default, it can be accessed only from:

- Inside the class in which it is declared.
- Inside a class specifically declared to be a `friend` of the class in which the member is declared. (Friend classes are examined more closely in Chapter 13.)

In Chapter 12, as you have seen, the member variables `strength`, `charisma`, `dexterity`, and `intelligence` are declared to be `private`. That means these variables cannot be directly accessed—and therefore cannot be inadvertently changed—by functions that are not members of the `PlayerAbils` class. However, they can be *indirectly* accessed from any function in the 1212.CPP program. Indeed, they are accessed from within the main function, as follows:

```
int main()
{
     myPlayer.GetAbils();
     myPlayer.PrintAbils();
     return 0;
}
```

This code segment indirectly accesses the private member variables `strength`, `charisma`, `dexterity`, and `intelligence` by calling the public member functions `PlayerAbils::GetAbils()` and `PlayerAbils::PrintAbils()`.

Because `PlayerAbils::GetAbils()` and `PlayerAbils::PrintAbils()` are member functions of the `PlayerAbils` class, both functions have access to the private member variables `strength`, `charisma`, `dexterity`, and `intelligence`. Therefore, you can use `PlayerAbils::GetAbils()` to obtain the values of the variables `strength`, `charisma`, `dexterity`, `intelligence`, and `armor`, and you can use `PlayerAbils::PrintAbils()` to write these values to the screen, in this format:

```
Strength: 24
Charisma: 29
Dexterity: 12
Intelligence: 2
```

**IMPORTANT**

Although `private` access makes a member inaccessible to portions of a program outside a class, it does not make the member invisible. Access specifiers were not designed to hide class members from prying eyes, but to safeguard them from being inadvertently changed by functions outside the classes in which they are defined.

Because access specifications are not airtight, you can override their effects in various ways. For instance, by recasting a pointer to a class object into a pointer to an `unsigned char`, you can gain access to the entire contents of the object, including its private and protected parts. In general, you should avoid using techniques such as this to defeat the purpose of access specifications. You might want to override access labels in writing code for utilities such as class browsers or debuggers, but not in the ordinary course of application development.

## The protected Access Specifier

A class member declared to be `private` within a base class is *not* recognized by classes that inherit from the base class. However, you can make a member of a base class accessible to functions in classes derived from the base class by declaring the member to be `protected`.

To understand how protected access works, it helps to have an understanding of class inheritance. Inheritance was introduced in Chapter 10 and is examined more closely in Chapter 19, "Inheritance and Polymorphism."

# Publicly and Privately Derived Objects

As you have seen, you can use the access specifiers `private`, `protected`, and `public` to permit, limit, or prohibit outside access to the member functions of a class. C++ provides a similar technique that lets you limit outside access to whole classes. A class that is accessible from any function in a program is called a *publicly derived* class. A class that has limited access is called a *privately derived* class.

> **ARE PRIVATELY DERIVED CLASSES REALLY NECESSARY?**
>
> Privately derived classes were created to make the access rules that C++ imposes on objects—which are pretty strict already—even tighter. Some C++ programmers feel that privately derived classes are overkill and never use them. In fact, I've never talked with a C++ programmer who used them very much. On the other hand, the designers of C++ must have thought that privately derived classes have some usefulness, or they wouldn't have included them in the language. So they're there if you need them, OK?

You can create a publicly derived class by using the keyword `public` in the class's declaration. You can create a privately derived class by using the keyword `private` in the declaration of the class.

In the Zalthar program, the keyword `public` is used to declare that the `Warrior` class is publicly derived from the `Player` class:

```
class Warrior: public Player
```

To make the `Warrior` class a privately derived class, you could declare it using the keyword `private`:

```
class Warrior: private Player
```

## Public Derivation

If a class is publicly derived from a parent class, the derived class begins its life as a duplicate of the parent class with a different name. Later, if you like, you can customize the derived class by adding new members to the derived class or by modifying members that the derived class inherits from its base class.

All the classes in the example programs that have been presented so far in this book are publicly derived classes. When a class is derived publicly, it can access the public and protected members of its base class, but it cannot access its base class's private members. Public members of the base class automatically become public members of the derived class, and protected members of the base class automatically become protected members of the derived class; you don't have to redefine them in the derived class.

Of course, because a derived class cannot access its parent class's private members, they do not become members of the derived class.

When a class is publicly derived from a parent class, the derived class is sometimes called "is-a" with respect to the parent class. The "is-a" description means that the derived class is a copy of the parent class.

For example, in the Zalthar program, the `Warrior` class "is-a" `Player`, and the `Gnome` class "is-a" `Warrior`. So the `Warrior` class inherits all public and protected members of the `Player` class, and the `Gnome` class inherits all public and protected members of the `Warrior` class.

## Private Derivation

When a class inherits a member variable from another class, the kind of derivation that takes place is called *private derivation*. When a subclass is privately derived from a base class, the public and protected members of the base class become *private* members of the derived class. So if the derived class is used as a base class for more derived classes, the classes that derive from it *do not have access to the public or protected members of the original base class.*

Figure 12.1 shows how public and private derivation work in C++. The class `highClass` has three member variables. The variable `spectacle` is public; the variable `vault` is protected; and the variable `keepOut` is private.

The class `middleClass` is publicly derived from `highClass`. So it inherits the public variable `spectacle` and the protected variable `vault`, but it doesn't inherit the variable `keepOut`, because `keepOut` is private.

The class `workingClass` is *privately* derived from `middleClass`. So `workingClass` inherits the public variable `spectacle` and the protected variable `vault`. However, in objects of the class `workingClass`, both `spectacle` and `vault` now become private variables.

Finally, the class `noClass` is derived from `workingClass`. Because `workingClass` has made the `spectacle` and `vault` variables private (because `workingClass` is privately derived from `middleClass`), the class `noClass` does not have access to the `workingClass` variables `spectacle` and `vault`.

Private derivation is sometimes called a "has-a" derivation. For example, in Figure 12.1, `middleClass` is publicly derived from `highClass`, so `middleClass` "is-a" `highClass`. However, `workingClass` is privately derived from `middleClass`, so `workingClass` "is-not-a" `middleClass`, and `middleClass` "is-not-a" `workingClass`. However, `middleClass` "has-a" `workingClass`.

# Creating Multiple Objects of a Class

When you have defined a class, you can declare multiple instances of a class in the same way that you declare multiple instances of a `struct`. When you create multiple instances of a class, each class that you define receives its own memory allocation.

## Creating Arrays of Objects

Sometimes it's useful to create an array of objects. Then, you can set up a loop to perform a particular action on every object in the array, for example, to assign a value to the same member variable of every object in the array.

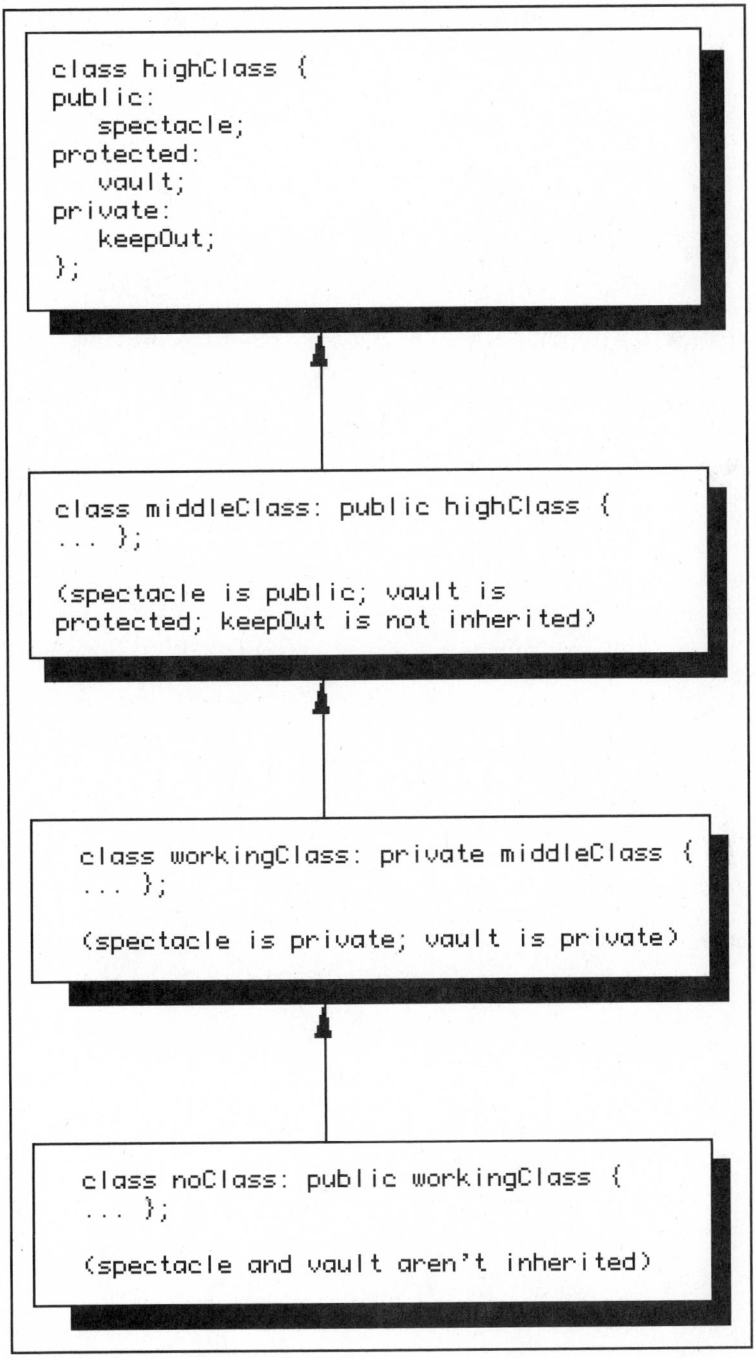
class highClass {
public:
spectacle;
protected:
vault;
private:
keepOut;
};
class middleClass: public highClass {
... };
(spectacle is public; vault is protected; keepOut is not inherited)
class workingClass: private middleClass {
... };
(spectacle is private; vault is private)
class noClass: public workingClass {
... };
(spectacle and vault aren't inherited)

*Figure 12.1. Public and private derivation.*

Arrays of objects are so useful in C++ that a special mechanism for initializing arrays of objects is provided. To instantiate an array of objects, all you have to do is define the class that you want to instantiate and then declare the array in a statement written in this format:

```
AClass anObject[12];
```

This statement initializes an array of 12 objects that are members of a class named `AClass`. The 12 objects in the array are named `anObject[0]` through `anObject[11]`.

When a program contains an array of class declarations like this one, the program calls the constructor of each object in the array—provided the class has a constructor. Every well-behaved object has a constructor, but if, by some chance, no constructor is available, the compiler creates a constructor for the class and creates the array of objects anyway.

The code in Listing 12.15 creates an array of objects and then uses a pair of loops to perform two kinds of actions on each member of the array. The first loop accesses each object in the array. Each time an object is accessed, the loop sets the value of the member variable named `strength` that belongs to each object. The second loop reads the value of each `strength` variable that has been set.

**Listing 12.15. Creating an array of objects.**

```
// 1215.CPP
// Creating an array of objects

#include <iostream.h>

char *className [3] = { "WARRIOR", "GNOME", "WIZARD" };

class Stamina {
private:
     int strength;
public:
     Stamina() { strength = 0; }
     Stamina(int s) { strength = s; }
     int GetValue() { return strength; }
     void SetValue(int s) { strength = s; }
};
```

```
Stamina players[3];

int playerStrength[3] = { 24, 28, 12 };

int main()
{
     int n;
     for (n = 0; n < 3; n++)
          players[n].SetValue(playerStrength[n]);
     for (n = 0; n < 3; n++) {
          cout << className[n] << ": ";
          cout << players[n].GetValue() << '\n';
          }
     return 0;
}
```

Listing 12.15 instantiates an array of objects that belong to a class called `Stamina`. The objects in the array are named `players[0]` through `players[2]`. This is the statement that creates the array:

```
Stamina players[3];
```

When the program in Listing 12.15 has created an array of objects, this loop sets the values of the member variables `players[0].strength`, `players[1].strength`, and `players[2].strength`:

```
for (n = 0; n < 3; n++)
     players[n].SetValue(playerStrength[n]);
```

Finally, this loop reads the value of each `strength` variable in the array:

```
for (n = 0; n < 3; n++) {
     cout << className[n] << ": ";
     cout << players[n].GetValue() << '\n';
     }
```

This is the program's output:

```
WARRIOR: 24
GNOME: 28
WIZARD: 12
```

The objects instantiated in Listing 12.15 were created by calling a class constructor that took no arguments. Listing 12.16 shows how to create an array of objects by calling a constructor that does take arguments. Then, a `for` loop is created to display the values of the member variables of each object in the array.

### Listing 12.16. Another array of objects.

```
// 1216.CPP
// An array of objects

#include <iostream.h>

class Abilities {
private:
     int strength;
     int dexterity;
     int charisma;
     int intelligence;
public:
     Abilities(int stren, int dext, int charis, int intel) :
          strength(stren), dexterity(dext), charisma(charis),
          intelligence(intel) {}
     ~Abilities() {}
     friend int main(); // give main() access to data
};

int main()
{
     Abilities myPlayer[3] = {
          Abilities(23, 26, 19, 12),
          Abilities(24, 19, 18, 32),
          Abilities(29, 30, 31, 28)
     };
     for (int n = 0; n < 3; n++) {
          cout << "\nPLAYER NO. " << n+1 << '\n';
          cout << "Strength: " << myPlayer[n].strength << '\n';
          cout << "Dexterity: " << myPlayer[n].dexterity << '\n';
          cout << "Charisma: " << myPlayer[n].charisma << '\n';
          cout << "Intelligence: "
               << myPlayer[n].intelligence << '\n';
     }
     return 0;
};
```

In Listing 12.16, this is the statement that initializes an array of objects:

```
Abilities myPlayer[3] = {
     Abilities(23, 26, 19, 12),
     Abilities(24, 19, 18, 32),
     Abilities(29, 30, 31, 28)
};
```

This is the loop that prints the values of the data members of objects in the array:

```
for (int n = 0; n < 3; n++) {
     cout << "\nPLAYER NO. " << n+1 << '\n';
     cout << "Strength: " << myPlayer[n].strength << '\n';
     cout << "Dexterity: " << myPlayer[n].dexterity << '\n';
     cout << "Charisma: " << myPlayer[n].charisma << '\n';
     cout << "Intelligence: "
          << myPlayer[n].intelligence << '\n';
}
```

The output of the program is:

```
PLAYER NO. 1
Strength: 23
Dexterity: 26
Charisma: 19
Intelligence: 12

PLAYER NO. 2
Strength: 24
Dexterity: 19
Charisma: 18
Intelligence: 32

PLAYER NO. 3
Strength: 29
Dexterity: 30
Charisma: 31
Intelligence: 28
```

## Creating Arrays of Pointers to Objects

By using pointers, you can access objects in an array very easily and conveniently. When you want to access data members of an array using pointers, the trick is to set up an array of *pointers* to an array of objects. Listing 12.17 shows how.

### Listing 12.17. An array of pointers to objects.

```
// 1217.CPP
// Creating an array with pointers

#include <iostream.h>

char *className [3] = { "WARRIOR", "GNOME", "WIZARD" };
```

*continues*

**Listing 12.17. continued**

```
class Brains {
private:
     int intelligence;
     friend int main();  // give main() access to data
public:
     Brains() {}
     ~Brains() {}
};

Brains players[3];
Brains *playerPtr[3];

int playerBrains[3] = { 24, 28, 12 };

int main()
{
     int n;
     for (n = 0; n < 3; n++)
          playerPtr[n] = &players[n];

     for (n = 0; n < 3; n++)
          playerPtr[n]->intelligence = playerBrains[n];
     for (n = 0; n < 3; n++) {
          cout << className[n] << ": ";
          cout << playerPtr[n]->intelligence << '\n';
          }
     return 0;
}
```

In Listing 12.17, these two statements instantiate an array of three objects and then create an array of pointers to those objects:

```
Brains players[3];
Brains *playerPtr[3];
```

When these two arrays have been created, the following statements use `for` loops to set and read the values of data members of the objects in the arrays:

```
for (n = 0; n < 3; n++)
     playerPtr[n]->intelligence = playerBrains[n];
for (n = 0; n < 3; n++) {
     cout << className[n] << ": ";
     cout << playerPtr[n]->intelligence << '\n';
     }
```

This is the output of the program:

```
WARRIOR: 24
GNOME: 28
WIZARD: 12
```

# Techniques for Designing Classes

There are several special techniques that you can use when you design classes for C++ programs. For example, you can create:

- *Nested classes.* When the definition of one class is placed inside the definition of another class, the inner class is called a nested class.
- *Composed classes.* When the *declaration* of one class appears inside the definition of another class, the outer class is called a composed class.
- *Friend classes.* In the definition of a class, you can declare a class to be a friend of another class. When a class grants friendship status to another class, the class designated as a friend has access to private and protected members of the other class.
- *Incomplete class declarations.* These declarations are provided so that a class can be referenced before it is fully defined.
- *Empty classes.* These classes don't do anything, but they can serve as placeholders during the development of a program.

## Nested Classes

In C++, you can place the definition of a class inside the definition of another class. A class defined inside the definition of another class is called a *nested class.* When you nest a class, the nested class is considered to be within the scope of the enclosing class.

> **A MICROSOFT FEATURE**
>
> In Visual C++, a nested class does not have any special privileges to access members of its enclosing class; for example, it can't access private members of its enclosing class. Some other implementations of C++ have different rules regarding nested classes. For example, in Borland C++, a nested class does have access to its enclosing class's private members.

Listing 12.18 shows how you can use a nested class in a C++ program. In the example, a class named `ClassB` is nested inside another class named `ClassA`.

**Listing 12.18. Using nested classes.**

```
// 1218.CPP

#include <iostream.h>

class ClassA {
private:
     int x;
public:
     class ClassB {
     private:
          int y;
     public:
          ClassB() {}                          // constructor
          void SetY() { y = 2; }
          int GetY() { return y; }
     };

     ClassA() {}                          // constructor
     void SetX() { x = 1; }
     int GetX() { return x; }
};

int main()
{
     ClassA    myObjectA;
     ClassA::ClassB myObjectB;

     myObjectA.SetX();    // initialize myObjectA.x (private)
     myObjectB.SetY();    // initialize myObjectA.myObjectB.y (private)

     int x = myObjectA.GetX();
     int y = myObjectB.GetY();      // y is in nested class ClassB

     cout << x << '\n';
     cout << y << '\n';

     return 0;
}
```

The program shown in Listing 12.18 contains an outer class named `ClassA` and a nested class named `ClassB`. The `main()` segment of the program creates an object belonging to `ClassA` by declaring the object. The program then creates an object that belongs to `ClassB` by using the scope resolution operator. The object that belongs to the outer class is named `myObjectA`, and the object that belongs to the nested class is named `myObjectB`.

These are the statements that create the two objects:

```
ClassA          myObjectA;
ClassA::ClassB       myObjectB;
```

After the object named `myObjectB` is created, its members can be accessed from the `main()` segment in the same way that members of `myObjectA` are accessed. For example, the first of these two statements calls a member function of `myObjectA`, and the second calls a member function of `myObjectB`:

```
int x = myObjectA.GetX();
int y = myObjectB.GetY();     // y is in nested class ClassB
```

Nested classes aren't terribly useful in C++ programming, because they seldom, if ever, offer any real benefits that couldn't be achieved more easily and more elegantly in other ways. For example, instead of nesting a whole class inside another class, you can simply place the *declaration* of a class inside the definition of another class. Then, you can place the *definition* of the declared class outside the definition of the other class.

## Composed Classes

When you place a declaration of another class inside the definition of another class, the class that contains the declaration is called a *composed class*. When an object belongs to a class that's declared inside another class, the object is called a *subobject*.

The technique of creating a composed class is illustrated in Listing 12.19.

### Listing 12.19. A composed class.

```
// 1219.CPP

#include <iostream.h>

class ClassB {
private:
     int y;
public:
     ClassB() {}                        // constructor
     void SetY() { y = 2; }
     int GetY() { return y; }
};
```

*continues*

**Listing 12.19. continued**

```
class ClassA {
private:
     int x;
public:
     ClassA() {}                              // constructor
     ClassB myObjectB;
     void SetX() { x = 1; }
     int GetX() { return x; }
     int GetY() { return myObjectB.GetY(); }
     void SetY() { myObjectB.SetY(); }
};

int main()
{
     ClassA     myObjectA;

     myObjectA.SetX();                   // initialize myObjectA.x (private)
     myObjectA.SetY();                   // initialize myObjectA.myObjectB.y

     int x = myObjectA.GetX();
     int y = myObjectA.GetY();

     cout << x << '\n';
     cout << y << '\n';

     return 0;
}
```

Listing 12.19 contains definitions of a class named `ClassA` and a class named `ClassB`. The definition of the class named `ClassB` appears outside the definition of `ClassA`. However, an object that belongs to a class named `ClassB` is declared inside the definition of `ClassA`. This object is named `myObjectB`.

Because the `myObjectB` object is declared inside the definition of `ClassA`, public member functions of `ClassB` can be accessed from within `ClassA` just as if they were member functions of `ClassA`. For example, these member functions of `ClassA` access public member functions of `ClassB`:

```
int GetY() { return myObjectB.GetY(); }
void SetY() { myObjectB.SetY(); }
```

Composed classes are used more often than nested classes because they make better use of the advantages of data encapsulation and data abstraction. When you have created a composed class that contains a declaration of another class, you can access all the members of both classes without knowing or caring whether they are defined in the composed (outer) class or in the class that's declared inside the composed class.

In Listing 12.19, for example, the function `SetY()` is defined inside the definition of `ClassB` but can be called from inside `ClassA` through another function also named `SetY()`. Because of this feature, the program's `main()` function does not have to initialize a `ClassB` object in order to call the `SetY()` function defined inside `ClassB`. Instead, the `main()` function calls the `ClassB::SetY()` function just as if the function were defined inside `ClassA`:

```
myObjectA.SetY();
```

## Local Classes

A class defined inside a function is called a *local class*. Because all the information about the class must appear inside the function in which the class is defined, you can't define a local class in one scope and then declare it in another. Furthermore, a local class can't access the automatic (local) variables of its enclosing function. Because of these limitations, local classes are usually used to perform simple chores that can be handled with short inline functions.

This short program shows the architecture of a local class:

```
main()
{
     class LocalClass {
          int x;
     public:
          LocalClass() {}
          int GetX() { return x; }
     };
     LocalClass myLocalClass;
     int a = myLocalClass.GetX();
     return 0;
}
```

Local classes aren't widely used in C++ programs. The consensus is that if you go to the trouble to create a class, you should go ahead and make it a full-fledged class that more than one function can access. If you don't do that, why bother?

## friend Classes

Another alternative to using nested classes is to make a class a *friend* of another class by writing a definition that begins with the keyword `friend`. When you declare a class to be a friend of another class, the class granted friendship status has access to all private and protected members of the other class. Functions can also be friends of classes.

Protected and public members of classes are described in more detail in the section of this chapter titled "Member Variables." Friend objects and friend classes are described in more detail in Chapter 13.

## Incomplete Class Declarations

A class, like a function, must be declared before it can be accessed by any other functions in a program. Sometimes, however, you may need to reference a class in a program before it is fully defined. This situation can arise when, for example, you want to reference a class, but the definition of the class appears in some other file.

In a case like this, you can place an incomplete declaration of the class in your program. An incomplete declaration of a class is a forward reference to the class; it works like a forward reference to a function works in a program written in a procedural language.

When you have placed a forward reference to a class in a program, you can declare a global pointer to the class. However, you can't reference the class directly because its members have not yet been defined, and its size is therefore not yet known.

This code fragment shows how an incomplete class declaration can be used in a C++ program:

```
// incomplete class declaration
// (forward reference to a class)
class ToComeClass;

// define a global pointer to the class
ToComeClass* globalPtr;

int main()
{
     // now we can declare the full class
     class ToComeClass {
```

```
    public;
          ToComeClass();
          ToComeClass* MemberFunction();
    };
    ToComeClass      myObject; // now a ToComeClass object ...
                              // ... can be declared
// more code
    return 0;
}
```

In this example, the first statement after the initial comments is an incomplete class declaration. That incomplete class definition serves as a forward reference to the class named `ToComeClass`. When the compiler reaches the statement in which the pointer is declared, the compiler doesn't know the size of the object that is the target of the pointer. But it does know that there is a class named `ToComeClass`, so the pointer to the class can be declared without generating a compiler error.

A compiler error is generated, however, if you try to instantiate an object belonging to a class that has been incompletely declared. Before you can create an object that belongs to a class, the class must be defined. In this example, once the class named `ToComeClass` has been defined, objects that belong to the class can be instantiated.

## Empty Classes

When software engineers develop a program in a procedural language, they often place functions called *stubs* in the program. A stub is a function that doesn't do anything, but is placed in a program as a placeholder, to be replaced with a real function later in the course of the program's developing.

In C++, you can place an empty class in a program, in the same way that you would place a function stub in a program written in a procedural language. An empty class doesn't do anything either, except it also serves as a placeholder to be replaced with a real class when the class that it represents is fully identified or fully implemented.

You can place an empty class in a program by placing this kind of class definition in a program:

```
class NoClass {};
```

When you have defined an empty class, you can declare objects of the class, even though they also will be nonfunctional:

```
int main()
```

```
{
    NoClass noObject;
    // more code ...
    return 0;
}
```

When you have defined an empty class in a program that's being developed and have placed a declaration of the object in the program, the declaration will create an object as soon as the object's definition is filled in.

# Scope and Linkage of Objects

Class objects follow the same scope rules as other data types. You can declare objects using the storage-class specifiers `static` and `extern`. An object declared to be `static` has a *static lifetime*, and an object declared to be `extern` has *external linkage*.

## Objects with External Linkage

An object with external linkage is accessible from any translation unit of a program. When an object in a program has external linkage, its name can appear in any translation unit in the program and is always guaranteed to refer to the same object.

An object that has external linkage comes into scope when a program begins and goes out of scope when the program ends. Thus, an object with external linkage also has static lifetime.

When you declare a global object—that is, when an object's declaration appears outside any function—the object's storage class specifier is `extern` by default.

If you want a local object to have external linkage, you must specifically declare it as `static` or `extern`.

## Objects with Static Duration

An object with *static duration* retains its value during the execution of a program. When a global object in a program has static storage class, the object is initialized at program startup and does not go out of scope until the program ends.

When a local object in a program is declared as `static`, the object is initialized the first time its declaration is encountered and stays in scope throughout the duration of the program.

Local objects must be explicitly declared as `static` or `extern` to have static storage class.

# The this Pointer

Listing 12.20 shows the use of the `this` pointer: a special pointer that C++ creates each time an object is instantiated in a program. Every member function of a class has a `this` pointer (except for *static member functions*, which are covered in more detail in Chapter 13).

When a `this` pointer for an object is created, the `this` pointer points to the object to which the member function belongs. Thus, the `this` pointer makes it possible for a member function to access any other member of the same class without using the dot (`.`) operator or the arrow (`->`) operator.

Because the `this` pointer is always available to a calling member function—and because it has a name (its name is `this`)—you can seize control of the `this` pointer and use it for your own purposes. Listing 12.20 shows how.

Listing 12.20 uses the `this` pointer to get and set the private member variables `a`, `b`, and `c`. It may also provide some helpful examples of how you can use references in a C++ program.

### Listing 12.20. Using the `this` pointer.

```
// 1220.CPP

#include <iostream.h>

class abc {
private:
     int a, b, c;
public:
     abc() {}        // constructor
     void getabc(int& x, int& y, int& z);
     void setabc(short a, short b, short c);
};
```

*continues*

**Listing 12.20. continued**

```
inline void abc::setabc(short a, short b, short c)
{
     this->a = a; this->b = b; this->c = c;
}

void abc::getabc(int& x, int& y, int& z)
{
     x = this->a;
     y = this->b;
     z = this->c;
}

int main()
{
     abc myabc;
     int a, b, c;

     int& aref = a;
     int& bref = b;
     int& cref = c;

     myabc.setabc(1, 2, 3);
     myabc.getabc(aref, bref, cref);
     cout << a << ' ' << b << ' ' << c;
     return 0;
}
```

Here is how the `this` pointer works: When a program calls a non-static member function, a hidden pointer to the current object is secretly passed to the member function. The member function can then use that unseen pointer to access any other member of its class.

This special pointer often appears in programs in the form `this->`, and that's why it's called the `this` pointer.

As you saw earlier in this chapter, a static member function is a member function that is not associated with any particular object of a class. That's why a static member function has no `this` pointer. Because a static member function has no `this` pointer, it can't access any non-static member variables or member functions of a class.

**NOW HEAR THIS**

In some implementations of C++, the `this` pointer behaves just like any other pointer—it can be assigned values, tempting clever programs to perform dangerous tricks. Visual C++ has removed such temptations by making the `this` pointer a `const` pointer. That means in Visual C++, you can't preempt the default behavior of `this` by assigning a value of your own to the `this` pointer. An even more dangerous practice—assigning a NULL value to the `this` pointer—has also been rendered impossible.

Before the security of the `this` pointer was tightened up, tricky programmers used to assign their own values to the `this` pointer or, even worse, assign a NULL value to the `this` pointer—in order to write their own memory-management functions. In Visual C++, you can't pull these kinds of tricks. If you want to write customized memory-allocation operations, you must do it by overloading the `new` and `delete` operators—a practice that C++ allows and supports. The `new` and `delete` operators are covered in more detail in Chapter 9 and Chapter 16, "Operator Overloading."

As noted previously, when you call a member function for an object, the compiler assigns the address of the object to the `this` pointer and then calls the function. Subsequently, every reference to a data member from within the member function implicitly uses the `this` pointer. The two output statements in the following example do the same thing.

Because the `this->` pointer is always available when a member function is executing, member functions don't have to use the dot (`.`) operator or the arrow (`->`) operator to access other members of their class. Therefore, if these two statements are executed from within the same member function—and if the string `aString` is also a member of the same class as the member function—the two statements have the same effect:

```
cout << aString;
cout << this->aString;
```

The effect is, of course, that both statements print `aString` to standard output, normally the screen.

**TECH TALK**

Internally, C++ defines `this` as a `const`. In a member function of a class named `T`, `this` is defined as follows:

```
T *const this;
```

Because `this` is declared as a `const`, you cannot alter its value by writing statements such as `this++` or `this--`. But you can obtain the address of `T` with the `this` pointer; for example, you can write a member function that returns a pointer to `this`, as follows:

```
return *this;
```

What's returned in this case is a pointer to the entire current object.

# Summary

Chapter 11 introduced classes, the blueprints of C++ programs. This chapter introduced objects, which are structures created in accordance with the descriptions that classes provide. This chapter explained how memory for objects is allocated, how access specifiers are used to enforce abstraction and encapsulation, and how public member functions can be used to access private member variables.

Other topics introduced in this chapter included the public and private derivation of objects, member functions and member variables, static member functions and member variables, arrays of objects, the scope and linkage of objects, and the `this` pointer.

Many of the topics introduced in this chapter will be covered in more detail in later chapters. For example, member functions are examined more closely in Chapter 13.

# Chapter 13

# Member Functions

A computer program that's written in a procedural language—C, for example—can usually be divided into two parts. One part is usually reserved for the storage of data, and the other part contains executable code—that is, functions.

C++ programs also contain data and functions, but the functions and data elements in a C++ program are usually arranged a little differently. In a well-designed C++ program, most functions and most data elements are members of classes. In other words, most of the data elements used in a C++ program are data members of classes, and most of the functions used in the program are *member functions*.

Data members—also known as member variables—were examined in Chapter 11, "Classes," and Chapter 12, "Objects." Member functions are the topic of this chapter.

# Capabilities of Member Functions

As you learned back in Chapter 12, member functions have one very special capability: A member function can be declared to be a public member function and can then be used to provide indirect access to private member variables of the class to which it belongs.

As you'll see in this chapter, member functions also have many other kinds of capabilities. For example, member functions can:

- Determine and control the access that derived classes have to base-class member functions.
- Grant special "friendship" status to specified classes and functions so that those classes and functions can obtain access to private and protected members of other functions.
- Return constant values, that is, variables whose values cannot be changed.
- Prevent data members of base classes from being changed by overriding functions in derived classes.
- Manipulate static member variables, that is, variables that are shared by all class objects in a program and exist for the life of the program.

This chapter covers all these capabilities of member functions.

# Kinds of Member Functions

Member functions can be divided into several categories. For example, member functions can include:

- *Inline member functions.* Functions defined inside class definitions are called inline functions. When you define a function inside a class definition, the compiler treats it as if it were preceded by the keyword inline—that is, the compiler treats it as an inline function. (Ordinary inline functions—functions defined with the keyword `inline`—were introduced in Chapter 2, "A Better C—Plus," and are examined in more detail in this chapter.)

- *Virtual functions.* A virtual function is a function declared inside the definition of a base class and is expected to be used by derived classes. (Derived classes can also use non-virtual functions. However, as explained later in this chapter, virtual functions are compiled in a way that makes their use by derived classes more efficient.)
- *Pure virtual functions.* A virtual function is a function declared inside the definition of a base class but can be used only by derived classes; a base class cannot use a virtual function under any circumstances, even though the function is declared within the base class's definition.
- *Friend functions.* A friend function is a function that is accessible both to its base class and to other classes specifically designated as friend classes.
- *Conversion functions.* Conversion functions are special functions that can convert data from one type to another. Conversion functions can operate on user-defined data types as well as fundamental data types. There are two kinds of conversion functions: *member conversion functions*, which are based on ordinary member functions, and *constructor conversion functions*, which are special-purpose constructors.
- *Constant member functions.* You can make a member function a constant by preceding the declaration of the function with the `const` keyword. When you declare a member function to be a constant, the function returns a `const`, that is, a variable whose value cannot be changed.
- *Member functions with constant `this` pointers.* By placing the `const` keyword *after* a function's declaration instead of before the function's declaration, you can declare that the function's `this` pointer is a constant. (If the function is not declared inline, the `const` keyword must also be placed after the function's *definition*.) When a function's `this` pointer is declared to be a constant, the member function cannot modify data members of the object to which it belongs and cannot call other member functions unless they are also declared to be member functions with constant `this` pointers. This procedure can prevent data members of base classes from being changed by overriding functions declared in derived classes.
- *Static member functions.* Static member functions are functions designed to access a special variety of variables called static member variables. Static member functions and static member variables are described under their own headings later in this chapter.

Constructor and destructor functions—which create and destroy objects—fall into a special category of their own and are not considered member functions. They are covered in Chapter 14, "Constructors and Destructors." All the varieties of member functions listed here are described in this chapter.

# Accessing Member Functions

If access to a member function is permitted by the rules of access currently in effect, you can call the member function from outside the class in which it is defined by using the dot operator (`.`) followed by the name of the function, or by using the arrow operator (`->`) followed by a pointer to the function.

You do not have to use these operators to call the member function from another member function of the same class.

The program presented in Listing 13.1 defines a class named `PlayerAbils`. The `PlayerAbils` class has two member functions: `GetAbils()` and `PrintAbils()`. (The class also has a constructor and a destructor, neither one of which is considered by C++ to be a member function.)

### Listing 13.1. Member functions.

```
// 1301.CPP
// Using member functions

#include <iostream.h>

class  PlayerAbils {
private:
     int  strength;
     int  charisma;
     int  dexterity;
     int  intelligence;
protected:
     char *armor;
public:
     PlayerAbils() {}                // constructor
     ~PlayerAbils() {}               // destructor
     void      GetAbils();
     void      PrintAbils();
};

void PlayerAbils::GetAbils()
{
```

```
        strength = 24;
        charisma = 29;
        dexterity = 12;
        intelligence = 2;
        armor = "chain mail";
}

void PlayerAbils::PrintAbils()
{
        cout << "\nStrength: " << strength << "\n";
        cout << "Charisma: " << charisma << "\n";
        cout << "Dexterity: " << dexterity << "\n";
        cout << "Intelligence: " << intelligence << "\n\n";
        cout << "Armor: " << armor << "\n\n";
}


int main()
{
        PlayerAbils myPlayer;

        myPlayer.GetAbils();
        myPlayer.PrintAbils();
        return 0;
}
```

In Listing 13.1, the member functions `GetAbils()` and `PrintAbils()` are declared inside the definition of the `PlayerAbils` class, but they are defined outside the `PlayerAbils` class definition.

The definition of the `GetAbils()` member function is quite straightforward; it merely assigns values to the member variables `strength`, `charisma`, `dexterity`, and `intelligence`. The `PrintAbils()` function uses the stream operator `cout <<` (described in detail in Chapter 20, "Streams") to print the contents of those four variables on-screen.

## Declaring and Defining Member Functions

These are the declarations of the `GetAbils()` and `PrintAbils()` member functions:

```
void       GetAbils();
void       PrintAbils();
```

And these are the definitions of the functions:

```
void PlayerAbils::GetAbils()
{
```

```
        strength = 24;
        charisma = 29;
        dexterity = 12;
        intelligence = 2;
        armor = "chain mail";
}

void PlayerAbils::PrintAbils()
{
        cout << "\nStrength: " << strength << "\n";
        cout << "Charisma: " << charisma << "\n";
        cout << "Dexterity: " << dexterity << "\n";
        cout << "Intelligence: " << intelligence << "\n\n";
        cout << "Armor: " << armor << "\n\n";
}
```

## Specifying Return Values of Member Functions

In Listing 13.1, the member functions `GetAbils()` and `PrintAbils()` are declared to have a return type of `void`. This brings up a rather odd convention of the C++ language. When a member function of a class has a `void` return type, the keyword `void` must precede the declaration of the function. However, when a member function has a return type of `int`, the keyword `int` does not have to precede the declaration of the function.

This convention of C++ is just the opposite of what a C programmer might expect. It means that when a member function of a class is declared inside the class's definition using the `void` keyword, like this:

```
void AVoidFunc();
```

the function can be defined outside the class definition without the void keyword, like this:

```
AVoidFunc()
{
        // place code here
}
```

In contrast, when a member function of a class is declared inside a class's definition without any return type specified, like this:

```
AnIntegerFunc();
```

the function's return type is presumed to be `int`, so it must be defined outside the class definition using this syntax:

```
int AnIntegerFunc()
{
    // place code here
}
```

This strange convention can generate error messages that may look puzzling when you're new to C++. The point to remember is this: If you declare a member function of a class without specifying the function's return type, the compiler assumes that the function's return type is `int`. The corollary: If you want to declare a member function that has a `void` return type, you must explicitly precede the declaration of the member function with the keyword `void`.

### WHAT'S IN A DOT—AND WHAT'S NOT

In the definition of the member function `PlayerAbils::GetAbils()`, the dot operator (`.`) is not used to show that the variables being set are members of the `PlayerAbils` class. The dot operator is not needed in the `GetAbils()` function definition because the `GetAbils()` function is a member function of the `PlayerAbils` class.

(From a more technical point of view, a pointer to the current object is secretly passed to every member function. Each time you seek to access a member of the current object, the compiler uses this implicit pointer to access the member. This pointer, as explained later in this section, is called the `this` pointer.)

Suppose you wanted to use the dot operator anyway. Could you? You bet. This version of the `PlayerAbils::GetAbils()` function produces the same result as the version used in Listing 13.1:

```
void PlayerAbils::GetAbils()
{
    PlayerAbils::strength = 24;
    PlayerAbils::charisma = 29;
    PlayerAbils::dexterity = 12;
    PlayerAbils::intelligence = 2;
    PlayerAbils::armor = "chain mail";
}
```

# The const and volatile Keywords

By preceding the declaration of a member function with the `const` keyword, you can declare a member function to be a `const`. When you declare a member function to be a constant, the function returns a `const`, that is, a variable whose value cannot be changed.

In the short program in Listing 13.2, the member function `GetX()` is a constant member function of a class named `TestClass`. The `GetX()` function is called from the program's `main()` segment. It returns a `const int` variable that has a value of 500.

#### Listing 13.2. A constant member function.

```
// 1302.CPP
// A constant member function

#include <iostream.h>

class TestClass {
private:
     int x;
public:
     void SetX(int valueOfX)  { x = valueOfX; }
     const int GetX() { return x; }
};

int main()
{
     TestClass s;
     TestClass *testClassPtr = &s;

     testClassPtr->SetX(500);
     const int a = testClassPtr->GetX();
     cout << a << '\n';
     return 0;
}
```

The program in Listing 13.2 generates this output:

```
500
```

## Member Functions with const this Pointers

As noted under the previous heading, you can make a member function a constant by preceding the declaration of the variable with the `const` keyword when you declare the function. Alternatively, you can place the `const` keyword *after* a function's declaration, but that has an effect that's quite different.

When you place the `const` modifier after the declaration of a member function, the result is that the function's `this` pointer is declared to be a `const`. (If the function is not declared inline, the `const` keyword must also be placed after the function's *definition*.)

When a function's `this` pointer is declared to be a constant, the member function cannot modify data members of the object to which it belongs, and cannot call other member functions unless they are also declared to be member functions with constant `this` pointers.

Member functions with constant `this` pointers are designed to be used by base classes. When you give a member function of a base class a constant `this` pointer, overriding functions in derived classes are prevented from modifying data members of the base class.

Some texts on C++ mistakenly refer to member functions with constant `this` pointers as constant member functions. But constant member functions and member functions with constant `this` pointers are actually quite different, and you now know what the difference between them is.

To declare a constant member function, you must place the keyword `const` *after* the member function's declaration, using this syntax:

```
void  PrintStrength() const;
```

When you have declared a constant member function, you must also place the `const` keyword in the function's definition, using this format:

```
void PlayerAbils::PrintStrength() const
{
     // body of function ...
}
```

or, alternatively, you can use this format to make the function a constant, if the function is defined inline:

```
int   GetStrength() const {return strength;}
```

When you have declared and defined a constant member function, you can call it as you would call any function. For Example:

```
pptr->GetStrength();
pptr->PrintStrength();
```

Listing 13.3 is a complete program in which the member functions `GetStrength()` and `PrintStrength()` are declared to be constant member functions.

### Listing 13.3. Member function with `const this` pointer.

```
// 1303.CPP
// Member function with const this pointer

#include <iostream.h>

class  PlayerAbils {
private:
     int  strength;
public:
     void SetStrength() { strength = 12; }
     void      PrintStrength() const;
     int  GetStrength() const {return strength;}
};

void PlayerAbils::PrintStrength() const
{
     cout << GetStrength() << '\n';
}

int main()
{
     PlayerAbils p;
     PlayerAbils *pptr = &p;

     pptr->SetStrength();
     pptr->PrintStrength();
     return 0;
}
```

In Listing 13.3, the `GetStrength()` function works as you would expect because it does not attempt to modify any private member functions and does not call any nonconstant member functions. The `PrintStrength()` function also has those characteristics and therefore can be declared as a constant member function.

However, the member function `SetStrength()` modifies the private member function `strength` and therefore can't be declared as a constant member function. If you tried to declare `SetStrength()` as a constant member function, the compiler would generate an error message.

## Member Functions with volatile this Pointers

In the same way that you can declare a member function with a `const this` pointer, you can declare a member function with a volatile `this` pointer. The syntax is the same, but the results are quite different. When a member function of a class has a volatile `this` pointer and you call the member function, the compiler regards all data members of the class as volatile variables.

As you may recall from Chapter 3, "Type Qualifiers," a volatile variable is a variable that is subject to unexpected modification by processes beyond the control of the currently executing program. The `volatile` type qualifier warns the compiler about the volatility of variables that are accessible from interrupt servicing routines (ISRs) as well as from the currently executing programs.

The `volatile` modifier instructs the compiler to make no assumptions about the value of such a variable during optimizations. Using `volatile` makes programs run slower, but ensures that the correct values of volatile variables are always used.

The program in Listing 13.4 contains three member functions with volatile `this` pointers. When you call any of these three functions, the compiler considers all data members of the `PlayerAbils` class to be volatile and therefore protects all data members of the class from being unexpectedly changed by outside routines such as ISRs.

### Listing 13.4. Member functions with volatile `this` pointers.

```
// 1304.CPP
// Member function with volatile this pointer

#include <iostream.h>

class  PlayerAbils {
private:
     int  strength;
```

*continues*

**Listing 13.4. continued**

```
public:
     PlayerAbils() {}
     ~PlayerAbils() {}
     void SetStrength(int n) volatile { strength = n; }
     void      PrintStrength() volatile;
     int  GetStrength() volatile const {return strength;}
};

void PlayerAbils::PrintStrength() volatile
{
     cout << GetStrength() << '\n';
}

int main()
{
     PlayerAbils p1;
     volatile PlayerAbils p2;

     p1.SetStrength(15);
     p2.SetStrength(16);

     p1.PrintStrength();
     p2.PrintStrength();

     return 0;
}
```

## Using volatile and const in the Same Statement

Notice that in Listing 13.4, the function named `GetStrength()` is defined as both a `const` function and a `volatile` function. That double construct means two things: That the function can be used with volatile objects, and that the function is used in objects that contain data that cannot be modified. This is the definition of the `GetStrength()` member function:

```
int  GetStrength() volatile const {return strength;}
```

In this function definition, the positions of the keywords `volatile` and `const` can be reversed without changing their meanings. Thus, this syntax is equivalent to the form shown above:

```
int  GetStrength() const volatile {return strength;}
```

Either way, the output of the program is:

```
15
16
```

## What's Permitted and What Isn't

In Listing 13.4, two objects of the `PlayerAbils` class are created. The object named `p2` is volatile, but the object named `p1` is not. Both objects contain volatile member functions, and the volatile member functions of both objects are called without generating any errors:

```
PlayerAbils p1;
volatile PlayerAbils p2;

p1.SetStrength(15);
p2.SetStrength(16);

p1.PrintStrength();
p2.PrintStrength();
```

It is not legal, however, to declare an object as `const` and then to call a volatile member function of that object. Thus, this sequence of statements is not permitted:

```
const PlayerAbils p3;
p3.SetStrength(17); // NO! NOT ALLOWED!
```

# Static and Non-Static Member Functions

A class definition can contain two kinds of member functions: *non-static member functions* and *static member functions*. A non-static member function can access any member of the class in which the function is declared. A static member function, in contrast, can access only the static member variables. Therefore, when you create a class that includes a static member variable, you can access that variable with a static member function.

When you declare a member function inside a class definition, you can make the function static by preceding its definition with the `static` keyword. If you do not declare a member function to be static, it is non-static by default.

For example, inside the definition of a class named `ObjectCount`, you can declare a static member function named `Count()` using this syntax:

```
class ObjectCount {
private:
     int x;
protected:
     static int ct;
public:
     static int Count()  // declaring static member function
};
```

In this class definition, the static member function `Count()` can access the static member variable `ct`, but it cannot access the non-static member variable `x`. That's because a static member function can access static member variables and other static member functions. A static member function cannot access non-static member variables or non-static member functions.

Another feature of a static member function is that it has no `this` pointer. (As noted in Chapter 12, the `this` pointer is a hidden pointer to the current object. The `this` pointer is secretly passed to the member function. The member function can then use that unseen pointer to access any other member of its class. Because a static member function is not associated with any particular object of a class, a static member function has no `this` pointer. So a static member function can't access any non-static member variables or member functions of a class.)

Static member functions are described in more detail under their own heading later in this chapter.

# Inline Member Functions

The program shown in Listing 13.5 shows how *inline member functions* are used in C++. In Listing 13.5, the definition of the `PlayerAbils` class contains a pair of member functions named `IncrementStrength()` and `GetStrength()`.

That's the only difference between the program in Listing 13.5 and the program in Listing 13.1. In C++, when a function is both declared and defined inside a class definition, the compiler treats the function as an inline member function.

**Listing 13.5. Using inline member functions.**

```
// 1305.CPP
// Inline functions

#include <iostream.h>
```

```
class  PlayerAbils {
private:
     int  strength;
     int  charisma;
     int  dexterity;
     int  intelligence;
protected:
     char *armor;
public:
     void      SetAbils();
     void      PrintAbils();
     void IncrementStrength() { strength++; }
     int  GetStrength() {return strength;}
};

void PlayerAbils::SetAbils()
{
     strength = 24;
     charisma = 29;
     dexterity = 12;
     intelligence = 2;
     armor = "chain mail";
}

void PlayerAbils::PrintAbils()
{
     cout << "\nStrength: " << strength << "\n";
     cout << "Charisma: " << charisma << "\n";
     cout << "Dexterity: " << dexterity << "\n";
     cout << "Intelligence: " << intelligence << "\n\n";
     cout << "Armor: " << armor << "\n\n";
}


int main()
{
     PlayerAbils    myPlayer;
     PlayerAbils    *playerPtr = &myPlayer;

     playerPtr->SetAbils();
     playerPtr->PrintAbils();
     playerPtr->IncrementStrength();
     cout << "Strength is now ";
     cout << playerPtr->GetStrength() << "\n\n";
     return 0;
}
```

As you have seen in other C++ programs presented in this volume, a member function must be *declared* inside a class definition, but can be *defined* either inside or outside the definitions of its class. In Listing 13.5, although the member functions `PlayerAbils::SetAbils()` and `PlayerAbils::PrintAbils()` are *declared* inside the definition of the `PlayerAbils` class, they are *defined* outside the definition of the class.

However, the member functions `GetStrength()` and `IncrementStrength()` are simultaneously declared and defined inside the definition of the `PlayerAbils` class. Therefore, the compiler treats them as inline member functions.

These are the definitions of the inline member functions `GetStrength()` and `IncrementStrength()`:

```
void IncrementStrength() { strength++; }
int  GetStrength() {return strength;}
```

`PlayerAbils::GetStrength()` is a public member function that accesses the private member variable `strength`. `PlayerAbils::IncrementStrength()` is a very short function that increments the `strength` variable.

## How Inline Member Functions Work

Inline functions, as you may recall from Chapter 2, are short, fast, efficient routines that can be used in the same way that macros are used in C. When you want to write a short routine that a program can call without the stack-manipulation overhead that functions require, you can write the routine as an inline function. Inline functions run much faster than ordinary functions do, usually at the cost of a slight increase in program size.

When a class definition contains an inline member function, the function often appears on a single line—which is the way the `IncrementStrength()` function is coded in the preceding example. This convention reinforces the idea that inline functions should be short. If a member function doesn't fit on a single line, that may be an indication that it's too long to be coded as an inline function.

## Accessing an Inline Member Function

When you have added the `PlayerAbils::IncrementStrength()` and `PlayerAbils::GetStrength()` member functions to the `PlayerAbils` class, you can access both functions from the program's `main()` function:

```
int main()
{
     PlayerAbils    myPlayer;
     PlayerAbils    *playerPtr = &myPlayer;

     playerPtr->SetAbils();
     playerPtr->PrintAbils();
     playerPtr->IncrementStrength();
     cout << "Strength is now ";
     cout << playerPtr->GetStrength() << "\n\n";
     return 0;
}
```

When the `main()` function has been modified to call the new `PlayerAbils::IncrementStrength()` and `PlayerAbils::GetStrength()` functions, the program prints this output to the screen:

```
Strength: 24
Charisma: 29
Dexterity: 12
Intelligence: 2

Armor: chain mail

Strength is now 25
```

In the program shown in Listing 13.5, the `main()` function prints the values of the member variables of the `PlayerAbils` class. Then, it increments the `Strength` variable and prints that variable's new value.

## Inline Member Functions and the Stack

When you define an inline function, the compiler does not call the function using the standard C calling convention, in which local variables are placed on the stack. Instead, if possible, the compiler makes a verbatim copy of the function each time the function is called in your program and places that copy at the point in the source code at which the function is called. Then, it executes the function *inline*, without touching the stack.

If the function is too long to be pasted into the program at each point where it's called, the compiler doesn't expand the function at the point where it is called. Instead, the compiler makes just one copy of the function and calls the function each time it appears using a stack-based calling method similar to standard C++ calling convention.

Because long inline functions aren't always declared inline, you shouldn't place long function definitions inside class declarations. An inline function that's defined within a class declaration—like an inline function that's defined with the `inline` keyword—should ideally be just one line long, and certainly no longer than two or three lines.

When you declare an inline function inside a class declaration, there's an additional reason to keep the function declaration short; class declarations full of long function definitions are hard to read. So keep your inline functions short, no matter how or where you declare and define them.

# Overloading Member Functions

In C++, you can overload a member function of a class, just as you can overload any other function—as long as each version of the overloaded function is distinguishable by its parameter list. To overload a member function of a class, you must declare a prototype of each version of the function in the class definition. Then, when you declare each version of the function, you must prefix the name of the function with the name of the class and the scope resolution operator (`::`).

For example, in Listing 13.6, the member function `SetCustName()` is overloaded—one version of the function has parameters, and one does not:

**Listing 13.6. Overloading a member function.**

```
// 1306.CPP

#include <iostream.h>

class Customer {
private:
     char *name;
public:
     Customer() {}
     void SetCustName(char *nm) { name = nm; }
     void SetCustName(void) { name = "Jerry\n"; }
     char *GetCustName() { return name; }
};
```

```
int main()
{
     Customer myCust;      // initialize object
     myCust.SetCustName("Dr. Strangelove\n");
     cout << myCust.GetCustName();
     myCust.SetCustName();
     cout << myCust.GetCustName();
     return 0;
}
```

When you execute this program, it calls both versions of the overloaded function and prints this output:

```
Dr. Strangelove
Jerry
```

## Overriding Member Functions

When you write multiple functions that have the same name, that's called *overloading*. When you replace a member of a function of a class by writing another function with the same name in a derived class, that's called *overriding*. In C++, you can replace any member function of a base class by defining a function with the same name and the same parameter list in the instantiation of a derived object. The virtual function is then said to be *overridden*.

# Virtual Functions

When you write a base-class member function that you expect to be overridden, you should declare the function to be a virtual function by preceding its definition with the keyword `virtual`, in this fashion:

```
virtual void VirtualValerie(void);
```

When you place a virtual function in a program, the compiler stores the function in a special memory location and then accesses the function through a table of pointers called a *v-table*. For the details of how v-tables work, see Chapter 19, "Inheritance and Polymorphism."

## Virtual Functions and Polymorphism

Virtual functions are the key to polymorphism. When you call a virtual member function through a pointer to a base class (a common practice in C++), the C++ compiler executes the derived class's version of the function. This is precisely the opposite of what happens when you call a non-virtual member function through a pointer to a base class.

When you declare a member function in a base class to be a virtual function, the function definition supplied in the base class declaration is not ordinarily used (although you can force it to be used by invoking the scope resolution operator (::), as explained in Chapter 12). When you define a virtual member function, the compiler expects the function to be overridden in a derived class.

When you write a virtual function, C++ does not force you to override the function in a derived class; if you don't override it, it will still work fine. However, it's a good idea to designate a base-class function as virtual when you think it might be overridden in a derived class. Some good reasons for doing that are outlined in Chapter 19.

You can define a member function of a class as a virtual function by preceding the name of the member function with the keyword `virtual` when the function is defined. For example:

```
class HighClass {
public:
     virtual void VirtualFunc1(char *aString);
     virtual void VirtualFunc2(int x);
};
```

Because the member functions `VirtualFunc1()` and `VirtualFunc2()` are declared to be virtual functions in the declaration of the class `HighClass`, they are expected to be (but don't have to be) overridden in objects derived from `HighClass`.

## Pure Virtual Functions

A member function that not only can be overridden, but also *must* be overridden, is called a *pure virtual function*. When you declare a pure virtual function in a base class, you are not only specifying that the member function must be overridden before it can be used, you are also specifying that the base class does not contain a definition of the function.

To turn a virtual member function into a pure virtual member function, assign the function a value of zero (effectively, a null pointer). In these two function definitions, `VirtualValerie` and `VirtualCalorie` are both declared to be pure virtual functions:

```
virtual void VirtualValerie(int x) = 0;
virtual void VirtualCalorie(double y) = 0;
```

For more detailed information about virtual functions and how they work, see Chapter 19.

# Friends

Some secrets are so important that they shouldn't be revealed to anyone, even within the family. In C++, those secrets are labeled `private`.

There are also secrets that can be shared with the family, but with no one else. C++ calls those kinds of secrets `protected`.

But have you ever had a friend you would trust with any secret, no matter what it was? C++ has those kinds of friends, too. In fact, that's what they're called—friends.

In C++, an object can grant *friendship* status to any function in a program by declaring that the function is a `friend`. Then, the `friend` function can access all private and protected members of the object.

An object can also grant friendship status to another object. In this case, too, the object that has been named a friend then has access to the other object's private and protected members.

Friend functions and friend objects can be useful when you want to relax the access rules that ordinarily apply to `private` and `protected` member variables. For example, suppose you write a program that has to execute a public member function of a class repeatedly because it needs access to a certain private data member of a class.

In such a situation—which arises often in C++ programming—each read or write of the desired data member requires the overhead that normally results from a call to a function. To eliminate this overhead, you can specify that the accessing function is a `friend` of the class that owns the desired member variable.

You can also use friend classes to prevent class descriptions from growing to unwieldy lengths. If there is a particular set of variables and functions that a class refers to only rarely, you can place them in a class and then make that class a friend of the class that refers to them from time to time. That way, the variables and functions that are accessed only from time to time can be kept separate from the class that sometimes accesses them.

## The friend Keyword

The `friend` keyword is usually used inside a class definition. You can use the `friend` keyword in three ways:

- When you declare that a class is a friend of another class, the class granted friendship status has access to all private and protected members of the class that contains the `friend` declaration.
- A class can also grant friendship status to a member function of another class. The class that is granted friendship status then becomes a friend of the class that you are defining. By preceding the declaration of the member function with the keyword `friend`, you can declare that the specified nonmember function is a friend of the class being defined.
- Finally, a class can grant friendship status to a function that is *not* a member of another class, that is, to a stand-alone function that appears anywhere in a program. If you specify an inside member function with the keyword `friend`, you can declare that the specified nonmember function is a friend of the class being defined.

To make a class a friend of the class being defined, all you have to do is precede the declaration of the friend class with the keyword `friend`, using this kind of syntax:

```
class HighClass {
private:
     friend FriendClass;
     int x;
     int y;
protected:
     friend void friendFunc(void);
     friend int OtherClass::FriendMembFunc(void);
     char *someString;
     double bigVar;
public:
     SetX();
     SetY();
};
```

In this class definition, these statements declare that the class named `HighClass` has three friends: another class named `FriendClass`, a class member function named `OtherClass::FriendMembFunc()`, and a stand-alone function named `FriendFunc()`.

```
friend FriendClass;
friend void FriendFunc(void);
friend int OtherClass::friendMembFunc(void);
```

You may notice that in the definition of `HighClass`, `friend` specifiers appear in two sections: under the `private` label and under the `protected` label. As you might guess, these placements are not significant; a `friend` declaration can be placed under a `public` label, under a `private` label, or under a `protected` label. Access specifiers don't affect `friend` declarations, so you can place a `friend` declaration under any access specifier you like.

Another important fact about `friend` labels is that they are effective in one direction only. In the preceding class definition, `FriendClass` is declared to be a friend of `HighClass`, and thus has access to all the private and protected members of `HighClass`. However, nothing in the definition of `HighClass` grants `HighClass` any access to private and protected members of `FriendClass`. If such access is to be granted, it must be granted inside the class definition of `FriendClass`.

### IS FRIENDSHIP DANGEROUS?

As you may know, the use of friendship has a reputation of being a controversial topic in the world of C++ programming. Some programmers claim that friendship is dangerous and can lead to severe abuse. Other programmers consider friendship a useful technique that is safe when used with the proper precautions.

The truth is that friendship is a powerful and useful mechanism that can be dangerous when it is used inexpertly, but not when it is used wisely. In some situations—for example, in many implementations of operator overloading—friendship is very useful, if not essential. In many other situations, it is a handy tool to have around. But, like any powerful tool, it can be dangerous if it is mishandled. Use friendship in the ways suggested in this book, and it can't hurt you or break your programs. Start using it unthinkingly, and you're on your own.

## friend Classes and friend Functions

Listing 13.7 shows how you can use friend classes safely. In this program, a class named `FriendlyClass` is granted friendship access to another class and to two functions. `FriendlyClass` then exercises its friendship rights by printing some privileged information to standard output, normally the screen.

### Listing 13.7. Using `friends`.

```
// 1307.CPP
// Demonstrating friend classes

#include <iostream.h>

class FriendlyClass {
private:
     friend void MakeAnObject(void);
     friend class FriendlyClass2;
     friend main();
     int privateVar;
     FriendlyClass():privateVar(500) {} // private constructor
public:
     int GetPrivateVar() { return privateVar; }
};

FriendlyClass *GlobalFriendlyClass;

void MakeAnObject(void)
{
     GlobalFriendlyClass = new FriendlyClass;
}

class FriendlyClass2 {
private:
     int privateVar2;
public:
     FriendlyClass2(FriendlyClass *x) :
          privateVar2(x->privateVar) {} // constructor
     int GetPrivateVar2() { return privateVar2; }
};

int main()
{
     int x, y;

     FriendlyClass myFriendlyClass;     // calling private constructor
     FriendlyClass2 myFriendlyClass2(&FriendlyClass);
```

```
    x = myFriendlyClass.GetPrivateVar();
    cout << x << '\n';

    y = myFriendlyClass2.GetPrivateVar2();
    cout << y << '\n';

    return 0;
}
```

In Listing 13.7, an object named `FriendlyClass` grants `friend` status to a class named `FriendlyClass 2` and also to two functions: the program's `main()` function and private member function named `MakeAnObject()`.

Because `FriendlyClass2` and `MakeAnObject()` are both private members of `FriendlyClass`, both `FriendlyClass2` and `MakeAnObject()` have access to a private member variable of `FriendlyClass` named `privateVar`. The `privateVar` variable is declared in the definition of `FriendlyClass`.

This program contains an interesting precaution that helps prevent misuse of its `friend` mechanisms. The safeguard is that the constructor function of `FriendlyClass` is labeled `private`. That means only friends of `FriendlyClass` can instantiate `FriendlyClass` objects.

Another special feature of the program is that the `main()` function is declared to be a friend of the class named `FriendlyClass`. This feature permits the `main()` function to create `FriendlyClass` objects.

When the program is executed, `FriendlyClass2` accesses `privateVar` and stores the variable's value in the member variable `FriendlyClass2::privateVar2`.

Next, the `main()` function (which, as you have seen, also has a friend of `FriendlyClass`) creates a `FriendlyClass` object by calling the private constructor of `FriendlyClass`. The `main()` function then calls the functions `myFriendlyClass.GetPrivateVar()` and `myFriendlyClass2.GetPrivateVar2()` to obtain the value of the private member variable `privateVar`.

When the `main()` function makes these two requests, the member function `myFriendlyClass.GetPrivateVar()` provides the `main()` function with direct access to `privateVar`. This causes no problems because `main()` is a friend of the class `FriendlyClass` and therefore has access to `privateVar`.

From the class named `myFriendlyClass2`, the `main()` function obtains the value of `privateVar` in a different way. The `main()` function does not ask `myFriendlyClass2` for the value of `myFriendlyClass.privateVar`, but instead calls the public function myFriendlyClass2.GetPrivateVar2(). That function provides main() with the value of the variable myFriendlyClass2.privateVar2, which contains a copy of the variable myFriendlyClass.privateVar.

The program concludes by printing the values of myFriendlyClass.privateVar and myFriendlyClass2.privateVar2 to standard output, which is probably your screen. Because each of these variables contains the value 500, the program's output is:

```
500
500
```

## Bridging friend Classes

The friend keyword is sometimes used to *bridge* classes, that is, to access the information in multiple classes simultaneously. The technique of bridging classes with the friend keyword is illustrated in Listing 13.8.

The program in Listing 13.8 defines two classes: Home, which keeps track of home finances, and Business, which keeps track of business finances. A stand-alone function named Print() is declared to be a friend of two classes: a class named Home and a class named Business.

#### Listing 13.8. Bridging classes with a friend function.

```
// 1308.CPP
// Bridging classes with a friend function

#include <iostream.h>

class Business;          // forward reference of a class

// home expenses

class Home {
private:
    float rent, car, groceries;
public:
    Home(float r, float c, float g)
          { rent = r; car = c; groceries = g;}
```

```
    friend void Print(Home&, Business&); // bridge function
};

        // business class

        class Business {
        float office, software, telecom;
        public:
        Business(float o, float s, float t)
          { office = o; software = s; telecom = t;}
        friend void Print(Home&, Business&);  // bridge function
};

        // bridge friend function

        void Print(Home& hm, Business& bz)
{
        cout << "\nRent: " << hm.rent;
        cout << "\nCar: " << hm.car;
        cout << "\nGroceries: " << hm.groceries;
        cout << "\nOffice: " << bz.office;
        cout << "\nSoftware: " << bz.software;
        cout << "\nTelecom: " << bz.telecom;

        float total = hm.rent + hm.car + hm.groceries
          + bz.office + bz.software + bz. telecom;

        cout << "\n\nTOTAL: " << total << '\n';
}

        int main()
{
        Home hm(270.00, 68.50, 317.92);
        Business bz(560.00, 129.72, 64.95);
        Print(hm, bz);
        return 0;
}
```

Because the `Print()` function is a friend to both the `Home` class and the `Business` class, it can be used to bridge the `Home` class and the `Business` class. And that's exactly what the program does; it accesses the private member variables of the `Home` class and the private member variables of the `Business` class and prints the values of all of them. Finally, the program adds up all home and business expenses and prints out a total.

### FORWARD REFERENCES TO CLASS DEFINITIONS

If a file in a C++ program refers to the name of a class before the class is defined, the reference to the class must be preceded by a forward definition of a class. In this respect, a class definition is similar to a function. As noted back in Chapter 2, a function in a C++ program must also have a forward declaration if it is referred to before it is defined.

In Listing 13.8, the definition of the `Home` class refers to the `Business` class before the `Business` class is defined. This reference appears in a statement that makes the `Print()` function a friend of the `Business` and `Home` classes:

```
Home(float r, float c, float g)

    { rent = r; car = c; groceries = g;}

friend void Print (Home&, Business &); //bridge function
```

Because the `Business` class has not yet been defined when this statement appears, a forward definition of the `Business` class precedes the definition of the `Home` class. This forward definition appears near the beginning of the program:

```
class Business;          // forward reference of a class
```

## Alternatives to Using Bridge Functions

Now that you know how bridge functions work, a word of caution is in order. An encapsulation purist might object to the use of bridge functions to access the private members of multiple classes simultaneously. True, a `friend` function can't pry into the contents of a private member variable unless the class that owns the variable specifically permits the practice. On the other hand, because the programmer is the person who oversees the granting of friend status, the program can also permit that status to be abused.

Unfortunately, bridge functions can be dangerous, and you should think twice about using them. With a little extra effort, you can eliminate the bridge function from Listing 13.8 by adding some public member functions to the definitions of the `Home` and `Business` classes. With the help of public member functions, you can indirectly access the private member variables of the `Home` and `Business` classes while safeguarding private member variables' unexpected changes by observing the principles of data encapsulation and data abstraction.

Listing 13.9 illustrates one way to access the private member variables of the `Home` and `Business` classes without using a bridge function. You may be able to figure out other alternatives.

### Listing 13.9. An alternative to using a `bridge` function.

```
// 1309.CPP
// An alternative to bridge functions

#include <iostream.h>

class Business;          // forward reference of a class

// home expenses

class Home {
private:
    float rent, car, groceries;
public:
        Home() { }
        void SetValues(float r, float c, float g)
           { rent = r; car = c; groceries = g; }
        float GetRent() { return rent; }
        float GetCar() { return car; }
        float GetGroceries() { return groceries; }
};

        // business class

        class Business {
        private:
        float office, software, telecom;
public:
        Business() {}
        void SetValues(float o, float s, float t)
           { office = o; software = s; telecom = t; }
        float GetOffice() { return office; }
        float GetSoftware() { return software; }
        float GetTelecom() { return telecom; }
};

        void Print(Home hm, Business bz)
{
        cout << "\nRent: " << hm.GetRent();
        cout << "\nCar: " << hm.GetCar();
        cout << "\nGroceries: " << hm.GetGroceries();
        cout << "\nOffice: " << bz.GetOffice();
        cout << "\nSoftware: " << bz.GetSoftware();
        cout << "\nTelecom: " << bz.GetTelecom();
```

*continues*

**Listing 13.9. continued**

```
     float total = hm.GetRent() + hm.GetCar() + hm.GetGroceries()
          + bz.GetOffice() + bz.GetSoftware() + bz.GetTelecom();

     cout << "\n\nTOTAL: " << total << '\n';
}

int main()
{
    Home hm;
     hm.SetValues(270.00, 68.50, 317.92);
     Business bz;
    bz.SetValues(560.00, 129.72, 64.95);
    Print(hm, bz);
     return 0;
}
```

# Static Member Functions

Static member variables—special variables shared by all objects in a class—were introduced in Chapter 12. As you may recall, when a class has a static member variable, only one copy of the variable exists, and that single copy of the variable is shared by all objects that belong to the class.

A static member function is a special kind of member function designed specifically to access static member variables.

In C++ programs, static member variables work much like global variables work in programs written in procedural languages. A static member variable, like a global variable, exists for the lifetime of a program.

But a static member variable, unlike a global variable, is a member of a class and therefore is subject to the usual rules of class member access. A static member variable, unlike a global variable, is always associated with a specific class and has a scope limited to the files in which the variable's class is defined and implemented.

Static member functions and static member variables have many different uses in C++ programs. For example, when a program contains a value that can be changed from outside the definition of a class and when you want that value to be accessible to all objects in a class, you can store the value in a static member variable, and you can access the static member variable with a static member function.

For example, static member functions and static member variables can help you keep track of the number of objects in a list. Static member functions and static member variables can also help you keep track of other kinds of changeable values, such as interest rates.

Listing 13.10—this chapter's version of The Wrath of Zalthar Program—shows how a static member variable can keep track of objects in a list, and can be accessed with static member variables. In Listing 13.10, a static variable named `count`—which is defined in the file named ZALTHAR.H—is used to keep track of the number of objects in the `Player` class. Each time a player is created, the `count` variable is incremented. Each time a `Player` object is destroyed, the variable is decremented. Thus, the `count` variable always contains the number of `Player` objects that are currently active.

The static member function `IncCount()` increments the `count` variable, and the static member function `DecCount()` decrements `count`. Another static member variable, `PrintCount()`, prints the contents of `count` to standard output, normally the screen.

#### Listing 13.10. Using static member functions.

```
// ZALTHAR.H
// Chapter 13 Version
// Copyright 1992, Mark Andrews

#if !defined( _ZALTHAR_H_ )
#define _ZALTHAR_H_

#include <iostream.h>

enum playerClasses { WARRIOR, GNOME, WIZARD };

char *className [3] = { "WARRIOR", "GNOME", "WIZARD" };

struct Abilities {
        int strength;
        int charisma;
        int dexterity;
        int intelligence;
};

String gClassName [3] = { "WARRIOR", "GNOME", "WIZARD" };
```

*continues*

**Listing 13.10. continued**

```
class Player {
private:
        int  playerClass;
        class String className;
        class String name;
        class String weapon;
        class String magic;
        Abilities playerAbils;
        static int count;
public:
        Player () { IncCount(); }
        ~Player () { DecCount(); }
        static int GetCount() { return count; }
        static void IncCount() { count++; }
        static void DecCount() { count—; }
        static void PrintCount();
        void SetPlayerClass(int pc) { playerClass = pc; SetClassStr(pc);
}
        void SetClassStr(int pc) { className = gClassName[pc]; }
        int GetPlayerClass() { return playerClass; }
        String GetClassName() { return className; }
        void SetName(String nm) { name = nm; }
        String GetName() { return name; }
        void SetWeapon(String wpn) { weapon = wpn; }
        String GetWeapon() { return weapon; }
        void SetMagic(String mag) { magic = mag; }
        String GetMagic() { return magic; }
        static void PrintTitle();
        virtual void PrintEntry() = 0;
        void SetData(int s, int c, int d, int i)
                { playerAbils.strength = s; playerAbils.charisma = c;
                  playerAbils.dexterity = d; playerAbils.intelligence =
i; }
        const Abilities GetAbils() { return playerAbils; }
        void PrintAbils();
};

class Warrior : public Player {
public:
        // default constructor
        Warrior () {}
        // warrior constructor
        Warrior(int pc, String nm, String wpn)
                { SetPlayerClass(pc); SetName(nm);
                  SetWeapon(wpn); }
        ~Warrior() {}  // destructor
        void PrintEntry();
};
```

```
class Gnome : public Warrior {
public:
        Gnome(int pc, String nm, String wpn, String mag) :
                Warrior(pc, nm, wpn)
                { SetMagic(mag); }
        ~Gnome() {}     // destructor
        void PrintEntry();
};

#endif // _ZALTHAR_H


// ZALTHAR.CPP

#include <iostream.h>
#include <string.h>
#include <stdio.h>
#include <stdlib.h>
#include "zalthar.h"

int Player::count = 0; // initialize nr of players to 0

String gClassName [3] = { "WARRIOR", "GNOME", "WIZARD" };

void FatalError()
{
    fprintf(stderr, "A fatal error has occurred\n");
    exit(1);
}

void Player::PrintTitle()
{
        cout << "\nTHE WRATH OF ZALTHAR\n";
        cout << "By [Your Name Here]\n";
};

void Player::PrintCount()
{
        cout << "\nNUMBER OF PLAYERS: " <<  Player::GetCount() << '\n';
};


void Player::PrintAbils()
{
        cout << "\nStrength: " << playerAbils.strength << '\n';
        cout << "Charisma: " << playerAbils.charisma << '\n';
        cout << "Dexterity: " << playerAbils.dexterity << '\n';
        cout << "Intelligence: " << playerAbils.intelligence << '\n';
}
```

*continues*

**Listing 13.10. continued**

```
void Warrior::PrintEntry()
{
        Abilities locAbils = GetAbils();

        cout << "\nClass: ";
        (this->GetClassName()).Display();
        cout << "\nName: ";
        (this->GetName()).Display();
        cout << "\nWeapon: ";
        (this->GetWeapon()).Display();
        cout << "\n";
        PrintAbils();
}

void Gnome::PrintEntry()
{
        Abilities locAbils = GetAbils();

        cout << "\nClass: ";
        (this->GetClassName()).Display();
        cout << "\nName: ";
        (this->GetName()).Display();
        cout << "\nWeapon: ";
        (this->GetWeapon()).Display();
        cout << "\nMagic: ";
        (this->GetMagic()).Display();
        cout << "\n";
        PrintAbils();
}


// MYSTRING.H

#ifndef _MYSTRING_H_
#define _MYSTRING_H_

#include <iostream.h>
#include "zalthar.h"

// String class
class String
{
public:
   String() : buf(0), length(0) {}
   String( const char *s );
   ~String() { delete buf; }
   // Copy constructor
   String( const String &other );
```

```
   // Assignment operator
   String &operator=( const String &other );
   void Display() const { cout << buf; }
private:
   int length;
   char *buf;
};

#endif  // _MYSTRING_H_
```

```
// MYSTRING.CPP

#include <string.h>
#include "mystring.h"

// Constructor that takes a parameter
String::String( const char *s )
{
    length = strlen( s );
    buf = new char[length + 1];
    strcpy( buf, s );
}

// Copy constructor
String::String( const String &other )
{
    length = other.length;
    buf = new char[length + 1];
    strcpy( buf, other.buf );
}

String &String::operator=( const String &other )
{
    if( &other == this )
        return *this;
    delete buf;
    length = other.length;
    buf = new char[length + 1];
    strcpy( buf, other.buf );
    return *this;
}
```

```
// MAIN.CPP

// The Wrath of Zalthar, Chapter 13 Version
// Copyright 1992 Mark Andrews.  All rights reserved.

#include <iostream.h>
#include "zalthar.h"
```

*continues*

**Listing 13.10. continued**

```
int main()
{
        // create players

        Warrior aWarrior;
        aWarrior.SetPlayerClass(WARRIOR);
        aWarrior.SetName("Bruno");
        aWarrior.SetWeapon("Sword");
        aWarrior.SetData(24, 16, 32, 19);

        Warrior bWarrior;
        bWarrior.SetPlayerClass(WARRIOR);
        bWarrior.SetName("GayLynn");
        bWarrior.SetWeapon("Crossbow");
        bWarrior.SetData(19, 22, 43, 21);

        Gnome aGnome(GNOME, "Glog", "Broadsword", "X-ray vision");
        aGnome.SetData(14, 15, 22, 32);

        // print report

        Player::PrintTitle();
        Player::PrintCount();

        aWarrior.PrintEntry();
        bWarrior.PrintEntry();
        aGnome.PrintEntry();

        return 0;
}
```

When you execute the program in Listing 13.10, it produces this printout:

```
THE WRATH OF ZALTHAR
By [Your Name Here]

NUMBER OF PLAYERS: 3


Class: WARRIOR
Name: Bruno
Weapon: Sword

Strength: 24
```

```
Charisma: 16
Dexterity: 32
Intelligence: 19


Class: WARRIOR
Name: GayLynn
Weapon: Crossbow

Strength: 19
Charisma: 22
Dexterity: 43
Intelligence: 21


Class: GNOME
Name: Glog
Weapon: Broadsword
Magic: X-ray vision

Strength: 14
Charisma: 15
Dexterity: 22
Intelligence: 32
```

## ZALTHAR REVISITED

The program in Listing 13.10 is yet another new and improved version of the adventure game The Wrath of Zalthar, which continues to evolve. This chapter's version of the program has a new private integer variable named `playerClass`—which identifies each player in the game as a warrior, a gnome, or a wizard. To set this variable, obtain its value, and print the appropriate player class on-screen, the program makes use of an enumeration class named `playerClasses` and an array of strings named `className`.

The `enum` list and the array contain the same list of classes, but the `enum` list expresses the classes as a series of numbers, whereas the array expresses the classes as a series of strings. The `PrintEntry()` function compares the contents of an `enum` element and its corresponding array element, and prints each character's class.

These mechanisms—defined in the file ZALTHAR.H and implemented in functions defined in the files ZALTHAR.H and ZALTHAR.CPP—are worth some study.

## The static Keyword

Listing 13.10 shows how you can make a function `static` by preceding its declaration with the `static` keyword. This statement, which appears in the definition of the `Player` class, declares a static member variable named `count`:

```
static int count;
```

When a static variable has been declared, it must be initialized. In Listing 13.10, the following statement in the ZALTHAR.CPP file initializes the static member variable `count`. This is the only format you can use to initialize a static member variable (although the initialization of the variable to a specific value is optional):

```
int Player::count = 0;    // initialize nr of players to 0
```

Although a static member variable (like any variable) can be initialized only once, you can assign a new value to a static member variable as many times as you want. For example, in the Zalthar program, the static member variable `count` is incremented each time a character is created and is decremented each time a character is destroyed. These incrementing and decrementing operations are carried out automatically by the constructor and destructor of the `Player` class, along with a `PrintCount()` function that prints the current number of players on-screen:

```
Player () { IncCount(); }
~Player () { DecCount(); }
static int GetCount() { return count; }
static void IncCount() { count++; }
static void DecCount() { count—; }
static void PrintCount();
```

## Initializing a Static Member Variable

As noted in Chapter 12, static member variables are initialized in an unusual way. Even if a static member variable is declared to be private, it can be (in fact must be) initialized from outside the class in which it is declared. This code fragment shows how the private static member variable `count` is initialized in the ZALTHAR.CPP file in Listing 13.10:

```
#include <iostream.h>
#include <string.h>
#include <stdlib.h>
#include "zalthar.h"

int Player::count = 0;    // initialize nr of players to 0
```

## Using Static Member Functions

As you now know, when a static member variable appears in a program, you can access the variable from a *static member function*. It is also possible to access a static member variable from a non-static member function. However, a static member function is specifically designed to access static member variables.

When you write a member function that accesses a static member variable, it's usually best to make the member function that accesses the variable a static member function. Then, when another programmer reads your code (or when you read it yourself after it gets cold), it's clear that the job of the function in question is to access a static member variable.

This point is illustrated in the latest version of the Zalthar program presented in Listing 13.10. In that program, in the definition of the `Player` class, the member functions `PrintCount()` and `PrintTitle()` are declared to be static member functions. That makes sense because neither of these functions has any special relationship to any particular object of the `Player` class:

```
static void PrintCount();
static void PrintTitle();
```

Later in the program—specifically, in the `main()` segment—these statements call the `PrintCount()` and `PrintTitle()` functions:

```
Player::PrintTitle();
Player::PrintCount();
```

In these preceding statements, the `PrintCount()` and `PrintTitle()` functions are not associated with any particular objects of the `Player` class. Instead, the scope resolution operator (`::`) associates both functions with the `Player` class itself. From this syntax, you can tell right away that the functions being called are static member functions.

From a technical point of view, the main feature of a static member function is that it has no `this` pointer. (As noted in Chapters 11 and 12, the `this` pointer is a hidden pointer to the current object and is secretly passed to the member function. The member function can then use that unseen pointer to access any other member of its class. Because a static member function is not associated with any particular object of a class, a static member function has no `this` pointer. So a static member function can't access any non-static member variables or member functions of a class.)

You can declare that a member function is static by preceding the declaration of the function with the keyword `static`. For example, the Zalthar program contains these static member functions:

```
static int GetCount() { return count; }
static void PrintCount();
static void PrintTitle();
```

# Pointers to Member Functions

In C language, pointers to functions have always had the potential of being very useful. However, because the syntax of pointers to member functions looks confusing and their behavior seems hard to understand, many C programmers have avoided using pointers to functions. Consequently, a powerful tool has been unavailable to legions of C programmers.

The reason that pointers to functions can be useful is that they are very versatile. When you have declared a pointer to a particular kind of function—for example, to a function that takes an integer variable as an argument and returns an integer function—you can set a pointer to point to any kind of function that has those characteristics. Then you can call the function. In this way, you can use the same pointer to call multiple functions.

Pointers to functions will probably remain neglected in C++, just as they have been in C. This is not as unfortunate in C++ as it has been in C, because C++ has new features that can replace pointers to functions in many situations. Furthermore, the alternatives supplied by C++ are more elegant than pointers to functions, as well as being easier to use and easier to understand.

In C++, when you encounter a situation where a pointer to a function might have come in handy, you can often use C++ alternatives such as overloading a function or overriding a virtual function, and thus sidestep the need for a pointer to a function. Because these kinds of alternatives are available in C++, pointers to functions are probably going to be even more rare in C++ than they have been in C.

Nonetheless, C++ does support pointers to functions. In fact, C++ provides even more support for member functions than C supplies. Not only does C++ support pointers to functions, it also supports pointers to member functions, pointers to static member functions, and arrays of pointers to member functions.

## Using Pointers to Ordinary Functions

If you're a C programmer and a pointers-to-functions guru, you may know that this is the syntax for declaring a pointer to a function in C:

```
int (*aFunc)();
```

The preceding statement creates a pointer to a function that takes no arguments and returns an integer value. The pointer is named `aFunc`. Once the above declaration has been placed in a program, the identifier `aFunc` can be used as a pointer to any function that takes no arguments and returns an integer value. For example, `aFunc` could be set to point to this function:

```
int MyFunc()
{
     return 500;
}
```

To make `aFunc` point to the above function, you could place this declaration in your program:

```
aFunc = MyFunc;
```

Then you could execute `MyFunc()` by calling this function:

```
int Test(int (*MyFunc)())
{
     int n = SameFunc();
     return n;
}
```

You could call the above function by placing this statement in your program:

```
int n = Test(aFunc);
```

That's all there is to it! Listing 13.11 combines all the preceding examples into a single program, and then prints the value returned by `MyFunc`:

```
500
```

### Listing 13.11. Using a pointer to a function.

```
// 1311.CPP
// Pointer to a member function

#include <iostream.h>

int (*aFunc)();
```

*continues*

**Listing 13.11. continued**

```
int MyFunc()
{
      return 500;
}

int Test(int (*MyFunc)())
{
      int n = MyFunc();
      return n;
}

int main()
{
      aFunc = MyFunc;

      int n = Test(aFunc);
      cout << n << '\n';
      return 0;
}
```

## Using Pointers to Member Functions

In C++, you can create and use a pointer to a member function in the same way that you would create and use a pointer to any other kind of function. The only difference is that when you want to use indirection (that is, a pointer) to access a member function of an object from outside the object, you must use the scope resolution operator (`::`) to tell the compiler where to find the function that you're referring to.

For example, this statement creates a pointer to a member function of a class named `Item`:

```
void (Item::*setPricePtr)(float p);
```

When this declaration has been placed in a program, you can use the pointer named `setPricePtr` to access any member function of the `Item` class that takes a `float` variable as an argument and returns no value. For example, this statement sets the pointer named `setPricePtr` to point to a member function of the `Item` class named `SetPrice()`:

```
setPricePtr= &Item::SetPrice;
```

Listing 13.12 is a program that uses pointers to access two member functions of a class named `Item`. The member functions are named `SetPrice()` and `GetPrice()`.

### Listing 13.12. Pointers to member functions.

```
// 1312.CPP
// Pointers to member functions

#include <iostream.h>

class Item {
private:
     float price;
public:
     float GetPrice() { return price; }
     void SetPrice(float p) { price = p; }
};

int main()
{
     // declare pointers to functions

     void (Item::*setPricePtr)(float p);
     setPricePtr= &Item::SetPrice;

     float (Item::*getPricePtr)() = &Item::GetPrice;

     // create an Item object
     Item i;

     // call Item::SetPrice()
     (i.*setPricePtr)(29.95);

     // call Item::GetPrice()
     float p = (i.*getPricePtr)();

     cout << "Price: $" << p << '\n';

     return 0;
}
```

The program shown in Listing 13.12 sets the price of an item and then obtains and prints out the price. This is the output of the program:

```
Price: $29.95
```

## Arrays of Pointers to Member Functions

Once you know how to create a pointer to a member function, you can create arrays of pointers to member functions. Listing 13.13 shows how.

### Listing 13.13. Arrays of pointers to member functions.

```
// 1313.CPP
// Arrays of pointers to member functions

#include <iostream.h>

class Account {
private:
        int card;
        int car;
        int mortgage;
public:
        Account() {}
        ~Account() {}
        void SetCardInt(int cc) {card = cc;}
        void SetCarInt(int c) {car = c;}
        void SetMortgageInt(int m) {mortgage = m;}
        // give main() access to private data
        friend int main();
};

// pointer to class function members
typedef void (Account::*FP)(int);
FP function [] = {
        &Account::SetCardInt,
        &Account::SetCarInt,
        &Account::SetMortgageInt
};

// initialize a global Account object
Account bills;

// call class member function with a pointer
void SetMember(void (Account::*callFunc)(int), int val )
{
        (bills.*callFunc)(val);
}

int interestList[] = { 21, 12, 9 };

int main()
{
```

```
        for (int c = 0; c < 3; c++)
                SetMember(function[c], interestList[c]);

        cout << "Credit Card: " << bills.card << '%' << '\n';
        cout << "Car: " << bills.car << '%' << '\n';
        cout << "Mortgage: " << bills.mortgage << '%' << '\n';

        return 0;
}
```

In Listing 13.13, the class named `Account` has three private member variables:

```
int card;
int car;
int mortgage;
```

To obtain and set the values of these variables, the `Account` class provides three member functions:

```
void SetCardInt(int cc) {card = cc;}
void SetCarInt(int c) {car = c;}
void SetMortgageInt(int m) {mortgage = m;}
```

When the three member functions shown here have been declared, this global function uses a pointer to a member variable to set up an array of pointers to member variables:

```
typedef void (Account::*FP)(int);
FP function [] = {
     &Account::SetCardInt,
     &Account::SetCarInt,
     &Account::SetMortgageInt
};
```

When this declaration has been placed in the program, an `Account` object named `bills` is defined, and a global function is set up to call class member functions:

```
// initialize an Account object
Account bills;

// call class member function with a pointer
void SetMember(void (Account::*callFunc)(int), int val )
{
     (bills.*callFunc)(val);
}
```

Next, a `for` loop is set up to assign values to the three member functions of the object named `bills`:

```
for (int c = 0; c < 3; c++)
     SetMember(function[c], interestList[c]);
```

And finally, the values of the member functions of the `bills` object are printed to the screen:

```
Credit Card: 21%
Car: 12%
Mortgage: 9%
```

## Pointers to Static Member Functions

Because C++ supports pointers to member functions (as explained under the previous heading), it should not be surprising that pointers to static member functions are also supported. Listing 13.14 shows how you can use pointers to static member functions in a C++ program.

### Listing 13.14. Pointers to static member functions.

```
// 1314.CPP
// Pointers to static member functions

#include <iostream.h>

class StaticTest {
private:
     static float amStatic;
     static float fmStatic;
public:
     static float AMTest();
     static float FMTest();
};

inline float StaticTest::AMTest() {
     return StaticTest::amStatic;
}
```

```
inline float StaticTest::FMTest() {
     return StaticTest::fmStatic;
}

// declare static member variables
float StaticTest::amStatic = 1620;
float StaticTest::fmStatic = 102.1;

int main()
{
     // print funny stuff
     cout << "This is a test.\n";
     cout << "This is only a test.\n\n";

     // declare function pointer
     float (*fptr)();

     // call member function by pointer
     fptr = &StaticTest::AMTest;
     cout << "AM Frequency: " << (*fptr)() << '\n';

     // change pointer and call function again
     fptr = &StaticTest::FMTest;
     cout << "FM Frequency: " << (*fptr)() << '\n';

     return 0;
}
```

As noted earlier in this chapter, a static member variable is a variable specially designed to access static member functions. The program in Listing 13.14 contains a class named `StaticTest` that has two static member variables: `amStatic` and `fmStatic`. The `StaticTest` class also contains two member functions: `AMTest()` and `FMTest()`. The `AMTest()` function returns the value of the `amStatic` variable, and the `FMTest()` function returns the value of the `fmStatic` variable.

When the `amStatic` and `fmStatic` variables have been initialized, the program's `main()` function uses pointers to print out the values of the two variables. This is the output of the program:

```
This is a test.
This is only a test.

AM Frequency: 1620
FM Frequency: 102.1
```

# Summary

Functions declared in the definition of a class are called member functions. Member functions of a class are often used to provide access to private member variables of the class. This chapter explores that topic, as well as a number of other important topics, including:

- Capabilities of member functions.
- Kinds of member functions.
- Accessing member functions.
- The `const` and `volatile` keywords.
- Static and non-static member functions.
- Inline member functions.
- Overloading member functions.
- Virtual and pure virtual functions.
- `friend` classes and functions.
- Static member functions.
- Pointers and arrays of pointers to member functions.

Besides member functions, a class usually has two kinds of special functions: a constructor function and a destructor function. Constructor and destructor functions are examined in Chapter 14.

Chapter 14

# Constructors and Destructors

There are two ways to initialize an object in C++. One technique is simply to declare the object, in the same way that you would declare an ordinary variable. The other way to initialize an object is to call a special kind of function called a *constructor*.

C++ does not require a constructor for every object, but constructors offer so many benefits that you should, as a matter of course, write a constructor for every object that you use in a program. A constructor can initialize data members of an object when the object is created and can ensure that member variables of an object being created are initialized with valid data.

Constructors also make it easier—and safer—to create objects and to destroy them when they are no longer needed.

Finally, constructors can perform special kinds of operations, such as converting data from one type to another and making copies of objects. Constructors are often used, for example, to make copies of strings that are implemented as objects.

Almost every object that has a constructor also has another special kind of function, called a *destructor*. When an object performs memory-allocation operations, a destructor can ensure that any memory that the object has allocated is deallocated when the object is destroyed.

Constructors and destructors are examined in depth in this chapter.

# Creating Constructors

Briefly, a constructor is a function that is invoked automatically when an object is created. A constructor function is easy to recognize because it always has the same name as the class in which it is declared.

To create a constructor, you must declare the construction inside the definition of a class. Then you must define the constructor, either inline (inside the class definition) or outside the class definition after the class has been defined.

A constructor never returns a value, and C++ does not allow you to specify a return type—not even `void`—when you define a constructor class.

Some constructors take arguments, and some do not. The following two statements are declarations of constructors. The first constructor has a parameter list, and the second does not:

```
AfterClass(char *nm);
InClass();
```

Figure 14.1 shows how a C++ program creates an object by invoking a constructor.

Using a Constructor

1. Declare class, including constructor.

```
class Player {
private:
   int strength, charisma, dexterity, intelligence;
public:
   Player(int, int, int, int);    // constructor
   ~Player();                     // destructor
   void PrintQuals();
};
```

2. Define constructor members and other class members.

```
Player::Player(int stren, int charac, int dext, int intell)
{
   strength = stren;
   charisma =  charac;
   dexterity = dext;
   intelligence = intell;
}

void Player::PrintQuals()
{
    cout << "\nStrength: " << strength << "\n";
    cout << "Charisma: " << charisma << "\n";
    cout << "Dexterity: " << dexterity << "\n";
    cout << "Intelligence: " << intelligence << "\n\n";
}
```

3. Call constructor to initialize values.

```
Player Player(int stren, int charac, int dext,
   int intell);
```

4. Call member functions.

```
thisPlayer.PrintQuals();
```

*Figure 14.1. Using a constructor.*

## Two Kinds of Constructors

Like any other function declared in a class definition, a constructor can be defined either inline or outside the class in which it is defined. The two constructor definitions shown previously are examples of constructors that are declared inside a class definition but are defined outside the class definition.

In contrast, the following two statements are inline function definitions:

```
AfterClass(char *nm) { memVar = nm; }
InClass() {}
```

When a class definition contains a constructor definition written in either of the previous formats, the compiler treats the constructor function as an inline function (for more information on inline functions, see Chapter 13, "Member Functions"). The function header is followed by curly brackets, and following the standard format for writing inline functions, the brackets are not followed by a semicolon.

## Creating Objects Without Constructors

When you instantiate an object in C++, the compiler always calls a constructor. If you don't provide a constructor in your program, the compiler creates a simple constructor when you declare the object. Then the compiler uses the constructor that it has created to initialize the object.

Because the compiler automatically creates a constructor when an object is declared, you can define, declare, and use a class without explicitly writing a constructor for the class.

But constructors that are created by the compiler are usually too primitive to be very useful. The easiest, most convenient, and safest way to allocate memory for an object is to write and call a constructor function.

In this chapter, you'll learn to write your own constructors. That will help you write better C++ programs. For reasons that will become clear as you read this chapter, constructors are so valuable that C++ programmers write explicit constructors for most C++ classes.

# Destructors

In the same way that you can use a constructor function to initialize an object, you can use another special kind of function—called a *destructor*—to deallocate memory and perform other housekeeping functions when an object is destroyed. A destructor, like a constructor, has the same name as the object with which it is associated. However, the name of a destructor is always preceded by the bitwise NOT operator (~), as in this example:

```
~AClass() {}
```

A destructor takes no arguments and returns no value. However, the declaration of a structure does not contain any return type—not even `void`. The `void` keyword is not required (in fact, is not *allowed*) because the compiler knows that destructors do not return values.

When an object that has a destructor goes out of scope, or for some other reason should be destroyed (see in later text), the object's destructor is automatically invoked. So you don't have to call the destructor explicitly when the object is no longer needed. When it's time to deallocate the object and any memory the object has allocated, C++ calls the destructor automatically.

## Using Destructors Safely

The main job of a destructor is to deallocate any memory that has been allocated by the object that is being destroyed. If an object has a member that is a non-null pointer, the object's destructor deletes the pointer and invokes the `delete` operator to deallocate any memory that is associated with the pointer.

Because a destructor automatically deletes any memory associated with a pointer, you should never create two objects that write to the same area of memory through a pointer.

If two objects have a pointer that points to the same memory address and each object can write to that memory address through its pointer, that can cause serious problems. If each of the objects has a destructor, and if both destructors are invoked when the objects are destroyed, the same block of memory is deleted twice. That can cause program crashes and other serious malfunctions.

To prevent this kind of disaster from happening, you should never create multiple objects that access the same location in memory through a pointer. Specifically, you must be careful when you write functions that make copies of objects. It is so important to make safe copies of objects in C++ that a whole chapter in this book—Chapter 18—deals solely with copying objects. In Chapter 18, you'll learn how to write functions that make safe copies of objects so problems won't arise when the objects are destroyed.

## How Destructors Are Invoked

A constructor does not necessarily have to be balanced by a destructor; you don't have to write a destructor for an object unless memory deallocation operations must be performed when the object is destroyed.

Although a program can explicitly call a destructor, destructors are usually invoked automatically by the compiler each time an object goes out of scope or is destroyed for some other reason. Specifically, when a class has a destructor, the destructor is called when:

- A local (automatic) object with block scope goes out of scope.
- The lifetime of a temporary object ends.
- A program ends and global or static objects exist.
- The destructor is explicitly called using the destructor function's fully qualified name.
- Memory for the object is deallocated using the `delete` operator. (Only an object constructed using the `new` operator can be explicitly destroyed with the `delete` operator. This topic is covered later in this chapter.)

## Using Destructors

A destructor is implemented as a class member function that is invoked each time an object goes out of scope. Each time an object goes out of scope, a destructor can be called to deallocate memory and perform other kinds of housekeeping operations. For example, destructors can decrease reference counts, uninstall interrupt handlers, output messages, save data in files, and so on.

Some classes don't require destructors, but most elaborate and tightly controlled classes rely on destructors to "clean things up" when objects go out of scope. Even when an object doesn't require a destructor, a null destructor can't hurt anything. So most C++ objects have destructors, whether the destructors accomplish any obvious aims or not.

A destructor, like a constructor, has the same name as the class with which it is associated. The name of a destructor, however, is always preceded by the symbol ~. For example, a destructor for a class named `HighClass` would be named `~HighClass`.

A destructor, like any other member function, can be defined inside or outside the definition of its class. When you define a destructor inside a class definition, the destructor has this kind of syntax:

```
virtual ~Player() {}
```

Alternatively, you can declare a function inside a class definition in this fashion:

```
~Warrior();
```

you can then define the destructor outside its class definition using this kind of format:

```
Warrior::~Warrior()
{
    delete name;
    delete weapon;
}
```

## Order of Destruction

When an object goes out of scope or is deleted, C++ follows a specific sequence of events to destroy the object and any other objects it has created. This sequence of events is carried out as follows:

1. If the class has a destructor, that destructor is called and executed.
2. Destructors for non-static member objects of a class are called in the reverse order in which they appear in the class's declaration.
3. Destructors for non-virtual base classes are called in the reverse order of the order in which they were declared.
4. Destructors for virtual base classes are called in the reverse order of the order in which they were declared.

This order of destruction is described in more detail in the Microsoft C++ *Language Reference* manual.

**RULES FOR WRITING DESTRUCTORS**

You must follow several rules when you write a destructor. For example:

- You can't pass arguments to a destructor.
- You cannot specify a return type for a destructor—not even `void`.
- A constructor cannot return a value.
- You cannot declare a constructor to be `const`, `volatile`, or `static`. However, a destructor can destroy objects that are declared to be `const`, `volatile`, or `static`.
- Destructors can be declared `virtual`, and they often are. With a virtual destructor, you can destroy objects without knowing their type; that's because a virtual destructor function automatically calls the correct destructor for the object being destroyed. In pure abstract classes, destructors can also be declared as pure virtual functions.
- A class can have only one destructor, but this doesn't necessarily mean that just one destructor is invoked when an object is destroyed. When an object is destroyed, the object's base class and its class's member objects are also destroyed, always in the reverse order in which they were constructed.

## Destructors in the Zalthar Program

In this chapter's version of the Zalthar program, the `Player`, `Warrior`, and `Gnome` classes have destructors that are defined in the ZALTHAR.CPP file. These are the definitions of those destructors:

```
virtual Player::~Player();    // destructor

virtual Warrior::~Warrior();  // destructor

virtual Gnome::~Gnome();      // destructor
```

These destructors are needed by the `Warrior` and `Gnome` classes because objects of both these classes allocate memory dynamically using the `new` operator. The destructor written for the `Player` class is an empty function.

All three destructors used in the Zalthar program are declared inside their class definitions; they are all defined outside the definitions of their classes. For example, this is the definition of the destructor written for the `Warrior` class:

```
// destructor
Warrior::~Warrior()
{
    delete name;
    delete weapon;
}
```

# How Constructors Work

A constructor is invoked whenever a constructor is explicitly called, or whenever an object of any of these types is created:

- *Global objects.* Externally linked objects or objects with file scope.
- *Local objects.* Objects declared within any code block.
- *Dynamically created objects.* Objects with memory allocated by the `new` operator.
- *Temporary objects.* Objects that are sometimes created by the compiler to initialize `const` data types, to store return values of functions, and to store the results of casts to user-defined data types (for more information on temporary objects, see the Microsoft C++ *Language Reference* manual).
- *Data members of classes.* When you create an object that belongs to a class, and the class type is made up of other class-type variables, the compiler calls a default constructor to initialize each object in the class.
- *Base-class subobjects of classes.* When you create an object of a derived class type, a constructor is created to initialize components of the base class.

Derived classes do not inherit constructors from their base classes. However, if you create an object that belongs to a derived class, the compiler calls any constructors that have been written for the object's base class before it calls the derived class's constructor.

# Kinds of Constructors

You can always tell a constructor from other member functions of a class because a constructor function has the same name as its class. Thus, if a class was named `AClass`, its constructor could be declared in this fashion inside the definition of the class:

```
AClass() {}
```

## Null Constructors

In the preceding example, the function named `AClass()` is an empty constructor, or a *null* constructor—in other words, a constructor that takes no parameters and performs no special initialization procedures specified by the programmer.

It is also an *inline* constructor because it is declared at the same time it is defined (or inline).

Although the constructor takes no arguments and contains no executable code, it is a complete inline function. It contains a pair of curly brackets—as all inline functions do—so even though its curly brackets have nothing between them, the constructor does not require a separate definition outside the class definition in which it is declared.

You can also write constructors that do take parameters. However, even a null constructor allocates memory for the object that it initializes and performs all other initialization and housekeeping operations that a constructor is supposed to perform.

This short program declares, defines, and calls a null constructor:

### Listing 14.1. A null constructor.

```
// 1401.CPP

#include <iostream.h>

class Customer {
private:
     char *name;
public:
     Customer();                // constructor
     void SetCustName(char *nm) { name = nm; }
     char *GetCustName() { return name; }
};

Customer::Customer() {}
```

```
int main()
{
     Customer myCust;     // initialize object; constructor called
     myCust.SetCustName("Dr. Strangelove\n");
     cout << myCust.GetCustName();
     return 0;
}
```

In the preceding example, the constructor for the `Customer` class is defined outside the `Customer` class definition, in this line:

```
Customer::Customer {}
```

A constructor that's defined outside a class definition consumes more space than a constructor that's defined inline, but constructors are often declared outside class definitions. This statement, in the program's `main()` function, invokes the following constructor:

```
Customer myCust;    // initialize object; constructor called
```

## Inline Constructors

As you have seen, a more efficient way to define the constructor for the `Customer` class would be to make it an inline constructor function, as in this example:

### Listing 14.2. An inline constructor.

```
// 1402.CPP

#include <iostream.h>

class Customer {
private:
     char *name;
public:
     Customer() {}       // inline constructor
     void SetCustName(char *nm) { name = nm; }
     char *GetCustName() { return name; }
};

int main()
{
     Customer myCust;    // initialize object; constructor called
     myCust.SetCustName("Dr. Strangelove\n");
     cout << myCust.GetCustName();
     return 0;
}
```

In this program, the `Customer` class has a constructor that is declared and defined in one step, or inline:

```
Customer() {}          // inline constructor
```

Because this constructor is declared inline, it does not have to be defined separately outside the definition of the `Customer` class.

### Defining a Constructor Outside a Class

If you want to define a constructor function *outside* a class definition, you can declare the constructor inside the definition of its class, using this format:

```
AClass(char *nm);
```

If the preceding constructor appears in a class definition, you can define the constructor outside the class definition, in this fashion:

```
AClass::AClass(char *nm)
{
      name = nm;
}
```

Notice that when a constructor for a class is defined outside the class's definition, the constructor's header consists of the name of the class, a scope resolution operator (`::`), and a standard function header—which also begins with the name of a class. When you see that kind of header at the beginning of a function in a C++ program, you can be sure that the function you're looking at is a constructor function.

## Invoking a Constructor

Once you have written a constructor for an object, you can invoke the constructor by simply writing a declaration for the object. For instance, assume this constructor definition appears inside a class definition:

```
Pals(char *nm, char *addr) { name = nm; address = addr; }
```

You can initialize the class named `AClass` by invoking the preceding constructor, in the same way that you would call any function. For example:

```
Pals("Darryl", "UC Berkeley");
```

If you write a constructor that takes parameters, as in the preceding example, the constructor can use the values of those parameters to perform any special kinds of initialization procedures that the object requires. For example, you can use the constructor's parameters to specify initialization values for member functions of the object being initialized. Of course you are responsible for providing the code that carries out any specialized operations that you want performed.

If you invoke a constructor directly—in other words, without using the `new` operator—you must invoke the constructor from inside a function. That means that when the function terminates, the object is destroyed.

## Other Ways to Invoke Constructors

To create an object with a longer lifetime—for example, the lifetime of a program—there are two other alternatives:

- You can invoke the object's constructor from within your program's `main()` function.
- You can invoke the constructor using the `new` operator.

This statement constructs an object by calling the `new` operator:

```
Pals *myObject = new Pals("Darryl", "UC Berkeley");
```

### ALLOCATING MEMORY WITH CONSTRUCTORS

As you may recall from Chapter 12, "Objects," there are two techniques for invoking a constructor to allocate memory for an object. You can create an object on a stack frame by calling the object's constructor from inside a function, or you can allocate memory for the object on your application's heap by invoking the `new` operator.

The primary advantage of using stack-frame allocation is that objects stored in stack frames don't have to be deallocated when they are no longer needed. When a function that contains a stack-frame object terminates, the memory that has been allocated for the object is deallocated automatically.

The main disadvantage of stack-frame allocation is that allocating and deallocating frame objects can slow a program down. Another potential problem is that stack-frame storage requires memory space on the stack, which may be in short supply.

These disadvantages can become particularly serious when a program stores large objects on stack frames. If a program creates and deletes stack-frame objects frequently, program execution can be slowed to a crawl. Still another shortcoming of variables stored in stack frames is that they cannot be used outside their scope.

In contrast, heap allocation requires no stack memory and makes programs run faster. The main disadvantage of heap allocation is that object variables stored in the heap aren't automatically deallocated when they're no longer needed. When you no longer need an object that's stored in the heap, you must remember to delete it by invoking the `delete` operator. And of course you must use pointers to access objects stored in the heap.

For more information on stack-frame allocation and heap allocation, see the section "Allocating Memory for Objects" in Chapter 12.

## Ground Rules for Using Constructors

As mentioned at the beginning of this chapter, a constructor never returns a value. And a constructor definition never specifies a return type—not even `void`, even though all constructors have a return value of `void` by default. If you define a return type for a constructor—even void—the compiler generates an error message.

Some other rules that govern constructors are the following:

- You can't obtain the address of a constructor.
- An object cannot inherit a constructor. C++ automatically creates a constructor when a class without a constructor is derived from a class with a constructor. However, when both a base class and a derived class have constructors, the base class's constructor is called first, and then the derived class's constructor is called.
- You can't declare a constructor to be `const` or `volatile`.
- You also can't declare a constructor as `static`. Member variables would not be accessible to a static constructor.
- A constructor cannot be virtual. C++ sees that all relevant constructors are invoked for every object.

- A constructor can't initialize static member variables in its initialization list. However, it can assign values to static member variables in its body. To initialize static member variables, use ordinary initializations.
- A class that has constructors can't be a member of a union, but a union can be a member of a class regardless of whether the class has constructors.

**TECH TALK**

Every constructor—even a constructor with no arguments—performs many kinds of tasks behind the scenes, even if you write no code for the constructor. For example, in Visual C++ (and in some other implementations of C++ as well), a constructor:

- Initializes the object's virtual base pointers, or v-table pointers. This step is performed if the class being constructed has virtual base classes. V-tables are responsible for providing the correct binding of virtual function calls to code. (V-tables are described in more detail in Chapter 19, "Inheritance and Polymorphism.")
- Calls base-class and member constructors.
- Executes the code (if there is any) in the body of the constructor function.

When a constructor completes these operations, the result is memory allocation for an object of the appropriate class type.

# Benefits of Using Constructors

Constructors are valuable because they give you control over what happens when an object is created. A constructor can initialize member variables of the object that it created, and it can even check to see if the values that are used to initialize those variables are within acceptable ranges.

If you want a constructor to perform custom operations, however, you must provide the code that carries out the operations you want to have performed.

Constructors have many other capabilities, too. For example, constructors can convert data from one type to another and can make copies of objects. And as you'll see in Chapter 18, "Copying Objects," constructors are particularly useful for creating, copying, and manipulating strings.

The main use of constructors, though, is to initialize objects. There are other ways to create objects, but they aren't nearly as convenient as using constructors, and they are more likely to cause programming errors.

## Constructors Can Help Manage Memory

Besides initializing data and performing error checking, if that is needed, a constructor can streamline memory management. Here's how:

When you instantiate an object in a C++ program, the compiler makes sure that enough memory will be available to contain the object's data members when the object comes into scope. However, the compiler does not initialize the object's data members when the object is instantiated.

When you call an object's constructor, the constructor can initialize any data members that you want to initialize. When the object initialized by the constructor goes out of scope, memory that has been allocated to the object's data members goes back to the system and becomes available for other uses.

## Constructors Can Initialize and Check Values

Constructors can initialize member variables of objects and can even check to see that the values used to initialize member variables fall into acceptable ranges. Listing 14.3 is a program that simulates the checking of a hospital patient's temperature.

### Listing 14.3. Using a constructor to check the value of a variable.

```
// 1403.CPP
// A constructor that checks a value

#include <iostream.h>

// forward declarations
class TempCheck     *tcPtr;         // forward class ptr declaration
```

```
void SetTemp(TempCheck *tcPtr);

class TempCheck {
private:
     double temp;
     char *charName;
public:
    TempCheck();          // default constructor
     double GetTemp() { return temp; }
     void TempIs(double v) { temp = v; }
};

TempCheck::TempCheck()        // constructor
{
     SetTemp(this);
     if (temp > 102)
          cout << "ALERT! Patient's temperature is "
               << temp << "!\n";
     else
          cout << "Patient's temperature is " << temp << ".\n";
};

void SetTemp(TempCheck *tcPtr)
{
     tcPtr->TempIs(98.6);
};

int main()
{
     TempCheck *takeTemp = new TempCheck();
     delete takeTemp;
     return 0;
}
```

Listing 14.3 creates a class named `TempCheck` to check the patient's temperature. The `TempCheck` class has a private member variable (`temp`) that can be set to the patient's temperature and a pair of public member functions (`GetTemp()` and `TempIs()`) that get and set the value of the `temp` variable.

Before the program creates a `TempCheck` object, it declares a global function that sets the patient's temperature (the member variable `TempCheck::temp`). The function that sets the value of the `temp` variable is named `TempIs()`:

```
void SetTemp(TempCheck *tcPtr)
{
     tcPtr->TempIs(98.6);
};
```

The program's `main()` function calls the constructor of the `TempCheck` class to create a `TempCheck` object named `takeTemp`. (Note that `takeTemp` is an intangible object. It represents a procedure (taking a temperature), not a tangible such as a game character or a table or chair.)

The `main()` function creates its `takeTemp` object by calling this constructor:

```
TempCheck::TempCheck()        // constructor
{
     SetTemp(this);
     if (temp > 102)
          cout << "ALERT! Patient's temperature is "
               << temp << "!\n";
     else
          cout << "Patient's temperature is " << temp << ".\n";
};
```

The `TempCheck` constructor sets the member variable `temp` by calling a global function named `SetTemp()`. In Listing 14.3, the `SetTemp()` function sets the value of the member variable `temp` to 98.6. The constructor then checks the value of `temp`.

If the value of the parameter is greater than 102, the constructor prints a warning message. Otherwise, the constructor simply prints a message reporting the patient's temperature.

Because a value of 98.6 is passed to the `TempCheck` constructor, the program prints this message to standard output:

```
Patient's temperature is 98.6
```

However, if you change the definition of the `SetTemp()` function to read:

```
void SetTemp(TempCheck *tcPtr)
{
     tcPtr->TempIs(102.4);
};
```

the program prints this message:

```
ALERT! Patient's temperature is 102.4!
```

## Conversion Constructors and Copy Constructors

Besides making it easier to allocate and deallocate the memory needed for objects, constructors have some special uses. For example, there's a special kind of constructor, called a *conversion constructor,* that can convert data from one type to another. There's also another kind of constructor, a *copy constructor,* that can make copies of objects.

You can use a conversion constructor to convert an object that belongs to one class into an object that belongs to another class (conversion constructors are examined in Chapter 17, "Conversion Functions"). With a conversion constructor, you can convert a user-defined class to a class that's built into C++, or *vice versa* (copy constructors are covered in Chapter 18, "Copying Objects").

## Initializing Variables with Constructors

As noted back in Chapter 4, "Variables," C++ makes a sharp distinction between initialization (which takes place when an object is created) and assignment (which assigns a value to an existing object). Nowhere is this distinction more sharply defined than in the writing of constructor functions.

In C++, you must initialize constants and references before they can be used. But once a constant or a reference has been initialized, you can't use an assignment statement to give it a new value.

This requirement can cause difficulties you may not expect when you write class definitions. For example, you can't initialize constants or references in class definitions, so this kind of coding is not allowed in C++:

```
class     Customer {
private:
     const long bombs = 100000; // NOT ALLOWED! You can't initialize..
     const long planes = 1000;  // ..constants in a class definition
public:
     // ... more stuff ...
};
```

### Initializing Constants and References

Although the preceding initializations are not allowed in C++, there is a legal syntax that yields the same result. Suppose, for example, that a class definition contained a constant named `bombs` and a reference to a constant that is named `planes`. You could initialize both the constant and the reference by writing a constructor using this format:

```
Customer::Customer() : bombs(100000), planes(1000) {}
```

When you write a constructor using this format, you place a colon after the name of the function to inform the compiler that initialization expressions follow. Each initialization expression consists of the name of a member variable and a parenthesized expression specifying the variable's initial value. These expressions are separated by commas.

The preceding constructor initializes the constant `bombs` by giving it a value of 100,000 and initializes a reference to a constant named `planes` by giving it a value of 1,000. This short program performs both initializations and then prints the results:

### Listing 14.4. Initializing constants and references.

```
// 1404.CPP

#include <iostream.h>

class Customer {
private:
        const long bombs;
        const long& planes;
public:
        Customer();                     // default constructor
        const long GetBombs() { return bombs; }
        const long GetPlanes() { return planes; }
};

long myPlanes = 1000;
Customer::Customer() : bombs(100000), planes(myPlanes) {}

int main()
{
        //instantiate object by calling constructor

        Customer myCust;
        cout << myCust.GetBombs() << '\n' << myCust.GetPlanes() << '\n';
        return 0;
}
```

Notice that in the preceding program, the function-style assignment operator was introduced by C++. When you execute the program, it prints these lines on-screen:

```
100000
1000
```

## Initializing Variables with Function-Like Statements

Although the syntax that produced the preceding printout is most often used to initialize constants, you can use it to initialize ordinary variables as well. In the following program, `bombs` and `planes` have become ordinary long variables. And although they are initialized with the values 100,000 and 1,000, respectively, these values are changed by statements in the `main()` function:

### Listing 14.5. Initializing variables.

```
// 1405.CPP

#include <iostream.h>

class Customer {
private:
        long bombs;
        long& planes;
public:
        Customer();                     // default constructor
        long GetBombs() { return bombs; }
        long GetPlanes() { return planes; }
        void SetBombs(long b) { bombs = b; }
        void SetPlanes(long p) { planes = p; }
};

long myBombs = 100000;
long myPlanes = 1000;
Customer::Customer() : bombs(myBombs), planes(myPlanes) {}

int main()
{
        //instantiate object by calling constructor

        Customer myCust;
        cout << myCust.GetBombs() << '\n' << myCust.GetPlanes() << '\n';
        myCust.SetBombs(4);
        myCust.SetPlanes(10);
        cout << myCust.GetBombs() << '\n' << myCust.GetPlanes() << '\n';
        return 0;
}
```

This version of the program produces this output:

```
100000
1000
4
10
```

# Default Constructors

A *default constructor* is a constructor that creates a default object of the appropriate class type.

A constructor that takes no arguments is always a default constructor. Surprisingly, a constructor that does take arguments can also be a default constructor—if the arguments are optional.

This is a typical declaration of a default constructor that takes no arguments:

```
class AClass {
public:
     AClass();
     // more code
};
```

This code fragment declares a default constructor that takes arguments and initializes them:

```
class AClass {
public:
     AClass(int x = 5, int y = 4);
     // more code
};
```

In the preceding constructor declaration, the arguments in the constructor's parameter list have default values and therefore do not have to be passed to the constructor when the constructor is called. If no arguments are passed to the constructor, the compiler uses the default values. Therefore, the constructor is considered a default constructor.

If an object has a default constructor and a program calls the object without specifying any values, the default constructor is invoked.

> **WHERE DECLARATIONS APPEAR, DEFINITIONS MUST FOLLOW**
>
> If declarations such as the previous ones appear in a program, the program must supply function definitions to go with the declarations. Otherwise, errors are returned.

> **DEFAULT CONSTRUCTORS AND NULL CONSTRUCTORS**
>
> It is important to note that default constructors and null constructors are not the same thing. A null constructor, as noted earlier in this chapter, is simply a constructor that does nothing. For example, a null constructor can be defined this way in a class definition:
>
> ```
> AClass() {}
> ```

## Calling a Default Constructor

When the declaration of a default constructor specifies default arguments, you don't have to pass those arguments to the constructor; you *call* the constructor. Suppose, for example, that a program contains this constructor:

```
anObject(int x = 1);     // default constructor with default argument
```

You can call the preceding default constructor without specifying any arguments, or you can call it by specifying a single `int` argument. Default arguments to a default constructor can also be pointers to members.

For more information on constructors with default parameters, see the Microsoft C++ *Language Reference Manual* that comes with the Professional Edition of Visual C++.

### When Default Constructors Are Invoked

If an object has a default constructor, the default constructor is invoked when:

- In the initialization list of a class's constructor, a member object is not explicitly initialized.
- In the initialization list of a derived class's constructor, a base class is not explicitly initialized.
- An object is dynamically allocated and arguments for the constructor are not specified.
- An array of objects is dynamically allocated. In this case, the default constructor is invoked for each element of the array.
- An array of objects is statically allocated, but some elements in the array lack initializers. In this case, the default constructor is invoked for the elements that are not explicitly initialized.

## Constructor Overloading

If more than one member function in a class definition has the same name as the class being defined, that means the class has more than one constructor. A class can have more than one constructor, provided each constructor has a unique parameter list. In other words, constructors—like other functions in C++—can be *overloaded*.

Because constructors can be overloaded, it naturally follows that a class can have more than one constructor—and that a class with multiple constructors can be initialized in more than one way, depending on which of its constructors is called.

When you overload an object's constructor, you can initialize it in different ways, depending on which constructor you call. When you call a constructor with multiple overloaded versions, the compiler executes the constructor with the parameter list that matches the parameters that are passed to the constructor.

The program in the next example has two constructors: a null constructor and a constructor that takes one parameter. You can call the program by invoking either constructor:

### Listing 14.6. Constructor overloading.

```
// 1406.CPP

#include <iostream.h>

class Customer {
private:
     char *name;
public:
     Customer() {}          // inline constructor
     Customer(char *nm);    // constructor with parameter
     void SetCustName(char *nm) { name = nm; }
     char *GetCustName() { return name; }
};

Customer::Customer(char *nm)
{
     name = nm;
}

int main()
{
     //instantiate object by calling constructor

     Customer myCust("Dr. Strangelove\n");
     cout << myCust.GetCustName();
     return 0;
}
```

If you call the program as shown in the example, the `name` variable is initialized with the string `Dr. Strangelove` when the program is executed. Consequently, this is the program's output:

```
Dr. Strangelove
```

Alternatively, you can create a `Customer` object by calling the inline empty constructor. Then you must call a separate function if you want to initialize the `name` variable:

```
Customer myCust;    // initialize object; constructor called
myCust.SetCustName("Dr. Strangelove\n");
```

These two statements also result in this output:

```
Dr. Strangelove
```

For more about constructor overloading, see Chapter 14, "Constructors and Destructors."

# Using Constructors

Listing 14.7—this chapter's version of the adventure-game program The Wrath of Zalthar—shows how constructors and destructors can be used in a C++ program. In this new version of the program, the `Player`, `Warrior`, and `Gnome` classes are all instantiated with constructors, and the `Warrior` and `Gnome` classes use overriding to create multiple constructors.

### Listing 14.7. The Wrath of Zalthar.

```
// ZALTHAR.H
// Chapter 14 Version
// Copyright 1992, Mark Andrews

#if !defined( _ZALTHAR_H_ )
#define _ZALTHAR_H_

// forward declarations

void FatalError(void);
void PrintTitle(void);

struct Abilities {
     int strength;
     int charisma;
     int dexterity;
     int intelligence;
};

class Player {
private:
     char *name;
     char *weapon;
     char *magic;
     Abilities playerAbils;
public:
     Player() { name = NULL; weapon = NULL; magic = NULL; }
     ~Player() { delete name; delete weapon; delete magic; }
     void SetName(char *nm) { name = DuplicateString(nm); }
     char *GetName() { return name; }
     void SetWeapon(char *wpn) { weapon = DuplicateString(wpn); }
     char *GetWeapon() { return weapon; }
     void SetMagic(char *mag) { magic = DuplicateString(mag); }
     char *GetMagic() { return magic; }
     virtual void PrintEntry() = 0;
     void SetData(int s, int c, int d, int i)
         { playerAbils.strength = s; playerAbils.charisma = c;
           playerAbils.dexterity = d; playerAbils.intelligence = i; }
```

```
     const Abilities GetAbils() { return playerAbils; }
     char *DuplicateString(char *aString);
     void PrintAbils();
};

class Warrior : public Player {
public:
     // default constructor
     Warrior () {}
     // warrior constructor
     Warrior(char *nm, char *wpn)
          { SetName(nm);
            SetWeapon(wpn); }
     ~Warrior() {}  // destructor
     void PrintEntry();
};

class Gnome : public Warrior {
public:
     Gnome(char *nm, char *wpn, char *mag) :
          Warrior(nm, wpn)
          { SetMagic(mag); }
     ~Gnome() {}     // destructor
     void PrintEntry();
};

#endif // _ZALTHAR_H
```

## ZALTHAR.CPP

```
// ZALTHAR.CPP

#include <iostream.h>
#include <string.h>
#include <stdio.h>
#include <stdlib.h>
#include "zalthar.h"

void FatalError()
{
    fprintf(stderr, "A fatal error has occurred\n");
    exit(1);
}

void PrintTitle()
{
     cout << "\nTHE WRATH OF ZALTHAR\n";
     cout << "By [Your Name Here]\n";
};
```

*continues*

**Listing 14.7. continued**

```
char *Player::DuplicateString(char *aString)
{
    char    *aCopy;
    aCopy = new char[strlen(aString) + 1];
    if (aCopy == NULL)
        FatalError();
    strcpy(aCopy, aString);
    return aCopy;
}

void Player::PrintAbils()
{
     cout << "\nStrength: " << playerAbils.strength << '\n';
     cout << "Charisma: " << playerAbils.charisma << '\n';
     cout << "Dexterity: " << playerAbils.dexterity << '\n';
     cout << "Intelligence: " << playerAbils.intelligence << '\n';
}

void Warrior::PrintEntry()
{
     Abilities locAbils = GetAbils();

     cout << "\nWARRIOR" << '\n';
     cout << "Name: " << this->GetName() << '\n';
     cout << "Weapon: " << this->GetWeapon() << "\n";
     PrintAbils();
}

void Gnome::PrintEntry()
{
     Abilities locAbils = GetAbils();

     cout << "\nGNOME" << '\n';
     cout << "Name: " << this->GetName() << '\n';
     cout << "Weapon: " << this->GetWeapon() << "\n";
     cout << "Magic: " << this->GetMagic() << '\n';
     PrintAbils();
}
```

### MAIN.CPP

```
// MAIN.CPP
// The Wrath of Zalthar, Chapter 14 Version
// Copyright 1992 Mark Andrews.  All rights reserved.

#include <iostream.h>
#include "zalthar.h"

int main()
{
```

```
    // create players

    Warrior aWarrior;
    aWarrior.SetName("Bruno");
    aWarrior.SetWeapon("Sword");
    aWarrior.SetData(24, 16, 32, 19);

    Warrior bWarrior;
    bWarrior.SetName("GayLynn");
    bWarrior.SetWeapon("Crossbow");
    bWarrior.SetData(19, 22, 43, 21);


    Gnome aGnome("Glog", "Broadsword", "X-ray vision");
    aGnome.SetData(14, 15, 22, 32);

    // print report

    PrintTitle();

    aWarrior.PrintEntry();
    bWarrior.PrintEntry();
    aGnome.PrintEntry();

    return 0;
}
```

This is the output of the program:

```
THE WRATH OF ZALTHAR
By [Your Name Here]

WARRIOR
Name: Bruno
Weapon: Sword

Strength: 24
Charisma: 16
Dexterity: 32
Intelligence: 19

WARRIOR
Name: GayLynn
Weapon: Crossbow

Strength: 19
Charisma: 22
Dexterity: 43
Intelligence: 21
```

*continues*

**Listing 14.7. continued**

```
GNOME
Name: Glog
Weapon: Broadsword
Magic: X-ray vision

Strength: 14
Charisma: 15
Dexterity: 22
Intelligence: 32
```

### OTHER NEW FEATURES OF THE ZALTHAR PROGRAM

Besides demonstrating the use of constructors and destructors, this chapter's version of the Zalthar program contains a number of other interesting new features. For example:

- The program now includes more inline functions (which simplify coding and improve execution speed).
- The abilities of the game's players are stored in a `struct` named `Abilities`. Then in this statement, an instance of that `struct`, named `playerAbils`, is declared as a member variable of the `Player` class:

  ```
  Abilities playerAbils;
  ```

- Some member functions have headers that make use of function-style initializer syntax (introduced in Chapter 2, "A Better C—Plus") to initialize variables. For example, this is one of the constructors of the `Warrior` class:

  ```
  Warrior(char *nm, char *wpn)
       { SetName(nm);
         SetWeapon(wpn); }
  ```

- Listing 14.7 is also the first version of The Wrath of Zalthar program that makes use of the `this` pointer—a special pointer that holds the address of the object that it belongs to. In C++, you can use the `this` pointer to access any member function of the object that is currently in scope. For example, these statements—which appear in a member function of the `Warrior` class—are used to call other member functions of the same class:

```
cout << "Name: " << this->GetName() << '\n';
cout << "Weapon: " << this->GetWeapon() << "\n";
```

For more information about the `this` pointer, see Chapter 12, "Objects."

## Classes with Multiple Constructors

In Listing 14.7, there are separate constructors for the `Player`, `Warrior`, and `Gnome` classes. Furthermore, the definitions of the `Warrior` and `Player` classes use overloading to provide multiple constructors. For example, these two constructors are defined for the `Warrior class` in the file ZALTHAR.CPP:

```
// default constructor
Warrior () {}
// warrior constructor
Warrior(char *nm, char *wpn)
     { SetName(nm);
       SetWeapon(wpn); }
```

As you can see, the `Warrior` class has a null constructor (a default constructor that takes no parameters), and a second constructor that does take parameters. When you initialize a `Warrior` object, the compiler decides which constructor to use by examining the parameters that you pass to the `Warrior` constructor. If you pass no parameters, the compiler invokes the default `Warrior` constructor. If you pass the parameters required by the `Warrior` class's second constructor, the compiler invokes the second constructor. If you try to instantiate a `Warrior` object with a parameter list that does not match either constructor's parameter list, an error message is returned.

Constructors can be overridden as well as overloaded. In The Wrath of Zalthar, the `Player` class—from which the `Warrior` class is derived—has its own constructor. The `Player` class's constructor initializes the string pointers `name`, `weapon`, and `magic` by giving them `NULL` values:

```
Player () { name = NULL; weapon = NULL; magic = NULL; }
```

### INITIALIZING POINTERS TO NULL

In the definition of the `Player` class's constructors, the `char` pointers `name`, `weapon`, and `magic` are initialized to the value `NULL`. That's done as a safety measure. Later in the Zalthar program, in the constructor for the `Warrior` class, strings are defined for the `char` pointers `name` and `weapon`, but no string is defined for the `char` pointer `magic`. That's because objects of the `Warrior` class don't have magical abilities; only objects of the `Gnome` class do. When you initialize a `Gnome` object, the constructor for the `Gnome` class does define a `magic` string.

When the Zalthar program creates a `name`, `weapon`, or `magic` string, it allocates memory for the string by calling the `new` operator. This allocation takes place in the `DuplicateString()` function in the file named ZALTHAR.CPP.

As you may recall from previous chapters, when you allocate memory with the `new` operator, you must deallocate the memory when it is no longer needed by invoking the `delete` operator. Otherwise, a *dangling pointer* (a pointer that points to an undefined value) remains. Dangling pointers can cause disasters, such as sudden and unexplained program crashes.

In the constructor for the `Player` class, the `char` pointers `name`, `weapon`, and `magic` are initialized to the value `NULL` to prevent the creation of dangling pointers. If you initialize a pointer to the value `NULL`, it's safe to make the pointer the target of a `delete` operation. When the compiler discovers that a pointer is a `NULL` pointer, it doesn't perform any deletion operator at all, so nothing harmful happens.

The Zalthar program initializes the `char` pointers `name`, `weapon`, and `magic` to `NULL` so that when the compiler deletes a `Warrior` object—which doesn't have a defined `magic` string—the compiler doesn't try to delete a nonexistent `magic` string. Instead, the compiler finds a `NULL` pointer where it expects to find a `char` pointer, and it isn't all that surprised. So all ends well.

> Because this scenario often occurs when strings appear in C++ program, the C++ language provides a simpler—and safer—way to manage memory that's allocated for strings. Most C++ class libraries, including the Microsoft Foundation Class library covered in Part III, contain definitions of string classes. When you treat a string as a class instead of as an ordinary C string, the compiler can use constructors and destructors to manage the memory for strings, and then you don't have to manage it yourself.
>
> String classes can also provide easy and efficient methods for performing common string operations, such as copying strings, searching strings for specified characters, and concatenating strings.
>
> In Chapter 18, "Copying Objects," you'll learn how to create a string class. In fact, in the version of the Zalthar program presented in Chapter 18, the `name`, `weapon`, and `magic` strings will be replaced by objects of a do-it-yourself `String` class.

# Order of Construction

When a base class has a constructor and a class derived from the base class also has a constructor, the compiler invokes both constructors. First, the compiler invokes the base class's constructor. Then it invokes the derived class's constructor.

If a derived class has a longer chain of inheritance, the compiler calls the constructors of each class in order, beginning with the first (most senior) parent class in the chain. Thus, the constructor for each class is assured that the class it initializes is completely constructed.

When a class definition contains a declaration of another class, the outer class is called a *composed class*. When a program creates an object of a composed class, the constructors for the contained classes are called before the composed class's own constructor is called.

## Construction by the Numbers

In all, four separate sets of constructors can be invoked when an object is created. When the creation of an object involves the invoking of more that one constructor, this is the order in which constructors are activated:

1. If the object has virtual base classes, they are activated first in the order in which they would be encountered in a left-to-right, depth-first traversal of the class hierarchy.

2. If the object has base class constructors, they are activated. This activation takes place in the left-to-right order in which the base classes appear in the header of the class's definition.

3. Constructors for member objects of the class are activated in the order in which the member objects are declared in the class's definition.

4. Finally, the constructor for the class itself is activated. This activation can rely on the activation of the earlier constructors. If the class has virtual member functions, the class's versions of these member functions are activated—not the versions of the functions defined inside the definition of the base class.

## Invoking Constructors in the Warrior Program

When you instantiate a `Warrior` object in the Zalthar program shown back in Listing 14.7, the compiler first calls the constructor for the `Player` class and then calls the constructor you specify when you instantiate your `Warrior` object. For example, this statement in the `main()` segment of the Zalthar program instantiates a `Warrior` object named `aWarrior`:

```
Warrior aWarrior;
```

The two `Warrior` constructors in this example create a pair of `Warrior` objects, each of which is derived from the `Player` class. That means that each `Warrior` object has data members. The `Gnome` constructor creates a `Gnome` object, which also has three data members.

The `Warrior` class, which is derived from the `Player` class, has a more complicated constructor. The `Warrior` constructor has a parameter list that contains two parameters:

```
Warrior(char *nm, char *wpn)
{ SetName9nm);
  SetWeapon(wpn); }
```

The `Gnome` class, which is derived from the `Warrior` class, has still another constructor. This one has a parameter list with three parameters:

```
Gnome(char *nm, char *wpn, char *mag):
      Warrior(nm, wpn)
      { SetMagic(mag); }
```

# Constructing a const Object

You can declare an object to be a constant by preceding the object's declaration with the `const` keyword. If an object declared to be a `const` has data members, they must be initialized when the object is created.

You can initialize a constant object and its data elements by writing a constructor that performs all necessary initialization at the same time. Listing 14.8 is a program that declares an object to be a `const` and then initializes the object and its data members.

> **CONSTANT MEMBERS OF OBJECTS**
>
> Besides declaring an object to be a `const`, you can declare member variables and member functions of classes to be constants. For more details on declaring member variables of classes to be `const` objects, see Chapter 3, "Type Qualifiers." Member functions that are constants are covered in Chapter 13, "Member Functions."

### Listing 14.8. A `const` object.

```
// 1408.CPP
// Constant objects

#include <iostream.h>
```

*continues*

**Listing 14.8. continued**

```
class PlayerAbils {
private:
     int  strength;
     int  charisma;
     int  dexterity;
     int intelligence;
public:
     PlayerAbils(int stren, int charis, int dext, int intel)
          { strength = stren; charisma = charis;
            dexterity = dext; intelligence = intel; }
     ~PlayerAbils() {}
     void      PrintAbils() const;
     int  GetStrength() const {return strength;}
};

void PlayerAbils::PrintAbils() const
{
     cout << "\nStrength: " << strength << "\n";
     cout << "Charisma: " << charisma << "\n";
     cout << "Dexterity: " << dexterity << "\n";
     cout << "Intelligence: " << intelligence << "\n\n";
}


int main()
{
     const PlayerAbils myPlayer(24, 29, 12, 2);
     myPlayer.PrintAbils();
     return 0;
}
```

In Listing 14.8, the following statement instantiates a `const` member of a class named `PlayerAbils` and initializes all the object's data members:

```
const PlayerAbils myPlayer(24, 29, 12, 2);
```

This is the constructor that the preceding statement invokes:

```
PlayerAbils(int stren, int charis, int dext, int intel)
     { strength = stren; charisma = charis;
       dexterity = dext; intelligence = intel; }
```

When you execute the program, it prints this text to standard output, normally the screen:

```
Strength: 24
Charisma: 29
Dexterity: 12
Intelligence: 2
```

### PROTECTING DATA MEMBERS OF CONST OBJECTS

In Listing 14.8, you may notice that the `const` keyword is used in the declarations of the functions named `PrintAbils()` and `GetStrength()`, but is situated in an odd place: *after* the name of each function:

```
void      PrintAbils() const;
int  GetStrength() const {return strength;}
```

When you place the `const` modifier after the declaration of a member function, the result is that the function's `this` pointer is declared to be a `const`. (If the function is not declared inline, the `const` keyword must also be placed after the function's *definition*.)

When a function's `this` pointer is declared to be a constant, the member function cannot modify data members of the object to which it belongs and cannot call other member functions unless they are also declared to be member functions with constant `this` pointers.

Member functions with constant `this` pointers are designed to be used by base classes. When you give a member function of a base class a constant `this` pointer, overriding functions in derived classes are prevented from modifying data members of the base class.

For more information about member functions with a `const this` pointer, see Chapter 13, "Member Functions."

# Summary

A constructor is a special kind of function that initializes an object. Usually, an object that has a constructor also has another special kind of function called a destructor. When an object with a destructor goes out of scope or is destroyed for any other reason, the destructor deallocates any memory that the object has allocated.

This chapter described constructors and destructors in more detail and explained how they are used in C++ programs. Major topics covered in this chapter included:

- Creating and using constructors and destructors.
- Kinds of constructors.
- Default constructors and null constructors.
- Benefits of using destructors.
- Invoking constructors and destructors.
- Preventing crashes and other program malfunctions that can occur when destructors are used incorrectly.
- Constructor overloading.
- Order of construction and destruction.
- Constructing a `const` object.

Two special kinds of constructors—conversion constructors and copy constructors—are covered in Chapter 17, "Conversion Functions," and Chapter 18, "Copying Objects."

Chapter 15

# Function Overloading

An old adage sums up the trouble with computers: "Computers do what you say, not what you mean."

Today, in the era of object-oriented programming, that statement isn't as true as it used to be. When you call a function or execute a statement in C++, the compiler can often figure out what you meant—and can do what you meant, not what you said.

One feature of C++ that helps your computer figure out what you meant is called *overloading*.

There are two kinds of overloading in C++: function overloading and operator overloading. Function overloading lets you define multiple meanings for the same function. Operator overloading lets you redefine the behaviors of arithmetic and logical operators so they can perform different kinds of operations in different kinds of situations.

You've encountered examples of both function overloading and operator overloading in earlier chapters of this book. Function overloading was introduced in Chapter 2, "A Better C—Plus," described in more detail in Chapter 13, "Member Functions," and used in many example programs in this volume.

This chapter explores the topic of function overloading in more detail. Operator overloading is examined more closely in Chapter 16, "Operator Overloading."

# How Function Overloading Works

Overloading is one of the features of C++ that makes the language emulate real-life situations. In English, as well as in other languages, words often have different meanings when they are used in different contexts. But when a word has multiple meanings, they are often similar. For example, you can *play* the violin, *play* poker, or *play* baseball.

In these three cases, a C++ programmer might say the word *play* is overloaded because you can use it to do three different—but similar—things.

In C++, overloading works in a similar way. The main benefit of overloading is that it adds flexibility to your C++ programs. Overloading lets you write code with less effort because it lets you use the same identifiers and symbols to perform different, but similar, actions.

Function overloading is a technique that lets you call a C++ function without having to supply the compiler with as many details as you might have to provide in C. In other words, a C++ compiler permits you to use variations when you make function calls.

When a function in a C++ program can accept more than one parameter list, it is said to be *overloaded* because the compiler loads the function definition according to the parameters passed to it. Then the compiler executes the function.

The major benefit of function overloading is that it lets you give the same name to functions that perform different, but similar, operations. Another important fact about function overloading is that it imposes almost no runtime penalty and requires practically no overhead.

With one exception—involving argument matching (see box, "Function Overloading and Return Types")—an overloaded function works like any other function. So you get all the benefits of overloading practically free of charge.

> **FUNCTION OVERLOADING AND RETURN TYPES**
>
> With one notable exception, function overloading never applies to the return type of a function. The one exception—which is specific to Microsoft C++—is the `operator new()` function, which was introduced in Chapter 9, "Managing Memory." In Visual C++, you can overload `operator new()` solely on the basis of return type—specifically, on the basis of the memory-model modifier that is specified.
>
> In every other kind of case, if you call a function that returns a value and your function call requires that the return value be cast to some data type other than the one that's returned, the compiler performs the necessary cast. But that casting operation has no relationship to function overloading.

## Ground Rules for Function Overloading

When you overload a function, the versions of the function that you supply the compiler must differ from each other in either or both of these ways:

- The functions must contain a different number of arguments.
- At least one of the arguments in the argument lists of the two functions must be different.

These three function declarations show how function overloading works in C++:

```
void PrintIt(char *name, char *weapon, Abils abilities);
void PrintIt(int n);
void PrintIt(char *message);
```

In a C++ program, the three functions shown above can be called using the following three statements:

```
PrintIt(name, weapon, abilities);
PrintIt(5000);
PrintIt("There is a boat on the horizon.\n");
```

Listing 15.1 is a program in which the three functions shown above are defined and called.

**Listing 15.1. Overloaded functions.**

```
// 1501.CPP
// Overloaded functions

#include <iostream.h>

// overloaded functions - forward declarations
void PrintIt(char *name, char *weapon, int ability);
void PrintIt(int n);
void PrintIt(char *message);

int main()
{
      // calling overloaded functions
      PrintIt("Marjorie", "dagger", 23);
      PrintIt(5000);
      PrintIt("Lo, the lightning has struck the postilion.\n");

      return 0;
}


// -- overloaded functions

void PrintIt(char *name, char *weapon, int ability)
{
      cout << name << '\n';
      cout << weapon << '\n';
      cout << ability << "\n\n";
}

void PrintIt(int n)
{
      cout << n << "\n\n";
}
void PrintIt(char & message)
{
      cout << message << "\n\n";
}
```

This is the output of the program shown in Listing 15.1:

```
Marjorie
dagger
23
```

```
5000

Lo, the lightning has struck the postilion.
```

In C, it wouldn't be possible to use three function calls to call the same function as shown in Listing 15.1. In an ANSI C program, a function always has a specific argument list, and when you call the function, you must pass it exactly the right number and types of arguments. You must always pass the function the same number of arguments, and each of those arguments must have a data type that exactly matches the data type that's called for in the function's formal parameter list.

In C++, as Listing 15.1 shows, the situation is entirely different. In a C++ program, a function can have many different definitions, provided each definition has a different argument list. When you call a function in C++, the compiler automatically executes the correct version of the function you are calling, depending on the number and types of parameters that you pass to the function when you call it.

### NAME DECORATION

When you write a function in C++, the compiler stores the name of the function in memory using a technique called *name mangling*—a term that is so offensive-sounding that some texts substitute the term *name decoration*.

Because of name mangling—or, if you prefer, name decoration—the compiler adds encoded symbols to the name of the function, depending on the number and types of arguments that are in the function's argument list. When the compiler or the linker returns a message that contains a mangled name, the message sometimes contains the symbols that have been added to the function's name, along with the name of the function itself.

Some browsers and debuggers used with C++ decode mangled names, but some don't. So you may sometimes see mangled names when you write and build a C++ program.

# Argument Matching

Sometimes an overloaded function call does impose some overhead. But that only happens when you call a function by passing arguments that don't quite match the required argument of any versions of the functions that are available.

When you call a function with an argument list that the compiler doesn't recognize, the compiler looks for a function that has arguments on which casting operations can be performed. If the compiler finds a function with an argument list that almost matches the argument that's being passed, the compiler does whatever casting is necessary to make the supplied argument list work with the desired function, if that is possible. If the compiler can't find a match that it considers close enough, it generates an error.

The process of trying to make a supplied argument list work with an overloaded function is called *argument matching*.

Listing 15.2 shows how argument matching works in a C++ program.

### Listing 15.2. Argument matching.

```
// 1502.CPP
// Argument matching

#include <iostream.h>

struct Fraction {
        int a;
        int b;
};

// This VagueFunc() function takes a Fraction parameter ...
// ... and a long parameter.
void VagueFunc(Fraction param1, long param2)
{
        cout << "First version of function called." << '\n';
}

// This VagueFunc() function takes a long parameter ...
// and an int parameter.
void VagueFunc(long param1, int param2)
{
        cout << "Second version of function called." << '\n';
}
```

```
int main()
{
        Fraction myFrac;

        int intVal = 23;

        VagueFunc(myFrac, intVal); // Force argument matching.
        VagueFunc(23, 24);

        return 0;
}
```

In Listing 15.2, there are two versions of the function named `VagueFunc()`. The first version takes an argument list made up of a struct named `Fraction` and a long data type. The second version takes an argument list made up of a `long` data type and an `int` data type.

In the program's `main()` function, there are two calls to `VagueFunc()`. The first call passes the function a `Fraction` struct and an `int`. The second call passes the function two integers.

Neither of the calls in the `main()` function has exactly the kind of argument list that `VagueFunc()` expects, so in each case, the compiler uses argument matching to determine which version of the function should be called.

In the first call, the `long` data type that `VagueFunc()` expects can be easily created. If the `int` value in the call's argument list is cast to a `long`, the argument list becomes a `Fraction` and a `long`, and the first version of `VagueFunc()` can be called. In the second call, if the first `int` value that is passed to the function is cast to a `long`, the argument list becomes a pair of `long` data types, and the second version of `VagueFunc()` can be called.

When you execute the program, those two casts are indeed performed, and the two calls in the `main()` function produce the expected results. This is the output of the program:

```
First version of function called.
Second version of function called.
```

If you overload a member function of a class and then attempt to call the function by passing it an argument list that it does not expect, the compiler attempts to call the function by performing an argument-matching operation. Listing 15.3 shows how you can force the compiler to resort to argument matching in a class-and-object context.

### Listing 15.3. Using argument matching with member functions.

```
// 1503.CPP
// Argument matching in a class context

#include <iostream.h>

struct Fraction {
        long a;
        long b;
};

class FunWithArgs
{
private:
        Fraction fracStruct;
        long aLongVar;
public:
        void VagueFunc(Fraction param1, long param2);
        void VagueFunc(long param1, int param2);
};

// First version of VagueFunc() member function.
void FunWithArgs::VagueFunc(Fraction param1, long param2)
{
        fracStruct = param1;
        aLongVar = param2;
        cout << "First version of member function called." << '\n';
}

// Second version of VagueFunc() member function.
void FunWithArgs::VagueFunc(long param1, int param2)
{
        fracStruct.a = param1;
        fracStruct.b = param2;
        cout << "Second version of member function called." << '\n';
}

int main()
{
        FunWithArgs myFun;
        Fraction myFrac = { 100, 200 };

        myFun.VagueFunc(myFrac, 23); // Force argument matching.
        myFun.VagueFunc(23, 24);

        return 0;
}
```

In Listing 15.3, a class named `FunWithArgs` contains two member functions named `VagueFunc()`. They take the same kinds of argument lists as the two `VagueFunc()` functions that were presented earlier in Listing 15.2. The first version takes an argument list made up of a struct named `Fraction` and a `long` data type. The second version takes an argument list made up of a `long` data type and an `int` data type.

In Listing 15.3, the `main()` function creates a `FunWithArgs` object name `myFun` and a `Fraction` struct named `myFrac`. Then the program makes two calls to `MyFun.VagueFunc()`. As in Listing 15.2, the first call passes the funtion a `Fraction` struct and an `int`, and the second call passes the function two integers.

The results are the same as those you saw in Listing 15.2. In the first call, the `int` data type that is passed to `VagueFunc()` is cast to a `long`. The argument list then becomes a `Fraction` and a `long`, and the first version of `VagueFunc()` is called. In the second call, the first `int` value that is passed to the function is cast to a `long`. That call's argument list becomes two `long` data types, and the second version of `VagueFunc()` can be called.

The output is the same as the output of the previous listing:

```
First version of function called.

Second version of function called.
```

## How Argument Matching Works

When the compiler resorts to argument matching to make a function call work, the compiler tries to select the version of the function that most closely matches the formal argument list that is supplied for the function. In other words, the compiler tries to find a function on a *best-match* basis.

To select a function on a best-match basis, the compiler scans the overloaded version of the function to see which function declaration in the current scope best matches the arguments supplied in the function call. If a suitable function is found, that function is called. To be considered suitable, a function must meet one of the following criteria:

- The function's formal argument list must exactly match the arguments that are passed to the function.
- The function must have a formal argument list that can be converted to the desired argument list with a standard conversion operation.

- The function must have a formal argument list that can be converted to the desired argument list with a user-defined conversion. The conversion that is used for this purpose can be either an operator conversion or a constructor conversion function.

If the calling function meets one of the above criteria, the compiler creates a list of "best-matching functions" for each argument. The compiler then executes the best-matching function with the greatest number of best-matched arguments.

If the compiler finds one or more best-matched functions, one of the functions that is found must be a better match than any other function that is found. If there is no clear winner, the compiler returns an error message.

## Argument Matching, Step by Step

When the compiler attempts to call a function by building a list of best-matching functions, ambiguities can arise. The compiler resolves any possible ambiguities by performing argument matching in this order:

1. *No conversions are necessary.* If the argument list that is passed to a function exactly matches the function's formal argument list that is passed, the function is executed. There are some conversions, called trivial conversions, that qualify as exact matches. There are two main kinds of trivial conversions: conversions to and from references and conversions that involve only the type qualifiers `const` and `volatile`. Trivial conversions are listed in Table 15.1.

**Table 15.1. Trivial conversions.**

| *Convert from* | *Convert to* |
|---|---|
| Type name | Reference (`typeName&`) |
| Reference (`typeName&`) | Type name |
| Array (`typeName[]`) | Reference to type name (`typeName*`) |
| Type name and argument list (*typeName(argumentList)*) | Reference type name and argument list (**typeName(argumentList)*) |
| Type name | `const` type name (`const typeName`) |

| *Convert from* | *Convert to* |
|---|---|
| Type name | `volatile` type name (`volatile` *`typeName`*) |
| Pointer to type name (*`typeName`*`*`) | Pointer to `const` type name (`const` *`typeName`*`*`) |
| Pointer to type name (*`typeName`*`*`) | `volatile` type name (`volatile` *`typeName`*`*`) |

2. *Argument promotions are needed.* If an argument list that is passed to a function contains an argument that can be "promoted" to match one of the formal arguments of the function being called, the promotion is performed and the function is called. A promotion is a conversion of a data type to a longer data type; for example, a conversion of a `char` data type to an `int` data type. The argument conversion shown in Listing 15.4 is a conversion of a `char` data type to an `int` data type.

#### Listing 15.4. Passing an integer when a `char` is expected.

```
// 1504.CPP
// Argument promotion

#include <iostream.h>

int intValue;

// SetVal() takes an int argument
void SetVal(int param) { intValue = param; }
int GetVal() { return intValue; }

int main()
{
        SetVal('a');                            // pass SetVal() a char
        cout << GetVal() << '\n';               // print int
        cout << (char) GetVal() << '\n';        // print char
        return 0;
}
```

In Listing 15.4, the declaration of the `SetVal()` function requires that the function take an `int` argument. But in the program's `main()` function, `SetVal()` is called with a `char` argument. When `SetVal()` is called, the compiler promotes the `char` that's passed to `SetVal()` to an `int`. The program then prints the value that was passed to `SetVal()` twice: first as an integer and then as a character. This is the result:

```
97
a
```

Figure 15.1 is a chart of data-type promotions that the compiler uses in argument matching. Any data type shown in Figure 15.1 can be promoted to any data type that appears above it. Conversions in the opposite direction—from a data type to a data type that lies below it—requires a cast. Cast operations used in argument matching are described in Item 3.

3. *Standard argument conversions are needed.* If an argument does not meet the criteria outlined in Items 1 or 2, the compiler attempts to cast the argument to the desired type using standard conversion operations (described in Chapter 17, "Conversion Functions."). In Listing 15.4, the definition of the `SetVal()` function calls for a `char` type, but the `main()` function passes an integer value to `SetVal()` when it calls the function. The compiler responds by casting the supplied argument to the expected data type, and then executing the function. The output of the program is:

```
97
a
```

4. *User-defined argument conversions are needed.* If an argument does not meet the criteria outlined in Items 1, 2, or 3, the compiler looks for a user-defined casting operation that can cast the argument to the desired type. (User-defined casts are described in Chapter 17.)

5. *The argument can be matched with an ellipsis.* You can place an ellipsis (`...`) in a function's argument list when you declare the function. The ellipsis means that varying numbers and types of arguments can be used to define the function. If the declaration of a function contains an ellipsis, the compiler considers the ellipsis to be a last-resort match.

Many other subtleties are involved in argument matching, and are comprehensively described in the Microsoft C++ *Language Reference* manual. But since ambiguities can arise from argument matching, and can have unexpected results, the best way to handle argument matching is to do your best to avoid it.

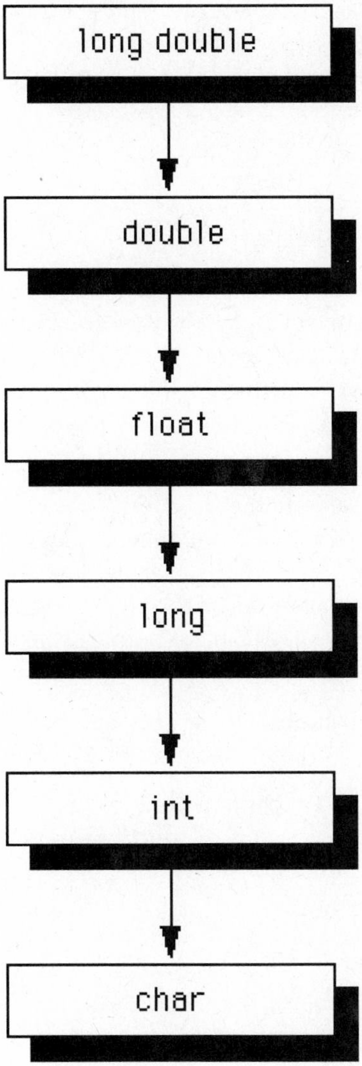


*Figure 15.1. Data-type promotions.*

That does not mean you should avoid using function overloading; on the contrary, function overloading is one of the most important features of C++, and you should take advantage of it in your programs. However, you should do your own argument-matching; forcing the compiler to perform argument-matching slows down the execution of your program and increases chances for programming errors.

When it's possible, declare and define functions that have clear and accurate argument lists, and then call your functions by passing the expected parameters. Then you won't have to worry about argument matching and the ambiguities that can affect the argument-matching process.

## Function Overloading and Scope

You can overload any function in C++, but an overloading operation is effective only inside the scope in which the function is defined. For example, any function defined outside any class and defined without the `static` keyword has file scope. Thus, all versions of the function that are created using operator overloading also have file scope. In Listing 15.4, the `GetVal()` and `SetVal()` functions both have file scope.

When more than one member function with the same name is declared in a class, the overloading of the function has class scope; that is, the function is overloaded only within the class in which the function is declared. Other classes might use the same name again, overloading it differently or even not overloading it at all. That's because classes have separate scopes in C++, and the compiler keeps those scopes separated.

Listing 15.5 illustrates the use of function overloading within class scope; that is, the overloading of a member function of a class.

In Listing 15.5, a function named `Value()` is overloaded in the definition of a class named `AClass`. One of the functions reads a value and the other writes the value, but the two functions have the same name. Overloading is often used for purposes such as this in C++.

### Listing 15.5. An overloaded member function.

```
// 1505.CPP
// Argument matching

#include <iostream.h>

class AClass {
private:
     char charVal;
public:
     void Value(char p1) { charVal = p1; }
     char Value() { return charVal; }
};
```

```
int main()
{
     AClass *anObject = new AClass;
     anObject->Value('a');          // force argument matching
     cout << anObject->Value() << '\n'; // print char
     return 0;
}
```

In Listing 15.5, the `main()` function calls both versions of the `Value()` function. One version reads the value of `anObject->charValue`, and the other version writes the value of the same variable to standard output, normally the screen.

## Overloading Constructors

As noted in Chapter 14, a *constructor* is a function that allocates memory for an object. When a class has a constructor, the constructor is declared inside the definition of the class. Although it's theoretically possible to create an object that doesn't have a constructor, constructors provide so many benefits to objects that it's conventional to provide a constructor for every object in a C++ program.

Constructors can be overloaded, and are often overloaded in C++ programs. For example, this code fragment contains a constructor that initializes objects of a class named `ExampleClass`:

```
class ExampleClass {
private:
     int x;
public:
     ExampleClass() {}              // constructor
     ~ExampleClass() {}             // destructor
};
```

In a class definition, you can overload a constructor in the same way you would overload any other kind of function. To provide a class with one or more overloaded constructors, all you have to do is make sure that each version of the class's constructor contains a unique parameter list. For example, this function definition contains three constructors for the class named `ExampleClass`:

```
class ExampleClass {
private:
     int x, y;
public:
     ExampleClass() {}              // constructor
     ExampleClass(int a) { x = a; }      // overloaded constructors ...
```

```
     ExampleClass(int a, int b) { x = a; y = b; }
     ~ExampleClass() {}            // destructor
};
```

For more information about constructors, see Chapter 14.

> **YOU CAN'T OVERLOAD DESTRUCTORS**
>
> There is no way to overload a destructor. Destructors don't take arguments, so there is only one way to call—and thus to define—a destructor.

## Overloading Functions in Derived Classes

When functions with the same names are declared in a base class and a derived class, any overloading that takes place in the derived class overrides the function that is declared in the base class. Listing 15.6 illustrates the overloading of member functions in base classes and derived classes.

### Listing 15.6. Function overloading in base and derived classes.

```
// 1506.CPP
// Overloading a function in base and derived classes

#include <iostream.h>

class AClass {
private:
     int aVal;
public:
     AClass() {}
     ~AClass() {}
     int Value(int n) { aVal = n + 1; return aVal; }
};

class BClass: public AClass {
private:
     float bVal;
public:
     float Value(float n) { bVal = n + 2; return bVal; }
};
```

```
int main()
{
     BClass anObject;
     cout << anObject.Value(100) << '\n';
     return 0;
}
```

In Listing 15.6, a class named `BClass` is derived from a class named `AClass`. The definition of `AClass` contains a function named `Value()`. The definition of `BClass` contains an overloaded version of the `Value()` function.

The `Value()` function declared inside the `AClass` definition is different from the `Value()` function that is declared inside the `BClass` definition. The `Value()` function that is defined by `AClass` is designed to manipulate variables of data type `int`. The `Value()` function that is defined by `BClass` is designed to manipulate variables of data type `float`.

There is also another difference between the `AClass` and `BClass` versions of the `Value()` function. The `AClass` version of the function adds 1 to the value that it's passed to it, and the `AClass` version adds 2 to the value that it's passed to it.

The `main()` function shown in Listing 15.6 calls the `Value()` function by passing an `int` variable. Since the version of `Value()` that is declared inside the `AClass` definition takes an `int` variable as an argument, that is the version of `Value()` that you might expect to be called.

However, when you execute the program, its output is:

```
102
```

That means that when you run the program, the compiler executes the `BClass` version of the `Value()` function—even though the `BClass` version requires an implicit conversion of an argument from an `int` type to a `float` type.

And why does that happen? Because the `AClass` version of the `Value()` function is not visible to an object that belongs to `BClass`. Even though `BClass` is derived from `AClass`, the version of the `Value()` function that is defined in the definition `BClass` obscures the version of the function that was originally declared in the definition of `AClass`.

Therefore, when the program in Listing 15.6 calls the `Value()` function, the only version of the function that can possibly be executed is the version that is declared inside the definition of `BClass`.

## The Scope Resolution Operator

If a member function that is declared by a subclass overrides a member function that is declared by a base class, you can access the member function declared in the base class by using the scope resolution operator (::). For example, suppose that you replace the `main()` function in Listing 15.6 with the following `main()` function:

```
int main()
{
     BClass anObject;
     cout << anObject.AClass::Value(100) << '\n';
     return 0;
}
```

In the `main()` function shown above, the statement

```
cout << anObject.AClass::Value(100) << '\n';
```

uses the scope resolution operator to call `AClass::Value()`. That changes the output of the program to

```
101
```

proving that the program now calls `AClass::Value()`.

## Overloading Virtual Functions

You can overload members of virtual functions, provided the usual rules of overloading are followed; an overloaded virtual function, like any overloaded function, must have an argument list that contains either a different number of arguments or at least one argument with a unique type.

When a virtual function is overloaded in a base class, you can call any version of the function in the same way that you would call it if it were overloaded in a derived class; just pass the function the kind of argument list that it expects, and the correct version of the function will be executed.

Listing 15.7 shows how you can overload virtual functions in a C++ program.

**Listing 15.7. Overloading virtual functions.**

```
// 1507.CPP
// Overloading virtual functions
```

```
#include <iostream.h>

class WindowRect {
protected:
    int h, v, hh, vv;
public:
    virtual void SetCoords(int     x, int y)
          { h = x; v = y; }
    virtual void SetCoords(int x, int y, int xx, int yy)
          { h = x; v = y; hh = xx; vv = yy; }
};

class MyWindowRect : public WindowRect {
public:
    void GetCoords(int *x, int *y, int *xx, int *yy)
     { *x = h; *y = h; *xx = hh; *yy = vv; }
};

int main()
{
    int x, y, xx, yy;

    MyWindowRect myWinRect;
    myWinRect.SetCoords(10,10);              // version 1
    myWinRect.SetCoords(20, 20, 100, 120);    // version 2
    myWinRect.GetCoords(&x, &y, &xx, &yy);

    cout << x << '\n';
    cout << y << '\n';
    cout << xx << '\n';
    cout << yy << '\n';

    return 0;
}
```

In Listing 15.7, a virtual function named `SetCoords()` is overloaded in the definition of the `WindowRect()` class. Both versions of the function are called in the program's `main()` segment, and they behave as expected. The output of the program is:

```
20
20
100
120
```

# Overloading Static Member Functions

Static member functions aren't overloaded in every C++ program, but it is certainly possible to overload a static member function. Listing 15.8, an example program that counts cats, contains an overloaded static member function.

### Listing 15.8. Overloading static member functions.

```
// 1508.CPP
// Overloading a static member function

#include <iostream.h>

class CatCount {
private:
    static int count;
public:
    CatCount() { count++; }    // constructor
    ~CatCount() { count --; } // destructor
    static int CountEm() { return count; }
    static void CountEm(int *x) { *x = count; }
};

int CatCount::count = 0;

int main()
{
    int x, y;

    CatCount cc;
    x = cc.CountEm();
    cout << x << '\n';

    cc.CountEm(&y);
    cout << y << '\n';

    return 0;
}
```

In Listing 15.8, a static member function `CountEm()` is overloaded. One version of the function takes no arguments but returns an integer. The other version takes a pointer as an argument, and returns no value; instead, it stuffs a value into the address that is passed to it as an argument. When you execute the program, it produces this output, showing you that both versions of the `CountEm()` function provide the `main()` function with the same value:

```
1
1
```

## Conversion Functions

In C, you can automatically convert data from almost any built-in type to another, provided the conversion makes sense. In C++, you can do more than that; you can create your own data types, and the compiler has no rules for converting them because there's no way that it can know what they are.

To create back and forth between a user-defined data type in C++, you must write a special kind of function called a conversion function. There are two kinds of conversion functions: *conversion constructors* and *member conversion functions.*

As you might guess from their names, conversion constructors and member conversion functions do their jobs in different ways. A conversion constructor is a special kind of a constructor. A member conversion function is a special kind of member function.

A conversion constructor is simply a constructor that converts an object of one type to an object of another type. To create a conversion constructor, you must use the function overloading technique that is described in this chapter. In fact, the overloaded constructor is the most commonly used mechanism for converting an object of one data type to an object of another type.

Conversion constructors are exceedingly versatile; you can convert anything to anything with a conversion constructor, provided the conversion makes sense to you. If it also makes sense to others, so much the better.

A conversion constructor always has just one parameter, and the data type of the parameter is the type of the source data that is being converted. For example, this conversion constructor converts a `double` variable named `amount` into an object named `Money`:

```
Money::Money(double x)              // conversion constructor--
{                                   // converts double to Money
     double y, n;
     double ct, dl;
     y = modf(x, &n);          // a math.h function
     ct = y * 100;             // frac comes back as .xx
     dl = n;                   // n comes back as a double
     dollars = dl;
     cents = ct;
}
```

To create a conversion constructor, all you have to do is declare the constructor using the *data type* of the value that you want converted as the single parameter to the conversion constructor.

Once you have defined a conversion constructor, you can invoke it by passing to the constructor the value that you want converted. The value that you pass to the conversion constructor must have the data type that the conversion constructor expects. The conversion constructor can then perform the requested conversion, using the constructor definition that you have provided.

Listing 15.9 shows how a conversion constructor can be used in a C++ program.

**Listing 15.9. A conversion constructor.**

```
// 1509.CPP
// A converter construction function

#include <iostream.h>
#include <math.h>

class Money {
private:
     double dollars;
     double cents;
public:
     Money() {}                       // default constructor
     ~Money() {}                      // destructor
     Money(double d, double c);       // another default const
     Money(double);                   // conversion from double
     double GetAmount(double &n);
};

Money::Money(double d, double c)
{
     dollars = d; cents = c;
}

Money::Money(double x)                // conversion constructor--
{                                     // converts double to Money
     double y, n;
     double ct, dl;
     y = modf(x, &n);            // a math.h function
     ct = y * 100;               // frac comes back as .xx
     dl = n;                     // n comes back as a double
     dollars = dl;
     cents = ct;
}
```

```
double Money::GetAmount(double &n)
{
     n = dollars;
     return cents;
}

double main()
{
     Money myCash(29.95);      // call conversion constructor
     double d, c;

     c = myCash.GetAmount(d); // check result of conversion
     cout << d << '\n';
     cout << c << "\n\n";

     return 0;
}
```

The program shown in Listing 15.9 converts a floating-point value—in this case, 29.95—to the long integers 29 and 95. The output of the program is:

```
29
95
```

Constructor conversion functions are described in more detail in Chapter 17.

> **CONVERSION OPERATIONS IGNORE MEMBER FUNCTIONS**
>
> When the C++ compiler carries out a conversion operation on an object, the compiler is concerned only with the object's data members. The object's member functions contain no data, so they are disregarded.
>
> Thus, for conversion purposes, the `Money` class is made up of just two member variables: the `double` variable `dollars` and the `double` variable `cents`. The object's member functions just don't count.

# Summary

There are two kinds of overloading in C++: function overloading and operator overloading. Function overloading lets you define multiple meanings for the same function. Operator overloading lets you redefine the behaviors of arithmetic and logical operators so that they can perform different kinds of operations in different kinds of situations.

When you overload a function, you can write code with less effort because overloading lets you use the same identifiers and symbols to perform different (but usually similar) actions.

This chapter covered function overloading. It explained how functions can be overloaded, how overloading works, and how overloading is used in C++ programs.

Operator overloading—the customizing of the operators used in C++—is covered in Chapter 16.

Chapter 16

# Operator Overloading

In C++, overloading is a very useful tool with a terrible-sounding name. To an audio engineer, an overloaded amplifier sounds awful. To an electrical engineer, an overloaded circuit means trouble. But to a C++ programmer, overloading is a useful tool that can add tremendous flexibility to an object-oriented program.

Overloading makes it easier to write C++ programs because it lets you use the same identifiers and symbols to perform different, but usually similar, actions.

There are two kinds of overloading in C++. As you learned in Chapter 15, *function overloading* lets you define multiple meanings for the same function. As you'll see in this chapter, *operator overloading* lets you extend the language by creating your own operators.

More specifically, operator overloading lets you redefine the behaviors of arithmetic and logical operators so that they can perform different kinds of operations in different kinds of situations.

# How Operator Overloading Works

An operator, as you may know, is a symbol that tells a compiler to perform a specific mathematical or logical operation. C++, like C, has three general classes of operators: *arithmetic operators*, *relational and logical operators*, and *bitwise operators*. In C++, you can overload all three kinds of operators to make them do what you want them to do instead of what they ordinarily do by default.

It's important to remember that when you overload an operator, the overloading operation that you execute affects only the scope in which the operation is executed. For example, if you overload an operator inside the definition of a class, the behavior of the operator is modified only within that class. The behavior of the operator in other parts of your program is not affected. And that's a good thing; if you could globally overload every operator in the C++ language, you could make the entire language behave in a very bizarre fashion, and that isn't what the creators of C++ intended when they decided to let you overload the language's operators.

## An Illustration of Operator Overloading

As an illustration of how operator overloading works, consider the operator +=, which is ordinarily used in this fashion:

```
int n = 100;
n += 200;
```

As you know, if the two statements shown above are executed in succession, the second statement evaluates to 300.

Now assume that you want to use the += operator to perform an addition operation on a pair of strings rather than on a pair of integers. In C++, you can do that, so you can overload the += to perform this kind of concatenation operation on two strings:

```
AString x = "Merry";
x += " Christmas";
// output desired: "Merry Christmas"
```

The preceding example illustrates an operation that you'd never be able to perform in a C program. But in C++, the preceding code fragment is all it takes to concatenate two strings. In fact, you usually don't even have to write the function that overloads the += operator. That's because most C libraries—including the Microsoft Foundation Class (MFC) library—contain string classes that let you perform many kinds of operations with strings that are similar to the one shown here.

By overloading operators in C++ programs, you can also write string classes of your own. With string objects—prewritten or homemade—you can overload functions to perform the kinds of string operations that are common in BASIC programs, and more; for example, you can create functions that can concatenate strings, find character patterns in strings, and copy strings from one memory location to another.

For more information about how you can overload operators to copy and manipulate strings, see Chapter 18, "Copying Objects."

## Using Operator Overloading in Math Operations

You can use operator overloading in mathematical operations too. For example, suppose you wanted to write a function that could tell you what the date would be three weeks from now. By creating a `Date` class and overloading the `+` operator, you could write a program that performed this kind of operation:

```
laterDate = todaysDate + weeks(3);
```

You could also use a `Date` class and operator overloading to calculate the difference between two dates. For example, you could overload the `<` operator to execute this kind of function:

```
if(oneDate < anotherDate)
   cout << "Due date has passed.\n";
```

C++ programmers often use operator overloading when they create classes that represent numeric types. For example, scientific programs often use complex numbers; that is, numbers with a real and an imaginary component. In C++, you can write a `Complex` class to represent these numbers (in fact, if you browse through the various class libraries on the market, you're likely to find that someone has written one for you).

In an old-fashioned C program—without a `Complex` class to help you out—you might perform tasks such as adding and multiplying complex numbers by writing functions with names like `add` and `mult`. This approach can result in long, complex statements that are hard to understand. For example:

```
x = mult( mult( add( y, z ), add( a, b ) ), c );
```

Statements such as the one shown above are difficult to write, and they can be even more difficult to figure out. Once more, C++ offers a better alternative. In C++, you can overload operators such as `+` and `*` so that they work on `Complex` objects—not in a weird or bizarre way, but in the way you would expect them to work.

When you use operator overloading to make the preceding statement more comprehensible, you might wind up with a statement that looks more like this:

```
x = ( y + z ) * ( a + b ) * c;
```

The preceding statement is obviously easier to read and easier to understand—not only for the programmer, but also for others who might later have the job of figuring out the equation.

# Writing Operator-Overloading Functions

To overload an operator, you must declare and define an operator-overloading function. Most operator-overloading functions are member functions of classes. But you also can overload an operator with a nonmember function.

A function that overloads an operator—whether it is a member function or a non-member function—always makes use of the keyword `operator`. For example, this is a declaration of a member function that overloads the + operator:

```
Money operator+(int);
```

When you have placed a declaration like the one shown above inside a definition of a class, you can define a function that overloads the + operator in the manner that is specified by the function's declaration. You can then use the overloaded function to add the class that is specified in the function declaration to the data type that is specified in the argument that is passed to the function (that data type can also be a class).

When you define a function that overloads an operator, the function that overloads the operator is called only when the operator is used with the data types that are specified in its header. If you want to overload the specified operator so that it behaves in a customized way when it is used with other data types, you must write another operator-overloading function that specifies those data types in its header.

## The Scope of Operator-Overloading Functions

When you overload an operator, normal scope rules apply; the operator is overloaded within the scope in which its overloading function appears. For example, suppose that a stand-alone function written in this syntax is used to overload the + operator:

```
Money operator+(int)
{
     // body of function
}
```

If the function definition that is shown above appears inside a program's `main()` function, the addition operator (+) is overloaded globally—that is, throughout the program—whenever it is used to add an object of the `Money` class to any integer.

If the preceding overloading function appears inside the definition of a class, its effect is the same but its scope is more limited; it creates a local addition operator for the `Money` class, and overloads that operator; it has no effect on the global addition operator that is defined by C++.

When you use an operator in an expression, the compiler checks to see whether the operator is overloaded locally for the operands that appear in the expression. If the operator is overloaded locally, the function that overloads it locally is executed.

Next, the compiler checks to see whether the operator is overloaded globally for the operands that are used in the expression. If the operator is overloaded locally, the function that overloads it locally is executed.

If the operator is not overloaded locally or globally, the expression that contains the operator is executed without any overloading.

Ordinarily, the order in which the compiler checks operator overloading makes no discernible difference in the execution of a program. However, if the same operator is overloaded with both a member function and a nonmember function, it is important to know that both operator-overloading functions are evaluated. That makes it possible to overload the same operator with both a member function and a nonmember function, as illustrated in the section on nonmember functions later in this chapter.

## The Format of an Operator-Overloading Function

When you declare a function that overloads an operator, the first word of the declaration is always the name of a class. Later, whenever the overloaded operator is used in an expression, the first operand of the expression is always the specified class. To use an overloaded operator with a different class, you must write another operator-overloading function that specifies the name of the class that is being overloaded.

In the declaration of an operator-overloading function, the second word is the keyword `operator`. The word `operator` is followed by the operator symbol that is being overloaded.

An operator-overloading function declaration—like any other function declaration—ends with a pair of parentheses and a semicolon. If the operator that is being overloaded takes a second parameter, that parameter's data type is placed between the parentheses.

## Overloading Binary and Unary Operators

There are two main kinds of operators in C++: binary operators, which have two operands, and unary operators, which have one operand. The + and - operators, which add and subtract numbers, are examples of binary operators. Examples of unary operators are the unary + and - operators, which precede positive and negative numbers, and the ++ and -- operators, which increment and decrement values.

You can overload both binary operators and unary operators in C++. This is a declaration of a member function that overloads the binary - operator:

```
Money operator-(int);
```

When you have placed a declaration like the one shown above inside a definition of a class, you can write a matching function that uses the overloaded - operator to subtract an integer from an object of the `Money` class.

This is a declaration of a member function that overloads the *unary* - operator:

```
Money operator-();
```

Notice that there is no data type inside the parentheses in the above expression. That means that the expression defines a function that overloads a unary operator. When you have placed a declaration like the one shown above inside a definition of a class, you can write a matching function that uses the overloaded - operator to negate the value of an object of the `Money` class.

Techniques for overloading most common binary and unary operators are presented in this chapter.

**TO OVERLOAD OR NOT TO OVERLOAD...**

Throughout this chapter, and throughout your C++ programming career, you should keep one important point in mind every time you overload an operator: Your motive in overloading an operator should never be to modify the operator's behavior in some strange, incomprehensible fashion, but to extend its capabilities so that it works in the expected way on user-defined data types.

In the previous example, the programmer resorted to function overloading because the C++ language defines operators such as + and * to work on built-in types, but don't work with user-defined types. When you overload the + and * operators so that they work in the expected way on complex numbers, you aren't really changing their default behavior; you're simply extending it so that it also works on complex numbers.

Often you must use discretion in deciding what kinds of overloading operations make sense, and what kinds don't. Most C++ programmers would agree that it probably makes sense to use the binary addition operator + to concatenate a pair of strings (as illustrated in an example earlier in this chapter). Most programmers would probably also agree that it would make no sense to overload the + operator to force it to perform a subtraction operation.

There's a lot of uncharted territory between these two extremes, and deciding where sensible overloading stops and weird overloading begins is strictly up to you; you're the programmer.

## Operators That Can Be Overloaded

In C++, you can overload any of the operators shown in Table 16.1.

**Table 16.1. Operators that can be overloaded.**

<table>
<tr><td>+</td><td>-</td><td>*</td><td>/</td><td>%</td><td>^</td><td>&</td><td>|</td></tr>
<tr><td>~</td><td>!</td><td>,</td><td>=</td><td><</td><td>></td><td><=</td><td>>=</td></tr>
<tr><td>++</td><td>--</td><td><<</td><td>>></td><td>==</td><td>!=</td><td>&&</td><td>11</td></tr>
<tr><td>+=</td><td>-=</td><td>*=</td><td>/=</td><td>%=</td><td>^=</td><td>&=</td><td>|=</td></tr>
<tr><td><<=</td><td>>>=</td><td>[]</td><td>()</td><td>-></td><td>->*</td><td>new</td><td>delete</td></tr>
</table>

### OVERLOADING AND THE IOSTREAM.H LIBRARY

Overloading can be used in countless ways in C++. For instance, the bitwise shift operators << and >> are overloaded in the IOSTREAM.H library to perform I/O operations. As you've seen in many of the example programs in this book, the IOSTREAM.H library has overloaded the >> operator to accept keyboard input, and has overloaded the << operator to print to standard output, normally the screen.

The IOSTREAM.H library is examined in detail in Chapter 20, "Streams."

## Operator Overloading: Tips and Techniques

If you carefully study the overloadable operators listed in Table 16.1, you might find some of them surprising. For example:

- `()`. The parentheses that are used in function calls in C++ constitute an overloadable operator. That means that in C++, a function call is overloadable. And that's why you can use a syntax that resembles the syntax of a function call syntax to perform operations on C++ classes.
- `[]`. Similarly, subscripting is overloadable in C++. So you can use C++'s standard element-of-array notation to implement operations such as bounds-checked array accesses.
- `=`. The assignment operator can be overloaded in C++, so you can use it to control the copying of objects.

- `->` and `->*`. The indirection operators are overloadable in C++. So you can overload these operators to perform more kinds of checking than ordinary pointers do.
- `,`. The comma, known technically as the sequential evaluation operator, is overloadable in C++. So, in a list of classes, objects, or members of classes, you can overload the comma operator so that it can separate the names of items in the list.
- `new` and `delete`. The `new` and `delete` operators can be overloaded in C++, so you can control storage allocation for a class.

For more information on all the operators shown on the chart, see the Microsoft C++ *Language Reference* manual.

## Operators that Can't Be Overloaded

There are some operators that can't be overloaded. Table 16.2 lists these operators and explains why they cannot be overloaded.

**Table 16.2. Operators that can't be overloaded.**

| *Operator* | *Name of Operator* | *Why Operator Can't Be Overloaded* |
|---|---|---|
| `?:` | Ternary operator | There is no syntax in C++ for defining a ternary operator. |
| `.` | Member-of operator | The designers of C++ considered it important to safeguard this operator's ability to access members. |
| `.*` | Member pointer operator | The designers of C++ also considered it important to safeguard this operator's ability to access members. |
| `::` | Scope resolution operator | The scope resolution operator is a special kind of operator. Syntactically, it resembles an ordinary operator, but its left operand, when present, is a type name, not an expression. |

*continues*

**Table 16.2. continued**

| *Operator* | *Name of Operator* | *Why Operator Can't Be Overloaded* |
|---|---|---|
| `sizeof` | sizeof operator | The `sizeof` operator, like the scope resolution operator, is an operator in name only. |

## UNARY AND BINARY OPERATORS

To understand how operator overloading works, it helps to know that a C++ operator can be *unary*, *binary*, or *ternary*. A unary operator, such as `++`, takes a single operand. A binary operator doesn't have anything to do with binary arithmetic; it's simply an operator, such as `+` or `-`, that takes two commands. The `?:` operator, which is used in conditional loops, takes three operands. So it's known as a ternary command.

In C++, unary and binary operators can be overloaded. The ternary operator `?:` cannot be overloaded and is not of any concern in this chapter.

Some operators can be used as either binary or unary operators. For example, the `-` operator executes a subtraction operation when you use it as a binary operator, but signifies negation when you use it as a unary operator.

Some operators can work with both unary and binary operands, and the same operator symbol can have different meanings, depending on whether it's being used as a unary operator or a binary operator. For example, the symbol `&` means "the address of" when it is used as a unary operator, but is the bitwise `AND` operator when it is used as a binary operator.

When an operator has both a unary and a binary usage, you can overload it to have different meanings in its different usages.

The unary operators shown in Table 16.1 are:

- ! (logical negation)
- & (address-of)
- * (pointer dereference; also used as binary multiplication operator)
- + (unary plus; also used as binary addition operator)
- ++ (increment)
- - (unary negation; also used as binary subtraction operator)
- -- (decrement)

All other operators shown in the table are binary operators.

# How C++ Implements Operator Overloading

To understand how operator overloading works, it helps to know something about how C++ implements operator overloading. This is a brief outline of how the operator-overloading process works:

In the C language, operators can perform operations only on variables and constants that belong to built-in data types. Furthermore, in C the meanings of operators are fixed.

In C++, you can define your own meanings for operators. When you redefine an operator, you can use algebraic notation to express operations on objects of user-defined classes.

When the C++ compiler evaluates an expression, it examines a series of values (both variables and constants) intermixed with operator symbols. When the compiler encounters an operator, it first determines whether the operator is being used as a unary operator or as a binary operator. Then the compiler evaluates the expression according to the rules of precedence and associativity, grouping operators and operands as those rules require.

Finally, the compiler determines the types of the operands of the operator it has encountered. Only then does the compiler know whether the expression is legal and, if it is, what code it should generate.

C++ allows only recognized C++ operators to be overloaded. Furthermore, when an operator is overloaded, the precedence and associativity that applies to the operator in C++ must be retained. If you could change the precedence and associativity of an operator when you overloaded, that might sometimes come in handy. But currently, there is no way to do either one of those things in a C++ program.

# Rules of Operator Overloading

Many different operators can be overloaded in many kinds of ways, so there is quite a large collection of rules and tips that you can use as guidelines when you overload operators. The following list contains both rules and tips for operator overloading:

- You cannot overload a unary operator when its operand is a built-in data type. And you cannot redefine the behavior of a binary operator when both of its operands are built-in data types. Before you can redefine the meaning of the operator, at least one operand must be an object. This restriction prevents you from fundamentally altering the meaning of the C++ language.
- If you want to write a statement in which an operator affects an object, you must overload the operator to make it work correctly with the object. If you try to use an object as an operand of an operator that hasn't been overloaded, the compiler returns an error.
- You can override only existing operators; you cannot extend the C++ language by inventing new operators. For example, you cannot turn the character combination `**` into a new operator. That character combination is not a legal operator in C++, and you can't turn it into one.
- You cannot change the number of operands that an operator takes (in more technical jargon, you can't change the operator's *arity*). For example, the logical-NOT operator (~) is a unary operator for built-in types, so you can't overload it to act as a binary operator in a user-defined class.
- You cannot change an operator's *precedence*. As you may recall from your C programming days, precedence governs the order in which subexpressions inside an expression are evaluated. For example, multiplication takes precedence over division, so the expression `200+30*40` is always evaluated as `200+(30*40)`, or 1,400. So, when you overload the `+` and `*` operators, you can't change their precedence to make an expression such as `200+30*40` evaluate to `(200+30)*40`.

- You cannot change an operator's *associativity*. When an operand appears between two operators that have the same precedence, the operand is associated with either one operator or the other, depending on its associativity. In a subtraction operation, for example, associativity always goes from left to right. So this expression

  ```
  x = 30 - 20 - 10;
  ```

  is evaluated as `(30-20)-10`, or `0`. (If the associativity of subtraction were right to left, the expression would evaluate to `30-(20-10)`, or `20`.)

  The associativity of most operators goes from left to right, so you cannot overload an operator to make its associativity go from right to left. Instead, you must use parentheses to alter the order of evaluation.

- You cannot change the way an operator works with built-in data types. For example, you cannot change the way the + operator works with a pair of integers.
- When an operator is implemented as a two-character combination (see Table 16.1), it is still just a single operator. Hence, the + operator is not part of the += operator. So, if you overload the + operator, that doesn't mean that the += operator is also overloaded. You can also overload += if you like, but that's a completely separate operation.
- Too many overloaded operators, or even just a few poorly chosen operators, can make your programs hard to read. So you should never overload an operator just to make it easier for you to type a program, or for any other trivial reason. The obfuscation that may result just isn't worth it. To sum up: Use common sense. Design your overloading operations carefully, and use them sparingly in your programs.
- As Table 16.1 shows, most C++ operators can be overloaded, including both the unary and the binary forms of operators that have both forms.

# Member Functions That Overload Operators

There are two ways to implement a function that overloads an operator. You can overload an operator with a member function of a class, or you can overload an operator by writing a stand-alone function. Usually—but not always—standalone functions that overload operators are implemented as friend functions.

The remainder of this section tells how member functions can overload operators in C++ programs. The next section tells how you can use stand-alone functions to overload operators.

## Overloading the ++ and -- Operators

In C++, as in C, ++ and -- are unary operators. The ++ operator increments a value, and the -- operator decrements a value. In C++, both operators can be overloaded, and the syntax for overloading them is identical.

As an illustration of how the ++ and - operators can be overloaded, assume that a program you're writing contains a class named `AClass`. To overload the unary operator ++ when it is used with an `AClass` object, you can place this statement in the definition of `AClass`:

```
AClass.operator++();
```

Once you have written a function declaration like the one shown above, you can define the function using this syntax:

```
AClass AClass::operator++()
{
      // body of function
}
```

Once a function-overloading member function has been declared and defined, the program can increment an object that belongs to `AClass` by simply executing a function written in this format:

```
++anObject;
```

Listing 16.1 shows how you can overload the ++ operator in a C++ program.

### Listing 16.1. Overloading the ++ operator.

```
// 1601.CPP
// Overloading the ++ operator

#include <iostream.h>
#include <math.h>
#include <stdlib.h>
#include <stdio.h>

class Money {
private:
```

```
    double dollars;
    double cents;
public:
    Money() {}                     // default constructor
    ~Money() {}                    // destructor
    Money(double d, double c);     // another const
    Money(double);                 // conversion from double
    Money operator++();            // operator overloading
    double GetAmount(double &n);
};

Money Money::operator++()
{
    ldiv_t result;

    cents++;

    if (cents > 99) {
        dollars++;
        cents = 0;
    }
    return *this;
}

Money::Money(double d, double c)
{
    dollars = d; cents = c;
}

Money::Money(double cash)       // conversion constructor--
{                               // converts fp to Money
    double frac, n;
    frac = modf(cash, &n);      // a math.h function
    cents = frac * 100;
    dollars = n;                // n comes back as a double
}

double Money::GetAmount(double &n)
{
    n = dollars;
    return cents;
}

int main()
{
    double c, d;
    Money myCash(2.99);

    c = myCash.GetAmount(d);
```

*continues*

**Listing 16.1. continued**

```
    cout << d << '\n';
    cout << c << '\n';

    ++myCash;

    c = myCash.GetAmount(d);

    cout << d << '\n';
    cout << c << '\n';

    return 0;
}
```

### CONVERSION CONSTRUCTORS

Listing 16.1 contains a conversion constructor that enables you to construct a `Money` object by passing the constructor a single floating-point value—which represents dollars and cents—instead of passing it a pair of values that express dollars and cents separately.

This is the conversion constructor that is used in the program:

```
Money::Money(double cash)      // conversion constructor--
{                              // converts fp to Money
    double    frac, n;
    frac = modf(cash, &n);     // a math.h function
    cents = frac * 100;
    dollars = n;               // n comes back as a double
}
```

Conversion constructors are described in more detail in Chapter 17, "Conversion Functions."

In the program shown in Listing 16.1, the unary operator ++ is overloaded to increment a class named `Money`. The `Money` class stores a monetary value as a pair of double (floating-point) types that represent dollars and cents. This is the function that overloads the ++ operator:

```
Money Money::operator++()
{
     ldiv_t result;

     cents++;

     if (cents > 99) {
          dollars++;
          cents = 0;
     }
     return *this;
}
```

The above function increments the `cents` variable, and then checks to see if `cents` has been incremented to a value that exceeds 99. If that's the case, `cents` is decremented back down to 99, and `dollars` is incremented by 1. The result is an incrementation that simulates a floating-point operation.

The output of the program is:

```
2
99
3
0
```

## OVERLOADING PREFIX AND POSTFIX OPERATORS

In C++, just as in C, the increment (++) and decrement (--) operators can be either *prefix* or *postfix* operators. If the ++ or -- operator precedes an operand, it's a prefix operator. When a prefix operator precedes an operand in an expression, the operator is applied to the operand before the expression is evaluated. When a postfix operator follows an operand in an expression, the operator is applied to the operand *after* the expression is evaluated.

Early versions of C++ had no mechanism for distinguishing between prefix and postfix operators in operator-overloading functions. Now that situation has been remedied: Visual C++ provides different formats for overloading prefix and postfix operators.

The ++ operator that is overloaded in Listing 16.1 is a prefix operator. When you want to overload a prefix operator using a member function, the syntax for declaring the function is:

```
Money operator++();
```

To write a member function that overloads a postfix operator, you must pass an integer argument to the function, using this format:

```
Money operator++(int x);
```

When you declare a function that overloads a postfix operator, you can define the function using this format:

```
Money Money::operator++(int x)
{
     cents++;
     if (cents > 99) {
          dollars++;
          cents = 0;
          return *this;
     }
}
```

When you use a function like the one shown above to overload a postfix operator, the value that is passed to the function does not affect the overloading operation. A null value (`0`) is usually passed to the function, but if you want, you can pass a value to the function. When you write the code for the function, you can use the value that's passed to the function in any way you like.

This is the format that is used most frequently to call a function that overloads a postfix operator:

```
++myCash(0);
```

## Overloading the Binary + and - Operators

Because a unary operation involves just one value and a binary operation affects two values, the formats of statements that carry out the two kinds of operations are different. For example, this is the syntax for declaring a function that overloads the binary + operator:

```
AClass.operator+(AClass);
```

If a declaration like the one shown above appears in the definition of a class—and is supported by a corresponding function definition—you can add two `AClass` objects by simply executing this kind of function:

```
aObject = aObject + bObject;
```

Listing 16.2 is a program that adds two `AClass` objects by overloading the binary + operator.

### Listing 16.2. Overloading the binary + operator.

```
// 1602.CPP
// Overloading a binary operator

#include <iostream.h>
#include <math.h>
#include <stdlib.h>

class Money {
private:
     double dollars;
     double cents;
public:
     Money() {}                        // default constructor
     ~Money() {}                       // destructor
     Money(double d, double c);        // another const
     Money(double);                    // conversion from double
     Money operator++();               // operator overloading
     Money operator+(Money m);         // operator overloading
     double GetAmount(double &n);
};

Money Money::operator+(Money m)
{
     ldiv_t result;

     cents += m.cents;
     dollars += m.dollars;

     if (cents > 99) {
         result = ldiv((long)cents, 100);
         dollars = dollars + result.quot;
         cents = (double)result.rem;
     }

     return *this;
}

Money::Money(double d, double c)
{
     dollars = d; cents = c;
}
```

*continues*

#### Listing 16.2. continued

```
Money::Money(double cash)      // conversion constructor--
{                              // converts fp to Money
     double  frac, n;
     frac = modf(cash, &n);    // a math.h function
     cents = frac * 100;
     dollars = n;              // n comes back as a double
}

double Money::GetAmount(double &n)
{
     n = dollars;
     return cents;
}

int main()
{
     double c, d;
     Money myCash(2.99);
     Money yourCash(5001.01);

     myCash = myCash + yourCash;

     c = myCash.GetAmount(d);

     cout << d << '\n';
     cout << c << '\n';

     return 0;
}
```

In Listing 16.2, a function that overloads the binary + operator is declared inside the definition of the `Money` class:

```
Money operator+(Money m);      // operator overloading
```

This is the definition of the function:

```
Money Money::operator+(Money m)
{
     ldiv_t result;

     cents += m.cents;
     dollars += m.dollars;

     if (cents > 99) {
         result = ldiv((long)cents, 100);
         dollars = dollars + result.quot;
```

```
            cents = (double)result.rem;
        }

        return *this;
}
```

The function shown above is called from the program's `main()` function. This is the calling function:

```
myCash = myCash + yourCash;
```

## Overloading the += Operator

In C++, as in C, the binary operator += can add two values or expressions using this syntax:

```
valueA += valueB;
```

In both C and C++, the preceding statement has the same effect as:

```
valueA = valueA + valueB;
```

Listing 16.3 is a program that adds two `AClass` objects by overloading the binary += operator.

### Listing 16.3. Overloading the += operator.

```
// 1603.CPP
// Overloading the += operator

#include <iostream.h>
#include <math.h>
#include <stdlib.h>

class Money {
private:
     double dollars;
     double cents;
public:
     Money() {}                      // default constructor
     ~Money() {}                     // destructor
     Money(double d, double c);      // another const
     Money(double);                  // conversion from double
     Money operator++();             // unary operator overloading
     Money operator+(Money m);       // binary operator overloading
     Money operator+=(Money m);      // binary operator overloading
```

*continues*

**Listing 16.3. continued**

```
     double GetAmount(double &n);
};

Money Money::operator+(Money m)
{
     ldiv_t result;

     cents += m.cents;
     dollars += m.dollars;

     if (cents > 99) {
         result = ldiv((long)cents, 100);
         dollars = dollars + result.quot;
         cents = (double)result.rem;
     }

     return *this;
}

Money Money::operator+=(Money m)
{
    ldiv_t result;

    cents += m.cents;
    dollars += m.dollars;
    if (cents > 99) {
     result = ldiv((long)cents, 100);
     dollars = dollars + result.quot;
     cents = (double)result.rem;
    }
    return *this;
}

Money::Money(double d, double c)
{
     dollars = d; cents = c;
}

Money::Money(double cash)      // conversion constructor--
{                              // converts fp to Money
     double  frac, n;
     frac = modf(cash, &n);    // a math.h function
     cents = frac * 100;
     dollars = n;              // n comes back as a double
}
```

```
double Money::GetAmount(double &n)
{
     n = dollars;
     return cents;
}

long main()
{
     double c, d;
     Money myCash(2.00);
     Money yourCash(3, 00);

     c = myCash.GetAmount(d);

     cout << d << '\n';
     cout << c << '\n';

     return 0;
}
```

In Listing 16.3, this is the declaration of the function that overloads the += operator:

```
Money operator+=(Money m);         // binary operator overloading
```

This is the definition of the function:

```
Money Money::operator+=(Money m)
{
    ldiv_t result;

    cents += m.cents;
    dollars += m.dollars;
    if (cents > 99) {
     result = ldiv((long)cents, 100);
     dollars = dollars + result.quot;
     cents = (double)result.rem;
    }
    return *this;
}
```

And this is the calling function:

```
myCash += yourCash;
```

The output of the program is:

```
2
0
```

# Overloading the = Operator

There are two ways to make a copy of an object in C++. One technique is to invoke a special kind of constructor called a *copy constructor*. The other way is to customize (or overload) the assignment operator = so that it can make an accurate copy of an object.

A copy constructor, as its name suggests, is a special kind of constructor that is specifically designed to copy objects. A copy constructor creates an object and initializes it with the contents of the object being copied.

An overloaded = operator, in contrast, does not create an object. Instead, it copies the contents of a source object to an existing target object. So you cannot use an overloaded = operator to create an object that is a copy of another object. An overload = operator can only assign the value of an existing object to another existing object. The target object should belong to the same class as the source object, or should be an object that is derived from the source object's class.

Copy constructors are covered in Chapter 18.

The following section focuses on overloading the = operator.

## Overloading the = Operator to Copy Strings

Because objects are often copied in C++ programs, applications written in C++ often contain assignment operators that have been overloaded to copy objects. One kind of object that is often copied in C++ programs is a string.

As C programmers know, strings can be difficult to manage in the C language because C strings are generally not accessed directly, but are controlled through pointers. So a statement such as

```
char *bString = aString;
```

doesn't actually copy a string. Instead, it merely sets up a *pointer* named `*bString`, and sets that pointer to point to the same array of characters that is pointed to by the pointer named `*aString`. If `aString` is destroyed or is moved to another memory location, the `*bString` pointer no longer points to `aString`, but to an area in memory that is now undefined. That turns `*bString` into a dangerous dangling pointer.

In C++, strings are often stored as objects because string objects can be manipulated more easily than conventional C-style strings. To store a string as a class, an application has to create a class that can store strings. Once a program has created a string class, it can create string objects that are members of the string class.

A string class usually includes several overloaded operators. String classes generally overload the = operator (to copy strings) and the + and += operators (to concatenate strings). When the =, +, and += operators are customized to manipulate strings, it becomes very easy to perform such tasks as copying and concatenating strings. For example, you can overload = operator in such a way that this statement

```
char *bString = aString;
```

actually does copy a string instead of merely copying a pointer to a string.

String classes are used so often in C++ programs that many C++ class libraries—including the Microsoft Foundation Class (MFC) library—contain prewritten string classes. When you have to access a string class that is provided in a C++ class library, you don't have to write your own string class.

Chapter 18 explores string classes and string objects in more detail. Chapter 18 also covers techniques for copying other kinds of objects that contain pointers. The remainder of this section focuses on a simpler problem: overloading the = operator to copy objects that do not contain pointers.

## Using operator= Functions

C++ programs often copy objects by overloading the assignment operator (=). A function that overloads the = operator takes a reference as an argument and returns a reference to a class. Because an `operator=` function returns a reference, it can be used to assign a value to chains of objects, as explained later in this section.

The following statement declares a function that overloads the = operator:

```
TestClass& operator=(&TestClass);
```

The statement shown above declares a function that can copy an object named `aObject` to a new object named `bObject`. You must provide the definition of the function that performs the object-copying operation.

## Letting the Compiler Generate an operator= Function

If a program uses the = operator to copy an object, and the compiler discovers that the program has not overloaded the = operator to make the requested copying operation possible, the compiler creates an `operator=` function and then uses that function to perform the requested copying operation.

It's important to note, though, that when the compiler generates an `operator=` function, the function may not perform the kind of copying operation that you want.

When the compiler creates an `operator=` function, the function performs a *memberwise* copy. That means that the compiler copies the source object to the target object verbatim, one member at a time.

That works fine, provided the class that the two objects belong to does not contain any members that are pointers. If the objects involved in the copy contain pointers, that can cause problems.

When a memberwise copy of an object is made, any pointer that is a member of the source object is copied to the target object verbatim. When the copy is complete, both objects contain a pointer that points to the same memory.

Subsequently, if one of the objects is destroyed—along with the data that its pointers access—the other object winds up pointing to an undefined area of memory. That can cause program crashes and other disasters. To prevent such problems, you should copy objects using your own `operator=` functions whenever possible.

## Declaring a Function That Overloads the = Operator

You can overload the = operator by placing a declaration like this inside the definition of a class:

```
Money& operator=(Money&);
```

The above declaration announces that the = operator is going to be overloaded in such a way that it can be used to add to objects of a class named `Money`. An `operator=` function usually (but not always) takes a reference to a class as an argument and returns a reference to a class.

Once a declaration like the one shown above has been placed in a class definition, an operation that overloads the = operator can be written. For example:

```
Money& Money::operator=(Money& m)
{
    dollars = m.dollars;
    cents = m.cents;
    return *this;
}
```

The function shown above overloads the = operator so it can be used to add two objects that belong to the `Money` class. The function appears in Listing 16.4.

**Listing 16.4. Overloading the = operator.**

```
// 1604.CPP
// Overloading the assignment operator

#include <iostream.h>
#include <math.h>
#include <stdlib.h>

class Money {
private:
     double dollars;
     double cents;
public:
     Money() {}                   // default constructor
     ~Money() {}                  // destructor
     Money(double d, double c);   // another const
     Money(double);               // conversion from double
     Money operator++();          // unary operator overloading
     Money operator+(Money m);    // binary operator overloading
     Money operator+=(Money m);   // binary operator overloading
     Money& operator=(Money&);    // assignment operator overload

     double GetAmount(double &n);
};

Money Money::operator+(Money m)
{
     ldiv_t result;

     cents += m.cents;
     dollars += m.dollars;

     if (cents > 99) {
         result = ldiv((long)cents, 100);
         dollars = dollars + result.quot;
         cents = (double)result.rem;
     }

     return *this;
}

Money Money::operator+=(Money m)
{
    ldiv_t result;

    cents += m.cents;
    dollars += m.dollars;
    if (cents > 99) {
```

*continues*

**Listing 16.4. continued**

```
     result = ldiv((long)cents, 100);
     dollars = dollars + result.quot;
     cents = (double)result.rem;
    }
    return *this;
}

Money& Money::operator=(Money& m)
{
    dollars = m.dollars;
    cents = m.cents;
    return *this;
}

Money::Money(double d, double c)
{
     dollars = d; cents = c;
}

Money::Money(double cash)      // conversion constructor--
{                              // converts fp to Money
     double  frac, n;
     frac = modf(cash, &n);    // a math.h function
     cents = frac * 100;
     dollars = n;              // n comes back as a double
}

double Money::GetAmount(double &n)
{
     n = dollars;
     return cents;
}

long main()
{
     double c, d;
     Money yourCash(2.16);

     Money myCash = yourCash;

     c = myCash.GetAmount;

     cout << d << '\n';
     cout << c << '\n';

     return 0;
}
```

As you can see by examining Listing 16.4, a `Money` object has two data members expressed as `double` values: `dollars` and `cents`. The `operator=` function shown above simply adds the `dollars` and `cents` members of one `Money` object to the `dollars` and `cents` members to another `Money` object. Then the function returns the result.

When you have overloaded the = operator, you can make a copy of an object by executing a function written in this syntax:

```
Money myCash = yourCash;
```

## CONVERSION FUNCTIONS

You can overload the = operator to convert objects from one data type to another, as well as to copy the contents of one object to an identical object. When you overload the = operator to convert one data type to another, the function that overloads the = operator is called a conversion version.

The class definition shown below declares two `operator=` functions. One declares a standard, object-to-object `operator=` function, and the other is a conversion function that converts a `double` data type to a `TestClass` object:

```
class TestClass {
private:
     // data members
public:
     TestClass& operator=(&TestClass);
     TestClass& operator=(double);
};
```

To implement the conversion function shown in the last line of the above code fragment, you must provide code that converts a `double` data type to an object of the class named `TestClass`. Conversion functions are the topic of Chapter 17.

## How the Program Works

In Listing 16.4, this statement initializes a `Money` object named `yourCash`:

```
Money yourCash(2.16);
```

This statement is then executed to create an object named `myCash`, which is a copy of `yourCash`:

```
Money myCash = yourCash;
```

Finally, the member function `GetAmount()` is called to print the contents of the member variables `myCash.dollars` and `myCash.cents`. The output of the program is:

```
2
16
```

### TIP—HELPFUL HINTS

When you make a copy of an object by using an overloaded assignment operator, there are some important facts that it may be helpful to remember. For example:

- An assignment operator function must be a class member function. Furthermore, it must be a nonstatic member function. You cannot implement an `operator=` function as a stand-alone function, or as a static member function.
- The argument that you supply to an `operator=` function is the argument that appears on the right side of the function's assignment expression. The value that an `operator=` function returns is the value of the left side of the expression after the assignment is complete.
- There is no restriction on the return type of an `operator=` function; in this respect, an `operator=` function is like any other function that overloads an operator. In practice, however, most user-defined binary operators return either a class type or a reference to a class type. This convention lets you write chains of assignment statements such as this using an overloaded = operator:

  ```
  objA = objB = objC;
  ```

An example of this kind of assignment chaining is presented under its own heading later in this chapter.

- For reasons outlined later in this chapter, an overloaded assignment operator function is not inherited by derived classes.
- An `operator=` function has some things in common with a constructor. For example, you can use the = operator to make a copy of an object without explicitly writing an `operator=` function. If a program uses the = operator to make a copy of an object, and the object doesn't have an `operator=` function, the compiler can generate an `operator=` function.

When you perform an assignment operation with an assignment-operator function that is generated by the compiler, the compiler performs what is known as a memberwise assignment. That means that the compiler makes a verbatim copy of every data member of the source object. That's fine, unless the object being copied contains data members that are referenced with pointers (a category that includes strings). That can cause problems because it means that when a copy is made of an object that contains a pointer, the pointers in both objects point to the same address. Usually, that's not what you want when you copy an object. Generally, what you want to do is make a copy of the information that is pointed to, and then set up a pointer in the target object to point to that information. To do that, you must either overload the = operator to make the kind of copy that you want or write a copy constructor that makes the correct kind of copy.

Copy constructors and pointer-copying operations are described in Chapter 18.

## Return Types

A function that overloads the = operator is not required to have any particular return type. Usually, however, the return type of an assignment operator function is a reference to the class object being created. When this convention is observed, it lets you write chains of assignments, as shown in Listing 16.5.

### Listing 16.5. `operator=` return types.

```
// 1605.CPP
// Demonstrating operator= return types

#include <iostream.h>

class TestClass {
private:
     int x, y;
public:
     TestClass() {}
     ~TestClass() {}
     TestClass& operator=(TestClass&);    // operator overload
     void TestFunc();
     void Values(int a, int b)
          { x = a; y = b; }
     int Values(int *a)
          { *a = y; return x; }
};

TestClass& TestClass::operator=(TestClass& t)
{
    x = t.x;
    y = t.y;
    return *this;
}

void PrintIt(int param1, int param2)
{
     cout << param1 << ", " << param2 << '\n';
}

int main()
{
     int value = 300;
     int tempVal;

     TestClass a, b, c, q;
     c.Values(100, 200);
     a = b = c;          // chain of assignments

     // get and print values of data members
     tempVal = a.Values(&value);
     PrintIt(tempVal, value);
     tempVal = b.Values(&value);
     PrintIt(tempVal, value);
     tempVal = c.Values(&value);
     PrintIt(tempVal, value);
```

```
    // create new object named q
    (q = a).Values(300, 400);
    tempVal = q.Values(&value);
    PrintIt(tempVal, value);

    return 0;
}
```

In Listing 16.5, a function for overloading the = operator is declared in the definition of a class named `TestClass`. This function is written in the conventional manner; it takes a reference to a class as an argument, and it also returns a reference to a class.

```
TestClass& operator=(TestClass&);
```

Later in the program, the function declared in the above statement is defined as follows:

```
TestClass& TestClass::operator=(TestClass& t)
{
    x = t.x;
    y = t.y;
    return *this;
}
```

When the `operator=` function has been declared and defined, four `TestClass` objects are created. These four objects are named `a`, `b`, `c`, and `q`. When the objects have been initialized, a member function named `Values()` is called to initialize two data members of the object named `c`:

```
TestClass a, b, c, q;
c.Values(100, 200);
```

When all these preparations are complete, this chain of assignments is executed to initialize the objects named `a` and `b`:

```
a = b = c;            // chain of assignments
```

The above statement works because a reference behaves like a pointer variable but can be treated like a nonpointer variable. If the `operator=` function were changed to return a void value, an assignment statement such as the one shown above would generate an error.

Besides the chain of assignments shown in the above code fragment, the `main()` segment of the program in Listing 16.5 contains this function:

```
(q = a).Values(300, 400);
```

This statement does two interesting things. First, it copies the data members of the `TestClass` object into a new `TestClass` object named `q`. Then it assigns the values `300` and `400` into the data members of the new `q` object.

Finally, when you execute the program, it prints the data members of all four of the objects that have been created:

```
100, 200
100, 200
100, 200
300, 400
```

Although a function that overloads the `operator=` function usually returns a reference to an object, it can return a variable of any type—or it can be a function that returns a `void` type, which is another way of describing a function that returns no data at all.

When you write an `operator=` function that has a return type of `void`, you can use the function in a statement like this:

```
TestClass a = b;
```

Listing 16.6 is a program that contains an assignment statement like the one shown above.

### Listing 16.6. An `operator=` function with a void return type.

```
// 1606.CPP
// An operator= function with a void return type

#include <iostream.h>

class TestClass {
private:
     int x, y;
public:
     TestClass(int a, int b)     // constructor
          { x = a; y = b; }
     ~TestClass() {}
     void operator=(TestClass&);    // operator overload
     void TestFunc();
     int Values(int *a)
          { *a = y; return x; }
};

void TestClass::operator=(TestClass& t)
{
```

```
        x = t.x;
        y = t.y;
}

void PrintIt(int param1, int param2)
{
        cout << param1 << ", " << param2 << '\n';
}

int main()
{
        int value = 300;
        int tempVal;

        TestClass b(100, 200);
        TestClass a = b;

        // get and print values of data members
        tempVal = a.Values(&value);
        PrintIt(tempVal, value);
        tempVal = b.Values(&value);
        PrintIt(tempVal, value);

        return 0;
}
```

In Listing 16.6, this is the definition of the function that overloads the assignment operator:

```
void TestClass::operator=(TestClass& t)
{
        x = t.x;
        y = t.y;
}
```

The program instantiates a `TestClass` object named `b`, and then invokes the = operator to create a second `TestClass` object named `a`. The statements that perform these two tasks appear in the program's `main()` function:

```
TestClass b(100, 200);
TestClass a = b;
```

The program then prints the values of the data members of the `a` and `b` objects:

```
100, 200
100, 200
```

## Compiler-Generated operator= Functions

As mentioned in passing earlier in this section, you can overload the = operator without writing an explicit definition of the function that overloads the operator. If you execute an assignment statement without writing an assignment-operator function or a copy constructor, the compiler can generate an assignment-operator function for you, as shown in Listing 16.7.

### Listing 16.7. A compiler-generated assignment-operator function.

```
// 1607.CPP
// Compiler-generated assignment-operator function

#include <iostream.h>

class TestClass {
private:
     int x, y;
public:
     TestClass() {}
     ~TestClass() {}
     void TestFunc();
     void Values(int a, int b)
          { x = a; y = b; }
     int Values(int *a)
          { *a = y; return x; }
};

void PrintIt(int param1, int param2)
{
     cout << param1 << ", " << param2 << '\n';
}

int main()
{
     int value = 300;
     int tempVal;

     TestClass a, b, c, q;

     c.Values(100, 200);

     a = b = c;          // chain of assignments

     // get and print values of data members
     tempVal = a.Values(&value);
     PrintIt(tempVal, value);
     tempVal = b.Values(&value);
```

```
    PrintIt(tempVal, value);
    tempVal = c.Values(&value);
    PrintIt(tempVal, value);

    // create new object named q
    (q = a).Values(300, 400);
    tempVal = q.Values(&value);
    PrintIt(tempVal, value);

    return 0;
}
```

The program in Listing 16.7 is identical to the program shown previously in Listing 16.6, except that it contains no explicit `operator=` function. The version of the program shown in Listing 16.7 shows how the compiler can generate an assignment-operator function when you don't bother to write your own.

When the compiler generates an `operator=` function, the function always makes what is known as a *memberwise copy* of the source object. That means that the function makes a verbatim copy of each data member of the object being copied. If the source object contains a data member that is a pointer, the function copies the pointer, not the data that is pointed to. That is usually not what you want when you make a copy of an object that contains pointer-type data members. When you want to make a copy of an object that contains pointer-type data members, you can write an operator-overloading function that copies pointer objects in a safer manner. Chapter 18 describes techniques for copying objects that contain pointers.

A compiler-generated `operator=` function is always public, and always returns a reference to the new object. For more information about object-copying functions that are generated by the compiler, see Chapter 18.

## Assignment Operations and Inheritance

A function that overloads the assignment operator cannot be inherited by derived classes. The only other kinds of functions that share this distinction are constructors and destructors. In all three cases, this is a logical restriction.

In C++, a base class is not expected to know about its derived classes. That means if an `operator=` function is declared inside the definition of a base class, the function has no way of knowing the details that might be needed to overload the = operator in such a way that it can make a complete copy of a derived class.

If a derived class can't inherit an overloaded assignment operator from a derived class, what happens when you attempt to copy a derived object with the = operator and the derived object doesn't have an `operator=` function of its own?

The answer: When a program uses the = operator to instantiate an object that has no `operator=` function, the compiler generates an `operator=` function for the object, and uses that. If a base class of the object being created has an `operator=` function, the `operator=` function that is generated by the compiler calls that function to build the base part of the object being created. However, the derived class does not directly inherit its base class's `operator=` function.

Listing 16.8 shows how this process works.

### Listing 16.8. Class derivation and the `operator=` function

```
// 1608.CPP
// Assignment and inheritance

#include <iostream.h>

class AClass {
private:
     int x;
public:
     AClass() { x = 500; }     // constructor
     ~AClass() {}                   // destructor
     AClass& operator=(AClass&);
     int GetVal() { return x; }
};

AClass& AClass::operator=(AClass&)
{
     cout << "Executing AClass 'operator=' function.\n";
     return *this;
}

class BClass : public AClass {
public:
     // BClass has no operator= function,
     // so the compiler generates one
     // when a BClass object is created.
};

int main()
{
     AClass objA1, objA2;
     objA2 = objA1;
```

```
    BClass objB1, objB2;
    objB2 = objB1;

    return 0;
}
```

In Listing 16.8, the base class named `AClass` has an `operator=` function, but the derived class named `BClass` has no `operator=` function and has no copy constructor. However, the `BClass` does not inherit the `operator=` function that is declared inside the definition of `AClass`. Instead, the compiler generates a new `operator=` function to create a `BClass` object.

In the program in Listing 16.8, this is the `operator=` function that is defined for the class name `AClass`:

```
AClass& AClass::operator=(AClass&)
{
    cout << "Executing AClass 'operator=' function.\n";
    return *this;
}
```

When the function definition shown above is executed, this line is printed to standard output (normally the screen):

```
Executing AClass 'operator=' function.
```

When you execute the program, the above line is printed twice: once when an `AClass` object named `objA1` is copied to an `AClass` object named `objA2`, and again when a `BClass` object named `objB1` is copied to a `BClass` object named `objB2`:

```
Executing AClass 'operator=' function.
Executing AClass 'operator=' function.
```

What does the program's output show? It shows that the `operator=` function that is defined for `AClass` is executed in two kinds of cases: when the = operator is used to copy an `AClass` object to another `AClass` object, and when the = operator is used to copy a `BClass` object to another `BClass` object. That proves that the compiler uses the = operator that is defined for `AClass` to copy `BClass` objects, as well as to copy `AClass` objects.

## Writing an operator= Function for a Derived Class

When you write an `operator=` function for a derived class, the `operator=` function that is defined for the derived class overrides the `operator=` function that is derived for the base class. Therefore, you can override the behavior illustrated in the preceding example by simply writing an `operator=` function for the derived class named `BClass`. Listing 16.9 shows what happens when a derived class has its own `operator=` function.

#### Listing 16.9. A derived class `operator=` function.

```
// 1609.CPP
// Assignment and inheritance

#include <iostream.h>

class AClass {
private:
     int x;
public:
     AClass() {}
     ~AClass() {}
     AClass& operator=(AClass&);
     int GetVal() { return x; }
};

AClass& AClass::operator=(AClass&)
{
     cout << "Executing AClass 'operator=' function.\n";
     return *this;
}

class BClass : public AClass {
public:
     BClass& operator=(BClass&);
};

BClass& BClass::operator=(BClass&)
{
     cout << "Executing BClass 'operator=' function.\n";
     return *this;
}

int main()
{
     AClass objA1, objA2;
     objA2 = objA1;

     BClass objB1, objB2;
     objB2 = objB1;

     return 0;
}
```

Listing 16.9 shows how a derived class behaves when it has its own `operator=` function. In Listing 16.9, a class named `BClass` is derived from a class named `AClass`, and each of those classes has an `operator=` function.

Because `BClass` has its own `operator=` function, the compiler does not have to use the `operator=` function that is defined for `AClass` when it is called upon to copy a `BClass` object. Instead, the compiler creates the object by simply invoking the `operator=` function that is declared inside the definition of `BClass`.

When you execute the program shown in Listing 16.9, its output shows that the `operator=` function that is defined for `ClassB` overrides the `operator=` function that is defined for `ClassA`:

```
Executing AClass 'operator=' function.
Executing BClass 'operator=' function.
```

## Overriding an Overloaded operator= Function

When an `operator=` function is defined for a base class, and another `operator=` function is defined for a derived class, it's often desirable to call both functions to make a copy of the derived object. That ensures that both the base part and the derived part of the object is copied correctly.

When you want to copy a derived object by executing both a base-class `operator=` function and a derived-class `operator=` function, you can use the scope resolution operator (`::`) to call the base class's `operator=` function from the derived class's `operator=` function. Listing 16.10 shows one technique for carrying out that kind of operation.

### Listing 16.10. Using two `operator=` functions.

```
// 1610.CPP
// Assignment and inheritance

#include <iostream.h>

class AClass {
private:
     int x;
public:
     AClass() {}
     ~AClass() {}
     AClass& operator=(AClass&);
     int GetVal() { return x; }
};
```

*continues*

**Listing 16.10. continued**

```
AClass& AClass::operator=(AClass&)
{
     cout << "Executing AClass 'operator=' function.\n";
     return *this;
}

class BClass : public AClass {
public:
     BClass& operator=(BClass&);
};

BClass& BClass::operator=(BClass& b)
{
     this->AClass::operator=(b);
     cout << "Executing BClass 'operator=' function.\n";
     return *this;
}

int main()
{
     BClass objB1, objB2;
     objB2 = objB1;

     return 0;
}
```

In the program shown in Listing 16.10, this `operator=` function—which is defined for a derived class named `ClassB`—calls a base-class `operator=` function that is defined for `ClassA`:

```
BClass& BClass::operator=(BClass& b)
{
     this->AClass::operator=(b);
     cout << "Executing BClass 'operator=' function.\n";
     return *this;
}
```

In the preceding code fragment, this is the line that calls the base class's `operator=` function:

```
this->AClass::operator=(b);
```

If you don't want to use the scope resolution operator, you can accomplish the same result by replacing the preceding statement with a statement that recasts the `this` pointer used by `BClass` objects into a pointer used by `AClass` objects.

For example:

```
*((AClass *)this) = b;
```

When the preceding change is made, the `operator=` function defined for `BClass` looks like this:

```
BClass& BClass::operator=(BClass& b)
{
     *((AClass *)this) = b;
     cout << "Executing BClass 'operator=' function.\n";
     return *this;
}
```

No matter which of these two `operator=` functions you use, the program in Listing 16.10 produces this output:

```
Executing AClass 'operator=' function.
Executing BClass 'operator=' function.
```

This output shows that the base class's `operator=` function calls the derived class's `operator=` function.

## Copying a Derived-Class Object

Listing 16.11 shows how you can use the techniques just described to copy a derived-class object to a base-class object. Most of the program in Listing 16.11 probably looks familiar by now; the part to focus your attention on is the `main()` function.

### Listing 16.11. Copying a derived-class object to a base-class object.

```
// 1611.CPP
// Assignment and inheritance

#include <iostream.h>

class AClass {
private:
     int x;
public:
     AClass() {}
     ~AClass() {}
     AClass& operator=(AClass&);
     int GetVal() { return x; }
};
```

*continues*

**Listing 16.11. continued**

```
AClass& AClass::operator=(AClass&)
{
     cout << "Executing AClass 'operator=' function.\n";
     return *this;
}

class BClass : public AClass {
public:
     BClass& operator=(BClass&);
};

BClass& BClass::operator=(BClass& b)
{
     *((AClass *)this) = b;
     cout << "Executing BClass 'operator=' function.\n";
     return *this;
}

int main()
{
     AClass objA1;
     BClass objB1;

     objA1 = objB1;

     return 0;
}
```

In Listing 16.11, the assignment statement that appears in the `main()` function does not work symmetrically; you can copy a base-class object to a derived-class object, but you can't do the reverse. So, if you rewrite the program's `main()` function to look like this, it doesn't work, but generates an error message:

```
int main()
{
     AClass objA1;
     BClassoobjB1;

     objB1 = objA1; // ERROR! Doesn't work!

     return 0;
}
```

But wait; with just one more change, you can make the `main()` segment work. All you have to do is use a cast:

```
int main()
{
     AClass objA1;
     BClassobjB1;

     (AClass&)objB1 = objA1;    // this works fine

     return 0;
}
```

## Overloading Relational Operators

The ==, <, and > operators are binary relational operators. Each returns a `true` or `false` value, depending on whether a specified value passes or fails a test. The == returns `true` if the tested value is equal to another specified value, and returns `false` otherwise. The < and > operators check to see whether the tested value is larger than or smaller than another value.

Besides the ==, <, and > operators, there are a number of two-character combinations that are also recognized as relational operators. Other relational operators include <=, >=, and `!=`. All relational operators can be overloaded to test objects instead of testing built-in data types.

Listing 16.12 is a program that shows how relational operators can be overloaded in C++. It overloads the == and < operators to compare the values of two `Money` objects.

### Listing 16.12. Overloading relational operators.

```
// 1612.CPP
// Overloading the == operator

#include <iostream.h>
#include <math.h>
#include <stdlib.h>

const int TRUE = 1;
const int FALSE = 0;

class Money {
private:
     double dollars;
     double cents;
```

*continues*

**Listing 16.12. continued**

```
public:
     Money() {}                        // default constructor
     ~Money() {}                       // destructor
     Money(double d, double c);        // another const
     Money(double);                    // conversion from double
     Money operator++();               // unary operator overloading
     Money operator+(Money m);         // binary operator overloading
     Money operator+=(Money m);        // binary operator overloading
     int operator==(Money& m);         // == operator overload
     int operator<(Money& m);          // < operator overload
     double GetAmount(double &n);
};

Money Money::operator+(Money m)
{
     ldiv_t result;

     cents += m.cents;
     dollars += m.dollars;

     if (cents > 99) {
         result = ldiv((long)cents, 100);
         dollars = dollars + result.quot;
         cents = (double)result.rem;
     }

     return *this;
}

Money Money::operator+=(Money m)
{
    ldiv_t result;

    cents += m.cents;
    dollars += m.dollars;
    if (cents > 100) {
     result = ldiv((long)cents, 100);
     dollars = dollars + result.quot;
     cents = (double)result.rem;
    }
    return *this;
}

inline int Money::operator==(Money& m)
{
    return this->dollars == m.dollars &&
     this->cents == m.cents;
}
```

```
int Money::operator<(Money& m)
{
    if (this->dollars < m.dollars)
     return TRUE;
    else if (this->cents < m.cents)
     return TRUE;
    else return FALSE;
}

Money::Money(double d, double c)
{
     dollars = d; cents = c;
}

Money::Money(double cash)      // conversion constructor--
{                              // converts fp to Money
     double    frac, n;
     frac = modf(cash, &n);    // a math.h function
     cents = frac * 100;
     dollars = n;              // n comes back as a double
}

double Money::GetAmount(double &n)
{
     n = dollars;
     return cents;
}

int main()
{
    Money hisCash(3.00); // call conversion constructor
    Money yourCash(4.00);

    if (yourCash < hisCash)
       cout << "Ask for a loan.\n";
    else cout << "Don't ask for a loan.\n";

    if (yourCash == hisCash)
       cout << "You have as much money as he has.\n";

    return 0;
}
```

Listing 16.12 defines two objects of the `Money` class: `yourCash` and `hisCash`. The program then overloads two relational operators,== and <,to compare `yourCash` with `hisCash`.

If `yourCash` is less than `hisCash`, the program prints this advice:

```
Ask for a loan.
```

If `yourCash` is greater than or equal to `hisCash`, the program prints a different message:

```
Don't ask for a loan.
```

If `yourCash` is exactly equal to `hisCash`, the program adds this explanation:

```
You have as much money as he has.
```

# Overloading the [] Operator

C-style arrays have numerous shortcomings. In C, there is no set place to store the size of an array, and there is no built-in mechanism that prevents a program from accidentally indexing past the end of the array.

In programs written in C++, you overcome these shortcomings by overloading the square brackets (`[]`) that delimit arrays. In C++, the left and right brackets that delimit an array are considered to be a single operator, which is called the subscript operator.

By overloading the subscript operator, you can create arrays that are safer and more powerful than C-style arrays. For example, you can create an array that automatically checks any value that is assigned to it to ensure that the value is within an acceptable range and does not index past the end of the array.

The most common way to overload the subscript operator is to create an array class. You can use array classes to create bounds—checked arrays, sparse arrays, virtual (disk-resident) arrays, associative arrays, dynamically sized arrays, and arrays of many other kinds.

## How to Overload the [] Operator

In C++, you can declare a function that overloads the `[]` operator by writing a statement using this syntax:

```
int &operator[](int index);
```

A function that overloads the `[]` operator must be implemented as a member function of a class, so a declaration like the one shown above must appear inside a class definition.

These are other rules to remember when you want to design an `operator[]` function:

- In an expression that creates an overloaded `[]` operator, the left operand is traditionally the name of the array that is being created (in the program shown in Listing 16.12, the name of the array is `aray`). The expression's right operand must be a data type that is compatible with types that are permitted by the `operator[]` member functions of the class.
- When you write a function that overloads the subscript operator, the function is always a nonstatic member function, and it always takes a single argument.

When you have written a declaration for an `operator[]` function, you can define the function by writing a block of code that allocates memory for the array and performs any other kinds of tasks, such as range-checking, that you want performed.

The definition of an `operator[]` function can take many forms. This is one example:

```
int &ArrayClass::operator[](int index)
{
     int nada;

     if (index < len)
          return aray[index];
     else {
          cout << "Error: Index out of range.\n";
          return nada;
     }
}
```

The program in Listing 16.13 uses the function that is defined above to overload an array. The program overloads the `[]` operator by creating an array class that is named (logically enough) `ArrayClass`. The class named `ArrayClass` overloads the `[]` operator to perform range checking.

**Listing 16.13. Overloading the `[]` operator.**

```
// 1613.CPP
// Overloading

#include <string.h>
#include <iostream.h>
```

*continues*

**Listing 16.13. continued**

```
class ArrayClass {
private:
     int len;
     int *aray;
public:
     ArrayClass(int ln);       // constructor
     ~ArrayClass() { delete aray; }      // destructor
     int GetLen() const { return len; }
     void SetLen(int ln) { len = ln; }
     int &operator[](int index);
};

ArrayClass::ArrayClass(int ln)
{
     if(ln > 0) {
          len = ln;
          aray = new int[ln];
          // initialize contents of array to zero
          // memset(aray, 0, sizeof(int) * ln);
     }
     else {
          ln = 0;
          aray = 0;
     }
}

int &ArrayClass::operator[](int index)
{
     int nada;

     if (index < len)
          return aray[index];
     else {
          cout << "Error: Index out of range.\n";
          return nada;
     }
}

int main()
{
     ArrayClass myArray(10);
     myArray[3] = 517;
     cout << myArray[3] << '\n';

     return 0;
}
```

In the `main()` function of the program shown in Listing 16.13, this statement instantiates an `ArrayClass` object—named `myArray`—that can hold ten integers:

```
ArrayClass myArray(10);
```

Next, this statement assigns a value of 517 to the array element that is designated `myArray[3]`:

```
myArray[3] = 517;
```

Finally, the program prints the contents of `myArray[3]`:

```
517
```

In Listing 16.13, the `operator[]` function checks to see whether a specified index value is within a specified range. If it is, the function returns a reference to the corresponding element in the array. If it isn't, the function prints an error message and returns a reference to a static integer.

This error-checking mechanism prevents out-of-range array references from overwriting other regions of memory. It is satisfactory for instructional purposes, but in a commercial-quality application, you would probably want to use a more sophisticated error-checking technique, such as one of the exception-handling procedures defined in the Microsoft Foundation Class (MFC) library.

## Advantages of Subscript Overloading

An array class such as the one created in Listing 16.13 has numerous advantages over the kinds of arrays that are conventionally used in C. For example:

- When you implement an array as a class, the definition of the class can provide a place in which you can store the size of the array. Thus, you can easily keep track of the size of the array, and you can prevent functions in your application from indexing past the limits of the array.
- When you implement an array as a class, the size of an array doesn't have to be a constant; you can determine the size of an array class at runtime without having to use memory-allocation operators such as `new` and `delete`.
- When the size of an array is stored in the array's class definition, you can pass the array to a function without having to pass the size of the array separately.

### Tips for Subscript Overloading

When you create an array that uses an overloaded `[]` operator, it may be helpful to keep these rules and miscellaneous facts in mind:

- Although the subscript operator is divided into two parts—a left bracket and a right bracket—it is considered a binary operator. (A binary operator, as noted earlier in this chapter, is an operator that takes two operands). When an overloaded `[]` operator is used in an expression, the operator's left bracket is placed between the operator's two operands, and the operator's right bracket is placed to the right of the right operand.
- In an expression that creates an overloaded `[]` operator, the left operand is traditionally the name of the array that is being created (in the program shown in Listing 16.13, the name of the array is `aray`). The expression's right operand must be a data type that is compatible with types that are permitted by the `operator[]` member functions of the class.
- When you write a function that overloads the subscript operator, the function is always a nonstatic member function, and it always takes a single argument.
- An `operator[]` function must be implemented as a member function of a class. The left operand of the function must be a class object. An `operator[]` function can have a single argument of any type, which is its right operand, and its return can be of any type.
- An `operator[]` function takes only one parameter. You cannot provide an `operator[]` function with multiple parameters to simulate a multidimensional array. However, you can simulate a multidimensional array by overloading the function-call operator—that is, the `()` operator—as explained under the next heading.

## Overloading the () Operator

In C++, the parentheses that delimit a function are known as the function call operator. And the function call operator—like the subscript operator—can be overloaded.

The function call operator is a unique feature; it is the only operator that can take multiple right-hand operands. Because of this feature, the function call operator has great flexibility. But it also has a potentially dangerous characteristic; when you use an overloaded function call operator, it looks just like a function.

So if you overload the `()` operator in a program, you should document your program carefully, particularly if your source code is ever going to be referred to by other programmers.

When you declare an `operator()` function, the syntax that you use is similar to the syntax of an `operator[]` declaration:

```
void operator()(int x, int y, char c);
```

When you have declared and defined an `operator()` function, you can overload the `()` with a statement like this:

```
aClass(0, 1, 'p');
```

In Listing 16.14, the statement shown above is used to overload the function call operator.

### Listing 16.14. Overloading the `()` operator.

```
// 1614.CPP
// Overloading the function call operator

#include <iostream.h>

const int coord1 = 10;
const int coord2 = 10;

class TestClass {
private:
    char aray [coord1] [coord2];
    friend int main();
public:
    void operator()(int x, int y, char c);
    char GetChar(int x, int y);
};

void TestClass::operator()
    (int x, int y, char c)
{
    aray [x] [y] = c;
}

char TestClass::GetChar(int x, int y)
{
    char c = aray [x] [y];
    return c;
}
```

*continues*

**Listing 16.14. continued**

```
int main()
{
    TestClass aClass;

    aClass(0, 1, 'p');
    char c = aClass.aray [0] [1];

    cout << c << '\n';

    return 0;
}
```

As noted under the previous heading, the C++ mechanism for overloading the subscript operator does not support multidimensional arrays. The program in Listing 16.14 overcomes this deficiency by overloading the `()` operator to manipulate a multidimensional array.

In Listing 16.14, a character array named `aray` is declared inside the definition of a class named `TestClass`. The array, which measures ten elements by ten elements, is declared in this statement (the coordinates of the array are set using a pair of integer constants named `coord1` and `coord2`:

```
char aray [coord1] [coord2];
```

Later in the program, this member function overloads the `()` operator by stuffing the `x` and `y` coordinates of the array named `aray` with a specified character (the coordinates and the character are passed to the function as arguments):

```
void TestClass::operator()
    (int x, int y, char c)
{
    aray [x] [y] = c;
}
```

In the `main()` function of the program, this statement places the character `p` in the array cell designated `aray[0][1]`:

```
aClass(0, 1, 'p');
```

The program then prints the value of `aray[0][1]`:

```
p
```

# Overloading the & Operator

You can overload the address-of (`&`) operator in C++, and that can sometimes come in handy. As Listing 16.15 illustrates, you can overload the `&` operator to make a pointer point to the address of an object that is an element in an array. Then, by using a loop to index through the array, you can change the address that the pointer points to without changing the name of the pointer.

### Listing 16.15. Overloading the & operator.

```
// 1615.CPP
// Overloading the & operator

#include <iostream.h>
#include <string.h>

class Pet {
    char petName[255];
public:
    char *operator&() { return this->petName; }
};

int main()
{
    Pet myPet[3];

    for (int n = 0; n < 3; n++)      {
          cout << "Type a pet's name: ";
          cin >> &myPet[n];
    }
    for (n = 0; n < 3; n++)
          cout << '\n' << &myPet[n];

    return 0;
}
```

The `main()` segment of Listing 16.15 declares an array of three `Pet` objects. These three objects are named `myPet[0]`, `myPet[1]`, and `myPet[2]`:

```
Pet myPet[3];
```

When you execute the program, it prompts you to type the names of three pets. Each name that you type is then stuffed into a string that is a data member of an object in the `myPet[]` array. The program then prints each name that you have typed in.

The main() segment of the program contains two loops: one that prompts you to type three names, and one that prints the names you have provided.

Each loop uses an overloaded & operator to access a data member of each object in the myPet[] array. The data member that the overloaded & accesses is a string named name. So, each time you use the & operator, it accesses the name variable of a myPet[] object. This is the function that overloads the & operator to perform that operation:

```
char *operator&() { return this->petName; }
```

To illustrate how this procedure works, suppose you provide this input during the first loop in the main() segment of the program:

```
Type a pet's name: Spot
Type a pet's name: Fluffy
Type a pet's name: Tweety
```

Given the above input, the second loop in the main() segment prints this output:

```
Spot
Fluffy
Tweety
```

Another way to access data members of objects in an array is to overload the -> operator, as shown in Listing 16.16 in the next section.

## Overloading the -> Operator

The pointer-to-member operator (->) is a unary operator that returns the address of an object. Alternatively, the -> operator can return an object by value, provided the object itself has an overloaded -> operator.

To use an overloaded -> operator in an expression, the left-hand value of the expression must be an object or a reference to an object. The function that overloads the -> operator can then ensure that the object pointed to has a value. By overloading the -> operator in this way, you can create a "smart pointer," that is, a pointer that always returns a safe value without being tested for a NULL value every time it's used.

## Testing a Pointer

Listing 16.16 shows how you can overload the -> operator to create a smart pointer. If the -> operator is used to access a Money object, but does not point to a valid address, the program prints a pair of zeroes. If the address is valid, the program prints the values of the data members of the specified Money object.

### Listing 16.16. Testing a pointer.

```
// 1616.CPP
// Overloading the -> operator

#include <iostream.h>
#include <math.h>
#include <stdlib.h>

class Money {
private:
     double dollars;
     double cents;
public:
     Money() {}                     // default constructor
     ~Money() {}                    // destructor
     Money(double d, double c);     // another constructor
     Money(double);                 // conversion from double
     void PrintIt()
          { cout << dollars << '\n' << cents << '\n'; }
};

Money::Money(double d, double c)
{
     dollars = d; cents = c;
}

Money::Money(double cash)      // conversion constructor--
{                              // converts fp to Money
     double    frac, n;
     frac = modf(cash, &n);    // a math.h function
     cents = frac * 100;
     dollars = n;              // n comes back as a double
}

// smart pointer class

class MoneyPtr {
    static Money *mp;
```

continues

**Listing 16.16. continued**

```
public:
    MoneyPtr() {}
    MoneyPtr(Money *m) { mp = m; }
    Money *operator->();
};

Money *MoneyPtr::mp;

Money *MoneyPtr::operator->()
{
    static Money nullVal(0,0);
    if (mp == NULL)    // if the pointer is NULL
     return &nullVal; // return the dummy address
    return mp; `       // otherwise return the pointer
}

int main()
{
    MoneyPtr mp;       // Money pointer with nothing in it
    mp->PrintIt();     // use smart pointer (returns zeros)
    Money mn(29.95);   // Money object with valid contents
    mp = &mn;          // set smart pointer to its address
    mp->PrintIt();     // display object via smart pointer

    return 0;
}
```

Listing 16.16 defines a pointer class as well as a `Money` class. The pointer class, named `MoneyPtr`, has two constructors: a default constructor that has an empty argument list, and a constructor that instantiates a `Money` object. When you instantiate a `MoneyPtr` object by invoking the constructor that instantiates a `Money` object, an object of the `Money` class is automatically created.

This is the constructor of the `MoneyPtr` class:

```
// smart pointer class

class MoneyPtr {
    static Money *mp;
public:
    MoneyPtr() {}
    MoneyPtr(Money *m) { mp = m; }
    Money *operator->();
{;
```

Notice that the `MoneyPtr` class has a static member variable that is a pointer to a `Money` object. That static member variable is named `mp`. When you invoke the `MoneyPtr` constructor that creates a `Money` object, the `MoneyPtr` constructor that you have invoked sets the `MoneyPtr::mp` variable to point to the `Money` object that the constructor creates.

In the `main()` function of the 1616.CPP program, two objects are created: a `MoneyPtr` object and a `Money` object. The `MoneyPtr` object, named `mp`, is created by invoking the default constructor of the `MoneyPtr` class. The `Money` object, named `mn`, is created by invoking the constructor of the `Money` class:

```
int main()
{
    MoneyPtr mp;          // Unitialized Money pointer
    mp->PrintIt();        // use smart pointer (returns zeros)
    Money mn(29.95);      // Money object with valid contents
    mp = &mn;             // set smart pointer to its address
    mp->PrintIt();        // display object via smart pointer

    return 0;
}
```

When the `MoneyPtr` object named `mp` is created, it is not initialized to point to a `Money` object. That means that it's a dangerous dangling pointer—the kind of pointer that doesn't point to anything, and can therefore cause a disastrous program crash.

When the dangling pointer `mp` has been created, the program attempts to print the contents of the object that `mp` points to by calling the function `mp->PrintIt()`. That's a risky thing to do, but the overloaded `->` operator in the second line of the program saves the day. The function that overloads the `->` operator detects the problem with the `mp` pointer, and simply prints a pair of zeroes to standard output.

When that has been done, the program creates a valid `Money` object and sets the pointer `mp` to point to that object. The program then calls the function `mp->PrintIt()` to print the contents of the object that `mp` points to. This time `mp` points to a valid object, so the program generates the expected output:

```
0
0
29
95
```

## Accessing Multiple Objects with ->

You can also overload the -> operator to let a single statement access multiple objects. In the main() function of Listing 16.17, the -> operator is used in a loop. When the program is executed, the -> operator lets the same statement access three different objects: sis[0], sis[1], and sis[2]. The program then prints a member variable of each object to standard output (generally the screen).

### Listing 16.17. Overloading -> to control access to an object.

```
// 1617.CPP
// Overloading the -> operator

#include <iostream.h>

const int MAX_NUM = 3;

class Sisters {
private:
     char *name;
    int dataMem;
    // private constructors
     Sisters(char *nm) { dataMem = 0; name = nm; }
public:
    char *GetName() { dataMem++; return name; }
    friend class PtrClass;
};

// set up a pointer class

class PtrClass {
private:
    Sisters *sis[MAX_NUM];
    int count;
public:
    PtrClass();                // constructor
    Sisters *operator->();     // -> operator overload
};

// PtrClass constructor sets up 3 Sisters objects

PtrClass::PtrClass() {
    sis[0] = new Sisters("Nyla");
    sis[1] = new Sisters("Tammy");
    sis[2] = new Sisters("Miriam");
    count = 0;
}
```

```
// create a "smart" -> operator

Sisters *PtrClass::operator->()
{
    // access each entry once
     return sis[count++];
}

int main()
{
    PtrClass myClass;

    int n;
    for (n = 0; n < MAX_NUM; n++)
          cout << myClass->GetName() << '\n';
    return 0;
}
```

The program in Listing 16.17 defines two classes: a class called `Sisters` and a pointer class. When you instantiate an object of the pointer class, the constructor of the pointer class automatically creates an array of `Sisters` objects: `sis[0]`, `sis[1]`, and `sis[2]`. The program's `main()` segment then prints the names of three sisters by writing the contents of three strings that contain names. Each of these three strings is a data member of a `Sisters` object.

One interesting feature of the program in Listing 16.17 is that the `Sisters` class has a private constructor. That means that a `Sisters` object can be created only by an object that belongs to a class that's designated as a friend. The `Sisters` class has only one friend class—named `PtrClass`—so there is only one way to create a `Sisters` object: You simply create a `PtrClass` object. The constructor that is defined for `PtrClass` then instantiates an array of three `Sisters` objects.

This is the constructor for the `PtrClass` class:

```
// PtrClass constructor sets up 3 Sisters objects

PtrClass::PtrClass() {
    sis[0] = new Sisters("Nyla");
    sis[1] = new Sisters("Tammy");
    sis[2] = new Sisters("Miriam");
    count = 0;
}
```

And this is the statement that overloads the `->` operator:

```
// create a "smart" -> operator
```

```
Sisters *PtrClass::operator->()
{
    // access each entry once
     return sis[count++];
}
```

When a `PtrClass` object has instantiated three `Sisters` objects, the program's `main()` segment uses the overloaded `->` operator to print each sister's name. Each name is obtained by a member function of the `Sisters` class called `GetName()`:

```
cout << myClass->GetName() << '\n';
```

As the following statement shows, the `Sisters::GetName()` function increments a member variable named `Sisters::dataMem` each time it obtains a name from a `Sisters` object:

```
char *GetName() { dataMem++; return name; }
```

The incrementing mechanism in the above statement causes the `GetName()` function to print the `name` variable of a different `Sisters` object each time it is called.

This is the output of the program:

```
Nyla
Tammy
Miriam
```

## Overloading Data Types

You can use the `operator` keyword to convert data from one type to another, as well as to overload operators. When objects of a class need to convert a variable from one data type to another, a function that performs that task can be defined within the definition of a class. For example, by writing a statement like this, you can define a member function of a class that converts variables of the `float` type to another data type:

```
operator float();    // member conversion function
```

Once you have written a function declaration like the one above, you can define a function that performs the necessary conversion—for example:

```
// member conversion function
Coins::operator float()
{
     int dollars, dimes, pennies;

     dollars = dl * 100;
```

```
        dimes = dm * 10;
        pennies = pn;
        float amount = (dollars + dimes + pennies);
        amount = amount / 100;
      return amount;
}
```

If a class definition contains a member function like the one defined above, you can use the function to convert any variable of the `float` type into a variable of another type. For example, the function that is defined above can convert any `float` variable to an object of the `Coins` class.

Technically, this use of the `operator` keyword is not operator overloading, but data-type overloading. However, because data-type overloading works so much like operator overloading, it is commonly placed in the same category as operator overloading.

For more information about data-type overloading, see Chapter 16, "Operator Overloading."

# Overloading new and delete

As you can see by consulting Table 16.1, the memory-allocation operators `new` and `delete` are operators that can be overloaded in C++. Procedures for overloading `new` and `delete` were outlined briefly in Chapter 9, "Managing Memory," and are described in more detail later in this chapter.

You can overload the `new` and `delete` operators when you want to perform customized memory-management operations. In fact, many commercial programs written in C++ use operator overloading to define their own class-specific `new` and `delete` operators.

## Reasons for Overloading new and delete

The `new` and `delete` operators are often overloaded because in some situations, customized allocation and deallocation operators can operate faster and more efficiently than the global `new` and `delete` operators provided by C++.

When you define your own memory allocation and deallocation operators, you can tell your `new` operator the size of an object being allocated, as well as how and when the object is to be deleted. You can even specify where in memory you want the object stored.

Therefore, by overloading `new` and `delete`, you can reduce problems caused by memory fragmentation, and you can speed up operations that allocate and deallocate memory.

More specific reasons for overloading `new` and `delete` include:

- *control over storage*. A customized `new` operator can place an object in a specified block of memory—such as a block of shared memory—instead of letting the C++ memory-management determine where the object is stored.
- *control over deleting objects*. When you create on object by invoking a constructor, C++ automatically deletes the object and deallocates its memory when the object is no longer needed. However, when you allocate memory dynamically—that is, with the `new` operator—you must deallocate it manually by using the `delete` operator. When you define your own `new` and `delete` operators, you can write memory-allocation functions that keep track of dynamically allocated memory. Then you can deallocate the memory with the `delete` operator when it is no longer needed.
- *easier debugging*. When you control the way memory is dynamically allocated and deallocated, your applications are easier to debug because you know more about how the `new` and `delete` operators are used, and more about what they do.

## Techniques for Overloading new and delete

An `operator new()` function always takes at least one argument: an operand that has a special data type called `size_t`. The `size_t` data type, defined in the header file STDDEF.H, specifies the size of the memory block that is required by the object being created. When you pass a `size_t` variable to an `operator new()` function, the compiler automatically sets the value of the function's `size_t` argument.

An `operator new()` function always has a return type of `void`. This is the syntax of an `operator new()` function:

```
void *operator new(size_t bufSize);
```

A function that overloads the `delete` operator can be defined to take either one or two arguments. The first argument is always a `void` pointer to the object that is being deleted. The second argument, which is optional, is the size of the object to be deleted.

If an `operator delete()` member function takes the size of an object as an argument, the overloading function's class should have a virtual destructor. This precaution ensures that the correct destructor is always called, and that the correct size is passed to `operator delete()` function.

An `operator delete()` function always has a return type of `void`. This is the syntax of an `operator delete()` function:

```
void operator delete(void *voidPtrType);
```

When a program dynamically allocates memory for an object, the compiler checks to see whether the definition of the object's class contains a customized `operator new()` function. If there is one, it is used; otherwise, C++ uses the global implementation `operator new()` function (which may also be overloaded). If no overloaded `operator new()` function is found, the compiler uses its default global `new` operator.

The compiler performs a similar procedure when a program deallocates memory for an object using the `delete` operator.

### USING THE NEW OPERATOR WITH CONSTRUCTORS

When a C++ program instantiates an object that belongs to a class, the statement that instantiates the object often contains both a call to a constructor and a `new` operator. In fact, as you may recall from Chapter 14, "Constructors and Destructors," that's the most common method for instantiating class objects. Typically, a statement that instantiates a class has this syntax:

```
AClass *anObject = new AClass;
```

When you allocate memory for a class object by using both the `new` operator and a constructor, as shown above, the `new` operator does not override the object's constructor; the constructor is still invoked.

It is also important to note that when you use both the `new` operator and a constructor to create a class object, it is not necessary to delete the object using the `delete` operator when the object is no longer needed. When an object is instantiated with both a constructor and a `new` operator, the object is automatically deleted and its memory is deallocated automatically when it is no longer needed.

Listing 16.18 is a program that overloads the `new` and `delete` operators. The program allocates memory for an array of characters, stuffs the memory locations in the allocated block with zeroes, prints the zeroes, and then deletes the memory that has been allocated.

### Listing 16.18. Overloading `new` and `delete`.

```
// 1618.CPP
// Overloading the new and delete operators

#include <iostream.h>
#include <stdlib.h>
#include <stddef.h>

// class definition
class AClass {
private:
     int *stuffVal;
public:
     void *operator new(size_t bufSize);
     void operator delete(void *voidPtrType)
          { free(voidPtrType); }
     void AllocMem(int val)
          { stuffVal = new int[val]; }
     void DeallocMem()
          { delete [] stuffVal; }
     void AClass::StuffIt(int val);
};

void *AClass::operator new(size_t bufSize)
{
    void *retVal = calloc(1, bufSize);
    return retVal;
}

void AClass::StuffIt(int val)
{
    for (int n = 0; n < val; n++)
        cout << " " << stuffVal[n];
}

// the main() function

int main()
{
     static int stuffVal = 16;

     AClass *myObject = new AClass;
```

```
    myObject->AllocMem(stuffVal);
    myObject->StuffIt(stuffVal);
    myObject->DeallocMem();
    return 0;
}
```

In Listing 16.18, the `new` and `delete` operators are overloaded inside the definition of a class named `AClass`. In the program's `main()` function, an `AClass` object named `myObject` is created. The statement that instantiates the object contains both a `new` operator and a constructor:

```
AClass *myObject = new AClass;
```

When `myObject` has been instantiated, these statements allocate a block of memory, stuff it with zeroes, print the zeroes, and deallocate the memory that was allocated:

```
myObject->AllocMem(stuffVal);
myObject->StuffIt(stuffVal);
myObject->DeallocMem();
```

## Rules for Overloading new and delete

When you overload the `new` operator in a program, you should also overload the corresponding `delete` operator. That way, the compiler's default `delete` operator can't make any false assumptions about your `new` operator, and therefore can't generate any unexpected errors.

These are some other rules, facts, and tips that may be helpful to remember when you want to overload the `new` and `delete` operators:

- A function that overloads the `new` or `delete` operator is always implemented as a member function; a nonmember function cannot be used to overload the `new` operator or the `delete` operator. However, you can redefine, or *overload*, the global `operator new()` and `operator delete()` functions that are defined by Visual C++, as explained in Chapter 15.
- A function that overloads the `new` operator or the `delete` operator is always a static member function. It is not necessary to use the `static` keyword in the declaration of an `operator new()` or `operator delete()` function; even if you don't use the `static` keyword, the compiler treats the function as a static member function.

- An `operator new()` or `operator delete()` function cannot be a virtual function.
- When the `new` and `delete` operators are overloaded, the overloaded versions of the operators are used only when individual objects are allocated dynamically. They are not used when arrays of objects are allocated, when automatic (local) variables are allocated on the stack, or when static global objects are created.

# Nonmember Overloading Functions

All the operator-overloading operations described in the preceding section have one thing in common; they are all implemented by member functions. And an operator that is overloaded with a member function has one shortcoming when you overload an operator with a member function, and then write an expression that makes use of the overloaded operator, the operator's left-hand operand cannot be a built-in data type; it must be a member of a class.

For example, this is a definition of a member function that overloads the + operator so a `Money` object can be added to an integer:

```
Money Money::operator+(double dubval)
{
     Money m;
     ldiv_t result;
     double     frac, n;

     frac = modf(dubval, &n); // a math.h function
     m.cents = frac * 100;
     m.dollars = n;            // n comes back as a double
}

     cents += m.cents;
     dollars += m.dollars;

     if (cents > 99) {
         result = ldiv((long)cents, 100);
         dollars = dollars + result.quot;
         cents = (double)result.rem;
     }

     return *this;
}
```

Once a member function like the one above is defined, the = operator that the member function overloads can be used in a statement like this:

```
myCash = myCash + 3.15;
```

However, because of the structure of the member function that overloads the + operator, the operator cannot be used in this kind of expression:

```
myCash = 3.15 + myCash;
```

Fortunately, this deficiency is easy to remedy; all you have to do is write a nonmember function that reverses the two operands in the statement shown above. The nonmember function that performs this operation must have access to private members of the `Money` class, so it must be designated as a `friend` function.

This is an example of a `friend` function that can perform the necessary operation:

```
friend Money operator+(double d, Money& mn) { return mn + d; }
```

Notice that the `friend` function shown above takes two arguments: a `double` variable and a variable that is an object of the `Money` class. That makes it a more versatile kind of function than an operator-overloading member function, which can take only one argument.

In the `friend` function shown above, the + operator is overloaded to reverse the operands of the expression shown in the preceding code fragment. The `friend` function that performs this operation is so simple that it is implemented as an inline function inside the definition of the `Money` class. The function merely reverses the operands of any statement that is written in this format:

```
myCash = 3.15 + myCash;
```

so that it becomes an expression that is written in this format:

```
myCash = myCash + 3.15;
```

Once the expression above has been built by a nonmember operator-overloading function, it can be executed by a second + operator that has been overloaded in standard fashion by a member `operator+` function.

## Writing a Nonmember Operator-Overloading Function

When a nonmember function is used to overload an operator, the overloading function usually does its work by manipulating private members of a class. Therefore, nonmember operating-overloading functions are usually `friend` functions.

However, that is not a strict requirement. If you write a nonmember operating-overloading function that does not require access to private members of a class, you do not have to make it a friend of any class.

As you saw in the previous section, when a member function of a class overloads an operator, the operator's left-hand operand must be a class object, and the compiler cannot apply any conversions to that object. Also, only one argument can be passed to the function. If an argument is passed to the function, that argument becomes the operator's right-hand operand.

When a nonmember function overloads an operator, the syntax of the function is quite different. Either one or two arguments can be passed to the function, and each argument can have any type. Each argument that is passed to the function can be a built-in data type, a user-defined data type, or a class. Furthermore, the computer can apply conversions to any argument that is passed to a nonmember operator-overloading function.

It's important to remember, though, that when you overload an operator using a nonmember function, at least one of the function's parameters must be an object. So you can't write a binary `operator+` function that takes two integers as parameters. This prevents you from redefining the meaning of operators on built-in types.

Also remember that you cannot use a nonmember function to overload the function call operator (written as parentheses), the assignment operator (=), the function-type operator, the subscript operator (`[]`), or the `new` or `delete` operator. To overload any of these operators, you must use member-style operator-overloading functions.

## Overloading a Unary Operator

When you use a nonmember function to overload a unary operator, only one argument to the function is required. For example, this statement declares a nonmember function that overloads the unary ++ operator:

```
operator++(AClass);
```

Similarly, this is a definition of a nonmember function that overloads the unary - operator when the operator is used with an object of the `Money` class:

```
inline Money operator-(Money &m)
{
    return Money(-m.dollars, m.cents);
}
```

### Overloading a Binary Operator

The syntax of a friend function that overloads a binary operator is similar to the syntax of a friend function that overloads a unary operator. This statement declares a friend function of `AClass` that overloads a binary operator:

```
operator++(AClass, BClass);
```

If a declaration like the one shown above appears in a function that is a friend of a class, and is supported by a corresponding function definition, you can call the `friend` function in the same way that you would call an operator-overloading member function:

```
cObject = aObject + BClass;
```

## An Operator-Overloading friend Function

Listing 16.19 is a program that overloads a binary operator using a `friend` function instead of a member function:

#### Listing 16.19. An operator-overloading `friend` function.

```
// 1619.CPP
// Overloading the + operator

#include <iostream.h>
#include <math.h>
#include <stdlib.h>

class Money {
private:
     double dollars;
     double cents;
public:
     Money() {}                      // default constructor
     ~Money() {}                     // destructor
     Money(double d, double c);      // another conrt
     Money(double);                  // conversion from double
     Money operator+(double dubval); // operator overloading
     double GetAmount(double &n);
     friend Money operator+(double d, Money& mn)
         { return mn + d; }
};
```

*continues*

**Listing 16.19. continued**

```
Money Money::operator+(double dubval)
{
     Money m;
     ldiv_t result;
     double     frac, n;

     frac = modf(dubval, &n); // a math.h function
     m.cents = frac * 100;
     m.dollars = n;            // n comes back as a double

     cents += m.cents;
     dollars += m.dollars;

     if (cents > 99) {
         result = ldiv((long)cents, 100);
         dollars = dollars + result.quot;
         cents = (double)result.rem;
     }

     return *this;
}

Money::Money(double d, double c)
{
     dollars = d; cents = c;
}

Money::Money(double cash)     // conversion constructor--
{                             // converts fp to Money
     double    frac, n;
     frac = modf(cash, &n);   // a math.h function
     cents = frac * 100;
     dollars = n;             // n comes back as a double
}

double Money::GetAmount(double &n)
{
     n = dollars;
     return cents;
}

int main()
{
     double c, d;
     Money myCash(2.99);

     myCash = 3.15 + myCash;

     c = myCash.GetAmount(d);
```

```
    cout << d << '\n';
    cout << c << '\n';

    return 0;
}
```

In Listing 16.19, the following definition of a `friend` function appears inside the definition of the `Money` class:

```
friend Money operator+(double d, Money& mn)
    { return mn + d; }
```

The above function is so short that it is declared and defined at the same time, inside the definition of the `Money` class. The function overloads the global + operator by simply reversing the order of the arguments that are passed to it. Then the function uses those same arguments to call another function: specifically, a standard operator-overloading member function that overloads the local + operator used by the `Money` class.

This is the member function that is called by the `friend` function shown in the previous code fragment:

```
Money Money::operator+(double dubval)
{
    Money m;
    ldiv_t result;
    double    frac, n;

    frac = modf(dubval, &n); // a math.h function
    m.cents = frac * 100;
    m.dollars = n;           // n comes back as a double

    cents += m.cents;
    dollars += m.dollars;

    if (cents > 99) {
        result = ldiv((long)cents, 100);
        dollars = dollars + result.quot;
        cents = (double)result.rem;
    }

    return *this;
}
```

This member function divides the long value that is passed to it into two parts—a pair of data members named `dollars` and `cents`. The function then adds this pair of values to the `dollars` and `cents` members of the `Money` object that is the other operand of the + function that is being overloaded. Finally, the function uses the MATH.H function `ldiv` to ensure that the `cents` member variable that has just been calculated contains a value of less than 100.

In this way, the `friend` function executes this expression, which appears inside the program's `main()` function:

```
myCash = 3.15 + myCash;
```

## Another Operator-Overloading friend Function

Although a nonmember `operator+` function can simply reverse the operands in an expression—as shown in Listing 16.19—that isn't the only way to write an operator-overloading `friend` function. Listing 16.20 shows another alternative.

### Listing 16.20. Another kind of operator-overloading `friend` function.

```
// 1620.CPP
// Overloading a binary operator

#include <iostream.h>
#include <math.h>
#include <stdlib.h>

class Money {
private:
    double dollars;
    double cents;
public:
    Money() {}                          // default constructor
    ~Money() {}                         // destructor
    Money(double d, double c);          // another const
    Money(double);                      // conversion from double
    friend Money operator+(double dubval, Money &m);
    double GetAmount(double &n);
    void SetAmount(double x, double y)
     { dollars = x; cents = y; }
};

Money::Money(double d, double c)
{
    dollars = d; cents = c;
}

Money::Money(double cash)       // conversion constructor--
{                               // converts fp to Money
```

```
    double frac, n;
    frac = modf(cash, &n);     // a math.h function
    cents = frac * 100;
    dollars = n;               // n comes back as a double
}

double Money::GetAmount(double &n)
{
    n = dollars;
    return cents;
}

// operator-overloading friend function

Money operator+(double dubval, Money &m)
{
    Money m2(dubval);     // call conversion constructor
    ldiv_t result;
    double c, d;

    c = m2.GetAmount;    // get m2 data members

    if (c > 99) {
          result = ldiv((long)c, 100);
          d = d + result.quot;
          c = (double)result.rem;
    }

    m2.SetAmount(m.dollars + d, m.cents + c);

    return m2;
}

int main()
{
     double c, d;
     Money yourCash(5000.00);

     Money myCash = 2.99 + yourCash;

     c = myCash.GetAmount(d);

     cout << d << '\n';
     cout << c << '\n';

     return 0;
}
```

The `friend` function in Listing 16.20 is more complicated than the `friend` function in the previous listing, but it doesn't do its job by calling an operator-overloading member function. Instead, it uses a conversion constructor to set up a local `Money` object, and then it adds that object to the `Money` object that is passed to it as a parameter.

```
Money operator+(double dubval, Money &m)
{
    Money m2(dubval);      // call conversion constructor
    ldiv_t result;
    double c, d;

    c = m2.GetAmount(d);    // get m2 data members

    if (c > 99) {
          result = ldiv((long)c, 100);
          d = d + result.quot;
          c = (double)result.rem;
    }

    m2.SetAmount(m.dollars + d, m.cents + c);

    return m2;
}
```

# Summary

This chapter covered operator overloading: it lets you extend the language by creating your own operators. By using operator overloading, you can redefine the behaviors of arithmetic and logical operators so they can perform different kinds of operations in different kinds of situations.

Topics covered in this chapter included:

- Using member functions and nonmember functions to overload operators.
- Overloading binary and unary operators.
- Overloading the assignment operator (=).
- Overloading relational operators.
- Overloading the subscript and function call (`[]` and `()`) operators.
- Overloading the address-of (`&`) operator.

- Overloading the pointer-to-member (`->`) operator.
- Overloading data types.
- Overloading the `new` and `delete` operators.

Chapter 17

# Conversion Functions

Computer programs often have a need to convert data from one type to another. To meet this need, C++ has built-in utilities that can automatically convert standard data types to other standard data types.

What happens, however, when a program must convert data to or from a user-defined data type, such as a class? No compiler can automatically convert data to or from a user-defined data type, because there is no way of knowing in advance what the structure of a user-defined data type is.

C++ does provide a mechanism for converting data to and from user-defined data types. To perform customized data conversions in C++, all you do is write a special kind of function called a *conversion function*.

There are two kinds of conversion functions in C++:

- *Member conversion functions*. Functions that use a mechanism similar to operator overloading to perform data-type conversions.
- *Conversion constructors*. Special constructors that can perform three tasks in a single step. A conversion constructor can initialize an object, convert a parameter that is passed to the constructor from one data type to another, and initialize a member variable of the new object with the data on which the conversion was performed.

This chapter explains how to write member conversion functions and conversion constructors and how to use both kinds of conversion functions to convert data to and from user-defined data types in C++ programs.

# How Conversion Functions Work

In C++, as in C, programs routinely convert data from one data type to another. For example, if you use an `int` variable in an expression that calls for a `long` variable, any C++ compiler can automatically apply built-in type conversion rules to convert the integer value that it is supplied with to the long format that the expression requires.

Of course, the kind of data conversion that the compiler is expected to perform must make sense; that is, the data types involved in the conversion must be compatible in the context of the conversion that is being attempted. If the data types in the expression don't mix, the compiler returns an error message.

The kind of conversion a C++ compiler performs automatically on standard data types is called a *standard conversion*. C++ provides standard conversions for all fundamental data types. The Visual C++ compiler can automatically perform a standard conversion when it detects a need to substitute one data type for another in an expression, an assignment, a function argument, a return value, or an initializer.

Sometimes, however, the compiler can't convert a type to another type without some extra help from the program being executed. For example, a C++ compiler can't perform a *mod* operation on a variable of type `float`; so if you want to mod a `float`, you must write an expression that *casts* your `float` variable to data of another type.

There are several techniques for converting data from one type to another. These techniques include *casting operations,* which have long been used in the C language, but are improved in C++; and *member conversion functions,* which are similar to conversion constructor functions, but with more limited capabilities.

# Casting

In C, as in C++, a cast is an operation that converts data of one type to data of another type:

```
float y = 17.49;
int x = (int) y % 4;
```

This code fragment casts the `float` variable `y` to an `int` and then performs a mod (`%`) calculation on `y`.

This example illustrates the traditional C syntax for executing a cast operation. In this syntax, a type specifier enclosed in parentheses is followed by an expression. When the expression is evaluated, it is converted to the specified data type.

In C++, there's an alternate syntax for performing casts, as you'll soon see as you read on.

## The Trouble with Casting

Although casts are sometimes necessary, unnecessary casting should be avoided. When you perform a cast, you are really circumventing safeguards that have been carefully built into your compiler to prevent compilation errors. The C language has long been criticized for weak type-checking, and cast operations water down type-checking even more.

C++ has strengthened C's type-checking system and, at the same time, has managed to reduce the need to cast. As you saw in Chapter 9, "Managing Memory," C++ has replaced the `malloc()` and `free()` family of memory-allocation functions with the `new` and `delete` pointers—which can allocate memory without relying on casting—and has also replaced other C-language mechanisms that used to require casting operations.

# Function-Style Casts

Paradoxically, while reducing the need to cast, C++ has introduced a new syntax that you can use when you do need to cast. In C++, you're not restricted to using the casting syntax that was described under the previous heading. Instead, you can use an alternate syntax that looks like a function. For example, this small program contains a C++-style cast operation that converts an integer data type to a double type:

```
// TEST2.CPP

#include <iostream.h>

int main()
{
      int i = 10;
      double d;
      d = double(10);
      cout << d << '\n';
      return 0;
}
```

In this new syntax for casting operations, a type name is followed by an expression—or by a list of expressions—that is converted to a class type (or class types). The preceding program generates this output (which, although you can't tell it by looking, is a double-data type):

```
10
```

This syntax for casting operations is related to C++'s function-style format for initializations, which was introduced in Chapter 2, "A Better C—Plus." To refresh your memory about how initialization operations work in C++, look at this old, conventional C-style initialization:

```
int x = 5;
```

In C++, you also can perform an initialization operation on a numeric variable by using this new alternate syntax.

```
int x(5);
```

The preceding statement has the same effect as the previous C-style initialization operation. As you can see, this alternate function-style format for initialization operations is similar to C++'s new function-style format for performing a cast:

```
d = double(10);
```

## Uses for Function-Style Casts

Although a function-style cast can perform the same job as a traditional C-style cast, C++ introduced the new syntax to fulfill a special need: the need for a casting format that can be used with multiple arguments. This is also the reason that C++ provides a new function-style format for the initialization of variables.

Because the new function-style syntax for casting can be used with multiple arguments, a function-style cast can be expanded into a special kind of function—called a *conversion function*—that can convert data into user-defined classes. Conversion functions are described in more detail later in this chapter.

> **TIP—SPECIAL REQUIREMENTS FOR CASTING**
>
> In C++, you must perform an explicit casting operation when you convert a pointer to a `void` data to a pointer to any other type. You must also use an explicit casting operation when you want to convert any integral type to an enumeration type.

## Rules for Using Function-Style Casts

No matter how you use a function-style cast—for a simple casting operation or as part of a more sophisticated conversion function—you must provide a type name for the type that you want to cast. To convert a simple data type to another simple type, you must only declare a variable to hold the result of your cast, as in this code fragment:

```
double d;
d = double(10);
```

To cast a variable to a more complex data type—such as a character pointer, a `struct`, or a class—you can declare a data type for the target of your cast by using keywords such as `typedef`, `struct`, or `class`, for example:

```
typedef point { int x, y; };
typedef void (*funcPtr) (void);
typedef char *chrPtr;
```

# Converting User-Defined Data Types

In C++, as in C, casting operations are provided so you can convert existing data types into other predefined types. Sometimes you may also need to convert data to or from a user-defined data type, such as a class.

When you want to convert data back and forth between user-defined types and other data types (which also may be user-defined), you must provide the necessary code, because C++ knows nothing about the data types you define for use in your programs. To perform conversions that involve user-defined data types, you can write special kinds of functions called, logically enough, *conversion functions.*

After you write a conversion function, the compiler can execute your function automatically when the syntax of a statement suggests the conversion should be performed, that is, when the compiler expects data of a particular type and encounters another data type instead. When that happens, the compiler automatically looks for user-written conversion functions. If it finds a conversion function that can perform the necessary conversion, the compiler automatically calls the appropriate conversion function.

There are two kinds of conversion functions in C++:

*Member conversion functions* are functions that use a mechanism similar to operator overloading (which was described in Chapter 16, "Operator Overloading") to convert data from one type to another. A member conversion can convert data from any built-in data type (such as `float`, `double`, or `int`) to a user-defined data type, such as a class.

*Conversion constructor functions* are special-purpose constructors. Conversion constructor functions are based on the function-style casting syntax described in the previous section. A conversion constructor can perform three tasks in a single step:

- Initialize an object.
- Convert a parameter that is passed to the object from any data type—including a user-defined type, such as a class—to any user-defined type, such as a class.
- Initialize a member variable of the new object with the data on which the conversion has been performed.

You can use a conversion constructor to convert any standard data type—such as a `double` variable—to a user-defined data type, such as a class (provided a `double` value can be converted to the structure of the target data type). You also can use a conversion constructor to convert any user-defined data type—such as a class—to any other user-defined data type (provided the source and target data types have structures that are compatible).

# Conversion Constructor Functions

A constructor that has only one entry in its parameter list is a *conversion constructor function*. A conversion constructor can convert a variable from any data type to any other type. In other words, a conversion constructor can convert data from either a fundamental data type or a user-defined type *to* either a fundamental data type or a user-defined type.

You can declare a conversion constructor inside a class declaration in the same way you define any member function. In a declaration of a conversion constructor, the name of the function is always the name of the data type to which the data passed to the function will be converted. A single parameter enclosed in parentheses follows the name of the function and specifies the type of data that will be passed to the function.

This is a declaration of a conversion constructor:

```
Money(float);        // conversion constructor
```

The preceding statement declares the existence of a conversion constructor that can convert a variable of type `float` to a class named `Money`. The name of the constructor function is `Money`, and the single parameter passed to the function is a variable of type `float`.

**NOTE—EITHER WAY IS OK**

Either element in the declaration of a conversion constructor can be the name of a built-in data type. Either element can also be the name of any user-defined data type, such as a class. For example, this is a declaration of a conversion constructor that converts a datum of class `Money` to a datum of type `float`:

```
zfloat(Money);       // conversion constructor
```

When you have declared a conversion constructor, you are responsible for writing the definition of the function. The function that you write must take a single parameter of the specified type and must return the data type that is specified by the name of the function.

Once you have written a conversion constructor, you can call it with a statement like this:

```
Money japanese(toYen);    // calling a conversion constructor
```

### NOTE—AN ALTERNATIVE FORMAT FOR A CONVERSION CONSTRUCTOR

You may recall that C++ provides two formats for writing casting operations: a function-style format that uses parentheses and an assignment-style format that uses the assignment operator (=). As you might guess, you can also use either of these two alternate formats when you write conversion constructors. You, thus, can also call a conversion constructor by using this syntax:

```
Money japanese = toYen; // calling a construction conversion function
```

The above statement declares that a conversion constructor function named `Money` will be defined, and that the function will convert a `long` data type to a user-defined class named `Money`.

### NOTE—A CURRENCY-CONVERSION PROGRAM

The previous declaration is taken from the program presented in Listing 17.1. This program converts dollars, which are expressed as type `float`, to Japanese yen, which are expressed as a user-defined class named `Money`. (When the program was written, a dollar was selling for 120.70 yen, so that's the ratio the program uses for its conversion.)

**Listing 17.1. A conversion constructor.**

```
// 1701.CPP
// Conversion constructor

#include <iostream.h>

class Money {
     int yen;
public:
    Money() {}             // null constructor
     Money(float);         // conversion constructor
     int GetYen() { return yen; }
};

// conversion constructor
Money::Money(float amount)
{
     float temp = amount * 120.70;
     yen = (int) temp;
     if (temp - yen > .49)
          yen = yen + 1;
}

int main()
{
     const float amtInDollars = 237.95;

     float toYen = amtInDollars;
     Money japanese(toYen);
     cout << "\n$" << amtInDollars << " = ";
     cout << japanese.GetYen() << " yen.\n";

     return 0;
}
```

## Defining a Class for a Conversion Function

When a program contains a conversion constructor function, the program is responsible for providing the code that performs the actual conversion. Because the program in Listing 17.1 converts a long data type to a user-defined class named `Money`, the executing program must define the `Money` class. The program defines the `Money` class as follows:

```
class Money {
     int yen;
public:
    Money() {}          // null constructor
     Money(float);       // conversion constructor
     int GetYen() { return yen; }
};
```

As you can see, the Money class—like most classes used in C++—contains both member variables and member functions. When a conversion function is used to convert data to or from a class type, however, the class's member variables are disregarded; only the class's data members are used in the conversion operation.

In the definition of the preceding Money class, the only member variable declared is an integer variable named yen. The conversion constructor

```
Money(float);
```

therefore converts a float value to a user-defined class named Money that contains one element, namely, an int variable named yen. You could also declare the conversion constructor using this format:

```
Money(float amount);
```

## Defining a Conversion Constructor

When you have declared a conversion constructor function, you must define it before you can use it. This is a definition of the construction conversion Money():

```
// conversion constructor
Money::Money(float amount)
{
     float temp = amount * 120.70;
     yen = (int) temp;
     if (temp - yen > .49)
          yen = yen + 1;
}
```

When you have written a conversion constructor, you can call it in the same way you call any class constructor. In Listing 17.1, the conversion function is called in the main() segment:

```
int main()
{
     const float amtInDollars = 237.95;

     float toYen = amtInDollars;
     Money japanese(toYen);
```

```
    cout << "\n$" << amtInDollars << " = ";
    cout << japanese.GetYen() << " yen.\n";

    return 0;
}
```

The above code fragment creates a `Money` object named `japanese` and declares a `float`-type variable named `toYen`. Then, this statement converts the variable `toYen` to a `Money` object named `japanese`:

```
Money japanese(toYen);
```

Finally, these two statements print the result of the conversion:

```
cout << "\n$" << amtInDollars << " = ";
cout << japanese.GetYen() << " yen.\n";
```

When you execute the 1701.CPP program, it prints this line on the screen:

```
$237.95 = 28721 yen.
```

The `Money()` function that performs the conversion operation in Listing 17.1 is a constructor as well as a conversion function. It actually performs two tasks: It initializes the `Money` object named `japanese`, and then it converts the `float` variable passed to it to a `Money` object.

The program shows how a conversion constructor can convert a basic data type to a user-defined class, but the class that is the target of the conversion has only one element.

## Converting a Variable to a Multi-Element Class

The program in Listing 17.2 performs a slightly more complex conversion. It converts a dollar-and-cents value that is expressed as a floating-point `double` type to a set of three integers that represents dollars, dimes, and pennies.

### Listing 17.2. Another conversion constructor.

```
// 1702.CPP
// Conversion constructor

#include <iostream.h>
#include <stdlib.h>
#include <math.h>
```

*continues*

#### Listing 17.2. continued

```
class Money {
    long pn, dm, dl;
public:
    Money() {}      // null constructor
    Money(double);  // conversion constructor
    void display(void);
};

// member function to display coins
void Money::display()
{
    cout << "\nDollars: " << dl << "\n";
    cout << "Dimes: " << dm << "\n";
    cout << "Pennies: " << pn << "\n";
}

// conversion constructor
Money::Money(double cash)
{
    double frac, frac2, n;
    ldiv_t ldiv_result;

    frac = modf(cash, &n); // break cash down into
                           // n and frac parts

    dl = n;   // n part of cash = dollars

    // — multiply frac part of cash by 10
    frac *= 10;

    frac2 = modf(frac, &n);   // break frac down into
                              // n and frac2 parts

    dm = n;    // n part of frac = dimes

    // — multiply frac2 part of frac by 10
    frac2 *= 10;    // pennies = frac2 * 10

    pn = (long)frac2;    // copy double type to long type
}

int main()
{
    double cash = 75535.91;
    Money myCash(cash);     // invoke the conversion constructor
    myCash.display();       // display money
    return 0;
}
```

The 1702.CPP program shows how a conversion constructor can convert a variable from its original data type into a multi-element, user-defined type such as a class.

The class that is the target of the conversion is named `Money`. This is the definition of the `Money` class:

```
class Money {
    int pn, dm, dl;
public:
    Money() {}              // null constructor
    Money(float);           // conversion constructor
    void display(void);
};
```

The program uses the `modf()` function in Visual C++'s MATH.H library to convert a floating-point variable of the `double` type to a user-defined class that contains three integer variables named `pn`, `dm`, and `dl`.

The `modf()` function separates the `double` value that is passed to the constructor (`75535.91`) into an integer part and a fraction part. The integer part of the double equates to a value expressed in dollars, and the fraction part equates to a value expressed in cents.

The 1702.CPP program stores the dollar part of the value passed to it in the member variable `dl`. Then, the program uses two multiplications by ten and a cast from a `double` data type to a `long` data type to convert the fraction part of the value passed to the constructor to dimes and pennies. The results of these calculations are stored in the member variables `dm` and `pn`.

Finally, the program prints this output:

```
Dollars: 75535
Dimes: 9
Pennies: 1
```

## A More Advanced Conversion Constructor

Listing 17.1 showed how a conversion constructor can convert a basic data type to a user-defined class, and Listing 17.2 demonstrated the conversion of a variable from its original data type to a multi-element class type.

The program in Listing 17.3 performs a conversion that is even more ambitious. It converts a value that is returned by the standard `time` function from a `time_t` data type (the data type the `time` function returns) to another kind of user-defined variable—in this case, a string. Next, the program stores the converted variable in a class data member that has been reserved for it. Finally, the program prints the result of its conversion.

**Listing 17.3. A more advanced conversion constructor.**

```
// 1703.CPP
// Class conversions

#include <iostream.h>
#include <time.h>

class Timestamp {
private:
    char *datebuf;  // buffer for date
    char *timebuf;  // buffer for time
public:
    Timestamp() {}      // default constructor
    Timestamp(time_t);  // conversion constructor
    void display(void); // function to display date & time
};

// member function to display date and time
void Timestamp::display()
{
   // display contents of datebuf
   cout << "Date: " << datebuf << "\n";

   // display contents of timebuf
   cout << "Time: " << timebuf;
}

// conversion constructor
Timestamp::Timestamp(time_t ltime)
{
    _strdate(datebuf);   // store date in datebuf
    _strtime(timebuf);   // store time in timebuf
}

int main()
{
    // get today's date and time
    time_t ltime = time((time_t *)NULL);

    Timestamp dt(ltime);   // invoke conversion constructor
    dt.display();          // display today's date
    return 0;
}
```

## Converting a Variable to a Multi-Element Class

The program in Listing 17.3 illustrates how a conversion constructor works. The program converts the value that is returned by the standard `time` function from a `time_t` data type (the data type that the `time` function returns) to a user-defined variable—in this case, a string. Next, the constructor stores the converted variable in a class data member that has been reserved for it.

When the conversion has been completed and the converted parameter has been stored away for safekeeping, the program shows you the results of the conversion by printing the converted variable—that is, by printing the `time_t` variable that has been converted to a string.

## Functions in the TIME.H Library

To understand how the 1703.CPP program works, you need to know a little about a set of time-related functions and data types that Microsoft provides in its C/C++ runtime library. These functions and data types are defined in the TIME.H header file as follows:

- The `time()` function returns the current data and time, as calculated by your computer's system clock, in a data type designated `time_t`. The `time_t` data type represents the current date and time as the number of seconds that have elapsed since midnight on December 31, 1899, Universal coordinated time.
- The `_strdate()` function converts the date portion of a `time_t` data type to a text string that has the form 00/00/00.
- The `_strtime()` function converts the time portion of a `time_t` data type to a text string that has the form 00:00:00.

Listing 17.3 makes use of these functions by defining a class named `Timestamp`. This is the definition of the `Timestamp` class:

```
class Timestamp {
private:
    char datebuf*;  // buffer for date
    char timebuf*;  // buffer for time
public:
    Timestamp() {}        // default constructor
    Timestamp(time_t);    // conversion constructor
    void display(void);   // function to display date & time
};
```

The `Timestamp` class contains:

- Two string buffers reserved for the `time()` function's output.
- A default (empty) constructor.
- A conversion constructor designed to convert a `time_t` data type to a string.
- A function that displays converted strings on the screen.

The `main()` function in Listing 17.3 initializes the `Timestamp` class with this conversion constructor:

```
Timestamp dt(ltime);            // invoke conversion constructor
```

This short statement, like the statement that called the `Money()` function in Listing 17.3, performs two distinct and remarkable tasks. First, it instantiates an object named `dt`, which is an instance of the `Timestamp` class. Second, it calls the `Timestamp` class's conversion constructor by passing a parameter of the `time_t` data type.

This is the conversion constructor the preceding statement calls:

```
// conversion constructor
Timestamp::Timestamp(time_t ltime)
{
    _strdate(datebuf);    // store date in datebuf
    _strtime(timebuf);    // store time in timebuf
}
```

Because this is a conversion constructor, it does more than initiate the `Data` object `dt`. It also calls two TIME.H functions: `_strdate()` and `_strtime()`. The `_strdate()` function converts the date portion of the constructor's `time_t` parameter to a text string that has the form 00/00/00. The `_strtime()` function converts the time portion of the same parameter to a text string that has the form 00:00:00. The date string is stored in the data member `datebuf`, and the time string is stored in the data member `timebuf`.

When these conversions are complete, the `main()` function calls the function `dt.Display()`, a member function of the `Timestamp` class. The `dt.Display()` function uses the `cout` operator to print the converted strings in `datebuf` and `timebuf` to the screen in this format:

```
Date: 10/20/93
Time: 08:46:46
```

## Conversion Constructors Step by Step

To sum up, these are the steps that the compiler carries out to perform a conversion constructor:

1. The compiler first checks to see how many parameters are in the constructor's parameter list. If only one element is in the constructor's parameter list, the compiler recognizes that the constructor is a conversion constructor.
2. When the compiler has detected that the constructor is a conversion function, the compiler performs another test. If the data type that is passed to the constructor is the same as the data type of the constructor's class, the constructor works like any other constructor. If, however, the value passed to the constructor is the data type you have specified for conversion, the compiler converts the value that is passed to the constructor to the specified data type.

### NOTE—FOOLING THE COMPILER WITH A CONVERSION FUNCTION

Conversion functions can be useful when you want to use a class type as a constant in an expression. In C++, this practice is not allowed outright, but by using a conversion function, you can pull a trick that has the same effective result. Here's how:

In C++, only built-in data types (such as `int`, `long`, and `double`) can appear in expressions; constants of class types cannot be used in expressions. (One reason is that classes often describe objects that are too complicated to be notated easily.)

When you want to use a class type as a constant in an expression, you can get around this restriction by converting the class to a built-in data type by using a conversion function. Then, you can declare the built-in type returned by the construction function to be a constant. That done, you can use the constant you indirectly derived from a class type in any expression. Because the compiler ensures that the data conversion is performed correctly, you also can be assured that the expression will behave correctly.

This code fragment shows how a member conversion function works; in the example, the built-in data types `long` and `double` are converted to a user-defined class type named `Cash`:

```
class Cash
{
public:
    Cash(long);
    Cash(double);
    // ...
    Cash operator + (const Cash&); // Overloaded addition
                                   // operator.
};
```

Notice that the last line of this class declaration uses a member conversion function to perform an addition operation on a constant. If a declaration such as this appears in a program, expressions such as these can be used to specify constant values:

```
Cash AccountBalance = 29.42;
Cash NewBalance = AccountBalance + 14L;
```

The second of these two lines requires the use of an overloaded addition operator—an instance of the kind of operator overloading covered in Chapter 16. Both of the preceding examples cause the compiler to convert the constants to the user-defined class type `Cash` before using them in the expressions.

# Member Conversion Functions

As explained at the beginning of this chapter, C++ supplies two kinds of functions that can convert one data type to another. Recall that a *conversion constructor* can convert a variable of any data type (including a user-defined type such as a class) from its original type to any other data type (also including a user-defined type such as a class).

The other kind of conversion function, called a *member conversion function,* is slightly more limited in its capabilities. A member conversion function can be used only to convert an object that belongs to a user-defined class to a predefined data type (such as a `float`, a `double`, or an `int`). Of course, the object that's being converted must be designed so that the specified conversion makes sense—and you are responsible for providing the code that performs the conversion.

You cannot use a member conversion to convert a class to another class, to an enumeration, or to any user-defined data type that's defined with the keyword `typedef`. For conversions that belong to any of those classes, you can use conversion constructor functions.

Member conversion functions do their work by using a technique similar to, but not identical with, operator overloading, which was the topic of Chapter 16.

### NOTE—OPERATOR OVERLOADING AND DATA-TYPE OVERLOADING

As noted in Chapter 16, C++ provides techniques for redefining, or *overloading,* the default functions of most built-in operators. For example, with operator overloading, you can write a code sequence that forces the arithmetic addition operator (+) to add times of day. It uses a base of 12 or 24 rather than the familiar decimal base of 10.

Fortunately, you don't have to overload an operator globally. That would interfere with the way the operator works every time it occurs in a program, which is usually not desirable because that would change the whole way C++ works. C++, therefore, enables you to overload an operator on a class-by-class basis, in accord with normal scope rules. You, therefore, can write a program that allows the + operator to work in its default fashion most of the time, but to perform special kinds of operations in specified blocks of code.

Although member conversion functions don't actually use the C++ technique called *operator overloading,* what they do is similar. A member conversion function doesn't overload an operator, but it does overload a *type specifier,* so that a variable can be converted from the specified data type to another data type. Operations that do overload operators—and, therefore, can be referred to more accurately as operator overloading—are described in Chapter 16.

## Writing a Member Conversion Function

A member conversion function is always a member function of a class, so the declaration of a member conversion function always appears inside a class definition. When you call a member conversion function, it converts the object to which it belongs to a built-in C++ data class.

To write a member conversion, you must declare a *typecasting operator:* an operator specifically designed for use in typecasting. A member conversion function that defines a typecasting operator looks like this:

```
operator float();     // member conversion function
```

As you can see by examining the preceding declaration, a member conversion function has two peculiarities:

- Its name is always the name of a data type.
- It has no explicit return type. However, it does have an *implicit* return type: the data type that a member conversion function returns is always the type specified by the name of the function.

## How Member Conversion Functions Work

This is how a member conversion function works: When you write a member conversion function, you place it in the definition of a class. When you call the function, it converts an object of the class to which it belongs to a variable of the data type specified by the name of the function.

Suppose a member conversion function named `operator float()` appears in the definition of a class named `Coins`, as in this code fragment:

```
class Coins {
    int dl, dm, pn;
public:
    Coins(int dol, int dim, int pen) { dl = dol, dm = dim, pn = pen; }
    operator float();     // member conversion function
};
```

After you write a class definition such as the preceding one, you can implement the member function `operator float()` by defining a function that performs the necessary conversion. For example:

```
// member conversion function
Coins::operator float()
{
     int dollars, dimes, pennies;
```

```
      dollars = dl * 100;
      dimes = dm * 10;
      pennies = pn;
      float amount = (dollars + dimes + pennies);
      amount = amount / 100;
     return amount;
}
```

When you have written the conversion function, you can call it from any other function in this fashion:

```
int main()
{
    Coins change(12, 3, 7);
    float result = change;
     cout << '\n' << "Result: $" << result << '\n';
     return 0;
}
```

Listing 17.4 combines all the preceding code fragments into a short program. This program reduces a random pocketful of pennies, nickels, and dimes to a more efficiently organized collection of coins that have the same types and values. For example, if the collection contains 177 pennies, the program reduces the bulk of the coins by converting them to one dollar, seven dimes, and seven pennies.

### Listing 17.4. A member conversion function.

```
// 1704.CPP
// Demonstrating a member conversion function

#include <iostream.h>

class Coins {
    int dl, dm, pn;
public:
    Coins(int dol, int dim, int pen) { dl = dol, dm = dim, pn = pen; }
    operator float();    // member conversion function
};

// member conversion function
Coins::operator float()
{
     int dollars, dimes, pennies;

     dollars = dl * 100;
     dimes = dm * 10;
     pennies = pn;
```

*continues*

**Listing 17.4. continued**

```
     float amount = (dollars + dimes + pennies);
     amount = amount / 100;
    return amount;
}

int main()
{
    Coins change(12, 3, 7);
    float result = change;
     cout << '\n' << "Result: $" << result << '\n';
     return 0;
}
```

## Using Member Conversion Functions

`Coins` is a class that has three private integer members: a variable named `dl` (for dollars), a variable named `dm` (for dimes), and a variable named `pn` (for pennies). The `Coins` class also includes a constructor that takes three arguments and the `operator float()` conversion function.

The program's `main()` function initializes an object of the class `Coins`, invokes the member conversion function `operator float()`, and returns a floating-point value:

```
int main()
{
   Coins change(12, 3, 7);
   float result = change;
     cout << '\n' << "Result: $" << result << '\n';
     return 0;
}
```

As you can see, to issue the function call shown in the preceding code fragment, you must pass a variable of the `Coins` type to the member conversion function `change()`. That is, you pass a three-element variable. In the previous example, this is the statement that invokes the `change()` function:

```
Coins change(12, 3, 7);
```

Here is the statement that invokes the member conversion function `operator`

```
float():

float result = change;
```

When you execute a call to a member conversion function, the function executes the conversion procedures you specified—which means, in this case, that the function assigns the value you specified to the member variables `dl`, `dm`, and `pn`. Finally, the function performs whatever conversion procedure you specified and returns the result of that conversion in the form of a floating-point variable:

```
Result: $12.37
```

### NOTE—IMPROVING THE 1704.CPP PROGRAM

1704.CPP would be a more elegant program if its output was formatted to print as a fixed-point number with two digits following the decimal point. The program wouldn't truncate round numbers by omitting trailing zeros, and its output would always look right to people who are accustomed to seeing all the zeroes printed in numbers that represent dollars and cents.

C++ does provide a way to do this, but this volume hasn't covered it yet. The technique is to use *manipulators:* functions that are provided by the IOSTREAM.H library to format text. You'll learn how to use manipulators and other IOSTREAM.H mechanisms in Chapter 20, "Streams," which covers C++'s IOSTREAM.H library in detail.

When `float` is redefined by the `operator float()` function, its new specifications are effective only within the scope in which the new version of `float` is defined. In this case, the overloading of `float` will be effective only within a class named `Coins`. When `Coins` goes out of scope, `float` will work the same way that it always did, and the task that it performed while `Coins` was in scope will be forgotten.

You'll see in a few moments exactly how this all works, and how the version of `float` that's recognized within the `Coins` class is redefined.

> **NOTE—OTHER NAMES FOR MEMBER CONVERSION FUNCTIONS**
>
> Because member conversion functions convert data from one type to another by using a technique similar to operator overloading, member conversion functions are sometimes referred to as *conversion operator functions*.
>
> Because member conversion functions use the `operator` keyword in a special way, you may also see them referred to in some texts as *special conversion functions*.
>
> As you no doubt have observed by now, I prefer to call them member conversion functions.

## Illustrating Member Conversion Functions

Listing 17.5 shows how a member conversion function can be used in a slightly more ambitious program. This program, named TIMESTAMP.CPP, converts data from a user-defined class named `Timestamp` to a structure type named `tm` that's defined in the Microsoft header file TIME.H.

### Listing 17.5. A member conversion function.

```
// 1705.CPP
// Conversion member function

#include <iostream.h>
#include <time.h>

class Timestamp {
    int mo, da, yr;
public:
    Timestamp(int m, int d, int y) { mo = m; da = d; yr = y; }
    operator struct tm();     // member conversion function
};

// member conversion function
Timestamp::operator struct tm()
{
    struct tm returnVal;
    returnVal.tm_mon = mo;
    returnVal.tm_mday = da;
```

```
    returnVal.tm_year = yr;

    return returnVal;
}

int main()
{
    Timestamp inputDate(7, 6, 65);
    struct tm theTimestamp = inputDate;
    cout << "Month: " << theTimestamp.tm_mon << "\n";
    cout << "Day: " << theTimestamp.tm_mday << "\n";
    cout << "Year: " << theTimestamp.tm_year << "\n";
    return 0;
}
```

In 1705.CPP, the `operator` keyword is used to declare a member conversion function named `tm()`. This conversion function is declared in the definition of the `Timestamp` class:

```
operator struct tm();     // member conversion function
```

When the `operator struct tm()` function has been declared, as the preceding code line shows, the function is defined as follows:

```
// member conversion function
Timestamp::operator struct tm()
{
    struct tm returnVal;
    returnVal.tm_mon = mo;
    returnVal.tm_mday = da;
    returnVal.tm_year = yr;

    return returnVal;
}
```

Next, an object of the `Timestamp` class is created, and the member conversion function is called:

```
Timestamp inputDate(7, 6, 65);
struct tm theTimestamp = inputDate;
```

In the preceding code fragment, this statement instantiates a `Timestamp` object named `inputDate`:

```
Timestamp inputDate(7, 6, 65);
```

This statement invokes the member conversion function `operator struct tm()`:

```
struct tm theTimestamp = inputDate;
```

When the `operator` function has executed, it returns a variable of the `struct` type.

## Data Types Used in 1705.CPP

The `tm` structure used in 1705.CPP is a data type defined by Microsoft in the header file TIME.H. A `tm struct` can store a series of time-related values that can represent a month, a day, a year, a time zone, and a number of other values related to dates and times. In the Microsoft *Run-Time Library Reference,* under the entry `localtime`, you can find descriptions of all the elements in a `tm` structure.

In the 1705.CPP program, only three elements of the `tm` class are used: `tm_mon`, `tm_mday` (the day of the month), and `tm_year`. The values of these three fields are set in the definition of a member conversion function named `Timestamp::operator`:

```
// member conversion function
Timestamp::operator struct tm()
{
    struct tm returnVal;
    returnVal.tm_mon = mo;
    returnVal.tm_mday = da;
    returnVal.tm_year = yr;

    return returnVal;
}
```

When the 1705.CPP program is executed, it writes the values of the `tm_mon`, `tm_day`, and `tm_year` fields to standard output, normally the screen:

```
Month: 7
Day: 6
Year: 65
```

# Summary

C++ can perform standard conversion operators to convert data to and from fundamental data types; however, to convert data to or from user-defined data types, such as classes, another mechanism is required.

To perform data conversions that involve user-defined data types, C++ supports two kinds of data conversion functions: member conversion functions, which can convert data from any fundamental data type to a user-defined data type, and conversion constructors, which can convert any data type (including a user-defined type) to any other data type (including a user-defined type).

This chapter describes member conversion functions and conversion constructor functions, explains how both kinds of functions work, and explains how you can use both kinds of functions in C++ programs.

Chapter 18

# Copying Objects

When you start developing programs in C++, you'll often encounter situations when you must make a copy of an object. For example, you might need to copy an object in the following cases:

- When you want an existing object to initialize a new object of the same type.
- When you want to pass an object to a function by value.
- When you want a function to return an object.
- When you want to make a copy of a sequence of data that is usually referred to through a pointer such as a string.

There are two ways to make a copy of an object in C++. One way is to overload the assignment `operator=`. The other way is to write a special kind of constructor called a *copy constructor*.

There is an important difference between a copy constructor and an operator-overloading function: A copy constructor *initializes* an object by making a copy of another object. In contrast, when you make a copy of an object by overloading the `(=)` operator, you perform an *assignment* operation; that is, you create a new object and then copy a set of values in the object's data members.

This is a significant difference because the results of initialization and assignment operations are quite different in C++. After you have initialized an object, you cannot initialize the object again. There is, however, no limit to the number of times you can assign values to an object's data members. Once you have overloaded the `=` operator so that it can make a copy of a given object, you can use that operator to assign values to the object's data members as many times as you like.

When creating an object that will be heavily used in a program, you may want to invoke a copy constructor because objects created with constructors (as explained in Chapter 14, "Constructors and Destructors") enjoy certain advantages over objects that don't have constructors.

On the other hand, if you want to make a temporary copy of an object—for example, a short-lived copy of a string object—you can use an overloaded assignment operator.

## Copy Constructors and operator= Functions

A copy constructor, as its name suggests, is a special kind of constructor specifically designed to copy objects. A copy constructor always takes one argument—a reference to a class—and, being a constructor, never returns a result. You can declare a copy constructor using this syntax:

```
TestClass& anObject(anObject&);
```

When you have declared a copy constructor, you can define it in the same way you define any constructor, for example:

```
TestClass::TestClass(TestClass& anObject)
{
     // body of copy constructor
}
```

The preceding code fragment defines a copy constructor that instantiates an object named `anObject`.

When you have declared and defined a copy constructor, you can invoke it by executing a statement that has this syntax:

```
TestClass objectA;               // initialize an object
TestClass objectB = objectA      // copy the objectA
```

## Writing an operator= Function

An `operator=` function is always declared in the definition of a class. You can declare a copy constructor by using this syntax:

```
TestClass& operator=(TestClass&);
```

When you have declared an `operator=` function, you can define it with this kind of syntax:

```
TestClass& TestClass::operator=(TestClass& anObject)
{
     // body of function goes here
     return *this;
}
```

With the `operator=` defined in the preceding code fragment, you can execute a statement that has this syntax:

```
TestCase objectA;      // initialize Object A
TestCase objectB       // initialize Object B
objectB = objectA;     // copy Object A to Object B
```

## Invoking a Copy Constructor

There are two ways to invoke a copy constructor. One way is to write your own copy constructor and use it to initialize an object. The other way is to let the compiler write one for you.

If you want the compiler to create a copy constructor for you, all you must do is write a statement like this:

```
objectB = objectA;
```

If a statement like the preceding one appears in a program and the program does not supply a copy constructor or an `operator=` function that can perform the requested copying operation, the compiler automatically creates and executes a copy constructor that makes a copy of `objectA` and names the new object, `objectB`.

To create `objectB`, the compiler makes what is known as a *memberwise copy* of `objectA`. A memberwise copy is a copy in which each member of the source object is copied verbatim to the target object, one member at a time.

That's a satisfactory arrangement, as long as the class that the two objects belong to does not contain members that are pointers. If the objects involved in the copy contain pointers—for example, pointers to strings—problems can result.

Serious problems can result if two objects have a pointer that points to the same memory address and if each object can write to that memory address through its pointer. If each of the objects has a destructor and if both destructors are invoked when the objects are destroyed, the same block of memory is deleted twice, which can cause program crashes and other malfunctions.

When an object has a destructor, as most C++ objects do, the destructor is automatically invoked when the object goes out of scope or is no longer needed for any other reason. (Chapter 14 describes destructors and explains how they are used in C++ programs.)

To prevent memory-deallocation problems when destructors are invoked, always write a constructor or an `operator=` function when you want to copy an object that contains a pointer. Don't rely on the compiler to do the job for you. Of course, you should also be sure your object-copying function copies the memory that's associated with the pointer—rather than perform a memberwise copy that can cause memory-deallocation difficulties.

## Destruction Problems Illustrated

Listing 18.1 shows how you should *not* write a program that makes a copy of an object. The `main()` function of the program invokes two destructors that cause difficulties in the deallocation of memory.

### Listing 18.1. A memory-deallocation problem.

```
// 1801.CPP
// How a destructor can cause memory-deallocation woes

#include <iostream.h>
#include <stdlib.h>
```

```
// forward declaration
void CopyObject();

class GameChar {
private:
     int strength;
     int charisma;
     int intelligence;
     char *charName;
public:
     // constructor that takes arguments
     GameChar(int str, int charis, int intel, char *name):
          strength(str), charisma(charis), intelligence(intel),
          charName(name) {}
     // default constructor with zero and null initializers
     GameChar():strength(0), charisma(0), intelligence(0)
          { charName = NULL; };
     ~GameChar() {} // destructor
     char *GetName() { return charName; }
     void SetName(char *n) { charName = n; }
};

GameChar firstChar(13, 14, 15, "Fred");

int main()
{
     CopyObject();
     return 0;
}

void CopyObject()
{
     GameChar otherChar = firstChar;     // DANGER! memberwise copy
}
```

The 1801.CPP program attempts to make a copy of an object that contains a string pointer without providing a proper object-copying function. Instead, the program relies on the compiler to create and execute a copy constructor that performs the copy. That questionable practice causes problems later on, as you will soon see.

## Starting at the Beginning

Before the `main()` function of the 1801.CPP program is executed, this statement creates a global object variable named `firstChar`, which is an instance of a class named `GameChar`:

```
GameChar firstChar(13, 14, 15, "Fred");
```

The program creates the `firstChar` object by invoking a constructor that is declared and defined in the definition of the class named `GameChar`. The `GameChar` class contains a string pointer named `charName`, so when `firstChar`'s constructor is called, it invokes the C++ `new` operator to allocate memory for a `nameChar` string. The string is then initialized with the word `Fred`.

When the program's `main()` function executes, it calls a function named `CopyObject()`:

```
void CopyObject()
{
    GameChar otherChar = firstChar;
}
```

## A Memberwise Operation

When the preceding defined function is called, the compiler discovers that the program has not provided a copy constructor that can make a copy of a `GameChar` object. The constructor, therefore, generates a copy constructor and then invokes that constructor to make a copy of the object named `firstChar`. The new object is named `otherChar`.

When the compiler copies the members of `firstChar` to the new object named `otherChar`, the copying operation the compiler performs is a *memberwise* operation. That means `firstChar`'s `charName` pointer is copied to the new object named `otherChar`. In accord with the rules of memberwise copying, the string that is pointed to—the string that reads `Fred`—is not copied. Only the pointer to the string is copied to the new `otherChar` object.

## Different Scopes

As you can see by examining Listing 18.1, the `firstChar` object is created in the program's `main()` function, but the `otherChar` object is created in the program's `CopyObject()` function. That means when the `CopyObject()` terminates, `otherChar` goes out of scope; therefore, when `CopyObject()` terminates, the `otherChar` object's destructor is invoked automatically.

When `otherChar` goes out of scope, `firstChar` does not because `firstChar` is defined as a global object variable. When `otherChar`'s destructor is invoked, however, the destructor deallocates the memory that is pointed to by `otherChar`'s `charName` pointer.

Unfortunately, as you have seen, the firstChar object contains a charName pointer that points to the same block of memory that otherChar's destructor has now deleted. When otherChar's destructor destroys otherChar, the destructor automatically deallocates the memory pointed to by firstChar's charName pointer.

When you execute the 1801.CPP program, the dangling pointer that firstChar is left with doesn't cause immediate problems. That's because the memory the firstChar.charName variable points to is not immediately erased. Because the memory has been deallocated, however, it can be reallocated for a new purpose at any time. That can result in serious memory-allocation problems.

Another problem can arise when the firstChar object goes out of scope. When that happens, the memory that was pointed to by otherChar's name pointer—and has now been deleted—is deleted again. This doesn't affect the 1801.CPP program because firstChar is a global variable that doesn't go out of scope until the program quits. If, however, both firstChar and otherChar appear in functions that could terminate at different times during the execution of the program, the memory pointed to by *charName will be deleted twice, with still more danger for program crashes and other disasters.

## Changing a Variable with the Wrong Pointer

When objects that point to the same block of memory have the same scope, a different kind of problem can occur. To see what would happen if firstChar and otherChar had the same scope, assume that the function named CopyObject() has been deleted from the program and that the program's main() function has been rewritten as follows:

```
GameChar firstChar(13, 14, 15, "Fred");

int main()
{
      cout << firstChar.GetName() << '\n';
      GameChar otherChar = firstChar;
      otherChar.SetName("Ginger");
      cout << firstChar.GetName() << '\n';
      cout << otherChar.GetName() << '\n';
      return 0;
}
```

In the preceding version of the main() function, the compiler still makes a memberwise copy of the firstChar object, and the name of the new object is still otherChar. This time, though, both objects have the same scope, and a member function named GetName() is called to change the name string that the otherChar object points to.

As you now know, `firstChar` and `otherChar` point to the same name string. When you change the contents of the name string that is associated with `otherChar`, you also change the contents of the name string that is associated with `otherChar`.

When you execute the program, it prints the string that `firstChar` is set to print. It then resets the string that is associated with `otherChar`. When that is done, the program prints the string `firstChar` now points to, followed by the string that `otherChar` has been set to. The program's printout clearly shows that resetting the `otherChar` object's string also changes the `firstChar` object's string:

```
Fred
Fred
Ginger
```

If you didn't know about memberwise copies, the preceding phenomenon would seem quite strange.

## Writing a Copy Constructor

The program in Listing 18.2 shows how a copy constructor can be used in a C++ program. The `main()` segment of the program initializes an object named `myCash` and then uses a copy constructor to make a copy of `myCash`. The copy of `myCash` is named `moreCash`.

### Listing 18.2. Demonstrating a copy constructor.

```
// 1802.CPP
// Demonstrating a copy constructor

#include <iostream.h>

class Money {
    long dl, pn;
public:
    Money() {}             // null constructor
     Money(Money&);        // copy constructor
     Money(int dol, int pen):dl(dol), pn(pen) {}
     int GetDol() { return dl; }
     int  GetPen() { return pn; }
};

Money::Money(Money& cash)
{
     dl = cash.dl;
```

```
     pn = cash.pn;
};

int main()
{
     Money myCash(29, 95);
     Money moreCash = myCash;
     int d = moreCash.GetDol();
     int p = moreCash.GetPen();
     cout << '$' << d << '.' << p << '\n';
     return 0;
}
```

Because the 1802.CPP program copies an object that contains no pointers, the copy constructor the program uses is straightforward:

```
Money::Money(Money& cash)
{
     dl = cash.dl;
     pn = cash.pn;
};
```

The program in Listing 18.3 copies a class named `GameChar`. The `GameChar` class contains a pointer to a string. The program's `main()` section creates a `GameChar` named `myChar` and a copy of the `myChar` class that is named `yourChar`.

## Listing 18.3. Copying an object that contains a string.

```
// 1803.CPP
// Demonstrating a copy constructor that contains a pointer

#include <iostream.h>
#include <stdio.h>
#include <stdlib.h>
#include <string.h>

void FatalError();     // forward declaration

class GameChar {
private:
     int strength;
     int charisma;
     int intelligence;
     char *charName;
public:
```

*continues*

**Listing 18.3. continued**

```
    GameChar();          // default constructor
     GameChar(int str, int charis, int intel, char *name):
          strength(str), charisma(charis), intelligence(intel),
          charName(name) {}
     GameChar(GameChar&);     // copy constructor
     char *DuplicateString(char *aString);
     char *GetName() { return charName; }
};

// constructor that's called for an unitialized GameChar
GameChar::GameChar()
{
     strength = 0; charisma = 0; intelligence = 0;
     charName = NULL;
}

char *GameChar::DuplicateString(char *aString)
{
    char    *aCopy;
    aCopy = new char[strlen(aString) + 1];
    if (aCopy == NULL)
        FatalError();
    strcpy(aCopy, aString);
    return aCopy;
}

GameChar::GameChar(GameChar& aChar)
{
     strength = aChar.strength;
     charisma = aChar.charisma;
     intelligence = aChar.intelligence;
     charName = DuplicateString(aChar.charName);
};

void FatalError()
{
    fprintf(stderr, "A fatal error has occurred\n");
    exit(1);
}

int main()
{
     GameChar myChar(13, 14, 15, "Rocky");
     GameChar yourChar = myChar;
     cout << yourChar.GetName() << '\n';
     return 0;
}
```

This is the copy constructor in Listing 18.3:

```
GameChar::GameChar(GameChar& aChar)
{
     strength = aChar.strength;
     charisma = aChar.charisma;
     intelligence = aChar.intelligence;
     charName = DuplicateString(aChar.charName);
};
```

This copy constructor makes a memberwise copy of each integer member of the `GameChar` class. The function then copies a string that is pointed to by a string pointer named `*charName`.

Notice that the copy constructor does not merely copy the pointer named `*charName`. Instead, it copies the actual `charName` string by calling a string-copying procedure named `DuplicateString()`.

When the program is executed, the copy constructor copies a `GameChar` object named `myChar` to a new `GameChar` object named `yourChar`. The program then prints the string that has been copied to `yourChar`:

```
Rocky
```

## How the operator= Function Works

When both a copy constructor and an object-copying `operator=` function appear in a C++ program, the compiler automatically selects the correct function when the program executes a command to copy an object. If the program executes an object-copying statement that requires a copy constructor, the compiler calls the object's copy constructor. If the program contains an object-copying statement that requires the use of the object's `operator=` function, the `operator=` function is called.

If a program attempts to invoke an object-copying `operator=` function and the function that is required does not exist, the compiler creates an `operator=` function that performs a memberwise copy. The compiler then performs the requested operation with the `operator=` function that it has created.

The `GameChar` class in Listing 18.4 has two object-copying functions: a copy constructor and an `operator=` function that copies objects. The program's `main()` function creates a `GameChar` object and then makes two copies of it. One copy is made with a conversion constructor, and the other is made with an `operator=` function.

A memberwise `operator=` function has the same limitations as a memberwise copy constructor. If the objects involved in the copy contain pointers, any pointer that is a member of the source object is copied to the target object verbatim. Subsequently, if one of the objects is destroyed along with the data that's associated with it, the other object is left with a member that is a dangling pointer. If that dangling pointer is referenced later in the execution of the program, the result can be a program crash or a badly malfunctioning program.

#### Listing 18.4. A program with two object-copying functions.

```
// 1804.CPP
// A copy constructor that contains a pointer

#include <iostream.h>
#include <stdio.h>
#include <stdlib.h>
#include <string.h>


void FatalError();  // forward declaration

class GameChar {
private:
     int strength;
     int charisma;
     int intelligence;
     char *charName;
public:
    GameChar() {}             // null constructor
     GameChar(int str, int charis, int intel, char *name):
          strength(str), charisma(charis), intelligence(intel),
          charName(name) {}
     // copy constructor
     GameChar(GameChar&);
     //overloaded = operator
     GameChar& operator=(GameChar&);
     char *DuplicateString(char *aString);
     char *GetName() { return charName; }
};

char *GameChar::DuplicateString(char *aString)
{
    char    *aCopy;
    aCopy = new char[strlen(aString) + 1];
    if (aCopy == NULL)
        FatalError();
    strcpy(aCopy, aString);
```

```
    return aCopy;
}

// Copy constructor
GameChar::GameChar(GameChar& aChar)
{
     cout << "Using copy constructor.\n";
     strength = aChar.strength;
     charisma = aChar.charisma;
     intelligence = aChar.intelligence;
     charName = DuplicateString(aChar.charName);
};

// Overloaded = operator
GameChar& GameChar::operator=(GameChar& aChar)
{
     cout << "Using operator= function.\n";
     strength = aChar.strength;
     charisma = aChar.charisma;
     intelligence = aChar.intelligence;
     charName = DuplicateString(aChar.charName);
     return *this;
};

void FatalError()
{
    fprintf(stderr, "A fatal error has occurred\n");
    exit(1);
}

int main()
{
     GameChar myChar(13, 14, 15, "Bullwinkle");
     GameChar hisChar = myChar;     // call copy constructor
     GameChar yourChar;
     yourChar = myChar;       // call operator= function
     cout << hisChar.GetName() << '\n';
     cout << yourChar.GetName() << '\n';
     return 0;
}
```

When you execute the program in Listing 18.4, the copy constructor defined for the `GameChar` class prints a message on the screen when called. The `operator=` function that's defined for the class also prints a message when called.

In the program's `main()` function, the copy constructor that is defined for the `GameChar` class is called first, and then the class's `operator=` function is called. This statement calls the copy constructor:

```
GameChar hisChar = myChar;     // call copy constructor
```

These statements call the `operator=` function:

```
yourChar = myChar;        // call operator= function
cout << hisChar.GetName() << '\n';
```

As it calls each object-copying function, the program prints a message stating that the function has been called. The string that has been copied to each new object is then printed twice: once by the new object that has been created with a copy constructor and again by the other new object. This is the output of the program:

```
Using copy constructor.
Using operator= function.
Bullwinkle
Bullwinkle
```

### NOTE—RULES FOR WRITING COPY CONSTRUCTORS

If you copy an object by invoking a copy constructor you have written, you determine the rules used to copy the object. If your program copies an object by invoking a copy constructor created by the compiler, the specified object is copied in accord with certain specific rules:

- If the object being copied doesn't have a copy constructor but is a member of a base class that has a copy constructor, the base class's copy constructor is invoked.
- If neither the source object nor its base class has a copy constructor, a copy constructor created by the compiler is invoked.
- If a copy constructor created by the compiler is used, the compiler's copy constructor initializes a new object with an architecture that is identical to the architecture of the object being copied.
- The compiler's copy constructor initializes each member of the new object by making a copy of the corresponding member of the existing object; in other words, the compiler performs what's known as a *memberwise* initialization. When a memberwise initialization is performed, each member of the source object is copied individually to its corresponding position in the target object.
- During a memberwise initialization, as each member of the source object is copied, C++ checks whether the member being copied has a constructor. If the member being copied has a constructor, that constructor is called to copy the member.

- If a member being copied has no constructor, the compiler performs a bit-by-bit copy, or a *bitwise* copy, of the member that is being copied.
- When all members of the source object are copied to the target object, the copy is complete.

# Copying Strings

Unless you overload the assignment `operator=`, you can't copy a C-style string merely by writing a statement like this:

```
char *bString = aString;
```

If you execute a statement like the preceding one, the statement works, but it doesn't actually copy the string named `aString`. Rather than make a copy of `aString` and call it `bString`, the statement sets up a *pointer* named `*bString` and sets that pointer to point to the same array of characters referenced by the pointer named `*aString`.

This arrangement works fine as long as `aString` remains in memory and stays at the address that is designated by the pointers `*aString` and `*bString`. If, however, `aString` is destroyed or moved to another memory location (which could easily happen when running Windows or another application with its own memory manager), the `*bString` pointer no longer points to `aString`. Rather, it designates an area in memory that is now undefined. This turns `*bString` into a dangling pointer, and dangling pointers can lead to disasters, such as programs that crash without warning.

## The strcpy() Function

Because you can't use the assignment `operator=` to copy a string in C, the STDIO.H library that's used in C contains many string-related functions. For example, you can use the STDIO.H function `strcpy()` to copy strings.

In Listing 18.5, the `DuplicateString()` function uses the `strcpy()` function to copy a string. Listing 18.5—this chapter's version of The Wrath of Zalthar program—also shows the use of the `strcpy()` function.

**Listing 18.5. The Wrath of Zalthar, Chapter 18 version.**

```
// ZALTHAR.H

// Chapter 18 Version
// Copyright 1992, Mark Andrews

#if !defined( _ZALTHAR_H_ )
#define _ZALTHAR_H_

// forward declarations

void FatalError(void);
void PrintTitle(void);

struct Abilities {
     int strength;
     int charisma;
     int dexterity;
     int intelligence;
};

class Player {
private:
     char *name;
     char *weapon;
     char *magic;
     Abilities playerAbils;
public:
     Player() { name = NULL; weapon = NULL; magic = NULL; }
     ~Player() { delete name; delete weapon; delete magic; }
     void SetName(char *nm) { name = DuplicateString(nm); }
     char *GetName() { return name; }
     void SetWeapon(char *wpn) { weapon = DuplicateString(wpn); }
     char *GetWeapon() { return weapon; }
     void SetMagic(char *mag) { magic = DuplicateString(mag); }
     char *GetMagic() { return magic; }
     virtual void PrintEntry() = 0;
     void SetData(int s, int c, int d, int i)
          { playerAbils.strength = s; playerAbils.charisma = c;
            playerAbils.dexterity = d; playerAbils.intelligence = i; }
     const Abilities GetAbils() { return playerAbils; }
     char *DuplicateString(char *aString);
     void PrintAbils();
};

class Warrior : public Player {
public:
     // default constructor
     Warrior () {}
     // warrior constructor
     Warrior(char *nm, char *wpn)
```

```
            { SetName(nm);
              SetWeapon(wpn); }
        ~Warrior() {}  // destructor
        void PrintEntry();
};

class Gnome : public Warrior {
public:
        Gnome(char *nm, char *wpn, char *mag) :
            Warrior(nm, wpn)
            { SetMagic(mag); }
        ~Gnome() {}    // destructor
        void PrintEntry();
};

#endif // _ZALTHAR_H
```

```
// ZALTHAR.CPP

#include <iostream.h>
#include <string.h>
#include <stdio.h>
#include <stdlib.h>
#include "zalthar.h"

void FatalError()
{
    fprintf(stderr, "A fatal error has occurred\n");
    exit(1);
}

void PrintTitle()
{
     cout << "\nTHE WRATH OF ZALTHAR\n";
     cout << "By [Your Name Here]\n";
};

char *Player::DuplicateString(char *aString)
{
    char    *aCopy;
    aCopy = new char[strlen(aString) + 1];
    if (aCopy == NULL)
        FatalError();
    strcpy(aCopy, aString);
    return aCopy;
}

void Player::PrintAbils()
{
```

*continues*

**Listing 18.5. continued**

```
     cout << "\nStrength: " << playerAbils.strength << '\n';
     cout << "Charisma: " << playerAbils.charisma << '\n';
     cout << "Dexterity: " << playerAbils.dexterity << '\n';
     cout << "Intelligence: " << playerAbils.intelligence << '\n';
}

void Warrior::PrintEntry()
{
     Abilities locAbils = GetAbils();

     cout << "\nWARRIOR" << '\n';
     cout << "Name: " << this->GetName() << '\n';
     cout << "Weapon: " << this->GetWeapon() << "\n";
     PrintAbils();
}

void Gnome::PrintEntry()
{
     Abilities locAbils = GetAbils();

     cout << "\nGNOME" << '\n';
     cout << "Name: " << this->GetName() << '\n';
     cout << "Weapon: " << this->GetWeapon() << "\n";
     cout << "Magic: " << this->GetMagic() << '\n';
     PrintAbils();
}


// MAIN.CPP

// The Wrath of Zalthar, Chapter 18 Version
// Copyright 1992 Mark Andrews.  All rights reserved.

#include <iostream.h>
#include "zalthar.h"

int main()
{

     // create players

     Warrior aWarrior;
     aWarrior.SetName("Bruno");
     aWarrior.SetWeapon("Sword");
     aWarrior.SetData(24, 16, 32, 19);

     Warrior bWarrior;
     bWarrior.SetName("GayLynn");
     bWarrior.SetWeapon("Crossbow");
     bWarrior.SetData(19, 22, 43, 21);
```

```
    Gnome aGnome("Glog", "Broadsword", "X-ray vision");
    aGnome.SetData(14, 15, 22, 32);

    // print report

    PrintTitle();

    aWarrior.PrintEntry();
    bWarrior.PrintEntry();
    aGnome.PrintEntry();

    return 0;
}
```

This is the output of the program in Listing 18.5:

```
THE WRATH OF ZALTHAR
By [Your Name Here]

WARRIOR
Name: Bruno
Weapon: Sword

Strength: 24
Charisma: 16
Dexterity: 32
Intelligence: 19

WARRIOR
Name: GayLynn
Weapon: Crossbow

Strength: 19
Charisma: 22
Dexterity: 43
Intelligence: 21

GNOME
Name: Glog
Weapon: Broadsword
Magic: X-ray vision

Strength: 14
Charisma: 15
Dexterity: 22
Intelligence: 32
```

## How the Program Works

In the version of the Zalthar program shown in Listing 18.5, each instantiation of a Player object invokes the constructor for the Player class, which is a base class. The constructor for the Player class sets up NULL pointers for the name, weapon, and magic strings so that any memory allocated for them later in the program can be deallocated safely with the delete operator. This is the constructor that assigns these NULL pointers:

```
Player () { name = NULL; weapon = NULL; magic = NULL; }
```

The preceding statement provides something of a safety net because it ensures that if one of these three strings becomes the target of a delete operator—as each one does later in the program—no damage will be done. This safeguard is built into the delete operator; when the delete operator encounters a NULL pointer, the operator is intelligent enough never to try to delete any memory.

When you create a Warrior or Gnome object in the Zalthar program, the program uses the C-language strcpy() function to copy the strings that are defined for the object being created. In the program, strcpy() is called from a member function named DuplicateString() that is defined in the ZALTHAR.CPP file:

```
char *Player::DuplicateString(char *aString)
{
    char    *aCopy;
    aCopy = new char[strlen(aString) + 1];
    if (aCopy == NULL)
        FatalError();
    strcpy(aCopy, aString);
    return aCopy;
}
```

Several member functions of the Player, Warrior, and Gnome classes call DuplicateString(). For example, all three of these inline member functions of the Player class call DuplicateString():

```
void SetName(char *nm) { name = DuplicateString(nm); }
void SetWeapon(char *wpn) { weapon = DuplicateString(wpn); }
void SetMagic(char *mag) { magic = DuplicateString(mag); }
```

Each of the preceding member functions calls DuplicateString(), which then invokes the new operator to copy a string. The three strings that are copied by the preceding functions are called name, weapon, and magic.

## Allocating Memory for Strings

Each time the Zalthar program calls the `DuplicateString()` function, `DuplicateString()` obtains a block of memory large enough to hold the string being copied by invoking the C++ memory-allocation operator `new` (which was introduced in Chapter 2, "A Better C—Plus" and was described in more detail in Chapters 9, "Managing Memory" and 15, "Function Overloading." If `DuplicateString()` can't find enough memory to hold the string, a function named `FatalError()` is called.

If the `DuplicateString()` function succeeds in finding the memory it needs, it uses C's `strcpy()` function to copy the string that is passed to it and returns a pointer to the string:

```
strcpy(aCopy, aString);
return aCopy;
```

This procedure for copying strings works well, but from the point of view of program development, it has some shortcomings. The main problem is that each time the `DuplicateString()` function copies a string, the function uses the `new` operator to allocate memory for the string being copied.

As noted earlier in this chapter, when you allocate a block of memory by invoking the `new` operator, you must be sure to deallocate the memory by invoking the `delete` operator when the object is no longer needed. That means, of course, that the Zalthar program must invoke the `delete` operator each time a string is no longer needed. To fulfill this requirement, the destructor for the `Player` class invokes the `delete` operator to deallocate the memory that has been allocated for each string. This destructor is defined in the definition of the `Player` class:

```
~Player () { delete name; delete weapon; delete magic; }
```

This destructor invokes the `delete` operator to deallocate memory for the strings `name`, `weapon`, and `magic`. (When a `Warrior` object is destroyed, it doesn't have a `magic` string to deallocate, but that's all right. The constructor for the `Player` class sets up `NULL` pointers for the `name`, `weapon`, and `magic` strings, and the `delete` operator causes no harm when it encounters a `NULL` pointer.)

## Memory-Allocation Alternatives

Even though a `NULL` pointer can prevent a `delete` operator from crashing a program, you can see how tricky it can be to keep track of `new` and `delete` operations when a lot of new and delete operators are used in a long program. That's why it's usually better to create and destroy objects by using constructors and destructors than it is to allocate and deallocate memory for objects by invoking the new and delete operators.

Of course, you can't use constructors and destructors to allocate and deallocate just any kind of memory. Constructors and destructors—unlike the new and delete operators—must be used to create and destroy class objects, not only blocks of memory.

## Adding a String Class to the Zalthar Program

A new and improved version of The Wrath of Zalthar is presented in Listing 18.6. In the previous version of the program, the new and delete operators were used only to allocate and deallocate memory for strings. In Listing 18.6, the strings in the Zalthar program are turned into classes, so memory for the name, weapon, and magic strings can be (and is) allocated with constructors and destructors, rather than with the new and delete operators.

**LISTING 18.6. The Wrath of Zalthar, Chapter 18 version 2.**

```
// ZALTHAR.H

// Chapter 18 Version 2
// Copyright 1992, Mark Andrews

#if !defined( _ZALTHAR_H_ )
#define _ZALTHAR_H_

#include <iostream.h>
#include "mystring.h"

enum playerClasses { WARRIOR, GNOME, WIZARD };

struct Abilities {
     int strength;
     int charisma;
     int dexterity;
     int intelligence;
};

class Player {
private:
     int  playerClass;
     class String className;
```

```
     class String name;
     class String weapon;
     class String magic;
     static class String gClassName[3];
     Abilities playerAbils;
public:
     Player () {}
     ~Player () {}
     void SetPlayerClass(int pc) { playerClass = pc; SetClassStr(pc); }
     void SetClassStr(int pc) { className = gClassName[pc]; }
     int GetPlayerClass() { return playerClass; }
     String GetClassName() { return className; }
     void SetName(String nm) { name = nm; }
     String GetName() { return name; }
     void SetWeapon(String wpn) { weapon = wpn; }
     String GetWeapon() { return weapon; }
     void SetMagic(String mag) { magic = mag; }
     String GetMagic() { return magic; }
     static void PrintTitle();
     virtual void PrintEntry() = 0;
     void SetData(int s, int c, int d, int i)
          { playerAbils.strength = s; playerAbils.charisma = c;
            playerAbils.dexterity = d; playerAbils.intelligence = i; }
     const Abilities GetAbils() { return playerAbils; }
     void PrintAbils();
};

class Warrior : public Player {
public:
     // default constructor
     Warrior () {}
     // warrior constructor
     Warrior(int pc, String nm, String wpn)
          { SetPlayerClass(pc); SetName(nm);
            SetWeapon(wpn); }
     ~Warrior() {}  // destructor
     void PrintEntry();
};

class Gnome : public Warrior {
public:
     Gnome(int pc, String nm, String wpn, String mag) :
          Warrior(pc, nm, wpn)
          { SetMagic(mag); }
     ~Gnome() {}    // destructor
     void PrintEntry();
};

#endif // _ZALTHAR_H
```

*continues*

**LISTING 18.6. continued**

```
// ZALTHAR.CPP

#include <iostream.h>
#include <string.h>
#include <stdio.h>
#include <stdlib.h>
#include "zalthar.h"

void FatalError()
{
    fprintf(stderr, "A fatal error has occurred\n");
    exit(1);
}

// Initializing static member variable.
String Player::gClassName[] = { "WARRIOR", "GNOME", "WIZARD" } ;

void Player::PrintTitle()
{
     cout << "\nTHE WRATH OF ZALTHAR\n";
     cout << "By [Your Name Here]\n";
};

void Player::PrintAbils()
{
     cout << "\nStrength: " << playerAbils.strength << '\n';
     cout << "Charisma: " << playerAbils.charisma << '\n';
     cout << "Dexterity: " << playerAbils.dexterity << '\n';
     cout << "Intelligence: " << playerAbils.intelligence << '\n';
}

void Warrior::PrintEntry()
{
     Abilities locAbils = GetAbils();

     cout << "\nClass: ";
     (this->GetClassName()).Display();
     cout << "\nName: ";
     (this->GetName()).Display();
     cout << "\nWeapon: ";
     (this->GetWeapon()).Display();
     PrintAbils();
}

void Gnome::PrintEntry()
{
     Abilities locAbils = GetAbils();
```

```
        cout << "\nClass: ";
        (this->GetClassName()).Display();
        cout << "\nName: ";
        (this->GetName()).Display();
        cout << "\nWeapon: ";
        (this->GetWeapon()).Display();
        cout << "\nMagic: ";
        (this->GetMagic()).Display();
        PrintAbils();
}
```

```
// MYSTRING.H

#ifndef _MYSTRING_H_
#define _MYSTRING_H_

#include <iostream.h>
#include "zalthar.h"

// String class
class String
{
public:
    String() : buf(0), length(0) {}
    String(const char *s);
    ~String() { delete buf; }
    // Copy constructor
    String(const String &other);
    // Assignment operator
    String &operator=(const String &other);
    void Display() const { cout << buf; }
private:
    int length;
    char *buf;
};

#endif  // _MYSTRING_H_
```

```
// MYSTRING.CPP

#include <string.h>
#include "zalthar.h"

// Constructor that takes a parameter
String::String(const char *s)
{
```

*continues*

**LISTING 18.6. continued**

```
    length = strlen( s );
    buf = new char[length + 1];
    strcpy( buf, s );
}

// Copy constructor
String::String(const String &other)
{
    length = other.length;
    buf = new char[length + 1];
    strcpy( buf, other.buf );
}

String &String::operator=(const String &other)
{
    if(&other == this)
        return *this;
    delete buf;
    length = other.length;
    buf = new char[length + 1];
    strcpy(buf, other.buf);
    return *this;
}


// MAIN.CPP

// The Wrath of Zalthar, Chapter 18 Version 2
// Copyright 1992 Mark Andrews.  All rights reserved.

#include <iostream.h>
#include "zalthar.h"

int main()
{
     // create players

     Warrior aWarrior;
     aWarrior.SetPlayerClass(WARRIOR);
     aWarrior.SetName("Bruno");
     aWarrior.SetWeapon("Sword");
     aWarrior.SetData(24, 16, 32, 19);

     Warrior bWarrior;
     bWarrior.SetPlayerClass(WARRIOR);
     bWarrior.SetName("GayLynn");
     bWarrior.SetWeapon("Crossbow");
     bWarrior.SetData(19, 22, 43, 21);
```

```
        Gnome aGnome(GNOME, "Glog", "Broadsword", "X-ray vision");
        aGnome.SetData(14, 15, 22, 32);

        // print report

        Player::PrintTitle();

        aWarrior.PrintEntry();
        bWarrior.PrintEntry();
        aGnome.PrintEntry();

        return 0;
}
```

## Output of the Program

The version of Zalthar shown in Listing 18.6 has this output:

```
THE WRATH OF ZALTHAR
By [Your Name Here]

Class: WARRIOR
Name: Bruno
Weapon: Sword

Strength: 24
Charisma: 16
Dexterity: 32
Intelligence: 19

Class: WARRIOR
Name: GayLynn
Weapon: Crossbow

Strength: 19
Charisma: 22
Dexterity: 43
Intelligence: 21

Class: GNOME
Name: Glog
Weapon: Broadsword
Magic: X-ray vision

Strength: 14
Charisma: 15
Dexterity: 22
Intelligence: 32
```

## How the New Zalthar Program Works

Because most C++ programs contain strings, almost any C++ program can benefit from the addition of a `String` class. In Listing 18.6, the strings that were used in the previous version of the program are replaced by objects of the `String` class. These `String` objects are initialized by the constructor for the `String` class.

When a string is no longer needed, it is destroyed automatically by a destructor. The program's source code, therefore, isn't peppered with `new` operators, `delete` operators, and `NULL` values that neutralize string pointers to prevent program crashes—for example, the constructor for the `Player` class, which looked like this in previous versions of the program,

```
Player () { name = NULL; weapon = NULL; magic = NULL; }
```

is now devoid of `NULL` assignments:

```
Player () {}
```

### An Alternative to DuplicateString

In another significant change, the `DuplicateString()` function, which previous versions of the program called to allocate memory,

```
void SetName(char *nm) { name = DuplicateString(nm); }
```

has now been replaced with assignment statements that use the overloaded assignment operator:

```
void SetName(String nm) { name = nm; }
```

Finally, the destructor for the `Player` class, which used three `delete` operators to deallocate memory used by strings,

```
~Player () { delete name; delete weapon; delete magic; }
```

contains no `delete` operators in the new version of the program:

```
~Player () {}
```

### Overloading the = Operator to Copy Strings

The new Zalthar program contains not only a copy constructor, but also a function that overloads the (=) to copy strings. The program's `operator=` function is defined in the file named MYSTRINGCPP. It copies strings using the `strcpy()`

function, exactly like the program's copy constructor does. This is the function that overloads the (=) operator:

```
String &String::operator=( const String &other )
{
    if( &other == this )
        return *this;
    delete buf;
    length = other.length;
    buf = new char[length + 1];
    strcpy( buf, other.buf );
    return *this;
}
```

> **NOTE—THE JOY OF ABSTRACTION**
>
> One more point about the new Zalthar program is worth noting: Thanks to the data abstraction and data encapsulation principles that are observed in C++, the `main()` segment of the Zalthar program requires no changes from previous versions; it works exactly like the `main()` segments of previous versions of the program.

# String Classes

The Zalthar program presented in Listing 18.6 isn't the first C++ program to contain a string class. Most C++ class libraries—including the Microsoft Foundation Class library introduced in Part III, "The MFC Library"—contain classes designed to help programs create, copy, and manipulate strings. In many courses on C++, a string class is one of the first kinds of classes students are asked to write.

If you're a C-language programmer, you can probably guess why. A robust string class can make string-manipulation operations much simpler than they were in C. A string class can provide a basic and elegant mechanism for operations such as searching strings, concatenating strings, and most important of all, for copying strings.

## How the String Class Works

The `String` class created for the Zalthar program in Listing 18.6—created in a file named MYSTRING.H—isn't sophisticated, as string classes go. It doesn't concatenate strings, check whether strings are equal, or search for words or character patterns in strings. (The string class that's supplied in the MFC library does all that and more, so if you really want a powerful string class, that's the one to use.) The String class in Listing 18.6 does contain everything you need to create string objects and everything you need to copy a string from one memory location to another.

The string class in Listing 18.6 has two private data members: a character buffer named `buf`, in which a string is stored, and an integer variable named `length`, which holds the size of the string.

The class also has several member functions, including two constructors—one that takes parameters and one that doesn't—a destructor, a copy constructor, a `Display()` function that prints information, and a customized assignment (=) operator that enables you to make a true copy of a string by writing an assignment statement, such as follows:

```
dark2 = dark1;
```

This is exactly the way you can make a direct copy of a simple data type such as an integer. As you'll see later in this section, the customized assignment operator that enables you to perform operations like the preceding one is created by using operator overloading.

## Using the String Class

Take a close look at the `main()` segment of Listing 18.6, and you'll see that the program enables you to create a string by using either of the two initialization formats recognized by C++:

```
String dark1("It was a dark \n");
String dark3 = "and stormy night.\n";
```

## Initializing a String Object with a Copy Constructor

Both of these statements create a `String` object by calling the constructor for the `String` class. The `String` constructor calls the standard library function `strlen()`

to calculate the length of the string that is passed to it. Then, the constructor places the specified string in the data member named `buf` (a string buffer), and places the length of the string in the data member named `length`:

```
// Constructor
String::String( const char *s )
{
    length = strlen( s );
    buf = new char[length + 1];
    strcpy( buf, s );
}
```

## Assignment Operator Overloading

As you learned in Chapter 16, "Operator Overloading," C++ enables you to customize or overload operators to give them special behaviors in special situations. When a function that overloads the assignment operator is overloaded in the definition of a class, the compiler automatically calls that function whenever the assignment operator is used to make a copy of an object that belongs to a class. When the assignment `operator=` is overloaded by a string class, each time the compiler encounters an assignment statement associated with a string class, such as

```
bString = aString;
```

the compiler executes the function that overloads the assignment operator and then uses the overloaded assignment operator to make the copy.

## Using Overloaded Assignment Operators

Listing 18.6 overloads the assignment operator in the definition of the `String` class. This is the declaration of the overloaded assignment operator in Listing 18.6:

```
String &operator=( const String &other );
```

The preceding statement is not an inline statement, so the definition of the function that overloads the assignment operator appears outside the `String` class definition, in the file named MYSTRING.CPP:

```
String &String::operator=( const String &other )
{
   if( &other == this ) // these 2 statements prevent...
       return *this;     // ... assigning an object to itself
   delete buf;
```

```
    length = other.length;
    buf = new char[length + 1];
    strcpy( buf, other.buf );
    return *this;
}
```

# Summary

There are two ways to copy an object in C++: with a special kind of constructor called a copy constructor, or with an overloaded assignment `operator (=)`. A copy constructor makes a copy of an object by initializing a new object. A function that overloads the assignment operator can copy the members of an object to an existing object. If you don't write an object-copying function, but attempt to call one anyway, the Visual C++ will generate a copy constructor or an object-copying `operator=` function for you. It's safer, however, to write your own object-copying functions, especially when you want to copy an object that contains pointers.

This chapter describes copy constructors and object-copying `operator(=)` functions, explains how they work, and tells how you can write them and use them in your C++ programs. The chapter also introduces string classes—classes that you can use to perform string-related operations such as string copying, string concatenation, and string searches.

Although you can write your own string classes, a much better alternative in Visual C++ programs is to use the extraordinarily robust `CString` class that is defined in the Microsoft Foundation Class (MFC) library. The `CString` class is equipped with many powerful capabilities, including not only string-manipulation facilities, but also support for reading and writing files and checking errors. Part III, which begins with Chapter 21, "The Microsoft Foundation Classes," introduces some of the most important classes in the MFC library.

Chapter 19

# Inheritance and Polymorphism

Two of the most important characteristics of C++ are *inheritance* and *polymorphism*. Inheritance is the feature that allows classes to inherit behaviors from other classes and to modify those behaviors. Polymorphism is the feature of the language that lets different objects call different functions using the same name. If C++ did not have the properties of inheritance and polymorphism, it would not be a full-featured object-oriented language.

In C++, inheritance and polymorphism are the two main mechanisms for describing and manipulating the relationships between classes. Inheritance enables programs to derive new classes from existing classes. Polymorphism lets programs call member functions of an object without specifying the object's exact type.

Inheritance and polymorphism were introduced in Chapter 10, "Object-Oriented Programming," and are examined more closely in this chapter. This chapter describes inheritance and polymorphism, explains how they work, and tells how you can use them in your C++ programs.

# Derived Classes

In C++, you can derive new classes from existing classes by using the mechanism of inheritance. A class from which another class is derived is called a *base class*.

When a class is derived from another class, the derived class inherits characteristics from its base class; specifically, a derived class inherits all `public` and `protected` member variables and member functions of its base class. However, a derived class does not inherit members of its base class that are labeled `private`.

In addition to the member variables and member functions that it inherits from its base class, a derived class can, of course, define its own member variables and member functions.

When a class is derived from another class, more classes can be derived from the derived class. Thus, a derived class can also be a base class. Multiple levels of classes that are derived from each other form a *class hierarchy*. In a class hierarchy, classes at the bottom of the hierarchy inherit all the `public` and `protected` (but not the `private`) member variables and member functions of their base classes.

## Reasons for Using Derived Classes

C++ programmers use inheritance to create derived classes for a number of reasons.

- When you derive a class from a base class, the result is a new data type that inherits all the qualities of the base class without disturbing its purpose to the rest of the program. If the base class is already in use in your program, its behavior remains intact for objects that already use it, but can be modified for use by objects that require different behaviors.
- When you want to derive a class from a base class, you don't need to have access to the source code for the base class. If you have access to the source code that defines a base class (which is usually stored in a header file), you have all you need to derive classes from that class.

- A class hierarchy can make use of *abstract classes*; that is, general-purpose classes that do nothing themselves, but are specifically designed to be used as base classes. The only purpose of an abstract class is to define the behavior of a generic data structure. Derived classes can then add the implementation details. For example, an abstract class might be defined to manage objects in a list. If you wrote such a base class, you could provide it with member functions that insert, change, delete, reorder, and search entries in the list without having to know any details about objects in the list. Such a class would probably be designed as an abstract class because it would have no usefulness unless it were associated with an actual list. Abstract classes are described in more detail later in this section.
- With class hierarchies made up of base classes and derived classes, you can make use of other properties of the object-oriented languages, such as polymorphism—that is, the capability of classes to modify their own behavior based on the characteristics of the subclasses that use them. In C++, class hierarchies make polymorphism possible by supporting the virtual function mechanism. You learn more about virtual functions later in the chapter, in the "Polymorphism" section.

## Benefits of Using Derived Classes

Two benefits can result from using derived classes in C++ programs. One advantage is that derived classes provide a means for building a well organized object-oriented class hierarchy in which user-defined data types descend from a common root class. Also, derived classes let you use the C++ property of inheritance; by deriving classes that inherit behaviors from other classes, you can create new classes that are similar to—but not identical to—other classes. Thus, inheritance provides a systematic, logical, easy-to-use mechanism for creating new classes with new behaviors.

Listing 19.1, this chapter's version of the program called *The Wrath of Zalthar*, shows how derived classes can be used in a C++ program. As you might notice, Listing 19.1 is quite different from earlier versions of the Zalthar program. One difference is that there is a new class, named `Character`. The `Character` class, as you will see later in the chapter, is an *abstract* class; that is, a class from which objects cannot be created. The `Player` class is now derived from the `Character` class. The `Player` class, unlike the `Character` class, is a *concrete* class; that is, a class from which objects *can* be created.

### Listing 19.1. The Wrath of Zalthar, Chapter 19 version.

#### MYSTRING.H

```
// MYSTRING.H

#ifndef _MYSTRING_H_
#define _MYSTRING_H_

#include <iostream.h>
#include "zalthar.h"

// String class
class String
{
public:
   String() : buf(0), length(0) {}
   String( const char *s );
   ~String() { delete buf; }
   // Copy constructor
   String( const String &other );
   // Assignment operator
   String &operator=( const String &other );
   void Display() const { cout << buf; }
private:
   int length;
   char *buf;
};

#endif  // _MYSTRING_H_
```

#### MYSTRING.CPP

```
// MYSTRING.CPP

#include <string.h>
#include "zalthar.h"

// Constructor that takes a parameter
String::String( const char *s )
{
    length = strlen( s );
    buf = new char[length + 1];
    strcpy( buf, s );
}

// Copy constructor
String::String( const String &other )
{
    length = other.length;
    buf = new char[length + 1];
```

```
    strcpy( buf, other.buf );
}

String &String::operator=( const String &other )
{
    if( &other == this )
        return *this;
    delete buf;
    length = other.length;
    buf = new char[length + 1];
    strcpy( buf, other.buf );
    return *this;
}
```

## ZALTHAR.H

```
// ZALTHAR.H
// Chapter 19 Version
// Copyright 1993, Mark Andrews

#if !defined( _ZALTHAR_H_ )
#define _ZALTHAR_H_

#include <iostream.h>
#include "mystring.h"

enum playerClasses { WARRIOR, WIZARD, PRIEST, ROGUE };
const String gClassName [] = { "Warrior", "Wizard", "Priest", "Rogue" };

enum playerRaces { DWARF, ELF, GNOME,
     HALF_ELF, HALFLING, HUMAN };
const String gRaceName [] = { "Dwarf", "Elf", "Gnome",
     "Half elf", "Halfling", "Human" };

class Abilities {
public:
     int strength;
     int dexterity;
     int constitution;
     int intelligence;
     int wisdom;
     int charisma;
public:
     Abilities() {}
     ~Abilities() {}
     // return a const pointer to an Abilities object
     const Abilities *GetAbils() { return this; }
     void SetAbils(int s, int d, int c, int i, int w, int ch)
          { strength = s; dexterity = d; constitution = c;
          intelligence = i; wisdom = w;  charisma = ch; }
};
```

*continues*

**Listing 19.1. continued**

```
class Character {
private:
     int  playerClass, playerRace;
     class String className, raceName;
     class String name;
     class String race;
     class String weapon;
     class String armor;
     class String magic;
     Abilities PlayerAbils;
     static int count;
public:
     Character() { IncCount(); }
     ~Character () { DecCount(); }
     static void PrintTitle();
     static int GetCount() { return count; }
     static void IncCount() { count++; }
     static void DecCount() { count--; }
     static void PrintCount();
     void SetPlayerClass(int pc) { playerClass = pc; SetClassStr(pc); }
     void SetClassStr(int pc) { className = gClassName[pc]; }
     void SetPlayerRace(int pr) { playerRace = pr; SetRaceStr(pr); }
     void SetRaceStr(int pr) { raceName = gRaceName[pr]; }
     int GetPlayerClass() { return playerClass; }
     String GetClassName() { return className; }
     int GetPlayerRace() { return playerRace; }
     String GetRaceName() { return raceName; }
     void SetName(String nm) { name = nm; }
     String GetName() { return name; }
     void SetRace(String rc) { race = rc; }
     String GetRace() { return race; }
     void SetWeapon(String wpn) { weapon = wpn; }
     String GetWeapon() { return weapon; }
     void SetArmor(String arm) { armor = arm; }
     String GetArmor() { return armor; }
     void SetMagic(String mag) { magic = mag; }
     String GetMagic() { return magic; }
     // initialize an Abilities object
     void SetAbils(int s, int d, int c, int i, int w, int ch)
          { PlayerAbils.SetAbils(s, d, c, i, w, ch); }
     // read contents of the PlayerAbils object
     const Abilities *GetAbils() { return (PlayerAbils.GetAbils()); }
     virtual void PrintEntry() = 0;
     void PrintAbils();
};

class Player : public Character {
```

```
public:
     Player(int pr) { SetPlayerRace(pr); }
     void PrintEntry();
};

class Warrior : public Player {
public:
     Warrior(int pr, String nm) : Player(pr)
          { SetPlayerRace(pr); SetPlayerClass(WARRIOR);
              SetName(nm); }
     void PrintEntry();
};

class Wizard : public Player {
public:
     Wizard(int pr, String nm, String mag) : Player(pr)
          { SetPlayerRace(pr); SetPlayerClass(WIZARD);
            SetName(nm); SetMagic(mag); }
     Wizard(int pr, String nm) : Player(pr)
          { SetPlayerRace(pr); SetPlayerClass(WIZARD);
            SetName(nm); }
     void PrintEntry();
};

class Priest : public Player {
public:
     Priest(int pr, String nm, String mag) : Player(pr)
          { SetPlayerRace(pr); SetPlayerClass(PRIEST);
            SetName(nm); SetMagic(mag); }
     Priest(int pr, String nm) : Player(pr)
          { SetPlayerRace(pr); SetPlayerClass(PRIEST);
            SetName(nm); }
     void PrintEntry();
};

#endif // _ZALTHAR_H
```

### ZALTHAR.CPP

```
// ZALTHAR.CPP

#include <iostream.h>
#include <string.h>
#include <stdio.h>
#include <stdlib.h>
#include "zalthar.h"

int Character::count = 0;     // initialize nr of players to 0
```

*continues*

**Listing 19.1. continued**

```
void FatalError()
{
    fprintf(stderr, "A fatal error has occurred\n");
    exit(1);
}

void Character::PrintCount()
{
     cout << "\nNUMBER OF PLAYERS: " <<  Character::GetCount() << '\n';
};


void Character::PrintAbils()
{
     const Abilities *locAbils = GetAbils();

     cout << "\nStrength: " << locAbils->strength << '\n';
     cout << "Dexterity: " << locAbils->dexterity << '\n';
     cout << "Constitution: " << locAbils->constitution << '\n';
     cout << "Intelligence: " << locAbils->intelligence << '\n';
     cout << "Wisdom: " << locAbils->wisdom << '\n';
     cout << "Charisma: " << locAbils->charisma << '\n';
}

void Player::PrintEntry()
{
     const Abilities *locAbils = GetAbils();

     cout << "\nNAME: ";
     (this->GetName()).Display();
     cout << "\nRace: ";
     (this->GetRaceName()).Display();
     cout << "\nClass: ";
     (this->GetClassName()).Display();
}

void Warrior::PrintEntry()
{
     const Abilities *locAbils = GetAbils();

     Player::PrintEntry();
     cout << "\nWeapon: ";
     (this->GetWeapon()).Display();
     cout << "\nArmor: ";
     (this->GetArmor()).Display();
     PrintAbils();
}
```

```
void Wizard::PrintEntry()
{
     const Abilities *locAbils = GetAbils();

     Player::PrintEntry();
     cout << "\nWeapon: ";
     (this->GetWeapon()).Display();
     cout << "\nMagic: ";
     (this->GetMagic()).Display();
     PrintAbils();
}

void Priest::PrintEntry()
{
     const Abilities *locAbils = GetAbils();

     Player::PrintEntry();
     cout << "\nWeapon: ";
     (this->GetWeapon()).Display();
     cout << "\nArmor: ";
     (this->GetArmor()).Display();
     cout << "\nMagic: ";
     (this->GetMagic()).Display();
     PrintAbils();
}
```

### MAIN.CPP

```
// MAIN.CPP

#include <iostream.h>
#include <string.h>
#include "zalthar.h"

int main()
{
     Player *playerPtr[3];

     playerPtr[0] = new Warrior(GNOME, "Bruno");
     playerPtr[0]->SetAbils(23, 18, 22, 12, 8, 16);
     playerPtr[0]->SetWeapon("Sword");
     playerPtr[0]->SetArmor("Chain Mail");

     playerPtr[1] = new Wizard(HUMAN, "Zalthar");
     playerPtr[1]->SetAbils(12, 16, 14, 22, 25, 20);
     playerPtr[1]->SetWeapon("Dagger");
     playerPtr[1]->SetMagic("Dancing Lights");

     playerPtr[2] = new Priest(ELF, "Fiar Truck", "Bless");
     playerPtr[2]->SetAbils(4, 23, 6, 21, 14, 8);
```

*continues*

**Listing 19.1. continued**

```
    playerPtr[2]->SetWeapon("Mace");
    playerPtr[2]->SetArmor("Leather");

    Player::PrintTitle();
    Character::PrintCount();

    for (int n = 0; n < 3; n++)
        playerPtr[n]->PrintEntry();

    return 0;
}
```

### NOTE—MORE IMPROVEMENTS IN THE ZALTHAR PROGRAM

Besides some new classes, this chapter's version of The Wrath of Zalthar has a long list of improvements over previous versions. In fact, it's beginning to look like a real C++ program.

Some of its new features:

- The `Abilities` structure has been promoted to a full-fledged class, complete with a constructor, a destructor, and a set of member variables and functions. Also, the `Abilities` class has been designated a friend of the `Character` class, so the `Character` class can have access to the private member variables of the `Abilities` class.
- The architecture of the `Character` class (formerly known as the `Player` class) has been redesigned to correspond more closely with the requirements of a real adventure game. Adventure games usually have non-playing characters as well as playing characters—so, later on in the development of the game, the abstract `Character` class can be extended to support a non-player subclass as well as the current `Player` subclass. Also, characters can now have races as well as classes.
- One advantage of polymorphism is that it enables a programmer to arrange objects into lists that can contain pointers to objects of different types. When such a list has been created, the objects in the list can be treated as objects of the same type for some purposes,

and as objects of different types for other purposes. For instance, in the Zalthar program, a single list of all the players in a game can be compiled, even though the objects in the list represent different kinds of characters with different kinds of attributes. In this chapter's version of the program, the `main()` segment creates an array of pointers to three player objects. Then, through the magic of polymorphism, a single function (named `PrintEntry()`) is called in a loop to print out three different kinds of lists!

## The New Zalthar Hierarchy

In the version of the Zalthar program presented in Listing 19.1, the `Player` class has three subclasses: `Warrior`, `Wizard`, and `Priest`. This is the hierarchy of the classes used in the program:

- `Character` is an abstract class; that is, a class from which no objects can be created.
- The `Player` class is a concrete class that is now derived from the `Character` class.
- The `Warrior`, `Wizard`, and `Priest` classes are concrete classes that are derived from the `Player` class.

You can determine the derivation of each class used in the program by examining the header line of the definition of each class. For example, the first line of the definition of the `Character` class shows that it is not derived from any other class:

```
class Character {
```

In contrast, the first line of the `Player` class definition shows that the `Player` class is derived from the `Character` class:

```
class Player : public Character {
```

Similarly, the first line of the `Warrior` class definition shows that the `Warrior` class is derived from the `Player` class:

```
class Warrior : public Player {
```

In the current stage of the Zalthar program's development, the `Character`, `Player`, `Warrior`, `Wizard`, and `Priest` classes all have short definitions. But each class has a separate `PrintEntry()` function, and every class except `Player` has its own constructor (or constructors). Reasons for these differences will be outlined later in this chapter.

> **NOTE—PUBLIC AND PRIVATE CLASS DERIVATION**
>
> As noted in Chapter 11, "Classes," classes can be *publicly* or *privately* derived from other classes. When a class is privately derived from a base class, members of the base class that are designated `public` and `protected` become private members of the derived class. When a class is publicly derived from a base class, members of the base class that are designated `protected` are also protected members of the derived class, and members of the base class that are designated `public` are also public members of the derived class.
>
> Because the `Warrior` class is publicly derived from the `Player` class, objects of the `Warrior` class inherit all the member functions of the `Player` class. Because all the member functions of the `Player` class are public, they remain public when they are inherited by the `Warrior` class.
>
> If you do not provide an access specifier when you define a derived class, the derived class is designated `private`. An exception to this rule is a class that is derived from a structure. In that case, the derived class is public by default.

## Inheritance Rules for Constructors and Destructors

Except for the `Player` class, each class that is defined in the Zalthar program has its own constructor (or constructors). As you may recall from Chapter 14, constructors and destructors of base classes are not considered member functions of their classes, and are not inherited by derived classes. Instead, when you instantiate an object of a derived class, the compiler invokes the constructors for all the classes in the object's class hierarchy, beginning with the object's root class and moving down the hierarchy until the object's own constructor is called.

When a derived class is created, its constructor sometimes has a parameter list that is different from the parameters of the object's base class. Because constructors are not inherited, the constructor that is defined for the derived class must tell the compiler what values to use as arguments when it invokes the constructor for the base class.

In such a case, the constructor of the derived class uses a special kind of declaration to specify the arguments that should be passed to the constructor that is defined for the base class. The format of such a statement is simple; the declaration of the constructor for the derived class is followed by a colon, and the colon is followed by a declaration of the constructor for the base class. For example, in Listing 19.1, this constructor initializes an object of the `Warrior` class by invoking the constructor of the `Player` class:

```
Warrior(int pr, String nm) : Player(pr)
          { SetPlayerRace(pr); SetPlayerClass(WIZARD);
            SetName(nm); }
```

Another feature of the newest Zalthar program is that the `Wizard` and `Priest` classes each have two constructors. In each case, one constructor sets a value for the member variable `magic`, and one doesn't.

When a class has more than one constructor function, the compiler decides which constructor to call by using argument matching; that is, by comparing the numbers and types of the arguments that are passed to the base class with the numbers and types of the arguments in the argument list of each constructor defined for the base class.

In Listing 19.1, the `Wizard` class has two kinds of constructors, and so does the `Priest` class. In each case, one constructor sets the value of the member variable `magic`, and one doesn't. These are the two constructors that are defined for the `Wizard` class:

```
Wizard(int pr, String nm, String mag) : Player(pr)
     { SetPlayerRace(pr); SetPlayerClass(WIZARD);
       SetName(nm); SetMagic(mag); }
Wizard(int pr, String nm) : Player(pr)
     { SetPlayerRace(pr); SetPlayerClass(WIZARD);
       SetName(nm); }
```

The program's `main()` segment instantiates a `Wizard` object using the version of the `Wizard` class constructor that doesn't set the value of `magic`:

```
playerPtr[1] = new Wizard(HUMAN, "Zalthar");
```

The `playerPtr[1]` object's `magic` variable is then set using a separate statement:

```
playerPtr[1]->SetMagic("Dancing Lights");
```

The other kind of constructor—the kind that sets the value of the `magic` data member—is used to create an object of the `Priest` class:

```
playerPtr[2] = new Priest(ELF, "Fiar Truck", "Bless");
```

When this kind of constructor is invoked, it isn't necessary to write a statement that sets the value of the `magic` variable. This is the program's output:

```
THE WRATH OF ZALTHAR
By [Your Name Here]

NUMBER OF PLAYERS: 3

NAME: Bruno
Race: Gnome
Class: Warrior
Weapon: Sword
Armor: Chain Mail
Strength: 23
Dexterity: 18
Constitution: 22
Intelligence: 12
Wisdom: 8
Charisma: 16

NAME: Zalthar
Race: Human
Class: Wizard
Weapon: Dagger
Magic: Dancing Lights
Strength: 12
Dexterity: 16
Constitution: 14
Intelligence: 22
Wisdom: 25
Charisma: 20

NAME: Fiar Truck
Race: Elf
Class: Priest
Weapon: Mace
Armor: Leather
Magic: Bless
Strength: 4
Dexterity: 23
Constitution: 6
Intelligence: 21
Wisdom: 14
Charisma: 8
```

## Accessing Objects Through Pointers

One powerful capability of C++ is that it allows you to create a pointer to an object of a base class, and then use that pointer to access an object of a derived class. The Zalthar program presented in Listing 19.1 illustrates this capability. The program's `main()` segment creates an array of three pointers to the `Player` class. Then all three pointers are set to point to objects of classes that are derived from the `Player` class:

```
Player *playerPtr[3];

playerPtr[0] = new Warrior(GNOME, "Bruno");
playerPtr[0]->SetAbils(23, 18, 22, 12, 8, 16);
playerPtr[0]->SetWeapon("Sword");
playerPtr[0]->SetArmor("Chain Mail");

playerPtr[1] = new Wizard(HUMAN, "Zalthar");
playerPtr[1]->SetAbils(12, 16, 14, 22, 25, 20);
playerPtr[1]->SetWeapon("Dagger");
playerPtr[1]->SetMagic("Dancing Lights");

playerPtr[2] = new Priest(ELF, "Fiar Truck", "Bless");
playerPtr[2]->SetAbils(4, 23, 6, 21, 14, 8);
playerPtr[2]->SetWeapon("Mace");
playerPtr[2]->SetArmor("Leather");
```

The preceding code fragment deserves careful study. When it has been executed, `playerPtr[0]` points to a `Warrior` object, while `playerPtr[1]` points to a `Wizard` object, and `playerPtr[2]` points to a `Priest` object! That's a remarkable capability; it means that the program can create a single array of pointers that point to objects of different types! All three objects have the same base type, but are actually objects of different types.

In a C++ program, this capability can be used in interesting ways. In this case, for example, there are three characters in a computer game: one character of type `Warrior`, one character of type `Wizard`, and one character of type `Priest`. By accessing all three varieties of characters through the same kind of pointer—a pointer to the `Player` base class—the program compiles a single list that keeps track of all the characters in the game, even though the characters are objects of different classes.

What makes this even more noteworthy is the fact that when list objects have been put together in this fashion, they can be manipulated in different ways by different functions that have the same function name. In Listing 19.1, for instance, a single function—`PrintEntry()`—is called in a loop to print out three different kinds of lists!

More information about how this is done will be presented later in this chapter.

> **TIP—DON'T LOOK BACK**
>
> Although a pointer to a base-class object can point to a derived-class object, a pointer to a derived-class object can't be set to point to a base-class object. That's logical because there's no way for a base class to be aware of the member functions and member variables that are added to its derived classes.

# Virtual Functions

Ordinarily, when a derived class has a member function that exactly matches an accessible member function of a base class (in terms of its name and argument list), you can't execute the version of the function that is defined for the derived class by calling the function through a pointer to the base class. Instead, when you call the function through a pointer to the base class, the compiler executes the base-class version of the function.

You can reverse this behavior by declaring a member function of a base class to be `virtual`. When a derived class has a member function that exactly matches a private or protected member function of a base class, and the base-class member function is designated `virtual`, the version of the function that is defined for the derived class is the version that is called; when the base-class version of the function is designated `virtual`, the version of the function that is defined for the derived class overrides the base class `virtual` function.

You may have to read those rules several times before they sink in. If they still sound fuzzy, be patient; they'll be illustrated with code samples later in this section.

## Calling Virtual Functions

When you call a *virtual* member function through a pointer to a base class (a common practice in C++), the C++ compiler executes the *derived-class* version of the function instead of calling the version of the function that is defined for the base class. To declare a virtual member function in the definition of a base class, all you have to do is precede the declaration of the function with the keyword `virtual`, as follows:

```
virtual void PrintUsefulStuff()
    { cout << "This is a base class function.\n"; }
```

In the preceding code fragment, a virtual member function named `PrintUsefulStuff()` is defined. Because the function is preceded by the keyword `virtual`, the definition of the function probably appears in the definition of a base class. In the function definition, the `virtual` keyword tells us (and also tells the compiler) that the `PrintUsefulStuff()` function is designed not to be used in the form shown in the preceding code fragment (which isn't very useful), but is intended to be overloaded by a derived class.

If a derived class fails to provide an overloaded version of the `PrintUsefulStuff()` function, the function won't print any useful stuff when it is called, but will merely print the message, "This is a base function." This is apparently an alert message, intended to warn the program designer that the function has not been overridden.

## Pure Virtual Functions

A member function that not only can be overridden, but *must* be overridden, is called a *pure virtual function*. When you declare a pure virtual function in a base class, you are not only specifying that the member function must be overridden before it can be used; you are also specifying that the base class does not contain a definition of the function.

To turn a virtual member function into a pure virtual member function, all you have to do is assign the function a value of zero (effectively, a null pointer). For example, in Listing 19.1, the `PrintEntry()` function is a pure virtual function. It is defined this way in the definition of the base class `Character`:

```
virtual void PrintEntry() = 0;
```

When a function is defined in a class definition using the format shown here, the compiler treats the function as a pure virtual function. A pure virtual function can appear only in the definition of a base class, and must be overridden in a derived class.

When a class contains at least one pure virtual function, the class is known as an *abstract* class. An abstract class, as noted earlier in this chapter, is a class from which objects cannot be created.

The only purpose of an abstract class is to serve as a foundation for derived classes. Similarly, the only purpose of a pure virtual function is to serve as a foundation for other functions. You cannot instantiate an object that belongs to an abstract class, and you cannot call a pure virtual function; you can, however, call an overridden version of a virtual function when the override is provided in the definition of a derived class.

> **WARNING—ABSTRACT-CLASS PITFALLS DEPT.**
>
> Although you can't instantiate an abstract class, you can declare a pointer to a base class, and that base class can be an abstract class. That opens the door to indirect manipulation of an abstract class, which can cause problems. If you access an abstract class through a pointer, and then try to invoke a member function of that class that is a pure virtual function, the result is an error that may not be detected until runtime.
>
> Consequently, when you access a function in an abstract base class through a pointer to the base class, you should always check to see if the function is a virtual function. If it is, you should make sure that the function is overridden in the derived class from which it is called. If it isn't, you may encounter problems at runtime.

## Classes That Inherit Pure Virtual Functions

If a class inherits a pure virtual function, but does not override that function, the class is considered an abstract class. That means that a class can be considered an abstract class even if the definition of the class does not contain a definition of a pure virtual function. In Microsoft Visual C++, if a class does not explicitly *provide* an implementation for a virtual function that it inherits, the class is considered an abstract class, and no objects that belong to the class can be created.

If a class inherits a pure virtual function, and you try to create an object of the derived class, the Visual C++ compiler returns an error informing you that you are trying to instantiate a member of an abstract class. If you aren't familiar with the rules that govern the implementation of pure virtual functions, you may not understand why an error is being returned. You can prevent such errors from occurring by making sure that *every virtual function that is defined in a base class is overridden by every class that is derived from that base class.*

## Pure Virtual Functions in Class Hierarchies

When you build a hierarchy of classes, it is particularly important to remember the rules that govern the inheritance of pure virtual functions. In Visual C++, when a class that is a member of a hierarchy defines a pure virtual function, every concrete class that appears in the lower hierarchy must override the function. If a derived class fails to the pure virtual function, that class becomes an abstract class from which objects cannot be created.

If a pure virtual function is defined in a base class and is then passed down through a hierarchy of classes, there may be classes in the hierarchy that have no particular need for the virtual function they have inherited. If a class inherits a pure virtual function, but must provide an implementation of the function anyway so that it won't be considered an abstract class, the class can implement the pure virtual function by defining it as a *null virtual function*.

A null virtual function is a virtual function with an empty parameter list. This is a definition of a null virtual function:

```
virtual void PrintSomeStuff() {}
```

A null virtual function is not the same as a pure virtual function. A null virtual function is simply a virtual function that does nothing. When you declare a pure virtual function in the base class of a class hierarchy, you can use null virtual functions as placeholders in intermediate classes in the hierarchy. The null virtual functions that are implemented in the hierarchy serve no purpose except to make the pure virtual function accessible to lower classes in the chain.

Listing 19.2 shows how a null virtual function can be used in a class hierarchy.

### Listing 19.2. A null virtual function.

```
// 1902.CPP
// Null Virtual Functions

#include <iostream.h>

class AClass {
public:
    virtual void PrintIt() = 0;
};

class BClass : public AClass {
```

*continues*

**Listing 19.2. continued**

```
public:
     virtual void PrintIt() {}
};

class CClass : public BClass {
public:
     void PrintIt() { cout << "This is CClass.\n"; }
};

int main()
{
     BClass *bClassObj = new BClass;
     CClass *cClassObj = new CClass;

     bClassObj->PrintIt();
     cClassObj->PrintIt();

     return 0;
}
```

### NOTE—A MICROSOFT FEATURE

In some implementations of C++, it isn't necessary to override a pure virtual function in every subclass that's derived from the class in which the function definition appears. Intermediate classes don't have to override the function in an unbroken chain; if one subclass overrides the pure virtual function, that's all that's required. But Microsoft Visual C++ *does* require a pure virtual function that's defined in a base class to be overrun in every derived class. So, null virtual functions are a handy tool for the Visual C++ programmer.

In Listing 19.2, a pure virtual function named `PrintIt()` is defined inside the definition of a base class named `AClass`. The function is implemented as a null virtual function in a derived class named `BClass`, and is then overridden as a real working function in a lower derived class named `CClass`. When the program is executed, this is its output:

```
This is CClass.
```

You may notice that when you run the program, this statement in the program's `main()` segment does nothing:

```
bClassObj->PrintIt();
```

This statement has no effect because the intermediate derived class named `BClass` defines `PrintIt()` as a null virtual function. Examine the definition of `BClass`, and you'll find this definition of the `PrintIt()` function:

```
virtual void PrintIt() {}
```

Although this definition of `PrintIt()` performs no action, the NULLVIRT.CPP program doesn't work without it. If you remove that line from the program, or comment it out, the Visual C++ compiler returns an error complaining that you have tried to instantiate an abstract class (`BClass`).

## Overriding Virtual Functions

You can override virtual functions in C++. If you couldn't, there wouldn't be much reason to use virtual functions.

Listing 19.2 shows how virtual functions and polymorphism can work together in a C++ program. In the `main()` segment of the program, as you saw earlier, three objects are created: a `Warrior` object, a `Wizard` object, and a `Priest` object. All three of these objects are accessed through pointers to player objects. The three `Player` pointers that point to the objects are named `PlayerPtr[0]`, `PlayerPtr[1]`, and `PlayerPtr[2]`

When the `PlayerPtr[0]`, `PlayerPtr[1]`, and `PlayerPtr[2]` pointers have been created, the program executes a loop that calls a function named `PrintEntry()` three times: once through each `Player` pointer. This is the loop:

```
for (int n = 0; n < 3; n++)
     playerPtr[n]->PrintEntry();
```

Because the `PrintEntry()` function that is defined for the `Character` class is a virtual function, this loop does not execute the `PrintEntry()` statement that is defined for the base class `Character`—even though each iteration of the loop calls `PrintEntry()` through a pointer to an object of the `Player` class.

The `Character` class version of `PrintEntry()` cannot be executed because `Character::PrintEntry()` is a pure virtual function. So, the program can't do anything but execute the versions of the function that are declared in the definitions of the `Warrior`, `Wizard`, and `Priest` classes. Consequently, this is the program's output:

```
THE WRATH OF ZALTHAR
By [Your Name Here]

NUMBER OF PLAYERS: 3

NAME: Bruno
Race: Gnome
Class: Warrior
Weapon: Sword
Armor: Chain Mail
Strength: 23
Dexterity: 18
Constitution: 22
Intelligence: 12
Wisdom: 8
Charisma: 16

NAME: Zalthar
Race: Human
Class: Wizard
Weapon: Dagger
Magic: Dancing Lights
Strength: 12
Dexterity: 16
Constitution: 14
Intelligence: 22
Wisdom: 25
Charisma: 20

NAME: Fiar Truck
Race: Elf
Class: Priest
Weapon: Mace
Armor: Leather
Magic: Bless
Strength: 4
Dexterity: 23
Constitution: 6
Intelligence: 21
Wisdom: 14
Charisma: 8
```

Notice that the `PrintEntry()` functions for the `Warrior`, `Wizard`, and `Priest` classes all produce different results. The warrior named Bruno and the priest named Fiar Truck have armor, but the wizard named Zalthar lacks armor. And, while the wizard and the priest are armed with magic spells, the fighter has no magic.

The printout shows, then, that polymorphism works. One function, `PrintEntry()`, performs three different operations for three different objects. That's polymorphism in action.

## The Scope Resolution Operator

When a virtual function appears in the definition of a base class, and is overridden in a derived class, can you call the version of the function that is defined for the base, overriding the derived class's override? Yes, you can. All you have to do is call the function using the scope resolution operator (`::`). Suppose you insert this line into the `main()` function of the Zalthar program:

```
playerPtr[2]->Player::PrintEntry();
```

This line calls the `Character` class version of the `PrintEntry()` function, instead of the version of the function that is defined for the `Priest` class. So the program prints this output:

```
NAME: Fiar Truck
Race: Elf
Class: Priest
```

## How Virtual Functions Work

As mentioned in Chapter 13, "Member Functions," virtual functions are the keys to polymorphism. When you define a virtual member function in a base class, the function's declaration notifies the compiler that the function may be overridden in base classes. Therefore, when you write a base-class function that you think you might override, it's a good idea to make the function a virtual function.

Except for the ironclad rules that govern the use of pure virtual functions, C++ is fairly forgiving about how you use virtual functions in your programs. When you write a base-class function and declare it to be a virtual function, C++ does not force you to override the function in derived classes; if you don't override the function, it still works fine in the base class in which it is defined.

Conversely, if you write a base-class function and don't make it virtual, C++ doesn't force you to override the function in a derived class. However, it's a good idea to designate a base-class function virtual when you think it might be overridden in a derived class. That's because C++ compiles virtual functions and non-virtual functions in very different ways. Virtual functions work more efficiently than non-virtual functions when they're overridden. More important, because of the way they're compiled, virtual functions are the key to polymorphism in the C++ language.

## Static and Dynamic Binding

Until object-oriented languages came along, programs called functions in a very straightforward way. When a procedural program called a function, the compiler knew exactly what function was being called, and knew exactly where in memory the function resided. Therefore, when an application called a function, the call to the function was simply built into the program when the program was compiled. Today, that technique is known as *early binding*, or *static binding*.

When a C++ program calls a non-virtual function, the function is called using static binding, in the same way that it would be called in a C program. However, when a C++ program calls a virtual function through a pointer to a class, the compiler calls the function using a different technique. That technique is called *late binding*, or *dynamic binding*.

When a program calls a virtual function through a pointer to a base class—that is, when a function calls a virtual function using dynamic binding—the compiler doesn't know at link time which version of the function will be called when the program is executed. That's because the program doesn't call the function through a pointer to a specific derived class, but rather through a pointer to a base class that can (and usually does) have multiple derived classes.

Because the compiler doesn't know which version of the function to access when the program is linked, the program itself must evaluate the calling statement at runtime, when it can determine which version of the function to call. Thus, when a program uses dynamic binding to call a function through a pointer to an object, the calling statement is evaluated at runtime.

One important advantage of dynamic binding is that it lets you call functions that are individually tailored for individual objects, even when functions have the same names. That capability, as demonstrated in Listing 19.2, is what polymorphism is all about.

Another advantage of dynamic binding is that it lets you modify the behavior of code that has already been compiled. That means you can use dynamic binding to provide extensible class libraries to other programmers.

By calling functions using dynamic binding, you can let other programmers derive new classes from classes that you have defined and redefine the virtual functions in your classes, even if you don't give them access to your source code. You can keep your source code private and distribute only your header files (.H files), along with the compiled object code (.OBJ or .LIB files) for the hierarchy of classes you've written and the functions that use those classes. Other programmers can then derive new classes from your classes, and can redefine virtual functions that you have declared.

## V-Tables

Dynamic binding wouldn't be very useful in commercial-quality applications if it were an inefficient mechanism requiring a lot of overhead. Fortunately, virtual functions are very efficient; calling a virtual function takes only slightly longer than calling a normal function.

To implement dynamic binding, C++ uses *virtual function tables*, or *v-tables*. A v-table is an array of function pointers that the compiler constructs for every class that uses virtual functions. For example, in the Zalthar program, the compiler sets up separate v-tables for the `Player` class, the `Warrior` class, and the `Gnome` class.

When you compile a C++ program, the compiler stores the program's v-tables in a location that is accessible to all of the objects in the program. When you create a class that accesses virtual functions in a parent class, the code for each instance of the class contains a hidden pointer to the v-table of the class. The v-table for each object is built at runtime so that references can be resolved when the program that contains the object is executed.

Figure 19.1 shows how a v-table works in C++. Suppose that, at runtime, a program encounters a reference to a virtual function. When the reference is encountered, the object on the left is in scope, and the object's v-table pointer contains the address of an entry in the object's v-table.

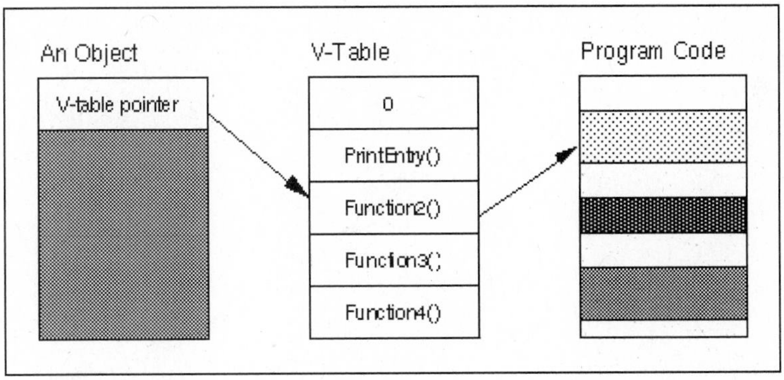


*Figure 19.1. Using a V-Table.*

Now assume that when a reference to a virtual function is encountered, the object's v-table pointer points to the second entry in the object's v-table. In Figure 19.1, the second entry in the object's v-table is the `PrintEntry()` function. So the `PrintEntry()` function, which resides in the code segment of the program, is called.

Because the call to a virtual function is indirect—through a pointer to an object—the code for the implementation of a virtual function does not have to be in the same code segment as the caller of the virtual function.

A v-table that is set up for a class contains one function pointer for each virtual function in the class. For example, in this chapter's version of the Zalthar program, the `Warrior` class and the `Gnome` class have separate v-tables for the `PrintEntry()` function. The v-table for the `Warrior` class contains a pointer to the `Warrior::PrintEntry()` function, whereas the v-table for `Gnome` class contains a pointer to the `Gnome::PrintEntry()`. But, as you have seen, both functions can be called through a pointer to a `Player` class.

When a program that is being executed calls the `PrintEntry()` function, the pointer to the function points to the version of the function that is appropriate to the class that is currently in scope. Thus, the correct function is called.

## Virtual Functions: Pros and Cons

Although dynamic binding is a powerful feature of C++, it doesn't mean that all functions in a program should be designated virtual functions. Because virtual functions are called indirectly, they add some overhead to an application, and therefore slightly slow down its execution speed. So, when you design a class, you should use the `virtual` keyword only for virtual functions that you expect to be overridden.

If you make a function virtual, and discover later that there is little chance of its being overridden, you can remove the `virtual` keyword from the declaration of the function and save a little overhead. But nothing bad will happen if you fail to notice that the function isn't overridden and forget to remove its `virtual` designation.

# Multiple Inheritance

Many pages ago, back in Chapter 10 ("Object-Oriented Programming"), you saw how a C++ object can inherit behaviors from more than one class. The derivation of a class from multiple base classes is known as *multiple inheritance*.

# Multiple Inheritance Illustrated

Multiple inheritance is more common in nature than it is in C++. Figure 19.2 (a portion of Figure 10.5, which appeared back in Chapter 10) shows how multiple inheritance works in the field of biology. Specifically, it shows how a duckbilled platypus—a beaked, fur-bearing creature that lays eggs—inherits characteristics from both the mammal and bird classes.

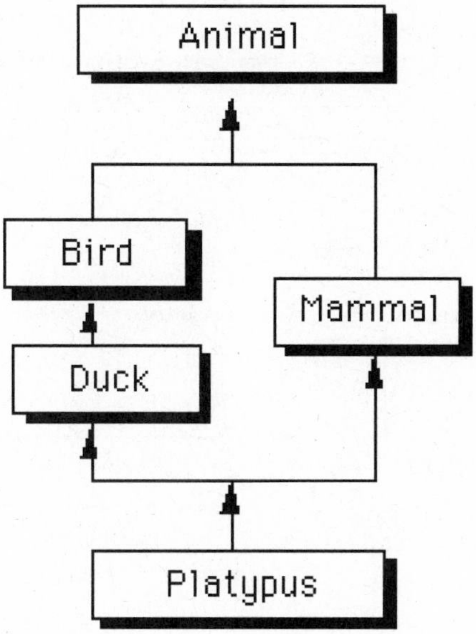


*Figure 19.2. Multiple inheritance.*

## Single Inheritance and Multiple Inheritance

In Figure 19.2, there is one root class, named `Animal`, from which every other class is derived. Every derived class except the `Platypus` class has a single base class. The `Mammal` and `Bird` classes are derived from the `Animal` class, and the `Duck` class is derived from the `Bird` class. So each of those classes is created in a simple way, using *single inheritance.*

The `Platypus` class is created differently. It has two base classes: `Mammal` and `Duck` classes. Because the `Platypus` class has two parent classes instead of one, you can say that it is derived using *multiple inheritance.*

### Using More than Two Base Classes

When you derive a class using multiple inheritance, the derived class is not limited to having two base classes. In Figure 19.3, which shows how rock music evolved in the 1950s, three classes are derived from a base class named `Music`. Those classes are named `Pop`, `R&B` (rhythm and blues), and `Country`. Finally, another subclass, named `Rock`, is derived from the `Pop`, `R&B`, and `Country` classes.

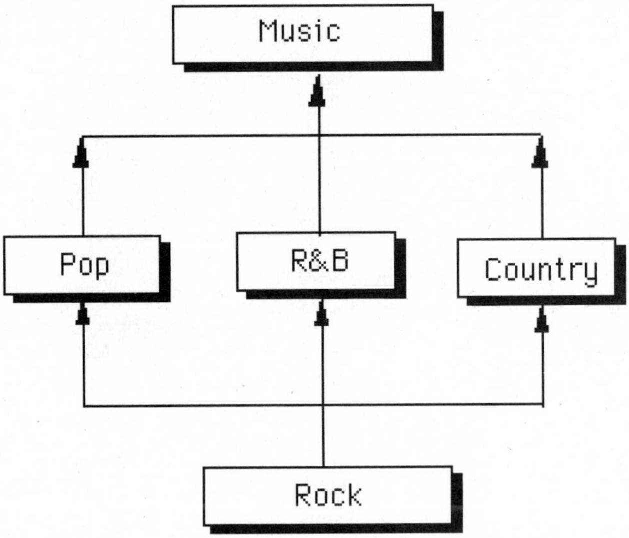


*Figure 19.3. Multiple inheritance.*

## Multiple Inheritance in the Animal Kingdom

When you define a class in a C++ program, and you want the new class to inherit member variables or member functions from more than one base class, you can create the new class by using multiple inheritance. To create a class that inherits data or behaviors using multiple inheritance, all you have to do is specify the base classes of the new class in the heading of its definition, as shown in this example:

```
class Platypus: public Mammal, public Duck {
public:
     void What()
          { cout << "What am I?\n"; }
     void Conclusion()
          { cout << "I'm a duckbilled platypus.\n"; }
};
```

The preceding code fragment, which appears in the program shown Listing 19.3, defines an object named `Platypus`. The program corresponds with the class diagram shown in Figure 19.2. The program uses the C++ principle of multiple inheritance to print out some facts about the duckbilled platypus.

#### Listing 19.3. Multiple inheritance.

```
// 1903.CPP
// Demonstrating Multiple Inheritance

#include <iostream.h>

class Animal {
public:
     void General()
          { cout << "I'm a sentient creature.\n"; }
};

class Bird: virtual public Animal {
public:
     void Mouth()
          { cout << "I have a beak.\n"; }
     void BirthMethod()
          { cout << "I lay eggs.\n"; }
};

class Duck: public Bird {
public:
     void Mouth()
          { cout << "I have a bill.\n"; }
};

class Mammal: virtual public Animal {
public:
     void Coat()
          { cout << "I have fur.\n"; }
};

class Platypus: public Mammal, public Duck {
public:
     void What()
          { cout << "What am I?\n"; }
     void Conclusion()
          { cout << "I'm a duckbilled platypus.\n"; }
};
```

*continues*

**Listing 19.3. continued**

```
int main()
{
      Platypus mysteryBeast;

      mysteryBeast.What();
      mysteryBeast.General();
      mysteryBeast.Coat();
      mysteryBeast.Mouth();
      mysteryBeast.BirthMethod();
      mysteryBeast.Conclusion();

      return 0;
}
```

The program in Listing 19.3 corresponds exactly to the class diagram shown in Figure 19.2. Every class that is defined in the program inherits from a single base class named `Animal`. The `Mammal` and `Bird` classes are derived from the `Animal` class, and the `Duck` class is derived from the `Bird` class. So each of those classes is created using single inheritance.

In Listing 19.3, just as in Figure 19.2, the `Platypus` class has two base classes: `Mammal` and `Duck` classes. So the `Platypus` class is defined using multiple inheritance.

When you execute the program, this is its output:

```
What am I?
I'm a sentient creature.
I have fur.
I have a bill.
I lay eggs.
I'm a duckbilled platypus.
```

## Virtual Base Classes

Because computers do what you say, not what you mean, there are some precautions that you have to exercise when you use multiple inheritance in a C++ program. For example, when a derived class inherits member functions from multiple base classes, you must make sure that there are no ambiguities in the names of the functions.

One common technique for avoiding ambiguities in function names is to create virtual base classes. In the definition of a derived class, you can declare a base class to be a virtual base class by preceding the name of the base class with the keyword `virtual`.

In the 1903.CPP program, for example, the definitions of the `Bird` and `Mammal` classes declare the `Animal` class to be a virtual base class. These are the lines in the program in which the `Animal` class is declared to be virtual:

```
class Bird: virtual public Animal {
/ ...
class Mammal: virtual public Animal {
```

When a derived class declares a base class to be virtual, the `virtual` keyword instructs the compiler to construct only one subobject of the base class. In the 1903.CPP program, if the `Animal` class were not declared to be `virtual`, the program's class hierarchy would not be constructed as shown back in Figure 19.2. Instead, it would look like the hierarchy shown in Figure 19.4.

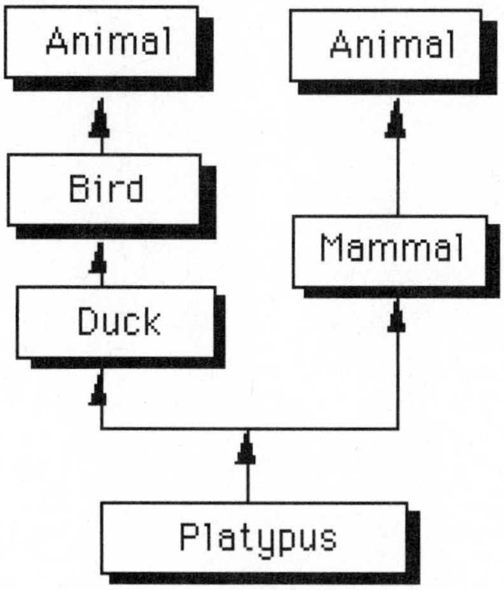


*Figure 19.4. Multiple inheritance without virtual base classes.*

In Figure 19.4, because the `Animal` class is not designated `virtual`, there are two subobjects of the `Animal` class. One is created when the `Bird` class is instantiated, and another is created when the `Mammal` class is instantiated.

When two subobjects of the `Animal` class exist, an ambiguity arises when the `main()` section of the program calls the `General()` function, a member function of the `Animal` class. In the program architecture shown in Figure 19.4, because there are two `Animal` subobjects, there also are two copies of the `Animal::General()` function. Both copies are identical, but the compiler has no way of knowing that. It simply detects an ambiguity and returns an error message.

You can resolve this ambiguity by simply declaring the `Animal` class to be a virtual base class. When you make the `Animal` class a virtual base class, the compiler creates only one copy of `Animal` subobjects, no matter how many objects of the class are instantiated. Then the compiler accesses the class object through a table of addresses, in much the same way that virtual member functions are accessed through v-tables.

Because the `Animal` class is designated a virtual class in Listing 19.3, the inheritance architecture of the 1903.CPP program does not look like the setup shown in Figure 19.4. Instead, it reflects the architecture shown earlier in Figure 19.2. Thus, in the 1903.CPP program, there are no ambiguity problems.

## Function-Name Ambiguities in the Inheritance Chain

When you use multiple inheritance in a program, you can't resolve all possible function-name ambiguities by merely declaring base classes with multiple subclasses to be virtual. Ambiguities can also arise when names of functions are duplicated in subclasses.

When multiple functions that have the same name appear in different objects in a multiple-inheritance architecture, the compiler tries to avoid function-name ambiguities through argument matching; that is, by checking the parameters of functions that have the same name to see if ambiguities can be resolved.

The compiler also uses another test to see if function-name collisions can be avoided. For example, if a member function is overridden by more than one object in a straight chain of inheritance, and is then called from an object lower in the chain, the compiler executes the function that is closest in the chain to the calling object—that is, the one that appears just above the calling object in the inheritance chain.

If ambiguities in function names cannot be resolved through argument matching, or by using the "closest function" mechanism, the compiler returns an error.

Listing 19.4 is almost identical to the program presented earlier in Listing 19.3. But two function-name ambiguities, clearly marked with `WARNING` comments, have been intentionally added to Listing 19.4

**Listing 19.4. Multiple inheritance: ambiguities in function names.**

```
// 1904.CPP
// Demonstrating Multiple Inheritance

#include <iostream.h>

class Animal {
public:
     void General()
          { cout << "I'm a sentient creature.\n"; }
};

class Bird: virtual public Animal {
public:
     void Mouth()
          { cout << "I have a beak.\n"; }
     void BirthMethod()
          { cout << "I lay eggs.\n"; }
     void Coat()
          { cout << "I have feathers.\n"; }
};

class Duck: public Bird {
public:
     void Mouth()
          { cout << "I have a bill.\n"; }
     void Coat()
          { cout << "I have oiled feathers.\n"; } // WARNING: Ambiguity!
};

class Mammal: virtual public Animal {
public:
     void Coat()
          { cout << "I have fur.\n"; }     // WARNING: Ambiguity!
};

class Platypus: public Mammal, public Duck {
public:
     void What()
          { cout << "What am I?\n"; }
     void Conclusion()
          { cout << "I'm a duckbilled platypus.\n"; }
};

int main()
{
     Platypus mysteryBeast;
```

*continues*

**Listing 19.4. continued**

```
    mysteryBeast.What();
    mysteryBeast.General();
    mysteryBeast.Coat();
    mysteryBeast.Mouth();
    mysteryBeast.BirthMethod();
    mysteryBeast.Conclusion();

    return 0;
}
```

In Listing 19.4, the `Coat()` function in the `Duck` class collides with the `Coat()` function in the `Mammal` class, so the compiler doesn't know which `Coat()` function it should compile. A compiler error is returned.

If you remove the `Coat()` function from the `Duck` class, and then try to compile the program, the `Coat()` function in the `Bird` class collides with the `Coat()` function in the `Mammal` class, so the compiler still doesn't know which `Coat()` function to compile. So, again, a compiler error is returned.

If you remove the `Coat()` function from the `Animal` class, but leave it standing in the `Bird` and `Duck` classes, no ambiguity arises. The compiler simply executes the `Coat()` function that's closest to the calling object in the inheritance chain. It ignores the `Bird` class version of the `Coat()` function, and executes the version that is defined by the `Duck` class. This is the printout that results:

```
What am I?
I'm a sentient creature.
I have oiled feathers.
I have a bill.
I lay eggs.
I'm a duckbilled platypus.
```

Everything seems to be working fine now—until you read the preceding printout. There's something wrong there. The third line says that a platypus has oiled feathers, and that isn't right; a platypus has fur, as the program correctly asserted before we started fooling with it. Now, although the program's code contains no function-name ambiguities, the program itself produces an incorrect result.

To sum up: Multiple inheritance can be a powerful tool, but be careful with it. In a C++ program, as in life, the more power you have at your disposal, the easier it is to misuse it, and the more serious a mistake can be.

# Summary

This chapter covered two very important C++ features: inheritance and polymorphism. Inheritance is the feature of C++ that allows classes to inherit behaviors from other classes and to modify those behaviors. Polymorphism is the feature of the language that lets different objects call different functions using the same name. This chapter is a closeup examination of inheritance and polymorphism. Major topics covered in this chapter included:

- *derived classes*: the keys to inheritance.
- *virtual functions* (functions that can be overridden): virtual functions are the key to polymorphism.
- *multiple inheritance*: a feature that lets objects inherit from more than one class.

This chapter completes the portion of this volume that covers the object-oriented features of C++. There is one more chapter in Part II—Chapter 20—but it deals with the Visual C++ `iostream` library, a special C++ library that contains input and output classes. It does not introduce any more features of the C++ language.

Chapter 20

# Streams

The C language has always handled input and output in an odd way, and C++ continues that tradition.

As you know if you're a C programmer, C doesn't have any built-in input or output capabilities—and neither does C++. To manage disk, display, and keyboard input and output in C, you must use the functions in C's familiar (and, some might say, infamous) run-time I/O library: functions such as `printf()`, `scanf()`, `_open()`, `_read()`, `fwrite()`, and `getchar()`. C++ handles I/O operations differently.

To manage input and output, C++ uses a special kind of mechanism called a *stream*. A stream is a series of bytes that can be used as either a source or a destination for data.

The `iostream` classes supplied with C++ are easier to use than the `printf()` and `scanf()` family of functions that are used for file management in C. The `iostream` classes also have stricter type-checking mechanisms than the functions in C's `printf()` and `scanf()` family, and therefore cause fewer programming errors.

Streams have one other advantage over C-style output functions. Streams make use of class inheritance and polymorphism, so when you manage I/O with member functions of `iostream` classes, you can use fewer functions to perform more actions.

When you use streams, you don't have to use one function (for example, `printf()`) to write data to an output device and another function (for example, `fprintf()`) to send output to a file. With stream-based I/O, you can use the same function (for example, `cout.write()`) to perform both kinds of operations.

With the I/O classes provided by C++, an application can do the following:

- Read data from standard input, such as the keyboard, a device driver, or a communications port.
- Write data to standard output, such as a monitor, a printer, or a communications device.
- Direct I/O errors and direct error messages to an output device such as a monitor or printer.
- Manage buffered and unbuffered input and output.
- Format text output so that different data types (including user-defined data types) are printed correctly and in a readable form.
- Print formatted columns in various widths, with left or right justifications, and using any desired padding character, in accordance with instructions provided in the application being executed.
- Print floating-point numbers using a specified number of decimal places.
- Print non-floating-point numbers using a specified number of significant digits.
- Read input and write output in accordance with special instructions, such as instructions to recognize or skip over white space, or instructions to recognize or skip over specified end-of-line characters.
- Perform various kinds of file-related input and output operations.

This chapter explains how the `iostream` classes perform these kinds of operations, and how you can use the `iostream` classes in your applications.

# How the iostream Classes Work

All C++ compilers—including the Visual C++ compiler—come bundled with a prewritten package of C++ classes that can be used to manage I/O using streams. Not surprisingly, these classes are known as `iostream` classes.

The `iostream` classes manage input and output by using various tools, such as:

- *Stream operators* such as `cin >>` and `cout <<`.
- *Manipulators,* or special members of stream classes that provide various text-formatting capabilities.
- *Member functions* of stream classes.

It's important to note, however, that the `iostream` classes are designed mainly to support text-based input and output, not Windows-based operations. The `iostream` classes work well in DOS-based programs. The classes also work well in Visual C++ programs that are compiled and linked using the Microsoft QuickWin library (as explained in Chapter 1, "Microsoft Visual C++").

Suppose you want to develop Windows-based programs with Visual C++—using the broad range of graphics tools that Windows offers. You'll probably find that it's easier to ignore the I/O classes and to handle input and output with the I/O-related classes that Microsoft supplies in another C++ library: the Microsoft Foundation Class (MFC) library.

The MFC library—described in Part III of this book—was designed specifically to support the creation of Windows-based, object-oriented programs. Generally speaking, the classes supplied in the MFC library are better tools for writing Windows-based programs than the `iostream` classes are.

With the classes defined in the MFC library, applications can perform interactive I/O with the computer user by displaying dialog boxes, menus, and other interactive tools. To manage file and disk I/O, and to move data into and out of memory, the MFC library supplies a base class named `CFile`, which has many subclasses that can be used for memory- and disk-based I/O operations.

Because most kinds of I/O operations can be performed by the classes in the MFC library, you'll probably use the `iostream` classes only when you want to write prototype or test programs using the QuickWin library, or when you want to handle file or disk I/O at a lower level than you can with the classes in the MFC library.

Nonetheless, the information in this chapter is valuable—not only because you may someday have a use for an `iostream` class, but also because many of the features of the I/O classes in the MFC library are modeled after features in the `iostream` classes. In fact, the I/O classes in the MFC library use the `iostream` classes internally, so learning about the `iostream` classes can help you understand how the classes in the Microsoft Foundation Class library manage I/O.

Because the `iostream` classes are used only for special purposes in Windows-related programs, this chapter provides only a general overview of the Microsoft `iostream` class library. More detailed information on `iostream` classes is provided in books about text-based implementations of C++. Many general books about C++ are listed in the Bibliography.

### THE IOSTREAM LIBRARY AND VISUAL C++

Although the classes in the `iostream` library are generally more useful in text-based programs than they are in Windows-based programs, the `iostream` library can be used in Windows-based programs under some circumstances.

You may occasionally want to use an `iostream` object in a Windows-based program because the `iostream` classes can sometimes control I/O operations at a lower level than the I/O classes supplied in the MFC library. If you know how the I/O stream classes work, you can do that easily, because Windows-based applications can use string- and file-related `iostream` classes without any restrictions in Windows-based programs.

Other kinds of `iostream` objects—such as the character-mode objects `cin` and `cout`—are more difficult to use in Windows-based programs. However, you can override the extraction (>>) and insertion (<<) operators by writing customized functions that make calls to the Windows system. By overriding the >> and << operators, you can use the `iostream` classes to support graphical-user interfaces such as Windows, or even to manage communications between Windows processes. One possible reason for overriding the >> and << operators might be to port an old application written for a text-based implementation of C++.

Another possible way to use `cin` and `cout` in a Windows-based program might be to create document windows in which the user can type text. That's a technique that might come in handy if, for example, you wanted to write a text-editor application in Visual C++.

The most important thing to remember about the `iostream` classes is that they offer object-oriented *alternatives* to the I/O classes defined in the MFC library, as well as alternatives to the standard C-language I/O functions (such as `printf()` and `_read`) that are defined in the STDIO.H library. There is no rule that you have to use the `iostream` classes in your Visual C++ programs, but there's also no rule that says you can't. So don't ignore the `iostream` classes completely; they may come in handy one day when you want to do something special in a Visual C++ program.

# The iostream Library

The `iostream` classes that are supplied with C++ manage input and output operations using mechanisms that are similar to those used in file-management operations. The `iostream` classes, however, extend the concept of a file to include I/O devices such as keyboards, monitors, printers, and even communication ports.

In the `iostream` system, all these sources and destinations of data are grouped together in a single category: the *stream*. The `iostream` classes are simply classes that are designed to interact with streams.

## Stream-Related Header Files

The input and output functions that are used most often in C-language programs are defined in a header file named STDIO.H; therefore, most applications that are written in C include the STDIO.H library.

Most of the `iostream` classes that are used in C++ are defined in a header file named IOSTREAM.H. Similarly, the `iostream` file that is most often included in C++ programs is IOSTREAM.H.

To use the classes that are defined in the Microsoft `iostream` library, you must include the appropriate header files in your applications. The IOSTREAM.H is included in most C++ programs because it defines the most commonly used `iostream` objects: `cin`, `cout`, `cerr`, and `clog`. Another file that's often included in programs is IOMANIP.H, which defines a set of data members called *manipulators* that you can invoke to perform various kinds of formatting functions. Manipulators are described in more detail under a separate heading in this section.

Other libraries that applications often include are FSTREAM.H file, which contains member functions for performing file I/O operations, and STRSTREAM.H, which provides classes for performing string manipulations.

STRSTREAM.H, FSTREAM.H, and IOMANIP.H all include the IOSTREAM.H file; therefore, if you include STRSTREAM.H or IOMANIP.H in an application, the application does not have to include the IOSTREAM.H file separately.

## The Microsoft iostream Class Library

The version of the `iostream` library that comes with Visual C++ is officially known as the Microsoft `iostream` Class Library. The Microsoft `iostream` Class Library contains more classes than the `iostream` library that is supplied with most implementations of C++. These classes extend the capabilities of C++'s `iostream` classes so they can be used to perform more kinds of operations than the classes defined in most other C++ packages.

For example, the Microsoft `iostream` Class Library contains classes that support reading from memory and writing to memory using the same syntax that can be used to manage disk I/O. The Microsoft `iostream` library also offers more sophisticated buffering capabilities than the `iostream` libraries that are provided with most other implementations of C++.

## The iostream Hierarchy

The Microsoft `iostream` Class Library is arranged in two separate hierarchies, which are illustrated in Figure 20.1. The more complex of the two hierarchies, which appears at the top of Figure 20.1, is used for formatted I/O. The other hierarchy, in the lower left-hand part of the illustration, manages unformatted I/O.

The `ios` class is the base class for formatted I/O classes. The `streambuf` class is the base class for unformatted I/O classes.

A class named `iostream_init`, which falls into neither hierarchy, is shown in the bottom right-hand corner of the diagram. The `iostream` class library uses the `iostream_init` class internally to initialize the stream objects `cin`, `cout`, `cerr`, and `clog`.

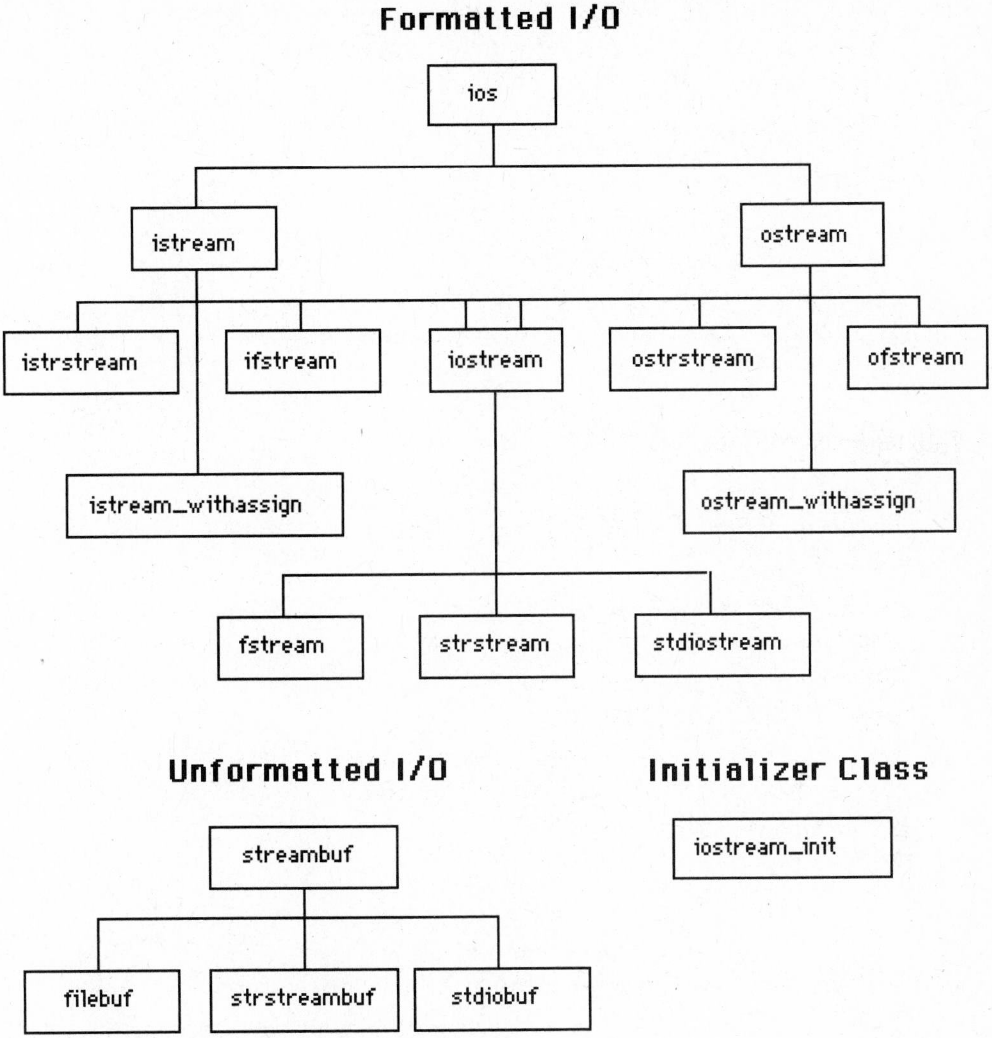


*Figure 20.1. The iostream library.*

## The ios Class and Its Subclasses

Two classes descend directly from the `ios` class: the `istream` class, which provides classes that manage only input, and the `ostream` class, which contains classes that manage only output.

When you need a single class that can perform both input and output operations, you must move one step down the `iostream` tree and find an object of the `iostream` class—which inherits from both the `istream` and `ostream` classes.

Besides classes that perform input and output, the `iostream` class libraries contain classes that are specially designed to

- Perform file I/O.
- Perform operations using I/O streams of character arrays.
- Interface stream-classes with the C-style I/O operations defined in the STDIO.H library.

## The cin and cout Objects

Although it's possible to create your own `iostream` classes, it's far more common to manage I/O with predefined objects that are provided in the Microsoft `iostream` Class Library.

For instance, the stream objects `cin` and `cout`—which are often used in C++ programs—are *predefined stream objects*. The `cin` class is derived from an `istream` subclass named `istream_withassign`, and the `cout` class is derived from an `ostream` subclass named `ostream_withassign`.

> **CONSTRUCTING STREAM OBJECTS**
>
> If you use only predefined stream objects such as `cin` and `cout` objects in your programs—which is likely—you'll never have to worry about writing a constructor or a destructor for stream objects. If you use file streams or string streams, however, you'll have to construct objects.

## The istream and ostream Classes

The `ios` class—the base class in the formatted I/O hierarchy—contains status flags, format flags, operator functions, and many member variables and member functions that are inherited by other classes. Applications do not usually construct `ios` objects, but they do use many member variables and member functions that are inherited by subclasses.

Two classes—`istream` and `ostream`—inherit from the `ios` class. The `istream` and `ostream` classes have subclasses that are specially designed to handle file and string-array input and output. One subclass, `iostream`, is derived from both the `istream` class and the `ostream` class. The `iostream` class has three subclasses of its own that can manage file input and output and string-array input and output.

## The iostream Hierarchy Illustrated

Table 20.1 lists and describes classes that perform formatted I/O. Table 20.2 lists and describes classes used for unformatted I/O.

The `streambuf` class, the base class in the unformatted I/O hierarchy, has three subclasses:

- `filebuf`, which provides a buffer for file input and output;
- `strstreambuf`, which provides a buffer for string-array input and output;
- `stdiobuf`, which provides a buffer that is compatible with the C-style I/O functions defined in the STDIO.H header file.

**Table 20.1. Classes for performing formatted I/O.**

| *Class* | *Description* |
|---|---|
| `ios` | The `ios` class is the base class from which all formatted I/O classes are derived. Although `ios` is not technically an abstract class, applications do not ordinarily construct `ios` objects or derive classes directly from `ios`. Instead, applications usually use classes derived from `istream`, `ostream`, or other sublcasses of `ios`. From the `ios` base class, these subclasses are derived: |
| `istream` | The `istream` class, a subclass of `ios`, overloads the extraction operator (>>) to read data from standard input. The `istream` class supplies overloaded >> operators that can read all the standard C++ data types. The >> operator can also be overloaded to read data from user-defined objects. |

*continues*

**Table 20.1. continued**

| *Class* | *Description* |
|---|---|
| `ostream` | The `ostream` class, derived from the `ios` class, manages stream output in the same way that the `istream` class manages input. It overloads the insertion operator (<<) to write data to standard output using the `cout`, `cerr`, and `clog` classes. The `cout`, `cerr`, and `clog` classes are defined by the `ostream_withassign` class, a subclass of `ostream` (see next entry). The `ostream` class supplies overloaded << (insertion) operators for formatting all the standard C++ data types. The << operator can also be overloaded to write formatted output defined by user-defined objects. |
| `istream_withassign` | The `istream_withassign` class, a subclass of `istream`, defines the stream object `cin`—which reads data for standard output using the extraction operator (>>). |
| `ostream_withassign` | The `ostream_withassign` class, a subclass of `ostream`, defines the stream objects `cout`, `cerr`, and `clog`. Objects of the `clog` class write to the standard error device using buffered output. (Buffered output is handled by the `filebuf` class, described in a separate item later in this list). Objects of the `cerr` class write to the standard error device using unbuffered output. The `cout`, `cerr`, and `clog` classes use the << operator (see previous entry) to write data to standard output. |
| `istrstream` | The `istrstream` class, derived from the `istream` class, manages stream input from character arrays. Before you construct an `istrstream` object, you must allocate a character array. You can then use `istrstream` operators and member functions to retrieve character data stored in that array. |

| *Class* | *Description* |
|---|---|
| `ifstream` | The `ifstream` class is an `istream` subclass designed for disk-file input. (Combined disk-file input and output is provided by the `fstream` class, described in a following separate entry.) The `ifstream` class provides the `istream` class with pointers for retrieving data from buffers. The buffers themselves and the functions used for opening and closing files are provided by the `filebuf` class (see Table 20.2). |
| `ostrstream` | The `ostrstream` class, derived from the `ostream` class, manages stream out for character arrays. Before you construct an `ostrstream` object, you can either allocate a character array or let the `ostrstream` constructor allocate an expandable array. You can then use `ostrstream` operators and member functions to fill that array. |
| `ofstream` | The `ofstream` class is an `ostream` subclass designed for performing disk-file output. (Combined disk-file input and output is provided by the `fstream` class, described in a following separate entry.) When you create an `ofstream` object, the object's constructor creates an object of the `filebuf` class (see Table 20.2) and associates that object with a stream. The buffer area itself is provided by the `filebuf` object. The `ofstream` class provides the `ostream` class with pointers for storing data in the buffer provided by the `filebuf` object. |

*continues*

**Table 20.1. continued**

| *Class* | *Description* |
|---|---|
| `iostream` | The `iostream` class, a subclass of both `istream` and `ostream`, provides the `iostream` classes with their basic capabilities for both sequential and random-access I/O. The `iostream` class works in conjunction with the `streambuf` class (see Table 20.2); in fact, although `ios` classes supply the programming interface and all formatting features for I/O operations, objects of the `streambuf` class and its subclasses do most of the work. Applications do not usually deal directly with the `iostream` class in basic I/O operations. Instead, they generally interface with the `fstream` class (see next entry), which derives from `iostream`. |
| `fstream` | The `fstream` class, derived from `iostream`, is an `iostream` subclass that is specialized for combined disk-file input and output. When you create an `fstream` object, the object's constructor creates an object of the `filebuf` class (see Table 20.2) and associates that object with a stream. The `fstream` class provides the `iostream` class with pointers that can be used for storing data in buffers provided by the `filebuf` class and for retrieving data from those buffers. The buffers themselves and the functions used for opening and closing files are provided by the `filebuf` class (see Table 20.2). |
| `stdiostream` | The `stdiostream` class, a subclass of `iostream`, can be used to interface `iostream` classes with standard C-language I/O functions defined in the STDIO.H file. Objects of the `stdiostream` class make I/O calls through the `stdiobuf` class (see separate entry) to the standard C-language I/O system. Calls, thus, that are defined STDIO.H, such as `printf()`, can be mixed with `stdiostream` I/O calls. |

**Table 20.2. Unformatted I/O classes.**

| *Class* | *Description* |
|---|---|
| `streambuf` | The `streambuf` class is the base class in a hierarchy of unformatted I/O classes. Objects derived from the `streambuf` class and its subclasses do the actual I/O processing for all subclasses of the base class `ios`. When you use an `ios`-derived object to manage I/O, an associated `streambuf` object is always constructed. That object supplies a stream connection in the form of an I/O buffer that can be partitioned into read and write areas. Objects of the `streambuf` class also contain read and write pointers, input and output mechanisms, functions to move the read and write pointers, and functions for basic reporting and error reporting. When you read or write data using an `ios`-derived object, the `ios` hierarchy supplies the programming interface and all formatting features, but the `streambuf` class and its subclasses do the actual I/O work. The `streambuf` class is an abstract class; applications ordinarily access the functionality of `streambuf` through three `streambuf` subclasses: `filebuf`, `strstreambuf`, and `stdiobuf`. |
| `filebuf` | The `filebuf` class, a subclass of `streambuf`, is the buffer class for disk-file I/O. The `filebuf` class supplies the `streambuf` class with memory areas that are used for file buffering and with functions for opening and closing files. |
| `strstreambuf` | The `strstreambuf` class, a subclass of `streambuf`, provides and manages a text buffer for storing strings. The file classes `ostrstream`, `istrstream`, and `strstreambuf` (see separate entries) use member functions of `strstreambuf` to fetch and store characters. Some of these member functions are virtual member functions of the `streambuf` class. |
| `stdiobuf` | The `stdiobuf` class, a subclass of `streambuf`, provides `streambuf` with an interface to the standard C-language I/O functions defined in the header file STDIO.H. The `stdiobuf` supplies `streambuf` with buffers that are specially designed to handle buffering to and from pointers to the `FILE` data types used by the standard C-language I/O system. |

# Using Streams

Besides defining special classes that can be used in I/O operations, the `iostream` library overloads the C-language operators >> and << to give them special behaviors when they are used in I/O operations.

In C, as you may know, >> and << are *bitwise operators;* they are used to shift the bits in a binary value to the right or to the left. In C++, the >> and << operators work the same as they do in C, but only when they are called on to perform their traditional bit-shifting operations. When the >> and << operators are used with `iostream` objects such as `cout` and `cin`, they become `iostream` operators and take on completely different behaviors.

When >> is used as an extraction operator by a stream class, it reads (or *extracts*) data to a stream from standard output. Similarly, when << is used as an insertion operator, it writes (or *inserts*) data to a stream and generates standard output.

The >> (extraction) operator is used to read data *from* standard input, normally the keyboard. You can read text that the user keys in by following the name of the `cin` object with the >> operator, as in this example:

```
cin >> x;
```

The << (insertion) operator is used to write data *to* standard input, such as a monitor, a printer, or a communications port. The extraction operator is often used with the `iostream` object `cin`, which reads data from standard input, normally the keyboard. The insertion operator (<<) is used most often with the `iostream` object `cout`, which writes data to standard output, usually a printer, a communications port, or the screen.

As you have seen in many example programs in this book, you can display text on the screen by following the word `cout` with the << operator and the text that you want displayed:

```
cout << "Hello, Visual C++";
```

### THE CERR AND CLOG OBJECTS

In text-based implementations of C++, the stream objects `cerr` and `clog` are often used with the insertion operator (<<) to write error messages to a specified error device. The stream object `cerr` can write messages to an error device using unbuffered output, and the object `clog` can write messages to an error device using buffered output.

The cerr and clog objects were designed for text-based implementations of C++ and are rarely used in Windows-based programs. The MFC library supplies an exception-handling utility that is better suited to Windows programming than cerr and clog, and is also more powerful.)

## Mixing Data Types in Streams

When you use the insertion operator (<<) in a C++ statement, you can follow it with any built-in data type. The extraction operator recognizes all built-in data types and can format them correctly when it generates its output. When you want to write multiple data types to the same output stream, all you have to do is use a separate insertion operator for each data type that you use. For example, the program in Listing 20.1 writes a string, an integer, and another string (which contains a period and a newline character).

**Listing 20.1. Mixing data types in a stream.**

```
#include <iostream.h>

int main()
{
     int price = 65;

     cout << "The price is $" << price << ".\n";

     return 0;
}
```

In Listing 20.1, notice that the strings to be written are enclosed in double quotation marks—the standard syntax for placing strings in statements in C++ and C. When the insertion operator is followed by a series of characters enclosed in double quotation marks, the compiler knows that the characters should be printed as a string. The output of the preceding program is therefore:

```
The price is $65.
```

If the insertion operator is followed by a character enclosed in single quotation marks—the standard syntax for placing a character in a C or C++ statement—

the compiler prints a character. Listing 20.2, thus, prints the character `C`, followed by a newline character (`\n`):

**Listing 20.2. Printing a single character.**

```
#include <iostream.h>

int main()
{
     cout << 'C' << '\n';

     return 0;
}
```

## Formatting Output

The stream object `cout`—like the `printf()` function used in C—can produce formatted output. To control the output of the `cout` object, you can set or clear 15 different flags that are defined by the `ios` class. Some of these flags, such as `hex`, `dec`, `scientific`, and `fixed` define the format that is used to write a single value. Other flags perform other kinds of formatting operations. The 15 formatting flags provided by the `ios` class are listed in Table 20.3.

**Table 20.3. Formatting flags provided by the `ios` class.**

| *Flag* | *Description* |
|---|---|
| skipws | Skips white space. |
| left | Left-aligns output; pads on the right with a fill character. |
| right | Right-aligns output; pads on the left with a fill character (default alignment). |
| internal | Adds fill characters after any leading sign or base indication, but before the value being written. |
| dec | Formats numeric values as decimal (base 10) (default radix). |
| oct | Formats numeric values as octal (base 8). |
| hex | Formats numeric values as hexadecimal (base 16). |

| *Flag* | *Description* |
|---|---|
| showbase | Displays numeric constants in a format that can be read by the C++ compiler. |
| showpoint | Shows decimal point and trailing zeroes for floating-point values. |
| uppercase | Displays uppercase A through F for hexadecimal values and E for scientific values. |
| showpos | Shows plus sign (+) for positive values. |
| scientific | Displays floating-point numbers in scientific format. |
| fixed | Displays floating-point numbers in `fixed` format. |
| unitbuf | Causes the `ostream::osfx()` function (the *output suffix function,* called after every insertion) to flush the stream after each insertion (by default, `cerr` is unbuffered). |
| stdio | Causes `ostream::osfx` to flush `stdout` and `stderr` after each insertion. |

Each of the 15 flags listed in Table 20.3 is a bit in a `long` member variable of the `ios` class. By setting and clearing these bits, you can format the output of `cout`.

You can use two mechanisms to set or clear the `cout` flags provided by the `ios` class. One of these tools is a special kind of class member called a *manipulator*. Alternatively, you can set or clear the `ios` class's flags by calling member functions of the `ios` class.

## Manipulators

A *manipulator* is a word that you can place in a stream to tell the compiler how you want the next element in the stream formatted. You can place more than one manipulator in a statement that uses a `cout <<` operator; however, each time you use a manipulator in a statement, you must precede the manipulator with its own << operator. The manipulator then sets an `ios` flag to control the formatting of any data that follows.

In the Microsoft `iostream` Class Library, manipulators are defined by the `ios`, `istream`, and `ostream` classes. Table 20.4 lists and describes the `ios`, `istream`, and `ostream` manipulators used in Visual C++.

**Table 20.4. Stream manipulators.**

| *Class* | *Manipulator* | *Description* |
|---|---|---|
| ios | binary | Sets the stream's format mode to binary (the default mode is text). |
| ios | dec | Sets the stream's mode to decimal (base 10). |
| ios | hex | Sets the stream's mode to hexadecimal (base 16). |
| ios | oct | Sets the stream's mode to octal (base 8). |
| ios | resetiosflags | Resets the `ios` class's formatting flags (listed in Table 20.3). |
| ios | setfill | Sets the fill character to be used as padding between fields (default fill character is a space). |
| ios | setiosflags | Sets the `ios` class's formatting flags (listed in Table 20.3). |
| ios | setprecision | Sets the number of decimal places or the number of significant digits to be displayed. If the display format is scientific or fixed, `setprecision` sets the number of digits to be displayed after the decimal point. If the format is automatic—neither floating-point nor fixed—`setprecision` sets the number of significant digits. Default is six digits. |
| ios | setw | Sets the field width in characters. |
| ios | text | Sets the stream's format mode to text (the default mode). |
| istream | ws | Extracts leading white spaces from the stream. |
| ostream | endl | Inserts a newline character into the output stream and then clears the stream buffer. |
| ostream | ends | Inserts a null-terminator character into the output stream. |
| ostream | flush | Flushes the output stream buffer. |

### Using Manipulators

Listing 20.3 is a program that shows how you can use manipulators with the stream object `cout`.

#### Listing 20.3. Using manipulators.

```
#include <iostream.h>

unsigned int main()
{
     int value = 65535;

     cout << dec << value << ' ' << hex << value;
     cout << '\n';

     return 0;
}
```

The program in Listing 20.3 prints the decimal number `65535`, the same value expressed as a hexadecimal number (`ffff`), and a return character. The output of the program is as follows:

```
65535 ffff
```

### Defining Your Own Manipulators

In the Microsoft `iostream` Class Library, manipulators are defined using this syntax:

```
ios& hex {
     // body of definition
};
```

As you can see, the first line of a manipulator definition has two parts: a reference to the class that the manipulator belongs to and the name of the manipulator. The preceding code fragment shows the structure of the predefined manipulator `hex`, which is a member of the `ios` class.

If you don't find the manipulator that you need in the 15 predefined manipulators listed in Table 20.4, you can define your own manipulators. The procedure for defining customized manipulators is described in the *iostream Class Library Reference* that is supplied with Microsoft Visual C++.

## Member Functions of Stream Classes

Another way to control the output of cout is to call a member function of the cout class. Two cout member functions can format output: setf() and unsetf(). You can set a flag by passing it as a parameter to cout.setf(), and you can clear a flag by passing it as a parameter to cout.unsetf().

The member-function method of setting flags is wordier than the manipulator method, but you might prefer it in some circumstances—for example, when you want to make it clear in your source code that a particular flag has a particular setting.

Listing 20.4 uses the cout.setf() and cout.unsetf() member functions to print a number in both the decimal and hexadecimal formats. It also issues the call cout.setf(ios::uppercase) to make the hexadecimal letters A through F print in uppercase.

### Listing 20.4. Using setf() and unsetf().

```
#include <iostream.h>

int main()
{
     unsigned int value = 65535;

     cout.setf(ios::dec);
     cout << value << '\n';
     cout.unsetf(ios::dec);
     cout.setf(ios::hex);
     cout.setf(ios::uppercase);
     cout << value << '\n';

     return 0;
}
```

The output of the program in Listing 20.4 is as follows:

```
65535
FFFF
```

When you use member functions rather than manipulators to set and clear ios flags, you must clear any flag that is set before you set another flag. That's why the preceding program calls the unset() function to clear the ios::dec flag before it calls the set() function to set the ios::hex flag. If that step is not taken, the ios::hex flag is not set.

To make it easier to clear flags before they are reset, the `ios` class provides a two-parameter version of the `cout.setf()` function. When you call `cout.setf()` with two parameters, the first parameter specifies the flag that you want set, and the second parameter is a 16-bit mask that you can use as a bit filter by placing a 1 in each bit field that is to be set. Listing 20.5 shows how you can use the bitwise OR operator (¦) to combine two or more values that are supplied for the second parameter.

### Listing 20.5. Mixing data types in a stream.

```
#include <iostream.h>

int main()
{
     unsigned int value = 65535;

     cout.setf(ios::dec);
     cout << value << '\n';
     cout.setf(ios::hex, ios::hex ¦ ios::dec);
     cout.setf(ios::uppercase);
     cout << value << '\n';

     return 0;
}
```

In Listing 20.5, the `ios` formatting flag is set for decimal output, and a value is then printed in decimal format:

```
cout.setf(ios::dec);
```

This statement clears the `ios` flag and resets it for hexadecimal output:

```
cout.setf(ios::hex, ios::hex ¦ ios::dec);
```

To understand how the preceding statement works, you have to understand how binary OR operations work. If binary math is not your strong point, you still have two other options for clearing and setting `ios` flags; you can use manipulators, or you can set and clear the flags manually, as demonstrated in the previous examples. The results are identical; in fact, the program in Listing 20.5 has the same output as the program presented earlier in Listing 20.4:

```
65535
FFFF
```

# Setting Output Width

You can specify a default width for each item displayed in an output stream by inserting the `setw` manipulator into the stream or by calling the `cout.width()` member function. When you invoke the `setw` manipulator or call `cout.width()`, the output of `cout` is right-aligned and can specify a column width of any size you want, expressed as a number of characters.

Both the `setw` manipulator and the `cout.width()` member function take a *width* parameter (expressed as a number of characters). The width of the output column is set to the number of characters specified by the *width* parameter.

## The cout.width() Function

The program in Listing 20.6 sets the width of an output stream by calling `cout.width()`.

**Listing 20.6. Setting output width with the `cout.width()` function.**

```
// 2006.CPP
// Using the cout.width() member function

#include <iostream.h>

int main()
{
    cout.setf(ios::fixed, ios::scientific);
    static double values[] = { 3.146, 32, 44.99, 98.6 };
    for (int i = 0; i < 4; i++)    {
          cout.width(10);
          cout << values[i] << "\n";
    }
    return 0;
}
```

This is the output of the program:

```
3.146
   32
44.99
 98.6
```

Notice that the numbers printed by Listing 20.6 are right-justified and have no set number of digits following the decimal point.

Before the program calls `cout.width()`, it makes a call to the two-parameter version of the `cout.setf()` function. As noted earlier in this section, when `cout.width()` is called with two parameters, the first parameter tells the compiler what bits to set, and the second parameter specifies flags that are to be cleared.

In this case, the first parameter calls for a `fixed` output, and the second parameter calls for a scientific output. The second parameter prevents the program from placing trailing zeroes after the numbers that are printed. If the `cout.setf()` function in Listing 20.6 is called *without* a second parameter, in this fashion

```
cout.setf(ios::fixed);
```

no flags will be cleared, so the output of Listing 20.6 will be

```
 3.146000
32.000000
44.990000
98.600000
```

## The setprecision Manipulator

If you like the looks of the preceding output, but would rather print fewer zeroes, you can invoke the `ios` class manipulator `setprecision`, which is described under a separate heading later in this chapter. With the `setprecision` manipulator, you can format `cout` to print floating-point numbers using as few (or as many) decimal places as you like. Listing 20.7 shows how you can use the `setprecision` manipulator in a Visual C++ program.

### Listing 20.7. The `setprecision` manipulator.

```
// 2007.CPP
// Using the cout.width() member function

#include <iomanip.h>

int main()
{
    cout.setf(ios::fixed);
    static double values[] = { 3.146, 32, 44.99, 98.6 };
    for (int i = 0; i < 4; i++)     {
          cout.width(10);
          cout << setprecision(2);
          cout << values[i] << "\n";
    }
    return 0;
}
```

This is the output of the program:

```
 3.15
32.00
44.99
98.60
```

## The setw Manipulator

If you don't want to use the `cout.width()` function, you can set the width of the output stream with the `ios` manipulator `setw`. The `setw` manipulator is more convenient than the `cout.width()` function in some situations, for example, when you want to print more than one column per line. Listing 20.8 shows how a Visual C++ program can use the `setw` manipulator.

**Listing 20.8. Setting output width with the `setw` manipulator.**

```
// 2008.CPP
// The setw manipulator

#include <iomanip.h>

int main()
{
    cout.setf(ios::hex);
    cout.setf(ios::uppercase);
    static int AGE[] = { 0x038, 0x036, 0x034, 0x042 };
    static char *names[] = {"Pam", "Mike", "Tanya", "Robert"};
    for (int i = 0; i < 4; i++)
          cout << setw(6)  << names[i]
              << setw(10) << SIZE[i] << '\n';
    return 0;
}
```

This is the output of the program in Listing 20.8:

```
   Pam       38
  Mike       36
 Tanya       34
Robert       42
```

> **FORMATTING NOTE**
>
> The `width()` function affects only one field: the field that immediately follows it. The same restriction applies when you use the `setw` manipulator. When one field has been printed, the field width reverts to its default behavior, which means that the fields have the same width as their contents. The `width()` function and the `setw` manipulator are the only stream-formatting options that have this behavior; all other stream-formatting options remain in effect until they are explicitly changed.

## Setting the Padding Character

When a field in a stream does not fill its allotted space, the default behavior of the `cout <<` operator is to pad the unfilled spaces with the space character. You can call the `cout.fill()` function to pad unfilled spaces in fields to a different character. Listing 20.9 shows how to change the padding character of the `cout <<` operator to an asterisk.

### Listing 20.9. Changing the padding character.

```
// 2009.CPP
// The setw manipulator

#include <iomanip.h>

int main()
{
    cout.setf(ios::hex);
    cout.setf(ios::uppercase);
    cout.fill('*');
    static int AGE[] = { 0x040, 0x038, 0x040, 0x032 };
    static char *names[] = {"Pam", "Mike", "Tanya", "Robert"};
    for (int i = 0; i < 4; i++)
          cout << setw(6)  << names[i]
                << setw(10) << SIZE[i] << '\n';
    return 0;
}
```

This is the output of the program in Listing 20.9:

```
***Pam*******40
**Mike*******38
*Tanya*******40
Robert*******32
```

# Alternatives to cin >> and cout <<

You may sometimes find that the `cin >>` and `cout >>` operators don't work exactly the way you want them to in a program. You may discover, for example, that `cin >>` handles spaces and return characters in ways that you may not expect.

When `cin >>` or `cout <<` don't give you the behavior you want, the `istream` class has several member functions you can use as alternatives to the `cin >>` and `cout <<` operators.

## Alternatives to the cin >> Operator

Listing 20.10 demonstrates one such problem. The program prompts you to type a certain number of names (you specify the number), and it echoes each name you type. When you finish typing names, the program prints the following:

```
That's all!
```

The 2010.CPP program works fine, as long as every name you type contains only a single word; the program can't handle multiple-word names. If you try to type a name that contains two or more words, the program interprets your entry as two names, and its counting system breaks down.

### Listing 20.10. A shortcoming of the `cin >>` operator.

```
// 2010.CPP
// Using the istream get member function

#include <iostream.h>

int main()
{
    char name[255];
    int x, n;
```

```
    cout << "How many names do you want to type? ";

    cin >> x;

    for (n = 0; n < x; n++) {
        cout << "Please type a name.\n";
        cin >> name;
        cout << "Name " << n+1 << " is " << name << '\n';
    }

    cout << "That's all!\a\n";

    return 0;
}
```

You can prevent the behavior shown in Listing 20.10 by rewriting the program to accept only one character of input at a time, as shown in Listing 20.11. Then, however, two other problems arise.

#### Listing 20.11. Solving one problem and creating two more.

```
// 2011.CPP
// The cout.get function

#include <iostream.h>

int main()
{
    char s[255], ch = 0, *cp;

    cout << " Type a sentence that ends with '.'\n>";
    cp = s;
    while (ch != '.')    {
        cin >> ch;
        *cp++ = ch;
    }

    *cp = '\0';
    cout << ' ' << s;

    return 0;
}
```

The program in Listing 20.11 works better than its predecessor, but it has two other shortcomings. One flaw is that you can't end a line of input with a return character. In this version of the program, the `cin >>` operator stops accepting input when it encounters a return character, so you must end the sentence you type with a period (`.`).

Another problem surfaces when you enter your line and the program prints what you've typed. When the program echoes your output, it drops spaces that you've typed. This sample session shows the output of 2011.CPP along with the user's input:

```
 Type a sentence that ends with '.'
>This sentence does that.
 Thissentencedoesthat.
```

In the preceding session log, the first line was generated by the computer; the second line was typed by the user; and the third line is the flawed echo printed by the program.

## The cin.get() Function

Listing 20.12 substitutes the `istream` member function `cin.get()` for the `cin >>` operator that was used in 2011.CPP. That solves one of the problems that arose in 2011.CPP, but the other problem remains.

### Listing 20.12. Solving one problem with `cin.get()`.

```
// 2012.CPP
// The cin.get function

#include <iostream.h>

int main()
{
    char s[255], ch = 0, *cp;

    cout << " Type a sentence that ends with '.'\n>";
    cp = s;
    while (ch != '.')    {
        cin.get(ch);
        *cp++ = ch;
    }

    *cp = '\0';
    cout << ' ' << s;

    return 0;
}
```

This is the output of the 2012.CPP program:

```
 Type a sentence that ends with '.'
>This sentence does that.
 This sentence does that.
```

As you can see, the 2012.CPP program doesn't strip the spaces out of its input, and that's an improvement. However, the other problem that was encountered in 2011.CPP still exists; when you respond to the prompt in 2012.CPP by typing a line of text, you still have to end the line with a period.

That's not the best way for the program to work; a period might be fine in some situations, but it is better if the program is versatile enough to enable you to end your input with a return character.

Fortunately, the `iostream` class library does provide a way to let a program treat a return character as an end-of-line character. In fact, there are several ways. Listing 20.13 shows one.

**Listing 20.13. Three problems solved.**

```
// 2013.CPP
// The cin.get function

#include <iostream.h>

int main()
{
    char line[255];

    cout << " Please type a line.\n>";
    cin.getline(line, 255, '\n');

    cout << ' ' << line;

    return 0;
}
```

## The cin.getline() Function

As you can see, the program in Listing 20.13 reads input by using the function `cin.getline()`, which takes three parameters: a `char` pointer, a string length (expressed in characters), and an end-of-line character. This log shows a sample of the program's output:

```
 Please type a line.
>George Washington Jefferson Clinton
 George Washington Jefferson Clinton
```

Although the `cin.getline()` function offers one solution to the previous problems involving spaces and return characters, the remedy shown in Listing 20.13 is not the only one. Both `cin.get()` and `cin.getline()` have several overloaded versions, and `cin.get()`, like `cin.getline()`, has several versions that can accept a return character as an end-of-line character.

In Listing 20.13, the `cin.getline()` function is used rather than `cin.get()` only because `cin.getline()` accepts a line of input more easily and elegantly than `cin.get()` can. All versions of the `cin.get()` and `cin.getline()` functions are listed in *iostream Class Library Reference.*

### The cin.read() Function

The `cin.read()` function is another `istream` member function that does not skip over white space. Unlike `cin.get()` and `cin.getline()`, the `cin.read()` function reads input data into a buffer. You can then write the contents of the buffer to some other output, such as the screen.

The `cin.read()` function is used most often with file-related operations, for example, to read data from a structure. A `cin.read()` function that reads data from a structure is written using this syntax:

```
cin.read((char *) &myStruct, sizeof myStruct);
```

If a statement like the preceding one appears in a program, all the data from `myStruct` is read into a buffer. The size of the structure is calculated by the `sizeof` keyword. When the data in the structure has been read, input stops.

## Alternatives to cout <<

The output of the `cout <<` operator is usually satisfactory for printing text to the screen; however, two `ostream` member functions `cout.put()` and `cout.write()` can be useful alternatives to `cout <<` in some situations. The `ostream` member functions `cout.put()` and `cout.write()` are used most often to write output to files.

## The cout.put() Function

The `cout.put()` member function writes a single character to the output stream. That means these two statements yield results if default formatting options are in effect.

```
cout.put('A');
cout << 'A';
```

If the formatting parameters *width* and *fill* are set to their default values (to the width of each field's contents and to spaces padded with the space character), the two preceding statements print a single character `A` to standard output. If the *width* and *fill* formatting parameters are set to nondefault values, they apply to the second statement, but not to the first one.

## The cout.write() Function

The `cout.write()` function writes a block of data to the output stream in binary format. The `cout.write()` function, thus, has a behavior similar to the `cout <<` operator. The `cout <<` operator, however, stops writing data when encountering a null character (`'0'`). In contrast, the `cout.write()` function takes the length of a block as a parameter and writes the specified number of characters, even if the data being written contains null characters. That means the `cout.write()` function can be useful when you need to write binary data to stream files.

The `cout.write()` function is used primarily in file-related operations. This is its syntax:

```
cout.write(char *dataPtr, int dataSize);
```

You can use C's `sizeof` function to calculate the value of the `dataSize` parameter, as in this example:

```
cout.write(char *dataPtr, sizeof myData);
```

If a statement like the preceding one appears in a program, the block of data that begins at the address specified by `dataPtr` is written to standard output. The `dataSize` parameter specifies the number of characters that are written. The `cout.write()` function writes the specified number of characters, even if the data being written includes return characters.

> **IMPORTANT**
>
> The first parameter passed to the `cout.write()` function must be either a pointer to a character or a pointer to an unsigned character. If you want `cout.write()` to write noncharacter data, you must cast the first parameter that you pass to the function as a pointer to a character or a pointer to an unsigned character, for example:
>
> ```
> cout.write((char *) &dataPtr, int dataSize);
> ```

# Overloading << and >>

The << and >> operators can format all predefined C++ data types. They can also be overloaded to format user-defined data types. (Overloading is covered in detail in Chapter 16, "Operating Overloading.")

## Overloading the << Operator

The program in Listing 20.14 overloads the << operator to format and print an object that belongs to a class named `Money`. The `Money` class has two data members that are integers. The program formats the data members of a `Money` object as a dollars-and-cents figure, and prints the result.

**Listing 20.14. Overloading the << operator.**

```
// 2014.CPP
// Overloading the << operator

#include <iostream.h>

class Money {
    int dollars, cents;
public:
    Money(int d, int c) { dollars = d; cents = c; }
    friend ostream& operator<< (ostream& os, Money& csh);
};
```

```
ostream& operator<< (ostream& os, Money& csh)
{
    os << '$' << csh.dollars << '.' << csh.cents;
    return os;
}

int main()
{
    Money csh(29, 95);
    cout << csh;
    return 0;
}
```

The output of the program in Listing 20.14 is as follows:

```
$29.95
```

## Overloading the >> Operator

You can overload the >> operator by writing a function that can read, recognize, and format the data members of a class. The program in Listing 20.15 reads, recognizes, and formats an object that belongs to the `Money` class. The program prompts the user to type two integers: one representing dollars and the other representing cents. The integers that the user types are then stored as the two data members of an object of the `Money` class.

### Listing 20.15. Overloading the >> operator.

```
// 2015.CPP
// Overloading the >> operator

#include <iostream.h>

class Money {
    int dollars, cents;
public:
    Money() {}
    friend ostream& operator<< (ostream& os, Money& csh);
    friend istream& operator>> (istream& is, Money& csh);
};
```

*continues*

**Listing 20.15. continued**

```
ostream& operator<< (ostream& os, Money& csh)
{
    os << '$' << csh.dollars << '.' << csh.cents;
    return os;
}

istream& operator>> (istream& is, Money& csh)
{
    is >> csh.dollars >> csh.cents;
    return is;
}

int main()
{
    Money csh;
    cout << "Please type two integers (xx xx): ";
    cin >> csh;
    cout << csh;
    return 0;
}
```

This is a sample of the input and output of the program in Listing 20.15:

```
Please type two integers (xx xx): 29 95
$29.95
```

# File I/O

Although the `iostream` class library has many classes and member functions that can manage file I/O, it's usually better to handle I/O in Visual C++ programs with the classes and functions in the MFC library. The MFC I/O classes are specially designed to manage I/O in Windows-based programs, and they offer many features that the `iostream` classes lack.

For example, when you manage I/O by using the MFC classes, you can use *serialization*: an MFC mechanism that can save an object to a disk file and then read it back with little or no intervention on the part of the calling program.

When you manage I/O by using the MFC classes, objects can serialize themselves to and from disk files. Collections of objects, such as lists and arrays, can automatically serialize themselves, reducing the act of serializing a collection of objects with a single function call. Furthermore, MFC serialization supports the use of pull-down file menus and standard file dialog boxes.

Because most users of Visual C++ will never have to use a file-related `iostream` class or function, this section provides only a general overview of the file-related capabilities of `iostream` classes. If you need more information about file-related `iostream` I/O, you can find it in *iostream Class Library Reference*.

## Opening, Using, and Closing a Stream File

These are the steps required to create, open, use, and close a file by using the `iostream` class library:

1. Declare an object that belongs to the `ifstream`, `ofstream`, or `fstream` class.
2. Open the file.
3. Read from or write to the file.
4. Close the file.

## File Streams

The `ifstream`, `ofstream`, and `fstream` classes are descended from the `istream`, `ostream`, and `iostream` classes. The `ifstream` class is derived from the `istream` class. The `ofstream` class is derived from the `ostream` class, and the `fstream` class is derived from the `iostream` class.

The `iostream` file stream classes inherit all the characteristics of the classes from which they are derived. Files, however, have special requirements that character devices such as screens, printers, and keyboards do not have; and the file stream classes are designed to support those needs.

The `iostream` file classes have special features that permit them to manage file-related I/O. For example, the file stream classes support these special characteristics of files:

- Files have distinct names.
- A program can append data to an existing file.
- A program can seek to a specified position in a file.

## The ofstream and ifstream Classes

With the `ofstream` class, you can create objects that can then be treated as files. When you have created an `ofstream` file, you can write to the file by using the << operator, in the same way you would write to a standard output device such as a printer or a monitor. You can also write to an `ofstream` object by using `ostream` member functions such as `cout.write()` and `cout.put()`.

When you have created an `ofstream` file, you can read its contents by opening it as an `ifstream` object. When you have opened an `ifstream` file, you can read from the file by using the >> operator, in the same way you would read from a standard input device such as a keyboard. You can also read from an `ifstream` object by using `istream` member functions such as `cout.read()`, `cout.get()`, and `cout.getline()`.

Listing 20.16 creates an `ofstream` file and then writes to the file and closes it. The program then opens the file as an `ifstream` object, reads the file, and closes it.

### Listing 20.16. Using the `ofstream` and `ifstream` classes.

```
// 2016.CPP
// Overloading the >> operator

#include <fstream.h>

class Money {
    int dollars, cents;
public:
    Money(int d, int c):dollars(d), cents(c) {}
    friend ostream& operator<< (ostream& os, Money& csh);
    // friend istream& operator>> (istream& is, Money& csh);
};

ostream& operator<< (ostream& os, Money& csh)
{
    os << '$' << csh.dollars << '.' << csh.cents;
    return os;
}

int main()
{
    Money cash(199, 95);
    Money cash2(0, 0);

    // create a file object
    ofstream wrFile;
    // open the file for writing & name it MyAcct.dat
    wrFile.open("MyAcct.dat");
```

```
    // write to the file
    wrFile.write((char *) &cash, sizeof cash);
    // close the file
    wrFile.close();

    // open the 'MyAcct.dat' file for reading
    ifstream rdFile("MyAcct.dat");
    // read file contents into the Money object cash2
    rdFile.read((char *) &cash2, sizeof cash2);
    // close the file
    rdFile.close();
    // read data from Money object cash2
    cout << cash2;

    return 0;
}
```

Because the program in Listing 20.16 uses file streams, it includes the FSTREAM.H file rather than the IOSTREAM.H file (it isn't necessary to include both files because FSTREAM.H includes IOSTREAM.H).

The program has two parts. The first part of the program creates and writes to a file named MYACCT.DAT. The second part of the program opens the same file and prints its contents.

The first part of the program instantiates two objects of the `Money` class: `cash` and `cash2`. The data members of the `cash` object are initialized to hold the values 199 and 95, and the data members of the `cash2` object are initialized to hold a pair of zeroes.

When two `Money` objects have been created, the program creates an `ofstream` object named `wrFile` and opens the `wrFile` object as a file named MYACCT.DAT. The program then calls the member function `wrFile.write()` to copy the contents of the `Money` object named `cash` into MYACCT.DAT. That done, the program closes the MYACCT.DAT file.

The second part of the program opens the MYACCT.DAT file as an `fstream` object named `rdFile`. The program then calls the member function `rdFile.read()` to copy the contents of the MYACCT.DAT file into the `Money` object named `cash2`. The program then prints the contents of the `cash2` object.

## The fstream Class

The `fstream` class supplies file objects that can be used for both input and output. An `fstream` object is a single stream with two logical substreams, one for input and one for output. Each of the two substreams that make up an `fstream` object has its own position pointer. The input pointer is defined by the `ifstream` class, and the output pointer is defined by the `ofstream` class. An `fstream` object, therefore, is almost like two objects: an `ostream` object and `istream` object rolled into one.

Listing 20.17 is a basic example of a program that creates and uses an `fstream` file. The program opens a file, writes some data to it, reads out the data, and closes the file.

### Listing 20.17. Using the `fstream` class.

```
// 2017.CPP
// Using an fstream object

#include <fstream.h>
#include <ctype.h>

int main()
{
    fstream myFile("TestFile.txt", ios::in | ios::trunc);
    if (myFile.fail())
        cout << "ERROR! Could not open file.";

    else {

        myFile.clear();
        myFile << "This life is a test. It is only a test.\n"
               << "If it were a real life, you would have\n"
               << "been provided with more instructions.";

        myFile.seekp(0);

        while (!myFile.eof()) {
            char chr;
            myFile.get(chr);
            if (!myFile.eof())
            cout << chr;
        };

        myFile.close();

    }
    return 0;
}
```

This is the output of the program in Listing 20.17:

```
This life is a test. It is only a test.
If it were a real life, you would have
been provided with more instructions.
```

The 2017.CPP program creates an `fstream` object with this constructor:

```
fstream myFile("TestFile.txt", ios::in | ios::trunc);
```

## fstream Masks

The preceding constructor creates an `fstream` object named `myFile`. The first parameter passed to the constructor specifies the name of the file (TESTFILE.TXT). The second parameter is a *mask,* also known as an *`ios` enumerator*—that is, a set of `ios` flags that provide the compiler with various specifications for the `fstream` object that is being constructed.

In this case, the mode specifiers passed to the `fstream` constructor are the `ios::in` enumerator, which causes the file to be opened for input, and the `ios::trunc` enumerator, which causes the contents of the file to be erased each time it is opened. The bitwise OR operator (|) is used to combine the two enumerators.

If the `ios::trunc` enumerator is not used, the file will be opened in *append* mode, and the data written to the file will be appended to the file's existing data.

In all, there are eight enumerators that can be passed to an `fstream` constructor. They are listed in Table 20.5.

**Table 20.5. `fstream` enumerators.**

| *Enumerator* | *Description* |
|---|---|
| ios::app | Causes text to be written to the end of the `fstream` file. |
| ios::ate | Sets a position pointer to the end of the `fstream` file. When the first new byte is written to the file, it is appended to the end, but subsequent bytes are written starting at the current position. |
| ios::in | The file is opened for input. The original file, if there is one, is not truncated. |

*continues*

**Table 20.5. continued**

| *Enumerator* | *Description* |
|---|---|
| ios::trunc | If the file already exists, its contents are discarded. |
| ios::nocreate | If the file does not already exist, the function fails. |
| ios::noreplace | If the file already exists, the function fails. |
| ios::binary | Opens the file in binary mode (the default mode is text). |

## Testing an Object's Error Flags

The `ios` class provides three member functions that can test for errors in I/O stream operations. Each `iostream` object has a set of condition flags that change according to the object's current state, and the three test functions of the `ios` class—named `ios::bad()`, `ios::fail()`, and `ios::good()`—can test the object's flags when a function that affects the flags has been executed. You can use the `ios` class's three test functions to determine whether a function called to create a stream has returned an error, has failed, or has succeeded.

In Listing 20.17, these two lines test the attempt to create an `fstream` object:

```
if (myFile.fail())
     cout << "ERROR! Could not open file.";
```

The `ios::bad()` function returns a `true` value if a program attempts to do something illegal, such as seek beyond the end of a file. The `ios::fail()` function returns a `true` value under the same conditions that trigger `ios::bad()` and also returns `true` when valid operations fail—for example, when an attempt is made to open an unavailable file or to write to a disk device that is full. The `ios::good()` function returns `true` when a call succeeds.

Another test function `ios::eof()` returns a nonzero value if the end of a file has been reached.

## Clearing and Flushing the Stream Buffer

The `ios` class and its subclasses not only provide member functions that can be used for testing, but also supply member functions that can perform various operations related to stream buffers, for example:

- `ios::clear()`. Returns 0 if all error bits are cleared; otherwise, error bits are set according to the following masks (which can be combined by using the bitwise OR operator (¦)).
- `ios::goodbit`. No error condition noted (no error bits set).
- `ios::eofbit`. End of file reached.
- `ios::failbit`. A formatting or conversion error that may be recoverable.
- `ios::badbit`. A severe I/O error.
- `ios::fill()`. Specifies a fill character to be used as padding between fills.
- `ios::rdbuff()`. Returns a pointer to the `streambuf` object that is associated with a stream.
- `ostream::flush()`. Function flushes the buffer associated with a stream.

In Listing 20.17, this line calls the `ios::clear()` function:

```
myFile.clear();
```

The preceding statement appears in the program because the stream is at end-of-file when the `myFile` object is created. The `myFile.clear()` function clears the end-of-file marker and all other indicators, enabling the program to proceed with its output.

## Seeking a Position in a Stream

An `fstream` object has two member functions that can set file markers in a stream. By calling these functions—called *seeking* functions—you can cause a read or write operation to start at a specific point in a file.

One of the two seeking functions available to a `stream` object is the `seekg()` function, a member function inherited from the `istream` class. The other seeking function is the `seekp()` function, a member function inherited from the `ostream` class.

The `seekg()` function sets the position of the next input operation. The `seekp()` function sets the position of the next output operation. In Listing 20.17, this statement calls the `seekp()` member function:

```
myFile.seekp(0);
```

The preceding statement sets the position of the next output operation to the beginning of `myFile`. Because of that procedure, the file is read using the `while` loop that starts on the next line. If the `seekp(0)` function is not called, the read operation starts at the end of the file, and no characters are read.

Both the `seekp()` function and the `seekg()` function can be called with either one or two parameters. If the second parameter is missing (as it is in Listing 20.17), the seek operation sets the file marker to the beginning of the file.

The first parameter of a `seekp()` or `seekg()` function is an integer. When there is only one parameter, the integer specifies an offset, expressed in characters, from the beginning of a stream. The file marker is set to the position that the offset specifies.

When a `seekp()` or `seekg()` function has two parameters, the second parameter can be one of these enumerators:

- `ios::beg`. Causes a seek operation to begin at the beginning of a stream.
- `ios::cur`. Causes a seek operation to begin at the current position in a stream.
- `ios::end`. Causes a seek operation to begin at the end of a stream.

These lines show how the `seekg()` or `seekp()` function can be used in a program:

```
myFile.seekg(12, ios::beg);    // starts a seek at the 12th character
                               // in a stream

myFile.seekg(2, ios::cur);     // starts a seek two characters past the
                               // current position in a stream

myFile.seekg(-12, ios::end);   // starts a seek 12 characters prior to
                               // the last character in a stream
```

# Summary

The MFC's I/O classes are so much more powerful than C++'s `iostream` classes, and so much more convenient to use, that you'll probably never have to use the file-related `iostream` classes except under the rarest of circumstances.

If you ever have to write a special kind of printer driver or a communications program with unusual requirements, you might need to use some of the file-handling functions defined in the `iostream` class library. Otherwise, you'll almost always be better off handling I/O with classes and functions in the MFC library.

Nevertheless, the information in this chapter is valuable and shouldn't be ignored. That's because many of the features of the I/O classes in the MFC library are modeled after features in the `iostream` classes; indeed, the I/O classes in the MFC library use the classes in the `iostream` class library internally.

So, if you know how to handle I/O using the `iostream` classes, it will be easier for you to learn how the classes in the MFC library manage I/O. For more information about file-related I/O by using the `iostream` classes, refer to *iostream Class Library Reference.*

It should also be noted that the Microsoft `iostream` Class Library has many features and capabilities that were not covered in this chapter. For example, there is a set of classes that support in-memory formatting in much the same way that C's `sprintf()` and `sscanf()` functions of C do, but with the additional support of the C++ insertion and extraction operations and member functions of the `iostream` classes.

There are several ways to manage input and output in a Visual C++ program. If you restrict yourself to writing QuickWin programs and aren't interested in learning anything new, you can use the I/O functions supplied in C's STDIO.H library. (If you own the Professional Edition of Visual C++, you can also use C's I/O functions to write MS-DOS programs.)

If you're a little more ambitious, you can write QuickWin (and MS-DOS) programs using the classes in the Visual C++ `iostream` class library—an improved and expanded version of the original `iostream` library designed by the original creators of C++.

If you want to write full-scale Windows applications, the best way to manage I/O is with the input and output classes provided in the MFC library.

The classes in the Visual C++ `iostream` library can come in handy when you want to write a short QuickWin program (like the example programs presented so far in this book), a prototype function, or when you want to test a piece of code.

The `iostream` library is also a good training tool. It provides solid, tested examples of routines that overload functions, and it shows how class libraries can improve and enhance the capabilities of the C++ language.

This chapter—the last one in Part II of this volume—introduced the `iostream` class library supplied with Visual C++ and explained how you can use the Visual C++ `iostream` classes in your QuickWin and MS-DOS programs.

Part 3, "The MFC Library," which introduces the Microsoft Foundation Class library, begins with Chapter 21, "The Microsoft Foundation Classes."

# III

# The MFC Library

Chapter 21

# The Microsoft Foundation Classes

When Microsoft engineers began demonstrating Visual C++ to the press, the most popular part of the presentation came when the spokesperson launched the Visual Workbench editor, selected AppWizard from the Project menu, waited for an application to be created, and then announced: "See? We've created a Window application without writing a line of code."

That was true, but there was a catch. When you create a Visual C++ application without writing a line of code, what you get is an application that doesn't execute a line of user-written code—although an application generated by

AppWizard does display a window on the screen. To create an application that does anything more than that, there's no getting around the fact that you have to write some code. That's what you'll get a chance to do in this chapter.

This chapter introduces Version 2 of the Microsoft Foundation Class (MFC) library: a set of more than 100 classes designed specifically to help Visual C++ programmers write Windows-based programs.

Version 2 of the MFC library, which totals more than 60,000 lines of code, provides software developers with complete access to the Windows API from Visual C++ programs. It is backward-compatible with Version 1 of the MFC library, but it is written specifically for the Visual Workbench and all other interactive Windows-based tools that come with Visual C++.

The classes and functions in the MFC library are pretested, debugged abstractions that do all kinds of useful jobs. There are string classes, collection classes, time classes, and much more. There's even a `CObject` class that some have called "the mother of all classes" because it truly is the parent class of most other classes used in Visual C++.

In this chapter, you'll get a chance to build a program that creates objects from several of the most important classes in the MFC library. The program you'll be dealing with is a new and greatly improved version of The Wrath of Zalthar: the first version of the game that makes use of the classes in the MFC library. The source-code listing of this chapter's Zalthar program is too long to fit comfortably inside the text of the chapter, so it's supplied at the end of the chapter, in Listing 21.1.

The Zalthar application in Listing 21.1, like earlier versions of the program, is a QuickWin application. The program's I/O operations, however, are grouped together in two files—INTERFACE.H and ZALTHAR.H—so the parts of the application that are unique to a text-based interface are easy to find.

That new organization will come in handy in later chapters in which the Zalthar program's text-based I/O operations will be replaced with an interface that enables the user to interact with the program by selecting commands from pull-down menus and dialog boxes. When those changes are made, you'll have an opportunity to upgrade The Wrath of Zalthar from a QuickWin application to a full-scale Windows program.

**NOTE—THE NEW ZALTHAR PROGRAM**

Many of the code samples in this chapter can be found in the newest version of The Wrath of Zalthar, which is presented at the end of this chapter in Listing 21.1. This new Zalthar program is full of improvements and changes. Some of its enhancements were added to make it compatible with the MFC library. Others were added simply to make it a better program.

Listing 21.1 is the first version of the Zalthar program that has made use of the Microsoft Foundation Classes. As you'll see in this chapter, MFC-based classes have many useful features that will probably make your Visual C++ classes much more powerful than they would ever be if you wrote all your classes yourself. They're also easier to use than homemade classes because expert programmers have written them for you, have thoroughly debugged them, and have carefully designed them to work together in Windows-based programs.

Classes based on MFC classes can automatically write data to a disk and read it from a disk, a handy feature in many kinds of programs, such as database applications (and games like The Wrath of Zalthar). MFC-based classes also have many handy features that can help you debug programs and can even trap errors and other unforeseen events at runtime. You'll learn how some of these features work later in this chapter.

The newest version of The Wrath of Zalthar is described in more detail in the section "The Example Program" at the end of this chapter.

# General Purpose Classes

This chapter introduces several of the most important general-purpose classes in the MFC library. By convention, the names of classes that are derived MFC classes begin with a capital C, so it isn't difficult to detect the classes that have been converted to MFC-derived classes in this chapter's version of the Zalthar program. Besides the classes in the program that have been upgraded to MFC-based classes, the program also contains some new MFC-derived classes that are making their appearance in the game for the first time. The MFC-based classes in Listing 21.1 include:

- *CCharacter*. A base class that was formerly known as Character. The CCharacter class has been renamed because it is now derived from the CObject class: a base class from which most MFC classes are derived. The main reason that CCharacter is now derived from CObject is that child classes of CObject can *serialize* data, or read and write data to and from a disk. You'll see how data serialization works later in this chapter.

- *CPlayer, CWarrior, CPriest, CThief,* and *CWizard*. CPlayer has a C-name because it is derived from CCharacter. CWarrior, CPriest, CThief, and CWizard are all derived from CPlayer.

- *CPlayerList*. A new class derived from an MFC class named CObList. CObList is a collection class (a class in which objects are grouped together) that is derived in turn from CObject. C++ programmers find that it's often convenient to arrange a set of objects together in a list so that the objects can be managed as a unit, and classes that do that job are known as *collection classes*. In previous chapters, you saw how objects could be grouped into simple lists. The MFC library supplies several powerful list classes that make it convenient to work with groups of objects arranged into various kinds of lists.

- *CString*. One of the OOP (object-oriented programming) world's most powerful string classes. In previous chapters, you saw how string classes can help you manage strings much more easily than they can be managed in C. The CString class defined in the MFC library can do much more than the small string classes presented in previous chapters. With the MFC's CString class, you not only can perform operations such as copying and concatenating strings, but you also can search for strings, search for patterns in strings, modify sequences of characters in strings, and much more.

- *CFile*. The base class for Microsoft Foundation file classes. The CFile class provides direct, unbuffered, binary disk input and output services. It also indirectly supports text files and memory files through its derived classes. CFile works in conjunction with the CArchive class (see next item) to support serialization of MFC objects. With the CFile class and its derived classes, a program can operate on many kinds of file objects through a polymorphic interface. For example, CFile can make a memory file behave like a disk file. Normally, a disk file is opened automatically when a CFile object is constructed and is closed when the object's destructor is invoked. CFile also provides static member functions that enable you to examine a file's status without opening the file.

- `CArchive`. A class that enables you to save complex objects in a permanent binary form (usually disk storage) that persists after those objects are deleted. Later, you can load the objects from disk and back into memory. This process of making data persistent is called *serialization*.
- `CDataBase`. A class derived from `CObject`.

The next section describes the `CObject` class, the most important base class in the MFC library. The other classes in the preceding list are described under separate headings later in this chapter.

# The CObject Class

Most of the classes in the MFC library are derived from the `CObject` class. When you develop programs in Visual C++, you'll undoubtedly want to derive many of your own program objects from the `CObject` class, too. The benefits of classes derived from `CObject` include support for serialization, availability of runtime class information, and printing of diagnostic information that can be useful in debugging.

You don't have to pay a high price for these benefits; the cost of deriving your class from `CObject` is minimal. The only overhead for a derived class is a total of four virtual functions and a single `CRuntimeClass` object.

Although the `CObject` class contains many useful member functions, Visual C++ programs usually override some of `CObject`'s member functions to handle specific needs of user-defined classes. For example, the `Dump()` function defined by `CObject` is generally used to provide class-specific debugging operations. (For details about how to override `Dump()`, see the heading "The Dump() Function" later in this chapter.

Another `CObject` member function that is often overridden is `AssertValid()`. For a description of how to override `AssertValid()`, see the material on `AssertValid()` later in this chapter.

## Benefits of Using the CObject Class

There are many reasons for using objects that are derived from the `CObject` class. Some of the benefits of using the `CObject` class are summarized in the following list and are examined more closely later in this section. The advantage of using `CObject` objects include these:

- *Serialization*. Serialization is the process of writing or reading an object to or from a persistent storage medium, such as a hard disk. The MFC library offers built-in support for automatic serialization of objects that belong to the `CObject` class. That means when you derive an object from `CObject`, the object can store its member variables on a disk and then read them back into memory with little or no effort on your part. To use the serializing capabilities of the `CObject` class, you must call a macro named `DECLARE_SERIAL` in the declaration of the object that you want to serialize, and you must call another macro named `IMPLEMENT_SERIAL` in the code that implements objects of the class. These two macros are used extensively in this chapter's version of the Zalthar program.

- *Dynamic creation of objects*. In C++, objects are often created dynamically—that is, at runtime. For example, when objects are serialized from disk, they must be dynamically created. To support the dynamic creation of objects at runtime, the MFC library provides a macro named `DECLARE_DYNCREATE`. When you want a program to create an object dynamically, you can call the `DECLARE_DYNCREATE` macro in the declaration of the `CObject` that you want to create. You must also call a corresponding macro named `IMPLEMENT_DYNCREATE` from the class's implementation (.CPP) file. These two macros are also used in this chapter's version of the Zalthar program.

- *Availability of runtime class information*. When you're debugging a program, it's sometimes helpful to be able to obtain information about a class at runtime. In programs written in Visual C++, you can access class information at runtime by calling the `DECLARE_DYNAMIC` macro in the class's definition and calling the `IMPLEMENT_DYNAMIC` macro in the code that implements the class.

- *Assertion*. You can use two MFC macros, `ASSERT` and `ASSERT_VALID`, to test the validity of objects during the debugging stage or program development. The `ASSERT` macro can evaluate any specified expression (even expressions that include pointer values). The `ASSERT_VALID` macro can check to see whether a pointer to a specified object is valid. `ASSERT` returns a Boolean value that can test the validity of pointers and can also test your assumptions about the validity of an object's internal state.

- *Tracing*. The `TRACE` macro is a debugging macro that writes debugging data to standard output by using the same format that the `printf()` function generates in C-language programs.

- *Dump()*. `Dump()` is a member function of `CObject` that you can override to print information about an object during the debugging stage of program development. The `Dump()` function is not used in The Wrath of Zalthar program; for more information on the `Dump()` function, see the Class Library Reference supplied with Visual C++.
- *Exception handling*. When a C++ program runs into abnormal conditions, it responds by doing what software developers refer to as "throwing an exception." When a program throws an exception, you can force it to jump to a special routine called an exception handler and to execute that function rather than the function it would otherwise attempt to execute. Here are four macros that you can use to create exception handlers in Visual C++: `TRY`, `CATCH`, `AND_CATCH`, and `END_CATCH`.
- *Compatibility with selected collection classes*. The MFC library supplies a set of collection classes—such as `CObArray`, `CObList`, `CMapStringToOb`, and `CMapWordToOb`—that accept `CObject` pointer elements and can therefore store collections of objects derived from the `CObject` class. When you archive such a collection or use it to print debugging information, the MFC library classes can handle all necessary serialization tasks automatically.

## Serialization

One of the most useful capabilities of the `CObject` class is its capacity to read and write file information automatically. The process of writing or reading an object to or from a persistent storage medium, such as a disk file, is called *serialization*.

By using the MFC library's serialization tools to read and write data, you can transfer any serializable object to disk with only one line of code. Even a whole collection of serializable objects can be serialized simply, conveniently, and with a small amount of code.

To make use of the serializing capabilities of the `CObject` class, you must first derive a class from the `CObject()` class. Then, you must call a macro named `DECLARE_SERIAL` in the declaration of the object that you want to serialize (that is, in your class's .H file), and you must call another macro named `IMPLEMENT_SERIAL` in the class's implementation (.CPP) file. Finally, if you have added new data members in your derived class, you must override a `CObject` member function named `Serialize()` with your own `Serialize()` function.

The DECLARE_SERIAL and DECLARE_DYNCREATE macros generate all the header code and implementation code that is needed to create a serializable CObject subclass. DECLARE_SERIAL contains all the functionality of the DECLARE_DYNAMIC and DECLARE_DYNCREATE macros, so if you call DECLARE_SERIAL in a class definition, you don't have to call DECLARE_DYNAMIC or DECLARE_DYNCREATE.

## Formats of the Serialization Macros

The syntax of the DECLARE_SERIAL macro is

```
DECLARE_SERIAL(className)
```

where *className* is the name of the class that is to have serialization capability.

The syntax of the IMPLEMENT_SERIAL macro is as follows:

```
IMPLEMENT_SERIAL(className, baseClassName, schemaNumber)
```

In the preceding syntax, *className* is the name of the class being serialized, *baseClassName* is the name of that class's base class, and *schemaNumber* is a version number that you can assign to objects in the class being serialized.

Each time you modify a class, you can assign it a higher schema number. When the class is being serialized from storage to memory, if the schema number of the object on the disk does not match the version number of the class in memory, an exception is thrown. This can help prevent the serialization to disk of an incorrect version of an object.

Schema numbers must be 0 or greater; numbers of less than zero are not permitted.

## Using the Serialization Macros

In this chapter's version of The Wrath of Zalthar program, presented in Listing 21.1, the DECLARE_SERIAL and IMPLEMENT_SERIAL macros are used to make the CPlayer class serializable. In the definition of the CPlayer class, which appears in the ZALTHAR.H file, the DECLARE_SERIAL statement appears as follows:

```
DECLARE_SERIAL(CPlayer)
```

The IMPLEMENT_SERIAL statement that corresponds to the preceding declaration statement appears at the beginning of the ZALTHAR.CPP file, which contains the implementation of the CPlayer class and its subclasses:

```
IMPLEMENT_SERIAL(CPlayer, CObject, 1)
```

Later in the ZALTHAR.CPP file, this function definition overrides the `Serialize()` function that is defined for the `CObject` class:

```
// Serialization function
void CCharacter::Serialize(CArchive& archive)
{
   ASSERT_VALID(this);
   //Call base class function first
   CObject::Serialize(archive);

   //Dump data for CPlayer class
   if (archive.IsStoring()) {
      TRACE( "Serializing a CPlayer out.\n" );
      archive << m_class << m_race
            << m_s << m_d << m_c << m_i << m_w << m_ch
            << m_name << armor
            << weapon << magic;
   }
   else {
      TRACE( "Serializing a CPlayer in.\n" );
      archive >> m_class >> m_race
            >> m_s >> m_d >>m_c >> m_i >> m_w >> m_ch
            >> m_name >> armor
            >> weapon >> magic;
   }
}
```

**NOTE—ORDERLY SERIALIZATION**

When you write a `Serialize()` function that writes a class's member variables to disk, you should write them in the same order in which they appear in the object's definition when the object is defined. Conversely, when your function serializes a class's member variables from disk, they should be extracted in the same order that they were inserted. That way, you can ensure that each member variable that is written to disk is correctly matched with each member variable that is read from disk when the data is deserialized.

## The IsStoring() Function

When you override the `CObject` class's `Serialize()` member function, your `Serialize()` function—like the preceding one—must call a member function for the `CArchive` class called `IsStoring()`. The `IsStoring()` function checks to see whether information about a specified object is being read from disk or written to disk.

In a `Serialize()` function, the serialization of data to and from disk is handled by a pair of operators that are defined by a class named `CArchive`. The two operators are named `archive` << and `archive` >>.

The `CArchive::archive` << operator and the `CArchive::archive` >> operator work much like the `iostream` operators `cout` << and `cin` >>. The `archive` << operator is the *archive insertion operator*; it reads archived data from a disk. The `archive` >> operator is the *archive extraction operator;* it writes data to a disk archive.

## NOTE—RESTRICTIONS ON DATA TYPES IN ARCHIVING OPERATIONS

Although the `archive` << and `archive` >> operators work much like `cout` << and `cin` >>, they are much more sensitive about the kinds of data they can handle. The only primitive data types that the `archive` << and `archive` >> operators can serialize are `BYTE`, `WORD`, `DWORD`, and `DLONG`. That means if you try to serialize even such a common data type as an `int`, the compiler returns an error.

Because of this limitation, the member variables of the `CCharacter` class have all been converted to integers in the version of the Zalthar program that is presented in Listing 21.1. In the definition of the `CCharacter` class, which you can find in the file ZALTHAR.H, all member variables that were previously defined as integers have now been converted to the WORD data type, which is a serializable type. This is a fragment of the `CCharacter` class definition that appears in the ZALTHAR.H file:

```
class CCharacter : public CObject {
protected:
   WORD m_class;
   WORD m_race;
   WORD m_s;
   WORD m_d;
   WORD m_c;
   WORD m_i;
   WORD m_w;
   WORD m_ch;
   class CString m_name;
   class CString weapon;
```

```
    class CString armor;
    class CString magic;
    static int count;
public:
    CCharacter() {}
    ~CCharacter () {}
    static int GetCount() { return count; }
    static void IncCount() { count++; }
    // More definitions
}
```

If a program is writing to disk—that is, storing data to an archive—the archive insertion operator (`archive <<`) is used to write data about the object being serialized to the file associated with the archive. If the program is reading data from an archive, the archive extraction operator (`archive >>`) is used to read each member variable of the object being serialized.

When you use the insertion and extraction operators in a `Serialize()` function, they perform all the operations necessary to be sure the member variables are correctly written or read.

## Reading Files and Writing Files

An object of class `CArchive` always encapsulates one disk file. The `archive >>` operator writes data to disk file (represented as a `CArchive` object) and the `archive <<` reads data from a file (represented as another `CArchive` object).

When you create a `CArchive` object, you can use it either for reading a disk file or for writing a disk file; you can't use it for both purposes. If you want to read data from a file and write data to the same file, you must create two `CArchive` objects—one for reading and one for writing.

You can create a `CArchive` object that reads a disk file by placing a statement like this in a program:

```
CArchive archive( pFile, CArchive::load );
```

To create a `CArchive` object that writes data to a disk, you can execute this kind of statement:

```
CArchive archive( pFile, CArchive::store );
```

## Serializing a Whole Object

When you have made an object serializable—that is, when you have written a `Serialize()` function that manages the serialization of the object's member functions—you can serialize the entire object by invoking only one `archive <<` or `archive >>` operator. In Listing 21.1, for example, a serializable collection class named `CPlayerList` is used to create a list of players. Then, the whole list is written to disk in a one-step serializing operation.

To make that kind of operation possible, the Zalthar program defines a `CObject` subclass named `CDataBase`. In the definition of the `CDataBase` class, two `CPlayerList` objects are declared. One of these `CPlayerList` objects holds the data for all the players in the game, and another holds data for players that have been located by using search operations (the `CPlayerList` class is a subclass of the `CObList` class, so `CObList` member functions can be used to search for players in the list).

Inside the definition of the `CDataBase` class, pointers to two `CPlayerList` objects are declared in a straightforward manner.

```
CPlayerList* m_pDataList;
CPlayerList* m_pFindList;
```

On the basis of these two declarations, two `CPlayerList` objects are created: one to hold all player objects in the game and the other to hold player objects that have been found using search operations and are subject to modification.

`CPlayerList` objects are serializable because the `DECLARE_SERIAL` macro is invoked for the `CPlayerList` class in the file LINKLIST.H, and the `IMPLEMENT_SERIAL` macro is invoked for `CPlayerList` objects in the file LINKLIST.CPP. No `Serialization()` function is in the LINKLIST.CPP file. It is not needed; a `CPlayerList` object is only a collection of `CPlayer` objects—and, as you have seen, objects that belong to the `CPlayer` class are already serializable.

Because a `CDataBase` object consists only of a pair of `CPlayerList` objects, nothing special must be done to make a `CDataBase` object serializable. When you execute a command to serialize a `CDataBase` object, the command simply serializes a pair of `CPlayerList` objects.

When an object has been made serializable or belongs to a class that is serializable in its own right, you can write the whole object to a disk file in a single step by executing a pair of statements like this:

```
CArchive archive( pFile, CArchive::store );
archive << pNewDataBase;
```

Going in the other direction, you can read the object from a disk file by executing a pair of statements written in this format:

```
CArchive archive( pFile, CArchive::load );
archive >> pNewDataBase;
```

In Listing 21.1, both the preceding pairs of statements appear in the file named DATABASE.CPP.

## Serialization Step by Step

In a nutshell, this is how you can implement serialization in your programs:

1. Derive a class from `CObject`.
2. Place a call to the `DECLARE_SERIAL` macro in the class's declaration.
3. Define a default constructor for the class (a constructor with no arguments).
4. Call the `IMPLEMENT_SERIAL` macro in the class's implementation file.
5. Write a `Serialize()` member function for your class that overrides the `CObject` class's `Serialize()` member function.

## The IsKindOf() Function

With the `CObject` class's `IsKindOf()` member function, you can test any object to see if it belongs to a particular class. To use the `CObject::IsKindOf()` function, follow these steps:

1. Be sure the class has runtime class support. To have runtime class support, a class must be derived from `CObject`, and you must call either the `DECLARE_SERIAL` and `IMPLEMENT_SERIAL` macros or the `DECLARE_DYNAMIC` and `IMPLEMENT_DYNAMIC` macros in the appropriate places in your program (as explained earlier in this chapter).
2. When you are sure a class has runtime class support, call the appropriate `IsKindOf()` member function for objects of that class.

The `IsKindOf()` function uses a macro named `RUNTIME_CLASS` to obtain information about the specified class. This code fragment shows how you can use the `IsKindOf()` function in a program:

```
if(myObject->IsKindOf(RUNTIME_CLASS(CMyClass))) {
   CMyClass* pMyObject = (CMyClass*) pMyObject;
}
```

The `IsKindOf()` function returns `true` if an object is a member of the specified class or of a class derived from the specified class. It works properly only in single-inheritance hierarchies.

The Zalthar program in Listing 21.1 does not use the `IsKindOf()` function. For more information about `IsKindOf()`, see the *Class Library User's Guide*.

## The DYNCREATE Macros

A dynamically created object is an object that is created at runtime. Dynamically created objects are often used when, for example, a program reads an object from a disk or when the program *serializes* the object. The C++ language does not directly support the dynamic creation of objects, but the MFC library does. The `DECLARE_DYNCREATE` and `IMPLEMENT_DYNCREATE` macros enable you to dynamically create objects that are derived from the `CObject` class.

Objects are dynamically created by the `CreateObject()` member function of a class named `CRuntimeClass`. The `DECLARE_DYNCREATE` and `DECLARE_DYNCREATE` macros override the `CreateObject()` function.

To create an object dynamically, you must call the `DECLARE_DYNCREATE` macro in the declaration of the `CObject` that you want to create, and you must call another macro named `DECLARE_DYNCREATE` when you implement objects of the class. The document, view, and frame classes that typically make up a Windows application should support dynamic creation because, as you'll see in later classes, the MFC framework often needs to create those classes dynamically.

### Formats of the DYNCREATE Macros

The syntax of the `DECLARE_DYNCREATE` macro is

```
DECLARE_DYNCREATE(className)
```

where *`className`* is the name of the class that is to have serialization capability.

The syntax of the `IMPLEMENT_DYNCREATE` macro is

```
IMPLEMENT_DYNCREATE(className, baseClassName)
```

where *`className`* is the name of the class being serialized and *`baseClassName`* is the name of that class's base class.

The Zalthar program in Listing 21.1 does not use the DYNCREATE macros. Instead, it uses the DECLARE_SERIAL and IMPLEMENT_SERIAL macros, which contain all the functionality of the DYNCREATE macros.

# The DYNAMIC Macros

The DECLARE_DYNAMIC and IMPLEMENT_DYNAMIC macros enable you to access information about classes dynamically, that is, at runtime. The ability to determine the class of an object at runtime can come in handy when you have function arguments that need extra type-checking or when you must write special-purpose code based on the class of an object.

When you derive a class from CObject and call the DECLARE_DYNAMIC and IMPLEMENT_DYNAMIC macros from the appropriate spots in your program (those locations are described later in this section), you can use member functions to access at runtime:

- The name of the class.
- The classes above it in the derivation hierarchy.

You can also retrieve class information for any CObject-base class that is declared in your program. This information enables you to cast safely a generic CObject pointer to a derived-class pointer. For example, suppose that in a Windows-based program, you want to process the child windows in a frame window. In this case, you can use the frame window's GetWindow() member function to return a generic CWnd pointer for each child window. You can obtain the child window's specific class by calling CObject member functions, such as IsKindOf(), described earlier in this chapter under the heading "The IsKindOf() Function."

Any class derived from class CObject can supply you with runtime information about itself and its base class, provided you invoke the DECLARE_DYNAMIC macro from the class's header file and call the IMPLEMENT_DYNAMIC macro from the class's implementation file. These two macros add code to your class to enable dynamic runtime information.

## Formats of the DYNAMIC Macros

The syntax of the DECLARE_DYNAMIC macro is

```
DECLARE_DYNAMIC(className)
```

where *className* is the name of the class that is to have serialization capability.

The syntax of the `IMPLEMENT_DYNAMIC` macro is

```
IMPLEMENT_DYNAMIC(className, baseClassName)
```

where `className` is the name of the class being serialized and `baseClassName` is the name of that class's base class.

> **CAUTION**
>
> The `IMPLEMENT_DYNAMIC` macro should be evaluated only once during any one compilation. That means you should not use `IMPLEMENT_DYNAMIC` in an interface file that can be included in more than one file. The safest policy is to be sure you always put `IMPLEMENT_DYNAMIC` in the implementation file (.CPP) for the class it's associated with.

## How the DYNAMIC Macros Work

When you have placed calls to the `DECLARE_DYNAMIC` and `IMPLEMENT_DYNAMIC` macros in a program and have derived a class from `CObject`, you can call the `RUNTIME_CLASS` macro and the `CObject::IsKindOf()` function at runtime to obtain information about your `CObject` subclass. With the `RUNTIME_CLASS` macro and the `CObject::IsKindOf()` function, you can determine the exact class of an object at runtime, and you can find out what base class it was derived from.

The `RUNTIME_CLASS` macro works by extracting the runtime class information for the specified class derived from `CObject`. The macro returns an object of the class `CRuntimeClass`.

A `CRuntimeClass` structure has member variables that contain the name of the class, the size of the object, the schema number, the object's base class, and other information—all of which you can access directly. `CRuntimeClass` is defined in the header file AFX.H.

You can also use the `IsKindOf()` member function of class `CObject` to determine whether an object belongs to a specified class. For more information about the `RUNTIME_CLASS` macro and the `IsKindOf()` member function, see the *Class Library User's Guide.*

The `DYNAMIC` macros are not used in the Zalthar program in Listing 21.1. Instead, Listing 21.1 uses the `DECLARE_SERIAL` and `IMPLEMENT_SERIAL` macros, which encapsulate all the functionality of the `DYNAMIC` macros.

## Diagnostic Aids

The MFC library comes with many classes, functions, and macros that can help you debug your Visual C++ programs. Debugging aids supplied by the MFC library range from features that can track memory allocations to assertion testing (described earlier in this chapter) that can cause your program to abort and print an error message when errors or other unforeseen problems are encountered.

Diagnostic aids provided by the MFC library include the following:

- The `ASSERT` and `ASSERT_VALID` macros, which can test the validity of objects and can also test the validity of assumptions that you make in your program.
- The `Dump()` member function of the `CObject` class, which can print information about objects during the debugging of programs (see the Visual C++ Class Library Reference for more information on the `Dump()` function).

### The ASSERT Macro

`ASSERT` is a powerful MFC macro that can help you test code when you're writing and debugging a Visual C++ program.

The `ASSERT` macro evaluates a specified expression. If the expression evaluates to `false`, the macro prints a diagnostic message (consisting of the source filename and line number) and aborts the program. If the expression evaluates to `true`, `ASSERT` takes no action.

When Windows is running, `ASSERT` displays its messages in a pop-up dialog box.

When you use `ASSERT` in a program, the Visual C++ compiler uses the macro only in the debugging environment. When you compile the release version of your program, the compiler does not evaluate `ASSERT` expressions and therefore does not interrupt the program if they evaluate to `false`. If you use the `VERIFY` macro (instead of `ASSERT`), the results will depend upon whether you are in Debug or Release mode. Using `VERIFY` in Debug mode will produce the same results as `ASSERT`. In Release mode, however, the expression will be evaluated, but the terminating action will not occur, regardless of the expression's evaluated result.

### Format of the ASSERT Macro

The syntax of the `ASSERT` macro is

```
ASSERT(booleanExpression)
```

where *booleanExpression* is an expression (which can include pointer values) that evaluates to `true` or `false`. If the result of the evaluation is `false`, the macro prints a diagnostic message and aborts the program. If the result is `true`, `ASSERT` takes no action.

The `ASSERT` macro appears several times in Listing 21.1. For example, this code fragment is from the DATABASE.CPP:

```
//  Look up a player by index.
CPlayer* CDataBase::GetPlayer( int nIndex )
{
   ASSERT_VALID( this );
   ASSERT( m_pDataList != NULL );

   if ( m_pFindList != NULL )
      return (CPlayer*)m_pFindList->GetAt( m_pFindList->FindIndex(
nIndex ) );
   else
      return (CPlayer*)m_pDataList->GetAt( m_pDataList->FindIndex(
nIndex ) );
}
```

When `ASSERT` detects an error or an expression evaluates to `FALSE`, the Visual C++ compiler generates an error message written in this format:

```
assertion failed in file <name> in line <number>
```

where *name* is the name of the source file and *num* is the line number of the assertion that failed in the source file.

When you are debugging a program written in Windows, `ASSERT` displays its output in a dialog box.

## The ASSERT_VALID Macro

`ASSERT_VALID` is another MFC macro that can help you test code when you're writing and debugging a program. The `ASSERT_VALID` macro can check whether an object is valid and also can evaluate expressions that you provide to determine whether assumptions you are making in your program are valid.

The `ASSERT_VALID` macro calls a `CObject` member function named `AssertValid()`. You can customize the `AssertValid()` function by overriding it in your own class definitions.

When you have overridden the AssertValid() function, you can call the ASSERT_VALID macro to test your assumptions about the validity of an object's internal state. When you pass an object's pointer to ASSERT_VALID, the macro checks the validity of the pointer and then calls your overridden AssertValid() function. If the pointer is not valid or fails tests you have supplied in your AssertValid() function, the ASSERT_VALID macro displays a diagnostic message.

In the Windows environment, ASSERT_VALID displays its messages in a pop-up dialog box.

You can use ASSERT_VALID to make any kind of test of an object. For example, ASSERT_VALID can test the validity of data that an object contains or can check whether an object is placed in the correct position in a list.

### Format of the ASSERT_VALID Macro

You call the ASSERT_VALID macro using the syntax

```
ASSERT_VALID(object)
```

where *object* is an object of a class derived from CObject.

The Zalthar program uses the ASSERT_VALID macro liberally, as in this example from the file ZALTHAR.CPP:

```
void CCharacter::PrintAbils()
{
   ASSERT_VALID( this );
   cout << '\n';
   cout << "Strength: " << GetStrength() << '\n';
   cout << "Dexterity: " << GetDexterity() << '\n';
   cout << "Constitution: " << GetConstitution() << '\n';
   cout << "Intelligence: " << GetIntelligence() << '\n';
   cout << "Wisdom: " << GetWisdom() << '\n';
   cout << "Charisma: " << GetCharisma() << '\n';
}
```

When ASSERT returns a diagnostic message, the format of the message is

```
assertion failed in file <name> in line <number>
```

where *name* is the name of the source file and *number* is the line number of the assertion that failed in the source file.

When you are programming in a Windows environment (even with QuickWin), ASSERT prints its output in a dialog box.

## The TRACE Macro

The TRACE macro prints information to standard output during the debugging phase of a program. TRACE works just like C's print() function, except that it has no effect in release versions of programs. In the Windows environment, TRACE writes its output to the CodeView debugger if it is present; otherwise, output is written to diagnostic output. You can prevent the output of the TRACE macro from being activated in release versions of your program by bracketing the statements that call the macro with the preprocessor directives #ifdef _DEBUG, and #endif. The TRACE macro is used extensively in Listing 21.1, particularly in the function named TestTheProgram(), which appears in the program's main() segment. For example, this statement causes the line "Creating a database" to be printed to standard output in the debugging versions of the program, but not in the release program:

```
TRACE("\nCreating a database.\n");
```

### NOTE—THE _DEBUG DIRECTIVE

When you compile a Visual C++ with debugging options on (by selecting the Debug Specific button in the Compiler Options dialog box), the compiler sets a variable named `_DEBUG` to `TRUE`. Then, when you are writing and debugging your program, you can use the preprocessor directive `#ifdef` to check the `_DEBUG` variable before you write statements that are intended for diagnostic output.

The preceding three code fragments use the `#ifdef` directive to test the `_DEBUG` variable. For example, if a debugging version of the program is being built, the `#ifdef` directive shown in the last of the three examples causes the compiler to include this statement:

```
TRACE("\nCreating a database.\n");
```

However, if a release version of the program is being built—that is, if the program is compiled with debugging options off—the preceding statement is not compiled, and the `TRACE` macro is not called.

### The VERIFY Macro

As explained earlier in this chapter, the `ASSERT` macro can evaluate an expression. If the condition is `false`, the macro prints the source filename and the line number and then terminates the program. The `ASSERT` macro is recognized only in the debugging versions of a program; in the release environment, the statement has no effect.

`VERIFY` is a companion macro to `ASSERT`. `VERIFY` works like `ASSERT`, but is active in both the debugging and release versions of your program. The difference is in the Release version of your program. The expression will be evaluated, but no action will be taken if the result is `false`.

When Windows is running, `VERIFY` displays its messages in a pop-up dialog box.

## Exception Handling

The MFC library uses macros to implement exception handling. Exceptions are represented as objects derived from an abstract class named `CException`. These macros manage exception handling in a way that is similar to the exception-handling functions provided by many other implementations of C++.

With the MFC library's exception-managing macros, you can set up exception handlers before you write or call functions that you think might encounter abnormal situations. Then, if your program runs into abnormal conditions, it throws an exception. When an exception is thrown, program execution jumps to the exception handler and resumes there.

In Visual C++, exceptions are represented as objects derived from the abstract class `CException`. The MFC library provides several predefined kinds of exceptions, and you can add your own.

Many classes and functions in the MFC library use exceptions to report abnormal conditions—especially the MFC classes and functions that deal with files and serialization. In your own programs, when you notice a function that might throw an exception, you may want to use an exception handler.

In general, this is how you can manage exception-handling in Visual C++:

1. When you spot a function in your code that might throw an exception, use the `TRY` macro to set up a `TRY` block. Execute any program statements that might throw an exception within a `TRY` block.

2. Use the CATCH macro to set up a CATCH block. Put your exception-handling code in your CATCH block. The code in the CATCH block is executed only if the code in the TRY block throws an exception of the type specified in the CATCH statement.

3. The CATCH macro takes an argument that holds a pointer to a CException object (or an object derived from a CException object, such as a CMemoryException object). Depending on the kind of exception that is encountered, you can examine the data members of the exception object to try to find out the cause of the exception.

The exception-handling macros defined in the MFC library are equipped with a large set of helper functions. These functions—with names like AfxCheckMemory, AfxThrowMemoryException, and AfxAbort—are described in detail in the *Class Library Reference*. Each function throws a preallocated exception object of a specified type.

When an exception is thrown, execution of the currently executing function is aborted, and the program jumps directly to the CATCH block of the innermost exception frame. It's important to remember that the exception mechanism bypasses the normal exit path from a function. Be sure to delete those memory blocks that would be deleted in a normal exit.

In Listing 21.1, the TRACE macro appears in this function in the file ZALTHAR.CPP:

```
{
   ASSERT_VALID(this);
   //Call base class function first
   CObject::Serialize(archive);

   //Dump data for CPlayer class
   if (archive.IsStoring()) {
      TRACE( "Serializing a CPlayer out.\n" );
      archive << m_class << m_race
            << m_s << m_d << m_c << m_i << m_w << m_ch
            << m_name << armor
            << weapon << magic;
}
else {
      TRACE( "Serializing a CPlayer in.\n" );
      archive >> m_class >> m_race
            >> m_s >> m_d >>m_c >> m_i >> m_w >> m_ch
            >> m_name >> armor
            >> weapon >> magic;
   }
}
```

As the preceding code fragment illustrates, the exception-handling process starts with the interruption of normal program execution in response to a THROW statement (that is, the invocation of the macro TRY). Execution resumes at the next CATCH statement. This exception-handling technique eliminates the need for extensive error testing after every call to a library function.

### Using Exception-Handling

The TRY and CATCH macros can help you detect out-of-memory and disk-full conditions, which can occur any time during program execution. When such conditions occur, a TRY/CATCH sequence at the top level of a program can provide a warning message, followed by a graceful exit.

At lower levels of applications, other kinds of file exceptions can occur. For example, if a program attempts to open a nonexistent file, a TRY/CATCH code block can inform the user or take other corrective action. A better alternative might be an explicit test for the file's presence.

# Other MFC Classes

Besides the CObject class described in the preceding major section, the MFC library contains a number of other useful general-purpose classes. The general-purpose classes in the MFC library include file classes, collection classes, a string class, time-related classes, diagnostic classes, and exception-handling classes.

## File Classes

The file classes in the MFC library can handle both standard-variety file I/O and serialization—the automatic reading and writing of disk data by objects derived from the CObject class. The file classes supplied in the MFC library include CArchive, CFile, CStdioFile, and CMemFile. Other file services are provided by the Serialize() member function of the CObject class and by the DECLARE_SERIAL and IMPLEMENT_SERIAL macros.

## The CArchive Class

`CArchive` is an MFC that provides a context for reading and writing object data to and from a disk file. The `CArchive` class is the class that makes serialization possible.

The `CArchive` class overloads the insertion and extraction operators (<< and >>) to write and read object data to and from the storage media. Although an archive uses the same overloaded operators as the general-purpose C++ I/O stream objects such as `cin` and `cout`, it's important to note that a `CArchive` object is different from an I/O stream.

An archive object works much like an input/output stream, but handles binary data. Like a binary I/O stream, an archive is associated with a file and permits the buffered writing and reading of data back and forth between the file and persistent (usually disk) storage. An archive processes binary object data in much the same way that a stream process text data, in an efficient, nonredundant format.

## The CFile Class

Before you can create a `CArchive` object, you must instantiate a `CFile` object (described earlier in this chapter). Also, you must ensure that the archive's load/store status is compatible with the file's open mode; if you want to load an archive into memory, the file object that it's associated with must be opened for reading, and if you want to store an archive, the file that it is to be stored in must be opened for writing. A file can be associated with only one active archive.

When you have constructed a `CArchive` object, you can attach it to an object of class `CFile` (or a class derived from `CFile`) that represents an open file. You must specify whether you want to use the archive for loading or storing information. Then, you can use the archive for the purpose you have specified.

The `CArchive` class overloads the extraction (>>) and insertion (<<) operators to provide a convenient way to serialize data.

`CArchive` objects can serialize primitive data types—such as words, longs, and binary types—as well as objects derived from the `CObject` derived classes designed for serialization. A serializable class must have a `Serialize()` member function and must use the `DECLARE SERIAL` and `IMPLEMENT SERIAL` macros, as described earlier in this chapter. The `Serialize()` function takes one argument: the `CArchive` object in which serialized data is stored.

By using the MFC library's serialization macros to read and write data, you can ensure that all the contents of the base-class portion of your object are correctly serialized. If the base class is itself a derived class, the `DECLARE_SERIAL` and `IMPLEMENT_SERIAL` macros also call the `Serialize()` function for the base class that is being serialized. The `Serialize()` function, therefore, is called for all classes in the hierarchy above the class that is being serialized. Serialization is examined more closely in the section "How Serialization Works."

### The CMemFile Class

The `CFile` classes in the MFC library provide a C++ programming interface to operating-system files. `CFile` is the base class for all file classes, so it provides a polymorphic programming interface for file I/O operations. For example, when a `CStdioFile` file is opened, its object pointer can be used by a pair of virtual member functions—`Read()` and `Write()`—which are defined for the `CFile` class.

The `CArchive` class, described earlier in this chapter, depends on the `CFile` class for input and output.

The `CFile` class offers access to low-level binary files, and the `CStdioFile` class—a subclass of `CFile`—provides access to buffered (standard I/O) files. `CStdioFile` files are often processed in text mode, which means each newline character is converted to a carriage return-plus-linefeed combination during write operations.

Another `CFile` subclass, named `CMemFile`, supports data that is stored in memory, but is treated as if it is stored in a file. Such "in-memory" files behave much like disk files, but actually are made up of bytes stored in RAM. An in-memory file is a useful means of transferring raw bytes or serialized objects between independent processes.

## Collection Classes

In object-oriented programming terminology, classes that group objects together in various kinds of lists and maps are known (collectively) as *collection classes.*

The MFC library contains 14 different kinds of collection classes, grouped into three categories:

- *Arrays.* The MFC library supplies classes that can be used to create arrays of bytes, words, double words, objects, pointers to objects, and strings.

- *Linked lists*. With the linked list classes in the MFC library, you can create lists of pointers, objects, and strings. The `CObList` class—the parent class of the `CCharacter` class used in the Zalthar program—can store collections of `CObjects` or objects derived from `CObjects`.
- *Maps*. A map is a collection that maps one kind of data to another. For instance, the `CMapToOb` class can store objects that map strings to objects of the `CObject` class. Then, you can look up the object with string-style key values.

The MFC library contains a number of ready-to-use list arrays and maps that are referred to as "collection classes." A collection is an extremely useful programming idiom for holding and processing groups of objects or standard types. C++ makes a collection appear as a single object, so collection member functions can operate on all elements of the collection.

All collections can be archived or written to any diagnostic output. Collections of `CObject` pointers have `Serialize()` and `Dump()` member functions that can call the corresponding functions for each of their elements. The MFCs contain 16 standard kinds of collections, and if you need a list, array, or map that is not included among these 16 collections, you can create your own collection classes.

## Array Classes

An array is a dynamically sized grouping of elements that are directly accessible through a zero-based integer subscript. In the MFC array classes, if a new element is inserted into an array, the elements above the insertion point are moved up. If an element above the current array bound is to be set, the programmer can specify whether the array is to grow automatically. You can use the subscript operator (`[]`) to set or retrieve array elements.

The MFC library contains array classes that can store bytes, words, double words, `CString` objects, `CObject` pointers, and `void` pointers.

## List Classes

A list is an ordered grouping of elements. New elements can be added at the head or tail of a list, or before or after a specified element. List objects created from the collection classes in the MFC library can be traversed in forward or reverse sequence, and you can remove elements. Also, you can search for elements with zero-based indexes or by value, but the find operation requires a sequential scan of the list.

The MFC library provides list classes for `CString` objects, `CObject` pointers, and `void` pointers.

When you don't have to "grow" a list, access to an MFC array collection is as fast as access to a standard C-language array. There is some extra storage overhead, but in practical terms it is insignificant.

### Maps

In collection-class terminology, a *map* is a kind of dictionary that can keep track of objects by using a key. For example, the MFC library contains one map class named `CMapWordToObj`. The `CMapWordToObj` class uses a `WORD` variable as a key to find a corresponding `CObject` pointer.

Map lookups are fast because they rely on a hashing technique. A map can be traversed, but retrieval sequences progress in indeterminate ways; therefore, when you want to iterate over a map collection, it makes sense to iterate over all the elements in the map.

The MFC library contains seven map classes; they support `CString` objects, words, `CObject` pointers, and `void` pointers.

## The CString Class

The MFC library supplies a powerful `CString` class that supports the dynamic manipulation of character strings. Strings stored as `CString` can be copied, concatenated, and even searched with simple operations reminiscent of those used in BASIC. These features make `CString` objects easier to use than C-style strings—which, as you know, are accessed or referenced with pointers and are notoriously difficult to manipulate.

When you implement a string as a `CString` object, you can manipulate it by using simple operations with overloaded operators. For example, using the plus operator (+), you can concatenate a pair of strings by "adding" them together, just as you can in BASIC.

`CString` can automatically grow and shrink to fill or save space without any intervention by the programmer. They also can be serialized. Furthermore, the `CString` class is equipped with conversion functions that can automatically convert back and forth between `CString` objects and conventional C-style strings.

For example, you can pass a `CString` object to a function that expects a pointer to a constant string (`const char*`) parameter. Conversely, you can pass a conventional C-style string pointer to a function that expects a `CString` object.

## Time-Related Classes

The MFC library supplies two time-related classes: `CTime` and `CTimeSpan`. A `CTime` object represents a specific time and date. A `CTimeSpan` object represents a time interval.

A `CTime` object encapsulates a time and date represented as a `time_t` data type—a data type standardized with an ANSI specification. A `CTime` object can represent any absolute date and time from January 1, 1900 to December 31, 2036.

The `CTime` class has runtime member functions that can convert back and forth between 24-hour time and a.m. and p.m. time and between the Julian and Gregorian calendars. Other member functions can convert a `time_t` value to integers that represent years, months, days, hours, minutes, and seconds. The `CTime` class has overloaded insertion and extraction operators for archiving and for diagnostic dumping.

The `CTimeSpan` class can represent time intervals. If one `CTime` object is subtracted from another, the result is a `CTimeSpan` object. You can add `CTimeSpan` objects to `CTime` objects, and you can subtract `CTimeSpan` objects from `CTime` objects. A `CTimeSpan` value is limited to the range of plus or minus 68 years, approximately.

# The Example Program

This chapter's version of The Wrath of Zalthar (in Listing 21.1) is the first version that has been designed to make use of classes in the MFC library.

Besides the enhancements in the program that are related to the MFC library, the program has a host of improvements that make it a better application, for example:

- Characters in the game now have both *races* (dwarf, elf, half-elf, human, and halfling) and *classes* (warrior, wizard, priest, and thief). This change makes The Wrath of Zalthar more closely resemble popular role-playing games.

- In another move aimed at bringing the Zalthar program more into line with existing games, the number of capabilities assigned to each character was increased to six. Each character now has scores for strength, dexterity, constitution, intelligence, wisdom, and charisma. More important, the characters are assigned their capabilities by a random-number algorithm that simulates a roll of a 20-sided die. If you're a quantum physicist, you may notice that the algorithm isn't elegant; you may be able to design a better one. But it works. You can find it in Listing 21.1 in the file named SETUP.CPP.
- In previous versions of the Zalthar program, characters' names and classes were hard-coded. This new version prompts you to type characters' names, classes, and races. Later, when you add dialog boxes to the program, it will become even more interactive.
- The program's files have been reorganized to make classes and functions easier to find, and to make the task of moving the game from a text base to an interactive base a little simpler.

Most of the application's I/O functions now reside in only two files—INTERFACE.CPP and ZALTHAR.CPP. When the time comes to upgrade the program to a WINDOWS.EXE application, it can be equipped with pull-down menus, and dialog boxes can be added easily. The encapsulation and abstraction features of C++ will simplify this job even more, as you'll see when the program starts getting transformed into a real Windows application in Chapters 22, 23, and 24.

**NOTE—ABOUT THIS CHAPTER'S ZALTHAR PROGRAM**

When Visual C++ succeeded Microsoft C/C++ Version 7, the C++ package contained a completely rewritten edition of the Microsoft C/C++ *Class Libraries User's Guide*. One significant change was that a program named Phone Book—a complete example of a basic object-oriented database—was replaced by a completely different kind of program named Scribble. Scribble is an easy-to-understand program that demonstrates the graphics capabilities of Visual C++ nicely, but from the point of view of data manipulation, it isn't as challenging or as useful an exercise as Phone Book, and it offers little functionality that is likely to be useful in most real-world applications.

> Although the Phone Book program is now history, some of the programming techniques it illustrated back in the days of Microsoft C/C++ Version 7 are reincarnated in the version of The Wrath of Zalthar that's presented in Listing 21.1. The data-management tools in that listing are modeled after parts of the Phone Book program in the old *Class Libraries User's Guide,* but they've been updated to take advantage of Visual C++ and Version 2 of the Microsoft Foundation Class library. If you examine them carefully, you can learn a lot about how object-oriented databases work, and you can easily incorporate them into your own programs.

## Architecture of the Example Program

Because the newest version of The Wrath of Zalthar was designed to make use of the MFC library and to be expanded into a full-scale Windows program beginning in Chapter 22, "The Visual Workbench," its architecture is more complex than the versions of the program that were presented in previous chapters.

Some of the files that make up the program were written by the author (that's me), and others were created by AppWizard, the application-generator tool that comes with Visual C++. In Chapter 22, you'll see how AppWizard was used to generate this new version of the Zalthar application.

The source-code files that were created by the author are as follows:

- *MAIN.CPP.* The MAIN.CPP segment of The Wrath of Zalthar contains two functions: the program's `main()` function and a longer function named `TestTheProgram()`. The `TestTheProgram()` function sets up a database and enables you to create a set of characters and enter them into the database. The function then writes the database to a file, closes the database, reopens the file that contains the database, and prints the contents of the database on the screen to show you that the database is working properly. The `TestTheProgram()` was written for testing purposes only and will not appear in the graphics-based versions of the program.
- *ZALTHAR.CPP and ZALTHAR.H.* In Listing 21.1, as in versions of the Zalthar program that appeared in previous chapters, the ZALTHAR.H file contains the definitions for the `CCharacter` class, a subclass of the MFC library's `CObject` class , and the `CPlayer` class, which is a subclass of `CCharacter`. The ZALTHAR.CPP file contains the implementations of the

classes defined in ZALTHAR.H. All character classes used in the game are objects of the `CCharacter` class, its derived `CPlayer` class, and subclasses of the `CPlayer` class.

- *SETUP.CPP and SETUP.H.* The SETUP.CPP file implements the function `CreatePlayers()`, which creates the characters used in the game, and the functions `SetRandomSeed()` and `RollDice()`, which calculate characters' ability scores. SETUP.CPP doesn't use `iostream` operators, so it can be ported to the graphics-based version of the Zalthar program intact. SETUP.H is the header file for SETUP.CPP.
- *INTRFACE.CPP and INTRFACE.H.* The INTRFACE.CPP file contains several functions that print information on the screen and several others that the user interacts with to create characters. Most of the functions in the INTRFACE.CPP file will be replaced with graphics-based functions in the forthcoming graphics-based version of the program. INTRFACE.H is the header file for INTRFACE.CPP.
- *LINKLIST.CPP and LINKLIST.H.* The LINKLIST.CPP file implements the `CPlayerList` class, which is derived from the `CObList` class. `CPlayerList` is a list class designed to hold a collection of `CPlayer` objects. LINKLIST.H is the header file for LINKLIST.CPP.
- *DATABASE.CPP and DATABASE.H.* The DATABASE.CPP file implements the `CDataBase` class, a subclass of the MFC library's `CObject` class. A `CDataBase` object is an encapsulated pair of player lists implemented as `CPlayerList` objects. One of the player lists in a `CDataBase` object is a complete list of players. The other list contains players that have been located with search operations. Player data that is on the "found" list is subject to modification and can be resaved. DATABASE.H is the header file for DATABASE.CPP.

  DATABASE.CPP implements the `CDataBase` member functions `AddPlayer()`, `DeletePlayer()`, `ReplacePlayer()`, `DoFind()` (which finds players by calling a LINKLIST.CPP function named `FindPlayer()`). DATABASE.CPP also implements functions that open and close a database and procedures that load and save a database.

The functions that find players in this chapter's Zalthar program are a little more robust than they have to be; they can find multiple players that meet search criteria that you specify. In this chapter's version of The Wrath of Zalthar—and in the Chapter 24 version, too—`DoFind()` and `FindPlayer()` are called upon to find just one player object at a time. But if you ever want them to exercise their ability to find multiple objects, they're right there in the program ready to use.

# Compiling the Example Program

As noted in Chapter 1, "Microsoft Visual C++"—and as you saw when creating the programming projects you've used so far in this book—projects are the cornerstone of Visual Workbench. A project keeps track of the various files and libraries needed to build a program or a library. Projects also contain information about compiler and linker options and even information stored in workspaces, such as the sizes and positions of Visual Workbench windows.

Projects speed up program development time by compiling only files that have changed since a program was last built or compiled—unless you choose otherwise. If you select Rebuild All from the Project menu, Visual Workbench rebuilds all files.

By creating a project and then selecting a project type, you can specify the kind of files you want to generate when you build a project. For instance, all the example programs presented in this book so far have been QuickWin applications that did not make use of the classes supplied in the MFC library.

In contrast, the version of the Zalthar program that's presented in Listing 21.1 is a QuickWin program that does make use of MFC classes. That means this chapter's version of the program will require a larger, more complex set of files that earlier versions required. The extra files that this new version of the program requires will be generated by AppWizard.

To compile this chapter's version of the Zalthar program, these are the steps to follow:

1. From the File Manager, create a directory for your application's project.
2. Copy this chapter's Zalthar program files from the program disk into your new application directory.
3. Launch Visual C++.
4. Select New from the Visual Workbench's Project menu.
5. When the New Project dialog box appears, choose "QuickWin Application (.EXE)" from the Project Type list box.
6. Click the Browse button.
7. When the Browse dialog box appears, select your application's directory from the Directories list box.
8. Close the Browse dialog box by clicking the Cancel button.

9. When the New Project dialog box reappears, type the word `zalthar` in the Project Name list box.
10. Close the New Project dialog box by clicking the OK button.
11. When the Edit dialog box appears, select your application's directory in the Directories list box.
12. Click the Add All button. That adds all your application's files to the "Files in Project" list box.
13. Click the Close button to close the Edit dialog box.
14. Select Project from the Options menu.
15. Click the Linker button.
16. From the Category list box, select Windows Libraries.
17. From the list box labeled Import Libraries and DLLs, select the COMMDLG and SHELL libraries.
18. Close the Linker Options dialog box by clicking the OK button.
19. Close the Project Options dialog box by clicking the OK button.
20. From the Project menu, select the command "Build ZALTHAR.EXE."
21. When a message box asks if you want to build your application, click the Yes button.
22. When your application has been built, execute it by selecting "Execute ZALTHAR.EXE" from the Project menu.

# Running the Example Program

When you execute the program in Listing 21.1, it prompts you for the number of game characters you want to create. You can then type in a name of each character you want to create, along with some other information about each character.

As you create each character, the program uses a pseudorandom number generator to generate information about each character's abilities. It places that information, along with information that you enter in a database. The program stores the database on disk as a text file, closes the file, reopens it, and then prints the information that has been stored in the file on your computer screen.

This chapter's version of The Wrath of Zalthar generates a text output. The next version of the program you see—Listing 22.1, in Chapter 22—generates a more sophisticated output using dialog windows. The final version of the program, presented in Chapter 24 (Listing 24.1), demonstrates the use of graphics in Visual C++ programs.

When you execute this chapter's version of the Zalthar program, you see a screen display like the one shown in Figure 21.1.

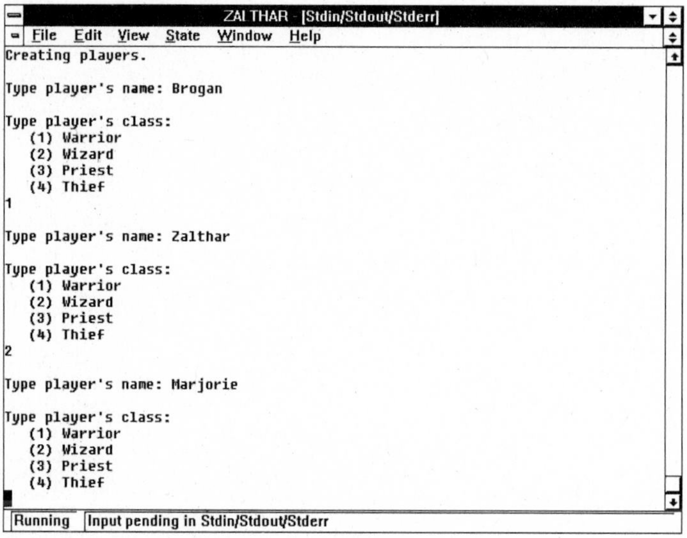


*Figure 21.1. The Wrath of Zalthar application.*

When you type in the names and classes of four players, the program creates your characters, saves them in a database, and then closes the database. Then, to show you that everything is working properly, it loads the same database into memory and prints the names and classes of the four characters you have created. The screen that the program displays when it has done all that is shown in Figure 21.2.

If you don't think the output of this chapter's version of The Wrath of Zalthar is very spectacular, consider what it does. It creates a database file, writes some information to the file, and saves the file. Then, it opens the database file, reads the data in the database, and displays that data in alphabetical order on the screen. Finally, it closes the database and prints a message informing you that the database is closed.

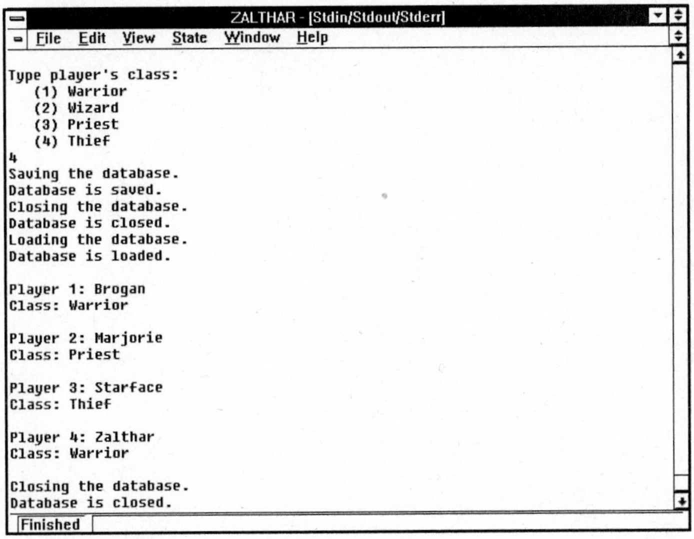


*Figure 21.2. The Wrath of Zalthar program's output.*

That isn't a bad day's work for a program that it took so little effort to create. Furthermore, thanks to inheritance, polymorphism, and various other capabilities of C++, the program is easily expandable. You'll see just how expandable when you encounter the next two installments of the program, presented in Chapters 22 and 24.

The program does have its shortcomings; it doesn't do any error-checking to speak of at runtime, and it isn't very versatile. But, at this stage of the program's development, that's fine.

At this point, the program is only a QuickWin prototype; it isn't even close to being a release version of an application. Its job is merely to confirm that the program's serialization functions work and that the database performs its loading and saving duties effectively.

The program has performed those tasks satisfactorily, and it is now time to move on to a version of the program that has a real user interface. That's the version of the program that you'll get a chance to examine (and execute) in Chapter 22.

**Listing 21.1. The Wrath of Zalthar, Chapter 21 version.**

**MAIN.CPP.**

```
// MAIN.CPP

#include <afxwin.h>
#include <afxcoll.h>
#include <iostream.h>
#include "setup.h"
#include "linklist.h"
#include "database.h"

// main function
int main()
{
   TestTheProgram();

   return 0;
}

// Routine to test the program
void TestTheProgram()
{
   const char fileName[] = "Zalthar.dat";
   CDataBase *pDataBase = new CDataBase;
   BOOL y;

   // Create database
   cout << "\nCreating a database.\n";
   y = pDataBase->New();
   ASSERT(y == TRUE);
   cout << "Database is created.\n";

   cout << "Creating players.\n";
   // Create players
   CreatePlayers(pDataBase);

   cout << "Saving the database.\n";
   y = pDataBase->DoSave(fileName);
   ASSERT(y == TRUE);
   cout << "Database is saved.\n";

   cout << "Closing the database.\n";
   pDataBase->Terminate();
   cout << "Database is closed.\n";

   cout << "Loading the database.\n";
   y = pDataBase->DoOpen(fileName);
   ASSERT(y == TRUE);
   cout << "Database is loaded.\n";
```

```
   for (int n = 0; n < 4; n++) {
      CPlayer *pPlayer = pDataBase->GetPlayer(n);
      cout << "\nPlayer " << n+1 << ": " <<
         pPlayer->GetName() << '\n';
      cout << "Class: "
         << pPlayer->GetClassName() << '\n';
   }

   cout << "\nClosing the database.\n";
   pDataBase->Terminate();
   cout << "Database is closed.\n";

}
```

### ZALTHAR.H

```
// ZALTHAR.H
// Chapter 19 Version
// Copyright 1993, Mark Andrews

#if !defined( _ZALTHAR_H_ )
#define _ZALTHAR_H_

#include <iostream.h>
#include <stdlib.h>
#include <afxwin.h>
#include <afxcoll.h>
#include <time.h>

void SetRandomSeed();
// void GetAbilScores();
int RollDice(int sides);

enum playerClasses { WARRIOR, WIZARD, PRIEST, THIEF };
const CString gClassName [] = { "Warrior", "Wizard", "Priest",
   "Thief" };

enum playerRaces { DWARF, ELF, GNOME,
   HALF_ELF, HALFLING, HUMAN };
const CString gRaceName [] = { "Dwarf", "Elf", "Gnome",
   "Half elf", "Halfling", "Human" };

enum playerAbils { STRENGTH, DEXTERITY, CONSTITUTION,
   INTELLIGENCE, WISDOM, CHARISMA };
const CString gAbilsName [] = { "Strength", "Dexterity",
    "Constitution", "Intelligence", "Wisdom",
    "Charisma" };

class CCharacter : public CObject {
protected:
   WORD m_class;
```

*continues*

**Listing 21.1. continued**

```
   WORD m_race;
   WORD m_s;
   WORD m_d;
   WORD m_c;
   WORD m_i;
   WORD m_w;
   WORD m_ch;
   class CString m_name;
   class CString weapon;
   class CString armor;
   class CString magic;
   static int count;
public:
   CCharacter() {}
   ~CCharacter () {}
   static int GetCount() { return count; }
   static void IncCount() { count++; }
   static void DecCount() { count—; }
   static void PrintCount();
   void SetPlayerClass(int pc) { ASSERT_VALID (this); m_class = pc; }
   void SetPlayerRace(int pr) { ASSERT_VALID (this); m_race = pr; }
   int GetPlayerClass() { ASSERT_VALID (this); return m_class; }
   int GetPlayerRace() { ASSERT_VALID (this); return m_race; }
   CString GetRaceName() { ASSERT_VALID (this);
      int r = m_race; return gRaceName[r]; }
   CString GetClassName() { ASSERT_VALID (this);
      return gClassName[m_class]; }
   void SetName(CString nm) { ASSERT_VALID (this); m_name = nm; }
   CString GetName() { return m_name; }
   void SetWeapon(CString wpn) { ASSERT_VALID (this); weapon = wpn; }
   CString GetWeapon() { return weapon; }
   void SetArmor(CString arm) { ASSERT_VALID (this); armor = arm; }
   CString GetArmor() { return armor; }
   void SetMagic(CString mag) { ASSERT_VALID (this); magic = mag; }
   CString GetMagic() { ASSERT_VALID (this); return magic; }
   // Set character's abilities
   void SetAbils(int st, int de, int co, int in,
      int wi, int ch)
      { m_s = st; m_d = de; m_c = co; m_i = in;
         m_w = wi; m_ch = ch; }
   // Get character's abilities
   void GetAbils(int *st, int *de, int *co, int *in,
      int *wi, int *ch)
      { *st = m_s; *de = m_d; *co = m_c; *in = m_i;
         *wi = m_w; *ch = m_ch; }
   // read contents of the PlayerAbils object
   int GetStrength() { return m_s; }
   int GetDexterity() { return m_d; }
   int GetConstitution() { return m_c; }
   int GetIntelligence() { return m_i; }
```

```
   int GetWisdom() { return m_w; }
   int GetCharisma() { return m_ch; }
   void SetStrength(int st) { m_s = st; }
   void SetDexterity(int de) { m_d = de; }
   void SetConstitution(int co) { m_c = co; }
   void SetIntelligence(int in) { m_i = in; }
   void SetWisdom(int wi) { m_w = wi; }
   void SetCharisma(int ch) { m_ch = ch; }
   virtual void PrintEntry() = 0;
   void PrintAbils();
   void SetAbilScores();
   //Override the CObject Serialize function
   virtual void Serialize(CArchive& archive);
#ifdef _DEBUG
   virtual void AssertValid() const;
#endif
};

class CPlayer : public CCharacter {
   DECLARE_SERIAL(CPlayer)
protected:
   CTime m_modTime;
   BOOL  m_bIsDirty;
public:
   CPlayer()
      { m_modTime = CTime::GetCurrentTime(); }
   ~CPlayer () {}
   CPlayer( const CPlayer& a );
   CPlayer(int pr) { SetPlayerRace(pr); }
   void PrintEntry();
   // Override the assignment operator
   CPlayer& operator=( const CPlayer& b );
   void SetDirty( BOOL bDirty )
      {   ASSERT_VALID( this );
         m_bIsDirty = bDirty; }

   BOOL GetDirty()
      {   ASSERT_VALID( this );
         return m_bIsDirty; }
   // Delete All deletes the Player objects as well as the pointers.
   void DeleteAll();
};

class CWarrior : public CPlayer {
public:
   CWarrior() {}
   CWarrior(int pr) : CPlayer(pr)
      { SetPlayerRace(pr); SetPlayerClass(WARRIOR); }
   void PrintEntry();
};
```

*continues*

**Listing 21.1. continued**

```
class CThief : public CPlayer {
public:
   CThief() {}
   CThief(int pr) : CPlayer(pr)
      { SetPlayerRace(pr); SetPlayerClass(WARRIOR); }
   void PrintEntry();
};

class CWizard : public CPlayer {
public:
   CWizard() {}
   CWizard(int pr) : CPlayer(pr)
      { SetPlayerRace(pr); SetPlayerClass(WIZARD); }
   CWizard(int pr, CString mag) : CPlayer(pr)
      { SetPlayerRace(pr); SetPlayerClass(WIZARD); SetMagic(mag); }
   void PrintEntry();
};

class CPriest : public CPlayer {
public:
   CPriest() {}
   CPriest(int pr) : CPlayer(pr)
      { SetPlayerRace(pr); SetPlayerClass(PRIEST); }
   CPriest(int pr, CString mag) : CPlayer(pr)
      { SetPlayerRace(pr); SetPlayerClass(PRIEST); SetMagic(mag); }
   void PrintEntry();
};

#endif // _ZALTHAR_H
```

### ZALTHAR.CPP

```
// ZALTHAR.CPP

#include <iostream.h>
#include <string.h>
#include <stdio.h>
#include <stdlib.h>
#include <afxwin.h>
#include <afxcoll.h>
#include "zalthar.h"
#include "intrface.h"

int CCharacter::count = 0;   // initialize nr of players to 0

IMPLEMENT_SERIAL(CPlayer, CObject, 1)
```

```
///////////////////////////////////////////////
//  CPlayer::operator=
//  Overloaded operator= to perform assignments.
//
CPlayer& CPlayer::operator=( const CPlayer& b )
{
   ASSERT_VALID( this );
   ASSERT_VALID( &b );
   int m_class = b.m_class;
   int m_race = b.m_race;
   int m_s = b.m_s;
   int m_d = b.m_d;
   int m_c = b.m_c;
   int m_i = b.m_i;
   int m_w = b.m_w;
   int m_ch = b.m_ch;
   class CString m_name = b.m_name;
   class CString weapon = b.weapon;
   class CString armor = b.armor;
   class CString magic = b.magic;
   m_modTime = b.m_modTime;
   return *this;
}

// function to set and get ability scores
void CCharacter::SetAbilScores()
{
   ASSERT_VALID( this );
   int abils[6];

   SetRandomSeed();
   for (int c = 0; c < 6; c++)
      abils[c] = RollDice(20);

   SetStrength(abils[0]);
   SetDexterity(abils[1]);
   SetConstitution(abils[2]);
   SetIntelligence(abils[3]);
   SetWisdom(abils[4]);
   SetCharisma(abils[5]);
}

void CCharacter::PrintAbils()
{
   ASSERT_VALID( this );
   cout << '\n';
   cout << "Strength: " << GetStrength() << '\n';
   cout << "Dexterity: " << GetDexterity() << '\n';
   cout << "Constitution: " << GetConstitution() << '\n';
   cout << "Intelligence: " << GetIntelligence() << '\n';
```

*continues*

**Listing 21.1. continued**

```
   cout << "Wisdom: " << GetWisdom() << '\n';
   cout << "Charisma: " << GetCharisma() << '\n';
}

// Serialization function
void CCharacter::Serialize(CArchive& archive)
{
   ASSERT_VALID(this);
   //Call base class function first
   CObject::Serialize(archive);

   //Dump data for CPlayer class
   if (archive.IsStoring()) {
      TRACE( "Serializing a CPlayer out.\n" );
       archive << m_class << m_race
          << m_s << m_d << m_c << m_i << m_w << m_ch
          << m_name << armor
          << weapon << magic;
   }
   else {
      TRACE( "Serializing a CPlayer in.\n" );
      archive >> m_class >> m_race
         >> m_s >> m_d >>m_c >> m_i >> m_w >> m_ch
         >> m_name >> armor
         >> weapon >> magic;
   }
}

void CPlayer::PrintEntry()
{
   ASSERT_VALID( this );
   cout << "\nNAME: ";
   cout << GetName();
   cout << "\nClass: ";
   cout << GetClassName();
   cout << "\nRace: ";
   cout << GetRaceName();
   cout << "\nWeapon: ";
   cout << GetWeapon();
   cout << "\nArmor: ";
   cout << GetArmor();
   PrintAbils();
}

void CWarrior::PrintEntry()
{
   ASSERT_VALID( this );
   cout << "\nNAME: ";
   cout << GetName();
```

```
    cout << "\nRace: ";
    cout << GetRaceName();
    cout << "\nClass: ";
    cout << GetClassName();
    cout << "\nWeapon: ";
    cout << GetWeapon();
    cout << "\nArmor: ";
    cout << GetArmor();
    PrintAbils();
}

void CThief::PrintEntry()
{
    ASSERT_VALID( this );
    cout << "\nNAME: ";
    cout << GetName();
    cout << "\nRace: ";
    cout << GetRaceName();
    cout << "\nClass: ";
    cout << GetClassName();
    cout << "\nWeapon: ";
    cout << GetWeapon();
    cout << "\nArmor: ";
    cout << GetArmor();
    PrintAbils();
}

void CWizard::PrintEntry()
{
    ASSERT_VALID( this );
    cout << "\nNAME: ";
    cout << GetName();
    cout << "\nRace: ";
    cout << GetRaceName();
    cout << "\nClass: ";
    cout << GetClassName();
    cout << "\nWeapon: ";
    cout << GetWeapon();
    cout << "\nMagic: ";
    cout << GetMagic();
    PrintAbils();
}

void CPriest::PrintEntry()
{
    ASSERT_VALID( this );
    cout << "\nNAME: ";
    cout << GetName();
    cout << "\nRace: ";
    cout << GetRaceName();
```

*continues*

**Listing 21.1. continued**

```
   cout << "\nClass: ";
   cout << GetClassName();
   cout << "\nWeapon: ";
   cout << GetWeapon();
   cout << "\nArmor: ";
   cout << GetArmor();
   cout << "\nMagic: ";
   cout << GetMagic();
   PrintAbils();
}

// An all-purpose AssertValid function

#ifdef _DEBUG

void CCharacter::AssertValid() const
{
   CObject::AssertValid();
}

#endif
```

### DATABASE.H

```
// database.h : Declares the interfaces for the CDataBase class.

#ifndef __DATABASE_H__
#define __DATABASE_H__

#include "zalthar.h"
#include "linklist.h"

// Definition of CDataBase Object
class CDataBase: public CObject {
private:
   CPlayerList* ReadDataBase( CFile* pFile );
   BOOL WriteDataBase( CFile* pFile );
   friend void TestTheProgram();
protected:
   CPlayerList* m_pDataList;
   CPlayerList* m_pFindList;
   CString m_szFileName;
   CString m_szFileTitle;
public:
   // constructor
   CDataBase();

   // Create/Destroy CPlayerLists
   BOOL New();
   void Terminate();
```

```
    // File handling
    BOOL DoOpen( const char* pszFileName );
    BOOL DoSave( const char* pszFileName = NULL );
    BOOL DoFind( const char* pszLastName = NULL );

    // Player Handling
    void AddPlayer( CPlayer *pNewPlayer );
    CPlayer* GetPlayer( int nIndex );

    // Database Attributes
    int GetCount();
    const char* GetName();
    CString GetTitle();
    void SetTitle( const char* pszTitle );

#ifdef _DEBUG
public:
    void AssertValid() const;
#endif
};


#endif // __DATABASE_H__
```

## DATABASE.CPP

```
// DATABASE.CPP -- Implements the CDataBase class.

#include <string.h>
#include "database.h"
#include "linklist.h"

const char szUntitled[] = "Untitled";

CDataBase::CDataBase() {
    m_pDataList = NULL;
    m_pFindList = NULL;
    m_szFileName = "";
    m_szFileTitle = "";
}

//  Initialize the database.
BOOL CDataBase::New()
{
    ASSERT_VALID( this );

    // Close database if not closed already.
    Terminate();

    m_pDataList = new CPlayerList;
```

*continues*

**Listing 21.1. continued**

```
   return ( m_pDataList != NULL );
}

//  Clean up the database.
void CDataBase::Terminate()
{
   ASSERT_VALID( this );

   if ( m_pDataList != NULL )
      m_pDataList->DeleteAll();

   delete m_pDataList;
   delete m_pFindList;

   m_pDataList = NULL;
   m_pFindList = NULL;

   m_szFileName = szUntitled;
   m_szFileTitle = szUntitled;
}

//  Look up a player by index.
CPlayer* CDataBase::GetPlayer( int nIndex )
{
   ASSERT_VALID( this );
   ASSERT( m_pDataList != NULL );

   if ( m_pFindList != NULL )
      return (CPlayer*)m_pFindList->GetAt
      ( m_pFindList->FindIndex( nIndex ) );
   else
      return (CPlayer*)m_pDataList->GetAt
         ( m_pDataList->FindIndex( nIndex ) );
}

// Add a player to the database
void CDataBase::AddPlayer( CPlayer* pNewPlayer )
{
   ASSERT_VALID( this );
   ASSERT_VALID( pNewPlayer );
   ASSERT( pNewPlayer != NULL );
   ASSERT( m_pDataList != NULL );

   POSITION pos = m_pDataList->GetHeadPosition();

   while ( pos != NULL &&
         _stricmp( ((CPlayer*)m_pDataList->
         GetAt(pos))->GetName(),
         pNewPlayer->GetName() ) <= 0 )
      m_pDataList->GetNext( pos );
```

```
    if ( pos == NULL )
       m_pDataList->AddTail( pNewPlayer );
    else
       m_pDataList->InsertBefore( pos, pNewPlayer );
}

//  Call FindPlayer() or clear find data.
BOOL CDataBase::DoFind( const char* pszName /* = NULL */ )
{
    ASSERT_VALID( this );
    ASSERT( m_pDataList != NULL );

    if ( pszName == NULL )
    {
       delete m_pFindList;
       m_pFindList = NULL;
       return FALSE;
    }

    // Prevent a second find to occur if
    // we already have one.
    ASSERT( m_pFindList == NULL );
    return ( ( m_pFindList = m_pDataList->
       FindPlayer( pszName ) ) != NULL );
}

//  Open the database and read data.
BOOL CDataBase::DoOpen( const char* pszFileName )
{
    ASSERT_VALID( this );
    ASSERT( pszFileName != NULL );

    CFile file( pszFileName, CFile::modeRead );

    // Read the object data from file
    CPlayerList* pNewDataBase = ReadDataBase( &file );

    file.Close();

    // Get rid of current database if new one is OK
    if ( pNewDataBase != NULL )
    {
       Terminate();
       m_pDataList = pNewDataBase;

       m_szFileName = pszFileName;
       return TRUE;
    }
    else
```

*continues*

**Listing 21.1. continued**

```
      return FALSE;
}

//  Save data to a file.
BOOL CDataBase::DoSave( const char* pszFileName /* = NULL */ )
{
   ASSERT_VALID( this );

   // store objects name.
   if ( pszFileName != NULL )
      m_szFileName = pszFileName;

   CFileStatus status;
   int nAccess = CFile::modeWrite;

   // Call GetStatus, which returns true if specified
   // file exists, false if it doesn't.
   if ( !CFile::GetStatus( m_szFileName, status ) )
      nAccess |= CFile::modeCreate;

   CFile file( m_szFileName, nAccess );

   // Write database to a file
   if ( WriteDataBase( &file ) )
   {
      file.Close();
      return TRUE;
   }
   else
   {
      file.Close();
      return FALSE;
   }
}

//  Write data to a file.
BOOL CDataBase::WriteDataBase( CFile* pFile )
{
   ASSERT_VALID( this );
   ASSERT( m_pDataList != NULL );

   // Create a archive from theFile for writing
   CArchive archive( pFile, CArchive::store );

   // Archive out, or catch the exception.
   TRY
   {
      archive << m_pDataList;
   }
```

```
    CATCH( CArchiveException, e )
    {
        // Throw this exception again for the benefit
        // of the caller.
        THROW_LAST();
    }
    END_CATCH

    // Exit here if no errors or exceptions.
    archive.Close();
    return TRUE;
}

//  Read data from the database.
CPlayerList* CDataBase::ReadDataBase( CFile* pFile )
{
    ASSERT_VALID( this );
    CPlayerList* pNewDataBase = NULL;

    // Create a archive from pFile for reading.
    CArchive archive( pFile, CArchive::load );

    // Deserialize the new data base from the archive,
    // or catch the exception.

    TRY
    {
        archive >> pNewDataBase;
    }
    CATCH( CArchiveException, e )
    {
        archive.Close();

        // If we got part of the database, delete it.
        if ( pNewDataBase != NULL )
        {
            pNewDataBase->DeleteAll();
            delete pNewDataBase;
        }

        // Caught an exception—but we throw it again so
        // the caller of this function can also catch it.
        THROW_LAST();
    }
    END_CATCH

    // Exit here if no errors or exceptions.
    archive.Close();
    return pNewDataBase;
}
```

*continues*

**Listing 21.1. continued**

```
#ifdef _DEBUG
void CDataBase::AssertValid() const
{
   if ( m_pDataList != NULL )
   {
      ASSERT_VALID( m_pDataList );
      if ( m_pFindList != NULL )
         ASSERT_VALID( m_pFindList );
   }
   else
      ASSERT( m_pFindList == NULL );
}
#endif

// Get number of players in currently active list.
int CDataBase::GetCount()
{
   ASSERT_VALID( this );
   if ( m_pFindList != NULL )
      return m_pFindList->GetCount();
   if ( m_pDataList != NULL )
      return m_pDataList->GetCount();
   return 0;
}

const char* CDataBase::GetName()
{
   ASSERT_VALID( this );
   return m_szFileName;
}

CString CDataBase::GetTitle()
{
   ASSERT_VALID( this );
   return  "Phone Book - " + m_szFileTitle;
}

void CDataBase::SetTitle( const char* pszTitle )
{
   ASSERT_VALID( this );
   m_szFileTitle = pszTitle;
}
```

### INTRFACE.H

```
// intrface.h
// header file for intrface.cpp module
```

```
#include <stdlib.h>
#include <afxwin.h>
#include <afxcoll.h>
#include "zalthar.h"
#include "linklist.h"

#if !defined( _INTRFACE_H_ )
#define _INTRFACE_H_

// Well, the file is here if we ever need to
// put something in it.

#endif // _INTRFACE_H_
```

## INTRFACE.CPP

```
// Intrface.cpp
// Setup Module for The Wrath of Zalthar
// Copyright 1993, Mark Andrews

#include <iostream.h>
#include <string.h>
#include <afxwin.h>
#include <afxcoll.h>
#include "zalthar.h"
#include "setup.h"
#include "linklist.h"

/////////////////////////////////////////////////////////////////
// The following functions are user interface functions
// and I/O functions. Later on, they'll make use of dialog boxes.
/////////////////////////////////////////////////////////////////

// function to print title screen

// Prompt user for number of characters to create
int GetNrOfChars()
{
   int n;
   cout << "How many characters do you want to create? ";
   cin >> n;
   cout << '\n';
   return n;
}

// Set new character's name
void SetPlayerName(CPlayer *playerPtr)
{
   char playerName[128];
```

continues

**Listing 21.1. continued**

```
   cout  << "\nType character's name: ";
   cin >> playerName;
   playerPtr->SetName(playerName);

}

// Set new player's race
int SetPlayerRace()
{
   int playerRace = 0;
   while (playerRace < 1 || playerRace >6) {
      cout << "\nSelect character's race: "
          << "\n(1) Dwarf"
          << "\n(2) Elf"
          << "\n(3) Gnome"
          << "\n(4) Half-elf"
          << "\n(5) Halfling"
          << "\n(6) Human\n\n";
      cin >> playerRace;
   }
   playerRace--;         // index from zero
   cout << "\nPlayer's race is " << gRaceName[playerRace];
   return playerRace;
}

// Set new player's class
int SetPlayerClass(int playerRace)
{
   int playerClass;
   cout << "\n\nSelect character's class: ";
      if (playerRace == HUMAN || playerRace == ELF
      || playerRace == HALF_ELF) {
         playerClass = 0;
         while (playerClass < 1 || playerClass >4) {
            cout << "\n(1) Warrior";
            cout << "\n(2) Wizard";
            cout << "\n(3) Priest";
            cout << "\n(4) Thief\n\n";
            cin >> playerClass;
         }
         playerClass--;   // index from zero
      }
      else if (playerRace == DWARF || playerRace == GNOME
      || playerRace == HALFLING) {
         playerClass = 0;
         while (playerClass < 1 || playerClass >3) {
            cout << "\n(1) Warrior";
            cout << "\n(2) Priest";
            cout << "\n(3) Thief\n\n";
            cin >> playerClass;
```

```
            }
            if (playerClass == 1)
               playerClass—;    // 2 and 3 already decremented
         }
      cout << "\nPlayer's class is " << gClassName[playerClass];
      return playerClass;
}
```

### LINKLIST.H

```
// LINKLIST.H

#if !defined( _LINKLIST_H_ )
#define _LINKLIST_H_

#include <afxwin.h>
#include <afxcoll.h>
#include "zalthar.h"

class CPlayerList : public CObList {
   DECLARE_SERIAL(CPlayerList)
public:
   void DeleteAll();
   CPlayerList() {}

   // Add new functions
   CPlayerList* FindPlayer( const char * szTarget );

};

#endif  // _LINKLIST_H_
```

### LINKLIST.CPP

```
// linklist.cpp

#include <iostream.h>
#include <stdlib.h>
#include <afxwin.h>
#include <afxcoll.h>

#include "linklist.h"

IMPLEMENT_SERIAL( CPlayerList, CObList, 0 )

// string const for untitiled database
extern const char szUntitled[];

//  Delete all objects in the list.
void CPlayerList::DeleteAll()
{
```

*continues*

**Listing 21.1. continued**

```
   ASSERT_VALID( this );
   POSITION pos = GetHeadPosition();

   while (pos != NULL)
      delete GetNext(pos);
   RemoveAll();
}

///////////////////////////////////////////////
//  CPlayerList::FindPlayer
//
CPlayerList* CPlayerList::FindPlayer( const char * szTarget )
{
   ASSERT_VALID( this );

   CPlayerList* pNewList = new CPlayerList;
   CPlayer* pNext = NULL;

   // Start at front of list
   POSITION pos = GetHeadPosition();

   // Iterate over whole list
   while( pos != NULL )
   {
      // Get next element (note cast)
      pNext = (CPlayer*)GetNext(pos);

      // Add current element to new list if it matches
      if ( _strnicmp( pNext->GetName(), szTarget, strlen( szTarget ) )
            == 0 )
         pNewList->AddTail(pNext);
   }

   if ( pNewList->IsEmpty() )
   {
      delete pNewList;
      pNewList = NULL;
   }

   return pNewList;
}
```

### SETUP.H

```
// Setup.h
// Module for The Wrath of Zalthar
// Copyright 1993, Mark Andrews

#include <afxwin.h>
#include <afxcoll.h>
```

```
#include "zalthar.h"
#include "database.h"
#include "linklist.h"

// forward declarations
void CreatePlayers(CDataBase *pDataBase);
void TestTheProgram();
```

## SETUP.CPP

```
// Setup.cpp
// Setup Module for The Wrath of Zalthar
// Copyright 1993, Mark Andrews

#include <iostream.h>
#include <string.h>
#include <afxwin.h>
#include <afxcoll.h>
#include "zalthar.h"
#include "setup.h"
#include "zalthar.h"
#include "linklist.h"

// Forward declarations.
int RollDice(int nrOfSides);
void SetRandomSeed(void);

//////////////////////////////////////////////////////////////
// This function creates the game's characters.
// It's called from main().
//////////////////////////////////////////////////////////////

void CreatePlayers(CDataBase *pDataBase)
{
   CString playerName;
   CPlayer *playerPtr;
   char pName[64];
   int pClass;

   for (int n = 0; n < 4; n++) {
      cout << "\nType player's name: ";
      cin >> pName;
      cout << "\nType player's class:\n"
         << "   (1) Warrior\n"
         << "   (2) Wizard\n"
         << "   (3) Priest\n"
         << "   (4) Thief\n";
      cin >> pClass;
      —pClass;
```

*continues*

**Listing 21.1. continued**

```
        switch (pClass) {
           case 0: {
              playerPtr = new CWarrior;
              break;
           }
           case 1: {
              playerPtr = new CWizard;
              break;
           }
           case 2: {
              playerPtr = new CPriest;
              break;
           }
           case 3: {
              playerPtr = new CThief;
              break;
           }
        }
        playerPtr->SetName(pName);
        playerPtr->SetPlayerClass(pClass);
        pDataBase->AddPlayer(playerPtr);
     }
}

// seed the random number generator with current time
void SetRandomSeed()
{
   srand((unsigned)time(NULL));
}

// function to roll dice
int RollDice(int nrOfSides)
{
   div_t div_result;   // struct used in dividing
   int randNr, randNr2;

   randNr = rand();           // get random number
   switch (nrOfSides) {
      case 4: {
         randNr = randNr & 0xFFF0;    // nr now 16 or less
         randNr /= 4;                 // nr now 4 or less
         randNr++;                    // start at 1 sted 0
         break;
      }
      case 8: {
         randNr = randNr & 0xFFF0;    // nr now 16 or less
         randNr /= 2;                 // nr now 8 or less
         randNr++;                    // start at 1 sted 0
         break;
```

```
        }
        case 10: {
           randNr = randNr & 0xFFF0;      // nr now 16 or less
           if (randNr > 9) {              // if nr is 10 or more
              div_result = div(randNr, 10);
              randNr = div_result.rem;
           }                              // nr is now in range 0-9
           break;
        }                                 // (that's ok for 10-sided die)
        case 12: {
           randNr = randNr & 0xFFF0;      // nr now 16 or less
           randNr2 = rand();              // get 2d random number
           randNr2 = randNr2 & 0xFFF0; // nr2 now 16 or less
           randNr2 /= 4;                  // nr2 now 4 or less
           randNr += randNr2;             // add the random nrs
           randNr++;                      // start at 1 sted 0
           break;
        }
        case 20: {
           randNr = randNr & 0x000F;      // nr now 0 to 15
           randNr2 = rand();              // get random number
           randNr2 = randNr2 & 0x0004; // nr2 now 0 to 4
           randNr += randNr2;             // add the 2 rand nrs
           randNr++;                      // start at 1 sted 0
           break;
        }
     }
     return (randNr);
}
```

# Summary

This chapter described in detail some of the most important classes in the MFC library. The most important class in the MFC library is the `CObject` class, from which most classes used in C++ programs are derived.

To show how MFC classes are used, the chapter presented a new and improved version of The Wrath of Zalthar program, updated to make use of several of the most important MFC classes. More MFC-related features will be added to the program in later chapters.

You're not required to derive classes from the `CObject` class, but classes that are derived from `CObject` have many important and powerful features and functionalities. For example, classes derived from `CObject` have serialization capabilities; that is, they can read or write information to and from disk storage with little or no intervention on the part of the programmer.

They can also supply many valuable diagnostic tools that can be useful during the debugging stage of program development.

This chapter described the capabilities of `CObject` subclasses in some detail and also introduced some other important MFC classes, such as file-related classes, collection classes, the `CString` class, and time-related classes.

Other kinds of MFC classes—including classes used in creating dialog boxes, menus, and graphics elements—are introduced in Chapters 22, 23, and 24.

Chapter 22

# The Visual Workbench

If you're an experienced Windows programmer, you know that the pre-C++ Windows API contains hundreds of C-language functions for managing Windows components such as windows, dialog boxes, device contexts, graphics tools such as brushes and pens, controls, and other standard Windows-related items.

The Microsoft Foundation Class (MFC) library supplies most of the functionality of the Windows API as C++ abstractions, that is, as C++ classes and functions. So, if you're an experienced Windows programmer, you already know a lot of what you need to know to start writing Visual C++ programs by using the classes and member functions in the MFC library.

There's still new material to learn, however—even if you've written programs for Windows by using Microsoft C/C++ Version 7. That's because Visual C++ comes with a new version of the MFC library: Version 2. This new version of the

MFC library is specially designed to work with Visual C++ and with the application framework. It has some new classes—for example, a new `CDocument` class—and in a behind-the-scenes kind of way, the MFC library supports a lot of the work that AppWizard does to create application frameworks.

As you saw in Chapter 21, "The Microsoft Foundation Classes," an application framework is a skeleton (but working) application you can construct with the AppWizard tool. When you have generated a framework application with AppWizard, you can expand it into any kind of Windows program you like.

This chapter is a general outline of how you use the programming tools provided in the Visual Workbench—App Studio, AppWizard, and ClassWizard—to write a Visual C++ program. The chapter describes the overall architecture of a Visual C++ program and explains how App Studio, AppWizard, and ClassWizard can help you write Windows applications in Visual C++. When you've learned how to use these new tools, you'll be ready to start Chapter 23, "Windows and Views," and to start writing Windows-based Visual C++ programs.

# Visual Workbench Components

If you have typed and executed example programs in this book, you have used one Visual Workbench tool—the Visual Workbench editor—extensively. This chapter introduces three other Visual Workbench tools: AppWizard, App Studio, and ClassWizard.

In a nutshell, here are the functions of these three tools:

- AppWizard is the tool that creates an application framework.
- App Studio is an interactive tool for creating user interface objects.
- ClassWizard is an interactive tool that can "bind," or connect, user interface objects with the commands and functions that make the objects work during the execution of a program.

You'll learn much more about AppWizard, App Studio, and ClassWizard later in this chapter.

# Message-Driven Programs

If you're a Windows programmer, you know that Windows programs are *message-driven*. That is, when a user runs a Windows-based program—no matter what language it's written in—a message loop continuously cycles, monitoring not only actions taken by the user, but also many other kinds of events (such as interrupts) that can occur during the running of the program. Every time the user moves the mouse, clicks a mouse button, or presses a key on the keyboard, Windows dispatches a message to the part of the program that controls the window in which the action has taken place.

In Visual C++, just as in older Windows programming environments, various kinds of objects—such as documents, views, windows, and even your application (which is an object itself)—have built-in capabilities for handling messages. Every object that is designed to handle messages has a member function that is known as a *message handler function*, or more succinctly, as a *message handler*. Each time an object receives a message, the Windows system routes the incoming message from one object to another in a carefully orchestrated sequence until it finds an object that can handle the message. The object then carries out the instructions contained in the message, and the program continues.

Many messages that Windows processes fall into a special category called *commands*. A command is a message that is dispatched to an application when the user selects a menu item, clicks a toolbar button, or presses an accelerator key. In other words, a command is simply an instruction to a program to perform a certain action. Unlike a function call, which is not related to a specific object, a command is a kind of message because it is directed at a specific target.

When a user action or a program event causes Windows to generate a message, the message is routed in a specific sequence to one target object after another. Each object that receives the message has an opportunity to respond to it. When the message reaches an object in the chain that has the capability of carrying out the message, that object "handles" the message and the chain stops.

As you may know if you are already a Windows programmer, commands are based on the Windows message `WM_COMMAND`. In Visual C++, you can send commands to frame windows, documents, views, your application, and other kinds of target objects.

> **NOTE—WE DON'T DO WINDOWS**
>
> To understand the material in this chapter, you must be familiar with the basic principles of Windows programming. This chapter reviews some of those principles, but it doesn't teach them. To learn how to write Windows programs, you'll need a supplementary text, such as *Programming Windows 3.1* by Charles Petzold (which is considered the standard text on Windows programming) or one or two of the other Windows programming books listed in the Bibliography.

# C++ Program Architecture

Before you start using AppWizard, App Studio, and ClassWizard, it's important to understand the relationship between the application framework AppWizard creates and the source code that you write to fill out the framework that AppWizard provides.

When a user executes your application, most of the program's flow of control is managed by the code AppWizard generates when it creates the application framework. For instance, the framework created by AppWizard manages the program's main *message loop*, which dispatches messages that inform the Windows system when the user performs actions such as selecting menu commands or editing data in a window. (You'll learn more about messages and message loops later in this chapter, in the section "The `WinMain()` Function."

Events that your application's framework can handle by itself don't rely on your code at all. For example, the framework knows how to close windows and how to exit your application in response to user commands. As it handles these tasks, the framework uses message handlers and C++ virtual functions to give you opportunities to respond to these events as well. You, however, don't have to write any code to perform these routine kinds of tasks. The application framework handles all that.

Your role in writing a Visual C++ program is to supply the application-specific source code and to connect the components by defining what messages and commands they respond to. You use the C++ language and standard C++ techniques to derive your own application-specific classes from those supplied by the class library and to override and augment the base behavior of the base classes that are provided in the MFC library.

## The WinMain() Function

A Visual C++ program, like any program for Windows, always has a main function named, logically enough, `WinMain()`. In a Visual C++ application, however, you don't write the `WinMain()` function; it is supplied by the MFC library and is called when the application starts up. In Visual C++, as in other languages that are used for writing Windows programs, `WinMain()` performs standard services such as registering window classes. Then, it calls member functions of your application, which is treated as a C++ object, to initialize and run the application.

A Visual C++ application always has one (and only one) *application object*. An application object is an object that is derived from the MFC library class `CWinApp`. In a Visual C++ application, the application object controls all the program's document and view objects, and manages various housekeeping chores for the program, such as initialization and cleanup. The application object also creates and manages *document templates* for any document types that the application supports.

A *document template* is an object that creates and manages all open documents of one type. It manages the creation of documents, views, and frame windows. Applications that support multiple kinds of documents have multiple document templates. The MFC library has a `CSingleDocTemplate` class that you can use for SDI (single document interface) applications and a `CMultiDocTemplate` that you can use for MDI (multiple document interface) applications.

To initialize your application, the `WinMain()` function calls two member functions of your application object: `InitApplication()` and `InitInstance()`. `WinMain()` runs the application's message loop by calling a member function named `Run()`. When it's time for your application to quit, `WinMain()` calls a member function of the application object named `ExitInstance()`.

You don't have to write the code that does any of those things, however. AppWizard generates all the code for you when it creates your application framework.

## Documents and Views

A typical Visual C++ application is built around a pair of objects called a *document* and a *view*. A document is an object that manages the data used by an application. A view is an object that manages the display of that data on the screen.

Typically, a Windows program creates a document when the user of a program selects the New or the Open command from the application's File menu. Most applications can save documents in files when the user of a program selects the Save command or the Save As command from the File menu.

As all this takes place, a view object usually displays the information that is being loaded or saved.

Document objects are derived from the MFC library class `CDocument`. A document object encapsulates an application's data. View objects are derived from the MFC library class `CView`.

When a user launches your application, its view object is the user's window into the program's data. The view object determines how the user sees the data in the program's document object and how the user interacts with that data.

Many applications can show the data in documents by using more than one view. You can give an application the capability of showing information in various formats by equipping it with multiple view objects.

If you need a view that scrolls, you can derive a view object from the MFC library class `CScrollView` rather than from `CView`. If your view has a user interface that is laid out in a way that is tailored for entering data—such as in a database—you can create a form-like screen display by deriving a view object from a class named `CFormView`. For a simpler display of text data, you can derive a display from another class named `CEditView`.

Visual C++ displays views inside windows called *document frame windows.* In an SDI application, which has just one window, the document frame window is also the application's *main frame window.* In an MDI application, which supports multiple windows, document windows are *child windows* that are displayed inside a main frame window.

The class that supplies a program's main frame window specifies the styles and other characteristics of the frame windows that contain the program's views. When you write an SDI program, you should derive your main frame window from the MFC library class `CFrameWnd`. When you write an MDI application, you should derive your main frame window from the `CMDIFrameWnd` class. MDI applications can also derive classes from the `CMDIChildWnd` class to create various other kinds of document frame windows.

## Message Maps

When an object receives a command, it determines whether it can handle the command by checking a sequence of code called a *message map.* Every class that can be a target of a command contains a definition of a message map. A message map contains an entry for each command (or other kind of message) that the target class can handle. A message map is easy to spot because it is always bracketed by the words BEGIN_MESSAGE_MAP and END_MESSAGE_MAP.

The message map for a class usually appears in the source code file that implements the class's member functions. For example, in this chapter's version of The Wrath of Zalthar (which appears in Listing 22.1 at the end of this chapter), this message map for the CMainFrame class appears in the file ZALTHDOC.CPP:

```
BEGIN_MESSAGE_MAP(CZaltharDoc, CDocument)
     //{{AFX_MSG_MAP(CZaltharDoc)
     ON_COMMAND(ID_CHARACTERS_CREATE_ONE, OnCharactersCreateOne)
     ON_COMMAND(ID_CHARACTERS_FIND, OnCharactrersFind)
     //}}AFX_MSG_MAP
END_MESSAGE_MAP
```

When a message map appears in the source file that implements a class, a call to the macro DECLARE_MESSAGE_MAP must appear in the class's header file. However, when you write a Visual C++ program, you don't ordinarily have to worry about that; when AppWizard and ClassWizard create the message maps that are needed by command-handling classes, they also take care of placing the necessary DECLARE_MESSAGE_MAP calls in the classes' header files.

Until the advent of Visual C++, it was the C++ programmer's responsibility to write a message map for every class that could handle messages. With Visual C++, that is no longer true. When AppWizard generates a C++ application framework, it produces message maps for all message-handling classes in the framework. Then, when you start creating more message-handling classes with ClassWizard, the ClassWizard tool generates the message maps that those new classes require.

### Comments in Message Maps

In the preceding example, two comment lines are written in a special format:

```
//{{AFX_MSG_MAP(CMainFrame)
//}}AFX_MSG_MAP
```

When comments written in the preceding format bracket a section of text in a C++ program, you should never write or change any text that appears between them. That's because it is not your responsibility to write message maps; that is ClassWizard's job. When ClassWizard is binding commands, it uses comments like those shown previously to find and write message maps, and if you disturb the code sandwiched between the comments, it's very likely your program will no longer compile properly.

### The Three Parts of a Message Map

The message map shown in the preceding example specifies that the `CZaltharDoc` class, which is derived from the `CDocument` class, can handle two command messages: `ID_CHARACTERS_CREATE_ONE` and `ID_CHARACTERS_FIND()`.

As the prior code fragment shows, each entry in a message map has three parts:

- The words `ON_COMMAND`. This is the name of a macro that Windows calls when it generates a command message.
- A *command ID*. This is a constant that represents the ID number of a resource type such as a menu, a menu item, a dialog box, a dialog box control, or an accelerator key. The message map shown previously contains two command IDs: `ID_CHARACTERS_CREATE_ONE` and `ID_CHARACTERS_FIND`. In the Zalthar program, both those ID constants are assigned to dialog boxes. `ID_CHARACTERS_CREATE_ONE` is a dialog box that the program uses to create characters one at a time, and `ID_CHARACTERS_FIND` is a dialog box that the program uses to find characters in search operations.
- The name of the message handler (or message-handling function) that carries out the messages the target object receives. Each message-handling function that appears in a message map is the name of a member function of the class receiving the message. In the Zalthar program, the message map shown in the preceding example causes the program's document class to call a message-handling function named `OnCharactersCreateOne()` whenever an `ID_CHARACTERS_CREATE_ONE` message is received. The message map also tells the program to call a message-handling function named `OnCharactersFind()` whenever an `ID_CHARACTERS_FIND` message is received.

When you write a Visual C++ program, it is your responsibility to write the functions that your program's functionality requires. However, ClassWizard can show you exactly where to put those functions in your program's source code, as you'll see later in this chapter.

When a target object receives a command message, it checks to see whether the message matches any of the kinds of messages that its message map says it can handle. If the command received matches an entry that appears in the class's message map, Windows calls the specified member function of the target class to handle the incoming message.

### Target Objects

Many kinds of objects can receive and respond to commands. In this chapter's version of the example program—the first version of The Wrath of Zalthar to qualify as a full-fledged application—several kinds of dialog boxes receive and respond to a variety of menu commands.

In Visual C++, target objects are always derived from the MFC library class `CCmdTarget`. Objects derived from `CCmdTarget` contain their own message maps and message-handler functions. You can find a complete list of target objects in the *Class Library Reference* that comes with Visual C++.

### How Visual C++ Handles Messages

Programs written in Visual C++ process messages just like other Windows programs, but the Visual C++ framework supplies some special enhancements that make it much easier to write Windows programs than before. These tools are known collectively as the Visual Workbench.

# The Visual Workbench Tools

This section introduces the three Visual Workbench tools that C++ provides to help you create applications: AppWizard, App Studio, and ClassWizard. As noted earlier in this chapter, AppWizard is the tool that creates an application framework; App Studio is an interactive tool for creating user interface objects; and ClassWizard is an interactive tool that can "bind," or connect, user interface objects with the commands and functions that make the objects work during the execution of a program.

This section briefly describes the operations of AppWizard, App Studio, and ClassWizard. You'll have an opportunity to use all three of these tools later in this chapter.

## AppWizard

The first step in writing a Visual C++ application is to create an application framework. When you start using AppWizard, you'll see that it's incredibly easy to use this tool to produce an application framework; all you must do is select the

AppWizard command from the Visual Workbench editor's Project menu, click an OK button in a dialog box, and wait a few seconds. While you wait, AppWizard creates an application framework.

When you have created an application framework—with more than a little help from AppWizard—you can use two more Visual Workbench tools to expand your framework into a full-scale Windows application. Then, with another Visual Workbench tool—App Studio—you can create all the user interface objects your application requires: menus, dialog boxes, bitmaps, icons, tables of often used strings, and accelerator keys.

### NOTE—WHAT'S A RESOURCE?

Every Windows program contains one or more files that create resources: special objects such as menus, dialog boxes, and icons that the program requires. There are two ways to create a resource. You can write a definition for the resource (in a special language called a resource-definition language) and place that definition in a special kind of source file called a *resource definition file*. When you program in Visual C++, there is also an easier way. You can design your resource interactively with a resource-creating tool such as App Studio. Either way, you wind up with a resource that your program can access when the resource is needed at runtime.

When you create an application framework with the tools supplied in the C++ Visual Toolbox, AppWizard places the definitions of the program's resources in a source file that has the filename suffix .RC. For example, the resource definition file that AppWizard created for the Zalthar program is named ZALTHAR.RC.

When you compile a Visual C++ program, the resources defined in the program's resource definition file are compiled into object-code modules with filenames that have various filename extensions, such as .ICO (for an icon resource), .BMP (for a bitmap resource), and .RC2 (for resources such as menus and dialog boxes that you create for your applications). When you execute your application, your program manages these resources dynamically, loading them when they are needed and unloading them when they are not required.

## How AppWizard Works

With AppWizard, you can create an executable Windows function complete with a menu bar and a window at the touch of a menu command.

When AppWizard creates a framework for an application, it defines the program's application object (an object derived from the MFC library class `CWinApp`). AppWizard also generates an implementation file that contains the following:

- An empty constructor for the program's application class.
- A variable that declares the one (and only one) object of the application class.
- A message map for the program's application object.
- A standard implementation of the application's `InitInstance()` member function.

AppWizard places the definition of the application class in a header (.H) file that has the same name as the application's Visual C++ project. The program's application object is placed in an implementation (.CPP) file that has the same name as the application's project.

In this chapter's version of the Zalthar program, presented in Listing 22.1, the name of the program's application class is `CZaltharApp`. The definition of the `CZalthar` class, which was created and placed in the file ZALTHAR.H by AppWizard, looks like this:

```
class CZaltharApp : public CWinApp
{
public:
     CZaltharApp();
// Overrides
     virtual BOOL InitInstance;

// Implementation

     //{{AFX_MSG(CZaltharApp)
     afx_msg void OnAppAbout();
          // NOTE - the ClassWizard will add and remove member functions
// here. DO NOT EDIT what you see in these blocks of generated
// code!
     //}}AFX_MSG
     DECLARE_MESSAGE_MAP()
};
```

The application class that AppWizard typically generates for a class (with a definition like the preceding one) is adequate for many purposes; however, you can modify the class if you like. In fact, you must override the `CWinApp` class's `InitInstance()` function.

`InitInstance()` is a function that the `WinMain()` function calls every time a new instance of the application starts. The standard `InitInstance()` implementation created by AppWizard performs these tasks:

- Opens either a document specified by the program or the user or a new, empty document.
- Loads standard file options from an .INI file, including the names of the most recently used files.
- Registers one or more document templates that in turn create documents, views, and frame windows. (Document templates are described in more detail later in this chapter.)

If an MDI application is running, `InitInstance()` also creates a main frame window.

Applications can override `InitInstance()` to perform such tasks as opening, displaying, and updating windows. Listing 22.1 doesn't do anything special with `InitInstance()`, but does override the function to do nothing, as you can see by examining the previous class definition.

When you override `InitInstance()` in your programs, be sure not to disturb the portion of the code bracketed by the comments `//{{ . . . //}}`, which is the exclusive property of AppWizard!

## Member Functions of CWinApp Objects

Besides `InitInstance()`, `CWinApp` also provides several other important member functions that can also be overridden. These functions include `ExitInstance()`, `OnIdle()`, and `Run()`.

### ExitInstance( )

The Windows system enables you to run more than one copy, or *instance*, of the same application. Each time an instance of an application terminates—usually because the user quits the application—the application calls the `ExitInstance()` member function of the `CWinApp` class.

When an application shuts down, the framework created by AppWizard takes care of most standard cleanup chores, such as gracefully shutting down documents and views. If your application requires any special kind of cleanup processing, however—such as releasing graphics device interface (GDI) resources or deallocating memory that has been used during the program's execution—you can override the `ExitInstance()` function.

### OnIdle()

When no Windows messages are being processed, the Visual C++ framework calls the `CWinApp` member function `OnIdle()`. The default version of `OnIdle()` updates the status of user interface objects such as toolbar buttons when the CPU is idle and performs cleanup operations involving temporary objects created by the framework as a program cycles through its main loop. You can override `OnIdle()` to perform any special background tasks that your program requires.

### Run()

A Visual C++ program typically spends most of its time in the `Run()` member function of the `CWinApp` class. As soon as the initialization phase of a program's processing is complete, the `WinMain()` function calls `Run()` to process the program's message loop.

The `Run()` function cycles through the program's message loop, checking a lineup of messages called the *message queue* to see if messages are waiting to be dispatched. If a message is waiting to be sent, `Run()` dispatches it.

If no messages are available, which often is the case, `Run()` calls `OnIdle()` to perform any background processing that the program or the framework may require. If no messages are waiting to be sent and there is no idle processing to do, the application waits until there is some work to do.

When the application quits, `Run()` calls `ExitInstance()` to terminate the program.

Besides running the message loop and giving you an opportunity to initialize the application and clean up after it, `CWinApp` provides several other services.

## How WinApp Objects Handle Documents

As the user of a program opens and closes files, the application object that the program has derived from the `CWinApp` class always keeps track of the four most recently used files. The names of these files are added to the File menu and are updated each time they change. The Visual C++ framework keeps track of these four filenames by storing them in an .INI file that has the same name as the application being executed. When the application quits and then starts up again, the framework reads the filenames from the .INI file that it maintains. When AppWizard creates an application framework, it overrides the `WinApp` class's `InitInstance()` function to include a call to another `CWinApp` member function named `LoadStdProfileSettings()`. When `LoadStdProfileSettings()` is called, it loads information from the .INI file, including the most recently used filenames.

### Document Templates

To manage the process of creating documents with their associated views and frame windows, the framework created by AppWizard uses two *document template* classes: `CSingleDocTemplate` for SDI applications and `CMultiDocTemplate` for MDI applications. From these two document template classes, you can create *document template objects*. The job of a document template object is to create and store documents.

As you might guess, an object that is derived from the `CSingleDocTemplate` class can create and store one type of document at a time, whereas an object created from the `CMultiDocTemplate` class can maintain a list of multiple open documents of the same type. If you want your application to support two or more document types, you must call a function named `AddDocTemplate()` for each kind of document you want to support.

Many applications support multiple document types. For example, you might write an application that supports both text documents and graphics documents. When the user of such an application selects the New command from the File menu, a dialog box might present a list of possible new document types to open. For each supported document type, your application could use a distinct document template object.

When an application is running, the application object derived from the `CWinApp` class creates and maintains document templates. When an application's `InitInstance()` function is called, one of its main tasks is to construct one or more document templates of whatever variety the application requires.

As each document template is created by the `InitInstance()` function, the application object stores a pointer to the template in a *template list* and sets up an appropriate interface that enables the user to add and remove document templates as required.

## Using AppWizard

The best way to learn about AppWizard is to use it. To create an application with AppWizard, follow these steps.

1. From the Windows File Manager, create a new folder. Name your project ZALTHAR.
2. Launch Visual C++.
3. Select AppWizard from the Visual Workbench's Project menu.
4. The Visual Workbench responds by displaying an MFC AppWizard dialog box like the one shown in Figure 22.1.

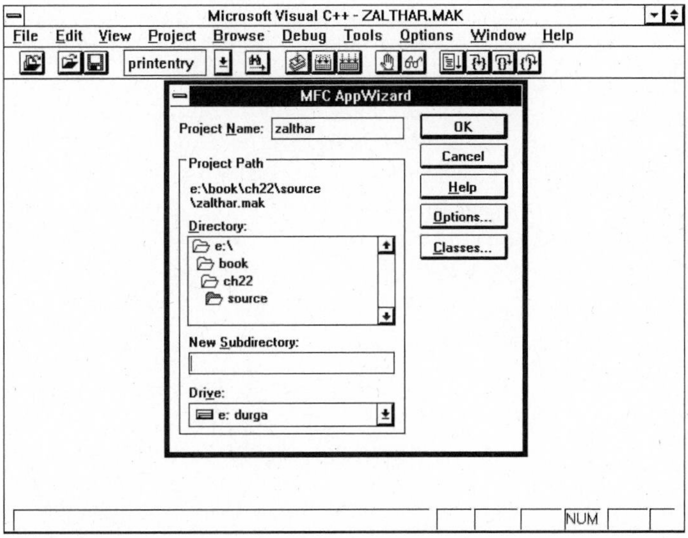


*Figure 22.1. The MFC AppWizard window.*

5. In the edit box labeled Project Name, type a name for your project. Give the project the same name as its folder: `zalthar` (you can't type uppercase letters in the MFC AppWizard window).
6. As you type your project's name, note that AppWizard echoes your typing in two locations in the MFC AppWizard window: in the static text item labeled Project Path and in the edit box named New Subdirectory. I don't know why AppWizard does this; the result is always more

subdirectories than I need. If you share my disdain for extra subdirectories, do this: When you have typed your project's name, delete the word *zalthar* from the New Subdirectory edit box. When you've done this, the MFC AppWizard dialog box should look like the one shown in Figure 22.1.

7. Close the MFC AppWizard dialog box by clicking the OK button.
8. When the New Application Information dialog box appears, you can read what it says. Then close the dialog box by clicking the Create button.
9. Wait a few seconds (that's all it takes) while AppWizard generates an application framework for a program named Zalthar.
10. When your application is ready, select Edit from the Project menu.
11. When the Project menu's Edit dialog box appears, navigate through the source files on the program disk that came with this book. Stop when you find the Chapter 22 version of the Zalthar program. Notice that there are two directories for the Chapter 22 version of the program: one labeled ZALTHDEM and one labeled ZALTHFIN. Open the ZALTHDEM folder; it contains a demonstration version of the program that you can work on as you complete this exercise. The ZALTHFIN directory contains a completed version of the program. When you have found the ZALTHDEM directory, select Open from the Visual Workbench Project menu and open the project named ZALTHAR.MAK.
12. When the names of the files in this chapter's Zalthar folder are displayed in the File Name list box, add them to your project by clicking the Add All button in the lower-right corner of the Edit window.
13. Close the Edit dialog box by clicking the Close button.
14. Now, you're ready to set some compiler and linker options for your new project. Start by selecting Project from the Options menu.
15. When the Project Options dialog box appears, be sure the project type that's selected in the Project Type list box is Windows application (.EXE) and that the box labeled Use Microsoft Foundation Classes is checked.
16. Click the Linker button in the Project Options dialog box.
17. When the Linker Options dialog box appears, check the boxes labeled Prevent Use of Extended Dictionary. These check boxes add the `/NOE` option to the Visual C++ linker's command line, preventing some symbols in the Visual C++ expanded dictionary from being defined more than once and instruct the compiler to ignore some other libraries that can cause linking errors.

18. Select Windows libraries from the Category list box, then select the COMMDLG and SHELL libraries from the list box labeled Import Libraries and DLLs.
19. Close the Linker Options dialog box by clicking the OK button.
20. When Project Options reappears, click the Compiler button.
21. When the Compiler Options dialog box opens, select Preprocessor from the Category list box.
22. Click the button labeled Use Project Defaults. That's a good step to take when you're compiling a new application for the first time. It ensures that any headers that have been precompiled for your application are deleted and that your application is recompiled from scratch.
23. Close the Compiler Options dialog box by clicking the OK button.
24. Close the Project Options dialog box by clicking its OK button.
25. Compile the Zalthar program by selecting Build ZALTHAR.EXE from the Project menu.

## App Studio

When you've compiled your application, you can add a user interface to it with the App Studio resource editor. App Studio is an interactive tool that you can use to design your application's user interface and create the user interface resources the program's interface requires: menus, dialog boxes, custom controls, accelerator keys, bitmaps, icons, cursors, and strings.

After you create a skeletal application with AppWizard, you can launch App Studio by selecting the App Studio command from the Visual Workbench's Tools menu. App Studio then displays a screen that enables you to select the kind of resource you want to create or edit (see Figure 22.2).

When you select a resource type—by choosing one of the icons shown in the list labeled Type on the left side of the screen—App Studio opens an interactive editor that's specially designed for the kind of resource you want to edit or create. Then, using standard point-and-click mouse commands, you can create your resource interactively.

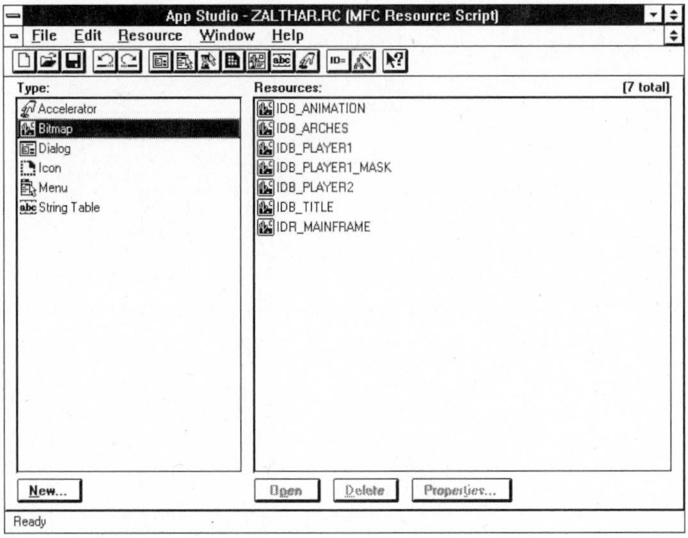


*Figure 22.2. The App Studio window.*

## Using App Studio

All the editors provided by App Studio enable you to use the map to edit and create resource objects interactively. For example, you can add controls to a dialog box by selecting a control icon on a control palette, dragging the control into the dialog box you are working on, and dropping it into place. You'll get a chance to design dialog boxes and menus with App Studio later in this chapter. Meanwhile, to use the App Studio bitmap editor, follow these steps:

1. Select the App Studio command from the Visual Workbench Tools menu. Visual Workbench responds by opening Studio App, which displays a window named the Resource Script window, shown previously in Figure 22.2.

2. Select the icon labeled Menu from the Type list or click the menu button on the App Studio toolbar.

3. Notice two menu IDs are in the Resources list on the right three-fifths of the screen. `IDR_MAINFRAME` is the menu resource for MDI windows when no documents are displayed in child windows. (Recall, MDI is the interface for programs that can have multiple windows. Under MDI, available menus vary depending on which windows are on the screen.)

IDR_ZALTHATYPE is a menu ID that AppWizard assigned to your project when your project was created. It is the menu resource for a frame window when a document in a child window has the focus. You'll be working with your project's menu bar in this exercise, so open the menu resource named IDR_ZALTHATYPE.

4. When you open the IDR_ZALTHATYPE menu resource, App Studio displays a menu-editing window like the one shown in Figure 22.3.

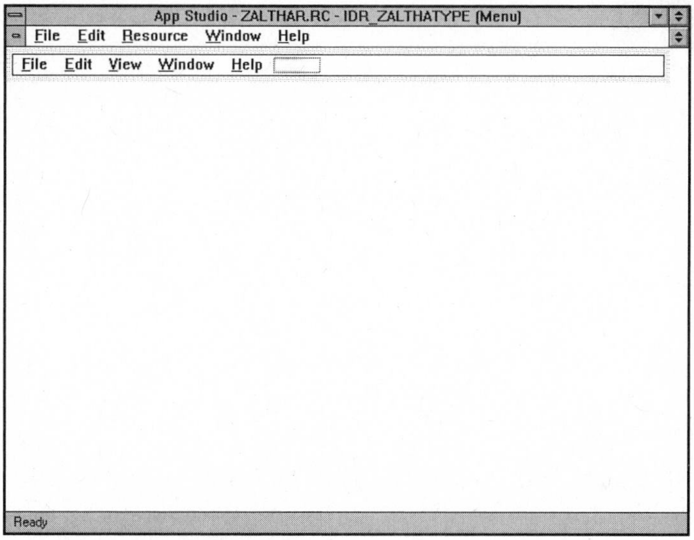


*Figure 22.3. App Studio Menu editor.*

5. In the menu-editing window, notice that a representation of a menu bar is displayed just underneath the toolbar. That's the menu bar your application will display when it is launched by the user. To edit your application's menu bar, double-click the Help menu. Then, double-click the Help menu item labeled About ZALTHAR.... App Studio responds by displaying a dialog box labeled Menu: Menu Item Properties. The dialog box looks like the one shown in Figure 22.4.

6. In the Caption text box of the Menu Item Properties dialog box, replace the word ZALTHAR... (typed in all uppercase letters) with the word Zalthar... (initial letter capitalized with others in lowercase) as shown in Figure 22.5. Leave the ampersand in front of the word About; that's what associates the About box with the accelerator key Alt-A.) As you type, notice that on the editable menu bar, the ZALTHAR... item under the Help menu also changes from ZALTHAR... to Zalthar.

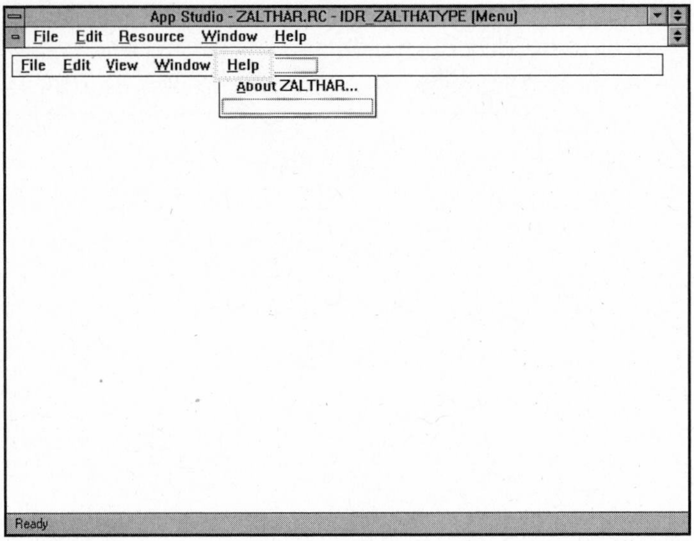


*Figure 22.4. The menu item Properties dialog box.*

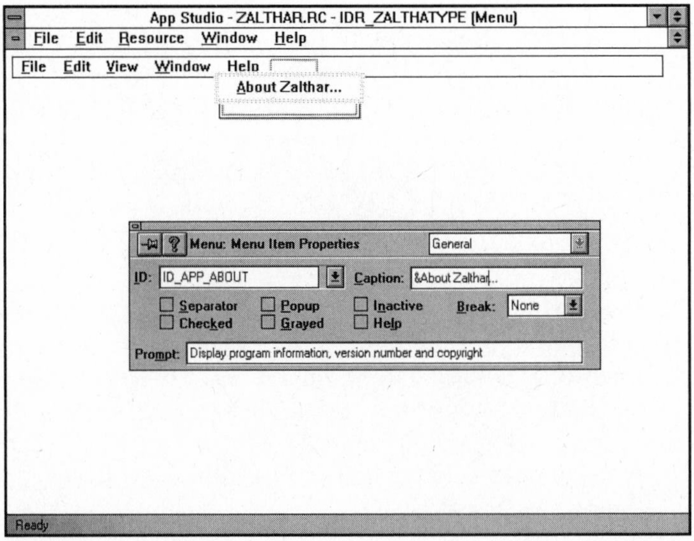


*Figure 22.5. Editing a menu item.*

7. You have now modified your application's menu bar to read About Zalthar... rather than About ZALTHAR.... As my pals back in New York might say, now was that easy, or what?

8. Highlight the word Help on the editable menu bar and press the Insert key. Notice that a space for a new menu appears to the left of the Help menu. Double-click that empty space. When the Properties dialog box appears, type the word Characters in the text box labeled Caption.
9. Be sure there is an X in the check box labeled Popup; that means you want to define some menu items for your new Characters menu.
10. Double-click the first item under your new Characters menu, and when the Properties dialog box appears, type the caption Create. The App Studio screen now resembles the one shown in Figure 22.6.

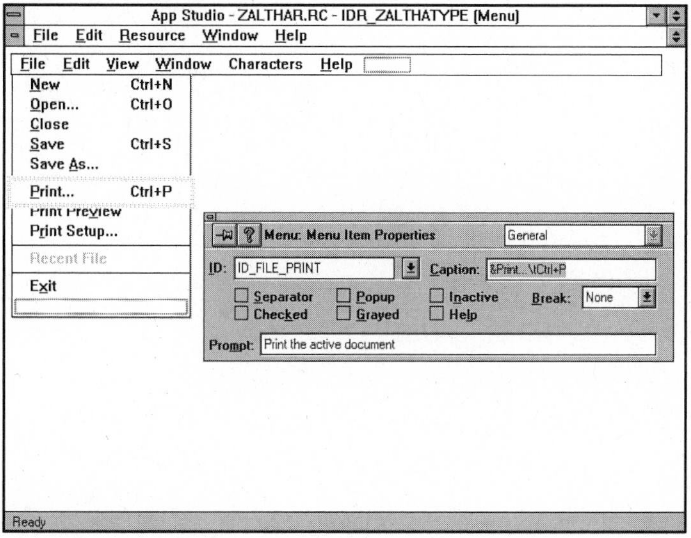


*Figure 22.6. The Create menu item.*

11. In the dialog box illustrated in Figure 22.6, select the button labeled Popup. App Studio responds by displaying an empty hierarchical menu item next to the Create item. Double-click the empty hierarchical menu item and when the item's Properties box appears, type the word One in the Caption box.
12. Notice that a second hierarchical item is now displayed under the new item that you have just created. Select that item and when its Properties box appears, type the word Multiple in the Caption box.

13. Double-click the Characters menu item again. Notice that there is a small arrow next to the name of the Create item under the Characters menu, as shown in Figure 22.7. That means Create is now a hierarchical menu with two subitems: one labeled One, and one labeled Multiple.

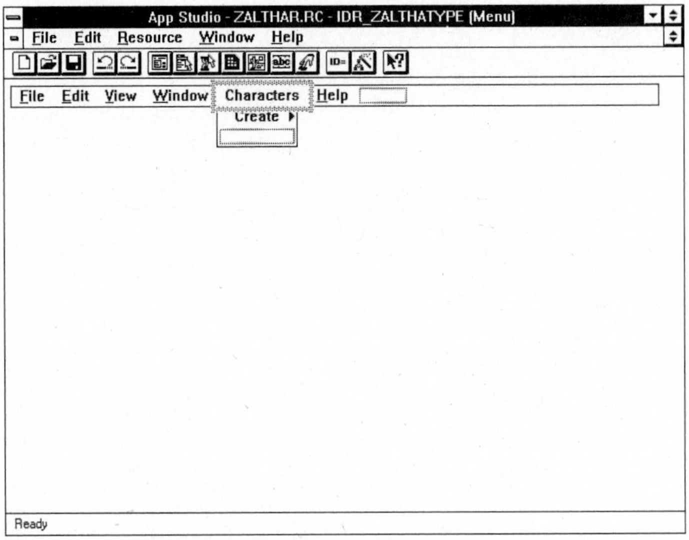


*Figure 22.7. Creating a hierarchical menu.*

14. There are several standard menu items the user may not need when he or she plays The Wrath of Zalthar. For example, at this stage of the program's development, there's no need to worry much about whether the game has printing capabilities (although, if you like, you can certainly add some when you start customizing the program). For the moment, you can practice disabling menu items by graying out the printing-related items under the File menu.

    To do that, double-click the File menu and select the Print item, as shown in Figure 22.8. When the Properties dialog box appears, select the check box labeled Grayed. Then, select the Print Preview and Print Setup menu items and do the same. The result is a menu with a trio of disabled (grayed-out) print-related items, as you can easily see by noticing how the appearance of the Print menu has changed.

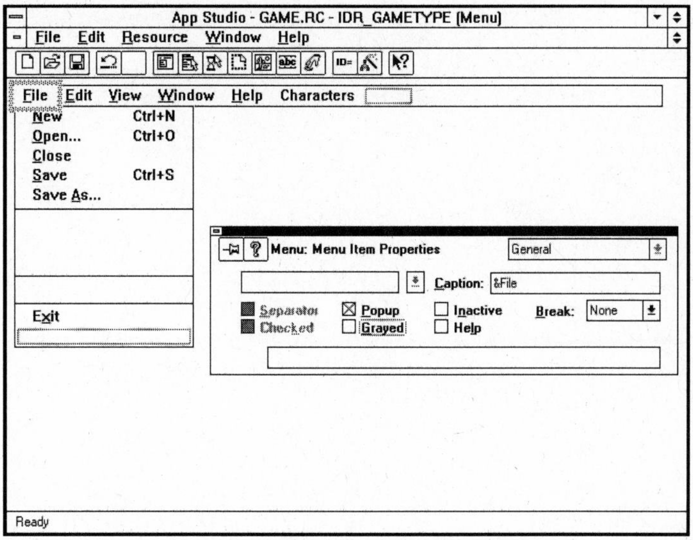


*Figure 22.8. Disabling the Print menu items.*

15. From the App Studio's File menu, select Save. That saves your new menu bar to the Zalthar program's resource definition file, named ZALTHAR.RC.

16. Close the App Studio window and return to Visual Workbench. Then compile and link the Zalthar program by selecting Build from the Project menu.

17. Launch the Zalthar program by selecting the Execute command from the Project menu. When the application displays its main frame window, select New under the File menu. A child window now appears, and its menu looks like the one shown in Figure 22.9.

18. Notice that your application now has a menu labeled Characters. Select the Create item under the Characters menu and you'll see that it is really a hierarchical menu, with a pair of submenus labeled One and Multiple. Notice that the menu labeled One is enabled, even though you haven't associated it with messages. That's because the program was designed to have a menu bar just like the one you created in this exercise, and the code needed to make the Characters/Create/One item operational was written before you started working on the program. Lucky you. The Characters/Create/Multiple item will become operational in Chapter 24.

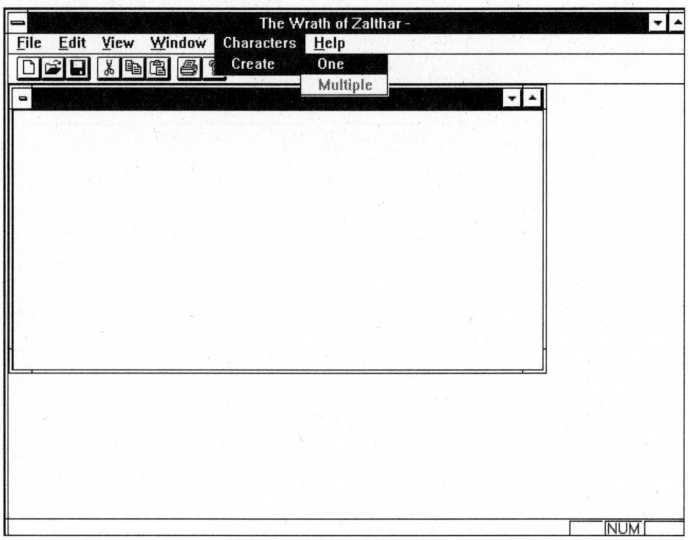


*Figure 22.9. Zalthar application with customized menu bar.*

## Creating a Dialog Box

In the previous exercise, you created a menu and an About box with App Studio. Now, you can use App Studio to create a dialog box of your own design. To do that, follow these steps:

1. From the Visual Workbench Tools menu, select the App Studio command. Visual Workbench again opens App Studio.

2. When the App Studio Resource Script Window opens, select the icon labeled Dialog from the Type list on the left side of the screen, or click the dialog button on the App Studio toolbar. In the large panel on the right side of the screen, Studio App now displays the names of four dialog boxes: your dialog box and three dialog boxes designed to handle the creation of game characters and the display of character-related data.

3. The screen that displays this information is shown in Figure 22.10. When that screen appears, select the icon next to the name `IDD_CREATE_CHAR`.

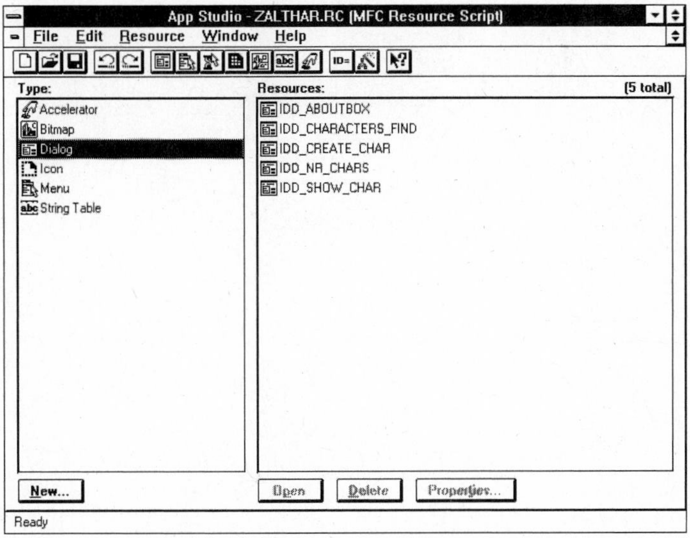


*Figure 22.10. The dialog-editing window.*

4. App Studio now opens a dialog editor—an interactive editor you can use to create your own custom-designed dialog boxes. Notice that the dialog editor window contains a ready-to-edit dialog box like the one shown in Figure 22.11. The dialog box is named Create a Character. As you might guess, this chapter's version of The Wrath of Zalthar uses the dialog to create game characters.

## How the Character-Creation Dialog Box Works

With the Create a Character dialog box, the user of the Zalthar program can create game characters and supply them with names, abilities, characteristics, equipment, treasures, and magical spells. Notice that on the left side of the dialog window, there is a group of static text items labeled Abilities. At the moment, there's a pair of zeroes next to each ability in that group. As soon as a character is created, the Zalthar program assigns the character a unique set of abilities, using the random-number generator that made its appearance in Chapter 21. You'll see how that works later in this chapter.

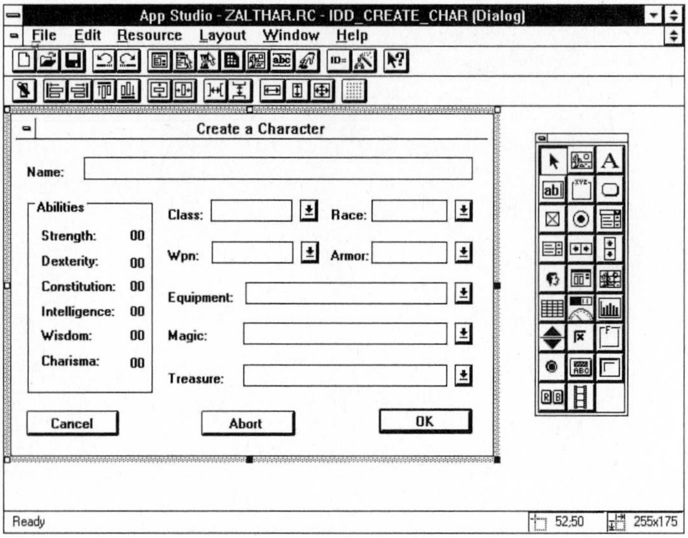


*Figure 22.11. The Create a Character dialog box.*

With the App Studio dialog editor, you can edit, add, and delete controls in dialog boxes by using click-and-drag mouse operations—and please feel free to try all the editor's features while you study the rest of this chapter. If you have a backup copy of your program disk, you can't ruin anything by experimenting with the dialog editor or any of the other editors that Studio App provides.

When a ready-to-edit dialog box is displayed in the dialog-editing window, you can edit the dialog box and its controls by using the dialog editor's control palette, which appears to the right of the Create a Character dialog box in Figure 22.11. If the control palette is not visible in the dialog editor window, you can display it by pressing F2 or choosing Show Control Palette from the Window menu.

With the dialog editor's control palette visible, you can add controls to the dialog box you are editing by clicking and dragging controls from the control palette into the dialog box. Studio App also provides many other tools for creating and adding controls to a dialog box and for drawing, editing, aligning, and deleting various kinds of dialog controls. All the editing tools supplied by the dialog editor are described in detail in the Visual C++ *App Studio User's Guide*. If you aren't familiar with the editing tools built into the dialog editor, you might want to read up on them before continuing this exercise.

# Using ClassWizard

When you have created a set of user interface objects with App Studio, you must connect the objects with the messages and functions that make your application work. ClassWizard is a Visual C++ tool that you can use to connect, or "bind," interface resources with the functions that make them operational.

You can launch ClassWizard from either the Visual Workbench or from App Studio. Either way, ClassWizard enables you to use pointing and clicking mouse operations to connect your application's interface resources with the functions that make the resources work. For example, the ClassWizard tool can connect, or "bind," Windows messages to message-handler functions. ClassWizard also can do the following:

- Connect user interface objects, such as menus and dialog boxes, to message-handler functions.
- Create new classes for dialog boxes, menus, icons, bitmaps, accelerator keys, and strings.
- Add member variables to dialog classes and determine how those variables are initialized and displayed.

## The ClassWizard Window

When you launch ClassWizard, the first thing you see is the main ClassWizard dialog box, which was shown in Figure 22.1 at the beginning of this chapter. The ClassWizard dialog window contains four drop-down lists and an assortment of buttons. By browsing through ClassWizard's drop-down lists, you can find all the classes in the program you are writing that can handle commands or Windows messages. When you select a class to which you want to map commands, a list box shows you all the visual objects associated with that class.

Various kinds of objects can appear in ClassWizard's drop-down lists. Those objects include the following:

- Classes, such as dialogs, views, and frame windows, that can receive standard Windows messages.
- Dialog box controls that can generate Windows control notification messages.
- Command IDs associated with menu items, toolbar buttons, or accelerator keys.

# How ClassWizard Works

From the list box at the top of the ClassWizard window, labeled Class Name, you can select the name of any class you have placed in your application by using ClassWizard. When you choose a class name from the Class Name list box, the list box on the left side of the ClassWizard dialog window—labeled Object IDs—displays the names of all object IDs that are available to objects of the specified class.

If you select an object ID from the Object ID list, ClassWizard presents a list of Windows messages that are associated with the specified object ID. That list, labeled Messages, is displayed to the right of the Object IDs list box. When an object ID has been bound to a message, a small hand icon appears next to the name of the message in the Messages list box.

If an object in the Object ID list box is not associated with a message, you can bind it to a message by clicking the button in the ClassWizard window labeled Add Function. ClassWizard then displays a dialog box named Add Class, which is shown in Figure 22.12.

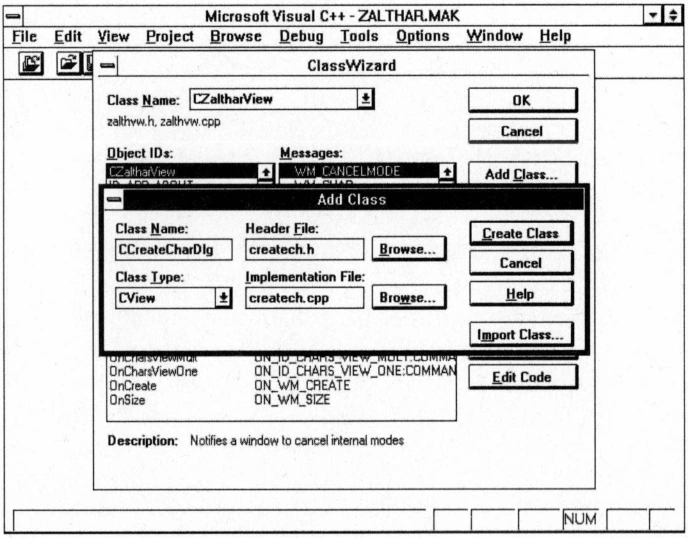


*Figure 22.12. The Add Class dialog box.*

When you have selected both an object ID shown in the Object ID window and a message displayed in the Messages window, you can use ClassWizard to create a member function of the object you have specified and to bind that member function to the Windows message that you have selected. When you have done that, the member function that you create will be called in your application every time Windows dispatches the message you have selected.

To create a member function of your selected object in the Object ID list box and to bind that member function to your selected Windows message in the Message list box, all you must do is click the ClassWizard button labeled Add Function. AppWizard then displays a dialog box named Add Member Function. The Add Member Function dialog box is shown in Figure 22.13.

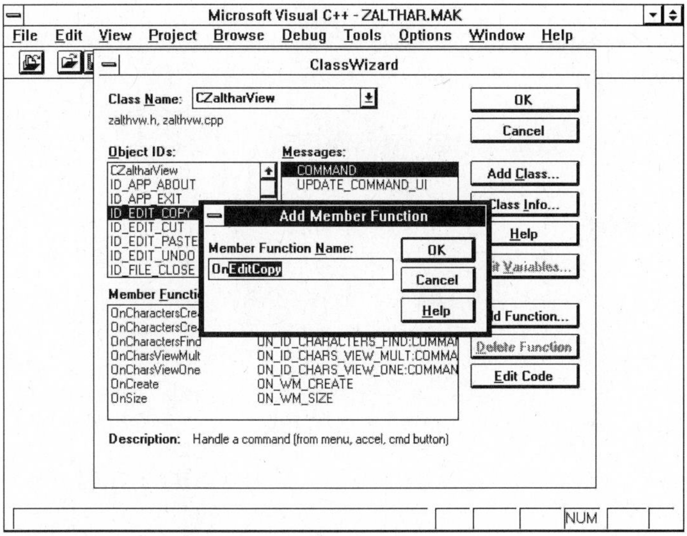


*Figure 22.13. The Add Member Function dialog box.*

When the Add Member Function dialog box appears, you can associate a message—and a member function—with the object ID that you have selected. When the Add Function dialog box appears, ClassWizard gives you a helping hand by suggesting a name for a new function that you are creating. You can accept the name that ClassWizard suggests, or you can type a name of your own choosing. The name that ClassWizard suggests appears in the edit box labeled Member Function Name.

When you have accepted the name that ClassWizard suggests or have typed a name of your own, you can close the Add Member Function dialog box by clicking the OK button. Then, you can take a look at the member function you have just created by clicking the button labeled Edit Code in the ClassWizard dialog window.

When you click the Edit Code button, Class Wizard carries out three operations in quick succession. It closes its main dialog window, opens the Visual Workbench editor, and jumps directly to the section of source code that contains the empty function definition that it has just created. You then can edit your new member function on the spot, adding any functionality you like. Any code you add to the function at this point will be executed every time Windows dispatches the message you have bound to the function.

## Command Binding

The job of associating an object ID with a Windows message and a member function is known as a *command binding*. When you perform a command-binding operation with ClassWizard, ClassWizard automatically writes an entry for the command you have chosen in the selected class's message map and adds a declaration for a new member function to the class's declaration.

ClassWizard also writes a *function template*—a function definition with an empty function body—in the source file that implements the specified member function in the specified class. When you write new functions, you then can use ClassWizard to edit existing message maps and message-handler functions. As Microsoft explains in the *App Studio User's Guide* that comes with Visual C++, "ClassWizard follows a conservative set of rules in writing to your files, writing only a few kinds of code to predictable places, so it's safe and easy to use."

Despite this assurance of safety, you must take some precautions when using ClassWizard. First, as noted earlier in this chapter, you should never disturb code that is placed in an `AFX_DATA_INIT` map, bracketed by comments written in the format `//{{` and `//}}`. That code is the exclusive property of AppWizard and ClassWizard, and Microsoft declares in its Visual C++ documentation that you should never change the code in any way. (As you'll see in Chapter 23, there is at least one exception to this rule. With Microsoft's blessing, you can initialize the contents of an item in a dialog box by inserting an initialization string in exactly the right spot in an `AFX_DATA_INIT` map. But that's the only time you should ever change a block of `AFX_DATA_INIT`, according to your Visual C++ documentation.)

One more warning: If you use ClassWizard to delete a command binding that has been created for a class, ClassWizard removes the class's message-map entry, but does not remove the message-handler function associated with the message or any other references you have made to the message handler in your other code. If such items exist, you must delete them by hand.

You should also know that when you use ClassWizard to perform class bindings, ClassWizard automatically writes all its work to disk. You don't have to do anything special to save the class bindings and function templates that ClassWizard creates—unless you do some file editing yourself, as you will when you fill in a function template that ClassWizard has created.

# Creating Dialog Boxes

When you start writing programs in Visual C++, you'll often find yourself moving back and forth between Studio App and AppWizard, designing graphics objects such as menus and dialog boxes with Studio App and then using AppWizard to connect the operations of objects, Windows messages, and member functions.

In the next exercise, you'll see how Studio App and AppWizard were used together to design and implement the dialog boxes used in this chapter's version of The Wrath of Zalthar. The dialog boxes in this chapter's edition of the program have already been designed and are already bound to menus and messages, so this will be an easy exercise.

You won't have to create dialog boxes yourself; in fact, you won't have to do much except click some buttons and see how everything that needs to be done has been done for you. To carry out the exercise, these are the steps to follow:

1. Select the Edit command from the Visual Workbench Project menu and be sure you are working with the Chapter 22 version of the Zalthar program. As you complete this exercise, you won't be changing anything in the program, so you can open its final version—the one in the ZALTHFIN directory.
2. Select ClassWizard from the Visual Workbench Browse menu. Studio App responds by launching AppWizard and displaying the AppWizard dialog window.
3. From the list box labeled Class Name, select the name of the class named `CZaltharView`.
4. Click the button labeled Add Class. In response, ClassWizard opens and displays a dialog box named Add Class, which was shown previously in Figure 22.12.

5. Select the class name `CDialog` from the list box labeled Class Type and type the word `CCreateCharDlg` in the text box labeled Class Name, as shown in Figure 22.12. Notice that as you type the class name `CCreateCharDlg`, the contents of the text boxes labeled Header File and Implementation File change automatically to keep up with the class name you are typing. When you are adding a new class to an application, you can edit the contents of those two boxes if you like, but for now, for the sake of simplicity, don't change them; just let AppWizard fill them in, no matter how strange the words in them might look. They'll work, even if they do look funny.

6. Click the button labeled Create Class. If you were actually creating a new class in this step, AppWizard would add a new class named `CCreateCharDlg` to your application. In this case, however, the `CCreateCharDlg` class has already been created, so AppWizard displays a message box telling you that.

7. Close the message box that AppWizard has just displayed by clicking the OK button. Then, close the Add Class dialog box. That leaves only the ClassWizard dialog window on the screen.

8. Confirm that a class named `CCreateCharDlg` does already exist by finding its name in the list box labeled Class Name, but don't select the `CCreateCharDlg` from the Class Name list box. Instead, select the name of the class `CZaltharView`. That's the class that is bound to the `CCreateCharDlg` class in this chapter's version of the Zalthar program.

9. In the Object IDs drop-down list, select the `ID_CHARACTERS_CREATE_ONE` command. (Part of the name is obscured, as shown in Figure 22.14, but the command you want is the second one that begins `ID_CHARACTERS_CREATE`.)

10. In the Messages drop-down list, select the message COMMAND. If you were creating a dialog box from scratch in this exercise, you would now click the button labeled Add Function, and ClassWizard would give you a chance to create a new member function. Your new menu function would then be bound to the Characters/Create menu command.

    In this exercise, however, you won't have to create a Characters/Create function because one has already been written for you. You can tell that's true because there is a small hand-shaped icon next to the word COMMAND, and when that icon appears next to the name of a message in the Messages list box, it means that the marked message is associated with a member function.

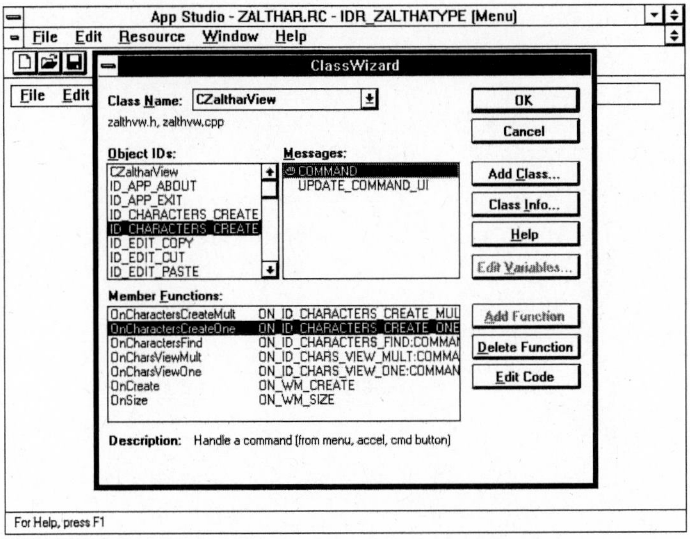


*Figure 22.14. Selecting a menu item in the Object IDs window.*

11. The member function associated with the `ID_CHARACTERS_CREATE_ONE` object is the `OnCharactersCreateOne` function, which is highlighted in the Member Function's list box near the bottom of the ClassWizard dialog window. You can examine the function by clicking the Edit Code button in the lower-right corner of the ClassWizard dialog window. Do that now.

12. Visual Workbench now displays a block of ready-to-edit source code on the screen, as shown in Figure 22.15. As you can see by examining the Visual C++ screen's title bar, the code that is displayed is from the file ZALTHVW.CPP—the file that implements the Zalthar program's dialog boxes. As you also can see by examining the code on the screen, Visual Workbench shows you exactly where you must add code to link your character-creating dialog box to its corresponding menu item.

13. When the ZALTHVW.CPP source file appears on the screen, you can see a block of source code that AppWizard has inserted into the file in accordance with your instructions. Specifically, these lines of code—created by AppWizard—now have become part of the ZALTHVW.CPP file:

```
void CZaltharView::OnCharactersCreateOne()
{

     // TODO: Add your command handler code here

}
```

After AppWizard added the preceding code fragment to the ZALTHVW.CPP file, some additional code was added by hand to implement the functionality of the `OnCharactersCreateOne()` member function. In its entirety, the function now looks like this:

```
void CZaltharView::OnCharactersCreateOne()
{
        // TODO: Add your command handler code here

        ASSERT_VALID(this);
        ASSERT_VALID(m_database);

        // Create a player

        m_player = new CWarrior;
        ASSERT_VALID(m_player);

        m_player->SetAbilScores();

        CCreateCharDlg dlg(m_player);
        if (dlg.Modal() == IDOK) {
             m_database->AddPlayer(m_player);
        }
        else {
             delete m_player;
        }

}
```

AppWizard has bound this function to the menu item Characters/Create/One, so the function is called when the user signals a desire to create a character by selecting the Create and One commands from the Characters menu. As you can see, the function creates a game character, sets the character's ability scores, and adds the character to The Wrath of Zalthar database. The function also does a considerable amount of error checking, and if the character can't be created, the function deletes the memory that has been assigned to the character from memory.

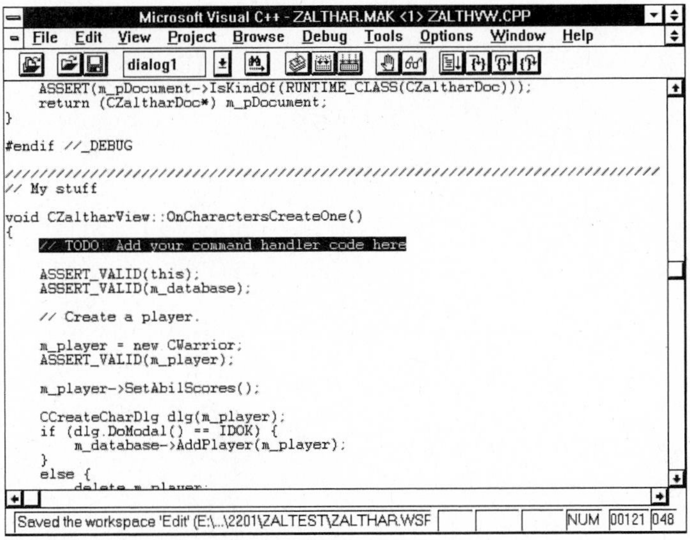


*Figure 22.15. Source code created by AppWizard.*

14. When you create a class using ClassWizard, both a header file and an implementation file are created for the class. When you finish creating a class with ClassWizard, you must always remember to include the class's header file in any other files that need to access it. Just to be sure you remember, scroll to the beginning of the ZALTHVW.CPP file and notice that this `#include` directive has been inserted into the file's heading section:

```
#include "createch.h"
```

# The Example Program

Listing 22.1 is the first graphically oriented, interactive version of The Wrath of Zalthar. That fact aside, this chapter's edition of the program has some truly remarkable features.

When you execute the program, you can use dialog boxes to create as many game characters as you like, with as many unique abilities, qualities, and possessions as you like. You can create characters one at a time, or all at once. Figure 22.16 shows the dialog box that the program uses to create game characters.

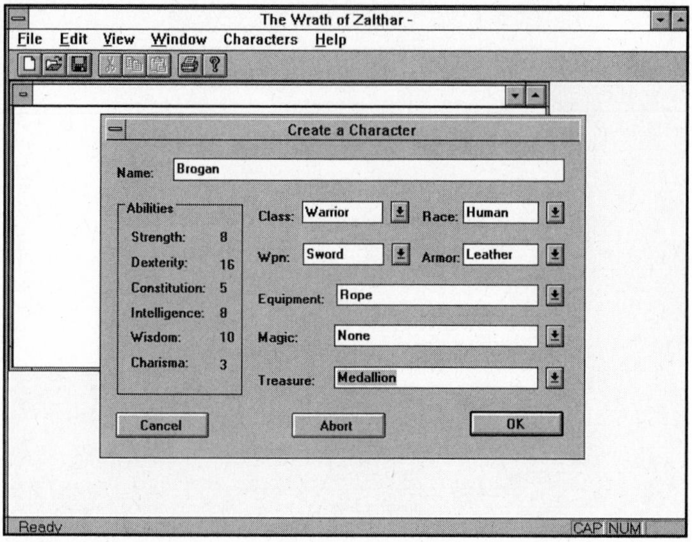


*Figure 22.16. Create a Character dialog box.*

If you want to examine all the data that pertains to an individual character, just choose Find from the Characters menu. When a dialog box like the one shown in Figure 22.17 appears, type the character's name. The program then searches through its database of characters, finds the character you have inquired about, and displays all the data that it has on file about the character you're looking for.

You can display an alphabetized list of characters by choosing the View and All commands from the Characters menu. When you do that, the dialog box the program displays is shown in Figure 22.18.

One of the most important features of this chapter's Zalthar program is its serialization capability. When you have created a collection of characters, you can save them in a database, and then you can retrieve the database at any time you like. If you have a modified database that hasn't been saved when you try to close a document or exit the program, the program warns you and asks if you want to save your work.

All these features are provided by the Visual C++ application framework. They use standard Windows dialog boxes that make your application look professional. You don't have to do much work to incorporate them into your programs.

Best of all, thanks to the magic of C++, most of the code in the Zalthar program continues to be reusable in other programs, as you'll see in the final version of the program, which is presented in Chapter 24.

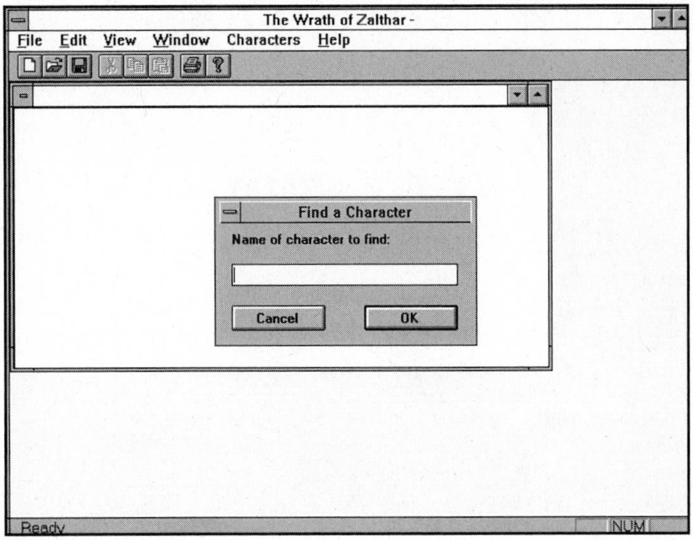


*Figure 22.17. Find a Character dialog box.*

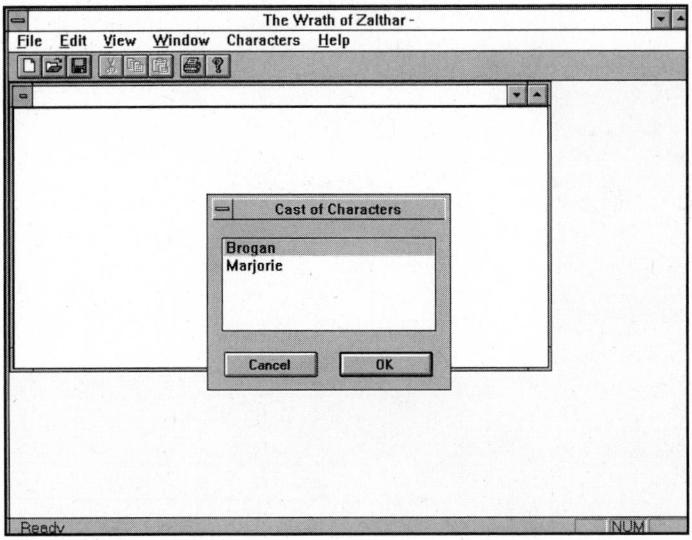


*Figure 22.18. View Cast of Characters dialog box.*

Listing 22.1 is a source code listing of this chapter's version of the Zalthar program.

**Listing 22.1. The Wrath of Zalthar, Chapter 22 version.**

### ZALTHAR.CPP

```
// zalthar.cpp : Defines the class behaviors for the application.
// Copyright 1993, Mark Andrews
//

#include "stdafx.h"
#include "zalthar.h"

#include "mainfrm.h"
#include "zalthdoc.h"
#include "zalthvw.h"

#ifdef _DEBUG
#undef THIS_FILE
static char BASED_CODE THIS_FILE[] = __FILE__;
#endif

/////////////////////////////////////////////////////////////////////////////
// CZaltharApp

BEGIN_MESSAGE_MAP(CZaltharApp, CWinApp)
     //{{AFX_MSG_MAP(CZaltharApp)
     ON_COMMAND(ID_APP_ABOUT, OnAppAbout)
          // NOTE - the ClassWizard will add and remove mapping macros
          // here. DO NOT EDIT what you see in these blocks of
          // generated code !
     //}}AFX_MSG_MAP
     // Standard file based document commands
     ON_COMMAND(ID_FILE_NEW, CWinApp::OnFileNew)
     ON_COMMAND(ID_FILE_OPEN, CWinApp::OnFileOpen)
     // Standard print setup command
     ON_COMMAND(ID_FILE_PRINT_SETUP, CWinApp::OnFilePrintSetup)
END_MESSAGE_MAP()

/////////////////////////////////////////////////////////////////////////////
// CZaltharApp construction

CZaltharApp::CZaltharApp()
{
     // TODO: add construction code here,
     // Place all significant initialization in InitInstance
}

/////////////////////////////////////////////////////////////////////////////
// The one and only CZaltharApp object

CZaltharApp NEAR theApp;
```

```
/////////////////////////////////////////////////////////////////////////////
// CZaltharApp initialization

BOOL CZaltharApp::InitInstance()
{
     // Standard initialization
     // If you are not using these features and wish to reduce the
     // size of your final executable, you should remove from the
     // following the specific initialization routines you do not
     // need.

     SetDialogBkColor();        // set dialog background color to gray
     LoadStdProfileSettings();  // Load standard INI file options
                                // (including MRU)

     // Register the application's document templates.  Document
     // templates serve as the connection between documents, frame
     // windows and views.

     AddDocTemplate(new CMultiDocTemplate(IDR_ZALTHATYPE,
               RUNTIME_CLASS(CZaltharDoc),
               RUNTIME_CLASS(CMDIChildWnd), // standard MDI childframe
               RUNTIME_CLASS(CZaltharView)));

     // create main MDI Frame window
     CMainFrame* pMainFrame = new CMainFrame;
     if (!pMainFrame->LoadFrame(IDR_MAINFRAME))
          return FALSE;
     pMainFrame->ShowWindow(m_nCmdShow);
     pMainFrame->UpdateWindow();
     m_pMainWnd = pMainFrame;

     ///////////////////////////////////////////////////////////////////
     //
     // COMMENTING OUT THE OnFileNew() CALL!
     //
     // AppWizard puts this function in, but watch out!
     //
     // COMMENT IT OUT IF YOUR APP CREATES ITS OWN DOCUMENTS!
     // (You can see that it's commented out here.)
     //
     // OnFileNew();
     //
     ///////////////////////////////////////////////////////////////////

     if (m_lpCmdLine[0] != '\0')
     {
          // TODO: add command-line processing here
     }
```

*continues*

**Listing 22.1. continued**

```
    return TRUE;
}

/////////////////////////////////////////////////////////////////////////////
// CAboutDlg dialog used for App About

class CAboutDlg : public CDialog
{
public:
    CAboutDlg();

// Dialog Data
    //{{AFX_DATA(CAboutDlg)
    enum { IDD = IDD_ABOUTBOX };
    //}}AFX_DATA

// Implementation
protected:
    virtual void DoDataExchange(CDataExchange* pDX); // DDX/DDV suppt
    //{{AFX_MSG(CAboutDlg)
        // No message handlers
    //}}AFX_MSG
    DECLARE_MESSAGE_MAP()
};

CAboutDlg::CAboutDlg() : CDialog(CAboutDlg::IDD)
{
    //{{AFX_DATA_INIT(CAboutDlg)
    //}}AFX_DATA_INIT
}

void CAboutDlg::DoDataExchange(CDataExchange* pDX)
{
    CDialog::DoDataExchange(pDX);
    //{{AFX_DATA_MAP(CAboutDlg)
    //}}AFX_DATA_MAP
}

BEGIN_MESSAGE_MAP(CAboutDlg, CDialog)
    //{{AFX_MSG_MAP(CAboutDlg)
        // No message handlers
    //}}AFX_MSG_MAP
END_MESSAGE_MAP()

// App command to run the dialog
void CZaltharApp::OnAppAbout()
{
    CAboutDlg aboutDlg;
    aboutDlg.DoModal();
```

```
}

///////////////////////////////////////////////////////////////////////////
// CZaltharApp commands
```

### ZALTHAR.H

```
// zalthar.h : main header file for the ZALTHAR application
// Copyright 1993, Mark Andrews
//

#ifndef _ZALTHAR_H_
#define _ZALTHAR_H_

#ifndef __AFXWIN_H__
     #error include 'stdafx.h' before including this file for PCH
#endif

#include "resource.h"          // main symbols

///////////////////////////////////////////////////////////////////////////
// CZaltharApp:
// See zalthar.cpp for the implementation of this class
//

class CZaltharApp : public CWinApp
{
public:
     CZaltharApp();

// Overrides
     virtual BOOL InitInstance();

// Implementation

     //{{AFX_MSG(CZaltharApp)
     afx_msg void OnAppAbout();
          // NOTE - the ClassWizard will add and remove member
          // functions here. DO NOT EDIT what you see in these blocks
          // of generated code !
     //}}AFX_MSG
     DECLARE_MESSAGE_MAP()
};


///////////////////////////////////////////////////////////////////////////

#endif // _ZALTHAR_H
```

*continues*

**Listing 22.1. continued**

### MAINFRM.CPP

```
// mainfrm.cpp : implementation of the CMainFrame class
// Copyright 1993, Mark Andrews
//

#include "stdafx.h"
#include "zalthar.h"

#include "mainfrm.h"

#ifdef _DEBUG
#undef THIS_FILE
static char BASED_CODE THIS_FILE[] = __FILE__;
#endif

/////////////////////////////////////////////////////////////////////////////
// CMainFrame

IMPLEMENT_DYNAMIC(CMainFrame, CMDIFrameWnd)

BEGIN_MESSAGE_MAP(CMainFrame, CMDIFrameWnd)
      //{{AFX_MSG_MAP(CMainFrame)
      ON_WM_CREATE()
      ON_WM_SIZE()
      //}}AFX_MSG_MAP
END_MESSAGE_MAP()

/////////////////////////////////////////////////////////////////////////////
// arrays of IDs used to initialize control bars

// toolbar buttons - IDs are command buttons
static UINT BASED_CODE buttons[] =
{
      // same order as in the bitmap 'toolbar.bmp'
      ID_FILE_NEW,
      ID_FILE_OPEN,
      ID_FILE_SAVE,
            ID_SEPARATOR,
      ID_EDIT_CUT,
      ID_EDIT_COPY,
      ID_EDIT_PASTE,
            ID_SEPARATOR,
      ID_FILE_PRINT,
      ID_APP_ABOUT,
};

static UINT BASED_CODE indicators[] =
{
```

```
        ID_SEPARATOR,               // status line indicator
        ID_INDICATOR_CAPS,
        ID_INDICATOR_NUM,
        ID_INDICATOR_SCRL,
};

///////////////////////////////////////////////////////////////////////
// CMainFrame construction/destruction

CMainFrame::CMainFrame()
{
        // TODO: add member initialization code here
}

CMainFrame::~CMainFrame()
{
}

int CMainFrame::OnCreate(LPCREATESTRUCT lpCreateStruct)
{
        if (CMDIFrameWnd::OnCreate(lpCreateStruct) == -1)
                return -1;

        SetWindowText("The Wrath of Zalthar");

        if (!m_wndToolBar.Create(this) ||
                !m_wndToolBar.LoadBitmap(IDR_MAINFRAME) ||
                !m_wndToolBar.SetButtons(buttons,
                  sizeof(buttons)/sizeof(UINT)))
        {
                TRACE("Failed to create toolbar\n");
                return -1;          // fail to create
        }

        if (!m_wndStatusBar.Create(this) ||
                !m_wndStatusBar.SetIndicators(indicators,
                  sizeof(indicators)/sizeof(UINT)))
        {
                TRACE("Failed to create status bar\n");
                return -1;          // fail to create
        }

        return 0;
}

///////////////////////////////////////////////////////////////////////
// CMainFrame diagnostics
```

*continues*

**Listing 22.1. continued**

```
#ifdef _DEBUG
void CMainFrame::AssertValid() const
{
     CMDIFrameWnd::AssertValid();
}

void CMainFrame::Dump(CDumpContext& dc) const
{
     CMDIFrameWnd::Dump(dc);
}

#endif //_DEBUG

/////////////////////////////////////////////////////////////////////////
// CMainFrame message handlers
```

## MAINFRM.H

```
// mainfrm.h : interface of the CMainFrame class
// Copyright 1993, Mark Andrews
//

class CMainFrame : public CMDIFrameWnd
{
     DECLARE_DYNAMIC(CMainFrame)
public:
     CMainFrame();

// Attributes
public:

// Operations
public:

// Implementation
public:
     virtual ~CMainFrame();
#ifdef _DEBUG
     virtual   void AssertValid() const;
     virtual   void Dump(CDumpContext& dc) const;
#endif


protected:     // control bar embedded members
     CStatusBar     m_wndStatusBar;
     CToolBar     m_wndToolBar;

// Generated message map functions
protected:
```

```
    //{{AFX_MSG(CMainFrame)
    afx_msg int OnCreate(LPCREATESTRUCT lpCreateStruct);
    afx_msg void OnSize(UINT nType, int cx, int cy);
    //}}AFX_MSG
    DECLARE_MESSAGE_MAP()
};

/////////////////////////////////////////////////////////////////////////////
```

### CHARLIST.CPP

```
// charlist.cpp : implementation file
// Copyright 1993, Mark Andrews

#include "stdafx.h"
#include "zalthar.h"
#include "charlist.h"
#include "zalthdoc.h"
#include "player.h"

#ifdef _DEBUG
#undef THIS_FILE
static char BASED_CODE THIS_FILE[] = __FILE__;
#endif

/////////////////////////////////////////////////////////////////////////////
// CCharList dialog

CCharList::CCharList(CZaltharDoc *pDataBase, CWnd* pParent /*=NULL*/)
    : CDialog(CCharList::IDD, pParent)
{
    m_database = pDataBase;

    //{{AFX_DATA_INIT(CCharList)
        // NOTE: the ClassWizard will add member initialization here
    //}}AFX_DATA_INIT
}

CCharList::OnInitDialog()
{
    RECT listRect = { 12,18,208,102 };
    RECT& rectPtr = listRect;

    m_charList.Create(LBS_SORT | LBS_HASSTRINGS | LBS_SORT |
                WS_CHILD | WS_VISIBLE | WS_VSCROLL |
                WS_TABSTOP, rectPtr, this, 500);
    m_charList.SetFocus();

    ASSERT_VALID(m_database);
    int ct = (m_database->GetCount());
```

*continues*

**Listing 22.1. continued**

```
	for (int n = 0; n < ct; ++n) {
		CPlayer *pPlayer = (m_database->GetPlayer(n));
		m_charList.AddString(pPlayer->GetName());
	}
	return FALSE;
}

void CCharList::DoDataExchange(CDataExchange* pDX)
{
	CDialog::DoDataExchange(pDX);
	//{{AFX_DATA_MAP(CCharList)
		// NOTE: the ClassWizard will add DDX and DDV calls here
	//}}AFX_DATA_MAP
}

BEGIN_MESSAGE_MAP(CCharList, CDialog)
	//{{AFX_MSG_MAP(CCharList)
		// NOTE: the ClassWizard will add message map macros here
	//}}AFX_MSG_MAP
END_MESSAGE_MAP()

/////////////////////////////////////////////////////////////////////////////
// CCharList message handlers
```

## CHARLIST.H

```
// charlist.h : header file
// Copyright 1993, Mark Andrews
//

/////////////////////////////////////////////////////////////////////////////
// CCharList dialog

#include "zalthdoc.h"

class CCharList : public CDialog
{
// Construction
private:
	CZaltharDoc *m_database;
	CListBox m_charList;
public:
	CCharList(CZaltharDoc *pDataBase, CWnd* pParent = NULL);
	virtual BOOL OnInitDialog();

// Dialog Data
	//{{AFX_DATA(CCharList)
	enum { IDD = IDD_DIALOG1 };
		// NOTE: the ClassWizard will add data members here
	//}}AFX_DATA
```

```
// Implementation
protected:
     virtual void DoDataExchange(CDataExchange* pDX);
     // DDX/DDV support

     // Generated message map functions
     //{{AFX_MSG(CCharList)
          // NOTE: the ClassWizard will add member functions here
     //}}AFX_MSG
     DECLARE_MESSAGE_MAP()
};
```

### CREATECH.CPP

```
// createch.cpp : implementation file
// Copyright 1993, Mark Andrews
//

#include "stdafx.h"
#include "zalthar.h"
#include "createch.h"
#include "zalthdoc.h"
#include "player.h"
#include "linklist.h"

#ifdef _DEBUG
#undef THIS_FILE
static char BASED_CODE THIS_FILE[] = __FILE__;
#endif

/////////////////////////////////////////////////////////////////////////////
// CCreateCharDlg dialog

// Original constructor created by AppWizard.
CCreateCharDlg::CCreateCharDlg(CWnd* pParent /*=NULL*/)
     : CDialog(CCreateCharDlg::IDD, pParent)
{
}

// Our constructor created by us.
CCreateCharDlg::CCreateCharDlg(CPlayer *pPlayer,
     CWnd* pParent /*=NULL*/)
     : CDialog(CCreateCharDlg::IDD, pParent)
{
     // copy the pPlayer parameter
     m_player = pPlayer;

     //{{AFX_DATA_INIT(CCreateCharDlg)
     m_name = "";
     m_armor = "Leather";
     m_class = "Warrior";
```

*continues*

**Listing 22.1. continued**

```
    m_equipment = "None";
    m_magic = "None";
    m_race = "Human";
    m_treasure = "None";
    m_weapon = "Sword";
    //}}AFX_DATA_INIT
}

void CCreateCharDlg::DoDataExchange(CDataExchange* pDX)
{
    CDialog::DoDataExchange(pDX);
    //{{AFX_DATA_MAP(CCreateCharDlg)
    DDX_Control(pDX, IDC_STATIC_WI, m_wisdom);
    DDX_Control(pDX, IDC_STATIC_ST, m_strength);
    DDX_Control(pDX, IDC_STATIC_IN, m_intelligence);
    DDX_Control(pDX, IDC_STATIC_DE, m_dexterity);
    DDX_Control(pDX, IDC_STATIC_CO, m_constitution);
    DDX_Control(pDX, IDC_STATIC_CH, m_charisma);
    DDX_Text(pDX, IDC_EDIT_NAME, m_name);
    DDV_MaxChars(pDX, m_name, 64);
    DDX_CBString(pDX, IDC_COMBO_ARMOR, m_armor);
    DDV_MaxChars(pDX, m_armor, 64);
    DDX_CBString(pDX, IDC_COMBO_CLASS, m_class);
    DDV_MaxChars(pDX, m_class, 64);
    DDX_CBString(pDX, IDC_COMBO_EQUIPMENT, m_equipment);
    DDV_MaxChars(pDX, m_equipment, 64);
    DDX_CBString(pDX, IDC_COMBO_MAGIC, m_magic);
    DDV_MaxChars(pDX, m_magic, 64);
    DDX_CBString(pDX, IDC_COMBO_RACE, m_race);
    DDV_MaxChars(pDX, m_race, 64);
    DDX_CBString(pDX, IDC_COMBO_TREASURE, m_treasure);
    DDV_MaxChars(pDX, m_treasure, 64);
    DDX_CBString(pDX, IDC_COMBO_WEAPON, m_weapon);
    DDV_MaxChars(pDX, m_weapon, 64);
    //}}AFX_DATA_MAP
}

BEGIN_MESSAGE_MAP(CCreateCharDlg, CDialog)
    //{{AFX_MSG_MAP(CCreateCharDlg)
    //}}AFX_MSG_MAP
END_MESSAGE_MAP()

//////////////////////////////////////////////////////////////////////////
// CCreateCharDlg message handlers

BOOL CCreateCharDlg::OnInitDialog()
{
    CDialog::OnInitDialog();
```

```
    // TODO: Add extra initialization here

    // char *aStr;

    m_player->SetAbilScores();        // Get a set of ability scores.

    // Set the ability scores in the dialog box
    // and in the m_player object

    m_player->SetRaceStr("Human");
    m_player->SetClassStr("Warrior");
    m_player->SetArmor("Leather");
    m_player->SetWeapon("Staff");
    m_player->SetMagic("None");
    m_player->SetEquipment("None");
    m_player->SetTreasure("None");

    SetDlgItemInt(IDC_STATIC_ST, m_player->GetStrength(), FALSE);
    SetDlgItemInt(IDC_STATIC_DE, m_player->GetDexterity(), FALSE);
    SetDlgItemInt(IDC_STATIC_CO, m_player->GetConstitution(), FALSE);
    SetDlgItemInt(IDC_STATIC_IN, m_player->GetIntelligence(), FALSE);
    SetDlgItemInt(IDC_STATIC_WI, m_player->GetWisdom(), FALSE);
    SetDlgItemInt(IDC_STATIC_CH, m_player->GetCharisma(), FALSE);

   m_race = m_player->GetRaceName();
   m_class = m_player->GetClassName();
   m_armor = m_player->GetArmor();
   m_magic = m_player->GetMagic();
   m_equipment = m_player->GetEquipment();
   m_treasure = m_player->GetTreasure();

   UpdateData(FALSE);

    return TRUE;  // return TRUE unless you set the focus to a control
}

void CCreateCharDlg::OnOK()
{
    // TODO: Add extra validation here
    const int sz = 64;
    char aStr[sz];

    GetDlgItemText(IDC_EDIT_NAME, aStr, sizeof(aStr));
    m_player->SetName(aStr);

    GetDlgItemText(IDC_COMBO_RACE, aStr, sizeof(aStr));
    m_player->SetRaceStr(aStr);

    GetDlgItemText(IDC_COMBO_CLASS, aStr, sizeof(aStr));
    m_player->SetClassStr(aStr);
```

*continues*

**Listing 22.1. continued**

```
    GetDlgItemText(IDC_COMBO_MAGIC, aStr, sizeof(aStr));
    m_player->SetMagic(aStr);

    GetDlgItemText(IDC_COMBO_ARMOR, aStr, sizeof(aStr));
    m_player->SetArmor(aStr);

    GetDlgItemText(IDC_COMBO_WEAPON, aStr, sizeof(aStr));
    m_player->SetWeapon(aStr);

    GetDlgItemText(IDC_COMBO_EQUIPMENT, aStr, sizeof(aStr));
    m_player->SetEquipment(aStr);

    GetDlgItemText(IDC_COMBO_TREASURE, aStr, sizeof(aStr));
    m_player->SetTreasure(aStr);

    CDialog::OnOK();     // this from ClassWizard
}
```

### CREATECH.H

```
// createch.h : header file
// Copyright 1993, Mark Andrews
//

/////////////////////////////////////////////////////////////////////////////
// CCreateCharDlg dialog

#include "player.h"
#include "linklist.h"
#include "zalthdoc.h"

class CCreateCharDlg : public CDialog
{
// Construction
private:
    CPlayer *m_player;
public:
    CCreateCharDlg(CWnd* pParent = NULL);   // standard constructor
    CCreateCharDlg(CPlayer *pPlayer, CWnd* pParent = NULL);

// Dialog Data
    //{{AFX_DATA(CCreateCharDlg)
    enum { IDD = IDD_CREATE_CHAR };
        // NOTE: the ClassWizard will add data members here
    CStatic   m_wisdom;
    CStatic   m_strength;
    CStatic   m_intelligence;
    CStatic   m_dexterity;
    CStatic   m_constitution;
    CStatic   m_charisma;
```

```
	CString   m_name;
	CString   m_armor;
	CString   m_class;
	CString   m_equipment;
	CString   m_magic;
	CString   m_race;
	CString   m_treasure;
	CString   m_weapon;
	//}}AFX_DATA


// Implementation
protected:
	virtual void DoDataExchange(CDataExchange* pDX);
	// DDX/DDV support

	// Generated message map functions
	//{{AFX_MSG(CCreateCharDlg)
	virtual BOOL OnInitDialog();
	virtual void OnOK();
	//}}AFX_MSG
	DECLARE_MESSAGE_MAP()
};
```

## FINDDLG.CPP

```
// finddlg.cpp : implementation file
// Copyright 1993, Mark Andrews
//

#include "stdafx.h"
#include "zalthar.h"
#include "finddlg.h"

#include "zalthdoc.h"
#include "player.h"

#ifdef _DEBUG
#undef THIS_FILE
static char BASED_CODE THIS_FILE[] = __FILE__;
#endif

/////////////////////////////////////////////////////////////////////////////
// CFindDlg dialog

CFindDlg::CFindDlg(CPlayer *pPlayer, CWnd* pParent /*=NULL*/) :
		CDialog(CFindDlg::IDD, pParent)
{
	//{{AFX_DATA_INIT(CFind)
```

*continues*

**Listing 22.1. continued**

```
    m_name = "";
    //}}AFX_DATA_INIT
}

CFindDlg::CFindDlg(CWnd* pParent /*=NULL*/) :
        CDialog(CFindDlg::IDD, pParent)
{
    //{{AFX_DATA_INIT(CFind)
    m_name = "";
    //}}AFX_DATA_INIT
}

void CFindDlg::DoDataExchange(CDataExchange* pDX)
{
    CDialog::DoDataExchange(pDX);
    //{{AFX_DATA_MAP(CFindDlg)
    DDX_Text(pDX, IDC_NAME, m_name);
    DDV_MaxChars(pDX, m_name, 64);
    //}}AFX_DATA_MAP
}

BEGIN_MESSAGE_MAP(CFindDlg, CDialog)
    //{{AFX_MSG_MAP(CFindDlg)
    //}}AFX_MSG_MAP
END_MESSAGE_MAP()

/////////////////////////////////////////////////////////////////////////////
// CFindDlg message handlers

void CFindDlg::OnOK()
{
    const int sz = 64;
    char aStr[sz];

    GetDlgItemText(IDC_NAME, aStr, sizeof(aStr));
    SetNameStr(aStr);

    CDialog::OnOK();
}
```

### FINDDLG.H

```
// finddlg.h : header file
// Copyright 1993, Mark Andrews
//

/////////////////////////////////////////////////////////////////////////////
// CFindDlg dialog
```

```
#include "zalthdoc.h"
#include "player.h"

class CFindDlg : public CDialog
{
// Construction
private:
     CPlayer* m_player;
     CZaltharDoc *m_database;
     CString m_playerName;

public:
     CFindDlg(CWnd* pParent = NULL);     // standard constructor
     CFindDlg(CPlayer *pPlayer, CWnd* pParent = NULL);

// Dialog Data
     //{{AFX_DATA(CFindDlg)
     enum { IDD = IDD_CHARACTERS_FIND };
     CString   m_name;
     //}}AFX_DATA

     CZaltharDoc *GetDataBase() { return m_database; }
     CPlayer* GetData() { return m_player; }
     CString& GetNameStr() { return m_playerName; }
     void SetNameStr(CString cs) { m_playerName = cs; }

// Implementation
protected:
     virtual void DoDataExchange(CDataExchange* pDX);  // DDX/DDV

     // Generated message map functions
     //{{AFX_MSG(CFindDlg)
     virtual void OnOK();
     //}}AFX_MSG
     DECLARE_MESSAGE_MAP()
};
```

## GETCHARD.CPP

```
// getchard.cpp : implementation file
// Copyright 1993, Mark Andrews
//

#include "stdafx.h"
#include "zalthar.h"
#include "getchard.h"
#include "zalthdoc.h"
#include "player.h"
```

*continues*

**Listing 22.1. continued**

```
#ifdef _DEBUG
#undef THIS_FILE
static char BASED_CODE THIS_FILE[] = __FILE__;
#endif

/////////////////////////////////////////////////////////////////////////////
// CGetCharData dialog

CGetCharData::CGetCharData(CPlayer *pPlayer, CWnd* pParent /*=NULL*/)
	: CDialog(CGetCharData::IDD, pParent)
{
	// copy the pPlayer parameter
	m_player = pPlayer;

	//{{AFX_DATA_INIT(CGetCharData)
		// NOTE: the ClassWizard will add member initialization here
	//}}AFX_DATA_INIT
}

void CGetCharData::DoDataExchange(CDataExchange* pDX)
{
	CDialog::DoDataExchange(pDX);
	//{{AFX_DATA_MAP(CGetCharData)
	DDX_Control(pDX, IDC_STATIC_WI, m_wi);
	DDX_Control(pDX, IDC_STATIC_WEAPON, m_weapon);
	DDX_Control(pDX, IDC_STATIC_TREASURE, m_treasure);
	DDX_Control(pDX, IDC_STATIC_ST, m_st);
	DDX_Control(pDX, IDC_STATIC_RACE, m_race);
	DDX_Control(pDX, IDC_STATIC_NAME, m_name);
	DDX_Control(pDX, IDC_STATIC_MAGIC, m_magic);
	DDX_Control(pDX, IDC_STATIC_IN, m_in);
	DDX_Control(pDX, IDC_STATIC_EQUIPMENT, m_equipment);
	DDX_Control(pDX, IDC_STATIC_DE, m_de);
	DDX_Control(pDX, IDC_STATIC_CO, m_co);
	DDX_Control(pDX, IDC_STATIC_CLASS, m_class);
	DDX_Control(pDX, IDC_STATIC_CH, m_ch);
	DDX_Control(pDX, IDC_STATIC_ARMOR, m_armor);
	//}}AFX_DATA_MAP
}

BEGIN_MESSAGE_MAP(CGetCharData, CDialog)
	//{{AFX_MSG_MAP(CGetCharData)
	//}}AFX_MSG_MAP
END_MESSAGE_MAP()

/////////////////////////////////////////////////////////////////////////////
// CGetCharData message handlers
```

```
BOOL CGetCharData::OnInitDialog()
{
     CDialog::OnInitDialog();

     // TODO: Add extra initialization here


     CDialog::OnInitDialog();  // This from ClassWizard.

     // Set dialog controls to player's characteristics

     SetDlgItemText(IDC_STATIC_NAME, m_player->GetName());
     SetDlgItemText(IDC_STATIC_RACE, m_player->GetRaceName());
     SetDlgItemText(IDC_STATIC_CLASS, m_player->GetClassName());
     SetDlgItemText(IDC_STATIC_WEAPON, m_player->GetWeapon());
     SetDlgItemText(IDC_STATIC_EQUIPMENT, m_player->GetEquipment());
     SetDlgItemText(IDC_STATIC_ARMOR, m_player->GetArmor());
     SetDlgItemText(IDC_STATIC_MAGIC, m_player->GetMagic());
     SetDlgItemText(IDC_STATIC_TREASURE, m_player->GetTreasure());

     SetDlgItemInt(IDC_STATIC_ST, m_player->GetStrength(),FALSE);
     SetDlgItemInt(IDC_STATIC_DE, m_player->GetDexterity(),FALSE);
     SetDlgItemInt(IDC_STATIC_CO, m_player->GetConstitution(),FALSE);
     SetDlgItemInt(IDC_STATIC_WI, m_player->GetIntelligence(),FALSE);
     SetDlgItemInt(IDC_STATIC_IN, m_player->GetWisdom(),FALSE);
     SetDlgItemInt(IDC_STATIC_CH, m_player->GetCharisma(),FALSE);

     return TRUE; // return TRUE unless you set the focus to a control
}
```

## GETCHARD.H

```
// getchard.h : header file
// Copyright 1993, Mark Andrews
//

#include "zalthdoc.h"
#include "player.h"

/////////////////////////////////////////////////////////////////////////////
// CGetCharData dialog

class CGetCharData : public CDialog
{
private:
     // Get a copy of the CPlayer object.
     CPlayer *m_player;
// Construction
public:
     CGetCharData(CPlayer *pPlayer, CWnd* pParent = NULL);
```

*continues*

**Listing 22.1. continued**

```
// Dialog Data
     //{{AFX_DATA(CGetCharData)
     enum { IDD = IDD_SHOW_CHAR };
     CStatic   m_wi;
     CStatic   m_weapon;
     CStatic   m_treasure;
     CStatic   m_st;
     CStatic   m_race;
     CStatic   m_name;
     CStatic   m_magic;
     CStatic   m_in;
     CStatic   m_equipment;
     CStatic   m_de;
     CStatic   m_co;
     CStatic   m_class;
     CStatic   m_ch;
     CStatic   m_armor;
     //}}AFX_DATA

// Implementation
protected:
     virtual void DoDataExchange(CDataExchange* pDX); // DDX/DDV

     // Generated message map functions
     //{{AFX_MSG(CGetCharData)
     virtual BOOL OnInitDialog();
     //}}AFX_MSG
     DECLARE_MESSAGE_MAP()
};
```

### LINKLIST.CPP

```
// linklist.cpp
// Copyright 1993, Mark Andrews

#include <iostream.h>
#include <stdlib.h>
// #include <afxwin.h>
// #include <afxcoll.h>

#include "linklist.h"
#include "player.h"

IMPLEMENT_SERIAL( CPlayerList, CObList, 0 )

// string const for untitiled database
extern const char szUntitled[];
```

```
//  Delete all objects in the list.
void CPlayerList::DeleteAll()
{
     ASSERT_VALID( this );
     POSITION pos = GetHeadPosition();

     while (pos != NULL)
          delete GetNext(pos);
     RemoveAll();
}

//////////////////////////////////////////////
//  CPlayerList::FindPlayer
//
//  Make a list of players found in a search operation --
//  Use this function when the search can find multiple objects.
//  The function returns the list.

CPlayerList* CPlayerList::FindPlayer( const char * szTarget )
{
     ASSERT_VALID( this );

     // Create a list of players.
     CPlayerList* pNewList = new CPlayerList;
     CPlayer* pNext = NULL;

     // Start at front of list
     POSITION pos = GetHeadPosition();

     // Iterate over whole list
     while( pos != NULL )
     {
          // Get next element (note cast)
          pNext = (CPlayer*)GetNext(pos);

          // Add current element to new list if it matches
          if ( _strnicmp( pNext->GetName(), szTarget,
                          strlen( szTarget ) )
                     == 0 )
               pNewList->AddTail(pNext);
     }

     if ( pNewList->IsEmpty() )
     {
          delete pNewList;
          pNewList = NULL;
     }

     return pNewList;
}
```

*continues*

**Listing 22.1. continued**

## LINKLIST.H

```
// LINKLIST.H
// Copyright 1993, Mark Andrews

#include "player.h"

#if !defined( _LINKLIST_H_ )
#define _LINKLIST_H_

#include <afxwin.h>
#include <afxcoll.h>
#include "zalthar.h"

class CPlayerList : public CObList {
     DECLARE_SERIAL(CPlayerList)
protected:
     BOOL  m_bIsDirty;
public:
     void DeleteAll();
     CPlayerList()
          { m_bIsDirty = FALSE; }

     // Add new functions
     CPlayerList* MakeFindList( const char * szTarget );
     CPlayerList* FindPlayer( const char * szTarget );

     void SetDirty( BOOL bDirty )
          {   ASSERT_VALID( this );
               m_bIsDirty = bDirty; }

     BOOL GetDirty()
          {   ASSERT_VALID( this );
               return m_bIsDirty; }

};

#endif  // _LINKLIST_H_
```

## NRCHARS.CPP

```
// nrchars.cpp : implementation file
// Copyright 1993, Mark Andrews
//

#include "stdafx.h"
#include "zalthar.h"
#include "nrchars.h"
```

```
#ifdef _DEBUG
#undef THIS_FILE
static char BASED_CODE THIS_FILE[] = __FILE__;
#endif

/////////////////////////////////////////////////////////////////////////////
// CNrChars dialog

CNrChars::CNrChars(CWnd* pParent /*=NULL*/)
     : CDialog(CNrChars::IDD, pParent)
{
     //{{AFX_DATA_INIT(CNrChars)
     m_nr_chars = 0;
     //}}AFX_DATA_INIT
}

void CNrChars::DoDataExchange(CDataExchange* pDX)
{
     CDialog::DoDataExchange(pDX);
     //{{AFX_DATA_MAP(CNrChars)
     DDX_Text(pDX, IDC_NR_CHRS, m_nr_chars);
     DDV_MinMaxUInt(pDX, m_nr_chars, 0, 9999);
     //}}AFX_DATA_MAP
}

BEGIN_MESSAGE_MAP(CNrChars, CDialog)
     //{{AFX_MSG_MAP(CNrChars)
          // NOTE: the ClassWizard will add message map macros here
     //}}AFX_MSG_MAP
END_MESSAGE_MAP()

/////////////////////////////////////////////////////////////////////////////
// CNrChars message handlers
```

## NRCHARS.H

```
// nrchars.h : header file
// Copyright 1993, Mark Andrews
//

/////////////////////////////////////////////////////////////////////////////
// CNrChars dialog

class CNrChars : public CDialog
{
// Construction
public:
     CNrChars(CWnd* pParent = NULL);     // standard constructor
```

*continues*

**Listing 22.1. continued**

```
// Dialog Data
	//{{AFX_DATA(CNrChars)
	enum { IDD = IDD_NR_CHARS };
	UINT m_nr_chars;
	//}}AFX_DATA

// Implementation
protected:
	virtual void DoDataExchange(CDataExchange* pDX);  // DDX/DDV

	// Generated message map functions
	//{{AFX_MSG(CNrChars)
		// NOTE: the ClassWizard will add member functions here
	//}}AFX_MSG
	DECLARE_MESSAGE_MAP()
};
```

## PLAYER.CPP

```
// PLAYER.CPP
// Copyright 1993, Mark Andrews

#include <iostream.h>
#include <string.h>
#include <stdio.h>
#include <stdlib.h>
#include <afxwin.h>
#include <afxcoll.h>
#include "player.h"

int CCharacter::count = 0;     // initialize nr of players to 0

IMPLEMENT_SERIAL(CPlayer, CObject, 1)

// Forward declarations.
void SetRandomSeed();
int RollDice(int sides);

//////////////////////////////////////////////
//  CPlayer::operator=
//  Overloaded operator= to perform assignments.
//
CPlayer& CPlayer::operator=( const CPlayer& b )
{
	ASSERT_VALID( this );
	ASSERT_VALID( &b );
	int m_class = b.m_class;
	int m_race = b.m_race;
	int m_s = b.m_s;
	int m_d = b.m_d;
```

```
    int m_c = b.m_c;
    int m_i = b.m_i;
    int m_w = b.m_w;
    int m_ch = b.m_ch;
    class CString m_name = b.m_name;
    class CString weapon = b.weapon;
    class CString armor = b.armor;
    class CString magic = b.magic;
    m_modTime = b.m_modTime;
    return *this;
}

// function to set and get ability scores
void CCharacter::SetAbilScores()
{
    ASSERT_VALID( this );
    int abils[6];

    SetRandomSeed();
    for (int c = 0; c < 6; c++)
        abils[c] = RollDice(20);

    SetStrength(abils[0]);
    SetDexterity(abils[1]);
    SetConstitution(abils[2]);
    SetIntelligence(abils[3]);
    SetWisdom(abils[4]);
    SetCharisma(abils[5]);
}

void CCharacter::PrintAbils()
{
    ASSERT_VALID( this );
    cout << '\n';
    cout << "Strength: " << GetStrength() << '\n';
    cout << "Dexterity: " << GetDexterity() << '\n';
    cout << "Constitution: " << GetConstitution() << '\n';
    cout << "Intelligence: " << GetIntelligence() << '\n';
    cout << "Wisdom: " << GetWisdom() << '\n';
    cout << "Charisma: " << GetCharisma() << '\n';
}

// Serialization function
void CCharacter::Serialize(CArchive& archive)
{
    ASSERT_VALID(this);
    //Call base class function first
    CObject::Serialize(archive);
```

*continues*

**Listing 22.1. continued**

```
    //Dump data for CPlayer class
    if (archive.IsStoring()) {
         TRACE( "Serializing a CPlayer out.\n" );
         archive << m_class << m_race
              << m_s << m_d << m_c << m_i << m_w << m_ch
              << m_classStr << m_raceStr
              << m_name << armor
              << weapon << magic
              << equipment << treasure;
    }
    else {
         TRACE( "Serializing a CPlayer in.\n" );
         archive >> m_class >> m_race
              >> m_s >> m_d >>m_c >> m_i >> m_w >> m_ch
              >> m_classStr >> m_raceStr
              >> m_name >> armor
              >> weapon >> magic
              >> equipment >> treasure;
    }
}

// Saving these in case we ever add print capabilities.

void CPlayer::PrintEntry()
{
    ASSERT_VALID( this );
    cout << "\nNAME: ";
    cout << GetName();
    cout << "\nClass: ";
    cout << GetClassName();
    cout << "\nRace: ";
    cout << GetRaceName();
    cout << "\nWeapon: ";
    cout << GetWeapon();
    cout << "\nArmor: ";
    cout << GetArmor();
    PrintAbils();
}

void CWarrior::PrintEntry()
{
    ASSERT_VALID( this );
    cout << "\nNAME: ";
    cout << GetName();
    cout << "\nRace: ";
    cout << GetRaceName();
    cout << "\nClass: ";
    cout << GetClassName();
    cout << "\nWeapon: ";
```

```
        cout << GetWeapon();
        cout << "\nArmor: ";
        cout << GetArmor();
        PrintAbils();
}

void CThief::PrintEntry()
{
        ASSERT_VALID( this );
        cout << "\nNAME: ";
        cout << GetName();
        cout << "\nRace: ";
        cout << GetRaceName();
        cout << "\nClass: ";
        cout << GetClassName();
        cout << "\nWeapon: ";
        cout << GetWeapon();
        cout << "\nArmor: ";
        cout << GetArmor();
        PrintAbils();
}

void CWizard::PrintEntry()
{
        ASSERT_VALID( this );
        cout << "\nNAME: ";
        cout << GetName();
        cout << "\nRace: ";
        cout << GetRaceName();
        cout << "\nClass: ";
        cout << GetClassName();
        cout << "\nWeapon: ";
        cout << GetWeapon();
        cout << "\nMagic: ";
        cout << GetMagic();
        PrintAbils();
}

void CPriest::PrintEntry()
{
        ASSERT_VALID( this );
        cout << "\nNAME: ";
        cout << GetName();
        cout << "\nRace: ";
        cout << GetRaceName();
        cout << "\nClass: ";
        cout << GetClassName();
        cout << "\nWeapon: ";
        cout << GetWeapon();
        cout << "\nArmor: ";
```

*continues*

**Listing 22.1. continued**

```
     cout << GetArmor();
     cout << "\nMagic: ";
     cout << GetMagic();
     PrintAbils();
}

// An all-purpose AssertValid function
#ifdef _DEBUG
void CCharacter::AssertValid() const
{
     CObject::AssertValid();
}
#endif

// seed the random number generator with current time
void SetRandomSeed()
{
     srand((unsigned)time(NULL));
}

// function to roll dice
int RollDice(int nrOfSides)
{
     div_t div_result;   // struct used in dividing
     int randNr, randNr2;

     randNr = rand();                  // get random number
     switch (nrOfSides) {
          case 4: {
               randNr = randNr & 0xFFF0;      // nr now 16 or less
               randNr /= 4;                   // nr now 4 or less
               randNr++;                      // start at 1 sted 0
               break;
          }
          case 8: {
          randNr = randNr & 0xFFF0;      // nr now 16 or less
          randNr /= 2;                   // nr now 8 or less
          randNr++;                      // start at 1 sted 0
               break;
     }
     case 10: {
          randNr = randNr & 0xFFF0;      // nr now 16 or less
               if (randNr > 9) {              // if nr is 10 or more
               div_result = div(randNr, 10);
               randNr = div_result.rem;
          }                                   // nr is now in range 0-9
               break;
          }                          // (that's ok for 10-sided die)
          case 12: {
```

```
            randNr = randNr & 0xFFF0;          // nr now 16 or less
                randNr2 = rand();              // get 2d random number
                randNr2 = randNr2 & 0xFFF0;    // nr2 now 16 or less
                randNr2 /= 4;                  // nr2 now 4 or less
                randNr += randNr2;             // add the random nrs
                randNr++;                      // start at 1 sted 0
                break;
            }
            case 20: {
            randNr = randNr & 0x000F;          // nr now 0 to 15
                randNr2 = rand();              // get random number
            randNr2 = randNr2 & 0x0004;        // nr2 now 0 to 4
                randNr += randNr2;             // add the 2 rand nrs
                randNr++;                      // start at 1 sted 0
                break;
            }
        }
        return (randNr);
}
```

## PLAYER.H

```
// PLAYER.H
// Copyright 1993, Mark Andrews

#if !defined( _PLAYER_H_ )
#define _PLAYER_H_

#include <afxwin.h>
#include <afxcoll.h>
#include <iostream.h>
#include <stdlib.h>
#include <time.h>

void SetRandomSeed();
// void GetAbilScores();
int RollDice(int sides);

enum playerClasses { WARRIOR, WIZARD, PRIEST, THIEF };
const CString gClassName [] = { "Warrior", "Wizard", "Priest",
    "Thief" };

enum playerRaces { DWARF, ELF, GNOME,
    HALF_ELF, HALFLING, HUMAN };
const CString gRaceName [] = { "Dwarf", "Elf", "Gnome",
    "Half elf", "Halfling", "Human" };

enum playerAbils { STRENGTH, DEXTERITY, CONSTITUTION,
    INTELLIGENCE, WISDOM, CHARISMA };
```

*continues*

**Listing 22.1. continued**

```
const CString gAbilsName [] = { "Strength", "Dexterity",
      "Constitution", "Intelligence", "Wisdom",
      "Charisma" };

class CCharacter : public CObject {
protected:
     WORD m_class;
     WORD m_race;
     WORD m_s;
     WORD m_d;
     WORD m_c;
     WORD m_i;
     WORD m_w;
     WORD m_ch;
     class CString m_classStr;
     class CString m_raceStr;
     class CString m_name;
     class CString armor;
     class CString weapon;
     class CString magic;
     class CString equipment;
     class CString treasure;
     static int count;
public:
     CCharacter() {}
     ~CCharacter () {}
     static int GetCount() { return count; }
     static void IncCount() { count++; }
     static void DecCount() { count--; }
     static void PrintCount();
     void SetPlayerClass(int pc) { ASSERT_VALID (this); m_class = pc;}
     void SetPlayerRace(int pr) { ASSERT_VALID (this); m_race = pr; }
     void SetClassStr(CString aStr)
          { ASSERT_VALID (this); m_classStr = aStr; }
     void SetRaceStr(CString aStr)
          { ASSERT_VALID (this); m_raceStr = aStr; }
     void SetClass(CString classString);
     void SetRace(CString raceString);
     int GetPlayerClass() { ASSERT_VALID (this); return m_class; }
     int GetPlayerRace() { ASSERT_VALID (this); return m_race; }
     CString GetRaceName() { ASSERT_VALID (this); return m_raceStr; }
     CString GetClassName() { ASSERT_VALID (this); return m_classStr;}
     void SetName(CString nm) { ASSERT_VALID (this); m_name = nm; }
     CString GetName() { return m_name; }
     void SetWeapon(CString wpn) { ASSERT_VALID (this); weapon = wpn; }
     CString GetWeapon() { return weapon; }
     void SetArmor(CString arm) { ASSERT_VALID (this); armor = arm; }
     CString GetArmor() { return armor; }
     void SetMagic(CString mag) { ASSERT_VALID (this); magic = mag; }
     CString GetMagic() { ASSERT_VALID (this); return magic; }
```

```
        void SetTreasure(CString tr)
            { ASSERT_VALID (this); treasure = tr; }
        CString GetTreasure() { ASSERT_VALID (this); return treasure; }
        void SetEquipment(CString eq)
            { ASSERT_VALID (this); equipment = eq; }
        CString GetEquipment() { ASSERT_VALID (this); return equipment; }
        // Set character's abilities
        void SetAbils(int st, int de, int co, int in,
            int wi, int ch)
            { m_s = st; m_d = de; m_c = co; m_i = in;
                m_w = wi; m_ch = ch; }
        // Get character's abilities
        void GetAbils(int *st, int *de, int *co, int *in,
            int *wi, int *ch)
            { *st = m_s; *de = m_d; *co = m_c; *in = m_i;
                *wi = m_w; *ch = m_ch; }
        // read contents of the PlayerAbils object
        int GetStrength() { return m_s; }
        int GetDexterity() { return m_d; }
        int GetConstitution() { return m_c; }
        int GetIntelligence() { return m_i; }
        int GetWisdom() { return m_w; }
        int GetCharisma() { return m_ch; }
        void SetStrength(int st) { m_s = st; }
        void SetDexterity(int de) { m_d = de; }
        void SetConstitution(int co) { m_c = co; }
        void SetIntelligence(int in) { m_i = in; }
        void SetWisdom(int wi) { m_w = wi; }
        void SetCharisma(int ch) { m_ch = ch; }
        virtual void PrintEntry() = 0;
        void PrintAbils();
        void SetAbilScores();
        //Override the CObject Serialize function
        virtual void Serialize(CArchive& archive);
#ifdef _DEBUG
        virtual void AssertValid() const;
#endif
};

class CPlayer : public CCharacter {
        DECLARE_SERIAL(CPlayer)
protected:
        CTime m_modTime;
        BOOL  m_bIsDirty;
public:
        CPlayer()
            { m_modTime = CTime::GetCurrentTime(); }
        ~CPlayer () {}
        CPlayer( const CPlayer& a );
```

*continues*

**Listing 22.1. continued**

```
     CPlayer(int pr) { SetPlayerRace(pr); }
     void PrintEntry();
     // Override the assignment operator
     CPlayer& operator=( const CPlayer& b );
     void SetDirty( BOOL bDirty )
          {   ASSERT_VALID( this );
               m_bIsDirty = bDirty; }

     BOOL GetDirty()
          {   ASSERT_VALID( this );
               return m_bIsDirty; }
     // Delete All deletes the Player objects as well as the pointers.
     void DeleteAll();
};

class CWarrior : public CPlayer {
public:
     CWarrior() {}
     CWarrior(int pr) : CPlayer(pr)
          { SetPlayerRace(pr); SetPlayerClass(WARRIOR); }
     void PrintEntry();
};

class CThief : public CPlayer {
public:
     CThief() {}
     CThief(int pr) : CPlayer(pr)
          { SetPlayerRace(pr); SetPlayerClass(WARRIOR); }
     void PrintEntry();
};

class CWizard : public CPlayer {
public:
     CWizard() {}
     CWizard(int pr) : CPlayer(pr)
          { SetPlayerRace(pr); SetPlayerClass(WIZARD); }
     CWizard(int pr, CString mag) : CPlayer(pr)
          { SetPlayerRace(pr);
            SetPlayerClass(WIZARD); SetMagic(mag); }
     void PrintEntry();
};

class CPriest : public CPlayer {
public:
     CPriest() {}
     CPriest(int pr) : CPlayer(pr)
          { SetPlayerRace(pr); SetPlayerClass(PRIEST); }
     CPriest(int pr, CString mag) : CPlayer(pr)
          { SetPlayerRace(pr); SetPlayerClass(PRIEST); SetMagic(mag);}
```

```
    void PrintEntry();
};

#endif // _PLAYER_H
```

**ZALTHDOC.CPP**

```
// zalthdoc.cpp : implementation of the CZaltharDoc class
// Copyright 1993, Mark Andrews
//

#include "stdafx.h"
#include "zalthar.h"

#include "zalthdoc.h"
// #include "database.h"
#include "linklist.h"

#ifdef _DEBUG
#undef THIS_FILE
static char BASED_CODE THIS_FILE[] = __FILE__;
#endif

//////////////////////////////////////////////////////////////////////
// CZaltharDoc

IMPLEMENT_DYNCREATE(CZaltharDoc, CDocument)

BEGIN_MESSAGE_MAP(CZaltharDoc, CDocument)
    //{{AFX_MSG_MAP(CZaltharDoc)
        // NOTE - the ClassWizard will add and remove mapping macros
        //      here. DO NOT EDIT what you see in these blocks of
        //      generated code !
    //}}AFX_MSG_MAP
END_MESSAGE_MAP()

//////////////////////////////////////////////////////////////////////
// CZaltharDoc construction/destruction

CZaltharDoc::CZaltharDoc()
{
    // TODO: add one-time construction code here
    m_pDataList = NULL;
    m_pFindList = NULL;
    m_szFileName = "";
    m_szFileTitle = "";
}

CZaltharDoc::~CZaltharDoc()
{
```

*continues*

**Listing 22.1. continued**

```
    // TODO: add reinitialization code here
    Terminate();   // Close down the database.
}

void CZaltharDoc::InitDocument()
{
    // TODO: add reinitialization code here
    New();     // Initialize the database.
}

BOOL CZaltharDoc::OnNewDocument()
{
    // TODO: add reinitialization code here
    if (!CDocument::OnNewDocument())
        return FALSE;
    InitDocument();
    return TRUE;
}

BOOL CZaltharDoc::OnOpenDocument(const char* pszPathName)
{
    // TODO: add reinitialization code here

    BOOL y = DoOpen(pszPathName);

    return y;
}

/////////////////////////////////////////////////////////////////////////////
// CZaltharDoc diagnostics

#ifdef _DEBUG
void CZaltharDoc::Dump(CDumpContext& dc) const
{
    CDocument::Dump(dc);
}
#endif //_DEBUG

#ifdef _DEBUG
void CZaltharDoc::AssertValid() const
{
    if ( m_pDataList != NULL )
    {
        ASSERT_VALID( m_pDataList );
        if ( m_pFindList != NULL )
            ASSERT_VALID( m_pFindList );
    }
    else
```

```
        ASSERT( m_pFindList == NULL );
}
#endif

//////////////////////////////////////////////////////////////////////
// My stuff

const char szUntitled[] = "Untitled";

//  This function initializes the database.
BOOL CZaltharDoc::New()
{
     ASSERT_VALID( this );

     // Clean up any old data.
     Terminate();

     m_pDataList = new CPlayerList;

     return ( m_pDataList != NULL );
}

//  Clean up the database.
void CZaltharDoc::Terminate()
{
     ASSERT_VALID( this );

     if ( m_pDataList != NULL )
          m_pDataList->DeleteAll();

     delete m_pDataList;
     delete m_pFindList;

     m_pDataList = NULL;
     m_pFindList = NULL;

     m_szFileName = szUntitled;
     m_szFileTitle = szUntitled;
}

// Count the players in the database.
int CZaltharDoc::GetCount()
{
     ASSERT_VALID( this );
     if ( m_pFindList != NULL )
          return m_pFindList->GetCount();
     if ( m_pDataList != NULL )
          return m_pDataList->GetCount();
     return 0;
}
```

*continues*

**Listing 22.1. continued**

```
// Miscellaneous document functions
//

const char* CZaltharDoc::GetName()
{
     ASSERT_VALID( this );
     return m_szFileName;
}

CString CZaltharDoc::GetTitle()
{
     ASSERT_VALID( this );
     return  "Zalthar - " + m_szFileTitle;
}

void CZaltharDoc::SetTitle( const char* pszTitle )
{
     ASSERT_VALID( this );
     m_szFileTitle = pszTitle;
}

// Add a player to the database
void CZaltharDoc::AddPlayer( CPlayer* pNewPlayer )
{
     ASSERT_VALID( this );
     ASSERT_VALID( pNewPlayer );
     ASSERT( pNewPlayer != NULL );
     ASSERT( m_pDataList != NULL );

     POSITION pos = m_pDataList->GetHeadPosition();

     while ( pos != NULL &&
               _stricmp(
                       ((CPlayer*)m_pDataList->GetAt(pos))->GetName(),
                         pNewPlayer->GetName() ) <= 0 )
          m_pDataList->GetNext( pos );

     if ( pos == NULL )
          m_pDataList->AddTail( pNewPlayer );
     else
          m_pDataList->InsertBefore( pos, pNewPlayer );

     SetModifiedFlag( TRUE );
}

//  Look up a player by index.
CPlayer* CZaltharDoc::GetPlayer( int nIndex )
{
```

```
    ASSERT_VALID( this );
    ASSERT( m_pDataList != NULL );

    if ( m_pFindList != NULL )
        return (CPlayer*)m_pFindList->GetAt
            ( m_pFindList->FindIndex( nIndex ) );
    else
        return (CPlayer*)m_pDataList->
            GetAt( m_pDataList->FindIndex( nIndex ) );
}

//  Remove a player from the database.
void CZaltharDoc::DeletePlayer( int nIndex )
{
    ASSERT_VALID( this );
    ASSERT( m_pDataList != NULL );

    POSITION el = m_pDataList->FindIndex( nIndex );
    delete m_pDataList->GetAt( el );
    m_pDataList->RemoveAt( el );
    SetModifiedFlag( TRUE );
}

//  Replace a player object with a new player object.
    void CZaltharDoc::ReplacePlayer( CPlayer* pOldPlayer,
    const CPlayer& rNewPlayer )
{
    ASSERT_VALID( this );

    ASSERT( pOldPlayer != NULL );
    ASSERT( m_pDataList != NULL );

    // Overloaded the new operator
    *pOldPlayer = rNewPlayer;
    SetModifiedFlag( TRUE );
}

//////////////////////////////////////////////////////
//  CZaltharDoc::DoFind
//  Do a FindPerson call, or clear the find data.
//
BOOL CZaltharDoc::DoFind( const char* pszName /* = NULL */ )
{
    ASSERT_VALID( this );
    ASSERT( m_pDataList != NULL );

    if ( pszName == NULL )
    {
        delete m_pFindList;
        m_pFindList = NULL;
```

*continues*

**Listing 22.1. continued**

```
            return FALSE;
        }

        // Prevents a second find to occur while
        // we already have one.
        ASSERT( m_pFindList == NULL );
        return ( ( m_pFindList = m_pDataList->
            FindPlayer( pszName ) ) != NULL );
}

//  Open the database and read a player list.
BOOL CZaltharDoc::DoOpen( const char* pszFileName )
{
        ASSERT_VALID( this );
        ASSERT( pszFileName != NULL );

        CFile file( pszFileName, CFile::modeRead );

        // read the object data from file
        CPlayerList* pNewDataBase = ReadDataBase( &file );

        file.Close();

        // get rid of current database if new one is OK
        if ( pNewDataBase != NULL )
        {
            Terminate();
            m_pDataList = pNewDataBase;
            SetModifiedFlag( FALSE );

            m_szFileName = pszFileName;
            return TRUE;
        }
        else
            return FALSE;
}

//  Save the database to a file.
BOOL CZaltharDoc::DoSave( const char* pszFileName /* = NULL */ )
{
        ASSERT_VALID( this );

        // store objects name.
        if ( pszFileName != NULL )
            m_szFileName = pszFileName;

        CFileStatus status;
        int nAccess = CFile::modeWrite;
```

```
        // Call GetStatus, which returns true if specified file exists,
        // false if it doesn't.
        if ( !CFile::GetStatus( m_szFileName, status ) )
            nAccess |= CFile::modeCreate;

        CFile file( m_szFileName, nAccess );

        // write database to a file and
        // mark the database clean if write is successful
        if ( WriteDataBase( &file ) )
        {
            SetModifiedFlag( FALSE );
            file.Close();
            return TRUE;
        }
        else
        {
            file.Close();
            return FALSE;
        }
}

//////////////////////////////////////////////////////////////////////
// CZaltharDoc serialization

void CZaltharDoc::Serialize(CArchive& ar)
{
        ASSERT_VALID( this );
        if (ar.IsStoring())
            {
            // TODO: add storing code here
            ::MessageBox(NULL, "Storing...", "CZaltharDoc", MB_OK);
            ASSERT( m_pDataList != NULL );
            // Archive out, or catch the exception.
            TRY
            {
                ar << m_pDataList;
            }
            CATCH( CArchiveException, e )
            {
                // Throw this exception again
                // for the benefit of the caller.
                THROW_LAST();
            }
            END_CATCH
            // ar.Close();

        }
        else {
```

*continues*

**Listing 22.1. continued**

```
        // TODO: add loading code here
        ::MessageBox(NULL, "Loading...", "CZaltharDoc", MB_OK);
        CPlayerList* pNewDataBase = NULL;

        // Deserialize the new data base from the archive,
        // or catch the exception.
        TRY
        {
            ar >> pNewDataBase;
        }
        CATCH( CArchiveException, e )
        {
            ar.Close();

            // If we got part of the database, delete it.
            if ( pNewDataBase != NULL )
            {
                pNewDataBase->DeleteAll();
                delete pNewDataBase;
            }

            // Caught an exception--but we throw it again so
            // the caller of this function can also catch it.
            THROW_LAST();
        }
        END_CATCH
        // ar.Close();
    }
}

//  Write data to a file.
BOOL CZaltharDoc::WriteDataBase( CFile* pFile )
{
    ASSERT_VALID( this );
    ASSERT( m_pDataList != NULL );

    // Create a archive from theFile for writing
    CArchive archive( pFile, CArchive::store );

    // Archive out, or catch the exception.
    TRY
    {
        archive << m_pDataList;
    }
    CATCH( CArchiveException, e )
    {
```

```
            // Throw this exception again
            // for the benefit of the caller.
            THROW_LAST();
        }
        END_CATCH

        // Exit here if no errors or exceptions.
        archive.Close();
        return TRUE;
}

//  Read data from a file.
CPlayerList* CZaltharDoc::ReadDataBase( CFile* pFile )
{
        ASSERT_VALID( this );
        CPlayerList* pNewDataBase = NULL;

        // Create an archive from pFile for reading.
        CArchive archive( pFile, CArchive::load );

        // Deserialize the new data base from the archive,
        // or catch the exception.

        TRY
        {
            archive >> pNewDataBase;
        }
        CATCH( CArchiveException, e )
        {
            archive.Close();

            // If we got part of the database, delete it.
            if ( pNewDataBase != NULL )
            {
                pNewDataBase->DeleteAll();
                delete pNewDataBase;
            }

            // Caught an exception--but we throw it again so
            // the caller of this function can also catch it.
            THROW_LAST();
        }
        END_CATCH

        // Exit here if no errors or exceptions.
        archive.Close();
        return pNewDataBase;
}
```

*continues*

### Listing 22.1. continued

**ZALTHDOC.H**

```
// zalthdoc.h : interface of the CZaltharDoc class
// Copyright 1993, Mark Andrews
//

#ifndef _ZALTHDOC_H_
#define _ZALTHDOC_H_

#include <afxwin.h>
#include <afxcoll.h>
#include "player.h"
#include "linklist.h"
// #include "database.h"

class CZaltharDoc : public CDocument
{
protected: // create from serialization only
     CZaltharDoc();
     DECLARE_DYNCREATE(CZaltharDoc)

// Implementation
public:
     virtual ~CZaltharDoc();
     // overridden for document I/O
#ifdef _DEBUG
     virtual   void AssertValid() const;
     virtual   void Dump(CDumpContext& dc) const;
#endif
protected:
     void InitDocument();
     virtual   BOOL OnNewDocument();
     virtual BOOL OnOpenDocument(const char* pszPathname);

// Generated message map functions
protected:
     //{{AFX_MSG(CZaltharDoc)
          // NOTE - the ClassWizard will add and remove member
          // functions here. DO NOT EDIT what you see in these blocks
          // of generated code !
     //}}AFX_MSG
     DECLARE_MESSAGE_MAP()

////////////////////////  My Stuff ////////////////////////////////

private:
     CPlayerList* ReadDataBase( CFile* pFile );
     BOOL WriteDataBase( CFile* pFile );
protected:
```

```
     CPlayerList* m_pDataList;
     CPlayerList* m_pFindList;
     CString m_szFileName;
     CString m_szFileTitle;
public:

     // Create/Destroy CPlayerLists
     BOOL New();
     void Terminate();

     // File handling
     void Serialize(CArchive& ar);
     BOOL DoOpen( const char* pszFileName );
     BOOL DoSave( const char* pszFileName = NULL );
     BOOL DoFind( const char* pszLastName = NULL );

     // Player Handling
     void AddPlayer( CPlayer *pNewPlayer );
     void ReplacePlayer( CPlayer* pOldPlayer, const CPlayer&
                         rNewPlayer );
     void DeletePlayer( int nIndex );
     CPlayer* GetPlayer( int nIndex );
     BOOL FindPlayer(const char *pName);

     // Database Attributes
     int GetCount();
     BOOL IsNamed();
     const char* GetName();
     CString GetTitle();
     void SetTitle( const char* pszTitle );

};

#endif // _ZALTHDOC_H_
```

## ZALTHVW.CPP

```
// zalthvw.cpp : implementation of the CZaltharView class
// Copyright 1993, Mark Andrews
//

#include "stdafx.h"
#include "zalthar.h"

#include "zalthdoc.h"
#include "zalthvw.h"
#include "player.h"
#include "createch.h"
#include "getchard.h"
#include "finddlg.h"
```

*continues*

**Listing 22.1. continued**

```
#include "charlist.h"
#include "nrchars.h"

#ifdef _DEBUG
#undef THIS_FILE
static char BASED_CODE THIS_FILE[] = __FILE__;
#endif

/////////////////////////////////////////////////////////////////////////////
// CZaltharView

IMPLEMENT_DYNCREATE(CZaltharView, CView)

BEGIN_MESSAGE_MAP(CZaltharView, CView)
     //{{AFX_MSG_MAP(CZaltharView)
     ON_COMMAND(ID_CHARACTERS_CREATE_ONE, OnCharactersCreateOne)
     ON_COMMAND(ID_CHARS_VIEW_ONE, OnCharsViewOne)
     ON_WM_SIZE()
     ON_WM_CREATE()
     ON_COMMAND(ID_CHARACTERS_FIND, OnCharactersFind)
     ON_COMMAND(ID_CHARS_VIEW_MULT, OnCharsViewMult)
     ON_COMMAND(ID_CHARACTERS_CREATE_MULT, OnCharactersCreateMult)
     //}}AFX_MSG_MAP
     // Standard printing commands
     ON_COMMAND(ID_FILE_PRINT, CView::OnFilePrint)
     ON_COMMAND(ID_FILE_PRINT_PREVIEW, CView::OnFilePrintPreview)
END_MESSAGE_MAP()

/////////////////////////////////////////////////////////////////////////////
// CZaltharView construction/destruction

CZaltharView::CZaltharView()
{
     // TODO: add construction code here
}

CZaltharView::~CZaltharView()
{
}

/////////////////////////////////////////////////////////////////////////////
// Get and store a pointer to the document
// associated with this view.

void CZaltharView::OnInitialUpdate()
{
     // TODO: add your code here
     m_database = GetDocument();
```

```
    ASSERT_VALID(m_database);
    OnUpdate(NULL, 0, NULL); // What basic function does
}

/////////////////////////////////////////////////////////////////////////////
// CZaltharView drawing

void CZaltharView::OnDraw(CDC* pDC)
{
    // m_database = GetDocument();

    // TODO: add draw code here
}

/////////////////////////////////////////////////////////////////////////////
// CZaltharView printing

BOOL CZaltharView::OnPreparePrinting(CPrintInfo* pInfo)
{
    // default preparation
    return DoPreparePrinting(pInfo);
}

void CZaltharView::OnBeginPrinting(CDC* /*pDC*/,
                                   CPrintInfo* /*pInfo*/)
{
    // TODO: add extra initialization before printing
}

void CZaltharView::OnEndPrinting(CDC* /*pDC*/, CPrintInfo* /*pInfo*/)
{
    // TODO: add cleanup after printing
}

/////////////////////////////////////////////////////////////////////////////
// CZaltharView diagnostics

#ifdef _DEBUG
void CZaltharView::AssertValid() const
{
    CView::AssertValid();
}

void CZaltharView::Dump(CDumpContext& dc) const
{
    CView::Dump(dc);
}

CZaltharDoc* CZaltharView::GetDocument() // non-debug version inline
{
```

*continues*

**Listing 22.1. continued**

```
    ASSERT(m_pDocument->IsKindOf(RUNTIME_CLASS(CZaltharDoc)));
    return (CZaltharDoc*) m_pDocument;
}

#endif //_DEBUG

/////////////////////////////////////////////////////////////////////////////
// My stuff

void CZaltharView::OnCharactersCreateOne()
{
    // TODO: Add your command handler code here

    ASSERT_VALID(this);
    ASSERT_VALID(m_database);

    // Create a player.

    m_player = new CWarrior;
    ASSERT_VALID(m_player);

    m_player->SetAbilScores();

    CCreateCharDlg dlg(m_player);
    if (dlg.DoModal() == IDOK) {
        m_database->AddPlayer(m_player);
    }
    else {
        delete m_player;
    }
}

void CZaltharView::OnCharsViewOne()
{
    // TODO: Add your command handler code here

    OnCharactersFind();

}

void CZaltharView::OnSize(UINT nType, int cx, int cy)
{
    CView::OnSize(nType, cx, cy);
}

int CZaltharView::OnCreate(LPCREATESTRUCT lpCreateStruct)
{
    if (CView::OnCreate(lpCreateStruct) == -1)
        return -1;
```

```
        SetWindowText("The Quest Begins.");

        // TODO: Add your specialized creation code here

        return 0;
}

void CZaltharView::OnCharactersFind()
{
        char *str1 =
              "Can't find any characters; please load or create a game!";
        char *str2 = "Woops!";

        int n = m_database->GetCount();
        if (n == 0)
             MessageBox( str1, str2,
                   MB_OK ¦ MB_ICONEXCLAMATION);
        else FindChar();      // Next function, see below.

}

void CZaltharView::FindChar()
{
        char *str1 = "Please create a character.";
        char *str2 = "Woops!";
        char *str3 = "Couldn't find your character!";
        char *str4 = "Sorry!";

        CFindDlg searchDlg;

        ASSERT_VALID(this);
        ASSERT_VALID(m_database);
        if (m_database->GetCount() == 0)
                  MessageBox( str1, str2,
                       MB_OK ¦ MB_ICONEXCLAMATION);
       else {
             // CFindDlg() just prompts for, gets,
             // and stores a character's name.
             if ( searchDlg.DoModal() == IDOK &&
                  searchDlg.GetNameStr().GetLength() != 0 ) {

                  // GetFindList() look for the name in the database.
                  if (m_database->DoFind(searchDlg.GetNameStr())) {
                       // Get 0th player in list
                            m_player = (m_database->GetPlayer(0));
                       // Call CGetCharDlg() to display
                       // data about the found character.
                       CGetCharData dlg(m_player);
                       dlg.DoModal();
```

*continues*

**Listing 22.1. continued**

```
                }
                else
                     MessageBox( str3, str4,
                     MB_OK ¦ MB_ICONEXCLAMATION);
                m_database->DoFind(); // Discard the find list.
           }
      }
}

void CZaltharView::OnCharsViewMult()
{
      // TODO: Add your command handler code here
      CCharList dlg(m_database, this);
      dlg.DoModal();
}


void CZaltharView::OnCharactersCreateMult()
{
      // TODO: Add your command handler code here
      CNrChars dlg(this);
      if (dlg.DoModal() == IDOK) {
           int n = dlg.m_nr_chars;
           for (int i = 0; i < n; i++) {
                OnCharactersCreateOne();
           }
      }
}
```

### ZALTHVW.H

```
// zalthvw.h : interface of the CZaltharView class
// Copyright 1993, Mark Andrews
//

#include "zalthdoc.h"
#include "linklist.h"
#include "player.h"

class CZaltharView : public CView
{
private:

      CPlayer *m_player;

      // The document associated with this view.
      CZaltharDoc *m_database;
```

```
protected: // create from serialization only
     CZaltharView();
     DECLARE_DYNCREATE(CZaltharView)
     void OnInitialUpdate();

// Implementation
public:
     virtual ~CZaltharView();
     virtual void OnDraw(CDC* pDC);  // overridden to draw this view
#ifdef _DEBUG
     virtual void AssertValid() const;
     virtual void Dump(CDumpContext& dc) const;
#endif

// My stuff
public:
     CZaltharDoc* GetDocument();
     void FindChar();

// Printing support
protected:
     virtual BOOL OnPreparePrinting(CPrintInfo* pInfo);
     virtual void OnBeginPrinting(CDC* pDC, CPrintInfo* pInfo);
     virtual void OnEndPrinting(CDC* pDC, CPrintInfo* pInfo);

// Generated message map functions
protected:
     //{{AFX_MSG(CZaltharView)
     afx_msg void OnCharactersCreateOne();
     afx_msg void OnCharsViewOne();
     afx_msg void OnSize(UINT nType, int cx, int cy);
     afx_msg int OnCreate(LPCREATESTRUCT lpCreateStruct);
     afx_msg void OnCharactersFind();
     afx_msg void OnCharsViewMult();
     afx_msg void OnCharactersCreateMult();
     //}}AFX_MSG
     DECLARE_MESSAGE_MAP()
};
```

# Summary

In this chapter, you created a Windows application, written in Visual C++, with the help of Visual C++'s trio of graphically oriented, interactive program-generation tools: AppWizard, Studio App, and ClassWizard. You learned that AppWizard is an automated tool for creating application frameworks, that

App Studio is an interactive tool for creating user interface objects, and that ClassWizard is an interactive tool that can "bind," or connect, user interface objects with the commands and functions that make the objects work during the execution of a program.

You became familiar with these three tools by using them to create and build this chapter's version of The Wrath of Zalthar, which appears in Listing 22.1. This chapter's edition of the Zalthar program, as you may have noticed, is the first version that you have compiled into a full-fledged Windows-based application.

Along with learning how AppWizard, ClassWizard, and App Studio work, you were introduced in this chapter to the structure of a Windows-based program written in Visual C++. You learned that Windows programs are message-driven, and you learned something about what that term means (although, if you're not familiar with Windows programming, you should learn more about it by reading texts that cover the topic in greater detail; a few are listed in the Bibliography).

This chapter also introduced you briefly to the `WinMain()` function, which every Windows program has; the application object, which every C++ Windows application has; the `CWinApp` class, from which all application objects are derived; and various other classes and member functions that are commonly used in Windows-based C++ programs.

The chapter covered many important elements of Windows programming in great detail, and most of the topics that it explored are illustrated in the Chapter 22 version of The Wrath of Zalthar. However, one important feature of most Windows programs is missing from the Zalthar program: a window.

That omission will be corrected in Chapter 23.

Chapter 23

# Windows and Views

In Chapter 22, "The Visual Workbench," you saw how to use the Visual Workbench to create menus, dialog boxes, and other kinds of user-interface objects. In Chapter 24, "Visual C++ Graphics," you'll see how to add eye-catching animation and graphics to the Windows program that you started designing in Chapter 22.

In this chapter, you'll see how it all fits together. You'll see how Visual C++ uses the ingredients it's handed by you and its team of Visual C++ tools—the Visual Workbench Editor, ClassWizard, AppWizard, and Studio App—to fashion an application.

In the beginning, when software engineers started writing Windows applications, things weren't too complicated. Writing Windows programs was more complicated than writing DOS programs, but things were relatively straightforward. To design a Windows application, you simply wrote your code for an interface that displayed things in a window.

Now, things are a little more complex. Today, when you develop a Windows application with Visual C++, it isn't just windows that you have to worry about. You have to write your program around *documents* and *views*.

Documents and views are so important in Visual C++ that every Visual C++ contains at least one pair of files that implements a document and one pair of files that implements a view. When you create the application framework for a Visual C++ program, AppWizard automatically creates a pair of document files named *YOURPROJECT*DOC.CPP and *YOURPROJECT*DOC.H and a pair of view files named *YOURPROJECT*VIEW.CPP and *YOURPROJECT*VIEW.H (or *YOURPROJECT*VW.CPP and *YOURPROJECT*VW.H, if the name of your project would result in a filename more than eight characters long).

When you start expanding a Visual C++ framework into a full-fledged Windows application, Microsoft recommends that you implement all your program's data in the *YOURPROJECT*DOC.CPP file that AppWizard has created and that you implement all your program's user-interface code in the *YOURPROJECT*VIEW.CPP. (If your program grows long and complex, you may split those files into smaller files, but it's still suggested that the overall architecture of document files and view files be preserved.)

If you're new to Visual C++ and are not yet familiar with the document-and-view paradigm, it may seem strange to you and you may be tempted to ignore it and continue designing programs the way you did before. If you feel that temptation, resist it! The architecture of the Visual C++ framework depends on the architecture of the document-and-view system. At least until you become so expert at using Visual C++ that you can start breaking the rules, I recommend that you follow the instructions. If you don't, there's no hint of a guarantee that your program will work as it is supposed to.

The Wrath of Zalthar program that was presented in Chapter 22, and will be completed in Chapter 24, follows Microsoft's suggested Visual C++ architecture to the letter. As you can see by examining Listing 22.1, the document files in the latest version of the Zalthar program are named ZALTHDOC.CPP and ZALTHDOC.H, and the program's view files are named ZALTHVW.CPP and ZALTHVW.DOC. The database that handles the program's game characters is encapsulated in the ZALTHDOC.CPP file, and all user-interface objects are accessed either in or through the ZALTHVW.DOC file. We'll take a closer look at both those files and how they work together later in this chapter.

# How Documents and Views Work

Because Visual C++ is a language based on classes and because most Visual C++ classes are defined in the Microsoft Foundation Class (MFC) library, it should not be a surprise that the documents in a Visual C++ program are objects of an MFC class named `CDocument` and that C++ views are objects of an MFC class named `CView`.

The `CDocument` and `CView` classes are closely related. To understand why, remember that a well behaved Visual C++ program encapsulates all its data in document objects and all its user-interface objects in view classes. The main job of a document object is to store data and make it available to the user, and the main job of a view object is to provide the user with an interface that can be used to manipulate the data in a document.

To get a perspective on how document and view objects work together, it might help to know that the `CDocument` class is derived from a class named `CCmdTarget` (which is specially designed to be a target of Windows messages) and that the `CView` class is derived directly from the `CWnd` class and that `CWnd`, like `CDocument`, is derived from the `CCmdTarget` class.

These derivations make sense because `CDocument` and `CView` objects are designed to facilitate communications between user-interface objects, data in documents, and Windows commands. This arrangement is illustrated in Figure 23.1.

### NOTE—ALL IN THE FAMILY

A `CView` object can be associated with only one `CDocument` object, but a `CDocument` object can be associated with multiple `CView` objects. When you think about it, that makes sense. The job of a view object is to display the data in a document object, and if more than one document is available, that can be confusing. But a document object might have multiple views; for instance, a database document might have a view that displays its entries in a list and another view that displays them individually.

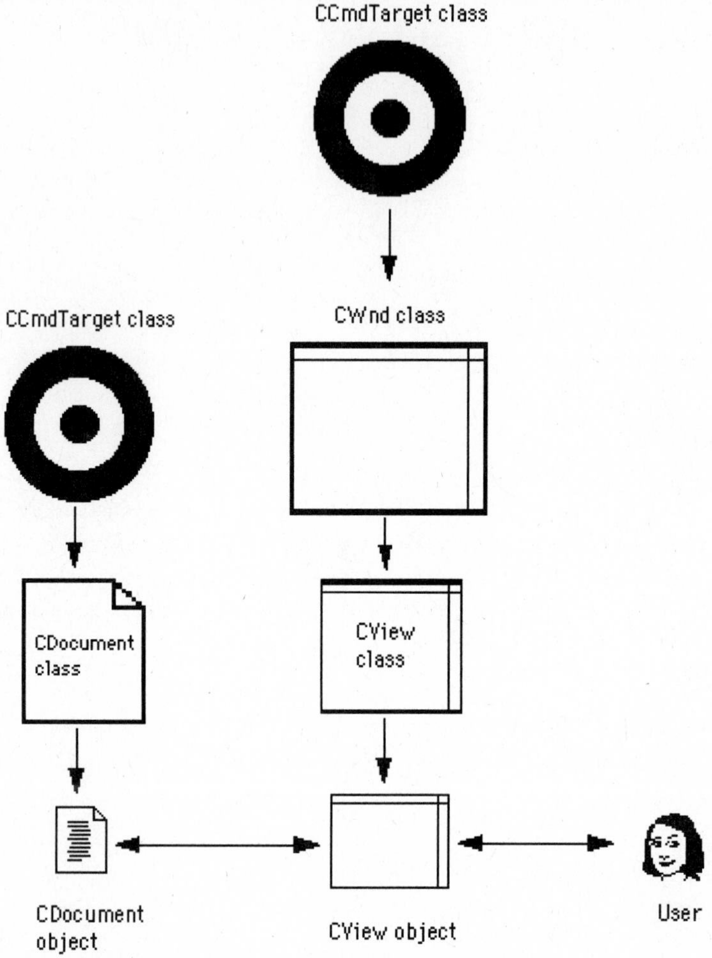


*Figure 23.1. Relationship between documents and views.*

Figure 23.1 shows how document objects descend from the `CCmdTarget` and `CDocument` classes and how view objects descend from the `CWnd` and `CView` classes. It also shows that although a view object descends from the `CWnd` class, that object is closely associated with a document object and serves as an interface between the data in a document object and the user of the program that manipulates the data.

> **NEW IN VISUAL C++: CDOCUMENT AND CVIEW**
>
> Both `CDocument` and `CView`, by the way, are new classes that have been added to the MFC library with the introduction of C++. They didn't exist in Microsoft C/C++ Version 7. That's one indication of how important documents and views have become in Visual C++; they now have their own classes in the MFC library.

## Features of the CDocument Class

A `CDocument` object has many powerful features for obtaining, storing, retrieving, and manipulating data. In Chapter 21, "The Microsoft Foundation Classes," you saw how a `CDocument` object can serialize (read and write) data to and from a disk and can even display those standard Windows dialogs that commercial programs use for loading and saving data. The `CDocument` class also has member functions for performing such tasks as adding more views, deleting views, and updating views—something that's often necessary when the data in a document changes.

Other useful `CDocument` member functions include `SetModifiedFlag()` and `SaveModified()`, which your application can use to be sure the data in a document is saved to disk when necessary.

## Features of the CView Class

The `CView` class has a set of features that supports its interaction with the `CDocument` class. For example, the `CView` class has a member function named `GetDocument()` that a `CView` object can use to obtain a pointer about the `CDocument` object with which it is associated.

Other useful member functions of the `CView` class include `OnActivateView()`, which is called when a view is activated; `OnDraw()`, which is called whenever a view needs to be redrawn on the screen; and `OnUpdate()`, which can be called to notify a view that its document has been modified.

The `CView` class also has several features that can control the printing of views on a printer.

## Using Documents

In Visual C++, a document is an object derived from the `CDocument` that encapsulates an application's data. When you create an application template with AppWizard, Visual C++ automatically provides the framework of a document object and places the code that implements it in a file named *YOURAPP*DOC.CPP (where *YOURAPP* is the name of your application). In the Chapter 21 version of the example program, The Wrath of Zalthar—and also in the final installment of the program, which is presented in Listing 24.1 at the end of Chapter 24—the document file created by AppWizard is named ZALTHDOC.CPP.

When you manage data in a Visual C++ program, the recommended practice is to manage it through objects derived from the `CDocument` class. That way, you can manage data serialization and other tasks by using the built-in capabilities of the `CDocument` class.

One special feature of the `CDocument` class is that it is specially designed to be used with programs created by AppWizard. When you use AppWizard to generate an application framework and instantiate an object inside the file *YOURAPP*DOC.CPP, AppWizard automatically connects the menu commands Save, Save As, and Open with your document object.

If you examine the file DATABASE.H in Listing 22.1, you'll see that the `CDataBase` object that made its debut in Chapter 21 (Listing 21.1) has been converted to an object of the `CDocument` class, so it can inherit the properties of documents. Furthermore, the `CDataBase` class that is implemented in Listing 22.1 is managed by a document class implemented in the ZALTHDOC.CPP file.

# How Windows Work in Visual C++

Because the `CView` class is derived from the `CWnd` class, one good way to start learning about view objects is to learn what you can about windows.

If you're an experienced Windows programmer, you'll be happy to learn that you already know much of what you need to know about how windows are used in Visual C++ programs. The engineers who designed the MFC library (Versions 1 and 2) have managed to retain the look and feel of the Windows interface while removing many of the design hurdles that made life unnecessarily difficult for pre-C++ designers of Windows software.

Many of the classes in the MFC library are patterned after similar functions in the familiar Windows API. In fact, many Windows-related member functions defined in the MFC library even have the same names as their counterpart functions in the standard Windows API.

On the other hand, there are abundant differences between programs for Windows that are written in Visual C++ and Windows programs that are written in more traditional languages. Most Windows programmers will welcome those differences. The following examples show some of the relative differences:

- Does not use switch statements for handling messages.
- Does not contain a `MakeProcInstance()` function.
- Has built-in type-checking safeguards that make it safer and easier to pass parameters to Windows-related functions.
- Can be built around an application framework that is generated automatically by AppWizard.
- Can be equipped with user-interface objects with the help of the App Studio and ClassWizard tools.
- Supports all the object-oriented features of the C++ language.

## Windows Classes

When you start writing Windows programs in Visual C++, you'll find that there are many Windows-related classes in the MFC library. All of them are derived from one monster class, `CWnd`, which has more than 100 member functions and more than a dozen children.

Of all the classes derived from `CWnd`, five are considered most important: `CWinApp`, `CFrameWnd`, `CMDIFrameWnd`, `CDialog`, and `CModalDialog`.

This section describes the MFC library class `CWnd`, its five most important subclasses, and several other Windows-related classes that you might find useful in your Visual C++ programs.

## The CWnd Class

`CWnd` is the root class of all the MFC library's Windows-related classes. It provides the base functionality of all window classes in the MFC library. Its subclasses include the five important classes mentioned at the beginning of this section, plus `CFrameWnd`, `CDialog`, `CStatic`, `CButton`, `CListBox`, `CComboBox`, `CEdit`, and `CScrollBar`.

It is possible to derive classes directly from the CWnd class, but it's much more common for Visual C++ programs to derive their classes from CWnd's child classes, such as CFrameWnd, CMDIFrameWnd, CDialog, and CModalDialog.

## CWnd Member Functions and the Windows API

About half the member functions of the CWnd class are straightforward replacements for familiar Windows functions (but CWnd's member functions are easier and safer to use than their Windows API counterparts, as you'll see later in this section). Experienced programmers will find them easy to spot because they have the same names as their Windows counterparts.

For example, the CWnd member function ShowWindow() has the same functionality as the native ShowWindow() function that is defined in the standard Windows API. Other CWnd member functions that have been borrowed from the Windows API with their names intact include the CScrollBar member functions GetScrollPos(), SetScrollPos(), GetScrollRange(), and SetScrollRange().

When you write a Windows-related program in Visual C++, you can call native Windows functions as well as the member functions of MFC library classes. To call a Windows API function when an object in your program is in scope, all you have to do is precede your function call with the scope resolution operator (::). For example, to call the native Windows function ShowWindow() when an object is in scope, just make a ::ShowWindow() call.

The other half (more or less) of CWnd's member functions are message handlers. These handlers are accessed through message maps, which were introduced in Chapter 22. A message-handling function is also easy to spot because it always begins with the word On. For example, the member function OnAbout(), which is executed when the user of an application chooses the About command from the program's menu, is a message-handling function. (You encountered many other message-handling functions when you learned how to use the ClassWizard tool in Chapter 22.)

## Message Handling: A Better Way

The member functions that the CWnd class has substituted for native Windows functions are safer and more convenient to use than the Windows functions that they have replaced. This is one of the most significant changes—and one of the most welcome improvements—that the MFC library has made in Windows programming.

In programs written in the original Windows programming environment, each Windows message has two parameters generally known as `wParam` and `lParam`. Unfortunately, these two parameters have no specific data types. Legions of Windows programmers have tried to work around this deficiency of the Windows API's design by resorting to using the macros `MAKELONG`, `HIWORD`, `LOWORD`, `LOBYTE`, and `HIBYTE` with the result that a badly engineered programming tool has often led to even worse program design.

The message-handling member functions of the `CWnd` class are strongly typed and therefore offer a much safer way to send and receive Windows messages. For example, the `OnKeyDown()` message handler has three parameters: `nChar`, `nRepCnt`, and `nFlags`. When you call `OnKeyDown()`, you can access the user's key repeat count simply by using the `nRepCnt` parameter; you don't have to consult Windows documentation to find out that the key count is stored in the `LOWORD` of `lParam`.

## The Big 5 Windows Classes

Although most Windows-related classes are derived from the `CWnd` class, you'll rarely, if ever, derive an object directly from `CWnd` in Visual C++ programs. In most Windows-based Visual C++ programs, you'll find yourself dealing instead with the five most important Window-related classes: `CWinApp`, `CFrameWnd`, `CMDIFrameWnd`, `CDialog`, and `CModalDialog`.

All five of these classes are derived directly from `CWnd`, and each one is important in Visual C++ Windows programming because each encapsulates a specific part of the standard Windows interface.

### CWinApp

`CWinApp`, as you learned in Chapter 22, is the base class for a special kind of object called an *application object,* which every Visual C++ program must have.

In a Visual C++ application, the application object controls all the program's document objects and view objects and also manages various housekeeping chores such as initialization and cleanup of the program. The application object takes care of many of the routine chores that the program must handle, that is, the aspects that are usually handled by `WinMain()` in a traditional nonobject-oriented Window program.

As you may recall from Chapter 22, the application object in a Visual C++ program always overrides the `InitInstance()` member function of `CWinApp` to perform routine but essential housekeeping tasks such as initializing data, creating the application's main window, and performing some cleanup of memory areas on shutdown.

The application object also controls all your application's document objects and view objects and creates and manages document templates for all document types that the application supports.

In the Chapter 22 version of The Wrath of Zalthar—and in the program's final installment, presented in Chapter 24—an application class named `CZaltharApp` is derived from the `CWinApp` class. An application object named `theApp` is then instantiated from the `CZaltharApp` class. (In Visual C++, you don't have to do any of this yourself; AppWizard creates an application object for you when it generates your program's application framework.)

In the installments of the Zalthar program presented in Chapters 22 and 24, the application class `CZaltharApp` is defined in the file ZALTHAR.H and is implemented in the file ZALTHAR.CPP.

In Listing 22.1, this is the declaration of the `CZaltharApp` class that appears in the file ZALTHAR.H:

```
class CZaltharApp : public CWinApp
{
public:
     CZaltharApp();

// Overrides
     virtual BOOL InitInstance();

// Implementation

     //{{AFX_MSG(CZaltharApp)
     afx_msg void OnAppAbout();
          // NOTE - the ClassWizard will add and remove member
          // functions here. DO NOT EDIT what you see in these blocks
          // of generated code !
     //}}AFX_MSG
     DECLARE_MESSAGE_MAP()
};
```

And this is the implementation of the `CZaltharApp` class, which appears in the file ZALTHAR.CPP:

```
CZaltharApp::CZaltharApp()
{
```

```
        // TODO: add construction code here,
        // Place all significant initialization in InitInstance
}
```

Also in the ZALTHAR.CPP file, this statement initializes the `CZaltharApp` object `theApp`:

```
CZaltharApp NEAR the App;
```

## The InitInstance() Function

As you may remember from Chapter 22, every Visual C++ program must override the `CWinApp` member function `InitInstance()`. This function definition, which also appears in the Chapter 22 version of ZALTHAR.CPP (Listing 22.2), overrides the `CWinApp` class's `InitInstance()` function:

```
BOOL CZaltharApp::InitInstance()
{
        // Standard initialization
        // If you are not using these features and wish to reduce the
        // size of your final executable, you should remove from the
        // following the specific initialization routines you do not need.

     SetDialogBkColor();        // set dialog background color to gray
     LoadStdProfileSettings();  // Load standard INI file options
(including MRU)

        // Register the application's document templates. Document
        // templates serve as the connection between documents, frame
        // windows and views.

     AddDocTemplate(new CMultiDocTemplate(IDR_ZALTHATYPE,
               RUNTIME_CLASS(CZaltharDoc),
               RUNTIME_CLASS(CMDIChildWnd),
        // standard MDI child frame
               RUNTIME_CLASS(CZaltharView)));

     CDataBase *gDataBase = new CDataBase;

        // create main MDI Frame window
     CMainFrame* pMainFrame = new CMainFrame;
     if (!pMainFrame->LoadFrame(IDR_MAINFRAME))
          return FALSE;
     pMainFrame->ShowWindow(m_nCmdShow);
     pMainFrame->UpdateWindow();
     m_pMainWnd = pMainFrame;
```

```
    // create a new (empty) document
    OnFileNew();

    if (m_lpCmdLine[0] != '\0')
    {
        // TODO: add command-line processing here
    }

    return TRUE;
}
```

The ZALTHAR.CPP file also contains this message map for the `CZaltharApp` class:

```
BEGIN_MESSAGE_MAP(CZaltharApp, CWinApp)
      //{{AFX_MSG_MAP(CZaltharApp)
      ON_COMMAND(ID_APP_ABOUT, OnAppAbout)
      // NOTE - the ClassWizard will add and remove mapping macros here.
      // DO NOT EDIT what you see in these blocks of generated code !
      //}}AFX_MSG_MAP
      // Standard file based document commands
      ON_COMMAND(ID_FILE_NEW, CWinApp::OnFileNew)
      ON_COMMAND(ID_FILE_OPEN, CWinApp::OnFileOpen)
      // Standard print setup command
      ON_COMMAND(ID_FILE_PRINT_SETUP, CWinApp::OnFilePrintSetup)
END_MESSAGE_MAP()
```

## CFrameWnd and CMDIFrameWnd

The MFC library class `CFrameWnd` creates a standard, framed, titled window like the main window that almost every Windows application has. The `CMDIFrameWnd` class implements the same kind of window, but `CFrameWnd` is designed to be used by single document interface (SDI) applications, whereas `CFrameWnd` is used by multiple document interface (MDI) applications. (An SDI application is a program that supports a single document window. An MDI program can support multiple document windows.)

The `CMDIFrameWnd` and `CFrameWnd` classes provide the windowing capabilities that are built into most C++ programs for Windows. Both classes are derived from the MFC library class `CWnd`, which has more than 100 window-managing functions.

Because `CMDIFrameWnd` and `CFrameWnd` are derived from `CWnd`, they inherit all its functionality and add some of their own. Extra capabilities offered by `CFrameWnd` and `CMDIFrameWnd` include support for an accelerator table and a `Create()` member function that is slightly more convenient than the `Create()` routine provided by the `CWnd` class.

## Using CFrameWnd and CMDIFrameWnd

When you write a Visual C++ program for Windows, you can create a frame window for your application by deriving a class from either `CFrameWnd` or `CMDIFrameWnd`. Then, you can add member variables to store data that is specific to your application.

You can also write message-handling member functions that specify what happens when messages are received by the `CFrameWnd` or `CMDIFrameWnd` that you define. For example, if you want your application to be capable of responding to a `WM_PAINT` message (which paints a window), you can derive a class from `CFrameWnd` or `CMDIFrameWnd` and equip it with an `OnPaint()` member function to handle the `WM_PAINT` message.

When AppWizard creates a framework for an application, it creates either a `CFrameWnd` object or a `CMDIFrameWnd` object, depending on which kind of document interface you select. When you launch AppWizard from the Visual Toolbox by selecting AppWizard from the Project menu, you can choose your application's document interface by clicking the Options button in the MFC AppWizard dialog box.

When AppWizard's Options dialog box appears, you can create an MDI application by leaving the MDI check box selected. If you remove the check from the box, AppWizard generates an SDI application.

## Creating a Frame Window

As experienced Windows programmers know, a conventional Windows program creates a Windows registration class by filling in a `WNDCLASS` structure and passing it to a function named `RegisterClass()`. In contrast, in Visual C++, you typically derive a window class from an existing MFC library class by using standard C++ syntax for class inheritance. For frame windows, the MFC library provides three base classes from which you can derive your frame window classes: `CFrameWnd` and `CMDIFrameWnd`, which have already been described, and `CMDIChildWnd`, a class for creating MDI child windows.

When you derive a frame window from an existing MFC library frame window class, you must take two main steps:

1. Define a constructor for the derived class.
2. Define message-handling functions and a message map for the derived class so that window messages that are received by the derived window can be correctly routed to the proper handler functions.

### Defining a Constructor

When you derive a window class from a window class defined in the MFC library, you must implement a constructor for your window class. To initialize the class, the constructor can call the `Create()` member function, which calls the Windows API function that actually creates the window you see on the screen.

Another alternative is to set up a message map that calls the `CWnd` member function `OnCreate()` when a window is to be created. This is the method used in the Zalthar program, as you'll see later in this section under the heading "Using `CMDIFrameWnd`: An Example."

### Switch Statements: The Visual C++ Alternative

When you define message-handling functions and a message map for a derived frame window class, your application's message handlers and message map take care of routing window messages received by the window to the appropriate handler functions.

There are three main categories of messages that must be handled:

- `WM_COMMAND` messages, which the user of your application generates by selecting a menu item or pressing an accelerator key.
- Notification messages that child windows dispatch. (These are also `WM_COMMAND` messages, but the window procedure arguments contain the control ID of the child window and an event code, such as `BN_CLICKED`, to identify why the child window is sending the notification.)
- Other `WM_` messages, such as `WM_PAINT`, that are generated by the system or user input.

In a traditional Windows program, a window procedure contains a message-handling switch statement, usually a large one. This switch statement examines each window message that arrives and determines what action to take.

In a Visual C++ program, this monster switch statement for handling Windows messages is replaced by a standard C++ derivation mechanism that is implemented in the MFC library. In a Visual C++ program, your derived Windows class inherits all the functionality of its base window class, including the base class's window-handling procedure. That procedure is where incoming window messages are processed.

When you write Windows programs in Visual C++, nothing prohibits you from overriding the window procedure for a window's base class and using switch statements to decode incoming window messages. If, however, you want to get the maximum benefit from the C++ style window-handling procedures defined in the MFC library and if you want to be sure your code is compatible with future enhancements to Visual C++, it's best to use the message-map mechanism provided in the MFC library.

### Message Handling Step by Step

This, then, is what you should do to use the message-map mechanism in your derived window classes:

1. Define all special message-handler member functions that your program uses in your derived window class.
2. Call the `DECLARE_MESSAGE_MAP` macro in your derived window class declaration. (AppWizard takes care of this step.)
3. Place the `BEGIN_MESSAGE_MAP`, `END_MESSAGE_MAP`, and any other message-specific macros that you need in the .CPP file that implements your derived window class. (AppWizard also takes care of this step.)

You can define message-handler functions as member functions for your derived window class. Typically, you define one message-handler function for each window message that you handle. The base window class from which you derive your window will handle all the other window messages that you don't explicitly handle.

### WM_COMMAND Messages

When a user of your application selects a menu item, Windows dispatches a WM_COMMAND message to the frame window that contains the menu item's menu bar. The arguments that accompany the WM_COMMAND message contain a menu item ID number. This ID number is defined in the resource definition file (.RC). (In a Visual C++ program, you typically define one message handler function for each menu item that a window supports. You associate these message-handler functions with specific menu item ID numbers by defining a message map.)

Handling menu command messages is a two-step process:

1. Define one message-handling function for each menu item.
2. Once the message-handler functions are defined and the message map is enabled by the `DECLARE_MESSAGE_MAP` macro, define the message map itself to indicate which message-handler functions are to be associated with which messages (AppWizard takes care of this step for you).

To illustrate these two steps, suppose your application's menu has the standard Open and Save commands with the ID numbers `IDM_OPEN` and `IDM_SAVE`. You can declare a window class using this format:

```
class CMyWnd : public CFrameWnd
{
     // Put your constructor here.
public:
     afx_msg void OnOpen();
     afx_msg void OnSave();
     DECLARE_MESSAGE_MAP()
};
```

The word `afx_msg` that appears in the preceding code fragment shows that the functions `OnOpen()` and `OnSave()` are called through the message-map mechanism. The prefix is not required, but is a Visual C++ programming convention.

Notice that these functions take no arguments and return no values. Because they are member functions of your window class, they have access to the other member functions and member variables of objects derived from that class so that they can obtain the information they need to perform their tasks.

Also notice the `DECLARE_MESSAGE_MAP` macro that appears after the two function declarations. This macro is required; it enables the class's message-map mechanism.

## Child Windows

In a Windows program, a main frame window often contains one or more child windows. For example, controls such as buttons or edit text fields are implemented as child windows.

Child windows communicate with their parent window by sending `WM_COMMAND` notification messages. For example, a child button control responds to a user mouse click by sending a `WM_COMMAND` message to its parent window. The arguments to the window message procedure contain the control ID of the button and the constant `BN_CLICKED`. Through this mechanism, the parent window gets a notification message that tells it the ID of the control and what happened to that control.

Visual C++ provides message maps for handling notification messages from child windows. These message maps, generated by AppWizard, support notification messages that are generated by standard control windows. For example, the message-map entry macro for a `BN_CLICKED` notification message is

ON_BN_CLICKED. Macros for other notification messages are formatted in a similar way. Message-map entry macros are listed in the header file AFXMSG.H.

For each message that a child window can dispatch, your program should provide a control ID number and a function pointer to the member function that is to be called when the message is received.

## Using CMDIFrameWnd: An Example

In Chapters 22 and 24, The Wrath of Zalthar program is compiled as an MDI application; therefore, the main frame window that AppWizard created for the program, named CMainFrame, is derived from the CMDIFrameWnd class.

In Listing 22.1, this definition of the CMainFrame class appears in the file MAINFRM.H:

```
class CMainFrame : public CMDIFrameWnd
{
     DECLARE_DYNAMIC(CMainFrame)
public:
     CMainFrame();

// Attributes
public:

// Operations
public:

// Implementation
public:
     virtual ~CMainFrame();
#ifdef _DEBUG
     virtual   void AssertValid() const;
     virtual   void Dump(CDumpContext& dc) const;
#endif


protected:     // control bar embedded members
     CStatusBar     m_wndStatusBar;
     CToolBar  m_wndToolBar;

// Generated message map functions
protected:
     //{{AFX_MSG(CMainFrame)
     afx_msg int OnCreate(LPCREATESTRUCT lpCreateStruct);
     afx_msg void OnDestroy();
     //}}AFX_MSG
     DECLARE_MESSAGE_MAP()
};
```

You can get a close look at how the program creates its main frame window by launching the Visual Workbench and selecting the ClassWizard command from the Visual Workbench's Project menu. When the ClassWizard dialog window appears, select the name of the `CMainFrame` class in the Class Wizard dialog box's Class Name text box. Select the `WM_CREATE` message in the Messages list box, and ClassWizard highlights the `OnCreate()` member function in the Member Functions list box, as shown in Figure 23.2.

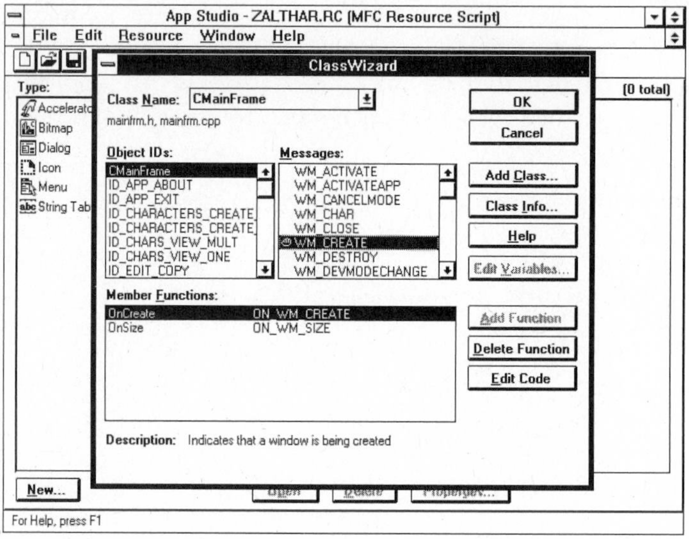


*Figure 23.2. Creating a main frame window.*

When ClassWizard highlights the `OnCreate()` member function, click the button labeled Edit Code. ClassWizard then opens the MAINFRM.CPP file and displays the source code that it has created for the `OnCreate()` member function, as shown in Figure 23.3.

As you can see from the source code in Figure 23.3, when the `CMainFrame` window is created, a `WM_CREATE` message is generated and the `CWnd` member function `OnCreate()` is called. That executes this function shown in Figure 23.2, which is defined in the MAINFRM.CPP file in Listing 22.1:

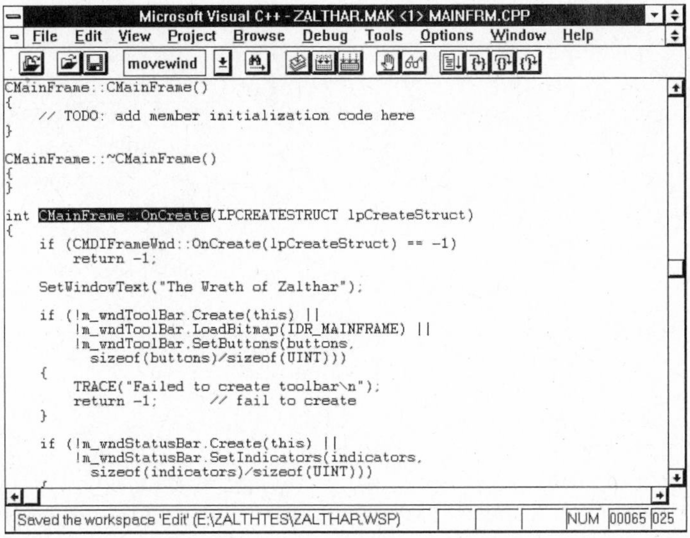


*Figure 23.3. Source code for the* `OnCreate()` *member function.*

```
int CMainFrame::OnCreate(LPCREATESTRUCT lpCreateStruct)
{
     if (CMDIFrameWnd::OnCreate(lpCreateStruct) == -1)
          return -1;

     if (!m_wndToolBar.Create(this) ¦¦
          !m_wndToolBar.LoadBitmap(IDR_MAINFRAME) ¦¦
          !m_wndToolBar.SetButtons(buttons,
            sizeof(buttons)/sizeof(UINT)))
     {
          TRACE("Failed to create toolbar\n");
          return -1;          // fail to create
     }

     if (!m_wndStatusBar.Create(this) ¦¦
          !m_wndStatusBar.SetIndicators(indicators,
            sizeof(indicators)/sizeof(UINT)))
     {
          TRACE("Failed to create status bar\n");
          return -1;          // fail to create
     }

     return 0;
}
```

This is the function that creates the program's main frame window.

> **NOTE—FROM WINDOWS TO VIEWS**
>
> Even though this chapter has gone into some detail about windows, don't forget that in a Visual C++ program, the most common way to access windows is through views. In Chapter 24, you'll see how views are used to add graphics features to the final version of The Wrath of Zalthar program.

# Dialog Boxes

A dialog box is a special kind of window that accepts and interprets user input. In Chapter 22, you used Studio App and ClassWizard to design several dialog boxes for that chapter's version of The Wrath of Zalthar program. This section provides some information about how dialog boxes work in Visual C++ programs.

There are two main kinds of dialog boxes: modal dialog boxes and modeless dialog boxes. A *modal* dialog box is one that does not allow any mouse events outside it to take place until it is closed. A *modeless* dialog box works more like an ordinary document window, enabling the user to work in other windows while it remains on the screen.

Many dialog boxes used in windows have characteristics of both modal and modeless dialog boxes. These hybrid modal/modeless dialog boxes behave like modal dialog boxes in some ways and like modeless dialog boxes in others. The dialog boxes that were created in Chapter 22 were of the modal/modeless variety.

When you create a modal/modeless dialog box, you can move it around on the screen as if it were modeless, but you can't perform any mouse-click actions outside it; if you try, your computer just beeps.

## The CDialog Class

All dialogs, modal and modeless, are objects of the `CDialog` class. The `CDialog` class descends directly from the `CWnd` class. The `CWnd` class, as noted earlier in this chapter, is descended from `CCmdTarget`, a class that is designed to be the target of Windows messages.

When you use a dialog box in a Visual C++ application, the dialog box is treated as an object and information associated with its controls can be stored as member variables. For example, an application can use a Boolean member variable to store the state of a radio button or a check box, or use a text or integer variable to store information that the user types in an edit box or selects in a list box.

When the user of a program closes a dialog box by clicking its OK button or its go-away box, the information stored in the dialog's controls can be recorded and then can be used in any way that the application requires.

If you want to initialize the contents of a dialog window's member variables before the dialog appears on the screen, you can do that by overriding a member function named `OnInitDialog()`. In installments of the Zalthar program in Chapters 22 and 24, the `OnInitDialog()` function is overridden to initialize most of the "Create a Character" dialog's controls.

You can create a modal dialog box—or a hybrid modal/modeless dialog box—by constructing a `CDialog` object on the stack and then calling the `CDialog` member function `DoModal()`. The `DoModal()` function creates the dialog box, manages it until the user clicks the OK button, and then closes it.

You can create a modeless dialog box by constructing a `CDialog` object and calling the `Create()` function in the constructor of your object.

# How Dialog Boxes Work

When the user of your application closes a *modal* dialog box by clicking the OK button, a `CModalDialog` member function named `OnOK()` is called. `OnOK()` can be overridden to retrieve data from the dialog's controls and store it in member functions. When the user closes the dialog by clicking the Cancel button, a function named `OnCancel()` is called. If you don't override `OnCancel()`, it does nothing.

## Modal and Modeless Dialog Boxes

Modal dialog boxes and modeless dialog boxes each have advantages and disadvantages. Modal dialog boxes are a little easier to program, but modeless dialogs are a little more convenient for the user. For instance, when you create a modeless dialog box, you have to call a member function named `Create()`, a finicky call with parameters that are difficult to get just right. There's also a sensitive `DestroyWindow()` call that you must make when it's time to close a modeless dialog.

Also, the procedure for collecting data from a *modeless* dialog is somewhat complicated. A modeless dialog doesn't prohibit all mouse clicks outside its borders when it is on the screen, so an application must collect data from a modeless dialog's controls continuously by tracking each control with a separate message handler and by changing its corresponding member function each time a change in its data is detected.

Also, because modeless dialogs must share processing with other objects that are on the screen at the same time they are, modeless dialogs are more difficult to create and dispose of than modal dialogs are.

## Creating a Modal/Modeless Dialog Box

To create a modal/modeless dialog box, derive it from the `CDialog` class. Then, invoke its constructor. When you have done that, you can call the member function `DoModal()`, as if working with a modal dialog box.

You can see how modeless and modal/modeless dialog boxes are created by examining the source code for the dialog boxes that were created in the Chapter 22 version of The Wrath of Zalthar program, presented in that chapter in Listing 22.1. The dialog boxes used in that program are implemented in the files CHARLIST.CPP, CREATECH.CPP, FINDDLG.CPP, GETCHARD.CPP, and NRCHARS,CPP.

The dialog that creates characters in the Zalthar program is implemented in the CREATECH.CPP file in Listing 22.1. To display the dialog box, the program calls a function named `OnCharactersCreateOne()`, which is defined in the file ZALTHVW.CPP.

In that file, this block of code is executed to create a modal/modeless dialog box:

```
void CZaltharView::OnCharactersCreateOne()
{
     // TODO: Add your command handler code here

     ASSERT_VALID(this);
     ASSERT_VALID(m_database);

     // Create a player.

     m_player = new CWarrior;
     ASSERT_VALID(m_player);

     m_player->SetAbilScores();
```

```
        CCreateCharDlg dlg(m_player);
        if (dlg.DoModal() == IDOK) {
             m_database->AddPlayer(m_player);
        }
        else {
             delete m_player;
        }
}
```

This block of code creates a new character for the game. It creates a game character, calls a random-number algorithm that sets the character's ability scores, and then creates a modeless dialog box and calls the member function `DoModal()` to display the dialog box. If the user closes the dialog box by clicking the OK button, the `DoModal()` function returns the constant value `IDOK` and a new character is created. Otherwise, the game character that the block of code has created is deleted.

The dialog box created in the preceding example is an object of a user-defined class named `CCreateCharDlg`. The `CCreateCharDlg` class is created by AppWizard, but implementation code has been added by hand.

The code that creates the dialog box is in the file CREATECH.CPP. This is what it looks like:

```
// Original constructor created by AppWizard.
CCreateCharDlg::CCreateCharDlg(CWnd* pParent /*=NULL*/)
     : CDialog(CCreateCharDlg::IDD, pParent)
{
}

// Our constructor created by us.
CCreateCharDlg::CCreateCharDlg(CPlayer *pPlayer,
     CWnd* pParent /*=NULL*/)
     : CDialog(CCreateCharDlg::IDD, pParent)
{
     // copy the pPlayer parameter
     m_player = pPlayer;

     //{{AFX_DATA_INIT(CCreateCharDlg)
     m_name = "";
     m_armor = "Leather";
     m_class = "Warrior";
     m_equipment = "None";
     m_magic = "None";
     m_race = "Human";
     m_treasure = "None";
     m_weapon = "Sword";
     //}}AFX_DATA_INIT
}
```

In this example, notice the items in the `CCreateCharDlg` dialog box are listed in a block of code labeled `AFX_DATA_INIT`. That construct is something new that was introduced with the premiere of Visual C++.

In Visual C++, a block of code labeled `AFX_DATA_INIT` is known as a *data initialization map*. As you can see, it has created a member function with the name that you selected in Step 9.

### NOTE—READ MY LIPS

In Chapter 22, I warned that you should almost never change the code in a data initialization map, that is, code that is bracketed with comments written in the syntax `//{{` and `//}}`. Those kinds of comments, I explained, are generated by ClassWizard and should never be changed by hand—with one exception.

This is the exception: In an `AFX_DATA_INIT` map created by ClassWizard, you can type a value that initializes a dialog control, that is, a value that appears inside the control when the dialog opens. So, you could edit this function:

```
CreateCharDlg::CCreateCharDlg(CWnd* pParent /*=NULL*/) :
  CDialog(CCreateCharDlg::IDD, pParent)
{
  //{{AFX_DATA_INIT(CCreateCharDlg)
  m_name = "";
  //}}AFX_DATA_INIT

}
```

to read:

```
CreateCharDlg::CCreateCharDlg(CWnd* pParent /*=NULL*/) :
  CDialog(CCreateCharDlg::IDD, pParent)
{
  //{{AFX_DATA_INIT(CCreateCharDlg)
  m_name = "Brogan";
  //}}AFX_DATA_INIT
}
```

When AppWizard creates a data initialization map, it also creates a corresponding function that contains another kind of data map called a DDX (data exchange) data map. AppWizard places the DDX map that it creates in the same file that contains the data initialization map, in a function named `DoDataExchange()`. In the CREATECH.CPP file, it is the `DoDataExchange()` function that creates the `CCreateCharDlg` dialog box's DDX map:

```
void CCreateCharDlg::DoDataExchange(CDataExchange* pDX)
{
     CDialog::DoDataExchange(pDX);
     //{{AFX_DATA_MAP(CCreateCharDlg)
     DDX_Control(pDX, IDC_STATIC_WI, m_wisdom);
     DDX_Control(pDX, IDC_STATIC_ST, m_strength);
     DDX_Control(pDX, IDC_STATIC_IN, m_intelligence);
     DDX_Control(pDX, IDC_STATIC_DE, m_dexterity);
     DDX_Control(pDX, IDC_STATIC_CO, m_constitution);
     DDX_Control(pDX, IDC_STATIC_CH, m_charisma);
     DDX_Text(pDX, IDC_EDIT_NAME, m_name);
     DDV_MaxChars(pDX, m_name, 64);
     DDX_CBString(pDX, IDC_COMBO_ARMOR, m_armor);
     DDV_MaxChars(pDX, m_armor, 64);
     DDX_CBString(pDX, IDC_COMBO_CLASS, m_class);
     DDV_MaxChars(pDX, m_class, 64);
     DDX_CBString(pDX, IDC_COMBO_EQUIPMENT, m_equipment);
     DDV_MaxChars(pDX, m_equipment, 64);
     DDX_CBString(pDX, IDC_COMBO_MAGIC, m_magic);
     DDV_MaxChars(pDX, m_magic, 64);
     DDX_CBString(pDX, IDC_COMBO_RACE, m_race);
     DDV_MaxChars(pDX, m_race, 64);
     DDX_CBString(pDX, IDC_COMBO_TREASURE, m_treasure);
     DDV_MaxChars(pDX, m_treasure, 64);
     DDX_CBString(pDX, IDC_COMBO_WEAPON, m_weapon);
     DDV_MaxChars(pDX, m_weapon, 64);
     //}}AFX_DATA_MAP
}
```

This function automatically handles the exchange of dialog-control data between the dialog control you have chosen and the member function declared in the previous example.

When you have bound the controls in a dialog box to corresponding member functions, you are almost ready to use the dialog box for data exchange. Only one more tip is necessary: You should know that after you make your data exchange, you must call the `CWnd` member function `UpdateData()`, which tells the compiler whether you'll be transferring information from a member function to a dialog box control or from a control to a member function.

As you'll see in just a moment, the `UpdateData()` function takes one parameter: a Boolean value. Passing a `FALSE` parameter to `UpdateData()` means that you want to move data from a dialog box item to a member function. Passing a `TRUE` parameter (or no parameter at all, because the call's one parameter is `TRUE` by default) means that you want to transfer information from a member function to a dialog box control.

That's all there is to it. In this code fragment, a `CMainFrame` member function named `m_charName` receives a string value:

```
m_charName = "Maureen"; // get data for the control
UpdateData(FALSE); // move the data into the control
```

In this example, the string `Maureen` in being moved into a dialog box control named `m_charName`. To move the string in the other direction, you could pass a `TRUE` value to the `UpdateData()` function that follows the data exchange.

You, however, don't actually have to do that. If you activate the DDX system, after the user clicks the dialog's OK button, you can obtain the updated value of any dialog item by using the assignment operator to obtain the value of the member variable associated with the dialog item. For example, if a dialog box has a text box named `m_dlgItem1` and has been designed (with App Studio) to contain an integer value, after the user clicks OK, you can retrieve the value of the item by executing a statement written in this format:

```
int x = m_dlgItem1;
```

These techniques are shown in more detail in the various files that create dialog boxes in Listing 22.1.

## Retrieving Data the Old Way

With the advent of the DDX system introduced with Visual C++, it has become much easier than it used to be to retrieve data that the user enters in a dialog box. In previous versions of Microsoft C/C++, when you wanted to obtain the value of a dialog box control, it was necessary to call functions such as `GetDlgItemInt()` or `GetDlgItemTxt()`. Because these calls are complicated, they are less convenient than using the DDX system. For example, the syntax of a call to `GetDlgItemInt()` is as follows:

```
UINT GetItemInt(int nID, BOOL *lpTrans = NULL,
     BOOL bSigned = TRUE) const;
```

Although the DDX system is a simpler method for retrieving information from a dialog box, the old way still comes in handy sometimes. For example, as you can see by examining the code in Listing 22.1 that creates dialog boxes, you can't use the DDX system to assign initial values to static dialog items; you still must do that by hand.

You also might want to stick with the old method when you port code to Visual C++ from earlier versions of Microsoft C++. Because some of the code in The Wrath of Zalthar was written before Visual C++ was released and because "If it works, don't fix it" is often an excellent rule (especially when it comes to code reuse), some of the functions that get and set the data entered in the program's dialog boxes use the old system of data retrieval rather than the new one. That's OK, because the old way still works, too.

# Summary

In this chapter, you learned how to add windowing capabilities to a Visual C++ application. The chapter described the `CWnd` class, the root class for all Windows-related classes, and explained how the classes and member functions in the MFC library handle Windows-related operations.

This chapter also introduced modal and modeless dialog boxes and explained how C++ classes and member functions can be used to track and record data that the user of a program enters in dialog boxes by interacting with dialog box controls.

The topics introduced in this chapter were shown in the newest and most robust version of The Wrath of Zalthar program to be introduced so far. Even more features will be added to the program in Chapter 24, which describes how graphics capabilities can be incorporated into Visual C++ programs.

Chapter 24

# Visual C++ Graphics

This is the last chapter in this volume, and I think you will find that it's a chapter worth waiting for. In this chapter, you'll get a chance to add spectacular color graphics, and even animation, to a Visual C++ program.

Here is a brief summary of what you'll find in this chapter:

- An introduction to graphics programming for Windows in general and Visual C++ in particular.
- A description of the bitmap editor that's built into App Studio, and some tips about how to use it.
- The final "release" version of the example program named The Wrath of Zalthar, which appears in Listing 24.1.

# The CDC Class

Whether you're a newcomer or an old-timer in the world of Windows programming, knowing how to use the CDC class is a prerequisite for writing graphics programs for Windows with Visual C++.

The CDC class is a large class that is defined in the Microsoft Foundation Class (MFC) library. The CDC class has many member variables and member functions that you can use to manipulate various kinds of drawing and painting objects, such as pens, brushes, patterns, and bitmaps.

The CDC class is derived from the CObject class. CDC isn't quite as big a class as CWnd, but with several subclasses and more than 100 member functions, it still qualifies as an enormous class.

With objects derived from the CDC class, your applications can paint and draw many kinds of lines and shapes on graphical output devices such as monitor screens, printers, and fax modems. You also can do almost any kind of painting and drawing on a printout or a computer screen with objects derived from the CDC class.

One basic example of a CDC function is CDC::LineTo(), which can draw a straight line on an output device such as a screen or a printed page. As an example of how the LineTo() function works, suppose an application contains a CDC object named myObj and a pair of points named x and y. When this LineTo() function is executed, it draws a line from point x to point y:

```
myObj.LineTo(x, y);
```

The CDC class provides many other kinds of graphics-related functions. For instance, you can create CDC objects to do the following:

- Draw and paint many kinds of shapes, such as lines, rectangles, ellipses, polygons, and regions (irregularly shaped objects).
- Print text in color or black and white.
- Get and set the colors for objects and text and for background colors of windows.
- Scroll screen and text displays.
- Tell a program what parts of the screen should be updated because their contents have been changed.
- Provide important data, such as start-of-page and end-of-page information, for printers.

- Display metafiles (files that can display assorted bitmaps, shapes, text, and other objects on a screen or a printed page).

Besides all these functions, there's a `CDC` member function named `BitBlt()` (pronounced "bit blit") that can copy a bitmap from one location to another—for example, from one memory buffer to another or from a memory buffer to the screen.

To execute the `BitBlt()` function, you provide it with a pointer to the bitmap you want copied, along with the bitmap's measurements, the upper-left coordinates of the destination rectangle, and a copying mode (there are many copying modes for painting bitmaps in various kinds of opaque and transparent configurations). For example, this is a `BitBlt()` function that copies a bitmap from a memory buffer to the screen:

```
pDC->BitBlt(0, 0, m_bmWidth, m_bmHeight, &dcZalth, 0, 0, SRCCPOPY)
```

Other examples of the `BitBlt()` function, and of a similar function named `StretchBlt()`, are presented in Listing 24.1, this chapter's version of The Wrath of Zalthar program. `StretchBlt()` is a function that can resize a bitmap as the bitmap is copied from one location to another. Both functions are used in a file named ZALTHDOC.CPP in the Zalthar program.

Several copying modes are demonstrated in the Zalthar program, and more modes are listed and described in the *Class Library Reference* manual supplied with Visual C++.

## CDC Subclasses

Although the `CDC` class has many member functions, it has only a few subclasses. Those include `CPaintDC`, `CWindowDC`, `CClientDC` and `CMetaFileDC`.

The `CPaintDC` class is a `CDC` class that corresponds to the native Windows message `WM_PAINT`. `CPaintDC` is useful because it encapsulates calls to the Windows API calls `BeginPaint()` and `EndPaint()`, which prepare windows for painting operations and close the painting operations when those are done. When you write a Visual C++ program, rather than call `BeginPaint()` and `EndPaint()`, you call a function named `OnPaint()`—or if you're drawing in a view, an alternative function called `OnDraw()`. (More information about `OnPaint()` and `OnDraw()` is provided later in this chapter.)

Because `CDC` and `CDC` subclass objects can handle text as well as graphics images and because calling `CDC` and `CDC` subclass functions is the only approved technique for performing graphics operations in Windows applications, programs that don't perform graphics operations except drawing text often use CDC-derived objects.

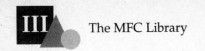

# The CGdiObject Class

Another important graphics-related class defined in the MFC library is the CGdiObject class. The CGdiObject class and the CDC class are closely related. In fact, objects of the CGdiObject class and objects of the CDC class rely on each other.

The CDC class, as you have seen, supplies a multitude of member functions for painting and drawing; however, the objects that are painted and drawn by CDC functions are members of the CGdiObject class.

The LineTo() function, which you encountered earlier in this chapter, is a member function of the CDC class. To draw a line with the LineTo() function, however, Visual C++ requires you to use a drawing object called a pen, and a pen is a member of a class called CPen, which is derived from the CGdiObject class.

The BitBlt() and StretchBlt() classes, also mentioned earlier in this chapter, are member functions of the CDC class, too. However, when you copy a bitmap with the BitBlt() function or the StretchBlt() function, the bitmap itself is a member of the CBitmap class—and the CBitmap class is derived from the CGdiObject class.

The CGdiObject class contains a CPen class for drawing lines, a CBrush class for filling shapes, and a CFont class to draw text. It also supplies a CBitmap class for creating bitmaps, a CPalette class for managing colors, and a CRegion class for drawing and painting regions (irregularly shaped objects).

These CGdiObject classes provide object-oriented graphics objects that are equivalent to the drawing tools provided by the standard Windows API. (The Windows tools that correspond to the graphics objects defined in the MFC library are HPEN, HBRUSH, HFONT, HBITMAP, HPALLETE, and HRGN.)

## Using the CDC and CGdiObject Classes

If you're an experienced Windows programmer, you have a head start on using objects derived from the CDC class. That's because the CDC class is based on the HDC structure that you may have used to write graphics programs by using the pre-C++ Windows API.

The `CDC` class, like the pre-C++ `HDC` structure, derives its name from the fact that it deals with *device-context objects,* that is, objects that are used to manipulate graphics images. The `CDC` class was designed because Windows-compatible computer systems use many different kinds of devices, such as monitors, printers, and other kinds of graphics devices.

The `CDC` class provides a common interface with all those kinds of devices, so you don't have to worry about the different kinds of characteristics they all have when you write programs for them.

The `CDC` class works because all Windows-compatible graphics devices are required to comply with a common graphics standard. That standard is a graphics programming language called the *Windows Graphical Device Interface,* or *GDI.* If a graphics device complies with the GDI standard, it can be accessed with Visual C++ objects that are derived from the `CDC` class.

## What's in a Name

The `CGdiObject` class derives its name from the fact that its objects are all GDI-compliant. Because all Windows-compatible graphics devices comply with the GDI standard and because the `CDC` class also follows that standard, you should use `CDC` member functions to perform all the graphics operations in your Visual C++ programs.

When you use a `CDC` object to perform a graphics operation—for example, to draw a line or a rectangle or to copy a bitmap to the screen—you can be confident that the operation will work on any Windows-compatible graphics device.

# Creating Graphics in Visual C++

Device-context objects are very useful because they provide a means for letting otherwise incompatible graphics devices work together. They, however, do introduce an extra level of complexity into Windows programs.

When you want to draw a shape in a Windows program, you can't just select a drawing object, such as a pen, and then draw a shape in the window. Instead, you must associate a pen with a device-context object or a `CDC` object, and then use the CDC object to draw the shape in the window (or, more often, in Visual C++ to draw the shape in a view).

In Visual C++ jargon, associating a drawing object with a CDC object is known as "selecting" the CDC object "into" the drawing object. To select a CDC object into a drawing object, you use a CDC member function named SelectObject(). To use the SelectObject() member function, you must execute a series of statements like this:

```
CPaintDC dc(this);
CPen newPen(PS SOLID, 2, RGB(0, 0, 255));
CPen* pOldPen = dc.SelectObject(&newPen);
```

The first line in this code fragment constructs a CDC object named dc. The CDC object that is constructed in this case is an object of the class CPaintDC, which is a subclass of CDC.

A CPaintDC object is an object that encapsulates two Windows functions that you may be familiar with if you've written Windows programs: the BeginPaint() function and the EndPaint() function. In pre-C++ Windows programs, you called BeginPaint() before you began a painting operation, and you called EndPaint() when you were done.

In Visual C++, the CPaintDC class makes both those calls for you. A CPaintDC object calls BeginPaint() when it is constructed and calls EndPaint() when its destructor is invoked. You don't have to make either of those calls yourself in your Visual C++ programs.

When you have instantiated a CPaintDC object to manipulate a drawing object, you can construct the drawing object. In the preceding example, the drawing object that is constructed is an object of the CPen class. In this example, this is the statement that creates a CPen object:

```
CPen newPen(PS SOLID, 2, RGB(0, 0, 255));
```

The CPen class is a subclass of the CGdiObject class. An object of the CPen class encapsulates the simplest kind of drawing object available in Visual C++—a pen. With a CPen object, you can draw lines on a printed page or on a screen.

In this example, once a CPen object has been instantiated, the CDC member function SelectObject() is called to select the CPen object that has just been created into the previously created CDC object. This is the statement that calls the SelectObject() function:

```
CPen* pOldPen = dc.SelectObject(&newPen);
```

The SelectObject() function takes a pointer to a CGdiObject as a pointer and returns a pointer to another CGdiObject. The pointer the function returns is always a pointer to whatever CGdiObject was currently active before the function was called.

When a program calls the SelectObject() function, the usual practice (and the recommended one) is to save the pointer SelectObject() returns. That way, when the program completes the drawing operation the SelectObject() call begins, the previously active CGdiObject can be restored when the drawing operation is complete. A program should always do that bit of cleaning up when it uses objects of the CDC and CGdiObject classes for drawing.

Now that you've had a step-by-step introduction to CDC and CGdiObject operations, you're ready to take an overall look at how the two classes work together. This code fragment shows how a program can use a CDC object and an object of the CGdiObject class to draw a line on the screen:

```
void CMainFrame::DrawALine()
{
     CPaintDC dc(this);
     CPen newPen(PS SOLID, 2, RGB(0, 0, 255));


// Change device context and save old pen
CPen* pOldPen = dc.SelectObject(&newPen);

// Do your drawing thing
     dc.MoveTo(6, 6);
     dc.LineTo(32, 6);
     // Restore old pen to the current device context.
     dc.SelectObject(pOldPen);
};
```

You also can use this kind of sequence to draw bitmaps on a screen in a Visual C++ program. That process, however, is a little more complicated, as you'll see later in this chapter.

## Visual C++ Graphics, Step by Step

As you have seen, Visual C++ programs never create objects of the CGdiObject class directly. Instead, they create objects from its derived classes: CBitmap, CBrush, CFont, CPalette, CPen, and CRgn.

These are the steps to follow to create a drawing in Visual C++:

1. Define an object that belongs to one of the graphics classes defined by the `CGdiObject` class. (Graphics objects usually are created on the stack frame—that is, as local objects—but nothing prevents you from creating a graphics object by using the `new` operator.)
2. Call the `SelectObject()` member function of the `CDC` class to place your object in the current device context. (If a previously selected graphics object is already in the current device context, `SelectObject()` saves the old graphics object automatically when you select your new one.)
3. When you have finished using your new graphics object, call the `CDC::SelectObject()` function to place the old graphics object back into the current device context. This step restores the current device context to its original state.
4. If you allocated your graphics object with the `new` operator, delete it with the `delete` operator. (If you created your object on the stack frame, it is deleted automatically when your program exits the scope in which the object was created.)

> **NOTE—ALLOCATING GRAPHICS OBJECTS IN InitInstance()**
>
> If your application uses a particular graphics object repeatedly, you can allocate the object just one time—for example, in your `CWinApp::InitInstance()` function—and then place the object in the current device context each time you want to use it. When you no longer need the object, you can delete it, typically just before your application terminates.

## The OnPaint() and OnDraw() Functions

As Windows programmers know, traditional Windows applications do most of their drawing in response to `WM_PAINT` messages. In a Visual C++ program, you don't have to work with Windows `WM_PAINT` messages directly. Instead, your application can handle `WM_PAINT` messages by calling either of two message-handling functions.

One of these message-handling functions is `OnPaint()`, a member function of the `CWnd` class. When your application needs to draw directly into a window, it can call the `OnPaint()` member function.

However, as you may recall from Chapter 22, "The Visual Workbench," and Chapter 23, "Windows and Views," Visual C++ applications rarely, if ever, do any drawing directly in a window. Instead, a Visual C++ program usually creates an object of the `CView` class, which is a subclass of the `CWnd` class, and then does all its drawing in that `CView` object.

In Visual C++, one difference betwen `CWnd` objects and `CView` objects is that you can't use the `OnPaint()` function to draw objects in a view. Instead, you use a similar function named `OnDraw()`, which is not available to `CWnd` objects because it is a member function of the `CView` class.

In Visual C++, the `CView` member function `OnDraw()` is called when an application needs to draw in a window. There is no default implementation of `OnDraw()`, so your application must override the `OnDraw()` function when it needs to draw on the screen.

In this chapter's version of the example program named The Wrath of Zalthar, the `OnDraw()` member function is overridden in the ZALTHVW.CPP file—the file in which the program's view class is implemented. This is the `OnDraw()` definition that appears in ZALTHVW.CPP:

```
void CZaltharView::OnDraw(CDC* pDC)
{
     CRect *rect;
   GetClientRect(rect);

     // m_database = GetDocument(); // We don't have to do this again!
     m_database->DrawBackdrop(pDC);
     m_database->DrawPlayer(pDC);
}
```

As you can see, this function definition is straightforward. It merely calls two longer functions: `m_database->DrawBackdrop()` and `m_database->DrawPlayer()`. The first of these functions draws a background that is used as a game-playing field. The second function draws a player in the foreground, over the playing field. You'll see the results of these operations later in this chapter.

The `m_database` pointer in the example points to the program's only document object, a member of a class named `CZaltharDoc`. The `m_database` pointer is a member function of a class named `CZaltharView`. The `CZaltharView` class is instantiated in the ZALTHVW.CPP file—the file in which the `OnDraw()` function appears.

The `CZaltharDoc` object that the `m_database` function points to is instantiated in a file named CZALTHARDOC.CPP. As you can see by examining the function definition, the `DrawBackdrop()` and `DrawPlayer()` functions are member functions of `CZaltharDoc`.

**NOTE—SECOND-GUESSING CLASSWIZARD**

You may notice that the first executable line in the example is preceded by a cryptic comment that says: "`We don't have to do this again!`" This is the line in which the comment appears:

```
// m_database = GetDocument(); // We don't have to do this again!
```

I placed the comment in the program after I deleted the statement that preceded it—specifically, the statement that said

```
// m_database = GetDocument();
```

I didn't want to erase this statement entirely because it was placed in the program by AppWizard. AppWizard put the comment there so that I would remember to call the `GetDocument()` member function, which obtains a pointer to a document associated with a `CView` object.

When I overrode my `CView` object's `OnDraw()` function, however, I didn't need to call `GetDocument()`. I had called `GetDocument()` already, back in my `CView` object's `OnInitialUpdate()` function, so I marked out the call to `GetDocument()` that appears in `OnDraw()`.

If you like, you can confirm that `GetDocument()` is called in my `CView` object's `OnInitialUpdate()` function by examining my `OnInitialUpdate()` function. It's in the ZALTHVW.CPP file.

## The OnDraw() Function, Step by Step

To sum up, this is how you can use the `OnDraw()` function to draw in a view in a Visual C++ program:

1. Derive your window class from one of the window classes derived from `CWnd` (such as `CFrameWnd` or `CMDIFrameWnd`).

2. Override the `CWnd` class's `OnPaint()` member function so that you can draw in your window any way you like.

3. Launch ClassWizard by selecting the ClassWizard command from the Visual Workbench's Project menu.

4. Select the class name `CMainFrame` from the Class Name edit box. (The `CMainFrame` class is a class that AppWizard sets up to handle your application's main frame window.)
5. Select the `WM_PAINT` message from the Member Functions list box.
6. Click the Add Function button. ClassWizard responds by adding an `OnPaint()` function to the Member Functions list box.
7. Click the Edit Code button. ClassWizard responds by opening your application's MAINFRM.CPP file and jumping to the `CMainFrame::OnPaint()` member function that it has just generated.
8. Place code that can draw your application's main window in the `CMainFrame::OnPaint()` member function that ClassWizard has written.

When you write an `OnPaint()` message handler for a window and bind it to Windows' `WM_PAINT` message with a message-map entry, Windows calls the function each time a `WM_PAINT` message is received.

## Drawing Text with CDC and GDI Objects

Recall that you can draw in a window by using an object of the `CGdiObject` as a drawing instrument and by using a `CDC` function as a drawing procedure. For example:

When you want to draw text in a view or a window, you can call the `CDC` member function `TextOut()`—the Visual C++ equivalent of the pre-C++ Windows function `TextOut()`. You can draw text in a view by executing a function such as this:

```
void CMainFrame::OnDraw()
{
     CString doit = "Print this, please.\n";
     CPaintDC dc (this);
     CRect rect;

     GetClientRect( &rect );
     dc.SetTextAlign( TA BASELINE I TA CENTER );
     dc.TextOut((rect.right / 2), (rect.bottom / 2),
          s, s.GetLength() );
};
```

This code sequence, like the previous example, is a function definition that overrides the `CView` class's member function `OnDraw()`. In the fourth line of the example, the statement

```
CPaintDC dc(this);
```

creates a `CPaintDC` object named `dc`, which can draw text on a screen. Next, the `CDC` member function `SetTextAlign()` is called to place the pen in the correct position on the screen. The text is then drawn by the `CDC` member function `TextOut()`.

# Creating and Deleting Graphics Objects

In Visual C++, there are two ways to create a graphics object. The first way is to write a constructor that instantiates and initializes the object in a single step. The second technique is to write a constructor that just creates the object and to initialize the object with a separate function.

The one-step procedure for creating graphics objects is concise and easy to use, but it can "throw an exception"—that is, result in a situation that your application may not be capable of handling—if an illegal parameter is passed to it or if there is a problem in allocating memory. The two-step method may be a hassle, but it is safer.

## One-Step Creation of a Graphics Object

Every graphics object defined in the MFC library has a constructor that can create and initialize the object in a single step. For example, you can instantiate and initialize a `CPen` object by invoking a constructor written in this format:

```
CPen myPen(PS_SOLID, 4, RGB(0,0,0);
```

The arguments passed to the preceding `CPen` constructor specify the style, the width, and the color that are to be used to create the pen. Constructors for other kinds of graphics arguments take different kinds of parameters. The *Visual C++ Class Library Reference* can supply you with the details.

When you have constructed a graphics object to draw with, you must place it in the current device context before you can use it. Procedures for placing an object in the current graphics context are described earlier in this section.

## Two-Step Creation of a Graphics Object

You can instantiate any graphics object by invoking a default constructor that takes no arguments. For example, you can create a `CPen` object without initializing it by invoking a default constructor written in either of these standard formats:

```
CPen myPen;
```

or

```
Cpen myPen = new CPen;
```

If you create an object by using either of these techniques, you must initialize it before you can use it in your application.

To initialize a graphics object that has been created without any initialization, you can choose from several initialization functions. The names of the initialization calls that you can use vary from object to object, but the choices that you are offered for each object are similar.

The functions that you can call to initialize a `CPen` object are `CreatePen`, which takes parameters that specify the pen's attributes; `CreatePenIndirect`, which enables you to specify pen attributes by passing a pointer to a structure; and `CreateStockObject`, a `CGdiObject` member function that enables you to specify attributes by passing a predefined constant.

The following code fragment shows how to construct a `CPen` object with a default constructor and then initialize it by using the `CreatePen()` function (the function's Boolean return value tells you whether your pen object is successfully initialized):

```
CPen aPen;
if(pPen.CreatePen(PS_SOLID, 4, RGB( 0, 0, 0 ));
    // Your code goes here.
```

## Placing a Graphics Object in a Device Context

Before you draw on a screen with a graphics object, you must place the object in a device context. When you place a graphics object into a device context, you modify the device context's drawing environment.

Each of the MFC library's device-context classes (`CPaintDC`, `CClientDC`, and `CWindowDC`) has a `SelectObject()` member function. To use the function, you supply a pointer to a graphics object. `SelectObject()` then places the specified object in the current device context and returns a pointer to the previous graphics object for the device context.

For example, if you call `SelectObject()` by using a parameter that is a pointer to a `CPen` object, `SelectObject()` returns a pointer to the pen that belonged to the previous device context. When you finish using your new pen, you can restore the old pen to the current device context by calling `SelectObject()` again.

The pointer that `SelectObject()` returns depends on the kind of graphics object you select. For example, `SelectObject()` returns a pointer to a `CFont` object when you select a new `CFont` object and returns a pointer to a `CBrush` object when you select a new `CBrush` object.

The following code fragment shows how you can create a `CPen` object, place it in the current device context, draw with the pen, and then return the original `CPen` to the current device context:

```
void CMainFrame::OnPaint()
{
     CPaintDC dc(this);
     CPen newPen(PS SOLID, 2, RGB(0, 0, 255));


// Change device context and save old pen
CPen* pOldPen = dc.SelectObject(&newPen);

// Do your drawing thing
     dc.MoveTo(6, 6);
     dc.LineTo(32, 6);
     dc.LineTo(32, 32);
     dc.LineTo(6, 32);
     dc.LineTo(6, 6);

     // Restore old pen
     dc.SelectObject(pOldPen);
};
```

# Using Bitmaps in Visual C++

When the `OnDraw()` function in the ZALTHVW.CPP file calls the `DrawBackdrop()` and `DrawPlayer()` functions in the ZALTHDOC.CPP file, the `DrawBackdrop()` and `DrawPlayer()` functions draw bitmaps on the screen.

In Visual C++, drawing a bitmap is not too different from drawing a line or a text string. The operation is just a bit more complicated.

## Creating a Bitmap Object

In a Visual C++ program, a bitmap usually starts its life as a block of data stored on a disk. Before you can use it in your application, you first must load it into memory.

When using a bitmap in a C++ program, the best way to store it on disk is to make it a `CBitmap` object. Then, you can instantiate the object by invoking the `new` operator, and when your bitmap object is instantiated, you can call the `CDC` member function `LoadBitmap()` to load the bitmap into memory.

In this chapter's version of the Zalthar program, the constructor of the program's document object instantiates three bitmaps. One bitmap is used to draw the playing field, another to draw a player, and a third to create a *mask* for the player so that the player can be drawn as an irregular object against a complex background (more information about using masks to draw irregular objects is presented later in this chapter).

In the file ZALTHDOC.CPP, this function is where these three bitmaps are created:

```
CZaltharDoc::CZaltharDoc()
{
     // TODO: add one-time construction code here
     m_pDataList = NULL;
     m_pFindList = NULL;
     m_szFileName = "";
     m_szFileTitle = "";

     // Create player and player mask bitmaps
     m_bmImage = new CBitmap;
     ASSERT_VALID(m_bmImage);
     m_bmBkg = new CBitmap;
     ASSERT_VALID(m_bmBkg);

     // Create a bitmap for the playing field
     m_pBitmap = new CBitmap;
     ASSERT_VALID(m_pBitmap);
}
```

A little later in the ZALTHDOC.CPP file, these same three bitmaps are loaded into memory. That happens in a `CZaltharDoc` member function named `InitDocument()`, which initializes the program's document object:

```
void CZaltharDoc::InitDocument()
{
     // TODO: add reinitialization code here
     New();     // Initialize the database.

     // Load the playing-field bitmap.
     int y = m_bmImage->LoadBitmap(IDB_PLAYER1);
     ASSERT(y != 0);
     y = m_bmBkg->LoadBitmap(IDB_PLAYER1_MASK);
     ASSERT(y != 0);
     y = m_pBitmap->LoadBitmap(IDB_ARCHES);
     ASSERT(y != 0);
```

```
    // Bitmap intializations
    m_bmWidth = 32;
    m_bmHeight = 32;
    m_startX = 5;
    m_startY = 5;

}
```

When the program's three bitmap objects have been instantiated and loaded into memory, they are ready to use. Earlier in this chapter, you saw how the `OnDraw()` member function of the `CZaltharView` class calls a pair of `CZaltharDoc` member functions named `DrawBackdrop()` and `DrawPlayer()`. The `DrawBackdrop()` member function draws the game's playing field, and the `DrawPlayer()` member function draws a player.

Both these member functions are implemented in the ZALTHDOC.CPP file. This is the definition of the `DrawBackdrop()` member function:

```
void CZaltharDoc::DrawBackdrop(CDC *pDC)
{
    CDC dcBackdrop;
    CBitmap *pOldMapZ;
    CBitmap Bitmap;
    int bmWidth = 123;
    int bmHeight = 160;

    // Create a bitmap of the right size.
    Bitmap.CreateCompatibleBitmap(pDC, bmWidth, bmHeight);

    // Create a device context that's
    // compatible with your bitmap.
    dcBackdrop.CreateCompatibleDC(pDC);

    // Select m_pBitmap into current device context,
    // and save previous bitmap in pOldMapZ.
    pOldMapZ = dcBackdrop.SelectObject(m_pBitmap);

    // Copy the bitmap to the screen.
    pDC->BitBlt(0, 0, bmWidth,
        bmHeight, &dcBackdrop, 0, 0, SRCCOPY);
    // DrawPlayer(pDC);

    // When it's over, return the saved bitmap to
    // the current device context.
    dcBackdrop.SelectObject(pOldMapZ);
}
```

When the `CView` member function `OnDraw()` calls the `CZaltharDoc` member function `DrawBackdrop()`, the `OnDraw()` function passes the `DrawBackdrop()` function a pointer to a `CDC` object. You don't have to worry about where `OnDraw()` gets this pointer; the Visual C++ framework obtains the pointer when it creates your program's CView object, and it makes sure that the pointer references an appropriate device-context object for the computer system that's running the program.

When the DrawBackdrop() function is called, it creates a bitmap that's compatible with the CDC object that it has been passed. This is the statement where that happens:

```
Bitmap.CreateCompatibleBitmap(pDC, bmWidth, bmHeight);
```

Next, the DrawBackdrop() function creates a CDC object that's compatible with its new bitmap:

```
dcBackdrop.CreateCompatibleDC(pDC);
```

You saw earlier in this chapter how the SelectObject() function can select an object of the CGdiObject class into a device context. In this statement, a CBitmap object is selected into the current device context:

```
pOldMapZ = dcBackdrop.SelectObject(m_pBitmap);
```

Notice that this statement also saves the previous device context in a variable named pOldMapZ.

When all these preparations are completed, the CDC member function BitBlt() is called to copy the playing field bitmap to the screen:

```
pDC->BitBlt(0, 0, bmWidth,
     bmHeight, &dcBackdrop, 0, 0, SRCCOPY);
```

When that's done, the previous device context is restored, and the DrawBackdrop() member function ends:

```
dcBackdrop.SelectObject(pOldMapZ);
```

## Drawing Irregular Shapes

Drawing the Zalthar game's background isn't too difficult because the bitmap that is used for the operation is rectangular. When you want to draw an irregularly shaped object against a complex background, the job of copying a bitmap to the screen gets a little more complicated.

In the ZALTHDOC.CPP file, there's a CZaltharDoc member function named DrawPlayer() that can copy an irregularly shaped bitmap to the screen. The bitmap that DrawPlayer() copies onto the screen is shown in Figure 24.1. The picture was created by using the bitmap editor that's built into Studio App, and the picture is a screen shot of the Studio App bitmap editor.

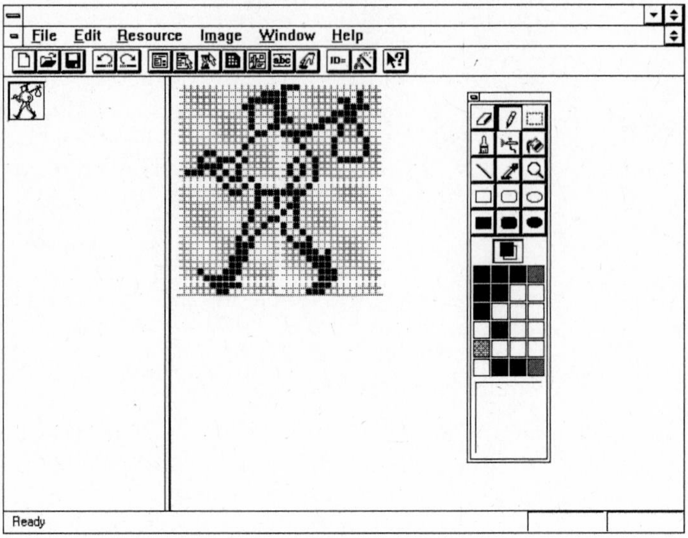


*Figure 24.1. The adventurer in The Wrath of Zalthar.*

The bitmap shown in Figure 24.1 is a picture of an adventurer. When the `OnDraw()` function calls the `DrawPlayer()` function, the picture of the adventurer is copied onto the playfield that was drawn by the member function `DrawBackdrop()` in the previous section.

You can get a close look at the adventurer bitmap by launching App Studio and selecting the Zalthar bitmap named `IDB_PLAYER1`. You also may want to take a look at two other bitmaps: `IDB_PLAYER_MASK`, which is a black mask with the same shape as the adventurer bitmap, and `IDB_PLAYER2`, which is a bitmap of a female adventurer.

The figure of the female adventurer is shown in Figure 24.2.

When you compile The Wrath of Zalthar, you can substitute the female adventurer shown in Figure 24.2 for the male adventurer shown in Figure 24.1. Just use the Studio App bitmap editor to draw a bitmap mask for her image.

Then, find the `CZaltharDoc::InitDocument()` function in the ZALTHDOC.CPP file and edit the source code so that it loads IDB_PLAYER2 and her mask into memory in place of IDB_PLAYER1 and IDB_PLAYER_MASK. That will take care of the change.

Of course the IDB_PLAYER1 and IDB_PLAYER2 bitmaps aren't the only two pictures that you can use in the Zalthar game. You can create and use as many others as you like in your copy of the Zalthar program.

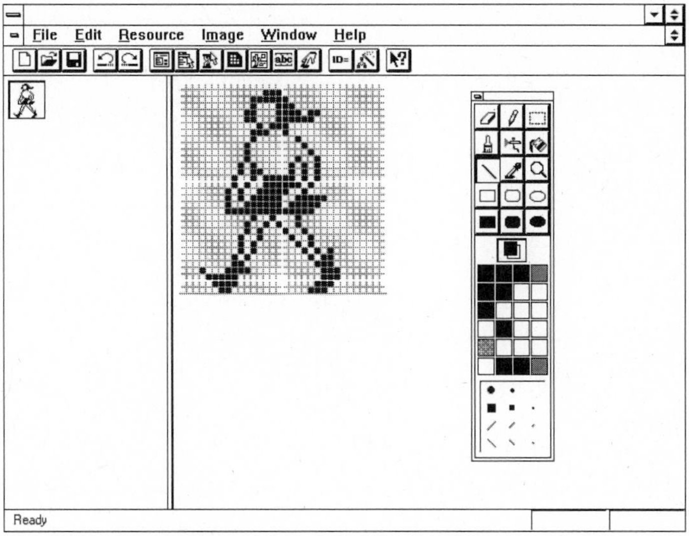


*Figure 24.2. A female adventurer.*

## Drawing the Zalthar Players

To draw the Zalthar game's adventurers on your computer screen, the `CZaltharView` member function `OnDraw()` calls the `CZaltharDoc` function `DrawPlayer()`. This is the definition of the `DrawPlayer()` member function:

```
void CZaltharDoc::DrawPlayer(CDC *pDC)
{
     CDC dcZalth, dcMask, memDC;
     CRect rect;
     CBitmap *pOldMapZ = NULL;
     CBitmap *pOldMapM = NULL;
     CBitmap *pOldBitmap = NULL;
     CBitmap Bitmap;
     int bigWidth = 123;
     int bigHeight = 160;

     // Create some device contexts that are
     // compatible with your system.
     dcZalth.CreateCompatibleDC(pDC);
     dcMask.CreateCompatibleDC(pDC);
     memDC.CreateCompatibleDC(pDC);

     // Create a bitmap of the right size.
     Bitmap.CreateCompatibleBitmap(pDC, m_bmWidth, m_bmHeight);
```

```
        // Select our bitmaps into current device context,
        // and save previous bitmaps.
        pOldMapZ = dcZalth.SelectObject(m_bmImage);
        pOldMapM = dcMask.SelectObject(m_bmBkg);
        pOldBitmap = memDC.SelectObject(&Bitmap);

        // Prepare a place for the player and the mask.
        memDC.Rectangle(m_startX-1, m_startY-1, m_bmWidth+2,
             m_bmHeight+2);

        // Copy mask into memory.
        memDC.BitBlt(0, 0, m_bmWidth,
             m_bmHeight, &dcMask, 0, 0, SRCCOPY);

        // Invert portion of screen.
        pDC->StretchBlt(m_startX, m_startY, m_bmWidth*2,
             m_bmHeight*2, pDC, 0, 0, m_bmWidth,
             m_bmHeight, DSTINVERT);

        // Draw mask to screen.
        pDC->StretchBlt(m_startX, m_startY, m_bmWidth*2,
             m_bmHeight*2, &memDC, 0, 0, m_bmWidth,
             m_bmHeight, SRCAND);

        // Copy player into memory.
        memDC.BitBlt(0, 0, m_bmWidth,
             m_bmHeight, &dcZalth, 0, 0, SRCCOPY);

        // Invert fragment of backdrop.
        // pDC->BitBlt(0, 0, m_bmWidth,
        //   m_bmHeight, pDC, 0, 0, DSTINVERT);

        // Draw player to screen and invert destination.
        pDC->StretchBlt(m_startX, m_startY, m_bmWidth*2,
             m_bmHeight*2, &memDC, 0, 0, m_bmWidth,
             m_bmHeight, SRCINVERT);

        // When it's over, return the saved bitmap to
        // the current device context.
        dcZalth.SelectObject(pOldMapZ);
        dcMask.SelectObject(pOldMapM);
        memDC.SelectObject(pOldBitmap);
}

// Update starting point for the player bitmap.
void CZaltharDoc::SetStartPoint(CPoint point)
{
        m_startX = point.x;
        m_startY = point.y;
        UpdateAllViews(NULL, 0, NULL);
}
```

The `DrawPlayer()` function is slightly more complicated than `DrawBackdrop()`. Rather than copying a bitmap directly to the screen, `DrawPlayer()` calls the `BitBlt()` and `StretchBlt()` functions several times each, using several different copying modes.

`DrawPlayer()` uses the `SRCCOPY` mode to copy the adventurer into memory, but uses the `SRCAND` mode to draw the player's mask to the screen. The `DSTINVERT` mode is used to invert a portion of the playing field before the player's mask is copied to the screen. After all drawing is completed, the `SRCINVERT` mode is used to draw the player to the screen and invert the destination bitmap again, restoring it to its original state.

When this is all done, `DrawPlayer()` finishes its job by doing the same kind of cleanup calls that `DrawBackdrop()` did.

Figure 24.3 is an illustration that can give you some idea of what `DrawBackdrop()` and `DrawPlayer()` do when they perform their bitmap-copying operations. Because of its lack of color and motion, however, the picture doesn't do justice to the output of those operations.

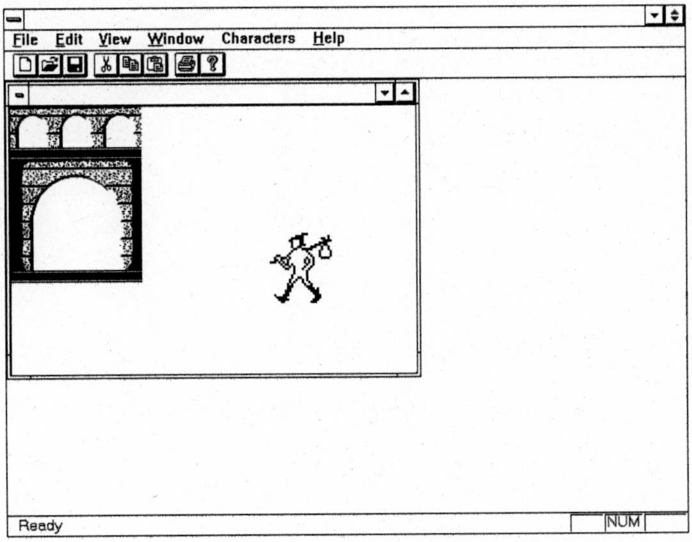


*Figure 24.3. An illustration created using `DrawBackdrop()` and `DrawPlayer()`.*

## Animation

This chapter's version of the Zalthar program introduces a basic kind of computer animation. The animation has purposely been kept simple to make the concept easy to understand. By investing a little time and effort, though, you can smooth it out until it looks quite professional.

As simple as the animation in the Zalthar program is, it is still impressive. It is built around a short function named `SetStartPoint()` in the ZALTHDOC.CPP file. This is the definition of the `SetStartPoint()` function:

```
void CZaltharDoc::SetStartPoint(CPoint point)
{
     m_startX = point.x;
     m_startY = point.y;
     UpdateAllViews(NULL, 0, NULL);
}
```

The `SetStartPoint()` function is called by a `CView` member function in the ZALTHVW.CPP file called `OnLButtonDown()`. The `OnLButtonDown()` function was inserted into the program with the help of ClassWizard. The function is a message handler that detects a click of the left mouse button. You can use ClassWizard to insert the `OnLButtonDown()` function into an application, and you then can override the function in whatever way you like.

In the Zalthar program, just one function call has been added to ClassWizard's version of `OnLButtonDown()`: a call to the `CZaltharDoc` member function `SetStartPoint()`. This enhancement causes the `OnLButtonDown()` function to call the `SetStartPoint()` function whenever the user of the Zalthar program presses the left mouse button.

This is the overridden version of `OnLButtonDown()`:

```
void CZaltharView::OnLButtonDown(UINT nFlags, CPoint point)
{
     // TODO: Add your message handler code here and/or call default

     // Set a new location for the player bitmap.
     m_database->SetStartPoint(point);

     // Frame says call the base function now.
     CView::OnLButtonDown(nFlags, point);
}
```

Now you can see how the animation works in the Zalthar program. When the user presses the left mouse button, Windows dispatches a message that causes the `OnLButtonDown()` message handler to be called. `OnLButtonDown()` then calls

SetStartPoint(), which sets a pair of coordinates to match the position of the mouse when its left button is pressed.

The next time the CView function OnDraw() is called, it draws the player bitmap at the mouse occupied when OnLButtonDown() and SetStartPoint() are called.

To draw the bitmap, OnDraw() calls DrawPlayer(). DrawPlayer() uses a black mask and some fancy bit-copying tricks to erase the player bitmap from its previous position and to draw it properly in its new position, redrawing part of the playing field so that the background is restored to its previous state before the player is redrawn.

As neat as this sequence of events is, it could be improved in two significant ways. First, there is a flashing of the background when the player is moved, and that could be fixed. Second, the player doesn't walk smoothly across the screen, but hops from one point to another. Although that might be perfectly acceptable in some situations, it might not be quite what you want in others.

I didn't make the animation in the Zalthar program complicated because that would have made the animation sections of the program even more difficult to puzzle out than they are now. Here are some ways you can smooth out the action:

- Open the *Class Library Reference* that came with your copy of Visual C++ and study the graphics-related member functions in the CWnd and CDC classes, particularly the CWnd member functions ValidateRect(), InvalidateRect(), and ExcludeClipRect(). By using these calls, you can limit the area of the screen that is redrawn every time OnDraw() is called, and that can reduce or eliminate background flashing.

- Study the CWnd member function OnTimer() and the CWinApp member function OnIdle(). You can use these functions to make bitmap figures and icons move smoothly across a screen rather than jump from one place to another. If you need assistance in figuring out how to use the OnTimer() and OnIdle() functions, see what Charles Petzold has to say about these functions in *Programming Windows 3.1* (see Bibliography).

- After practicing with OnTimer() and OnIdle(), launch Studio App and find the Zalthar bitmap named IDB_ANIMATION. The bitmap is an animation sequence; a portion of the sequence is shown in Figure 24.4.

When you've found the IDB_ANIMATION bitmap, copy the figures in the animation sequence into smaller, separate bitmaps of the same size. Draw a black mask that corresponds with each figure in the animation sequence. Then, write a loop that cycles through the animated figures when the `CZaltharDoc::DrawPlayer()` function is called. You'll have to know how to control the speed of your animation with the `OnTimer()` and `OnIdle()` functions to make this trick work. But try it; it will be worth the effort.

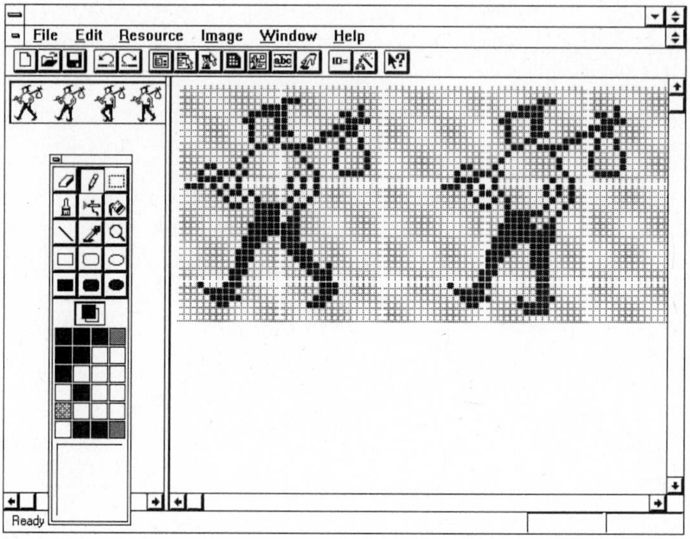


*Figure 24.4. Zalthar animation.*

# Zalthar: The Final Episode

Listing 24.1 is the final installment of The Wrath of Zalthar. Enjoy!

### Listing 24.1. The Wrath of Zalthar, final installment.

#### CHARLIST.CPP

```
// charlist.cpp : implementation file
// Copyright 1993, Mark Andrews
//

#include "stdafx.h"
#include "zalthar.h"
```

```
#include "charlist.h"
#include "zalthdoc.h"
#include "player.h"

#ifdef _DEBUG
#undef THIS_FILE
static char BASED_CODE THIS_FILE[] =__FILE__;
#endif

/////////////////////////////////////////////////////////////////////////
// CCharList dialog

CCharList::CCharList(CZaltharDoc *pDataBase, CWnd* pParent /*=NULL*/)
     : CDialog(CCharList::IDD, pParent)
{
     m_database = pDataBase;

     //{{AFX_DATA_INIT(CCharList)
          // NOTE: the ClassWizard will add member initialization here
     //}}AFX_DATA_INIT
}

CCharList::OnInitDialog()
{
     RECT listRect = { 12,18,208,102 };
     RECT& rectPtr = listRect;

     m_charList.Create(LBS_SORT ¦ LBS_HASSTRINGS ¦ LBS_SORT ¦
                  WS_CHILD ¦ WS_VISIBLE ¦ WS_VSCROLL ¦
                  WS_TABSTOP, rectPtr, this, 500);
     m_charList.SetFocus();

     ASSERT_VALID(m_database);
     int ct = (m_database->GetCount());
     for (int n = 0; n < ct; ++n) {
          CPlayer *pPlayer = (m_database->GetPlayer(n));
          m_charList.AddString(pPlayer->GetName());
     }
     return FALSE;
}

void CCharList::DoDataExchange(CDataExchange* pDX)
{
     CDialog::DoDataExchange(pDX);
     //{{AFX_DATA_MAP(CCharList)
          // NOTE: the ClassWizard will add DDX and DDV calls here
     //}}AFX_DATA_MAP
}
```

*continues*

**Listing 24.1. continued**

```
BEGIN_MESSAGE_MAP(CCharList, CDialog)
     //{{AFX_MSG_MAP(CCharList)
          // NOTE: the ClassWizard will add message map macros here
     //}}AFX_MSG_MAP
END_MESSAGE_MAP()

/////////////////////////////////////////////////////////////////////////////
// CCharList message handlers
```

## CHARLIST.H

```
// charlist.h : header file
// Copyright 1993, Mark Andrews
//

/////////////////////////////////////////////////////////////////////////////
// CCharList dialog

#include "zalthdoc.h"

class CCharList : public CDialog
{
// Construction
private:
     CZaltharDoc *m_database;
     CListBox m_charList;
public:
     CCharList(CZaltharDoc *pDataBase, CWnd* pParent = NULL);
     virtual BOOL OnInitDialog();

// Dialog Data
     //{{AFX_DATA(CCharList)
     enum { IDD = IDD_DIALOG1 };
          // NOTE: the ClassWizard will add data members here
     //}}AFX_DATA

// Implementation
protected:
     virtual void DoDataExchange(CDataExchange* pDX); // DDX/DDV suppt

     // Generated message map functions
     //{{AFX_MSG(CCharList)
          // NOTE: the ClassWizard will add member functions here
     //}}AFX_MSG
     DECLARE_MESSAGE_MAP()
};
```

## CREATECH.CPP

```
// createch.cpp : implementation file
// Copyright 1993, Mark Andrews
//

#include "stdafx.h"
#include "zalthar.h"
#include "createch.h"
#include "zalthdoc.h"
#include "player.h"
#include "linklist.h"

#ifdef _DEBUG
#undef THIS_FILE
static char BASED_CODE THIS_FILE[] = __FILE__;
#endif

//////////////////////////////////////////////////////////////////////
// CCreateCharDlg dialog

// Original constructor created by AppWizard.
CCreateCharDlg::CCreateCharDlg(CWnd* pParent /*=NULL*/)
     : CDialog(CCreateCharDlg::IDD, pParent)
{
}

// Our constructor created by us.
CCreateCharDlg::CCreateCharDlg(CPlayer *pPlayer,
     CWnd* pParent /*=NULL*/)
     : CDialog(CCreateCharDlg::IDD, pParent)
{
     // copy the pPlayer parameter
     m_player = pPlayer;

     //{{AFX_DATA_INIT(CCreateCharDlg)
     m_name = "";
     m_armor = "Leather";
     m_class = "Warrior";
     m_equipment = "None";
     m_magic = "None";
     m_race = "Human";
     m_treasure = "None";
     m_weapon = "Sword";
     //}}AFX_DATA_INIT
}

void CCreateCharDlg::DoDataExchange(CDataExchange* pDX)
{
     CDialog::DoDataExchange(pDX);
     //{{AFX_DATA_MAP(CCreateCharDlg)
```

*continues*

**Listing 24.1. continued**

```
    DDX_Control(pDX, IDC_STATIC_WI, m_wisdom);
    DDX_Control(pDX, IDC_STATIC_ST, m_strength);
    DDX_Control(pDX, IDC_STATIC_IN, m_intelligence);
    DDX_Control(pDX, IDC_STATIC_DE, m_dexterity);
    DDX_Control(pDX, IDC_STATIC_CO, m_constitution);
    DDX_Control(pDX, IDC_STATIC_CH, m_charisma);
    DDX_Text(pDX, IDC_EDIT_NAME, m_name);
    DDV_MaxChars(pDX, m_name, 64);
    DDX_CBString(pDX, IDC_COMBO_ARMOR, m_armor);
    DDV_MaxChars(pDX, m_armor, 64);
    DDX_CBString(pDX, IDC_COMBO_CLASS, m_class);
    DDV_MaxChars(pDX, m_class, 64);
    DDX_CBString(pDX, IDC_COMBO_EQUIPMENT, m_equipment);
    DDV_MaxChars(pDX, m_equipment, 64);
    DDX_CBString(pDX, IDC_COMBO_MAGIC, m_magic);
    DDV_MaxChars(pDX, m_magic, 64);
    DDX_CBString(pDX, IDC_COMBO_RACE, m_race);
    DDV_MaxChars(pDX, m_race, 64);
    DDX_CBString(pDX, IDC_COMBO_TREASURE, m_treasure);
    DDV_MaxChars(pDX, m_treasure, 64);
    DDX_CBString(pDX, IDC_COMBO_WEAPON, m_weapon);
    DDV_MaxChars(pDX, m_weapon, 64);
    //}}AFX_DATA_MAP
}

BEGIN_MESSAGE_MAP(CCreateCharDlg, CDialog)
    //{{AFX_MSG_MAP(CCreateCharDlg)
    //}}AFX_MSG_MAP
END_MESSAGE_MAP()

/////////////////////////////////////////////////////////////////////////////
// CCreateCharDlg message handlers

BOOL CCreateCharDlg::OnInitDialog()
{
    CDialog::OnInitDialog();

    // TODO: Add extra initialization here

    // char *aStr;

    m_player->SetAbilScores();      // Get a set of ability scores.

    // Set the ability scores in the dialog box
    // and in the m_player object

    m_player->SetRaceStr("Human");
    m_player->SetClassStr("Warrior");
    m_player->SetArmor("Leather");
```

```
     m_player->SetWeapon("Staff");
     m_player->SetMagic("None");
     m_player->SetEquipment("None");
     m_player->SetTreasure("None");

     SetDlgItemInt(IDC_STATIC_ST, m_player->GetStrength(), FALSE);
     SetDlgItemInt(IDC_STATIC_DE, m_player->GetDexterity(), FALSE);
     SetDlgItemInt(IDC_STATIC_CO, m_player->GetConstitution(), FALSE);
     SetDlgItemInt(IDC_STATIC_IN, m_player->GetIntelligence(), FALSE);
     SetDlgItemInt(IDC_STATIC_WI, m_player->GetWisdom(), FALSE);
     SetDlgItemInt(IDC_STATIC_CH, m_player->GetCharisma(), FALSE);

    m_race = m_player->GetRaceName();
    m_class = m_player->GetClassName();
    m_armor = m_player->GetArmor();
    m_magic = m_player->GetMagic();
    m_equipment = m_player->GetEquipment();
    m_treasure = m_player->GetTreasure();

    UpdateData(FALSE);

2    return TRUE;  // return TRUE unless you set
                   // the focus to a control
}

void CCreateCharDlg::OnOK()
{
     // TODO: Add extra validation here
     const int sz = 64;
     char aStr[sz];

     GetDlgItemText(IDC_EDIT_NAME, aStr, sizeof(aStr));
     m_player->SetName(aStr);

     GetDlgItemText(IDC_COMBO_RACE, aStr, sizeof(aStr));
     m_player->SetRaceStr(aStr);

     GetDlgItemText(IDC_COMBO_CLASS, aStr, sizeof(aStr));
     m_player->SetClassStr(aStr);

     GetDlgItemText(IDC_COMBO_MAGIC, aStr, sizeof(aStr));
     m_player->SetMagic(aStr);

     GetDlgItemText(IDC_COMBO_ARMOR, aStr, sizeof(aStr));
     m_player->SetArmor(aStr);

     GetDlgItemText(IDC_COMBO_WEAPON, aStr, sizeof(aStr));
     m_player->SetWeapon(aStr);
```

*continues*

**Listing 24.1. continued**

```
    GetDlgItemText(IDC_COMBO_EQUIPMENT, aStr, sizeof(aStr));
    m_player->SetEquipment(aStr);

    GetDlgItemText(IDC_COMBO_TREASURE, aStr, sizeof(aStr));
    m_player->SetTreasure(aStr);

    CDialog::OnOK();     // this from ClassWizard
}
```

## CREATECH.H

```
// createch.h : header file
// Copyright 1993, Mark Andrews
//

/////////////////////////////////////////////////////////////////////////////
// CCreateCharDlg dialog

#include "player.h"
#include "linklist.h"
#include "zalthdoc.h"

class CCreateCharDlg : public CDialog
{
// Construction
private:
    CPlayer *m_player;
public:
    CCreateCharDlg(CWnd* pParent = NULL);     // standard constructor
    CCreateCharDlg(CPlayer *pPlayer, CWnd* pParent = NULL);

// Dialog Data
    //{{AFX_DATA(CCreateCharDlg)
    enum { IDD = IDD_CREATE_CHAR };
        // NOTE: the ClassWizard will add data members here
    CStatic   m_wisdom;
    CStatic   m_strength;
    CStatic   m_intelligence;
    CStatic   m_dexterity;
    CStatic   m_constitution;
    CStatic   m_charisma;
    CString   m_name;
    CString   m_armor;
    CString   m_class;
    CString   m_equipment;
    CString   m_magic;
    CString   m_race;
    CString   m_treasure;
    CString   m_weapon;
    //}}AFX_DATA
```

```
// Implementation
protected:
     virtual void DoDataExchange(CDataExchange* pDX);  // DDX/DDV

     // Generated message map functions
     //{{AFX_MSG(CCreateCharDlg)
     virtual BOOL OnInitDialog();
     virtual void OnOK();
     //}}AFX_MSG
     DECLARE_MESSAGE_MAP()
};
// finddlg.cpp : implementation file
//

#include "stdafx.h"
#include "zalthar.h"
#include "finddlg.h"

#include "zalthdoc.h"
#include "player.h"

#ifdef _DEBUG
#undef THIS_FILE
static char BASED_CODE THIS_FILE[] = __FILE__;
#endif
```

## FINDDLG.CPP

```
/////////////////////////////////////////////////////////////////////////////
// CFindDlg dialog

CFindDlg::CFindDlg(CPlayer *pPlayer, CWnd* pParent /*=NULL*/) :
          CDialog(CFindDlg::IDD, pParent)
{
     //{{AFX_DATA_INIT(CFind)
     m_name = "";
     //}}AFX_DATA_INIT
}

CFindDlg::CFindDlg(CWnd* pParent /*=NULL*/) :
          CDialog(CFindDlg::IDD, pParent)
{
     //{{AFX_DATA_INIT(CFind)
     m_name = "";
     //}}AFX_DATA_INIT
}

void CFindDlg::DoDataExchange(CDataExchange* pDX)
{
```

*continues*

**Listing 24.1. continued**

```
	CDialog::DoDataExchange(pDX);
	//{{AFX_DATA_MAP(CFindDlg)
	DDX_Text(pDX, IDC_NAME, m_name);
	DDV_MaxChars(pDX, m_name, 64);
	//}}AFX_DATA_MAP
}

BEGIN_MESSAGE_MAP(CFindDlg, CDialog)
	//{{AFX_MSG_MAP(CFindDlg)
	//}}AFX_MSG_MAP
END_MESSAGE_MAP()

/////////////////////////////////////////////////////////////////////////////
// CFindDlg message handlers

void CFindDlg::OnOK()
{
	const int sz = 64;
	char aStr[sz];

	GetDlgItemText(IDC_NAME, aStr, sizeof(aStr));
	SetNameStr(aStr);

	CDialog::OnOK();
}
```

### FINDDLG.H

```
// finddlg.h : header file
//

/////////////////////////////////////////////////////////////////////////////
// CFindDlg dialog

#include "zalthdoc.h"
#include "player.h"

class CFindDlg : public CDialog
{
// Construction
private:
	CPlayer* m_player;
	CZaltharDoc *m_database;
	CString m_playerName;

public:
	CFindDlg(CWnd* pParent = NULL);	// standard constructor
	CFindDlg(CPlayer *pPlayer, CWnd* pParent = NULL);
```

```
// Dialog Data
     //{{AFX_DATA(CFindDlg)
     enum { IDD = IDD_CHARACTERS_FIND };
     CString   m_name;
     //}}AFX_DATA

     CZaltharDoc *GetDataBase() { return m_database; }
     CPlayer* GetData() { return m_player; }
     CString& GetNameStr() { return m_playerName; }
     void SetNameStr(CString cs) { m_playerName = cs; }

// Implementation
protected:
     virtual void DoDataExchange(CDataExchange* pDX);  // DDX/DDV

     // Generated message map functions
     //{{AFX_MSG(CFindDlg)
     virtual void OnOK();
     //}}AFX_MSG
     DECLARE_MESSAGE_MAP()
};
```

### GETCHARD.CPP

```
// getchard.cpp : implementation file
//

#include "stdafx.h"
#include "zalthar.h"
#include "getchard.h"
#include "zalthdoc.h"
#include "player.h"

#ifdef _DEBUG
#undef THIS_FILE
static char BASED_CODE THIS_FILE[] = __FILE__;
#endif

/////////////////////////////////////////////////////////////////////////////
// CGetCharData dialog

CGetCharData::CGetCharData(CPlayer *pPlayer, CWnd* pParent /*=NULL*/)
     : CDialog(CGetCharData::IDD, pParent)
{
     // copy the pPlayer parameter
     m_player = pPlayer;

     //{{AFX_DATA_INIT(CGetCharData)
          // NOTE: the ClassWizard will add member initialization here
```

*continues*

**Listing 24.1. continued**

```
     //}}AFX_DATA_INIT
}

void CGetCharData::DoDataExchange(CDataExchange* pDX)
{
     CDialog::DoDataExchange(pDX);
     //{{AFX_DATA_MAP(CGetCharData)
     DDX_Control(pDX, IDC_STATIC_WI, m_wi);
     DDX_Control(pDX, IDC_STATIC_WEAPON, m_weapon);
     DDX_Control(pDX, IDC_STATIC_TREASURE, m_treasure);
     DDX_Control(pDX, IDC_STATIC_ST, m_st);
     DDX_Control(pDX, IDC_STATIC_RACE, m_race);
     DDX_Control(pDX, IDC_STATIC_NAME, m_name);
     DDX_Control(pDX, IDC_STATIC_MAGIC, m_magic);
     DDX_Control(pDX, IDC_STATIC_IN, m_in);
     DDX_Control(pDX, IDC_STATIC_EQUIPMENT, m_equipment);
     DDX_Control(pDX, IDC_STATIC_DE, m_de);
     DDX_Control(pDX, IDC_STATIC_CO, m_co);
     DDX_Control(pDX, IDC_STATIC_CLASS, m_class);
     DDX_Control(pDX, IDC_STATIC_CH, m_ch);
     DDX_Control(pDX, IDC_STATIC_ARMOR, m_armor);
     //}}AFX_DATA_MAP
}

BEGIN_MESSAGE_MAP(CGetCharData, CDialog)
     //{{AFX_MSG_MAP(CGetCharData)
     //}}AFX_MSG_MAP
END_MESSAGE_MAP()

/////////////////////////////////////////////////////////////////////////////
// CGetCharData message handlers

BOOL CGetCharData::OnInitDialog()
{
     CDialog::OnInitDialog();

     // TODO: Add extra initialization here


     CDialog::OnInitDialog(); // This from ClassWizard.

     // Set dialog controls to player's characteristics

     SetDlgItemText(IDC_STATIC_NAME, m_player->GetName());
     SetDlgItemText(IDC_STATIC_RACE, m_player->GetRaceName());
     SetDlgItemText(IDC_STATIC_CLASS, m_player->GetClassName());
     SetDlgItemText(IDC_STATIC_WEAPON, m_player->GetWeapon());
     SetDlgItemText(IDC_STATIC_EQUIPMENT, m_player->GetEquipment());
     SetDlgItemText(IDC_STATIC_ARMOR, m_player->GetArmor());
```

```
        SetDlgItemText(IDC_STATIC_MAGIC, m_player->GetMagic());
        SetDlgItemText(IDC_STATIC_TREASURE, m_player->GetTreasure());

        SetDlgItemInt(IDC_STATIC_ST, m_player->GetStrength(),FALSE);
        SetDlgItemInt(IDC_STATIC_DE, m_player->GetDexterity(),FALSE);
        SetDlgItemInt(IDC_STATIC_CO, m_player->GetConstitution(),FALSE);
        SetDlgItemInt(IDC_STATIC_WI, m_player->GetIntelligence(),FALSE);
        SetDlgItemInt(IDC_STATIC_IN, m_player->GetWisdom(),FALSE);
        SetDlgItemInt(IDC_STATIC_CH, m_player->GetCharisma(),FALSE);

        return TRUE;  // return TRUE unless you set the focus to a control
}
```

## GETCHARD.H

```
// getchard.h : header file
//

#include "zalthdoc.h"
#include "player.h"

/////////////////////////////////////////////////////////////////////////////
// CGetCharData dialog

class CGetCharData : public CDialog
{
private:
        // Get a copy of the CPlayer object.
        CPlayer *m_player;
// Construction
public:
        CGetCharData(CPlayer *pPlayer, CWnd* pParent = NULL);

// Dialog Data
        //{{AFX_DATA(CGetCharData)
        enum { IDD = IDD_SHOW_CHAR };
        CStatic     m_wi;
        CStatic   m_weapon;
        CStatic   m_treasure;
        CStatic   m_st;
        CStatic   m_race;
        CStatic   m_name;
        CStatic   m_magic;
        CStatic   m_in;
        CStatic   m_equipment;
        CStatic   m_de;
        CStatic   m_co;
        CStatic   m_class;
        CStatic   m_ch;
```

*continues*

**Listing 24.1. continued**

```
    CStatic   m_armor;
    //}}AFX_DATA

// Implementation
protected:
    virtual void DoDataExchange(CDataExchange* pDX); // DDX/DDV

    // Generated message map functions
    //{{AFX_MSG(CGetCharData)
    virtual BOOL OnInitDialog();
    //}}AFX_MSG
    DECLARE_MESSAGE_MAP()
};
```

### LINKLIST.CPP

```
// linklist.cpp

#include <iostream.h>
#include <stdlib.h>
// #include <afxwin.h>
// #include <afxcoll.h>

#include "linklist.h"
#include "player.h"

IMPLEMENT_SERIAL( CPlayerList, CObList, 0 )

// string const for untitled database
extern const char szUntitled[];

//  Delete all objects in the list.
void CPlayerList::DeleteAll()
{
    ASSERT_VALID( this );
    POSITION pos = GetHeadPosition();

    while (pos != NULL)
        delete GetNext(pos);
    RemoveAll();
}

///////////////////////////////////////////////
//  CPlayerList::FindPlayer
//
//  Make a list of players found in a search operation --
//  Use this function when the search can find multiple objects.
//  The function returns the list.
```

```
CPlayerList* CPlayerList::FindPlayer( const char * szTarget )
{
     ASSERT_VALID( this );

     // Create a list of players.
     CPlayerList* pNewList = new CPlayerList;
     CPlayer* pNext = NULL;

     // Start at front of list
     POSITION pos = GetHeadPosition();

     // Iterate over whole list
     while( pos != NULL )
     {
          // Get next element (note cast)
          pNext = (CPlayer*)GetNext(pos);

          // Add current element to new list if it matches
          if ( _strnicmp( pNext->GetName(), szTarget,
                          strlen( szTarget ) )
                    == 0 )
               pNewList->AddTail(pNext);
     }

     if ( pNewList->IsEmpty() )
     {
          delete pNewList;
          pNewList = NULL;
     }

     return pNewList;
}
```

## LINKLIST.H

```
// linklist.h

#include "player.h"

#if !defined( _LINKLIST_H_ )
#define _LINKLIST_H_

#include <afxwin.h>
#include <afxcoll.h>
#include "zalthar.h"

class CPlayerList : public CObList {
     DECLARE_SERIAL(CPlayerList)
protected:
     BOOL  m_bIsDirty;
```

*continues*

**Listing 24.1. continued**

```
public:
     void DeleteAll();
     CPlayerList()
          { m_bIsDirty = FALSE; }

     // Add new functions
     CPlayerList* MakeFindList( const char * szTarget );
     CPlayerList* FindPlayer( const char * szTarget );

     void SetDirty( BOOL bDirty )
          {   ASSERT_VALID( this );
               m_bIsDirty = bDirty; }

     BOOL GetDirty()
          {   ASSERT_VALID( this );
               return m_bIsDirty; }

};

#endif  // _LINKLIST_H_
```

### MAINFRM.CPP

```
// mainfrm.cpp : implementation of the CMainFrame class
//

#include "stdafx.h"
#include "zalthar.h"

#include "mainfrm.h"

#ifdef _DEBUG
#undef THIS_FILE
static char BASED_CODE THIS_FILE[] = __FILE__;
#endif

/////////////////////////////////////////////////////////////////////////////
// CMainFrame

IMPLEMENT_DYNAMIC(CMainFrame, CMDIFrameWnd)

BEGIN_MESSAGE_MAP(CMainFrame, CMDIFrameWnd)
     //{{AFX_MSG_MAP(CMainFrame)
     ON_WM_CREATE()
     ON_WM_PAINT()
     //}}AFX_MSG_MAP
END_MESSAGE_MAP()
```

```
///////////////////////////////////////////////////////////////////////
// arrays of IDs used to initialize control bars

// toolbar buttons - IDs are command buttons
static UINT BASED_CODE buttons[] =
{
     // same order as in the bitmap 'toolbar.bmp'
     ID_FILE_NEW,
     ID_FILE_OPEN,
     ID_FILE_SAVE,
          ID_SEPARATOR,
     ID_EDIT_CUT,
     ID_EDIT_COPY,
     ID_EDIT_PASTE,
          ID_SEPARATOR,
     ID_FILE_PRINT,
     ID_APP_ABOUT,
};

static UINT BASED_CODE indicators[] =
{
     ID_SEPARATOR,                // status line indicator
     ID_INDICATOR_CAPS,
     ID_INDICATOR_NUM,
     ID_INDICATOR_SCRL,
};

///////////////////////////////////////////////////////////////////////
// CMainFrame construction/destruction

CMainFrame::CMainFrame()
{
     // TODO: add member initialization code here

     // Create a bitmap for the title screen.
     // m_pBitmap = new CBitmap;
     // ASSERT_VALID(m_pBitmap);
}

CMainFrame::~CMainFrame()
{
     // delete m_pBitmap;       // Delete title-screen bitmap.
}

int CMainFrame::OnCreate(LPCREATESTRUCT lpCreateStruct)
{
     if (CMDIFrameWnd::OnCreate(lpCreateStruct) == -1)
          return -1;

     SetWindowText("The Wrath of Zalthar");
```

*continues*

**Listing 24.1. continued**

```
    if (!m_wndToolBar.Create(this) ||
        !m_wndToolBar.LoadBitmap(IDR_MAINFRAME) ||
        !m_wndToolBar.SetButtons(buttons,
          sizeof(buttons)/sizeof(UINT)))
    {
        TRACE("Failed to create toolbar\n");
        return -1;          // fail to create
    }

    if (!m_wndStatusBar.Create(this) ||
        !m_wndStatusBar.SetIndicators(indicators,
          sizeof(indicators)/sizeof(UINT)))
    {
        TRACE("Failed to create status bar\n");
        return -1;          // fail to create
    }

    // Load title-screen bitmap.
    // BOOL y = m_pBitmap->LoadBitmap(IDB_TITLE);
    // ASSERT(y != 0);

    return 0;
}


//////////////////////////////////////////////////////////////////////
// CMainFrame diagnostics

#ifdef _DEBUG
void CMainFrame::AssertValid() const
{
    CMDIFrameWnd::AssertValid();
}

void CMainFrame::Dump(CDumpContext& dc) const
{
    CMDIFrameWnd::Dump(dc);
}

#endif //_DEBUG

//////////////////////////////////////////////////////////////////////
// CMainFrame message handlers


void CMainFrame::OnPaint()
{
    CPaintDC dc(this); // device context for painting
```

```
	// TODO: Add your message handler code here

	// DrawBackdrop(&dc);

	// Do not call CMDIFrameWnd::OnPaint() for painting messages
}
/////////////////////////////////////////////////////////////////////////////
// Function to draw playing field
//
void CMainFrame::DrawBackdrop(CDC *pDC)
{
	CDC dcBackdrop;
	CBitmap *pOldMapZ;
	CBitmap Bitmap;
	int bmWidth = 640;
	int bmHeight = 480;

	// Create a bitmap of the right size.
	Bitmap.CreateCompatibleBitmap(pDC, bmWidth, bmHeight);

	// Create a device context that's
	// compatible with your bitmap.
	dcBackdrop.CreateCompatibleDC(pDC);

	// Select m_pBitmap into current device context,
	// and save previous bitmap in pOldMapZ.
	pOldMapZ = dcBackdrop.SelectObject(m_pBitmap);

	// Copy the bitmap to the screen, several times.
	pDC->BitBlt(0, 0, bmWidth,
		bmHeight, &dcBackdrop, 0, 0, SRCCOPY);

	// When it's over, return the saved bitmap to
	// the current device context.
	dcBackdrop.SelectObject(pOldMapZ);
}
```

### MAINFRM.H

```
// mainfrm.h : interface of the CMainFrame class
//
/////////////////////////////////////////////////////////////////////////////

class CMainFrame : public CMDIFrameWnd
{
	DECLARE_DYNAMIC(CMainFrame)
private:
	CBitmap *m_pBitmap;
public:
	CMainFrame();
```

*continues*

**Listing 24.1. continued**

```
// Attributes
public:

// Operations
public:
     void CMainFrame::DrawBackdrop(CDC *pDC);

// Implementation
public:
     virtual ~CMainFrame();
#ifdef _DEBUG
     virtual     void AssertValid() const;
     virtual     void Dump(CDumpContext& dc) const;
#endif


protected:     // control bar embedded members
     CStatusBar     m_wndStatusBar;
     CToolBar  m_wndToolBar;

// Generated message map functions
protected:
     //{{AFX_MSG(CMainFrame)
     afx_msg int OnCreate(LPCREATESTRUCT lpCreateStruct);
     afx_msg void OnPaint();
     //}}AFX_MSG
     DECLARE_MESSAGE_MAP()
};
```

## NRCHARS.CPP

```
/////////////////////////////////////////////////////////////////////////////
// nrchars.cpp : implementation file
//

#include "stdafx.h"
#include "zalthar.h"
#include "nrchars.h"

#ifdef _DEBUG
#undef THIS_FILE
static char BASED_CODE THIS_FILE[] = __FILE__;
#endif

/////////////////////////////////////////////////////////////////////////////
// CNrChars dialog
```

```
CNrChars::CNrChars(CWnd* pParent /*=NULL*/)
     : CDialog(CNrChars::IDD, pParent)
{
     //{{AFX_DATA_INIT(CNrChars)
     m_nr_chars = 0;
     //}}AFX_DATA_INIT
}

void CNrChars::DoDataExchange(CDataExchange* pDX)
{
     CDialog::DoDataExchange(pDX);
     //{{AFX_DATA_MAP(CNrChars)
     DDX_Text(pDX, IDC_NR_CHRS, m_nr_chars);
     DDV_MinMaxUInt(pDX, m_nr_chars, 0, 9999);
     //}}AFX_DATA_MAP
}

BEGIN_MESSAGE_MAP(CNrChars, CDialog)
     //{{AFX_MSG_MAP(CNrChars)
          // NOTE: the ClassWizard will add message map macros here
     //}}AFX_MSG_MAP
END_MESSAGE_MAP()

/////////////////////////////////////////////////////////////////////////////
// CNrChars message handlers
```

## NRCHARS.H

```
// nrchars.h : header file
//

/////////////////////////////////////////////////////////////////////////////
// CNrChars dialog

class CNrChars : public CDialog
{
// Construction
public:
     CNrChars(CWnd* pParent = NULL);     // standard constructor

// Dialog Data
     //{{AFX_DATA(CNrChars)
     enum { IDD = IDD_NR_CHARS };
     UINT m_nr_chars;
     //}}AFX_DATA

// Implementation
protected:
     virtual void DoDataExchange(CDataExchange* pDX);  // DDX/DDV
```

*continues*

**Listing 24.1. continued**

```
     // Generated message map functions
     //{{AFX_MSG(CNrChars)
          // NOTE: the ClassWizard will add member functions here
     //}}AFX_MSG
     DECLARE_MESSAGE_MAP()
};
```

## PLAYER.CPP

```
// player.cpp

#include <iostream.h>
#include <string.h>
#include <stdio.h>
#include <stdlib.h>
#include <afxwin.h>
#include <afxcoll.h>
#include "player.h"

int CCharacter::count = 0;     // initialize nr of players to 0

IMPLEMENT_SERIAL(CPlayer, CObject, 1)

// Forward declarations.
void SetRandomSeed();
int RollDice(int sides);

///////////////////////////////////////////////
//  CPlayer::operator=
//  Overloaded operator= to perform assignments.
//
CPlayer& CPlayer::operator=( const CPlayer& b )
{
     ASSERT_VALID( this );
     ASSERT_VALID( &b );
     int m_class = b.m_class;
     int m_race = b.m_race;
     int m_s = b.m_s;
     int m_d = b.m_d;
     int m_c = b.m_c;
     int m_i = b.m_i;
     int m_w = b.m_w;
     int m_ch = b.m_ch;
     class CString m_name = b.m_name;
     class CString weapon = b.weapon;
     class CString armor = b.armor;
     class CString magic = b.magic;
     m_modTime = b.m_modTime;
     return *this;
}
```

```
// function to set and get ability scores
void CCharacter::SetAbilScores()
{
     ASSERT_VALID( this );
     int abils[6];

     SetRandomSeed();
     for (int c = 0; c < 6; c++)
          abils[c] = RollDice(20);

     SetStrength(abils[0]);
     SetDexterity(abils[1]);
     SetConstitution(abils[2]);
     SetIntelligence(abils[3]);
     SetWisdom(abils[4]);
     SetCharisma(abils[5]);
}

void CCharacter::PrintAbils()
{
     ASSERT_VALID( this );
     cout << '\n';
     cout << "Strength: " << GetStrength() << '\n';
     cout << "Dexterity: " << GetDexterity() << '\n';
     cout << "Constitution: " << GetConstitution() << '\n';
     cout << "Intelligence: " << GetIntelligence() << '\n';
     cout << "Wisdom: " << GetWisdom() << '\n';
     cout << "Charisma: " << GetCharisma() << '\n';
}

// Serialization function
void CCharacter::Serialize(CArchive& archive)
{
     ASSERT_VALID(this);
     //Call base class function first
     CObject::Serialize(archive);

     //Dump data for CPlayer class
     if (archive.IsStoring()) {
          TRACE( "Serializing a CPlayer out.\n" );
           archive << m_class << m_race
                << m_s << m_d << m_c << m_i << m_w << m_ch
                << m_classStr << m_raceStr
                << m_name << armor
                << weapon << magic
                << equipment << treasure;
     }
     else {
          TRACE( "Serializing a CPlayer in.\n" );
```

*continues*

**Listing 24.1. continued**

```
            archive >> m_class >> m_race
                 >> m_s >> m_d >>m_c >> m_i >> m_w >> m_ch
                  >> m_classStr >> m_raceStr
                 >> m_name >> armor
                 >> weapon >> magic
                  >> equipment >> treasure;
     }
}

// Saving these in case we ever add print capabilities.

void CPlayer::PrintEntry()
{
     ASSERT_VALID( this );
     cout << "\nNAME: ";
     cout << GetName();
     cout << "\nClass: ";
     cout << GetClassName();
     cout << "\nRace: ";
     cout << GetRaceName();
     cout << "\nWeapon: ";
     cout << GetWeapon();
     cout << "\nArmor: ";
     cout << GetArmor();
     PrintAbils();
}

void CWarrior::PrintEntry()
{
     ASSERT_VALID( this );
     cout << "\nNAME: ";
     cout << GetName();
     cout << "\nRace: ";
     cout << GetRaceName();
     cout << "\nClass: ";
     cout << GetClassName();
     cout << "\nWeapon: ";
     cout << GetWeapon();
     cout << "\nArmor: ";
     cout << GetArmor();
     PrintAbils();
}

void CThief::PrintEntry()
{
     ASSERT_VALID( this );
     cout << "\nNAME: ";
     cout << GetName();
     cout << "\nRace: ";
     cout << GetRaceName();
```

```
        cout << "\nClass: ";
        cout << GetClassName();
        cout << "\nWeapon: ";
        cout << GetWeapon();
        cout << "\nArmor: ";
        cout << GetArmor();
        PrintAbils();
}

void CWizard::PrintEntry()
{
        ASSERT_VALID( this );
        cout << "\nNAME: ";
        cout << GetName();
        cout << "\nRace: ";
        cout << GetRaceName();
        cout << "\nClass: ";
        cout << GetClassName();
        cout << "\nWeapon: ";
        cout << GetWeapon();
        cout << "\nMagic: ";
        cout << GetMagic();
        PrintAbils();
}

void CPriest::PrintEntry()
{
        ASSERT_VALID( this );
        cout << "\nNAME: ";
        cout << GetName();
        cout << "\nRace: ";
        cout << GetRaceName();
        cout << "\nClass: ";
        cout << GetClassName();
        cout << "\nWeapon: ";
        cout << GetWeapon();
        cout << "\nArmor: ";
        cout << GetArmor();
        cout << "\nMagic: ";
        cout << GetMagic();
        PrintAbils();
}

// An all-purpose AssertValid function
#ifdef _DEBUG
void CCharacter::AssertValid() const
{
        CObject::AssertValid();
}
#endif
```

*continues*

**Listing 24.1. continued**

```
// seed the random number generator with current time
void SetRandomSeed()
{
     srand((unsigned)time(NULL));
}

// function to roll dice
int RollDice(int nrOfSides)
{
     div_t div_result;                  // struct used in dividing
     int randNr, randNr2;

     randNr = rand();                   // get random number
     switch (nrOfSides) {
          case 4: {
               randNr = randNr & 0xFFF0;     // nr now 16 or less
               randNr /= 4;                  // nr now 4 or less
               randNr++;                     // start at 1 sted 0
               break;
          }
          case 8: {
          randNr = randNr & 0xFFF0;     // nr now 16 or less
          randNr /= 2;                  // nr now 8 or less
          randNr++;                     // start at 1 sted 0
               break;
     }
     case 10: {
          randNr = randNr & 0xFFF0;          // nr now 16 or less
               if (randNr > 9) {             // if nr is 10 or more
               div_result = div(randNr, 10);
               randNr = div_result.rem;
          }                                  // nr is now in range 0-9
               break;
          }                                  // (that's ok for 10-sided
die)
          case 12: {
          randNr = randNr & 0xFFF0;          // nr now 16 or less
               randNr2 = rand();             // get 2d random number
               randNr2 = randNr2 & 0xFFF0;   // nr2 now 16 or less
               randNr2 /= 4;                 // nr2 now 4 or less
               randNr += randNr2;            // add the random nrs
               randNr++;                     // start at 1 sted 0
               break;
          }
          case 20: {
          randNr = randNr & 0x000F;          // nr now 0 to 15
               randNr2 = rand();             // get random number
          randNr2 = randNr2 & 0x0004;        // nr2 now 0 to 4
               randNr += randNr2;            // add the 2 rand nrs
               randNr++;                     // start at 1 sted 0
               break;
```

```
            }
        }
        return (randNr);
}
```

### PLAYER.H

```
// player.h
// Chapter 24 Version
// Copyright 1993, Mark Andrews

#if !defined( _PLAYER_H_ )
#define _PLAYER_H_

#include <afxwin.h>
#include <afxcoll.h>
#include <iostream.h>
#include <stdlib.h>
#include <time.h>

void SetRandomSeed();
// void GetAbilScores();
int RollDice(int sides);

enum playerClasses { WARRIOR, WIZARD, PRIEST, THIEF };
const CString gClassName [] = { "Warrior", "Wizard", "Priest",
     "Thief" };

enum playerRaces { DWARF, ELF, GNOME,
     HALF_ELF, HALFLING, HUMAN };
const CString gRaceName [] = { "Dwarf", "Elf", "Gnome",
     "Half elf", "Halfling", "Human" };

enum playerAbils { STRENGTH, DEXTERITY, CONSTITUTION,
     INTELLIGENCE, WISDOM, CHARISMA };
const CString gAbilsName [] = { "Strength", "Dexterity",
      "Constitution", "Intelligence", "Wisdom",
      "Charisma" };

class CCharacter : public CObject {
protected:
     WORD m_class;
     WORD m_race;
     WORD m_s;
     WORD m_d;
     WORD m_c;
     WORD m_i;
     WORD m_w;
     WORD m_ch;
     class CString m_classStr;
```

*continues*

**Listing 24.1. continued**

```
     class CString m_raceStr;
     class CString m_name;
     class CString armor;
     class CString weapon;
     class CString magic;
     class CString equipment;
     class CString treasure;
     static int count;
public:
     CCharacter() {}
     ~CCharacter () {}
     static int GetCount() { return count; }
     static void IncCount() { count++; }
     static void DecCount() { count—; }
     static void PrintCount();
     void SetPlayerClass(int pc) { ASSERT_VALID (this);
                                   m_class = pc; }
     void SetPlayerRace(int pr) { ASSERT_VALID (this); m_race = pr; }
     void SetClassStr(CString aStr)
          { ASSERT_VALID (this); m_classStr = aStr; }
     void SetRaceStr(CString aStr)
          { ASSERT_VALID (this); m_raceStr = aStr; }
     void SetClass(CString classString);
     void SetRace(CString raceString);
     int GetPlayerClass() { ASSERT_VALID (this); return m_class; }
     int GetPlayerRace() { ASSERT_VALID (this); return m_race; }
     CString GetRaceName() { ASSERT_VALID (this); return m_raceStr; }
     CString GetClassName() { ASSERT_VALID (this);
                              return m_classStr; }
     void SetName(CString nm) { ASSERT_VALID (this); m_name = nm; }
     CString GetName() { return m_name; }
     void SetWeapon(CString wpn) { ASSERT_VALID (this); weapon = wpn; }
     CString GetWeapon() { return weapon; }
     void SetArmor(CString arm) { ASSERT_VALID (this); armor = arm; }
     CString GetArmor() { return armor; }
     void SetMagic(CString mag) { ASSERT_VALID (this); magic = mag; }
     CString GetMagic() { ASSERT_VALID (this); return magic; }
     void SetTreasure(CString tr) { ASSERT_VALID (this);
                                    treasure = tr; }
     CString GetTreasure() { ASSERT_VALID (this); return treasure; }
     void SetEquipment(CString eq) { ASSERT_VALID (this);
                                     equipment = eq; }
     CString GetEquipment() { ASSERT_VALID (this); return equipment; }
     // Set character's abilities
     void SetAbils(int st, int de, int co, int in,
          int wi, int ch)
          { m_s = st; m_d = de; m_c = co; m_i = in;
               m_w = wi; m_ch = ch; }
```

```
    // Get character's abilities
    void GetAbils(int *st, int *de, int *co, int *in,
         int *wi, int *ch)
         { *st = m_s; *de = m_d; *co = m_c; *in = m_i;
              *wi = m_w; *ch = m_ch; }
    // read contents of the PlayerAbils object
    int GetStrength() { return m_s; }
    int GetDexterity() { return m_d; }
    int GetConstitution() { return m_c; }
    int GetIntelligence() { return m_i; }
    int GetWisdom() { return m_w; }
    int GetCharisma() { return m_ch; }
    void SetStrength(int st) { m_s = st; }
    void SetDexterity(int de) { m_d = de; }
    void SetConstitution(int co) { m_c = co; }
    void SetIntelligence(int in) { m_i = in; }
    void SetWisdom(int wi) { m_w = wi; }
    void SetCharisma(int ch) { m_ch = ch; }
    virtual void PrintEntry() = 0;
    void PrintAbils();
    void SetAbilScores();
    //Override the CObject Serialize function
    virtual void Serialize(CArchive& archive);
#ifdef _DEBUG
    virtual void AssertValid() const;
#endif
};

class CPlayer : public CCharacter {
    DECLARE_SERIAL(CPlayer)
protected:
    CTime m_modTime;
    BOOL  m_bIsDirty;
public:
    CPlayer()
         { m_modTime = CTime::GetCurrentTime(); }
    ~CPlayer () {}
    CPlayer( const CPlayer& a );
    CPlayer(int pr) { SetPlayerRace(pr); }
    void PrintEntry();
    // Override the assignment operator
    CPlayer& operator=( const CPlayer& b );
    void SetDirty( BOOL bDirty )
         {   ASSERT_VALID( this );
              m_bIsDirty = bDirty; }

    BOOL GetDirty()
         {   ASSERT_VALID( this );
              return m_bIsDirty; }
```

*continues*

**Listing 24.1. continued**

```
     // Delete All deletes the Player objects as well as the pointers.
     void DeleteAll();
};

class CWarrior : public CPlayer {
public:
     CWarrior() {}
     CWarrior(int pr) : CPlayer(pr)
          { SetPlayerRace(pr); SetPlayerClass(WARRIOR); }
     void PrintEntry();
};

class CThief : public CPlayer {
public:
     CThief() {}
     CThief(int pr) : CPlayer(pr)
          { SetPlayerRace(pr); SetPlayerClass(WARRIOR); }
     void PrintEntry();
};

class CWizard : public CPlayer {
public:
     CWizard() {}
     CWizard(int pr) : CPlayer(pr)
          { SetPlayerRace(pr); SetPlayerClass(WIZARD); }
     CWizard(int pr, CString mag) : CPlayer(pr)
          { SetPlayerRace(pr); SetPlayerClass(WIZARD);
            SetMagic(mag); }
     void PrintEntry();
};

class CPriest : public CPlayer {
public:
     CPriest() {}
     CPriest(int pr) : CPlayer(pr)
          { SetPlayerRace(pr); SetPlayerClass(PRIEST); }
     CPriest(int pr, CString mag) : CPlayer(pr)
          { SetPlayerRace(pr); SetPlayerClass(PRIEST);
            SetMagic(mag); }
     void PrintEntry();
};

#endif // _PLAYER_H
```

## ZALTHAR.CPP

```
// zalthar.cpp : Defines the class behaviors for the application.
//
```

```
#include "stdafx.h"
#include "zalthar.h"

#include "mainfrm.h"
#include "zalthdoc.h"
#include "zalthvw.h"

#ifdef _DEBUG
#undef THIS_FILE
static char BASED_CODE THIS_FILE[] = __FILE__;
#endif

/////////////////////////////////////////////////////////////////////////////
// CZaltharApp

BEGIN_MESSAGE_MAP(CZaltharApp, CWinApp)
     //{{AFX_MSG_MAP(CZaltharApp)
     ON_COMMAND(ID_APP_ABOUT, OnAppAbout)
          // NOTE - the ClassWizard will add and remove mapping
          // macros here. DO NOT EDIT what you see in these blocks of
          // generated code !
     //}}AFX_MSG_MAP
     // Standard file based document commands
     ON_COMMAND(ID_FILE_NEW, CWinApp::OnFileNew)
     ON_COMMAND(ID_FILE_OPEN, CWinApp::OnFileOpen)
     // Standard print setup command
     ON_COMMAND(ID_FILE_PRINT_SETUP, CWinApp::OnFilePrintSetup)
END_MESSAGE_MAP()

/////////////////////////////////////////////////////////////////////////////
// CZaltharApp construction

CZaltharApp::CZaltharApp()
{
     // TODO: add construction code here,
     // Place all significant initialization in InitInstance
}

/////////////////////////////////////////////////////////////////////////////
// The one and only CZaltharApp object

CZaltharApp NEAR theApp;

/////////////////////////////////////////////////////////////////////////////
// CZaltharApp initialization

BOOL CZaltharApp::InitInstance()
{
```

*continues*

**Listing 24.1. continued**

```
    // Standard initialization
    // If you are not using these features and wish to reduce the
    // size of your final executable, you should remove from the
    // following the specific initialization routines you do not
    // need.

    SetDialogBkColor();          // set dialog background color to gray
    LoadStdProfileSettings();    // Load standard INI file options
                                 // (including MRU)

    // Register the application's document templates.  Document
    // templates serve as the connection between documents, frame
    // windows, and views.

    AddDocTemplate(new CMultiDocTemplate(IDR_ZALTHATYPE,
            RUNTIME_CLASS(CZaltharDoc),
            RUNTIME_CLASS(CMDIChildWnd), // standard MDI childframe
            RUNTIME_CLASS(CZaltharView)));

    // create main MDI Frame window
    CMainFrame* pMainFrame = new CMainFrame;
    if (!pMainFrame->LoadFrame(IDR_MAINFRAME))
        return FALSE;
    pMainFrame->ShowWindow(m_nCmdShow);
    pMainFrame->UpdateWindow();
    m_pMainWnd = pMainFrame;

    ////////////////////////////////////////////////////////////////////
    //
    // COMMENTING OUT THE OnFileNew() CALL!
    //
    // AppWizard puts this function in, but watch out!
    //
    // COMMENT IT OUT IF YOUR APP CREATES ITS OWN DOCUMENTS!
    // (You can see that it's commented out here.)
  //
    // OnFileNew();
  //
  ////////////////////////////////////////////////////////////////////

    if (m_lpCmdLine[0] != '\0')
    {
        // TODO: add command-line processing here
    }

    return TRUE;
}
```

```
/////////////////////////////////////////////////////////////////////////////
// CAboutDlg dialog used for App About

class CAboutDlg : public CDialog
{
public:
     CAboutDlg();

// Dialog Data
     //{{AFX_DATA(CAboutDlg)
     enum { IDD = IDD_ABOUTBOX };
     //}}AFX_DATA

// Implementation
protected:
     virtual void DoDataExchange(CDataExchange* pDX); // DDX/DDV
     //{{AFX_MSG(CAboutDlg)
          // No message handlers
     //}}AFX_MSG
     DECLARE_MESSAGE_MAP()
};

CAboutDlg::CAboutDlg() : CDialog(CAboutDlg::IDD)
{
     //{{AFX_DATA_INIT(CAboutDlg)
     //}}AFX_DATA_INIT
}

void CAboutDlg::DoDataExchange(CDataExchange* pDX)
{
     CDialog::DoDataExchange(pDX);
     //{{AFX_DATA_MAP(CAboutDlg)
     //}}AFX_DATA_MAP
}

BEGIN_MESSAGE_MAP(CAboutDlg, CDialog)
     //{{AFX_MSG_MAP(CAboutDlg)
          // No message handlers
     //}}AFX_MSG_MAP
END_MESSAGE_MAP()

// App command to run the dialog
void CZaltharApp::OnAppAbout()
{
     CAboutDlg aboutDlg;
     aboutDlg.DoModal();
}

/////////////////////////////////////////////////////////////////////////////
// CZaltharApp commands
```

*continues*

**Listing 24.1. continued**

### ZALTHAR.H

```
// zalthar.h : main header file for the ZALTHAR application
//

#ifndef _ZALTHAR_H_
#define _ZALTHAR_H_

#ifndef __AFXWIN_H__
     #error include 'stdafx.h' before including this file for PCH
#endif

#include "resource.h"          // main symbols

////////////////////////////////////////////////////////////////////////
// CZaltharApp:
// See zalthar.cpp for the implementation of this class
//

class CZaltharApp : public CWinApp
{
public:
     CZaltharApp();

// Overrides
     virtual BOOL InitInstance();

// Implementation

     //{{AFX_MSG(CZaltharApp)
     afx_msg void OnAppAbout();
          // NOTE - the ClassWizard will add and remove member
          // functions here. DO NOT EDIT what you see in these
          // blocks of generated code !
     //}}AFX_MSG
     DECLARE_MESSAGE_MAP()
};


////////////////////////////////////////////////////////////////////////

#endif // _ZALTHAR_H//Microsoft App Studio generated resource script.
//
```

### ZALTHDOC.CPP

```
// zalthdoc.cpp : implementation of the CZaltharDoc class
//
```

```
#include "stdafx.h"
#include "zalthar.h"
#include "zalthdoc.h"
#include "linklist.h"

#ifdef _DEBUG
#undef THIS_FILE
static char BASED_CODE THIS_FILE[] = __FILE__;
#endif

/////////////////////////////////////////////////////////////////////////////
// CZaltharDoc

IMPLEMENT_DYNCREATE(CZaltharDoc, CDocument)

BEGIN_MESSAGE_MAP(CZaltharDoc, CDocument)
     //{{AFX_MSG_MAP(CZaltharDoc)
          // NOTE - the ClassWizard will add and remove mapping macros
          // here. DO NOT EDIT what you see in these blocks of
          // generated code !
     //}}AFX_MSG_MAP
END_MESSAGE_MAP()

/////////////////////////////////////////////////////////////////////////////
// CZaltharDoc construction/destruction

CZaltharDoc::CZaltharDoc()
{
     // TODO: add one-time construction code here
     m_pDataList = NULL;
     m_pFindList = NULL;
     m_szFileName = "";
     m_szFileTitle = "";

     // Create player and player mask bitmaps
     m_bmImage = new CBitmap;
     ASSERT_VALID(m_bmImage);
     m_bmBkg = new CBitmap;
     ASSERT_VALID(m_bmBkg);

     // Create a bitmap for the playing field
     m_pBitmap = new CBitmap;
     ASSERT_VALID(m_pBitmap);
}

CZaltharDoc::~CZaltharDoc()
{
     // TODO: add reinitialization code here
     Terminate();     // Close down the database.
     delete m_pBitmap;
```

*continues*

**Listing 24.1. continued**

```
    delete m_bmImage;
    delete m_bmBkg;
}

void CZaltharDoc::InitDocument()
{
    // TODO: add reinitialization code here
    New();      // Initialize the database.

    // Load the playing-field bitmap.
    int y = m_bmImage->LoadBitmap(IDB_PLAYER1);
    ASSERT(y != 0);
    y = m_bmBkg->LoadBitmap(IDB_PLAYER1_MASK);
    ASSERT(y != 0);
    y = m_pBitmap->LoadBitmap(IDB_ARCHES);
    ASSERT(y != 0);

    // Bitmap intializations
    m_bmWidth = 32;
    m_bmHeight = 32;
    m_startX = 5;
    m_startY = 5;

}

BOOL CZaltharDoc::OnNewDocument()
{
    // TODO: add reinitialization code here
    if (!CDocument::OnNewDocument())
        return FALSE;
    InitDocument();
    return TRUE;
}

BOOL CZaltharDoc::OnOpenDocument(const char* pszPathName)
{
    // TODO: add reinitialization code here

    BOOL y = DoOpen(pszPathName);

    return y;
}

/////////////////////////////////////////////////////////////////////////////
// CZaltharDoc diagnostics

#ifdef _DEBUG
void CZaltharDoc::Dump(CDumpContext& dc) const
{
    CDocument::Dump(dc);
```

```
}
#endif //_DEBUG

#ifdef _DEBUG
void CZaltharDoc::AssertValid() const
{
      if ( m_pDataList != NULL )
      {
            ASSERT_VALID( m_pDataList );
            if ( m_pFindList != NULL )
                  ASSERT_VALID( m_pFindList );
      }
      else
            ASSERT( m_pFindList == NULL );
}
#endif

//////////////////////////////////////////////////////////////////////
// My stuff

const char szUntitled[] = "Untitled";

//  This function initializes the database.
BOOL CZaltharDoc::New()
{
      ASSERT_VALID( this );

      // Clean up any old data.
      Terminate();

      m_pDataList = new CPlayerList;

      return ( m_pDataList != NULL );
}

//  Clean up the database.
void CZaltharDoc::Terminate()
{
      ASSERT_VALID( this );

      if ( m_pDataList != NULL )
            m_pDataList->DeleteAll();

      delete m_pDataList;
      delete m_pFindList;

      m_pDataList = NULL;
      m_pFindList = NULL;
```

*continues*

**Listing 24.1. continued**

```
     m_szFileName = szUntitled;
     m_szFileTitle = szUntitled;
}

// Count the players in the database.
int CZaltharDoc::GetCount()
{
     ASSERT_VALID( this );
     if ( m_pFindList != NULL )
          return m_pFindList->GetCount();
     if ( m_pDataList != NULL )
          return m_pDataList->GetCount();
     return 0;
}

// Miscellaneous document functions
//

const char* CZaltharDoc::GetName()
{
     ASSERT_VALID( this );
     return m_szFileName;
}

CString CZaltharDoc::GetTitle()
{
     ASSERT_VALID( this );
     return  "Zalthar - " + m_szFileTitle;
}

void CZaltharDoc::SetTitle( const char* pszTitle )
{
     ASSERT_VALID( this );
     m_szFileTitle = pszTitle;
}

// Add a player to the database
void CZaltharDoc::AddPlayer( CPlayer* pNewPlayer )
{
     ASSERT_VALID( this );
     ASSERT_VALID( pNewPlayer );
     ASSERT( pNewPlayer != NULL );
     ASSERT( m_pDataList != NULL );

     POSITION pos = m_pDataList->GetHeadPosition();

     while ( pos != NULL &&
               _stricmp(
```

```
                    ((CPlayer*)m_pDataList->GetAt(pos))->GetName(),
                     pNewPlayer->GetName() ) <= 0 )
        m_pDataList->GetNext( pos );

    if ( pos == NULL )
        m_pDataList->AddTail( pNewPlayer );
    else
        m_pDataList->InsertBefore( pos, pNewPlayer );

    SetModifiedFlag( TRUE );
}

//  Look up a player by index.
CPlayer* CZaltharDoc::GetPlayer( int nIndex )
{
    ASSERT_VALID( this );
    ASSERT( m_pDataList != NULL );

    if ( m_pFindList != NULL )
        return (CPlayer*)m_pFindList->GetAt
            ( m_pFindList->FindIndex( nIndex ) );
    else
        return (CPlayer*)m_pDataList->
            GetAt( m_pDataList->FindIndex( nIndex ) );
}

//  Remove a player from the database.
void CZaltharDoc::DeletePlayer( int nIndex )
{
    ASSERT_VALID( this );
    ASSERT( m_pDataList != NULL );

    POSITION el = m_pDataList->FindIndex( nIndex );
    delete m_pDataList->GetAt( el );
    m_pDataList->RemoveAt( el );
    SetModifiedFlag( TRUE );
}

//  Replace a player object with a new player object.
    void CZaltharDoc::ReplacePlayer( CPlayer* pOldPlayer,
    const CPlayer& rNewPlayer )
{
    ASSERT_VALID( this );

    ASSERT( pOldPlayer != NULL );
    ASSERT( m_pDataList != NULL );

    // Overloaded the new operator
    *pOldPlayer = rNewPlayer;
    SetModifiedFlag( TRUE );
}
```

continues

**Listing 24.1. continued**

```
/////////////////////////////////////////////////////
//  CZaltharDoc::DoFind
//  Do a FindPerson call, or clear the find data.
//
BOOL CZaltharDoc::DoFind( const char* pszName /* = NULL */ )
{
     ASSERT_VALID( this );
     ASSERT( m_pDataList != NULL );

     if ( pszName == NULL )
     {
          delete m_pFindList;
          m_pFindList = NULL;
          return FALSE;
     }

     // Prevents a second find to occur while
     // we already have one.
     ASSERT( m_pFindList == NULL );
     return ( ( m_pFindList = m_pDataList->
          FindPlayer( pszName ) ) != NULL );
}

//  Open the database and read a player list.
BOOL CZaltharDoc::DoOpen( const char* pszFileName )
{
     ASSERT_VALID( this );
     ASSERT( pszFileName != NULL );

     CFile file( pszFileName, CFile::modeRead );

     // read the object data from file
     CPlayerList* pNewDataBase = ReadDataBase( &file );

     file.Close();

     // get rid of current database if new one is OK
     if ( pNewDataBase != NULL )
     {
          Terminate();
          m_pDataList = pNewDataBase;
          SetModifiedFlag( FALSE );

          m_szFileName = pszFileName;
          return TRUE;
     }
     else
          return FALSE;
}
```

```
//  Save the database to a file.
BOOL CZaltharDoc::DoSave( const char* pszFileName /* = NULL */ )
{
     ASSERT_VALID( this );

     // store objects name.
     if ( pszFileName != NULL )
          m_szFileName = pszFileName;

     CFileStatus status;
     int nAccess = CFile::modeWrite;

     // Call GetStatus, which returns true if specified file exists,
     // false if it doesn't.
     if ( !CFile::GetStatus( m_szFileName, status ) )
          nAccess |= CFile::modeCreate;

     CFile file( m_szFileName, nAccess );

     // write database to a file and
     // mark the database clean if write is successful
     if ( WriteDataBase( &file ) )
     {
          SetModifiedFlag( FALSE );
          file.Close();
          return TRUE;
     }
     else
     {
          file.Close();
          return FALSE;
     }
}

//////////////////////////////////////////////////////////////////////
// CZaltharDoc serialization

void CZaltharDoc::Serialize(CArchive& ar)
{
     ASSERT_VALID( this );
     if (ar.IsStoring())
          {
          // TODO: add storing code here
          ::MessageBox(NULL, "Storing...", "CZaltharDoc", MB_OK);
          ASSERT( m_pDataList != NULL );
          // Archive out, or catch the exception.
          TRY
          {
               ar << m_pDataList;
          }
```

*continues*

**Listing 24.1. continued**

```
        CATCH( CArchiveException, e )
        {
            // Throw this exception again
            // for the benefit of the caller.
            THROW_LAST();
        }
        END_CATCH
        // ar.Close();

    }
    else {
        // TODO: add loading code here
        ::MessageBox(NULL, "Loading...", "CZaltharDoc", MB_OK);
        CPlayerList* pNewDataBase = NULL;

        // Deserialize the new database from the archive,
        // or catch the exception.
        TRY
        {
            ar >> pNewDataBase;
        }
        CATCH( CArchiveException, e )
        {
            ar.Close();

            // If we got part of the database, delete it.
            if ( pNewDataBase != NULL )
            {
                pNewDataBase->DeleteAll();
                delete pNewDataBase;
            }

            // Caught an exception—but we throw it again so
            // the caller of this function can also catch it.
            THROW_LAST();
        }
        END_CATCH
        // ar.Close();
    }
}

//  Write data to a file.
BOOL CZaltharDoc::WriteDataBase( CFile* pFile )
{
    ASSERT_VALID( this );
    ASSERT( m_pDataList != NULL );

    // Create an archive from the File for writing
    CArchive archive( pFile, CArchive::store );
```

```
    // Archive out, or catch the exception.
    TRY
    {
        archive << m_pDataList;
    }
    CATCH( CArchiveException, e )
    {
        // Throw this exception again
        // for the benefit of the caller.
        THROW_LAST();
    }
    END_CATCH

    // Exit here if no errors or exceptions.
    archive.Close();
    return TRUE;
}

//  Read data from a file.
CPlayerList* CZaltharDoc::ReadDataBase( CFile* pFile )
{
    ASSERT_VALID( this );
    CPlayerList* pNewDataBase = NULL;

    // Create an archive from pFile for reading.
    CArchive archive( pFile, CArchive::load );

    // Deserialize the new database from the archive,
    // or catch the exception.

    TRY
    {
        archive >> pNewDataBase;
    }
    CATCH( CArchiveException, e )
    {
        archive.Close();

        // If we got part of the database, delete it.
        if ( pNewDataBase != NULL )
        {
            pNewDataBase->DeleteAll();
            delete pNewDataBase;
        }

        // Caught an exception—but we throw it again so
        // the caller of this function can also catch it.
        THROW_LAST();
    }
    END_CATCH
```

*continues*

**Listing 24.1. continued**

```
     // Exit here if no errors or exceptions.
     archive.Close();
     return pNewDataBase;
}

////////////////////////////////////////////////////////////////////////
// Function to draw playing field
//
void CZaltharDoc::DrawBackdrop(CDC *pDC)
{
     CDC dcBackdrop;
     CBitmap *pOldMapZ;
     CBitmap Bitmap;
     int bmWidth = 123;
     int bmHeight = 160;

     // Create a bitmap of the right size.
     Bitmap.CreateCompatibleBitmap(pDC, bmWidth, bmHeight);

     // Create a device context that's
     // compatible with your bitmap.
     dcBackdrop.CreateCompatibleDC(pDC);

     // Select m_pBitmap into current device context,
     // and save previous bitmap in pOldMapZ.
     pOldMapZ = dcBackdrop.SelectObject(m_pBitmap);

     // Copy the bitmap to the screen.
     pDC->BitBlt(0, 0, bmWidth,
          bmHeight, &dcBackdrop, 0, 0, SRCCOPY);
     // DrawPlayer(pDC);

     // When it's over, return the saved bitmap to
     // the current device context.
     dcBackdrop.SelectObject(pOldMapZ);
}

////////////////////////////////////////////////////////////////////////
// Function to draw a character
//
void CZaltharDoc::DrawPlayer(CDC *pDC)
{
     CDC dcZalth, dcMask, memDC;
     CRect rect;
     CBitmap *pOldMapZ = NULL;
     CBitmap *pOldMapM = NULL;
     CBitmap *pOldBitmap = NULL;
     CBitmap Bitmap;
     int bigWidth = 123;
     int bigHeight = 160;
```

```
// Create some device contexts that are
// compatible with your system.
dcZalth.CreateCompatibleDC(pDC);
dcMask.CreateCompatibleDC(pDC);
memDC.CreateCompatibleDC(pDC);

// Create a bitmap of the right size.
Bitmap.CreateCompatibleBitmap(pDC, m_bmWidth, m_bmHeight);

// Select our bitmaps into current device context,
// and save previous bitmaps.
pOldMapZ = dcZalth.SelectObject(m_bmImage);
pOldMapM = dcMask.SelectObject(m_bmBkg);
pOldBitmap = memDC.SelectObject(&Bitmap);

// Prepare a place for the player and the mask.
memDC.Rectangle(m_startX-1, m_startY-1, m_bmWidth+2,
     m_bmHeight+2);

// Copy  mask into memory.
memDC.BitBlt(0, 0, m_bmWidth,
     m_bmHeight, &dcMask, 0, 0, SRCCOPY);

// Invert portion of screen.
pDC->StretchBlt(m_startX, m_startY, m_bmWidth*2,
     m_bmHeight*2, pDC, 0, 0, m_bmWidth,
     m_bmHeight, DSTINVERT);

// Draw mask to screen.
pDC->StretchBlt(m_startX, m_startY, m_bmWidth*2,
     m_bmHeight*2, &memDC, 0, 0, m_bmWidth,
     m_bmHeight, SRCAND);

// Copy player into memory.
memDC.BitBlt(0, 0, m_bmWidth,
     m_bmHeight, &dcZalth, 0, 0, SRCCOPY);

// Invert fragment of backdrop.
// pDC->BitBlt(0, 0, m_bmWidth,
//   m_bmHeight, pDC, 0, 0, DSTINVERT);

// Draw player to screen and invert destination.
pDC->StretchBlt(m_startX, m_startY, m_bmWidth*2,
     m_bmHeight*2, &memDC, 0, 0, m_bmWidth,
     m_bmHeight, SRCINVERT);

// When it's over, return the saved bitmap to
// the current device context.
dcZalth.SelectObject(pOldMapZ);
```

*continues*

**Listing 24.1. continued**

```
     dcMask.SelectObject(pOldMapM);
     memDC.SelectObject(pOldBitmap);
}

// Update starting point for the player bitmap.
void CZaltharDoc::SetStartPoint(CPoint point)
{
     m_startX = point.x;
     m_startY = point.y;
     UpdateAllViews(NULL, 0, NULL);
}
```

## ZALTHDOC.H

```
// zalthdoc.h : interface of the CZaltharDoc class
//
/////////////////////////////////////////////////////////////////////////

#ifndef _ZALTHDOC_H_
#define _ZALTHDOC_H_

#include <afxwin.h>
#include <afxcoll.h>
#include "player.h"
#include "linklist.h"
// #include "database.h"

class CZaltharDoc : public CDocument
{
protected: // create from serialization only
      CZaltharDoc();
      DECLARE_DYNCREATE(CZaltharDoc)

// Graphics-related members.
private:
   CBitmap *m_pBitmap;
   BOOL    m_needsRedraw;
   BOOL    m_imageDrawn;
   int     m_bmX;          // Bitmap origin
   int     m_bmY;          // Bitmap origin
   int     m_bmWidth;      // Bitmap width
   int     m_bmHeight;     // Bitmap height
   CBitmap *m_bmImage;     // Image bitmap
   CBitmap *m_bmBkg;       // Image background
   // CDC   m_dcBackdrop; // DC for backdrop

     // int m_bigWidth;
     // int m_bigHeight;
     int m_startX;
```

```
     int m_startY;
     // int m_oldStartX;
     // int m_oldStartY;

private:
     // int m_xPrev;                    // Previous mouse position
      // int m_yPrev;
      // CRect m_rcClient;             // Client area bounding rectangle
public:
     /***
     void InitImageInfo (CWnd *pWnd, CBitmap *pBM, int nX, int nY);
     void SetImageDrawnFlag(BOOL theFlag) { m_imageDrawn = theFlag; }
     void DeleteImage (void);
     void DrawImage (CWnd *aView);
     BOOL IsSelected (int x, int y);
     void BeginDrag (CWnd *aView, int x, int y);
     void Drag (CWnd *aView, int x, int y);
     void EndDrag (CWnd *aView, int x, int y);
     ***/

     void SetStartPoint(CPoint point);
     // CPoint GetStartPoint();
     // CPoint GetOldStartPoint();

// Implementation
public:
     virtual ~CZaltharDoc();
     void DrawImage(CDC *pDC);
     void DrawPlayer(CDC *pDC);
     void DrawBackdrop(CDC *pDC);

#ifdef _DEBUG
     virtual   void AssertValid() const;
     virtual   void Dump(CDumpContext& dc) const;
#endif

protected:
     void InitDocument();
     virtual   BOOL OnNewDocument();
     virtual BOOL OnOpenDocument(const char* pszPathname);

// Generated message map functions
protected:
     //{{AFX_MSG(CZaltharDoc)
          // NOTE - the ClassWizard will add and remove member
          // functions here. DO NOT EDIT what you see in these
          // blocks of generated code !
     //}}AFX_MSG
     DECLARE_MESSAGE_MAP()
```

*continues*

**Listing 24.1. continued**

```
/////////////////////////  My Stuff ////////////////////////////////

private:
     CPlayerList* ReadDataBase( CFile* pFile );
     BOOL WriteDataBase( CFile* pFile );
protected:
     CPlayerList* m_pDataList;
     CPlayerList* m_pFindList;
     CString m_szFileName;
     CString m_szFileTitle;
public:

     // Create/Destroy CPlayerLists
     BOOL New();
     void Terminate();

     // File handling
     void Serialize(CArchive& ar);
     BOOL DoOpen( const char* pszFileName );
     BOOL DoSave( const char* pszFileName = NULL );
     BOOL DoFind( const char* pszLastName = NULL );

     // Player Handling
     void AddPlayer( CPlayer *pNewPlayer );
     void ReplacePlayer( CPlayer* pOldPlayer,
                         const CPlayer& rNewPlayer );
     void DeletePlayer( int nIndex );
     CPlayer* GetPlayer( int nIndex );
     BOOL FindPlayer(const char *pName);

     // Database Attributes
     int GetCount();
     BOOL IsNamed();
     const char* GetName();
     CString GetTitle();
     void SetTitle( const char* pszTitle );

};

#endif // _ZALTHDOC_H_
```

## ZALTHVW.CPP

```
// zalthvw.cpp : implementation of the CZaltharView class
//

#include "stdafx.h"
#include "zalthar.h"
```

```
#include "zalthdoc.h"
#include "zalthvw.h"
#include "player.h"
#include "createch.h"
#include "getchard.h"
#include "finddlg.h"
#include "charlist.h"
#include "nrchars.h"

#ifdef _DEBUG
#undef THIS_FILE
static char BASED_CODE THIS_FILE[] = __FILE__;
#endif

/////////////////////////////////////////////////////////////////////
// CZaltharView

IMPLEMENT_DYNCREATE(CZaltharView, CView)

BEGIN_MESSAGE_MAP(CZaltharView, CView)
     //{{AFX_MSG_MAP(CZaltharView)
     ON_COMMAND(ID_CHARACTERS_CREATE_ONE, OnCharactersCreateOne)
     ON_COMMAND(ID_CHARS_VIEW_ONE, OnCharsViewOne)
     ON_WM_CREATE()
     ON_COMMAND(ID_CHARACTERS_FIND, OnCharactersFind)
     ON_COMMAND(ID_CHARS_VIEW_MULT, OnCharsViewMult)
     ON_COMMAND(ID_CHARACTERS_CREATE_MULT, OnCharactersCreateMult)
     ON_COMMAND(ID_CHARS_DRAW_MAP, OnCharsDrawMap)
     ON_WM_LBUTTONDOWN()
     //}}AFX_MSG_MAP
     // Standard printing commands
     ON_COMMAND(ID_FILE_PRINT, CView::OnFilePrint)
     ON_COMMAND(ID_FILE_PRINT_PREVIEW, CView::OnFilePrintPreview)
END_MESSAGE_MAP()

/////////////////////////////////////////////////////////////////////
// CZaltharView construction/destruction

CZaltharView::CZaltharView()
{
     // TODO: add construction code here
}

CZaltharView::~CZaltharView()
{
}

/////////////////////////////////////////////////////////////////////
// Get and store a pointer to the document
// associated with this view.
```

*continues*

**Listing 24.1. continued**

```
void CZaltharView::OnInitialUpdate()
{
     // TODO: add your code here
     m_database = GetDocument();
     ASSERT_VALID(m_database);

     ShowWindow(SW_SHOWMAXIMIZED);

     OnUpdate(NULL, 0, NULL);     // What basic function does

     // UpdateWindow();
}

/////////////////////////////////////////////////////////////////////////////
// CZaltharView printing

BOOL CZaltharView::OnPreparePrinting(CPrintInfo* pInfo)
{
     // default preparation
     return DoPreparePrinting(pInfo);
}

void CZaltharView::OnBeginPrinting(CDC* /*pDC*/,
                                   CPrintInfo* /*pInfo*/)
{
     // TODO: add extra initialization before printing
}

void CZaltharView::OnEndPrinting(CDC* /*pDC*/, CPrintInfo* /*pInfo*/)
{
     // TODO: add cleanup after printing
}

/////////////////////////////////////////////////////////////////////////////
// CZaltharView diagnostics

#ifdef _DEBUG
void CZaltharView::AssertValid() const
{
     CView::AssertValid();
}

void CZaltharView::Dump(CDumpContext& dc) const
{
     CView::Dump(dc);
}

CZaltharDoc* CZaltharView::GetDocument() // non-debug version inline
{
```

```
        ASSERT(m_pDocument->IsKindOf(RUNTIME_CLASS(CZaltharDoc)));
        return (CZaltharDoc*) m_pDocument;
}

#endif //_DEBUG

//////////////////////////////////////////////////////////////////////
// My stuff

void CZaltharView::OnCharactersCreateOne()
{
        // TODO: Add your command handler code here

        ASSERT_VALID(this);
        ASSERT_VALID(m_database);

        // Create a player.

        m_player = new CWarrior;
        ASSERT_VALID(m_player);

        m_player->SetAbilScores();

        CCreateCharDlg dlg(m_player);
        if (dlg.DoModal() == IDOK) {
                m_database->AddPlayer(m_player);
        }
        else {
                delete m_player;
        }
}

void CZaltharView::OnCharsViewOne()
{
        // TODO: Add your command handler code here

        OnCharactersFind();

}

int CZaltharView::OnCreate(LPCREATESTRUCT lpCreateStruct)
{
        if (CView::OnCreate(lpCreateStruct) == -1)
                return -1;

        // TODO: Add your specialized creation code here

        return 0;
}
```

*continues*

**Listing 24.1. continued**

```
void CZaltharView::OnCharactersFind()
{
     char *str1 =
            "Can't find any characters; please load or create a game!";
     char *str2 = "Woops!";

     int n = m_database->GetCount();
     if (n == 0)
          MessageBox( str1, str2,
                MB_OK ¦ MB_ICONEXCLAMATION);
     else FindChar();     // Next function, see below.

}

void CZaltharView::FindChar()
{
     char *str1 = "Please create a character.";
     char *str2 = "Woops!";
     char *str3 = "Couldn't find your character!";
     char *str4 = "Sorry!";

     CFindDlg searchDlg;

     ASSERT_VALID(this);
     ASSERT_VALID(m_database);
     if (m_database->GetCount() == 0)
               MessageBox( str1, str2,
                     MB_OK ¦ MB_ICONEXCLAMATION);
    else {
          // CFindDlg() just prompts for, gets,
          // and stores a character's name.
          if ( searchDlg.DoModal() == IDOK &&
               searchDlg.GetNameStr().GetLength() != 0 ) {

               // GetFindList() look for the name in the database.
               if (m_database->DoFind(searchDlg.GetNameStr())) {
                    // Get 0th player in list
                         m_player = (m_database->GetPlayer(0));
                    // Call CGetCharDlg() to display
                    // data about the found character.
                    CGetCharData dlg(m_player);
                    dlg.DoModal();
               }
               else
                    MessageBox( str3, str4,
                    MB_OK ¦ MB_ICONEXCLAMATION);
               m_database->DoFind(); // Discard the find list.
          }
     }
}
```

```
void CZaltharView::OnCharsViewMult()
{
	// TODO: Add your command handler code here
	CCharList dlg(m_database, this);
	dlg.DoModal();
}


void CZaltharView::OnCharactersCreateMult()
{
	// TODO: Add your command handler code here
	CNrChars dlg(this);
	if (dlg.DoModal() == IDOK) {
		int n = dlg.m_nr_chars;
		for (int i = 0; i < n; i++) {
			OnCharactersCreateOne();
		}
	}
}

/////////////////////////////////////////////////////////////////////////////
// CZaltharView drawing

void CZaltharView::OnDraw(CDC* pDC)
{
	CRect *rect;
   GetClientRect(rect);

	// m_database = GetDocument(); // We don't have to do this again!
	m_database->DrawBackdrop(pDC);
	m_database->DrawPlayer(pDC);
}

void CZaltharView::OnCharsDrawMap()
{

}

void CZaltharView::OnLButtonDown(UINT nFlags, CPoint point)
{
	// TODO: Add your message handler code here and/or call default

	// Set a new location for the player bitmap.
	m_database->SetStartPoint(point);

	// Frame says call the base function now.
	CView::OnLButtonDown(nFlags, point);
}
```

*continues*

**Listing 24.1. continued**

## ZALTHVW.H

```
// zalthvw.h : interface of the CZaltharView class
//
/////////////////////////////////////////////////////////////////////////////

#include "zalthdoc.h"
#include "linklist.h"
#include "player.h"

class CZaltharView : public CView
{
private:

     CPlayer *m_player;

     // The document associated with this view.
     CZaltharDoc *m_database;

protected: // create from serialization only
     CZaltharView();
     DECLARE_DYNCREATE(CZaltharView)
     void OnInitialUpdate();

// Implementation
public:
     virtual ~CZaltharView();
     virtual void OnDraw(CDC* pDC);  // overridden to draw this view
#ifdef _DEBUG
     virtual void AssertValid() const;
     virtual void Dump(CDumpContext& dc) const;
#endif

// My stuff
public:
     CZaltharDoc* GetDocument();
     void FindChar();

// Printing support
protected:
     virtual BOOL OnPreparePrinting(CPrintInfo* pInfo);
     virtual void OnBeginPrinting(CDC* pDC, CPrintInfo* pInfo);
     virtual void OnEndPrinting(CDC* pDC, CPrintInfo* pInfo);

// Generated message map functions
protected:
     //{{AFX_MSG(CZaltharView)
     afx_msg void OnCharactersCreateOne();
     afx_msg void OnCharsViewOne();
```

```
    afx_msg int OnCreate(LPCREATESTRUCT lpCreateStruct);
    afx_msg void OnCharactersFind();
    afx_msg void OnCharsViewMult();
    afx_msg void OnCharactersCreateMult();
    afx_msg void OnCharsDrawMap();
    afx_msg void OnLButtonDown(UINT nFlags, CPoint point);
    //}}AFX_MSG
    DECLARE_MESSAGE_MAP()
};
```

# Summary

So ends this volume about object-oriented programming in Visual C++. In this chapter, as promised, you got a chance to compile and run a program that can serve as a foundation of a commercial-quality, world-class adventure game. You can design the game any way you like. You can create as many characters of as many kinds as you like, and you can create friends for them to pal around with, as well as monsters for them to fight.

You can design scenarios in which character meets character on the playing field, and whether they are friend or foe, you can use the abilities that the characters have to design algorithms that determine the outcome of their encounters.

By creating varieties of playing fields, you can send your characters to distant arid or beautiful lands.

In short, you can do what you want to do. It's your game.

Maybe you aren't the game-playing type. Perhaps you would prefer to use the databases and interface objects that were introduced in this volume to design other kinds of programs—databases, spreadsheets, and so on. Feel free. Thanks to the features of C++ code in this book and on its accompanying program disk, the concepts are easily reusable in whatever kind of program you decide to create.

I hope you enjoyed this book as much as I did, and I hope you enjoy programming with Visual C++. I know I do.

Appendix A

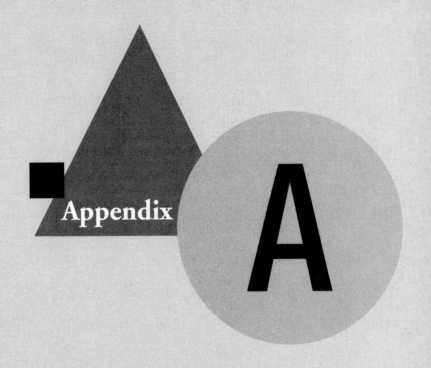

# ASCII Chart

ANSI Character Set (Character Codes 0-255)

| Dec | Hex | Char | Code† | Dec | Hex | Char | Dec | Hex | Char | Dec | Hex | Char |
|---|---|---|---|---|---|---|---|---|---|---|---|---|
| 0 | 00 | □ | NUL | 32 | 20 | (space) | 64 | 40 | @ | 96 | 60 | ` |
| 1 | 01 | □ | SOH | 33 | 21 | ! | 65 | 41 | A | 97 | 61 | a |
| 2 | 02 | □ | STX | 34 | 22 | " | 66 | 42 | B | 98 | 62 | b |
| 3 | 03 | □ | ETX | 35 | 23 | # | 67 | 43 | C | 99 | 63 | c |
| 4 | 04 | □ | EOT | 36 | 24 | $ | 68 | 44 | D | 100 | 64 | d |
| 5 | 05 | □ | ENQ | 37 | 25 | % | 69 | 45 | E | 101 | 65 | e |
| 6 | 06 | □ | ACK | 38 | 26 | & | 70 | 46 | F | 102 | 66 | f |
| 7 | 07 | □ | BEL | 39 | 27 | ' | 71 | 47 | G | 103 | 67 | g |
| 8 | 08 | □ | BS | 40 | 28 | ( | 72 | 48 | H | 104 | 68 | h |
| 9 | 09 | □ | HT | 41 | 29 | ) | 73 | 49 | I | 105 | 69 | i |
| 10 | 0A | □ | LF | 42 | 2A | * | 74 | 4A | J | 106 | 6A | j |
| 11 | 0B | □ | VT | 43 | 2B | + | 75 | 4B | K | 107 | 6B | k |
| 12 | 0C | □ | FF | 44 | 2C | , | 76 | 4C | L | 108 | 6C | l |
| 13 | 0D | □ | CR | 45 | 2D | - | 77 | 4D | M | 109 | 6D | m |
| 14 | 0E | □ | SO | 46 | 2E | . | 78 | 4E | N | 110 | 6E | n |
| 15 | 0F | □ | SI | 47 | 2F | / | 79 | 4F | O | 111 | 6F | o |
| 16 | 10 | □ | SLE | 48 | 30 | 0 | 80 | 50 | P | 112 | 70 | p |
| 17 | 11 | □ | CS1 | 49 | 31 | 1 | 81 | 51 | Q | 113 | 72 | q |
| 18 | 12 | □ | DC2 | 50 | 32 | 2 | 82 | 52 | R | 114 | 72 | r |
| 19 | 13 | □ | DC3 | 51 | 33 | 3 | 83 | 53 | S | 115 | 73 | s |
| 20 | 14 | □ | DC4 | 52 | 34 | 4 | 84 | 54 | T | 116 | 74 | t |
| 21 | 15 | □ | NAK | 53 | 35 | 5 | 85 | 55 | U | 117 | 75 | u |
| 22 | 16 | □ | SYN | 54 | 36 | 6 | 86 | 56 | V | 118 | 76 | v |
| 23 | 17 | □ | ETB | 55 | 37 | 7 | 87 | 57 | W | 119 | 77 | w |
| 24 | 18 | □ | CAN | 56 | 38 | 8 | 88 | 58 | X | 120 | 78 | x |
| 25 | 19 | □ | EM | 57 | 39 | 9 | 89 | 59 | Y | 121 | 79 | y |
| 26 | 1A | □ | SIB | 58 | 3A | : | 90 | 5A | Z | 122 | 7A | z |
| 27 | 1B | □ | ESC | 59 | 3B | ; | 91 | 5B | [ | 123 | 7B | { |
| 28 | 1C | □ | FS | 60 | 3C | < | 92 | 5C | \ | 124 | 7C | \| |
| 29 | 1D | □ | GS | 61 | 3D | = | 93 | 5D | ] | 125 | 7D | } |
| 30 | 1E |  | RS | 62 | 3E | > | 94 | 5E | ^ | 126 | 7E | ~ |
| 31 | 1F | □ | US | 63 | 3F | ? | 95 | 5F | _ | 127 | 7F | □ |

| Dec | Hex | Char | Dec | Hex | Char | Dec | Hex | Char | Dec | Hex | Char |
|---|---|---|---|---|---|---|---|---|---|---|---|
| 128 | 80 | □ | 160 | A0 | | 192 | C0 | À | 224 | E0 | à |
| 129 | 81 | □ | 161 | A1 | ¡ | 193 | C1 | Á | 225 | E1 | á |
| 130* | 82 | ‚ | 162 | A2 | ¢ | 194 | C2 | Â | 226 | E2 | â |
| 131* | 83 | ƒ | 163 | A3 | £ | 195 | C3 | Ã | 227 | E3 | ã |
| 132* | 84 | „ | 164 | A4 | ¤ | 196 | C4 | Ä | 228 | E4 | ä |
| 133* | 85 | … | 165 | A5 | ¥ | 197 | C5 | Å | 229 | E5 | å |
| 134* | 86 | † | 166 | A6 | ¦ | 198 | C6 | Æ | 230 | E6 | æ |
| 135* | 87 | ‡ | 167 | A7 | § | 199 | C7 | Ç | 231 | E7 | ç |
| 136* | 88 | ˆ | 168 | A8 | ¨ | 200 | C8 | È | 232 | E8 | è |
| 137* | 89 | ‰ | 169 | A9 | © | 201 | C9 | É | 233 | E9 | é |
| 138* | 8A | Š | 170 | AA | ª | 202 | CA | Ê | 234 | EA | ê |
| 139* | 8B | ‹ | 171 | AB | « | 203 | CB | Ë | 235 | EB | ë |
| 140* | 8C | Œ | 172 | AC | ¬ | 204 | CC | Ì | 236 | EC | ì |
| 141 | 8D | □ | 173 | AD | - | 205 | CD | Í | 237 | ED | í |
| 142 | 8E | □ | 174 | AE | ® | 206 | CE | Î | 238 | EE | î |
| 143 | 8F | □ | 175 | AF | ¯ | 207 | CF | Ï | 239 | EF | ï |
| 144 | 90 | □ | 176 | B0 | ° | 208 | D0 | Ð | 240 | F0 | ð |
| 145 | 91 | ‘ | 177 | B1 | ± | 209 | D1 | Ñ | 241 | F1 | ñ |
| 146 | 92 | ’ | 178 | B2 | ² | 210 | D2 | Ò | 242 | F2 | ò |
| 147* | 93 | “ | 179 | B3 | ³ | 211 | D3 | Ó | 243 | F3 | ó |
| 148* | 94 | ” | 180 | B4 | ´ | 212 | D4 | Ô | 244 | F4 | ô |
| 149* | 95 | • | 181 | B5 | µ | 213 | D5 | Õ | 245 | F5 | õ |
| 150* | 96 | – | 182 | B6 | ¶ | 214 | D6 | Ö | 246 | F6 | ö |
| 151* | 97 | — | 183 | B7 | · | 215 | D7 | × | 247 | F7 | ÷ |
| 152* | 98 | ˜ | 184 | B8 | ¸ | 216 | D8 | Ø | 248 | F8 | ø |
| 153* | 99 | ™ | 185 | B9 | ¹ | 217 | D9 | Ù | 249 | F9 | ù |
| 154* | 9A | š | 186 | BA | º | 218 | DA | Ú | 250 | FA | ú |
| 155* | 9B | › | 187 | BB | » | 219 | DB | Û | 251 | FB | û |
| 156* | 9C | œ | 188 | BC | ¼ | 220 | DC | Ü | 252 | FC | ü |
| 157 | 9D | □ | 189 | BD | ½ | 221 | DD | Ý | 253 | FD | ý |
| 158 | 9E | □ | 190 | BE | ¾ | 222 | DE | Þ | 254 | FE | þ |
| 159* | 9F | Ÿ | 191 | BF | ¿ | 223 | DF | ß | 255 | FF | ÿ |

□ Indicates that this character is not supported by Windows.
* Indicates that this character is available only in TrueType fonts.

† The "Code" column is meaningful only for characters 1–31.

For more information, see Appendix E in the C++ Language Reference.

Appendix B

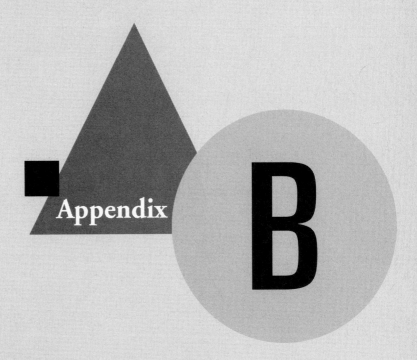

# The 80X86 Chip Family

The granddaddy of the 80X86 family was the Intel 8080 chip, an 8-bit microprocessor rarely found today except in computer museums. Introduced in 1974, it was packaged on a 40-pin DIP, the largest package used for an integrated chip at that time. Eight of its pins were used as a data bus for information going either in or out, and 16 other pins were used as an address bus for output only. The remaining 16 pins were used for power, clock, and various control signals.

In 1978, the 8080 was succeeded by a 16-bit chip, the Intel 8086. The next year, Intel introduced 8088, which powered the first IBM personal computers. Internally, the 8088 was like the 8086, but it had an 8-bit external data bus rather than a 16-bit external data bus—an architecture preferred by some manufacturers who wanted to keep their computers compatible with other peripheral hardware. If you look long enough, you can still find a few 8086- and 8088-equipped machines being used today.

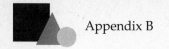

The next big evolutionary step in the 80X86 chip family was the development of the 16-bit Intel 80286, which became most popular as a CPU for laptop computers. Then came the 32-bit 80386 and 80486 chips, which are now more commonly referred to as the 386 and 486 microprocessors.

## The 8086 and 8088 Processors

The 8086 chip has a 16-bit data bus and a 20-bit address bus. As you know if you're familiar with hexadecimal arithmetic, a computer with a 20-bit address bus can access memory addresses that are up to 20 binary bits long. In decimal numbers, that means a 20-bit address bus can access 1,048,576 different memory addresses, or 1M of memory.

The next chip in the 80X86 family, the 8088, was a 16-bit chip with an 8-bit external data bus. Internally, the 8088 was like the 8086. The 8088, like its 8086 predecessor, had a 20-bit address bus, so it also could address 1M of memory.

## The 8086, the 8088, and Real Mode

The 8086 and 8088 were designed to access memory by using real mode. When an 80X86 chip operates in real mode, it accesses memory by using the segment:offset technique discussed in the following section. When an address is accessed by using the segment:offset system, a 16-bit segment address is combined with a 16-bit offset address to form an address known as a linear address. Segment:offset addressing is described in more detail under the next heading in this section.

Because most developers of the 80X86 software like to write programs that will run on any 80X86 computer—including the earliest 8086 models—real mode is still in widespread use. In fact, every chip in the 80X86 family "wakes up" in real mode when it is powered on. Only later can the chip be placed in another mode.

To understand how segment:offset addressing works, it helps to understand how the 8088 (or 8086) chip looks at memory.

# How Segment:Offset Addressing Works

Internally, the 8088 (like the 8086) is a 16-bit processor. That means the 8088 stores and manipulates information using 16-bit registers, or registers that can move data 16 bits at a time. A 16-bit register can hold a value of up to 64K, or a value ranging to 65,535. That means that one internal register in the 8088 (or the 8086) can hold a value ranging from 0 to 65,535. To store or manipulate larger values, additional registers are required.

Because the 8088 has registers that can store a value ranging from 0 to 65,535 but powers a line of computers with memory addresses ranging from 0 to 1,048,576, there's no way that one register can hold enough numbers to access all available memory locations. That is why the segment:offset addressing technique was created.

With the segment:offset addressing system, two 16-bit registers can be used together to access a 20-byte address. The scheme is simple: one register contains an offset address and the other word contains a segment address. Together the two registers can easily access 1M of memory.

# Segment Registers and Offset Registers

To make this system work, Intel created two kinds of CPU registers: segment registers and offset registers. A segment register always holds a segment value, that is, a value that specifies the beginning of a 64K memory segment. An offset register always holds an offset value, that is, a value that specifies a distance, or offset, into the segment specified by the segment register.

All chips in the 80X86 family have four segment registers in common: the CS, DS, SS, and ES registers.

The CS register holds the starting address of the currently executing program's code segment. The DS register holds the starting address of the current program's data segment. The stack segment register (SS) keeps track of values stored on the stack. The extra segment register (ES) helps to keep track of program data and helps to process data transfers between memory segments.

Because the 8086 and the 8088 are 16-bit chips, their segment and offset registers are 16-bit registers. That means an 8086/8088 offset register is just large enough to do its job. A 16-bit register can access up to 64K of memory, and an 80X86 memory segment is always 64K long, so that works out just right.

The operation of the segment register is a little more tricky. A segment register, like an offset register, is always 16 bits long. These two registers, placed end to end, can store a value of up to 32 bits. In practice, though, they are never called on to store that large a value. That's because the address capacity of an 8086/8088 computer is only 1M—a number whose maximum value, 1,048,576, fits into 20 bits. The segment and offset registers in the 8086/8088 chip never have to store a value more than 20 bits long; working together, they can store a 20-bit value with 12 bits to spare.

Because the 8086/8088 segment and offset registers have more capacity than they need to store 20-bit addresses, the chip designers at Intel devised a scheme that made it possible for the 8086/8088 to address 1M of memory while remaining compatible with an older microprocessor, the 8080. This was the plan: to shift the value stored in the segment register four bits to the left before adding it to the value stored in the address register. The idea worked, and it is still used in 80X86 chips today.

Here's the reason this system works: In hexadecimal arithmetic, shifting a value four bits to the left is equivalent to multiplying it by 16—in the same way that adding a zero to a decimal number is like multiplying it by 10.

Table B.1 shows how shifting a 16-bit value four bits to the left multiplies the value by 16 and results in a 20-bit value:

**Table B.1. Multiplying by bit-shifting.**

| | *Binary Value* | *Hex Value* |
|---|---|---|
| Before shifting | 00010010 00110100 | 3EB4 |
| After shifting | 00010010 00110100 0000 | 3EB40 |

In Table B.1, the value being bit-shifted is the hexadecimal value 3EB4. Shifting 3EB4 four bits to the left multiplies the value by 16 resulting in a hexadecimal value of 3EB40.

Figure B.1 shows how the segment:offset addressing technique uses bit-shifting to calculate an address.

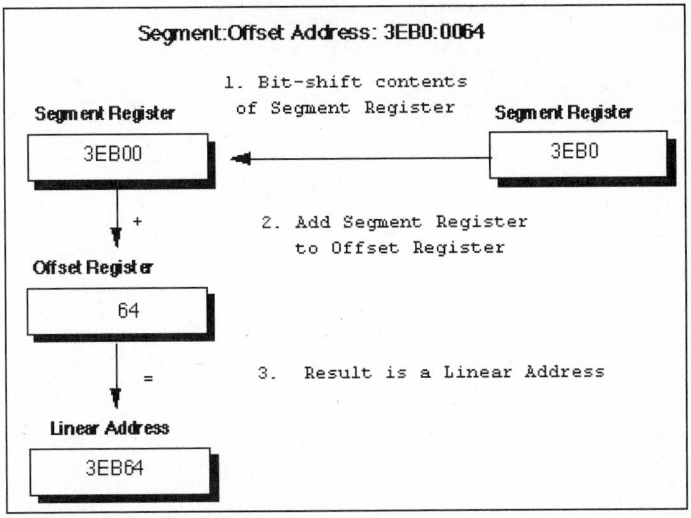


*Figure B.1. Segment:Offset addressing.*

In the operation shown in Figure B.1, a memory location with a segment:offset address of 3EB0:0064 is converted to a linear address of 3EB64.

In Step 1, a value stored in a segment register (3EB0) is shifted four bits to the left, resulting in a value of 3EB00.

In Step 2, the bit-shifted value 3EB00 is added to the value stored in the offset register, which is 64.

The result of this operation, as noted in Step 3, is a 20-bit value known as a linear address. In this example, the linear address is 3EB64.

When an 80X86 microprocessor is running in real mode—the only mode available in the 8086 and 8088—there is no difference between the physical address of a memory location and its linear address. When more advanced 80X86 chips run in other modes, however, there can be significant differences between the physical address and the linear address of a memory location. These differences are spelled out under the next heading.

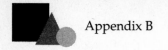

# Segment:Offset Addressing: A More Complex Example

The operation shown in Figure B.1 works out neatly because the value in the segment register does not end in a zero and the value in the offset register is only two hexadecimal digits long. In real-world segment:offset addressing, this situation is not the norm.

Figure B.2 shows how segment:offset addressing works when the value in the segment register does not end in zero and the value in the offset register is more than two hexadecimal digits long. There is no real difference in the way the operation works; the only reason the figures look more complicated is that the hexadecimal arithmetic involved is a little harder to carry out in one's head.

In Figure B.2, as in the previous example, the value stored in the segment register—in this case, 1234—is shifted four bits to the left. The value that results (12340) is then added to the contents of the offset register (5678), yielding a linear address (179B8).

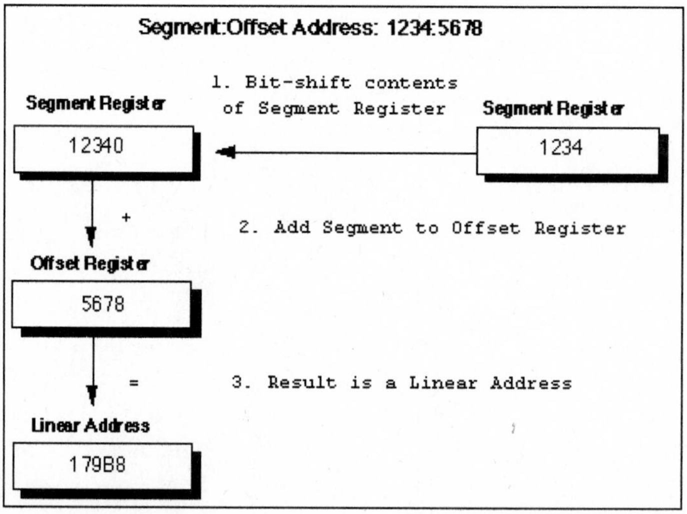


*Figure B.2. Segment:Offset addressing: a more complex example.*

# Ambiguities in Segment:Offset Addressing

From the point of view of chip compatibility, segment:offset addressing was a neat idea; it used CPU registers efficiently, and it could be used effectively by the 8080, 8086, and 8088 chips—at that time, the only processors in the 80X86 family. Unfortunately, there was a trade-off involved. Because the calculations that are used to obtain a linear address can start from anywhere in a computer's memory, many different linear addresses can represent the same physical address in a computer's memory. Figure B.3 shows how.

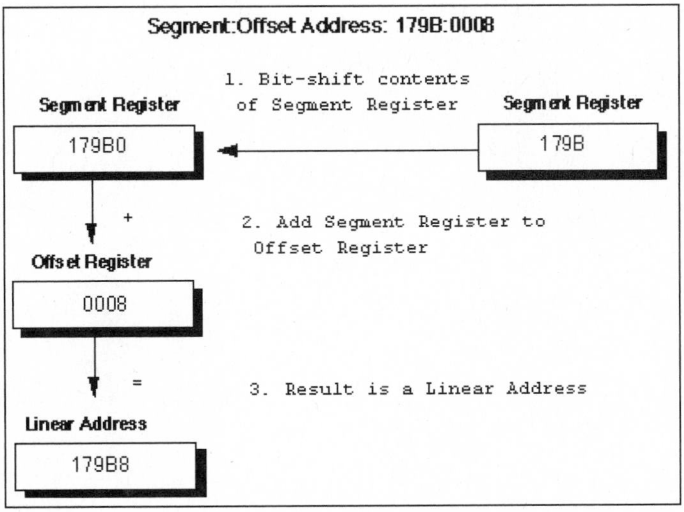


*Figure B.3. Ambiguities in segment:offset addressing.*

The operation shown in Figure B.3 works like the examples shown in the two previous illustrations. Notice that the value stored in the segment register—in this case, 179B—is shifted four bits to the left. The value that results (179B0) is then added to the contents of the offset register (0008), yielding a linear address (179B8).

This example has one unusual feature that may not be obvious at first glance. Although the values in the segment and offset registers shown in Figure B.3 are different from the values in the segment and offset registers shown in Figure B.2, the linear address that is generated in Figure B.3 is identical to the linear address shown in Figure B.2!

This occurrence is not a rarity in 80X86 programming; in fact, it happens so often that it could make a programmer's head spin. The reason is that in 8086/8088 math, any memory address that's divisible by 16 can be used as the starting address of a 64K memory segment. That means, of course, that memory segments overlap. Figure B.4 shows how.

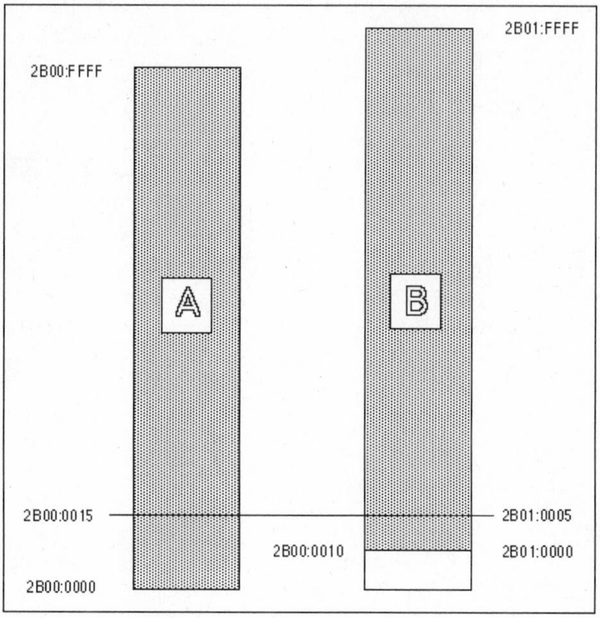


*Figure B.4. How memory segments overlap.*

Figure B.4 shows two memory 64K segments, labeled A and B. Memory segment A starts at memory address 2B00:0000, and memory segment B starts at 2B00:0010.

Because 2B00:0010 is the starting address of memory segment B, memory address 2B00:0010 also can be referred to as 2B01:0000. Each of these segment:offset addresses is made up of a segment address and an offset address. If you move each segment address four bits to the left and then add it to its corresponding offset address, you'll see that both physical addresses are the same.

Similarly, as Figure B.4 also shows, the segment:offset addresses 2B00:0015 and 2B01:0005 equate to the same physical addresses.

Although Figure B.4 shows only two segment:offset addresses for each physical address shown, every physical memory address in an 80X86 computer can be represented by many segment:offset addresses. By performing a little arithmetic, you can easily figure out how many segment:offset addresses a single physical memory location can have.

Because every 16th bit in memory marks the start of a new 64K memory segment, there are 65,536 memory segments in 1M of memory. In each memory segment, there are 65,536 addresses, for a combination of more than four billion segment:offset combinations. That means that every physical address on an 8086/8088 computer's memory map can be represented by 4,096 different segment:offset addresses!

## The 80286 Microprocessor

The Intel 80286 chip added two important new capabilities to the 8086: a 24-bit data bus and a protected addressing mode that supports multitasking and can access up to 16M of memory.

Because of its 24-bit data bus, the 80286 can manipulate data in larger chunks than its predecessors, the 8086 and 8088. The processor's protected mode supports multitasking by protecting programs from various kinds of disasters—such as memory-access errors and I/O errors—when multiple programs are running at the same time.

## Protected Mode and Segment:Offset Addressing

With the advent of protected mode, the segment:offset addressing technique was retained—and extended. In 80286 protected mode, a segment is not just any 64K region of memory that starts at a memory address that's divisible by 16. Instead, a segment is a variable-length region of memory.

Even better, protected-mode memory addresses are not restricted to a length of 1M. A protected-mode memory segment can start anywhere in an address range of 16M memory.

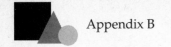

A protected-mode segment can have any length, ranging from a single byte all the way up to 64K. Each segment also carries some additional information called access rights. These bits are used to limit who can access this segment and for what purposes, and when a program that is in this segment may do I/O operations.

The 80286 protects active programs from each other by computing linear addresses in a new way. In real mode, as noted under the previous heading, you compute a memory address adding 16 times the value of the segment value to the offset to get a linear address. In protected mode, this computation is performed quite differently.

The 80286 chip's protected mode maintains the distinction between physical addresses and logical addresses (which are sometimes called virtual addresses). In protected mode, logical (or virtual) addresses are written in the segment:offset format, just as they are in earlier 80X86 processors. In protected mode, however, the segment part of the address (the part that precedes the colon) is used in a different way.

In 80286 protected mode, addresses are calculated by using indirection; the value in the segment register points to a number that is added to the value of the offset register to generate the linear address. The number that is added to the offset is known as the base address, and the number in the segment register is called a selector because it selects which segment is to be used.

In the 80286 processor's protected mode, as in 8086/8088 real mode, the values in the segment register and the offset register are 16 bits long. In protected mode, the base pointer that is pointed to by the selector is 24 bits long. This gives an 80286 running in protected mode an addressing capability of 16M, compared with an addressing limit of 1M in real mode.

Furthermore, the 80286 selector does not just point to a base address. It points to a line in a table called a descriptor table, which can track down any segment in a 16M range of memory. It is beyond the scope of this chapter to describe exactly how a descriptor table works, but if you're interested, you can read all about descriptor tables in books such as John M. Goodman's *Memory Management for All of Us,* which is listed in the Bibliography.

# The 386 Processor

The Intel 80386 (now more commonly called the 386) was the first true 32-bit computer in the 80X86 family; it has both a 32-bit address bus and a 32-bit address, so it can access 4G of memory.

Because the 386 is a true 32-bit chip, it presents a special challenge to software developers. The 386 can run two kinds of software: 16-bit programs that work on any IBM PC or PC-compatible and 32-bit programs that require the use of the Windows NT operating system and won't run on machines that are equipped with older microprocessors.

Programs specifically designed to run under Windows NT can be bigger and can run faster than programs designed to be downward-compatible with older machines. Also, programs written for Windows NT can take advantage of all the Win32 software development environment features.

Unfortunately, users of older machines can't run 32-bit programs written solely for Windows NT. There are, therefore, a lot of trade-offs to consider before you decide whether a program you're creating should be designed to run under MS-DOS, under Windows 3.X, or under Windows NT.

Along with its increased data-handling and addressing capabilities, the 386 introduced an important advancement called paging—another step in the evolution from the complex and time-consuming segment:offset addressing system used by the 8086 and 8088 chips to real physical addressing.

The 386 processor is fully backward-compatible with the earlier members of the 80X86 family. It supports all the instructions recognized by earlier 80X86 chips, and it can run in both an 8086/8088-style real mode and the protected mode introduced with the 80286 processor. The 386, however, also introduced two new operating modes: an advanced-style protected mode different from the protected mode used by the 80286 and a new "virtual-8086" mode.

# 386 Protected Mode

You probably won't be surprised to learn that the protected mode used by the 386 is different from the protected mode used by 80286, because 386 has a 32-bit data bus and a 32-bit address bus, whereas the 80286 has only a 16-bit data bus and a 24-bit address bus.

In 386 protected mode, logical addresses are still calculated by using a segment register value and an offset, but the 386 has a 32-bit offset register, so the offsets used in 386 protected mode can range up to a maximum of 4G. The 386's segment register (or selector) is still only 16 bits long, but the base address that the selector points to—like the contents of the 386 offset register—can be up to 32 bits long. The addressing range of the 386 chip can extend all the way up to 4G.

# Virtual-8086 Mode

The 386 chip also introduced another new operating mode called virtual-8086, or V86 mode. V86 mode lets the 386 chip emulate the 8086 chip while running in protected mode. By running in V86 mode, the 386 can execute multiple real-mode programs (such as old DOS programs) simultaneously, with all the memory-addressing and I/O protection offered by real mode.

# The 486 Processor

According to hardware experts, the 80X86 microprocessor finally reached maturity with the introduction of the 386, and the comparatively small differences between the 386 and 486 chips seem to back up this claim. The 486 has more than four times the complexity of the 386 chip, but breaks no significant new ground in chip architecture.

The most important feature of the 486 is that it incorporates into a single chip a great number of components that previously were spread all over a 80X86 PC's motherboard—for example, the 80387 math coprocessor and 8K of memory caching.

As for the 486 chip, it supports all the operating modes used by earlier chips in the 80X86 family, so it, too, can run in any of these modes: Real, 80286-protected, 386-protected, and virtual-8086.

# Using Pointers in C++ Programs

As noted in Chapter 4, "Variables," Visual C++ provides three kinds of pointers to access memory locations: near pointers, far pointers, and huge pointers. A near pointer is always 16 bits long. Pointers of the far and huge configurations are 32 bits long.

When you write a tiny-model program or a small-model program, every address in the program's code segment and every address in the program's data segment can be accessed with a 16-bit pointer. For this reason, a 16-bit pointer is called a near pointer, and 16-bit addressing is called near addressing.

When a program requires more than 64K for its code or its data, at least some of the pointers used in the program must be 32-bit pointers, or far pointers. Accessing an object with a far pointer is called far addressing.

A huge pointer is the only kind of pointer that can access memory locations in data segments longer than 64K. You can't use a huge pointer to access addresses in a code segment because 80X86 code segments cannot be longer than 64K.

A huge pointer—like a far pointer—contains 32 bits, expressed as a segment value and an offset value. The distinguishing feature of a huge pointer is that the address stored in the pointer is normalized.

To normalize the address stored in a huge pointer, the 386/486 chip performs a special mathematical conversion on the address stored in the pointer. The address is manipulated so that as much of the address as possible is stored in the segment part of the pointer. When this operation is complete, the offset part of the pointer contains a value ranging only from 0 to 16, or from 0 to F in hexadecimal notation.

Here is the difference between a far pointer and a huge pointer: When a memory address is stored in a far pointer, all addresses that can be accessed by the pointer must lie within the segment in which they start. Therefore, the pointer arithmetic used to create a far pointer operates only on the offset portion of the address.

When a memory address is stored in a huge pointer, the 386/486 chip performs pointer arithmetic on all 32 bits of the address, allowing data items referenced by the pointer to span more than one segment. Figure B.5 shows how the memory address in a huge pointer is normalized.

As Figure B.5 illustrates, this is how the 386/486 chip creates a huge pointer:

1. The address in the segment half of the pointer (3256 in Figure B.5) is moved four bits to the left, resulting in a multiplication by 16.
2. This left-shifted segment address (32560 in Figure B.5) is added to the address in the offset part of the pointer (00C4) in the illustration, producing a linear address. In this example, this linear address is 32624.
3. The linear address produced in Step 2 is now split into two parts: a 20-bit normalized segment address and a 4-bit normalized offset address. In Figure B.5, the normalized segment address is 32624 and the normalized offset address is 4.

A huge pointer can access memory addresses in segments longer than 64K, because the segment part of a value stored in a huge pointer changes when the address stored in the offset half crosses a 64K memory-segment boundary.

Because the segment values stored in huge pointers roll over in this way, a huge pointer can keep track of the memory addresses in data segments that are larger than 64K.

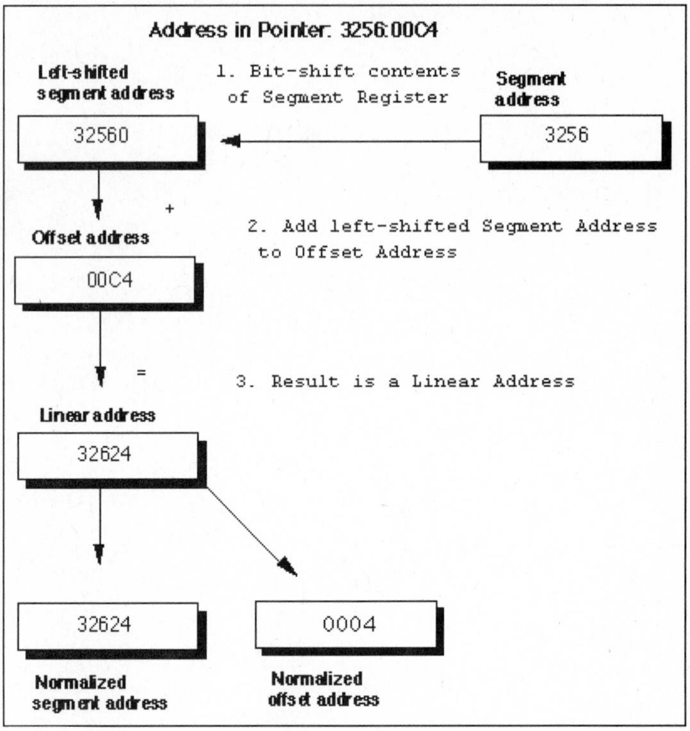


*Figure B.5. Normalizing the address in a huge pointer.*

A normalized huge pointer has two advantages over a far pointer. First, huge pointers that point to the same memory location are always equal, so you can logically compare the values of huge pointers. Second, you can perform mathematical operations on huge pointers more easily because the segment value of a huge pointer rolls over when an arithmetic operation requires the segment value to change.

The main disadvantage of using huge pointers is that the pointer arithmetic required to create and manipulate huge pointers requires extra overhead. Pointers of the huge variety therefore reduce processing speed.

# Bibliography


Atkinson, Lee, Mark Atkinson, and Ed Mitchell. *Using Microsoft C/C++ 7*. Carmel, Indiana: Que Corporation, 1992.

Barkakati, Nabajyoti. *Microsoft C/C++ 7 Developer's Guide*. Carmel, Indiana: Sams, 1992.

Barkakati, Nabajyoti. *Object-Oriented Programming in C++*. Carmel, Indiana: Sams, 1989.

Booch, Grady. *Object-Oriented Design*. Redwood City, California: Benjamin/Cummings, 1991.

Christian, Kaare. *The Microsoft Guide to C++ Programming*. Redmond, Washington: Microsoft Press, 1992.

Ellis, Margaret A., and Bjarne Stroustrup. *The Annotated C++ Reference Manual*. Reading, Massachusetts: Addison-Wesley, 1990.

Faison, Ted. *Borland C++ 3 Object-Oriented Programming*. Carmel, Indiana: Sams, 1989.

Goodman, John M. *Memory Management for All of Us*. Carmel, Indiana: Sams, 1992.

Hansen, Augie. *C Programming: A Complete Guide to Mastering the C Language*. Reading, Massachusetts: Addison-Wesley, 1989.

Hansen, Tony L. *The C++ Answer Book*. Reading, Massachusetts: Addison-Wesley, 1990.

Hunter, Bruce H. *Understanding C*. Berkeley: Sybex, 1984.

Kernighlan, Brian W., and Dennis M. Ritchie. *The C Programming Language*. 2d ed. Englewood Cliffs, New Jersey: Prentice Hall, 1985.

Klein, Mike. *DLLs and Memory Management*. Carmel, Indiana: Sams, 1992.

LaFore, Robert. *Object-Oriented Programming in Microsoft C++*. Corta Madera, California: Waite Group Press, 1991.

Lippman, Stanley B. *C++ Primer*, 2d ed. Reading, Massachusetts: Addison-Wesley, 1992.

Murray, William H. III, and Chris H. Pappas. *Microsoft C/C++ 7: The Complete Reference*. Berkeley: Osborne McGraw-Hill, 1992.

Petzold, Charles. *Programming Windows*. Carmel, Indiana: Sams, 1990.

Petzold, Charles. *Programming Windows 3.1*. Carmel, Indiana: Sams, 1992.

Prata, Stephen. *C++ Primer Plus*. Corta Madera, California: Waite Group Press, 1991.

Rector, Brent E. *Developing Windows 3.1 Applictions with Microsoft C/C++*. 2d ed. Carmel, Indiana: Sams, 1992.

Schildt, Herbert. *C: The Complete Reference*. 2d ed. Berkeley: Osborne McGraw-Hill, 1987.

Stevens, Al. *Teach Yourself C++*. New York: Management Information Source, Inc., 1991.

Stroustrup, Bjarne. *The C++ Programming Language*. 2d ed. Reading, Massachusetts: Addison-Wesley, 1990.

Tondo, Clovis L., and Scott E. Gimpel. *The C Answer Book*. Englewood Cliffs, New Jersey: Prentice-Hall, 1985.

Wiener, Richard S., and Lewis J. Pinson. *An Introduction to Object-Oriented Programming and C++*. Reading, Massachusetts: Addison-Wesley, 1988.

Wiener, Richard S., and Lewis J. Pinson. *The C++ Workbook*. Reading, Massachusetts: Addison-Wesley, 1990.

Winblad, Ann L., Samuel D. Edward, and David R. King. *Object-Oriented Software*. Reading, Massachusetts: Addison-Wesley, 1990.

## Symbols

## A

## B

## C

## D

## G

## H

## J–K

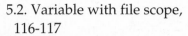

## M

## N

## O

## P

## Q–R

## S

## T

## U



## V

## W

## X–Z

## What's on the Disk

The disk contains source code for the book's programming examples, plus a complete Visual C++ application—The Wrath of Zalthar.

## Installing the Floppy Disk

The software included with this book is stored in compressed form. You cannot use the software without first installing it to your hard drive. The installation program runs from within Windows.

> To install the files on the disk, you'll need at least 2M of free space on your hard drive.

1. From File Manager or Program Manager, choose **File**¦**Run** from the menu.
2. Type `<drive>INSTALL` and press Enter. `<drive>` is the letter of the drive that contains the installation disk. For example, if the disk is in drive B:, type `B:INSTALL` and press Enter.

Follow the on-screen instructions in the install program. The files will be installed to a directory named \VCOOP, unless you changed this name during the install program.

The install program will display the file VCOOP.TXT when the installation is complete. This file contains information on the files and programs that were installed.

Book ISBN 0-672-30150-4